SHONEN JUMP MANGA

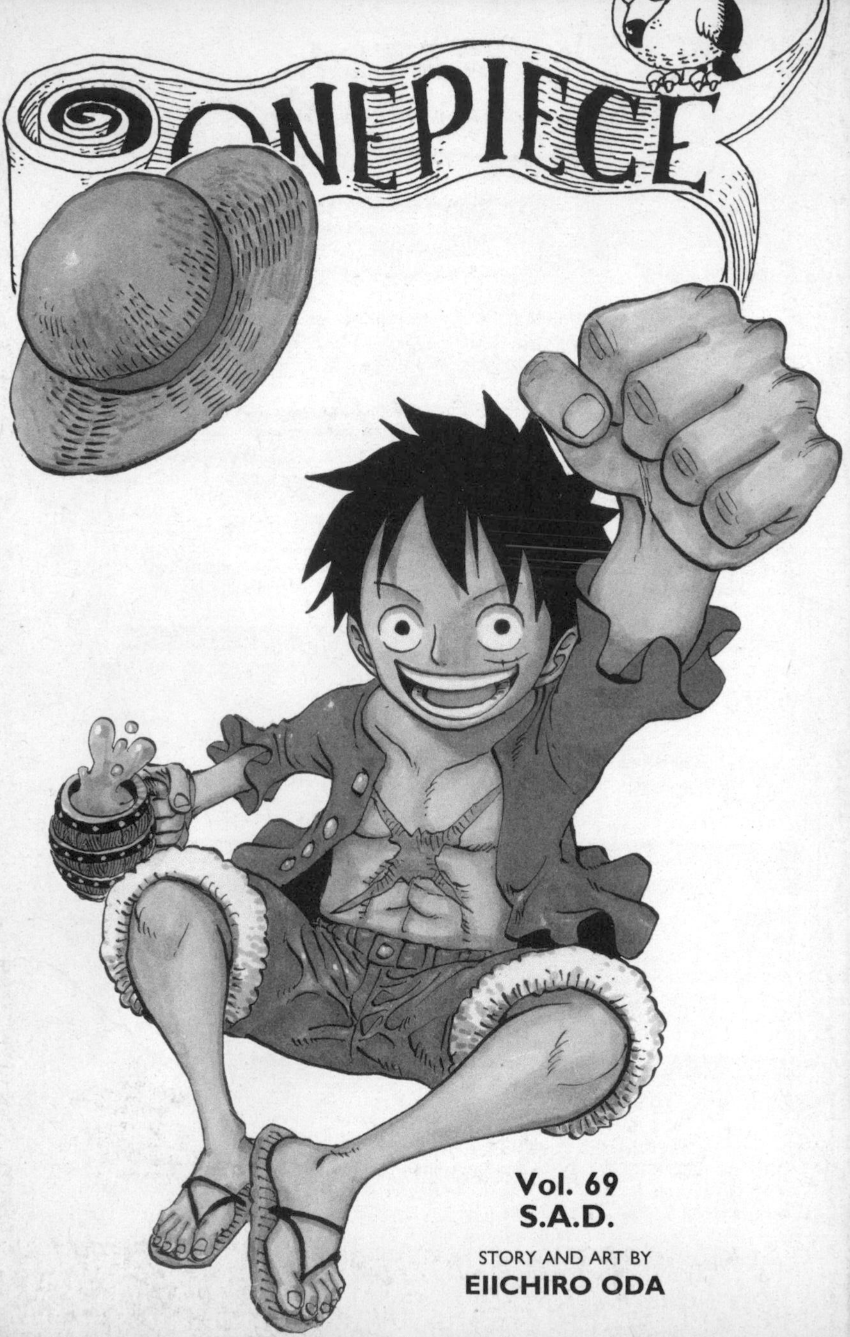
ONE PIECE

Vol. 69
S.A.D.

STORY AND ART BY
EIICHIRO ODA

The Straw Hat Crew

Monkey D. Luffy

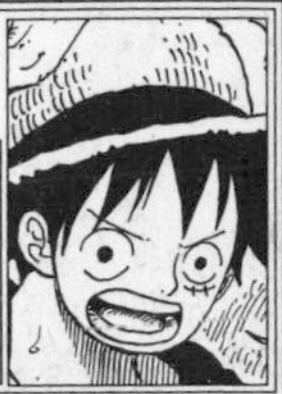

A young man who dreams of becoming the Pirate King. After training with Rayleigh, he and his crew head for the New World!

Captain, Bounty: 400 million berries

Roronoa Zolo

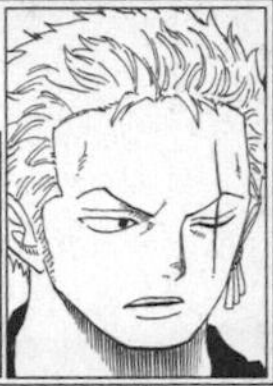

He swallowed his pride and asked to be trained by Mihawk on Gloom Island before reuniting with the rest of the crew.

Fighter, Bounty: 120 million berries

Tony Tony Chopper

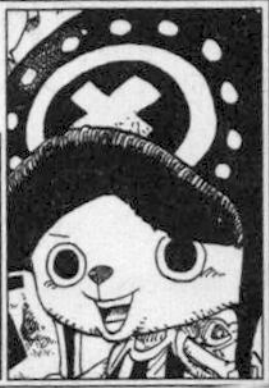

After researching powerful medicine in Birdie Kingdom, he reunites with the rest of the crew.

Ship's Doctor, Bounty: 50 berries

Nami

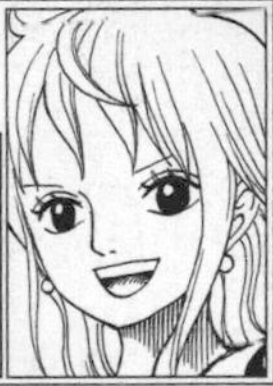

She studied the weather of the New World on the small Sky Island Weatheria, a place where weather is studied as a science.

Navigator, Bounty: 16 million berries

Nico Robin

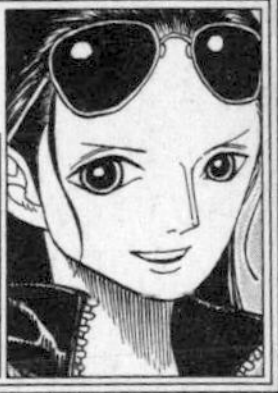

She spent her time in Baltigo with the leader of the Revolutionary Army: Luffy's father, Dragon.

Archeologist, Bounty: 80 million berries

Usopp

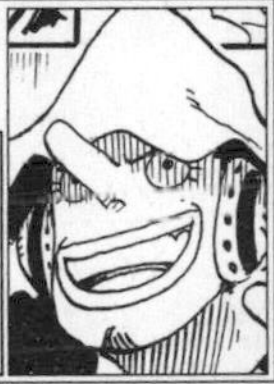

He trained under Heracles at the Bowin Islands to become the King of Snipers.

Sniper, Bounty: 30 million berries

Franky

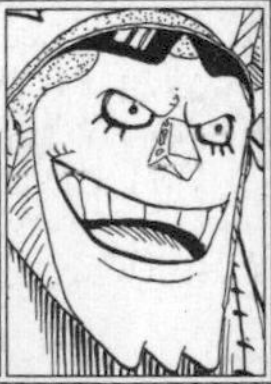

He modified himself in Future Land Baldimore and turned himself into Armored Franky before reuniting with the rest of the crew.

Shipwright, Bounty: 44 million berries

Sanji

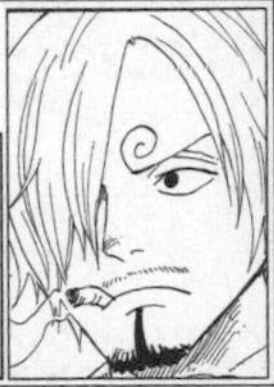

After fighting the New Kama Karate masters in the Kamabakka Kingdom, he returned to the crew.

Cook, Bounty: 77 million berries

Brook

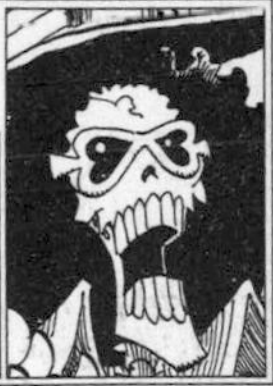

After being captured and used as a freak show by the Longarm Tribe, he became a famous rock star called "Soul King" Brook.

Musician, Bounty: 33 million berries

decide to join forces in a pirate alliance, but their plan to kidnap Caesar backfires. In captivity, they learn the terrible truth: Caesar's been developing deadly weapons in order to sell them to black market brokers. One of these brokers is the very man who helped kidnap the children: Doflamingo! Everything is going according to their nefarious plan until Law's clever liberation of the Straw Hats leads to an all-out counterattack!!

The story of ONE PIECE 1»69

Shanks

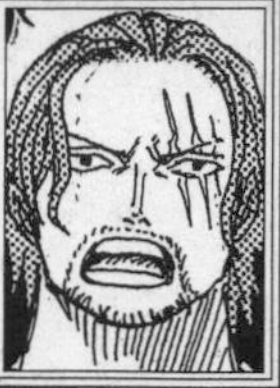

One of the Four Emperors. He continues to wait for Luffy in the second half of the Grand Line, called the New World.

Captain of the Red-Haired Pirates

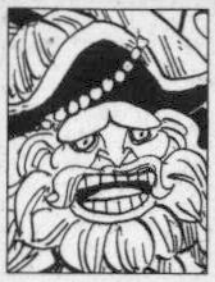

Brownbeard ("Boss")

Punk Hazard Patrol

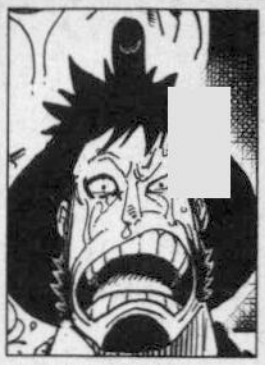

Foxfire Kin'emon

Samurai of Wano

Punk Hazard

Master Caesar Clown

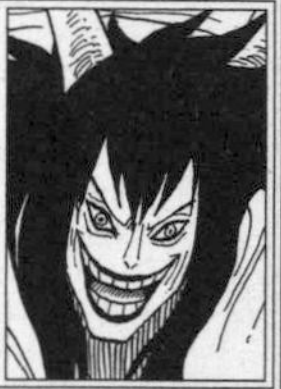

Dr. Vegapunk's former colleague. An authority on weapons of mass-murder, now wanted by the government.

Former gov't scientist

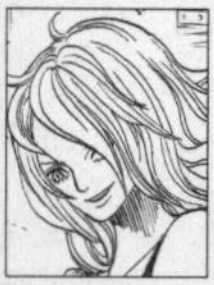

Monet

Harpy

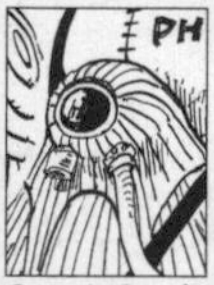
PH

Caesar's Guards

Caesar's followers

Naval G-5:

5th Branch of the Naval Grand Line

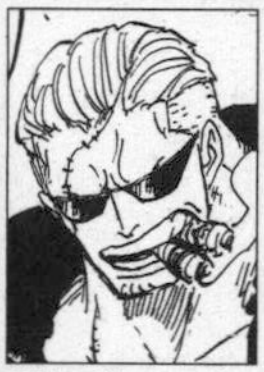

White Chase Smoker

G-5 Vice Admiral

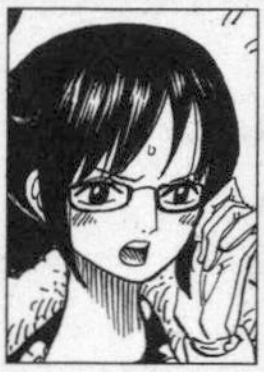

Tashigi

G-5 Captai

Vice Admiral Vergo

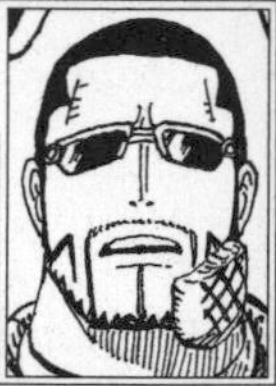

A Navy officer who secretly works for Doflamingo's organization. He helped orchestrate the child abductions.

G-5 Commander

Don Quixote Doflamingo (Joker)

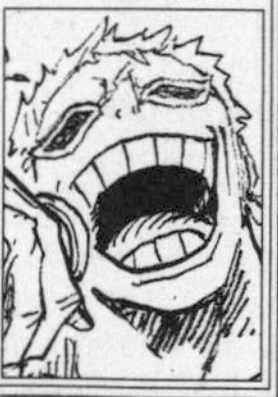

One of the Seven Warlords of the sea and a weapons broker. He works under the alias of "Joker."

Pirate, Warlord

Trafalgar Law

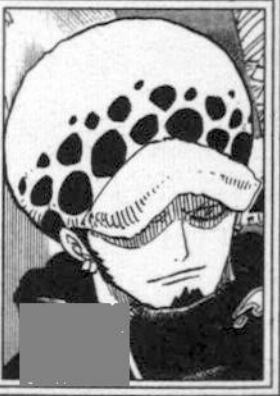

The Surgeon of Death, wielder of the Op-Op Fruit's powers. One of the Seven Warlords of the Sea.

Pirate, Warlord

Story

Having finished their two years of training, the Straw Hat crew reunites on the Sabaody Archipelago. They finally reach the final ocean, the New World, via Fish-Man Island!

The crew lands on Punk Hazard, where the mad scientist and wanted man Caesar Clown rules over the ruins of a government laboratory. With the arrival of the newly appointed Warlord of the Sea Trafalgar Law, the Straw Hats and the pursuing Navy, the island bursts into chaos! Luffy and Law

Vol. 69
S.A.D.

CONTENTS

Chapter 679:
THE G-5 SPIRIT

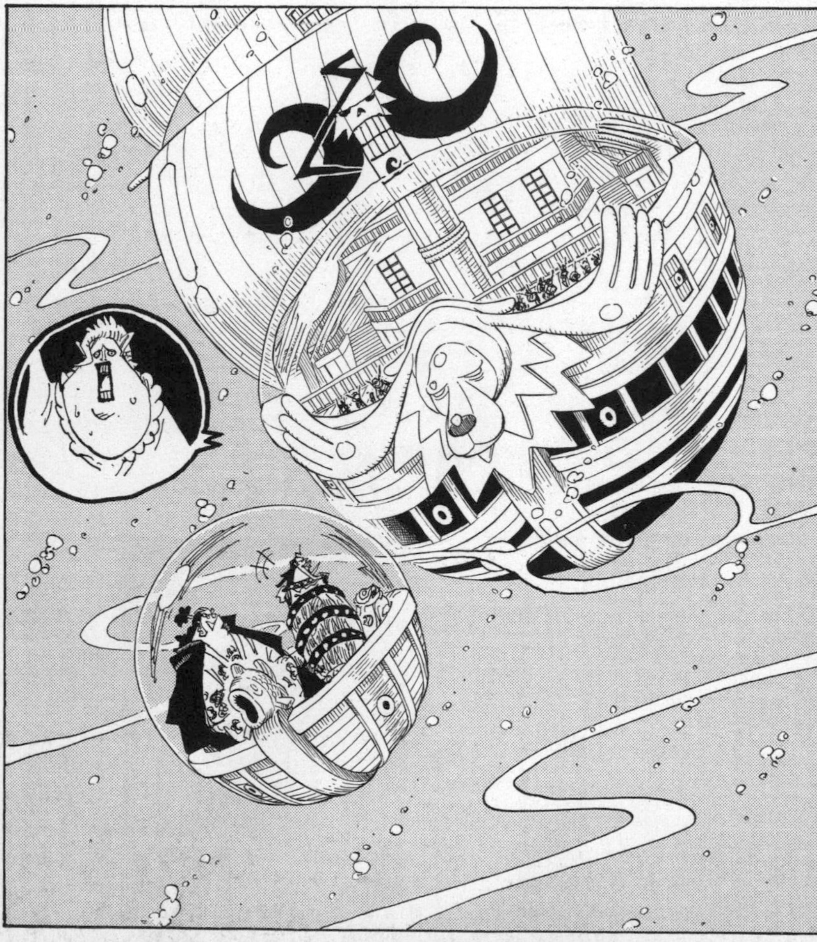

CARIBOU'S NEW WORLD KEE HEE HEE, VOL. 5:
"HERE COMES CORIBOU"

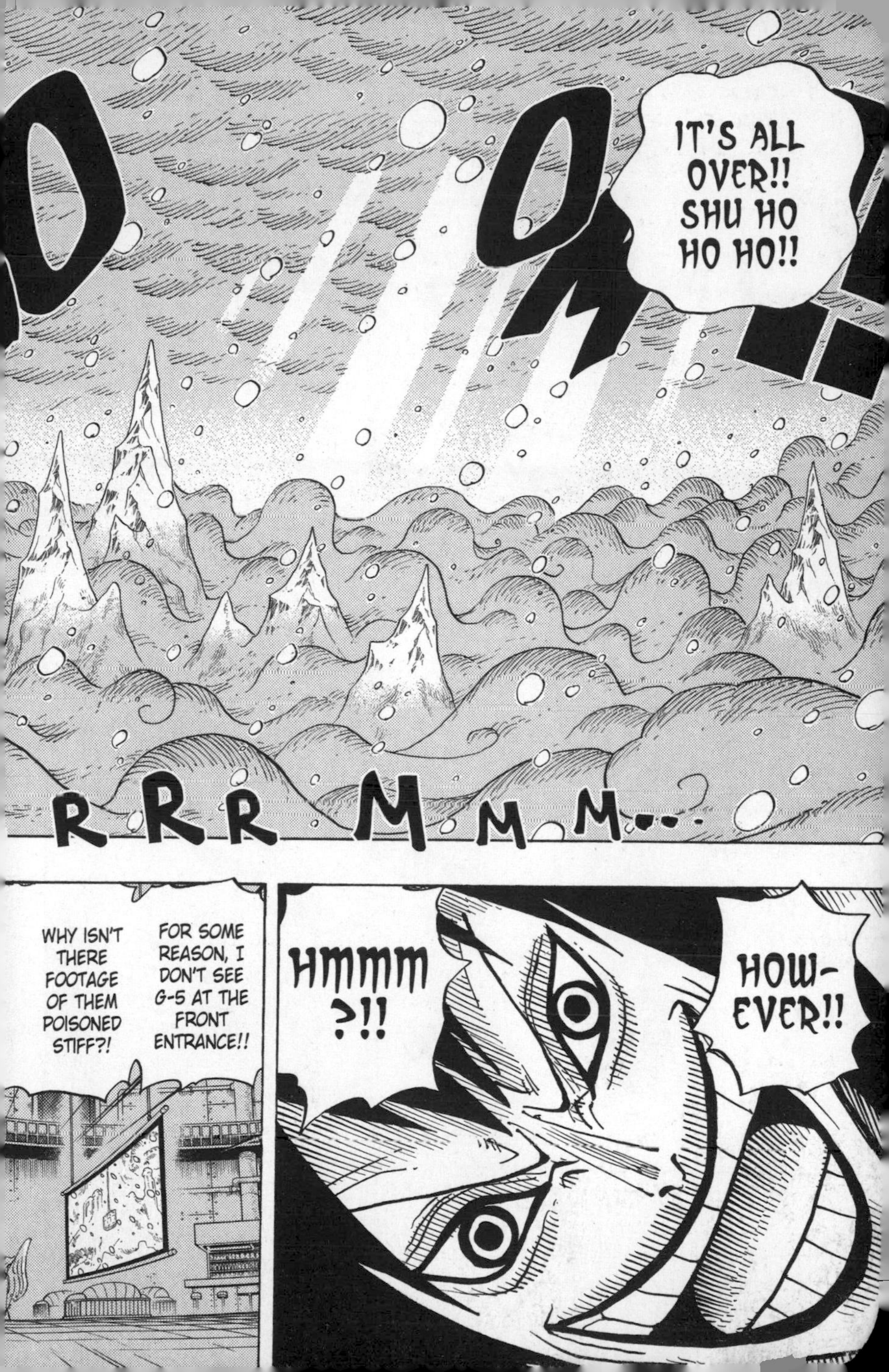
IT'S ALL OVER!! SHU HO HO HO!!
RRRMMM...
HOW-EVER!!
HMMM ?!!
FOR SOME REASON, I DON'T SEE G-5 AT THE FRONT ENTRANCE!!
WHY ISN'T THERE FOOTAGE OF THEM POISONED STIFF?!

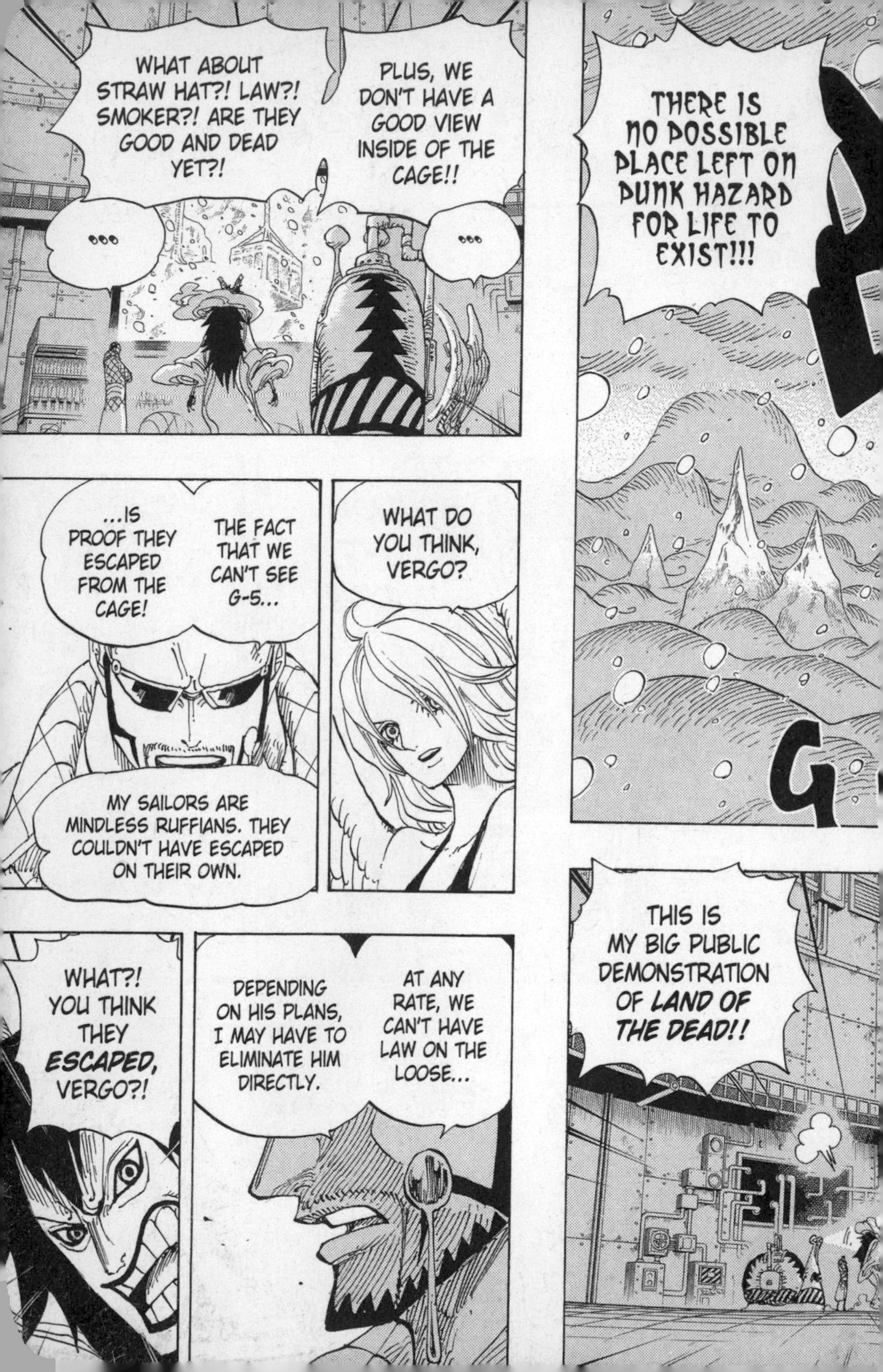
THERE IS NO POSSIBLE PLACE LEFT ON PUNK HAZARD FOR LIFE TO EXIST!!!
G
WHAT ABOUT STRAW HAT?! LAW?! SMOKER?! ARE THEY GOOD AND DEAD YET?!
PLUS, WE DON'T HAVE A GOOD VIEW INSIDE OF THE CAGE!!
...
...
WHAT DO YOU THINK, VERGO?
THE FACT THAT WE CAN'T SEE G-5...
...IS PROOF THEY ESCAPED FROM THE CAGE!
MY SAILORS ARE MINDLESS RUFFIANS. THEY COULDN'T HAVE ESCAPED ON THEIR OWN.
THIS IS MY BIG PUBLIC DEMONSTRATION OF *LAND OF THE DEAD!!*
AT ANY RATE, WE CAN'T HAVE LAW ON THE LOOSE...
DEPENDING ON HIS PLANS, I MAY HAVE TO ELIMINATE HIM DIRECTLY.
WHAT?! YOU THINK THEY *ESCAPED,* VERGO?!

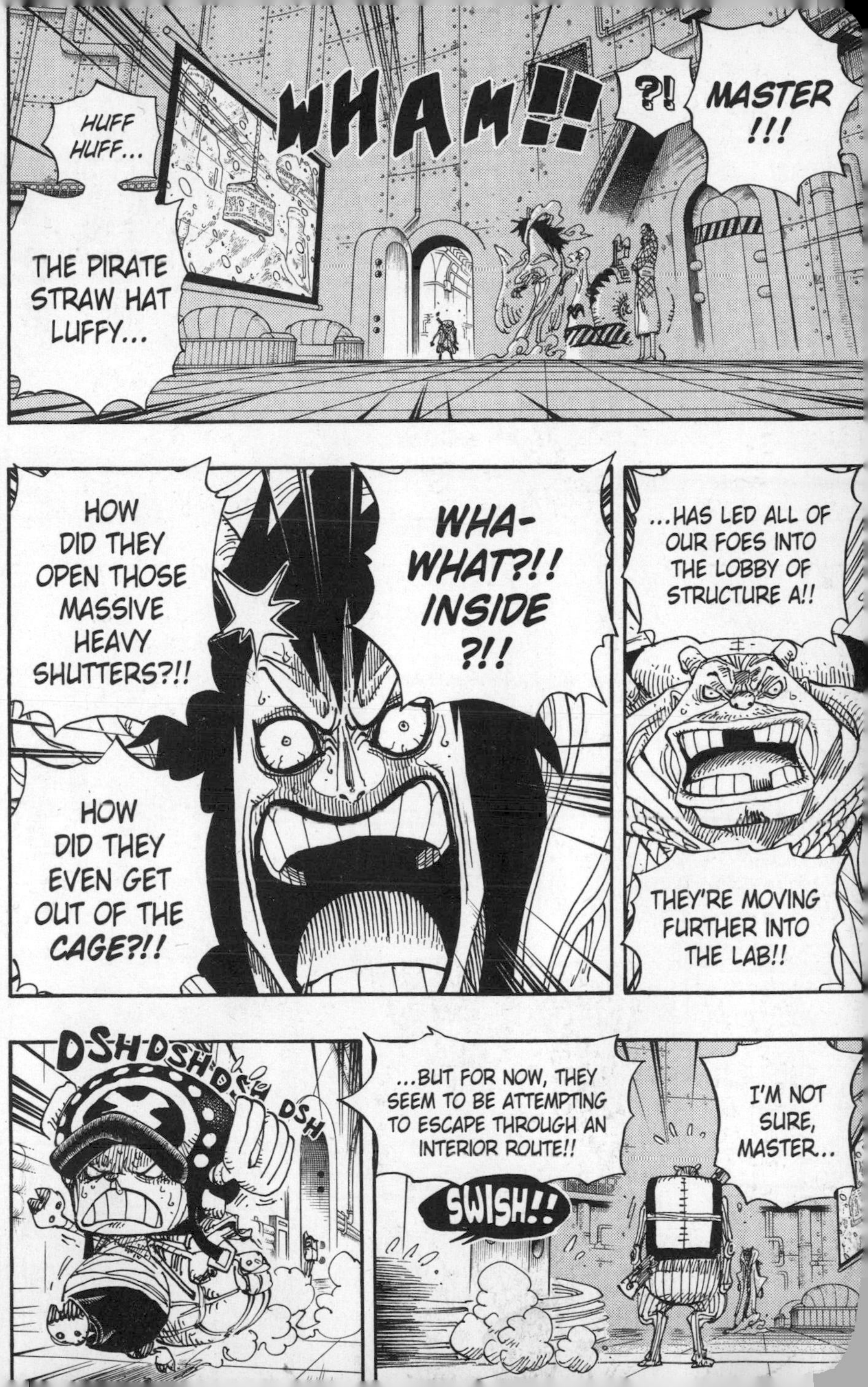
MASTER !!!
?!
WHAM!!
HUFF HUFF...
THE PIRATE STRAW HAT LUFFY...
...HAS LED ALL OF OUR FOES INTO THE LOBBY OF STRUCTURE A!!
THEY'RE MOVING FURTHER INTO THE LAB!!
WHA-WHAT?!! INSIDE ?!!
HOW DID THEY OPEN THOSE MASSIVE HEAVY SHUTTERS?!!
HOW DID THEY EVEN GET OUT OF THE CAGE?!!
I'M NOT SURE, MASTER...
...BUT FOR NOW, THEY SEEM TO BE ATTEMPTING TO ESCAPE THROUGH AN INTERIOR ROUTE!!
SWISH!!
DSH DSH DSH DSH DSH

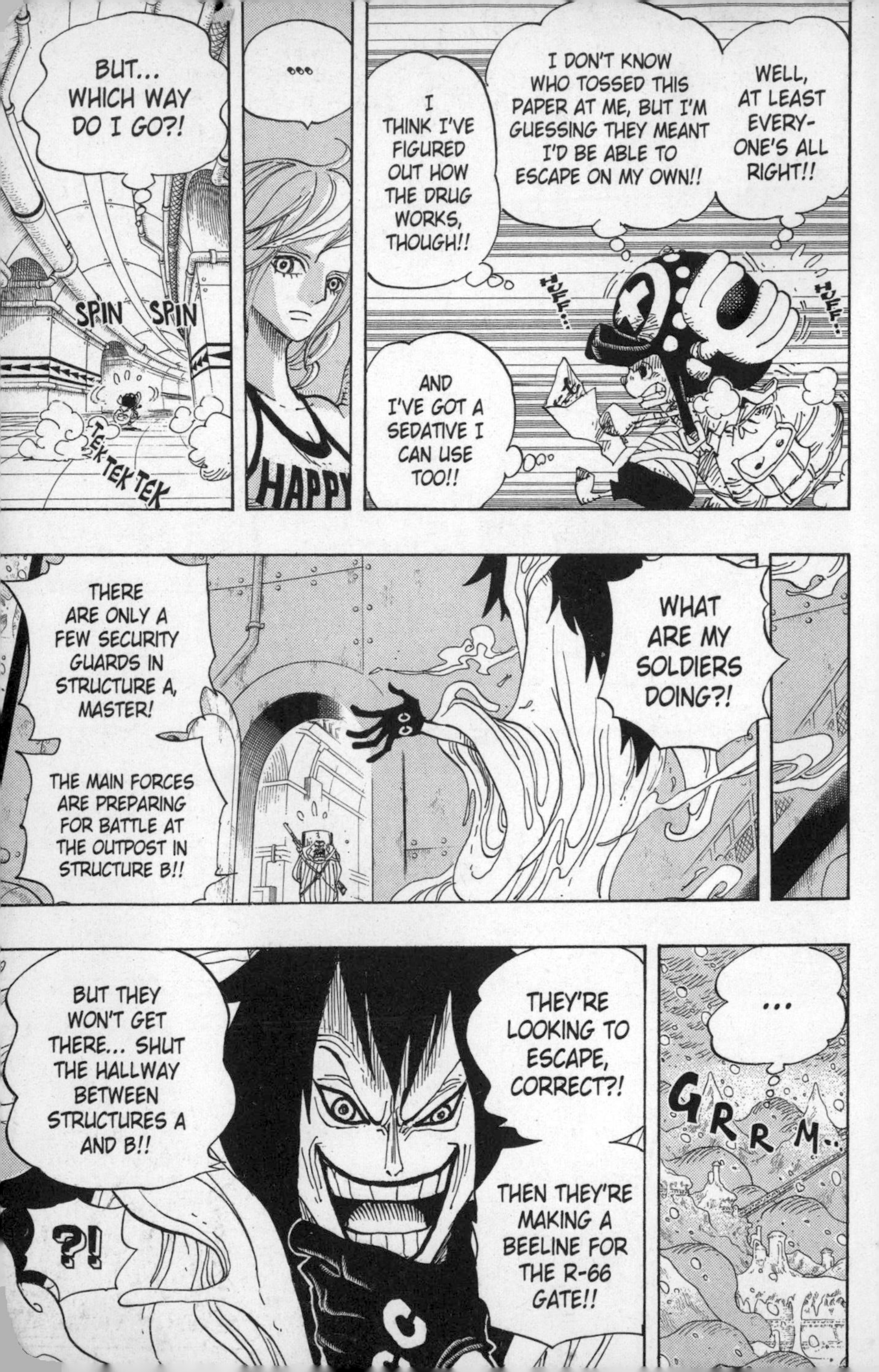
HUFF...
HUFF...
WELL, AT LEAST EVERY-ONE'S ALL RIGHT!!
I DON'T KNOW WHO TOSSED THIS PAPER AT ME, BUT I'M GUESSING THEY MEANT I'D BE ABLE TO ESCAPE ON MY OWN!!
I THINK I'VE FIGURED OUT HOW THE DRUG WORKS, THOUGH!!
AND I'VE GOT A SEDATIVE I CAN USE TOO!!
...
HAPPY
BUT... WHICH WAY DO I GO?!
SPIN SPIN
TEK TEK TEK
WHAT ARE MY SOLDIERS DOING?!
THERE ARE ONLY A FEW SECURITY GUARDS IN STRUCTURE A, MASTER!
THE MAIN FORCES ARE PREPARING FOR BATTLE AT THE OUTPOST IN STRUCTURE B!!
...
GRRRM..
THEY'RE LOOKING TO ESCAPE, CORRECT?!
THEN THEY'RE MAKING A BEELINE FOR THE R-66 GATE!!
BUT THEY WON'T GET THERE... SHUT THE HALLWAY BETWEEN STRUCTURES A AND B!!
?!

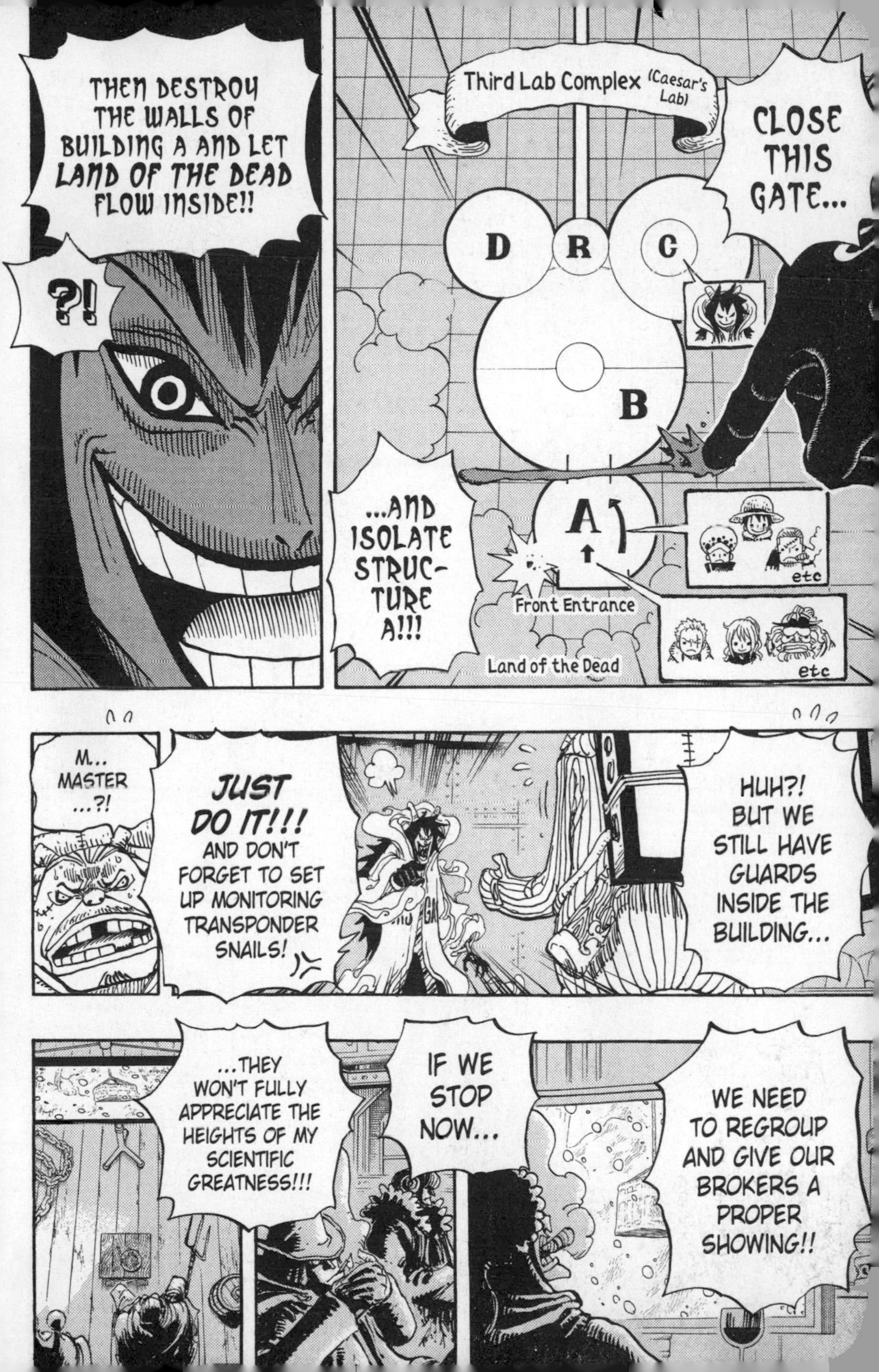
Third Lab Complex (Caesar's Lab)
CLOSE THIS GATE...
D
R
C
B
A
...AND ISOLATE STRUCTURE A!!!
Front Entrance
Land of the Dead
etc
etc
THEN DESTROY THE WALLS OF BUILDING A AND LET LAND OF THE DEAD FLOW INSIDE!!
?!
HUH?! BUT WE STILL HAVE GUARDS INSIDE THE BUILDING...
JUST DO IT!!! AND DON'T FORGET TO SET UP MONITORING TRANSPONDER SNAILS!
M... MASTER ...?!
WE NEED TO REGROUP AND GIVE OUR BROKERS A PROPER SHOWING!!
IF WE STOP NOW...
...THEY WON'T FULLY APPRECIATE THE HEIGHTS OF MY SCIENTIFIC GREATNESS!!!

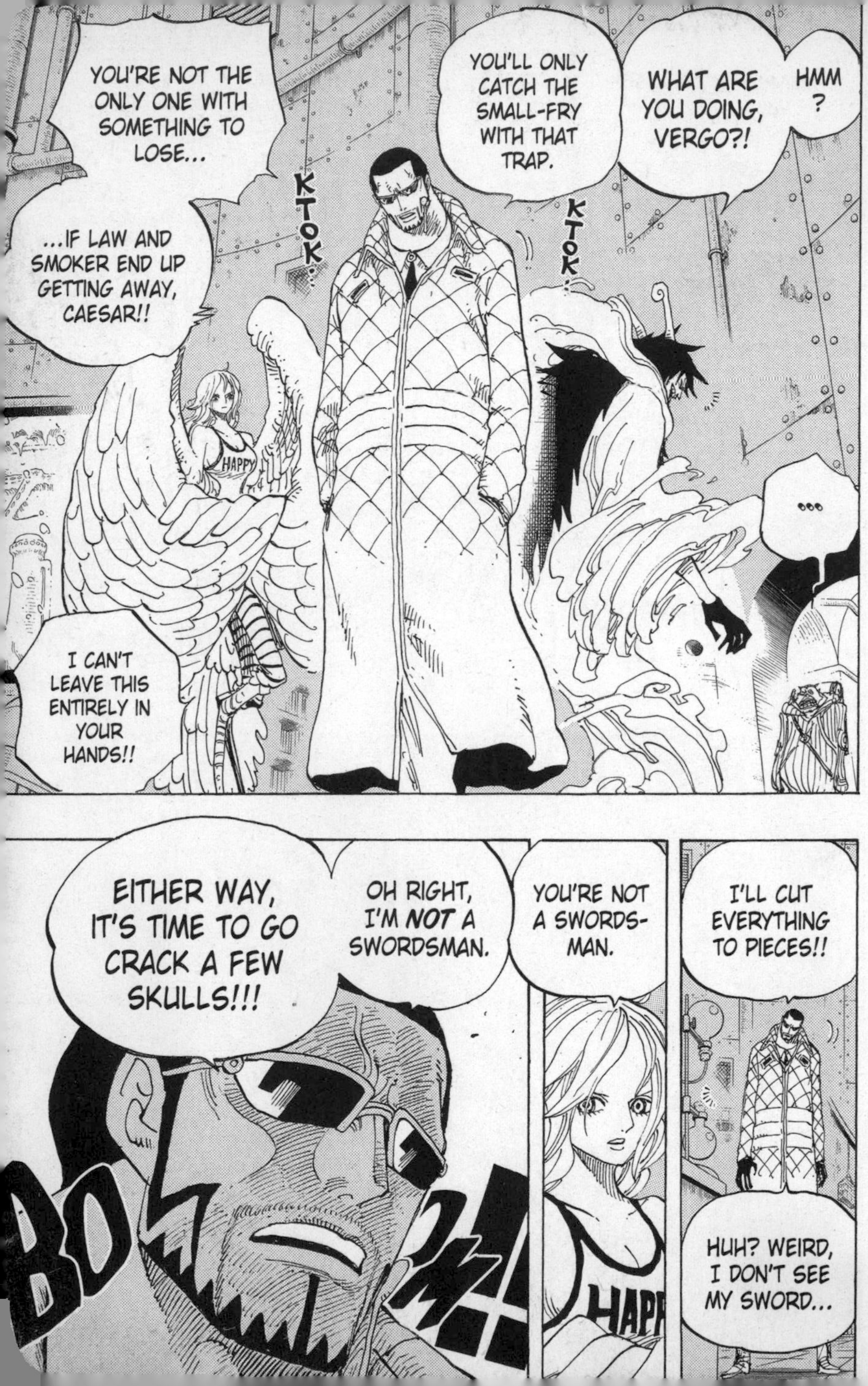
HMM ?
WHAT ARE YOU DOING, VERGO?!
YOU'LL ONLY CATCH THE SMALL-FRY WITH THAT TRAP.
KTOK
KTOK
YOU'RE NOT THE ONLY ONE WITH SOMETHING TO LOSE...
...IF LAW AND SMOKER END UP GETTING AWAY, CAESAR!!
...
I CAN'T LEAVE THIS ENTIRELY IN YOUR HANDS!!
I'LL CUT EVERYTHING TO PIECES!!
HUH? WEIRD, I DON'T SEE MY SWORD...
YOU'RE NOT A SWORDS-MAN.
OH RIGHT, I'M *NOT* A SWORDSMAN.
EITHER WAY, IT'S TIME TO GO CRACK A FEW SKULLS!!!

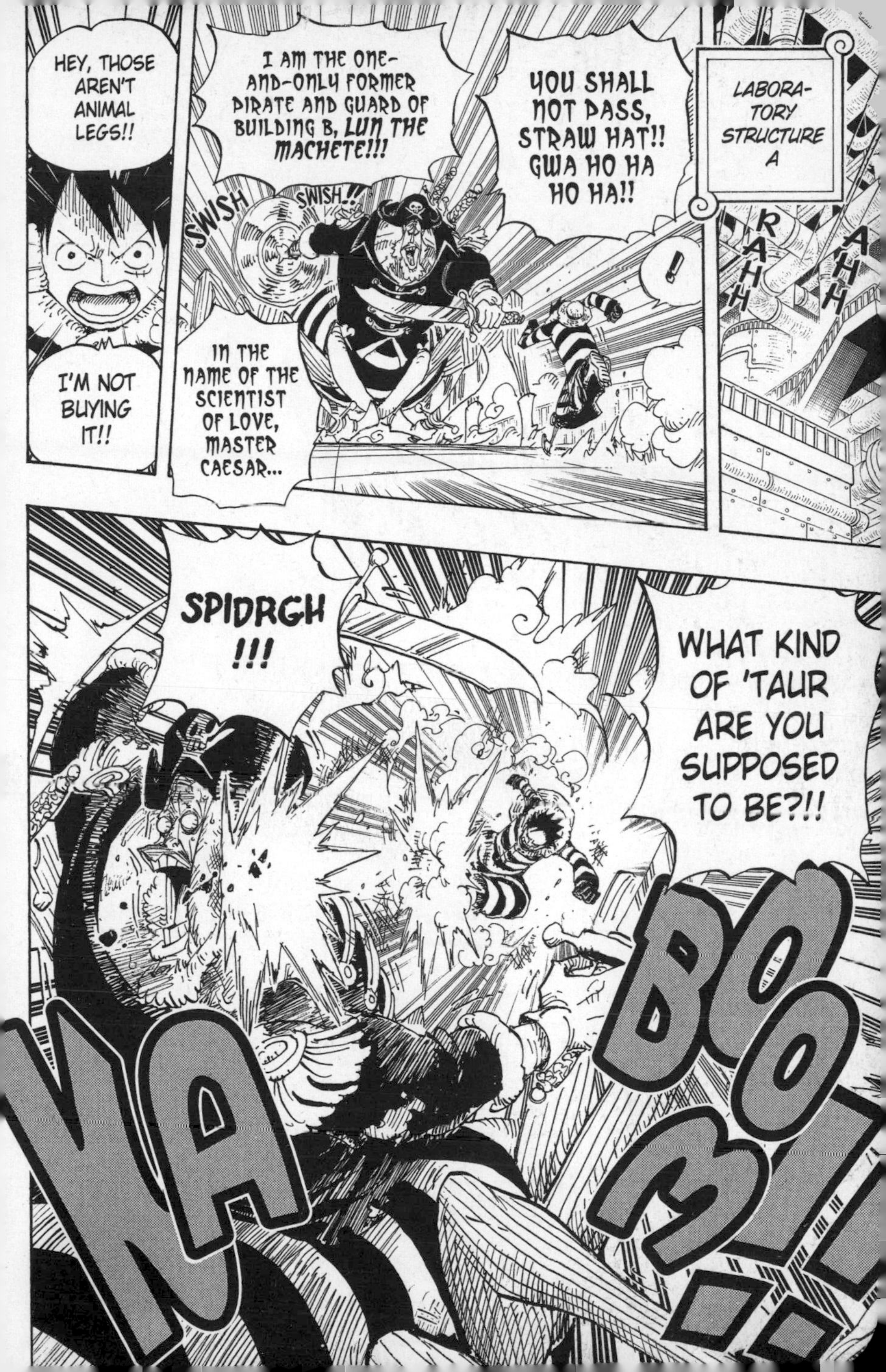
LABORA-TORY STRUCTURE A
RAHH
AHHH
YOU SHALL NOT PASS, STRAW HAT!! GWA HO HA HO HA!!
I AM THE ONE-AND-ONLY FORMER PIRATE AND GUARD OF BUILDING B, *LUN THE MACHETE!!!*
SWISH
SWISH!!
!
IN THE NAME OF THE SCIENTIST OF LOVE, MASTER CAESAR...
HEY, THOSE AREN'T ANIMAL LEGS!!
I'M NOT BUYING IT!!
WHAT KIND OF 'TAUR ARE YOU SUPPOSED TO BE?!!
SPIDRGH!!!
KA BOOM!!

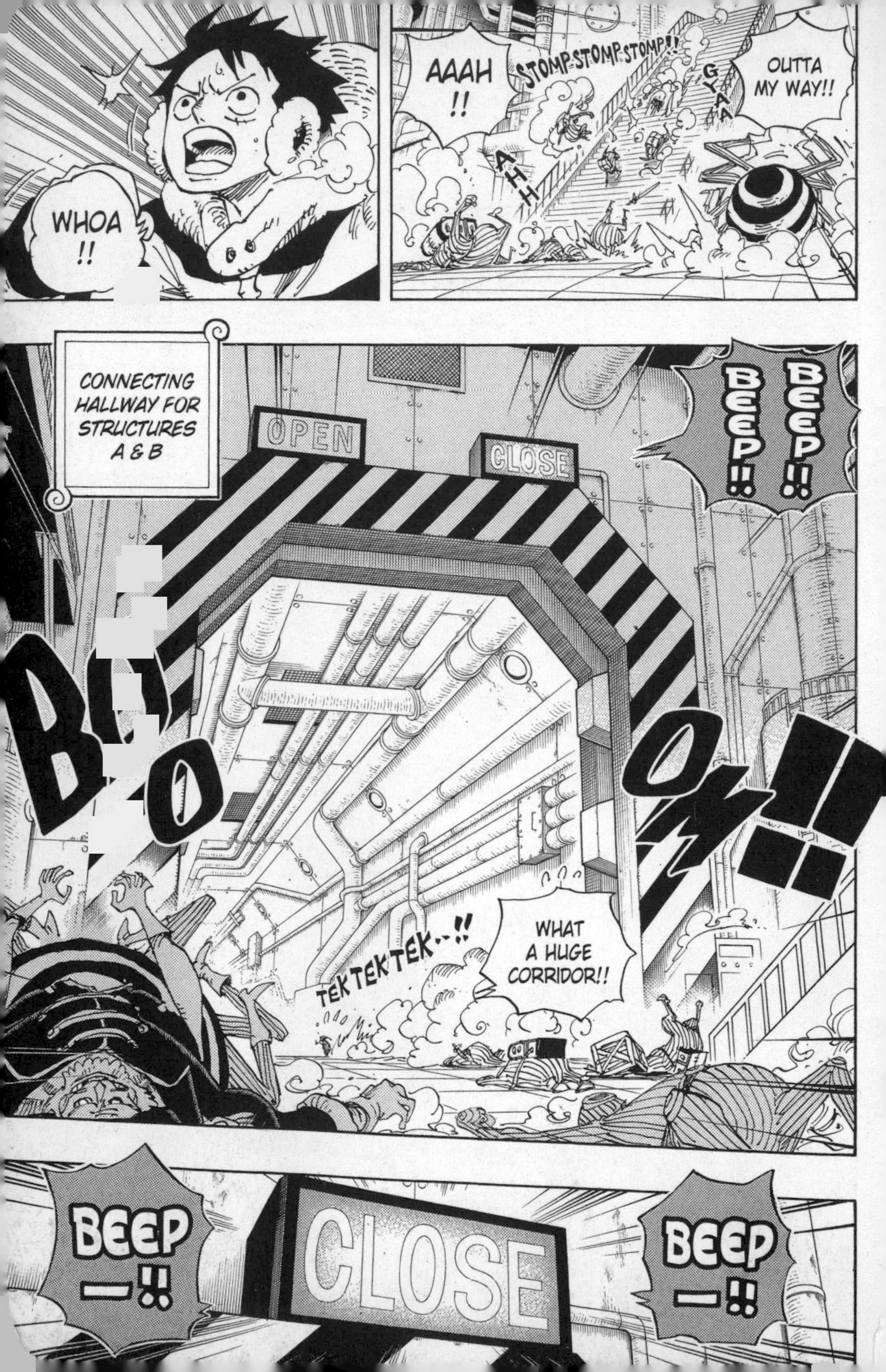
OUTTA MY WAY!!
GYAA
STOMP STOMP STOMP!!
AAAH!!
AHH
WHOA!!
BEEP!!
BEEP!!
CONNECTING HALLWAY FOR STRUCTURES A & B
OPEN
CLOSE
BOOOM!!
WHAT A HUGE CORRIDOR!!
TEKTEKTEK..!!
BEEP—!!
CLOSE
BEEP—!!

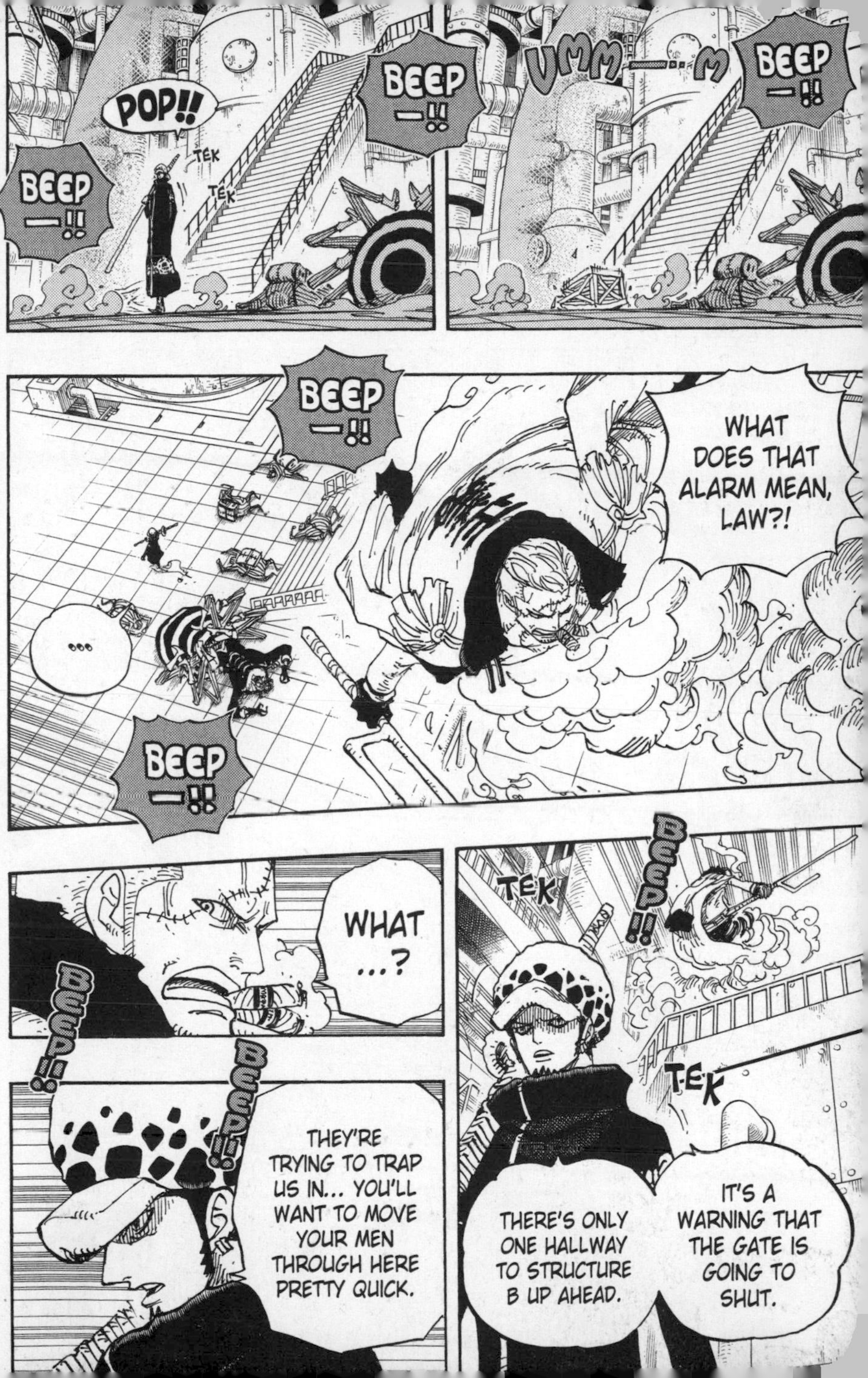
UMM—...M
BEEP —!!
BEEP —!!
POP!!
TEK
TEK
BEEP —!!
WHAT DOES THAT ALARM MEAN, LAW?!
BEEP —!!
...
BEEP —!!
BEEP!!
TEK
TEK
IT'S A WARNING THAT THE GATE IS GOING TO SHUT.
THERE'S ONLY ONE HALLWAY TO STRUCTURE B UP AHEAD.
WHAT ...?
BEEP!!
BEEP!!
THEY'RE TRYING TO TRAP US IN... YOU'LL WANT TO MOVE YOUR MEN THROUGH HERE PRETTY QUICK.

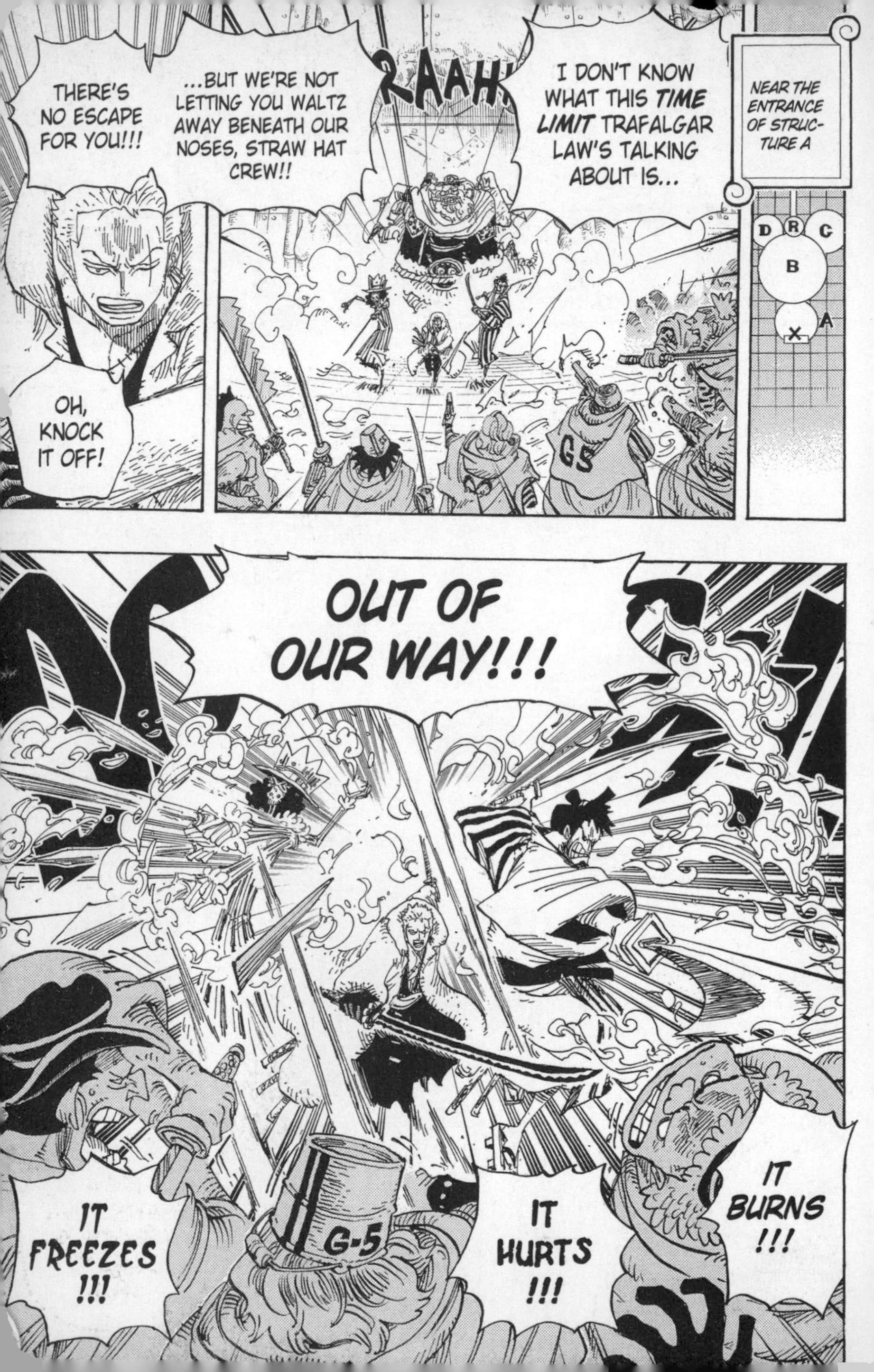
NEAR THE ENTRANCE OF STRUC- TURE A
D
R
C
B
A
I DON'T KNOW WHAT THIS TIME LIMIT TRAFALGAR LAW'S TALKING ABOUT IS...
RAAH!
...BUT WE'RE NOT LETTING YOU WALTZ AWAY BENEATH OUR NOSES, STRAW HAT CREW!!
THERE'S NO ESCAPE FOR YOU!!!
OH, KNOCK IT OFF!
G5
OUT OF OUR WAY!!!
IT BURNS !!!
IT HURTS !!!
G-5
IT FREEZES !!!

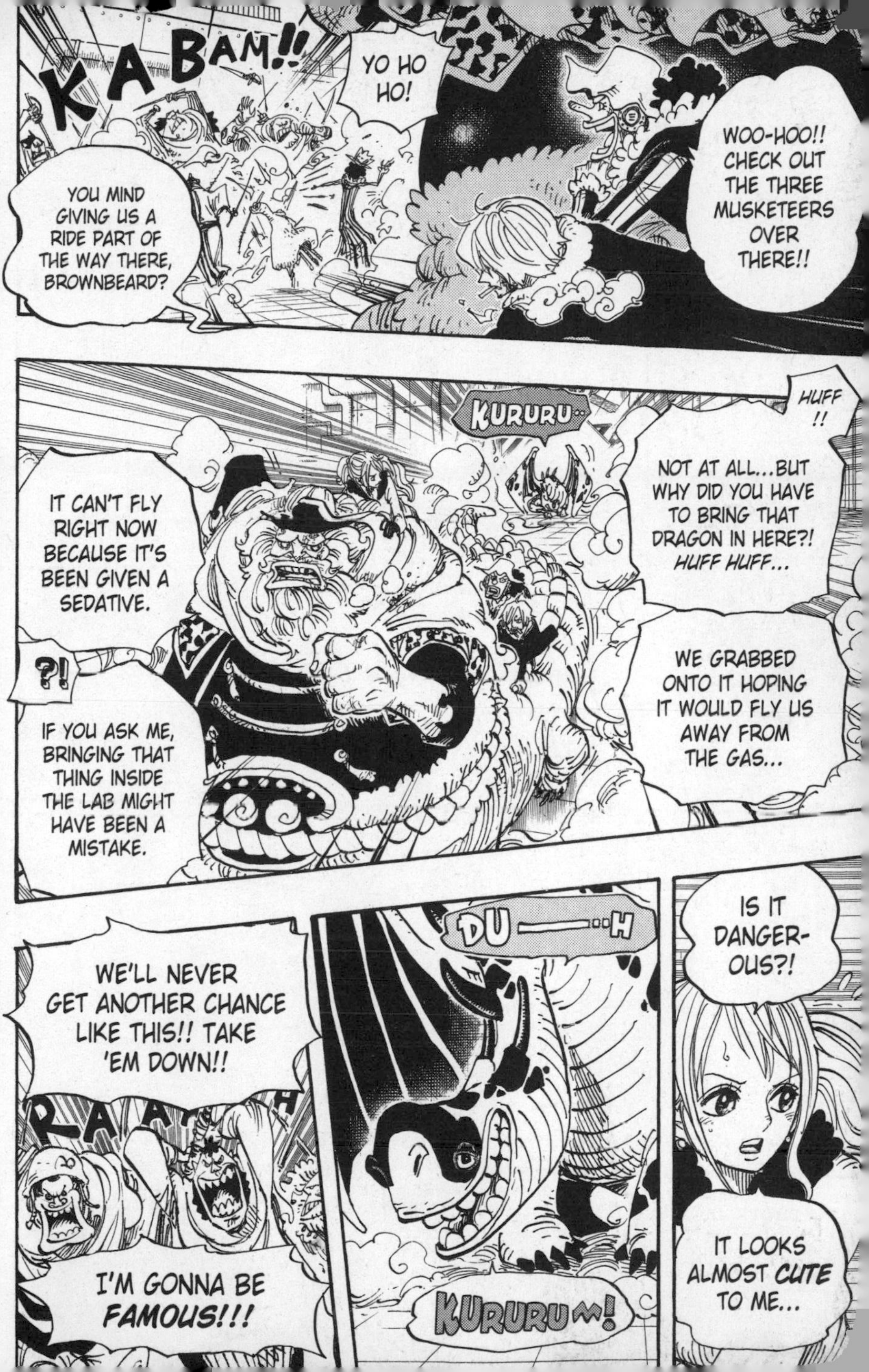
WOO-HOO!! CHECK OUT THE THREE MUSKETEERS OVER THERE!!
YO HO HO!
KABAM!!
YOU MIND GIVING US A RIDE PART OF THE WAY THERE, BROWNBEARD?
HUFF !!
NOT AT ALL...BUT WHY DID YOU HAVE TO BRING THAT DRAGON IN HERE?! *HUFF HUFF...*
KURURU..
IT CAN'T FLY RIGHT NOW BECAUSE IT'S BEEN GIVEN A SEDATIVE.
WE GRABBED ONTO IT HOPING IT WOULD FLY US AWAY FROM THE GAS...
?!
IF YOU ASK ME, BRINGING THAT THING INSIDE THE LAB MIGHT HAVE BEEN A MISTAKE.
IS IT DANGER-OUS?!
IT LOOKS ALMOST *CUTE* TO ME...
DU——H
KURURU~!
WE'LL NEVER GET ANOTHER CHANCE LIKE THIS!! TAKE 'EM DOWN!!
RAAAH
I'M GONNA BE *FAMOUS!!!*

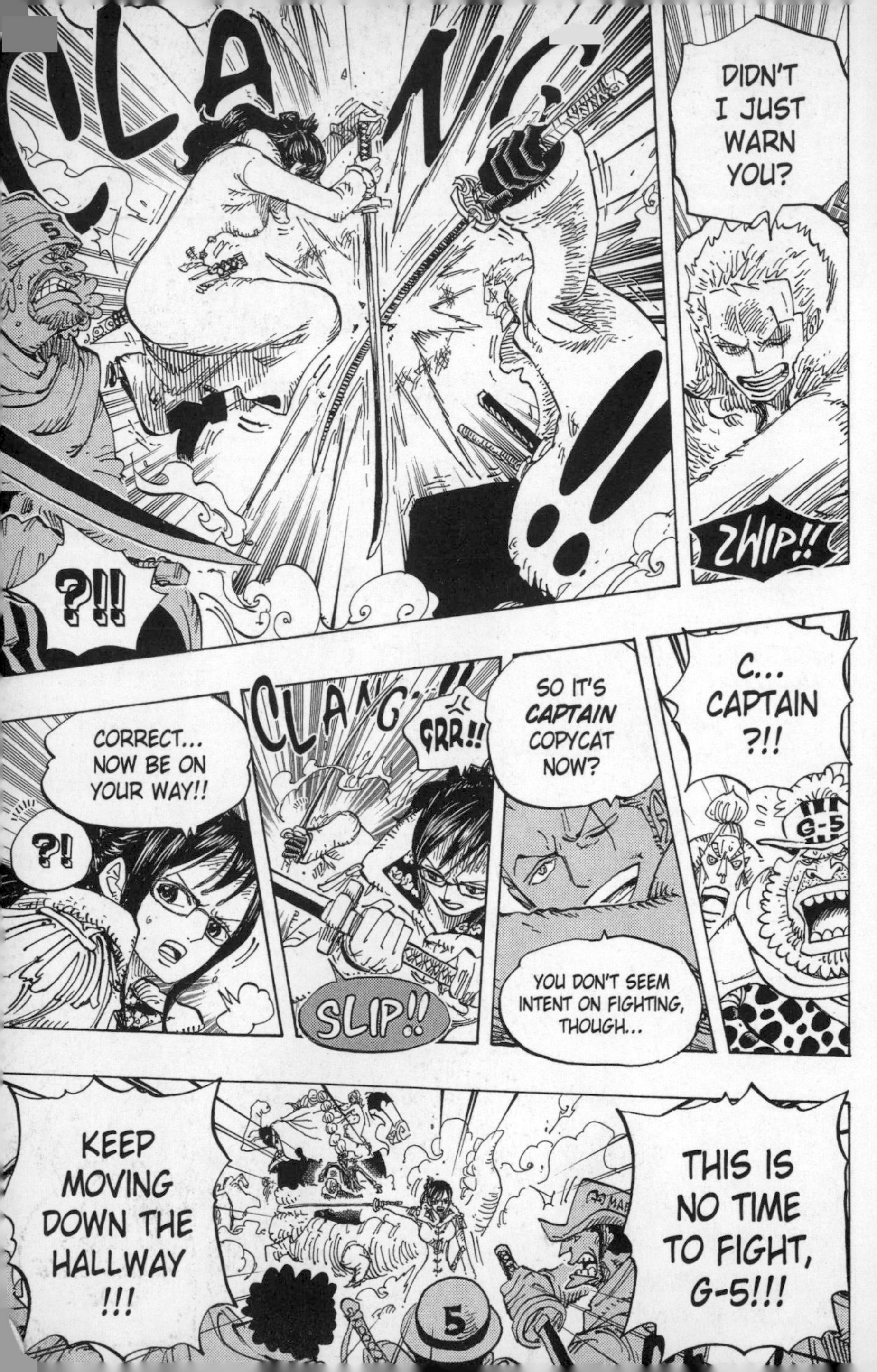
DIDN'T I JUST WARN YOU?
ZWIP!!
?!!
C... CAPTAIN ?!!
SO IT'S *CAPTAIN* COPYCAT NOW?
YOU DON'T SEEM INTENT ON FIGHTING, THOUGH...
GRR!!
SLIP!!
CORRECT... NOW BE ON YOUR WAY!!
?!
THIS IS NO TIME TO FIGHT, G-5!!!
KEEP MOVING DOWN THE HALLWAY!!!

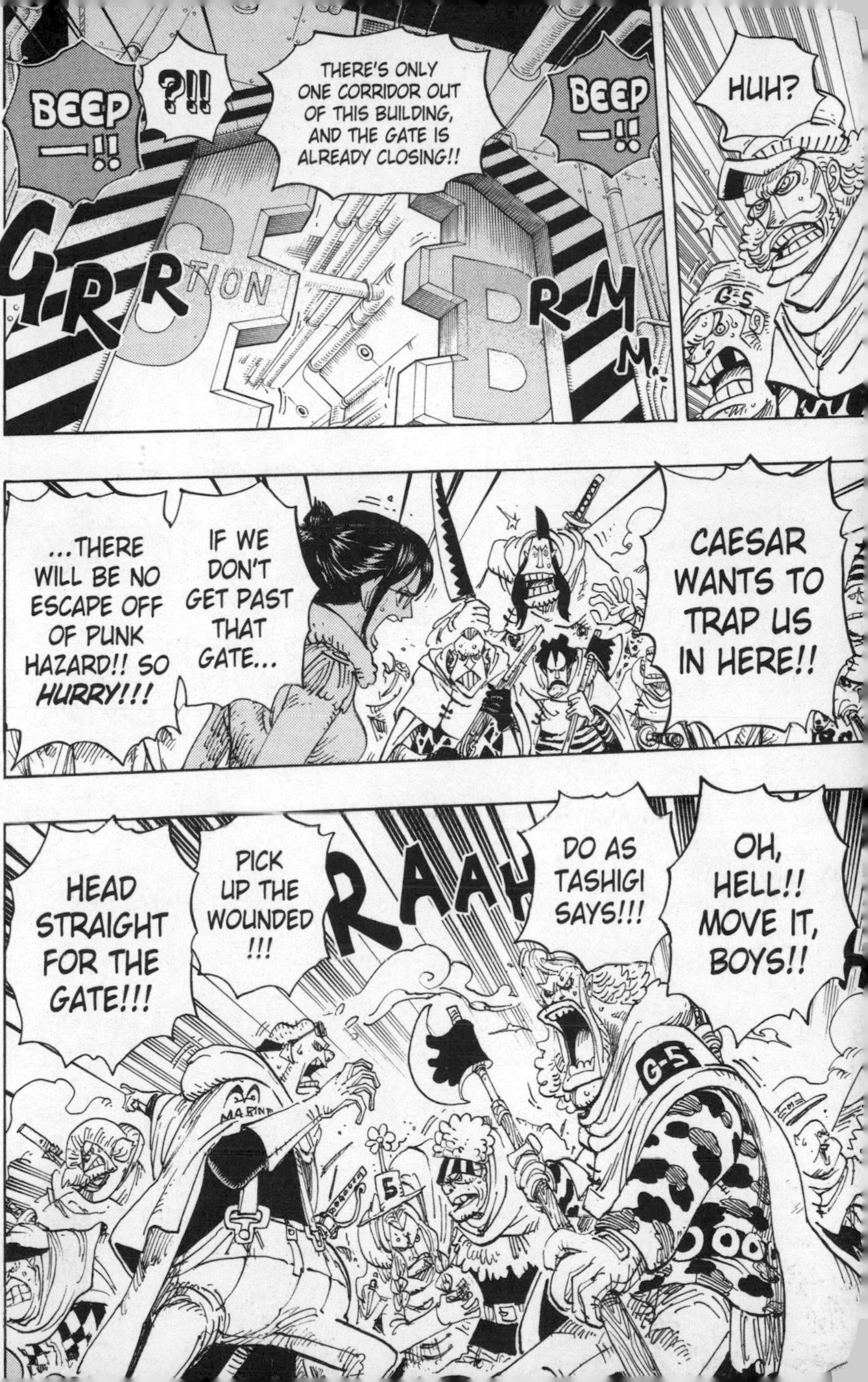
HUH?
BEEP—!!
THERE'S ONLY ONE CORRIDOR OUT OF THIS BUILDING, AND THE GATE IS ALREADY CLOSING!!
?!!
BEEP—!!
G-R-R-R
R-M-M-M.
CAESAR WANTS TO TRAP US IN HERE!!
IF WE DON'T GET PAST THAT GATE...
...THERE WILL BE NO ESCAPE OFF OF PUNK HAZARD!! SO *HURRY*!!!
OH, HELL!! MOVE IT, BOYS!!
DO AS TASHIGI SAYS!!!
RAAH
PICK UP THE WOUNDED!!!
HEAD STRAIGHT FOR THE GATE!!!

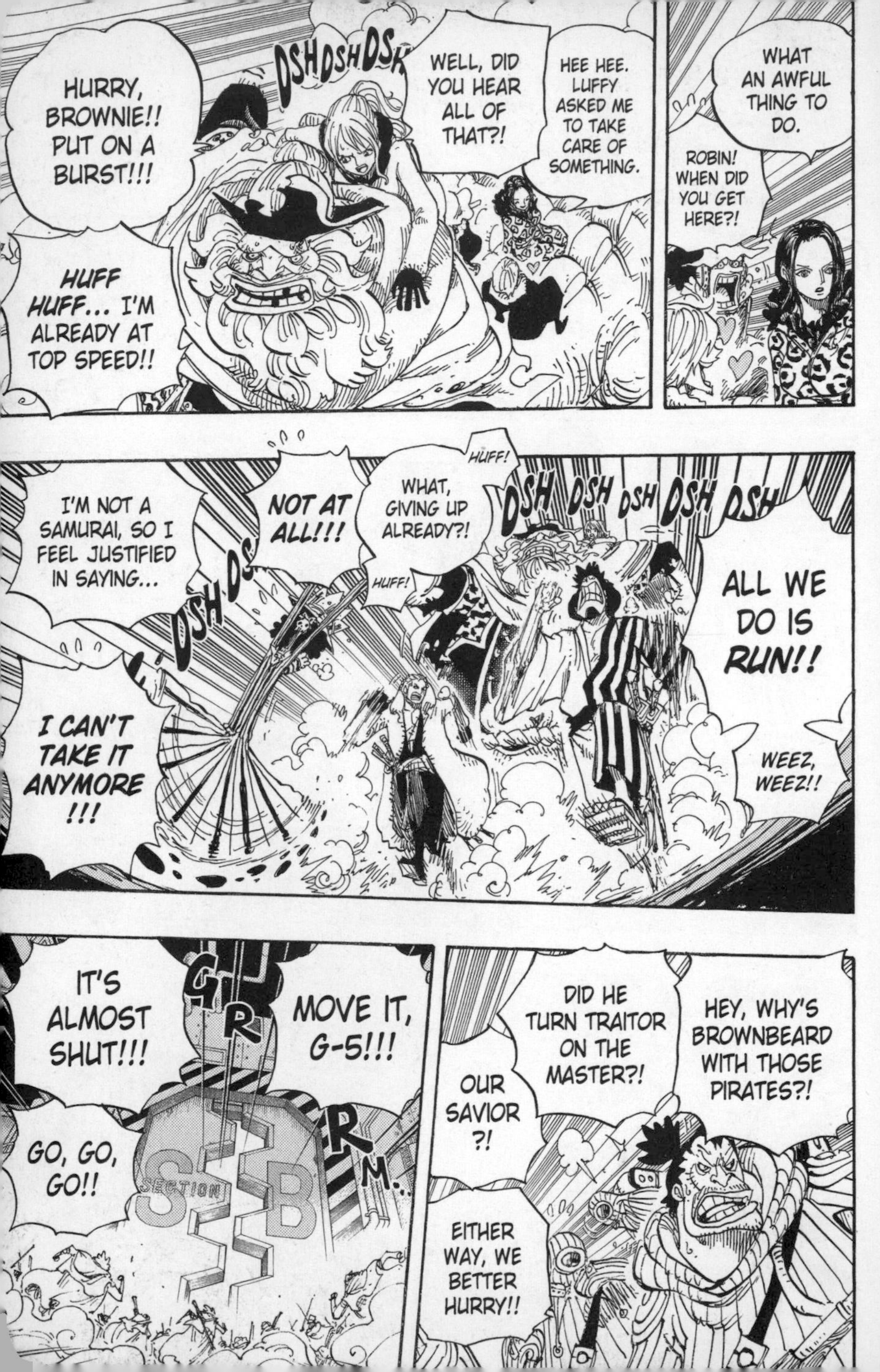
WHAT AN AWFUL THING TO DO.
ROBIN! WHEN DID YOU GET HERE?!
HEE HEE. LUFFY ASKED ME TO TAKE CARE OF SOMETHING.
WELL, DID YOU HEAR ALL OF THAT?!
DSHDSHDSH
HURRY, BROWNIE!! PUT ON A BURST!!!
HUFF HUFF... I'M ALREADY AT TOP SPEED!!
ALL WE DO IS RUN!!
WEEZ, WEEZ!!
DSH DSH DSH DSH DSH
HUFF!
WHAT, GIVING UP ALREADY?!
HUFF!
NOT AT ALL!!!
I'M NOT A SAMURAI, SO I FEEL JUSTIFIED IN SAYING...
DSH DSH
I CAN'T TAKE IT ANYMORE!!!
HEY, WHY'S BROWNBEARD WITH THOSE PIRATES?!
DID HE TURN TRAITOR ON THE MASTER?!
OUR SAVIOR?!
EITHER WAY, WE BETTER HURRY!!
MOVE IT, G-5!!!
IT'S ALMOST SHUT!!!
GRRRM..
GO, GO, GO!!
SECTION S-B

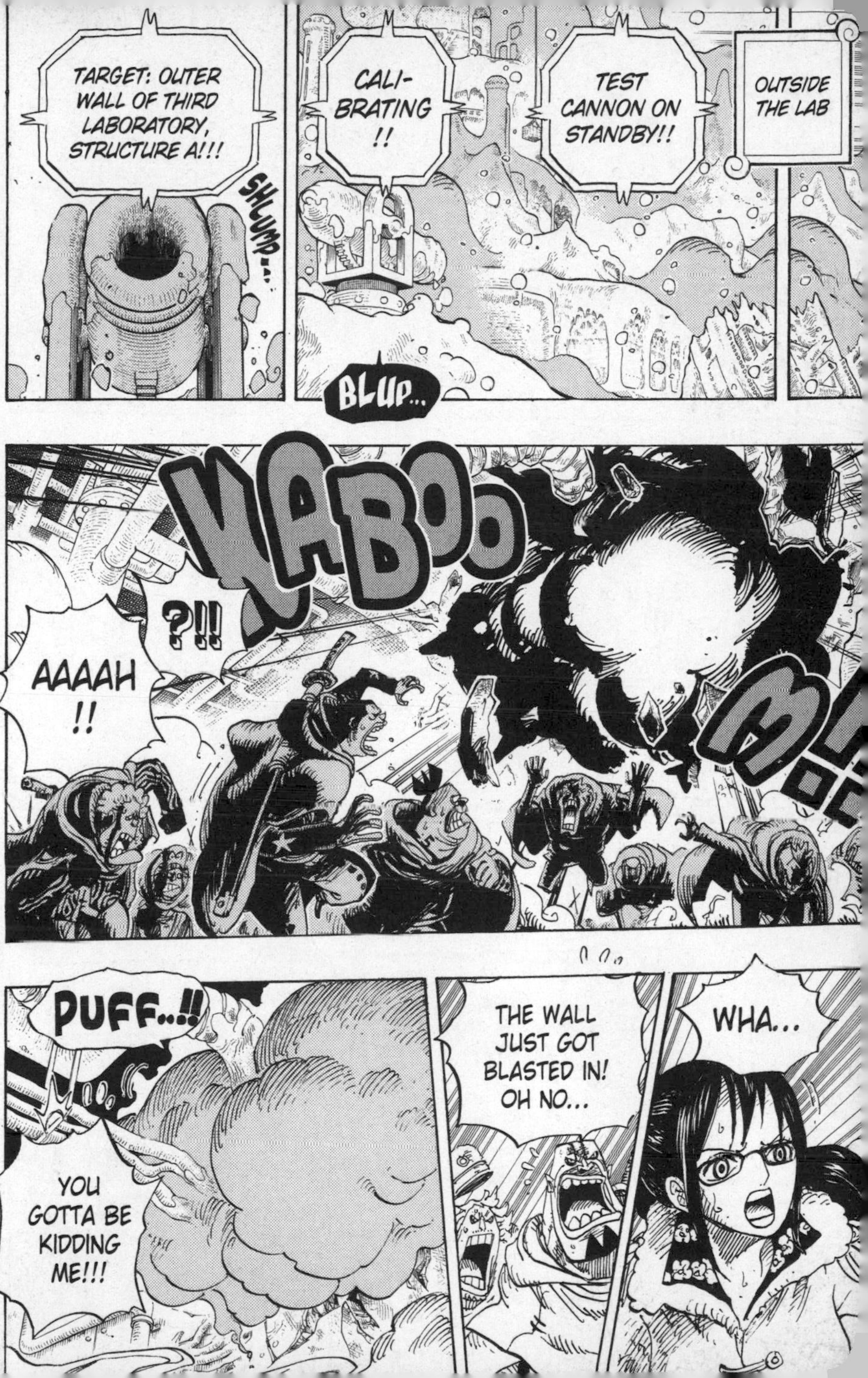
OUTSIDE THE LAB
TEST CANNON ON STANDBY!!
CALI-BRATING !!
TARGET: OUTER WALL OF THIRD LABORATORY, STRUCTURE A!!!
SHLUMP...
BLUP...
KABOOM!!
?!!
AAAAH !!
WHA...
THE WALL JUST GOT BLASTED IN! OH NO...
PUFF..!!
YOU GOTTA BE KIDDING ME!!!

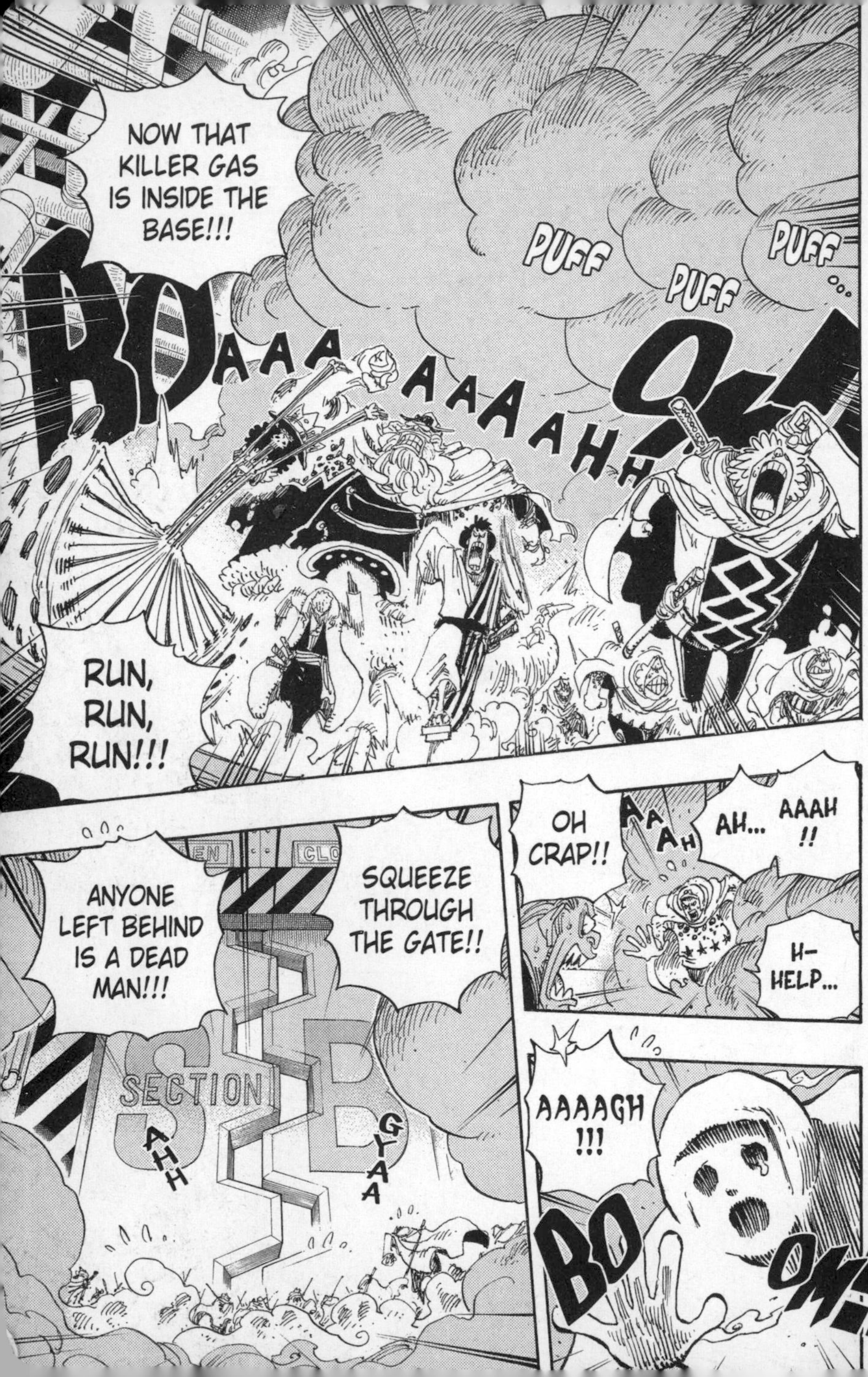
PUFF
PUFF
PUFF
NOW THAT KILLER GAS IS INSIDE THE BASE!!!
BO
AAAAAAAAHH
OM
RUN, RUN, RUN!!!
AAAH !!
AH...
AAAH
OH CRAP!!
H-HELP...
AAAAGH !!!
BO
OM!!
SQUEEZE THROUGH THE GATE!!
ANYONE LEFT BEHIND IS A DEAD MAN!!!
SECTION
GYAA
AHH

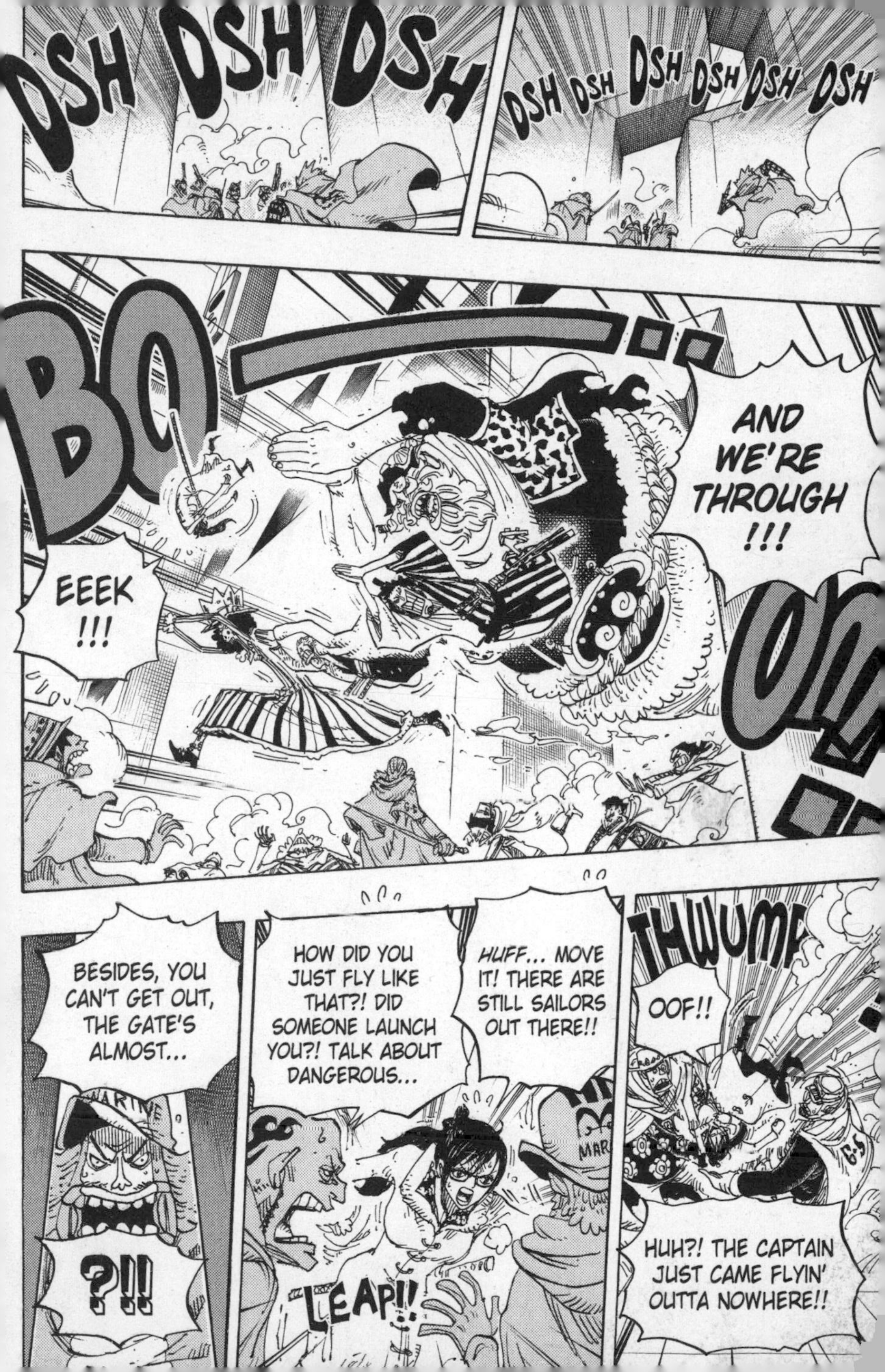
DSH DSH DSH DSH DSH DSH
DSH DSH DSH
AND WE'RE THROUGH !!!
BO
EEEK !!!
THWUMP
OOF!!
HUH?! THE CAPTAIN JUST CAME FLYIN' OUTTA NOWHERE!!
HUFF... MOVE IT! THERE ARE STILL SAILORS OUT THERE!!
HOW DID YOU JUST FLY LIKE THAT?! DID SOMEONE LAUNCH YOU?! TALK ABOUT DANGEROUS...
LEAP!!
BESIDES, YOU CAN'T GET OUT, THE GATE'S ALMOST...
?!!

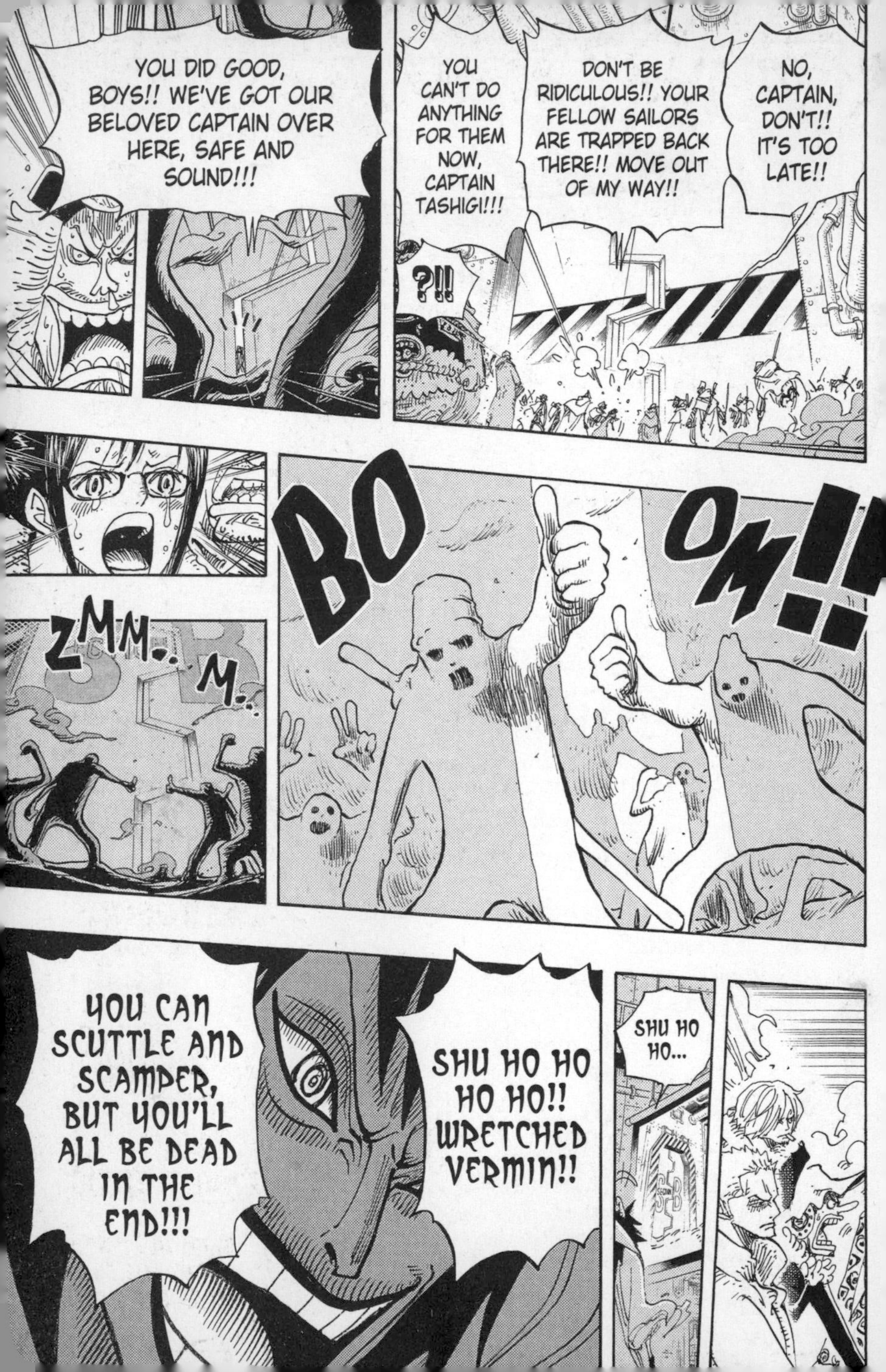
NO, CAPTAIN, DON'T!! IT'S TOO LATE!!
DON'T BE RIDICULOUS!! YOUR FELLOW SAILORS ARE TRAPPED BACK THERE!! MOVE OUT OF MY WAY!!
YOU CAN'T DO ANYTHING FOR THEM NOW, CAPTAIN TASHIGI!!!
?!!
YOU DID GOOD, BOYS!! WE'VE GOT OUR BELOVED CAPTAIN OVER HERE, SAFE AND SOUND!!!
BOOM!!!
ZMM..M..
SHU HO HO...
SHU HO HO HO HO!! WRETCHED VERMIN!!
YOU CAN SCUTTLE AND SCAMPER, BUT YOU'LL ALL BE DEAD IN THE END!!!

ヒゲから!?
エス
ビー
エス

(Haru, Nagano)

Q: Before we begin the SBS Corner, I, Eiichiro Oda, have an announcement to make. Finally, at long last, I have eaten the Perv-Perv Fruit! Gwehhehheh.

--I'm Green Peas

A: Stop trying to frame me!! "Gwehhehheh"? I sound like such a pig!

Q: Odacchi!! Can I ask a serious question? A really serious one? Are you sure? You don't mind? Here goes, then.

Do you like breast-bands?

--Chii-chan☆

OH DEAR.
NOT YOUR FAVORITE?
ON THE CONTRARY, I LOVE IT!!!

A: I love it!♡ Gwehhehheh.♡ Daah! Not again! Forget that! What sort of trap was that?! No, I just wear breast-bands like a normal person. Oh, right... Forgot to mention, the SBS is starting.

Q: Is Usopp's nose made of *chikuwa* fish sausage? Let's ask Usopp!!

--Howaichi

A: I don't think so. It's not chikuwa, right, Usopp?

Usopp: It's chikuwa.

A: It is?!! (Fifteen years, and I had no idea) Gwehhehheh.♡

Ⓐ
Ⓑ
Ⓒ

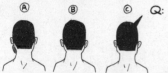

Q: Here's a quiz! Identify that silhouette! Which one is Vergo?
* Included among the others are Bon Clay and Lulu.

--N.I.K.U.

A: I've got the answer!
(A) Vergo with hamburger patty stuck to his face!
(B) Vergo after he ate the patty!
(C) Vergo with a shuriken stuck in his head!

Q: The answer is (A). B is Bon Clay, C is Lulu.

Chapter 680:
G-5 COMMANDER VERGO THE BAMBOO DEMON

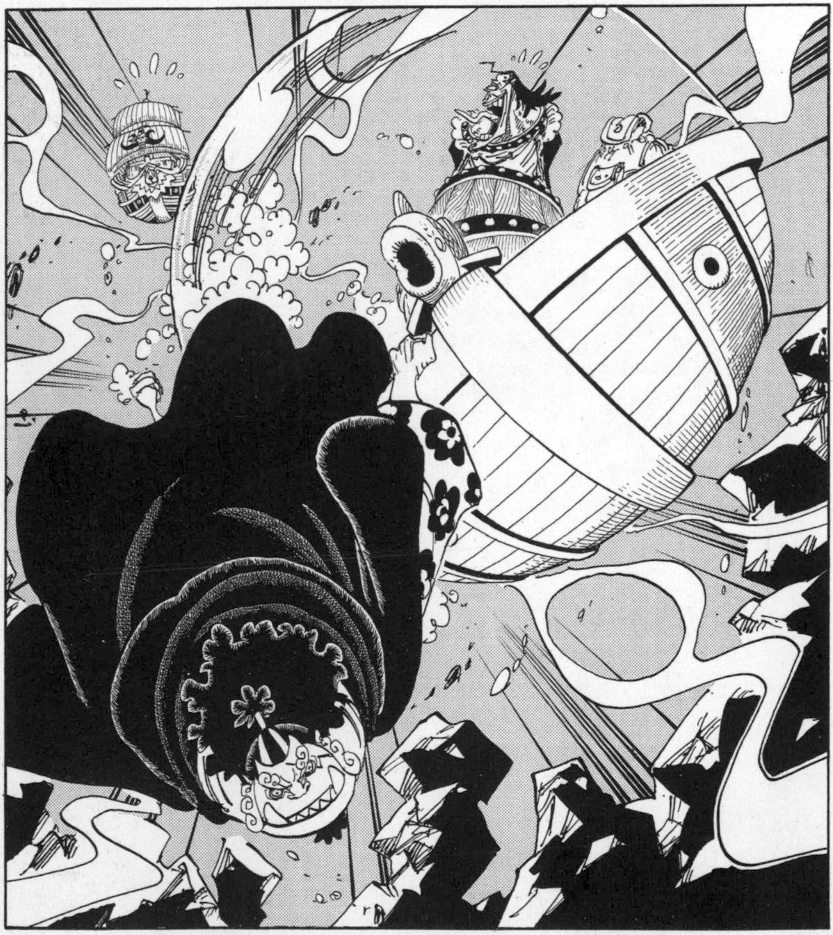

CARIBOU'S NEW WORLD KEE HEE HEE, VOL. 6:
"ACROSS THE SEA AT FISH-MAN SPEED!!"

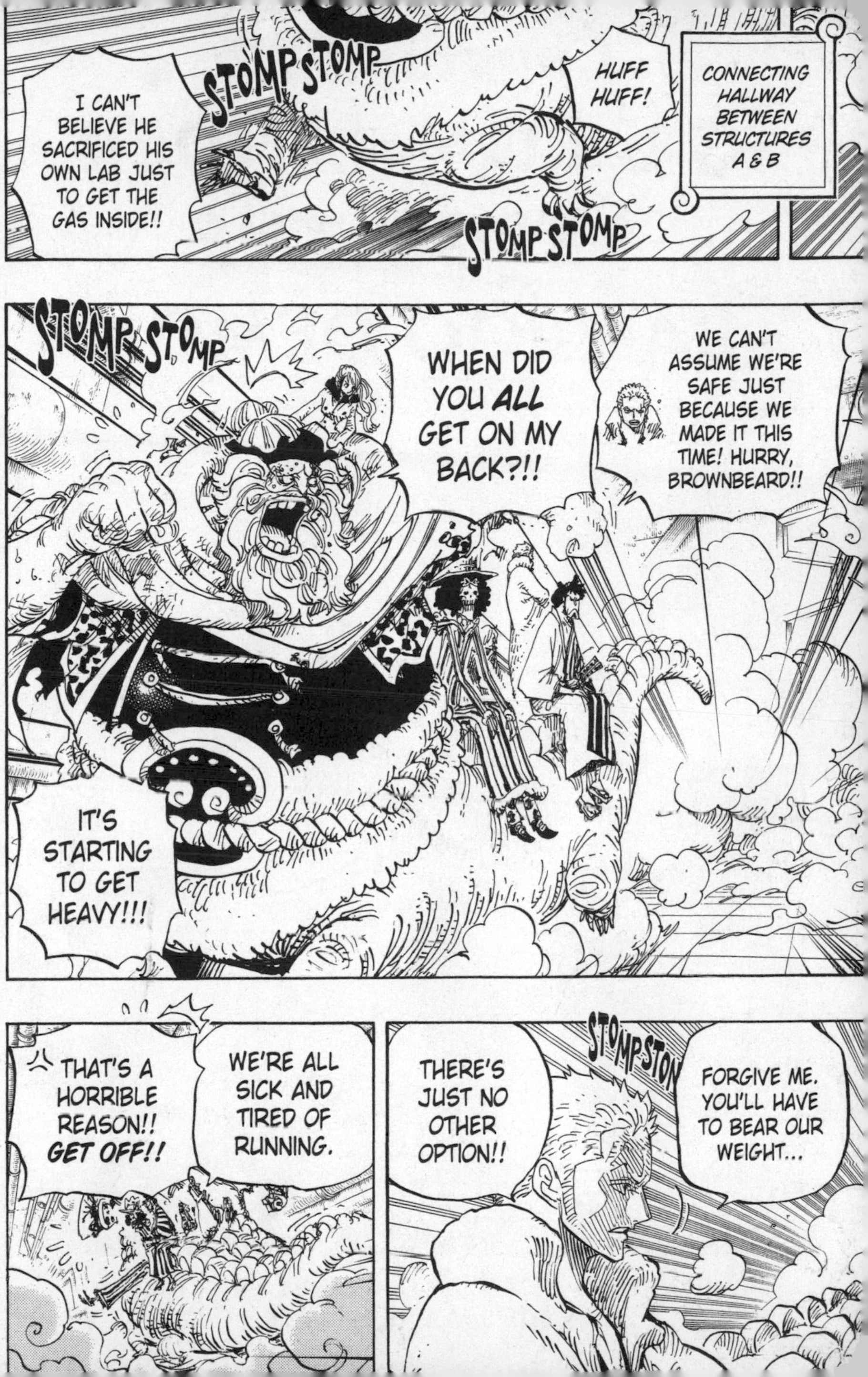
CONNECTING HALLWAY BETWEEN STRUCTURES A & B
HUFF HUFF!
STOMP STOMP
I CAN'T BELIEVE HE SACRIFICED HIS OWN LAB JUST TO GET THE GAS INSIDE!!
STOMP STOMP
WE CAN'T ASSUME WE'RE SAFE JUST BECAUSE WE MADE IT THIS TIME! HURRY, BROWNBEARD!!
WHEN DID YOU ***ALL*** GET ON MY BACK?!!
STOMP STOMP
IT'S STARTING TO GET HEAVY!!!
FORGIVE ME. YOU'LL HAVE TO BEAR OUR WEIGHT...
STOMP STOM
THERE'S JUST NO OTHER OPTION!!
WE'RE ALL SICK AND TIRED OF RUNNING.
THAT'S A HORRIBLE REASON!! ***GET OFF!!***

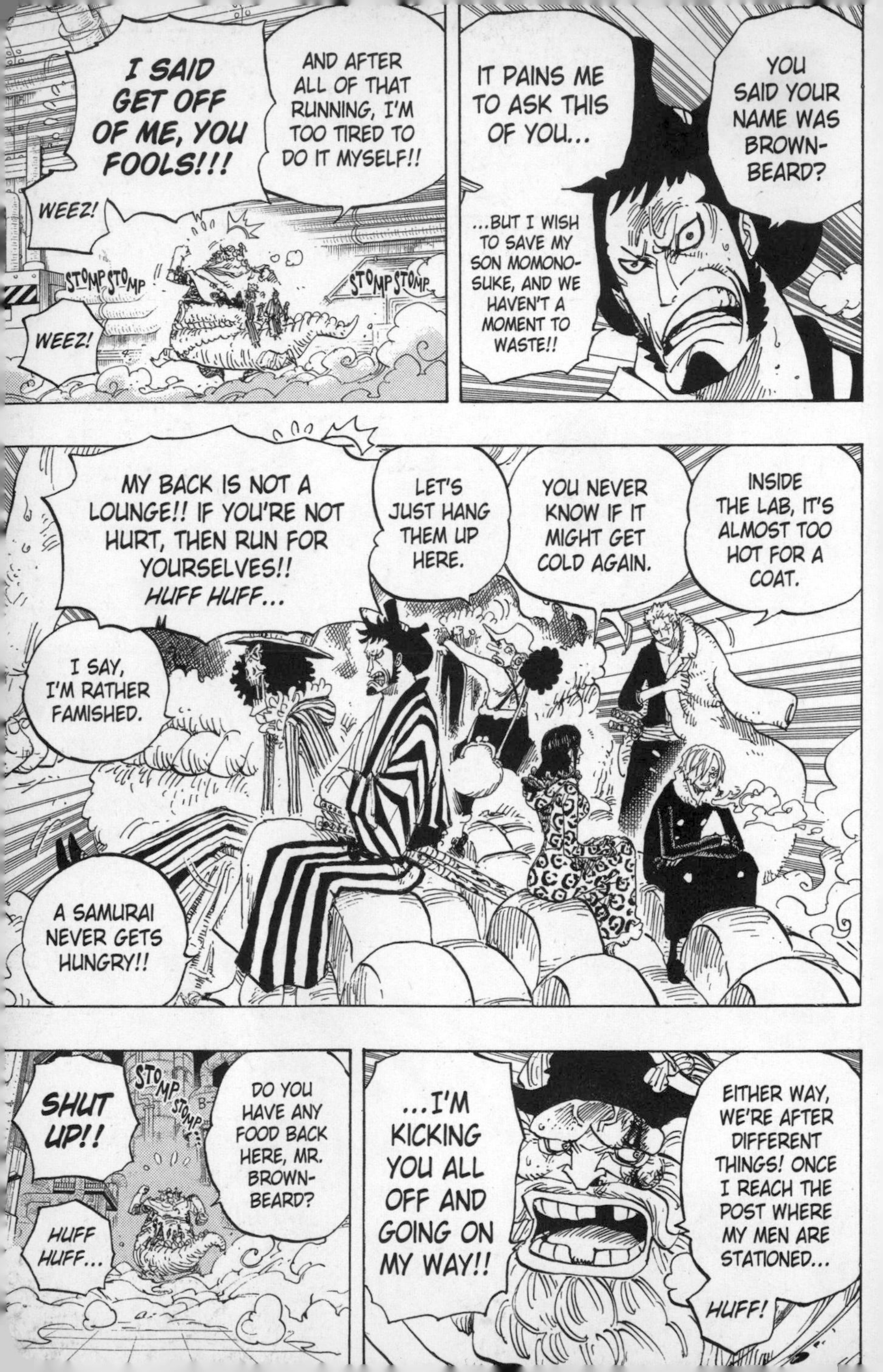
YOU SAID YOUR NAME WAS BROWN-BEARD?
IT PAINS ME TO ASK THIS OF YOU...
...BUT I WISH TO SAVE MY SON MOMONO-SUKE, AND WE HAVEN'T A MOMENT TO WASTE!!
AND AFTER ALL OF THAT RUNNING, I'M TOO TIRED TO DO IT MYSELF!!
I SAID GET OFF OF ME, YOU FOOLS!!!
WEEZ!
STOMP STOMP
STOMP STOMP
WEEZ!
INSIDE THE LAB, IT'S ALMOST TOO HOT FOR A COAT.
YOU NEVER KNOW IF IT MIGHT GET COLD AGAIN.
LET'S JUST HANG THEM UP HERE.
MY BACK IS NOT A LOUNGE!! IF YOU'RE NOT HURT, THEN RUN FOR YOURSELVES!! HUFF HUFF...
I SAY, I'M RATHER FAMISHED.
A SAMURAI NEVER GETS HUNGRY!!
EITHER WAY, WE'RE AFTER DIFFERENT THINGS! ONCE I REACH THE POST WHERE MY MEN ARE STATIONED...
HUFF!
...I'M KICKING YOU ALL OFF AND GOING ON MY WAY!!
DO YOU HAVE ANY FOOD BACK HERE, MR. BROWN-BEARD?
STOMP STOMP
SHUT UP!!
HUFF HUFF...

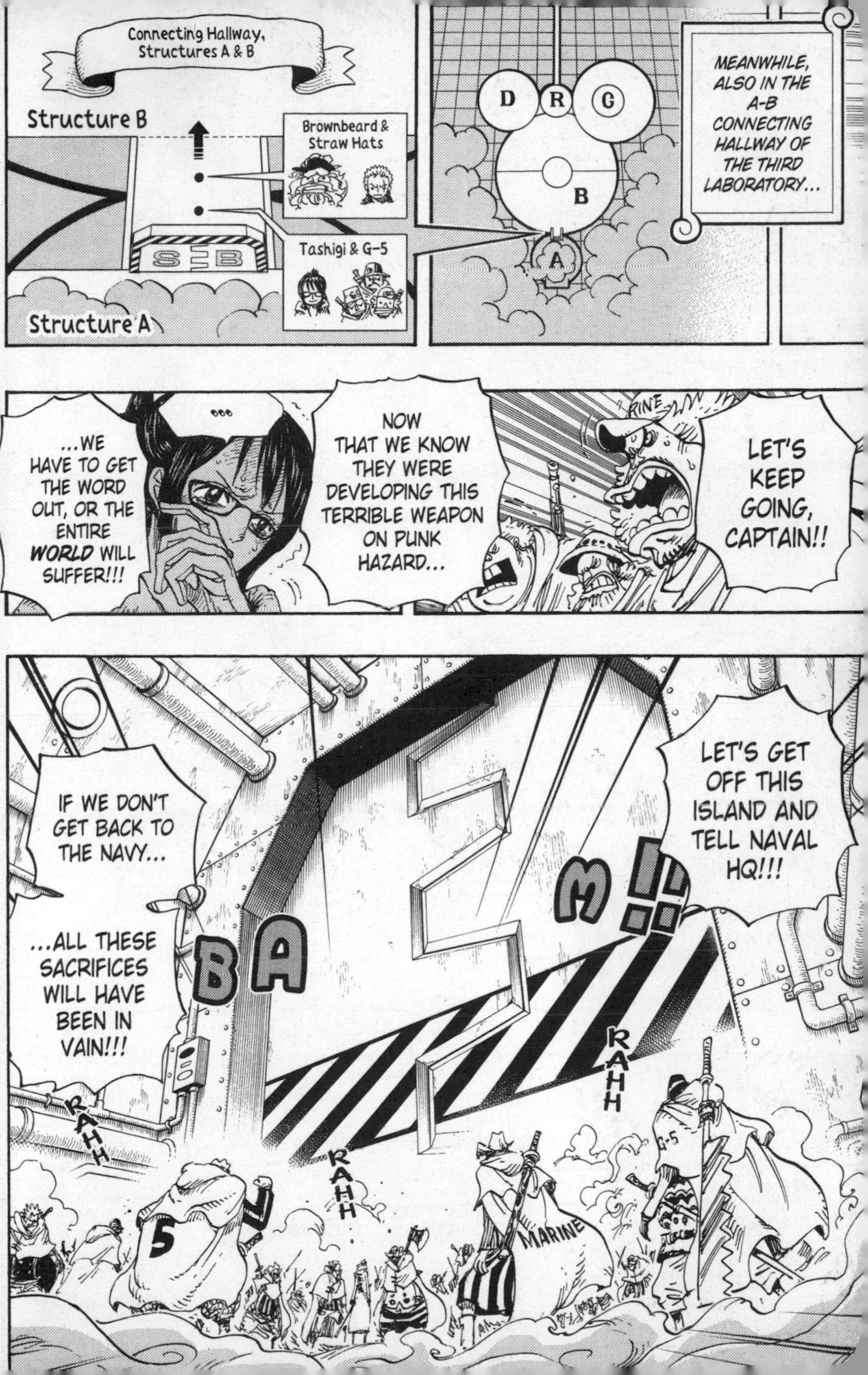
MEANWHILE, ALSO IN THE A-B CONNECTING HALLWAY OF THE THIRD LABORATORY...
D
R
C
B
A
Connecting Hallway, Structures A & B
Structure B
Brownbeard & Straw Hats
Tashigi & G-5
S B
Structure A
LET'S KEEP GOING, CAPTAIN!!
NOW THAT WE KNOW THEY WERE DEVELOPING THIS TERRIBLE WEAPON ON PUNK HAZARD...
...WE HAVE TO GET THE WORD OUT, OR THE ENTIRE *WORLD* WILL SUFFER!!!
LET'S GET OFF THIS ISLAND AND TELL NAVAL HQ!!!
IF WE DON'T GET BACK TO THE NAVY...
...ALL THESE SACRIFICES WILL HAVE BEEN IN VAIN!!!
BAM!!
RAHH
RAHH
RAHH
G-5
5
MARINE

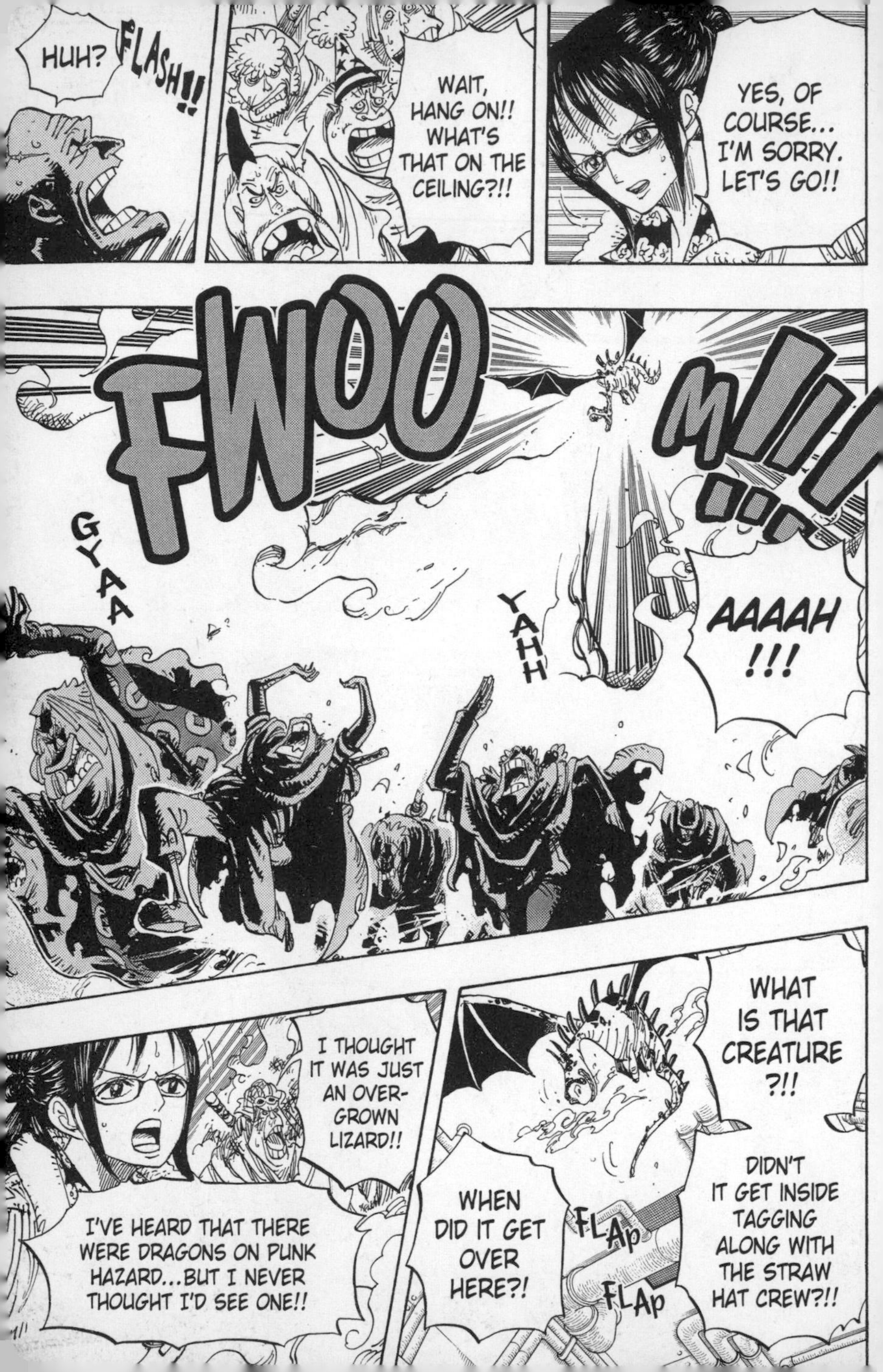
YES, OF COURSE... I'M SORRY. LET'S GO!!
WAIT, HANG ON!! WHAT'S THAT ON THE CEILING?!!
HUH?
FLASH!!
FWOOM!!!
AAAAH!!!
YAHHH
GYAA
WHAT IS THAT CREATURE?!!
DIDN'T IT GET INSIDE TAGGING ALONG WITH THE STRAW HAT CREW?!!
FLAp
FLAp
WHEN DID IT GET OVER HERE?!
I THOUGHT IT WAS JUST AN OVER-GROWN LIZARD!!
I'VE HEARD THAT THERE WERE DRAGONS ON PUNK HAZARD...BUT I NEVER THOUGHT I'D SEE ONE!!

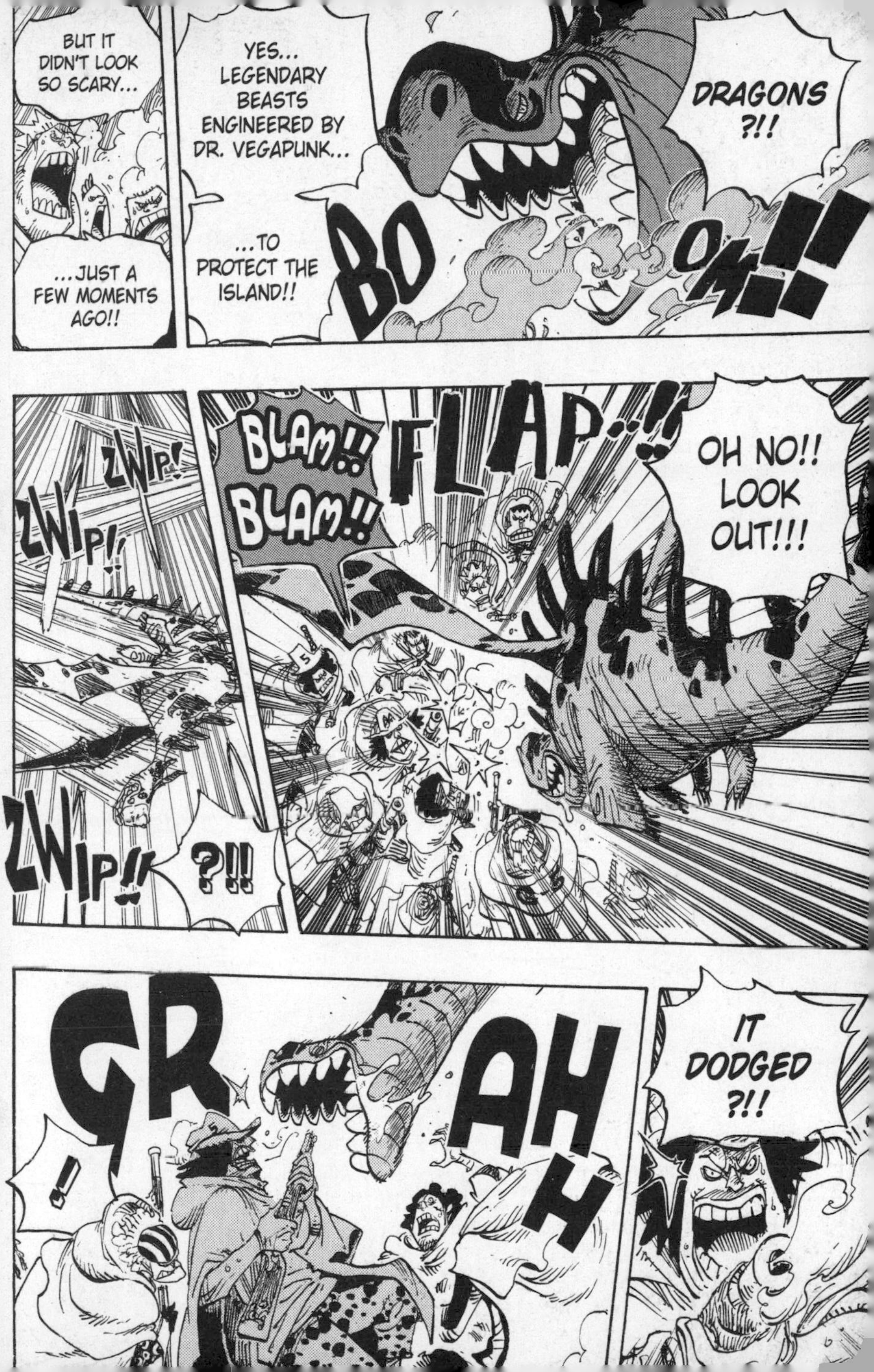
DRAGONS ?!!
BOOM!!
YES... LEGENDARY BEASTS ENGINEERED BY DR. VEGAPUNK...
...TO PROTECT THE ISLAND!!
BUT IT DIDN'T LOOK SO SCARY...
...JUST A FEW MOMENTS AGO!!
OH NO!! LOOK OUT!!!
FLAP!!
BLAM!! BLAM!!
ZWIP!
ZWIP!!
ZWIP!!
?!!
IT DODGED ?!!
GRAHH
!

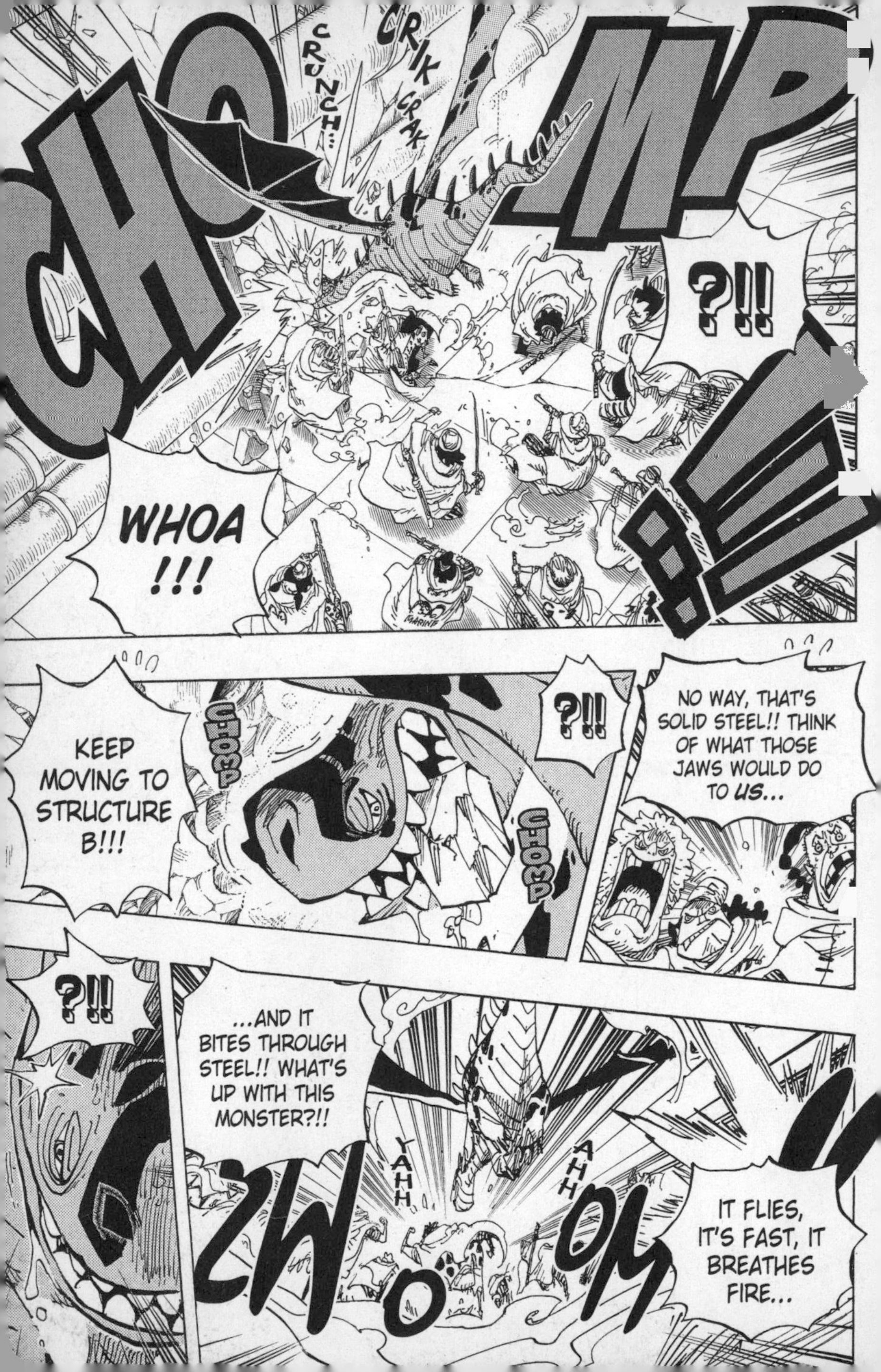
CHOMP!!
CRIK CRAK
CRUNCH...
?!!
WHOA !!!
NO WAY, THAT'S SOLID STEEL!! THINK OF WHAT THOSE JAWS WOULD DO TO US...
?!!
CHOMP
CHOMP
KEEP MOVING TO STRUCTURE B!!!
IT FLIES, IT'S FAST, IT BREATHES FIRE...
AHH
YAHH
ZHOOOM
...AND IT BITES THROUGH STEEL!! WHAT'S UP WITH THIS MONSTER?!!
?!!

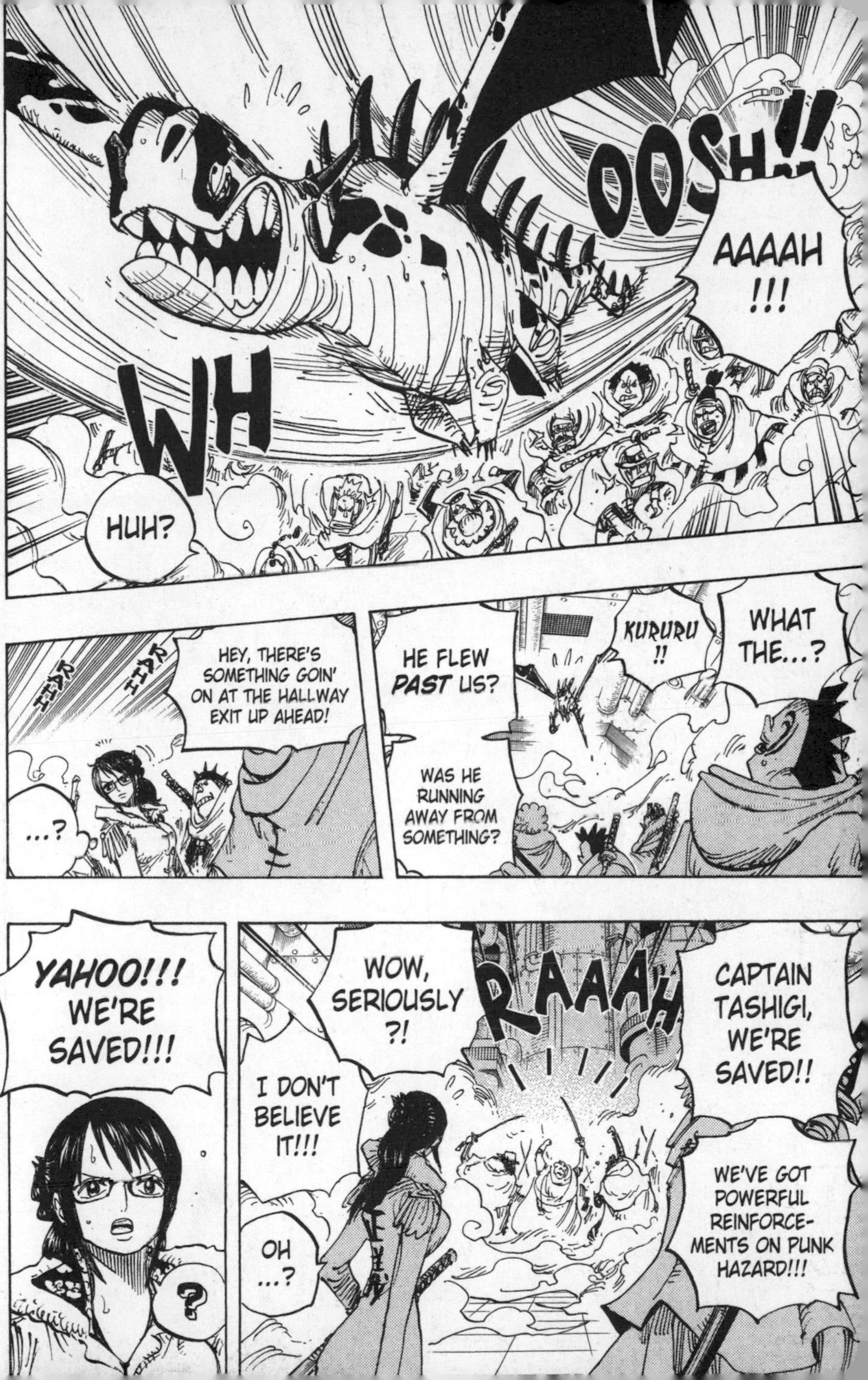
WHOOSH!!
AAAAH!!!
HUH?
WHAT THE...?
KURURU!!
HE FLEW *PAST* US?
WAS HE RUNNING AWAY FROM SOMETHING?
HEY, THERE'S SOMETHING GOIN' ON AT THE HALLWAY EXIT UP AHEAD!
RAHH RAHH
...?
CAPTAIN TASHIGI, WE'RE SAVED!!
RAAAH
WOW, SERIOUSLY?!
I DON'T BELIEVE IT!!!
WE'VE GOT POWERFUL REINFORCE-MENTS ON PUNK HAZARD!!!
OH...?
YAHOO!!! WE'RE SAVED!!!
?

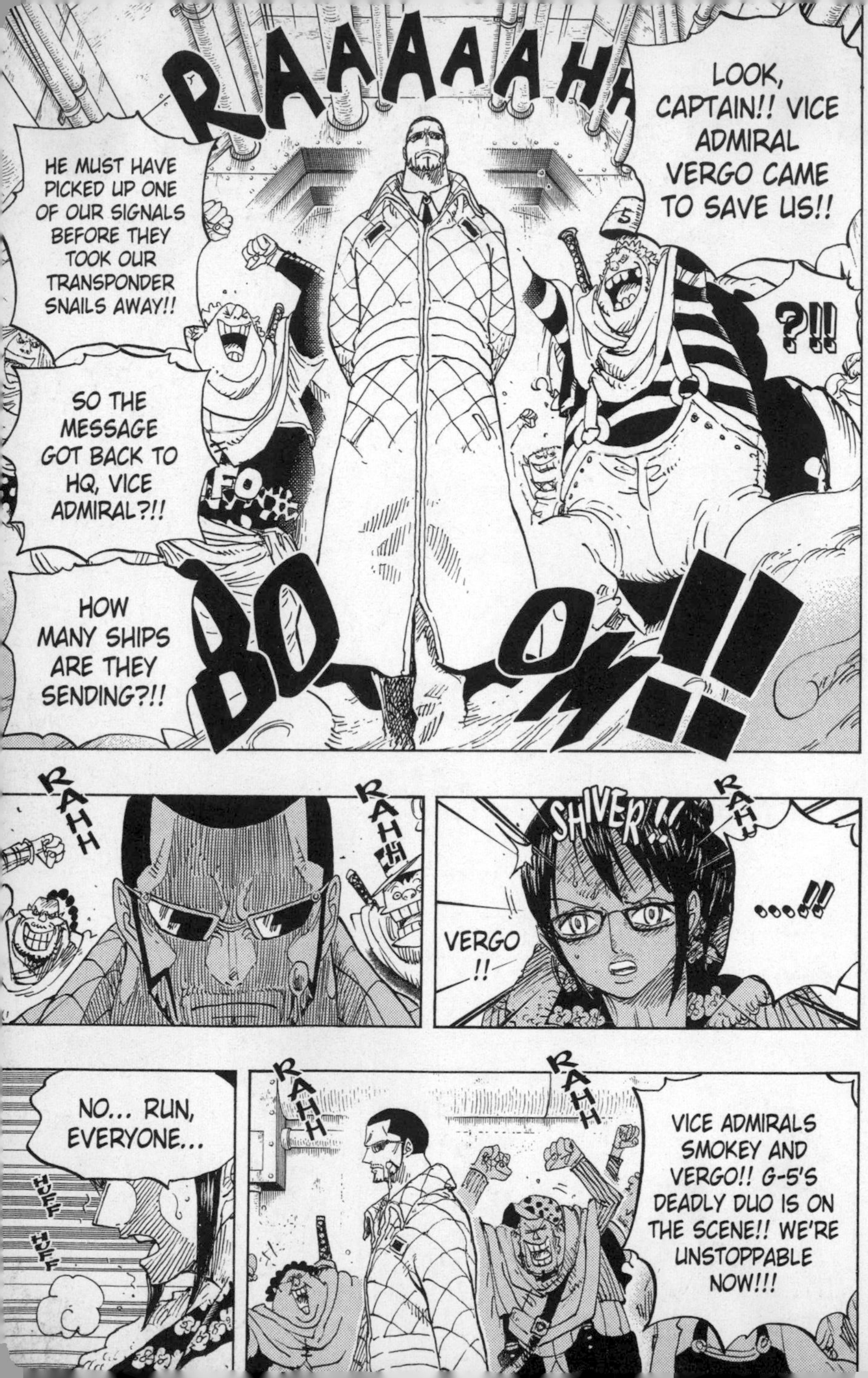
RAAAAAHH
LOOK, CAPTAIN!! VICE ADMIRAL VERGO CAME TO SAVE US!!
?!!
HE MUST HAVE PICKED UP ONE OF OUR SIGNALS BEFORE THEY TOOK OUR TRANSPONDER SNAILS AWAY!!
SO THE MESSAGE GOT BACK TO HQ, VICE ADMIRAL?!!
HOW MANY SHIPS ARE THEY SENDING?!!
BOOM!!
RAHH
SHIVER!!
...!!
VERGO!!
RAHH
RAHH
RAHH
RAHH
VICE ADMIRALS SMOKEY AND VERGO!! G-5'S DEADLY DUO IS ON THE SCENE!! WE'RE UNSTOPPABLE NOW!!!
NO... RUN, EVERYONE...
HUFF
HUFF

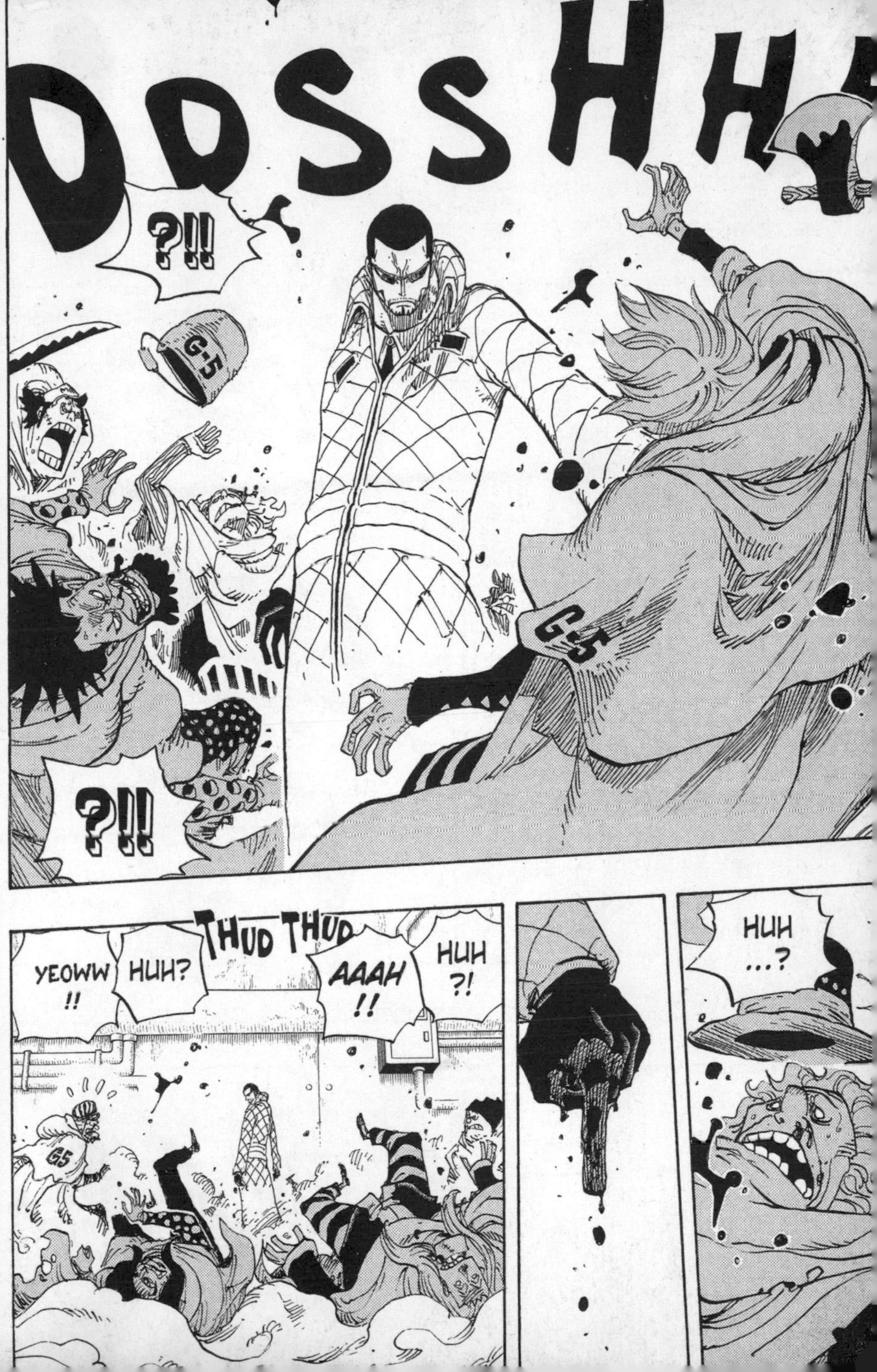
DDSSHH
?!!
?!!
HUH ...?
HUH ?!
AAAH !!
THUD THUD
HUH?
YEOWW !!
G-5
G-5
G5

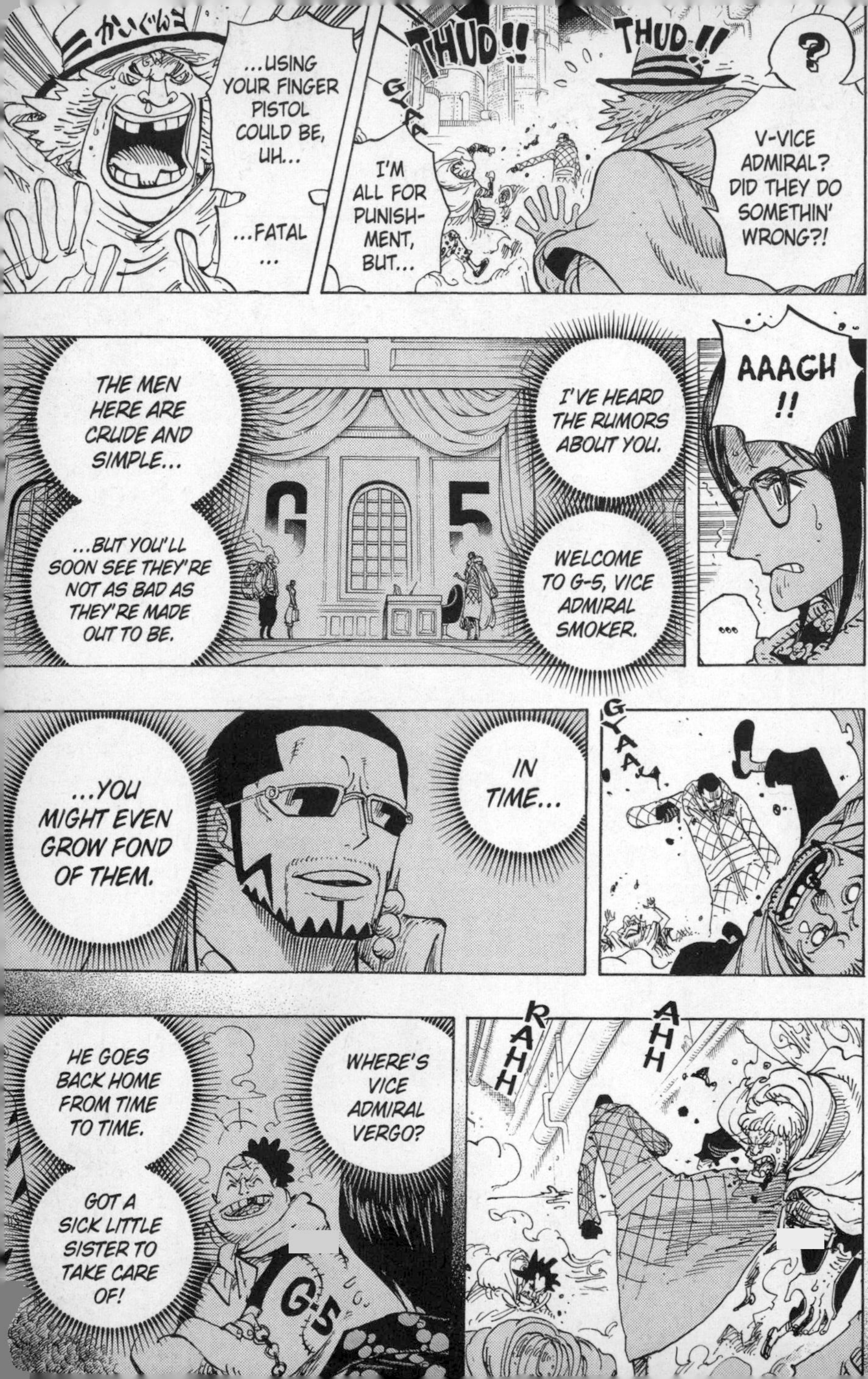
?
V-VICE ADMIRAL? DID THEY DO SOMETHIN' WRONG?!
THUD!!
THUD!!
GYAA
I'M ALL FOR PUNISH-MENT, BUT...
...USING YOUR FINGER PISTOL COULD BE, UH...
...FATAL ...
AAAGH !!
...
I'VE HEARD THE RUMORS ABOUT YOU.
WELCOME TO G-5, VICE ADMIRAL SMOKER.
THE MEN HERE ARE CRUDE AND SIMPLE...
...BUT YOU'LL SOON SEE THEY'RE NOT AS BAD AS THEY'RE MADE OUT TO BE.
G 5
GYAA
IN TIME...
...YOU MIGHT EVEN GROW FOND OF THEM.
AHH
RAHH
WHERE'S VICE ADMIRAL VERGO?
HE GOES BACK HOME FROM TIME TO TIME.
GOT A SICK LITTLE SISTER TO TAKE CARE OF!
G-5

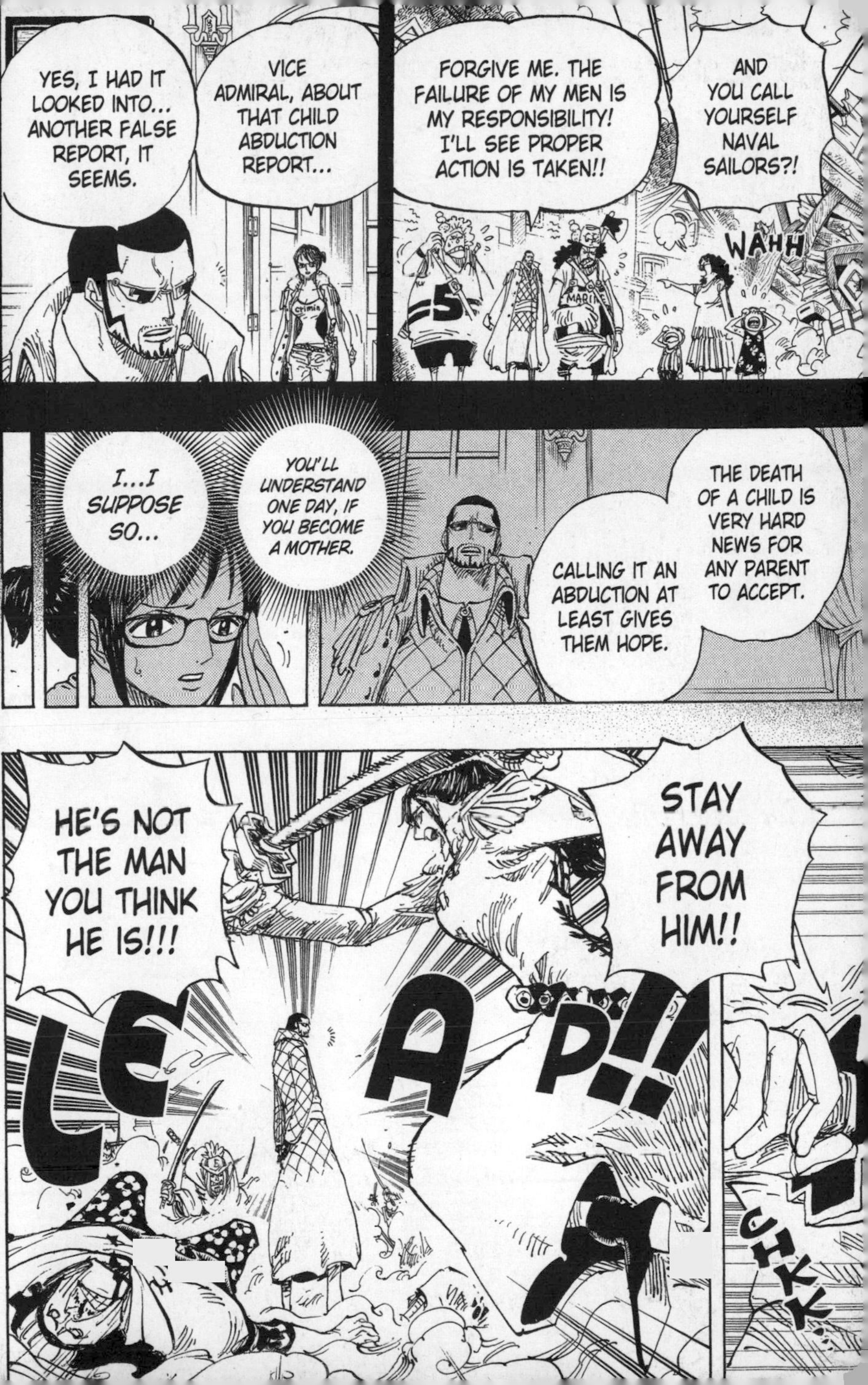
AND YOU CALL YOURSELF NAVAL SAILORS?!
WAHH
FORGIVE ME. THE FAILURE OF MY MEN IS MY RESPONSIBILITY! I'LL SEE PROPER ACTION IS TAKEN!!
VICE ADMIRAL, ABOUT THAT CHILD ABDUCTION REPORT...
YES, I HAD IT LOOKED INTO... ANOTHER FALSE REPORT, IT SEEMS.
THE DEATH OF A CHILD IS VERY HARD NEWS FOR ANY PARENT TO ACCEPT.
CALLING IT AN ABDUCTION AT LEAST GIVES THEM HOPE.
YOU'LL UNDERSTAND ONE DAY, IF YOU BECOME A MOTHER.
I...I SUPPOSE SO...
STAY AWAY FROM HIM!!
HE'S NOT THE MAN YOU THINK HE IS!!!
LEAP!!
CHKK

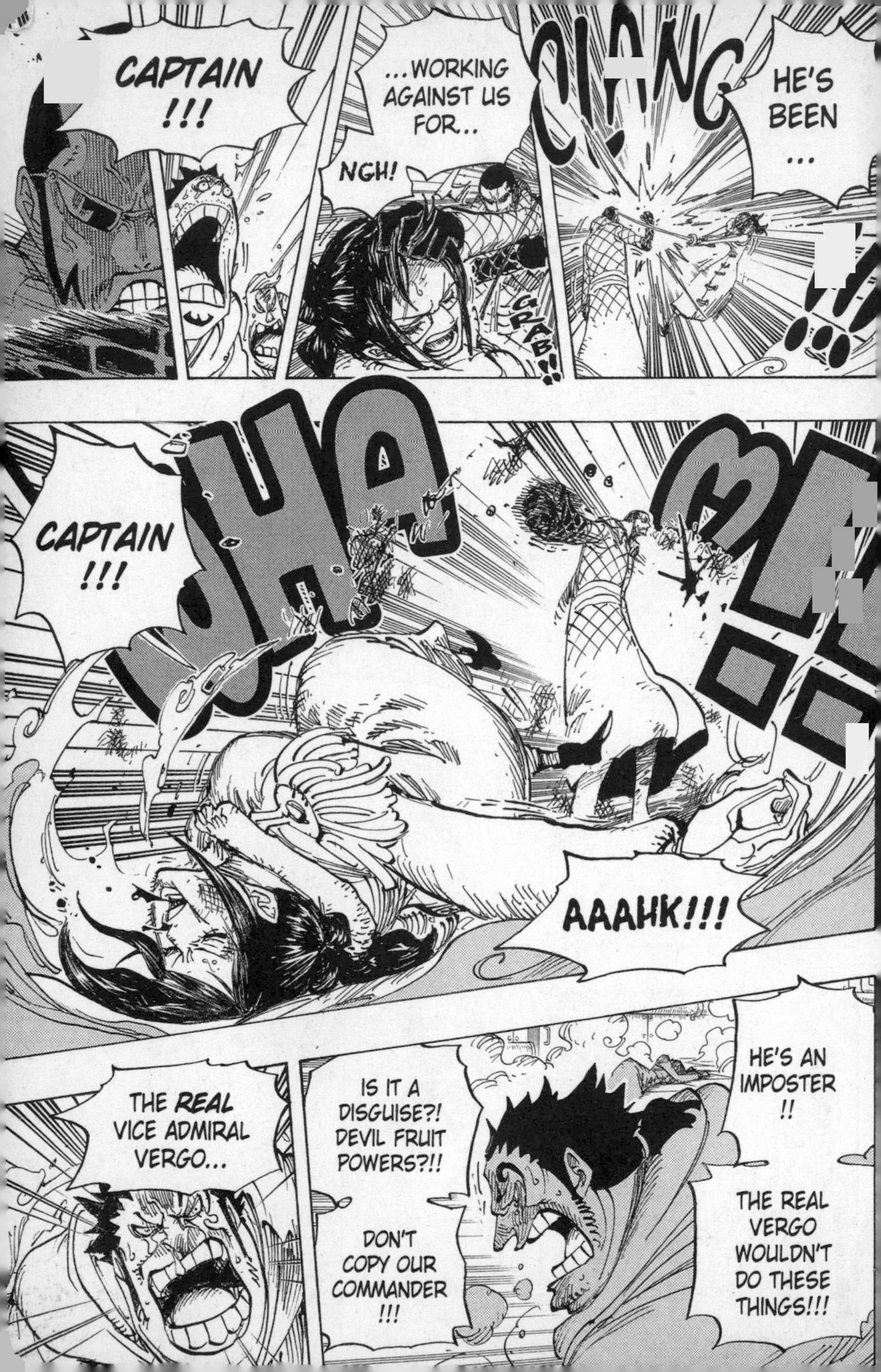
HE'S BEEN ...
CLANG
...WORKING AGAINST US FOR...
NGH!
GRAB!!
CAPTAIN!!!
CAPTAIN!!!
AAAHK!!!
HE'S AN IMPOSTER!!
THE REAL VERGO WOULDN'T DO THESE THINGS!!!
IS IT A DISGUISE?! DEVIL FRUIT POWERS?!!
DON'T COPY OUR COMMANDER!!!
THE REAL VICE ADMIRAL VERGO...

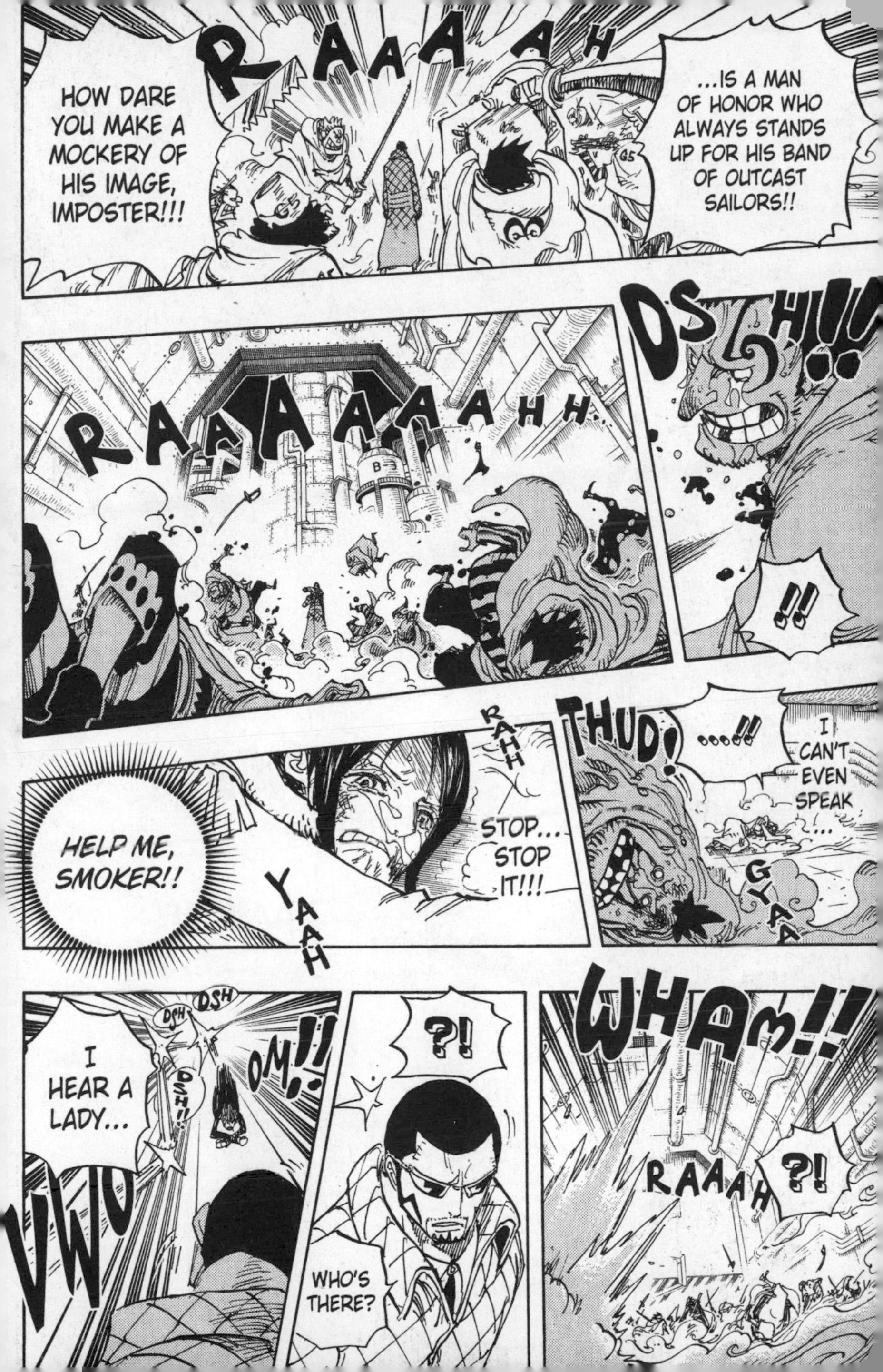
...IS A MAN OF HONOR WHO ALWAYS STANDS UP FOR HIS BAND OF OUTCAST SAILORS!!
RAAAAH
HOW DARE YOU MAKE A MOCKERY OF HIS IMAGE, IMPOSTER!!!
DSHH!!
!!
RAAAAAAHH...
I CAN'T EVEN SPEAK...
....!!
THUD!
GYAA
RAHH
STOP... STOP IT!!!
YAAH
HELP ME, SMOKER!!
WHAM!!
?!
RAAAH
?!
WHO'S THERE?
OM!!
DSH
DSH
DSH!!
I HEAR A LADY...
VWO

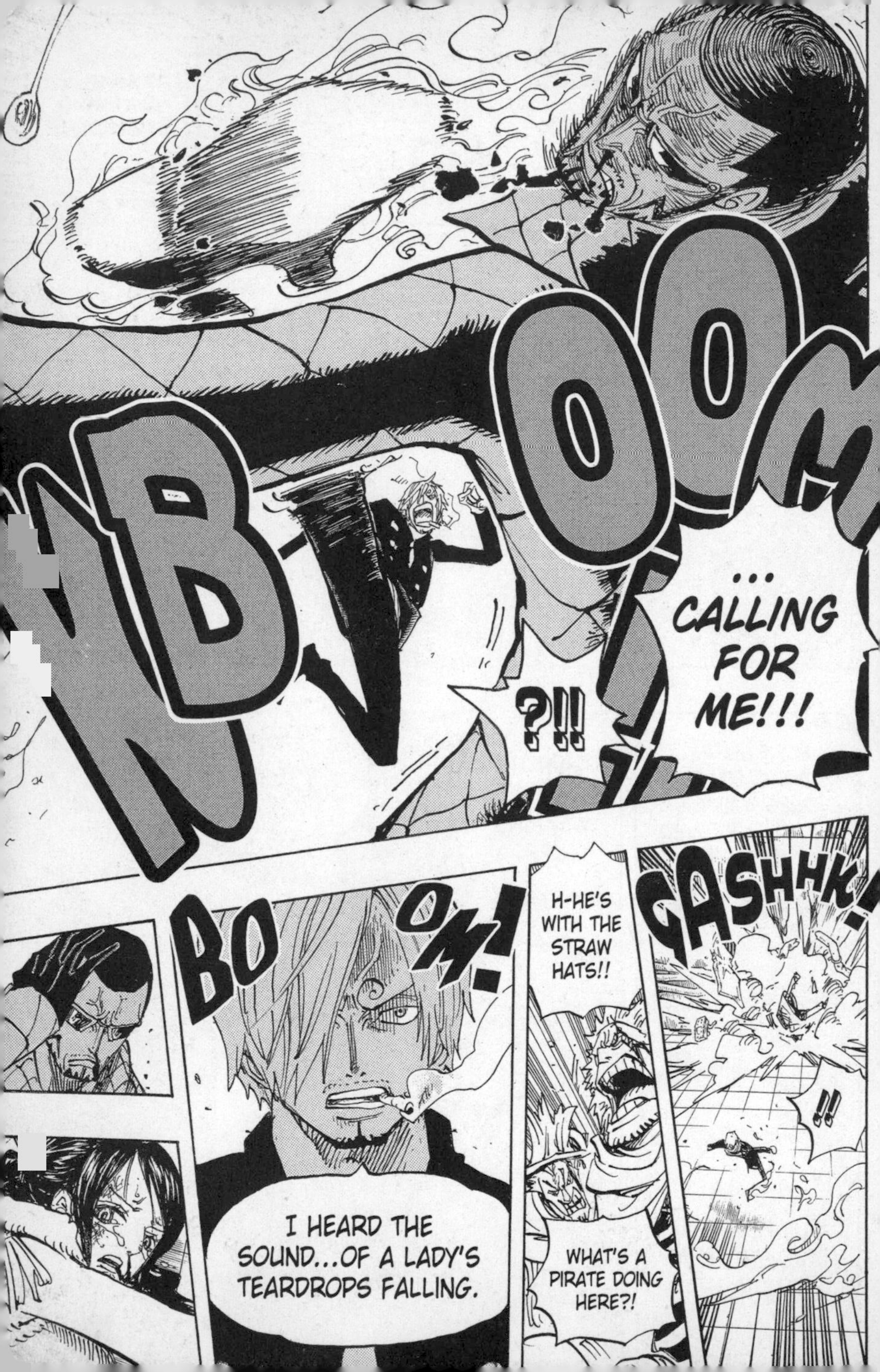
?!!
...CALLING FOR ME!!!
GASHHK!!
!!
H-HE'S WITH THE STRAW HATS!!
WHAT'S A PIRATE DOING HERE?!
BOOM!
I HEARD THE SOUND...OF A LADY'S TEARDROPS FALLING.

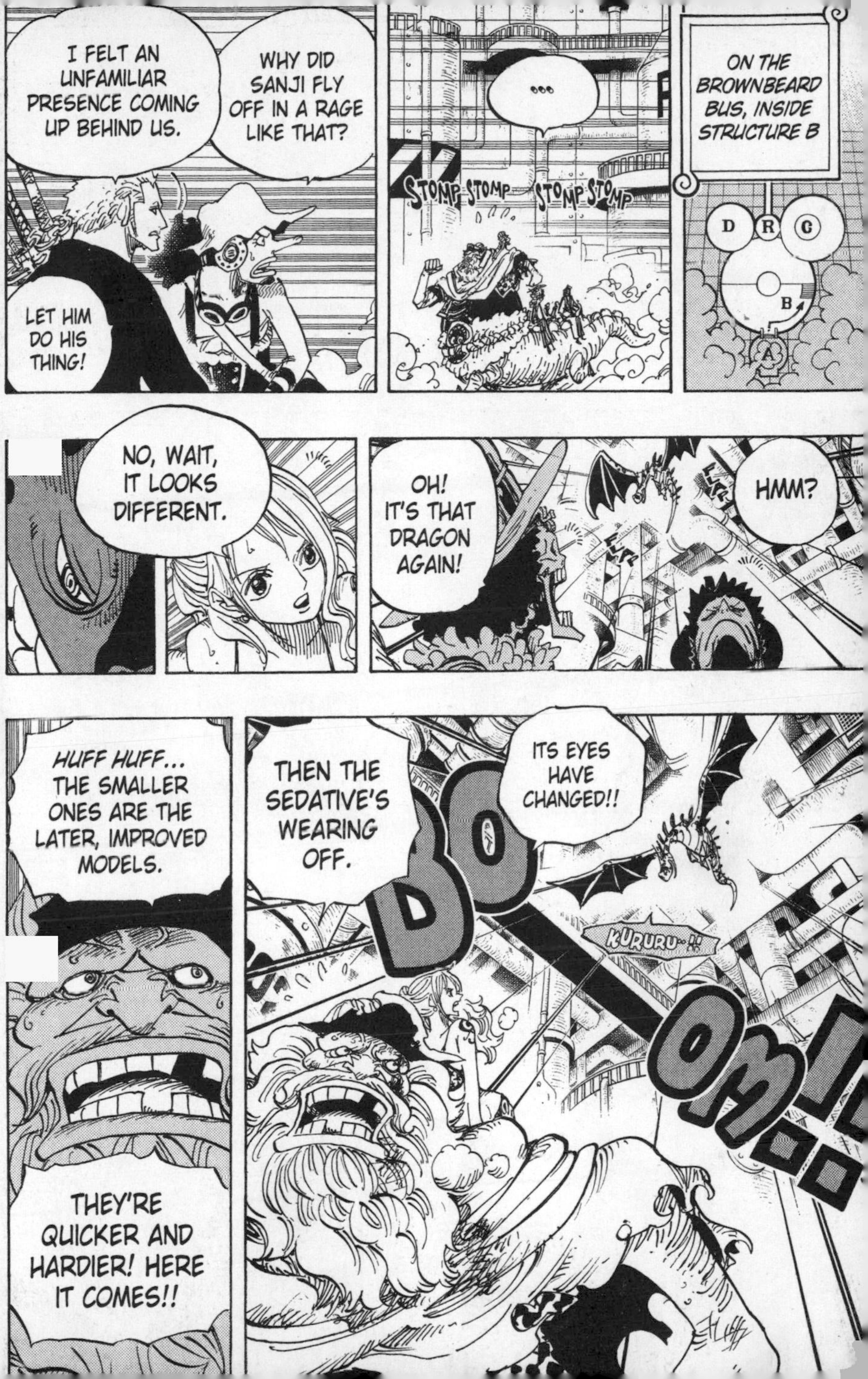
ON THE BROWNBEARD BUS, INSIDE STRUCTURE B
D
R
C
B
A
...
STOMP STOMP
STOMP STOMP
WHY DID SANJI FLY OFF IN A RAGE LIKE THAT?
I FELT AN UNFAMILIAR PRESENCE COMING UP BEHIND US.
LET HIM DO HIS THING!
HMM?
OH! IT'S THAT DRAGON AGAIN!
NO, WAIT, IT LOOKS DIFFERENT.
ITS EYES HAVE CHANGED!!
THEN THE SEDATIVE'S WEARING OFF.
BOOM!!
KURURU..!!
HUFF HUFF... THE SMALLER ONES ARE THE LATER, IMPROVED MODELS.
THEY'RE QUICKER AND HARDIER! HERE IT COMES!!

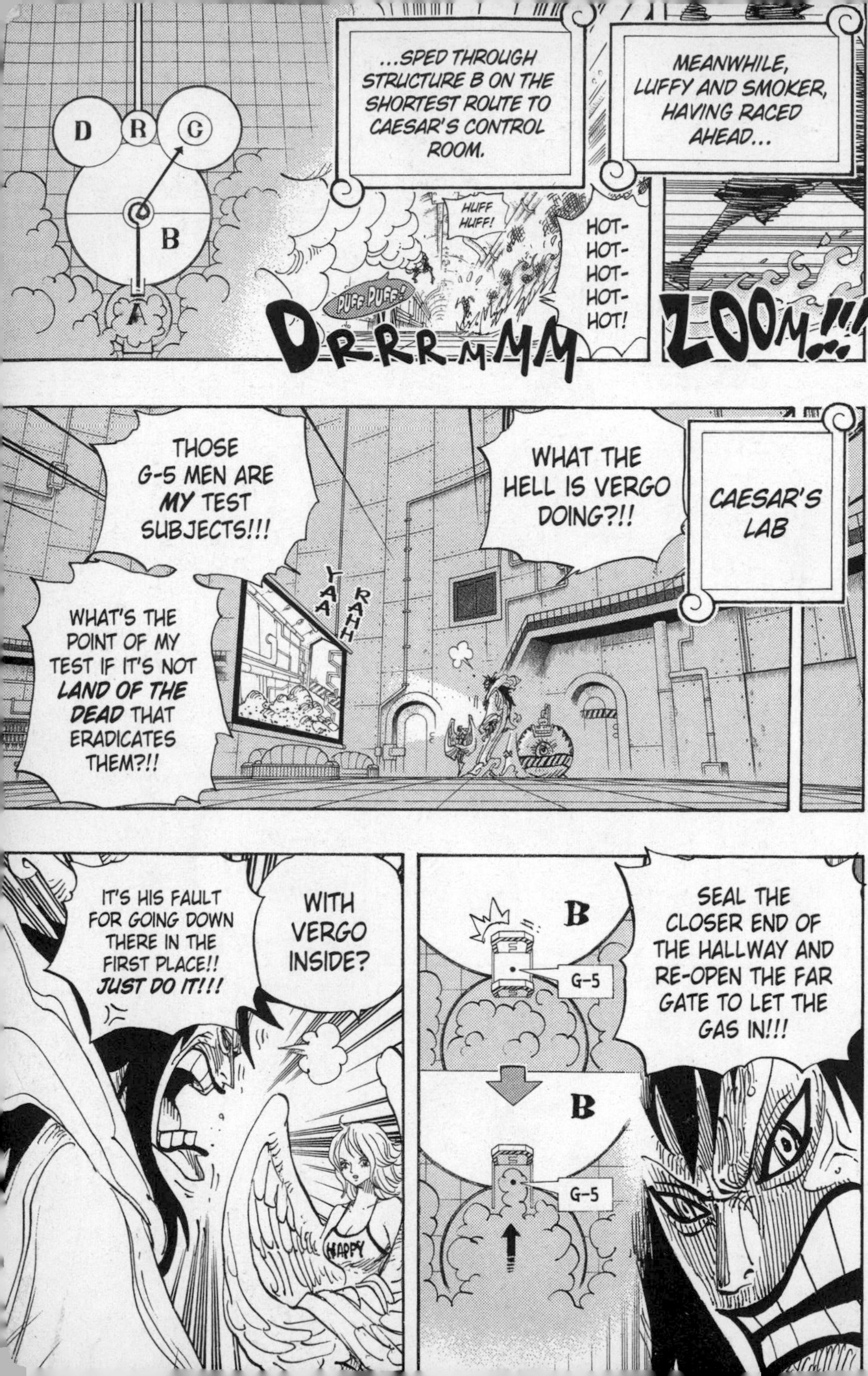
MEANWHILE, LUFFY AND SMOKER, HAVING RACED AHEAD...
ZOOM!!!
...SPED THROUGH STRUCTURE B ON THE SHORTEST ROUTE TO CAESAR'S CONTROL ROOM.
HUFF HUFF!
HOT-HOT-HOT-HOT-HOT!
PUFF PUFF!
DRRRRMMM
D
R
G
B
A
CAESAR'S LAB
WHAT THE HELL IS VERGO DOING?!!
THOSE G-5 MEN ARE *MY* TEST SUBJECTS!!!
YAAA
RAHHH
WHAT'S THE POINT OF MY TEST IF IT'S NOT *LAND OF THE DEAD* THAT ERADICATES THEM?!!
SEAL THE CLOSER END OF THE HALLWAY AND RE-OPEN THE FAR GATE TO LET THE GAS IN!!!
B
G-5
B
G-5
WITH VERGO INSIDE?
IT'S HIS FAULT FOR GOING DOWN THERE IN THE FIRST PLACE!! *JUST DO IT!!!*
HAPPY

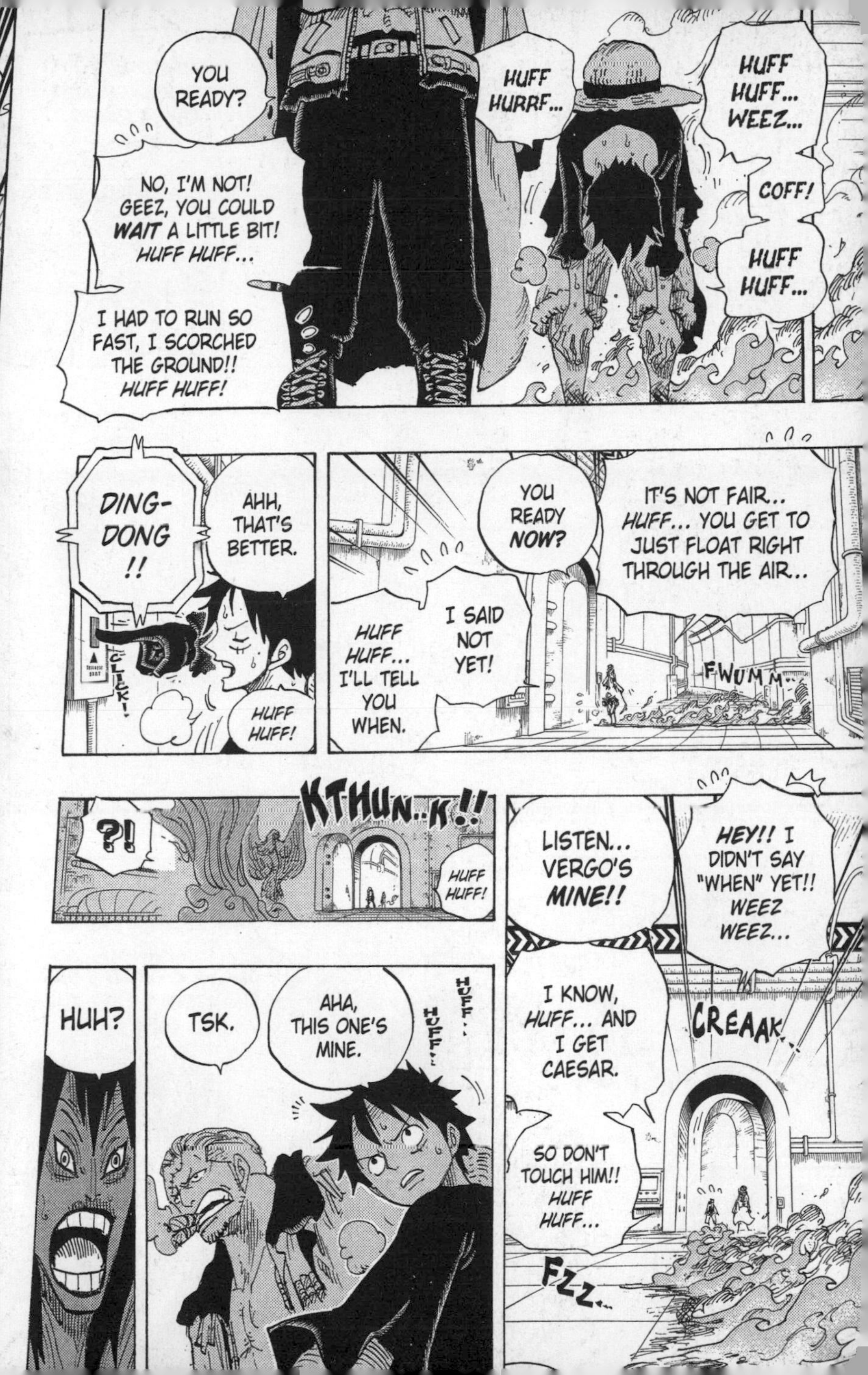
HUFF HUFF... WEEZ...
COFF!
HUFF HUFF...
HUFF HURRF...
YOU READY?
NO, I'M NOT! GEEZ, YOU COULD WAIT A LITTLE BIT! HUFF HUFF...
I HAD TO RUN SO FAST, I SCORCHED THE GROUND!! HUFF HUFF!
YOU READY NOW?
I SAID NOT YET!
HUFF HUFF... I'LL TELL YOU WHEN.
IT'S NOT FAIR.. HUFF... YOU GET TO JUST FLOAT RIGHT THROUGH THE AIR..
FWUMM
AHH, THAT'S BETTER.
DING-DONG !!
CLICK!
HUFF HUFF!
HEY!! I DIDN'T SAY "WHEN" YET!! WEEZ WEEZ...
LISTEN... VERGO'S MINE!!
I KNOW, HUFF... AND I GET CAESAR.
SO DON'T TOUCH HIM!! HUFF HUFF...
CREAAK
FZZ...
KTHUN..K!!
?!
HUFF HUFF!
AHA, THIS ONE'S MINE.
HUFF HUFF..
TSK.
HUH?

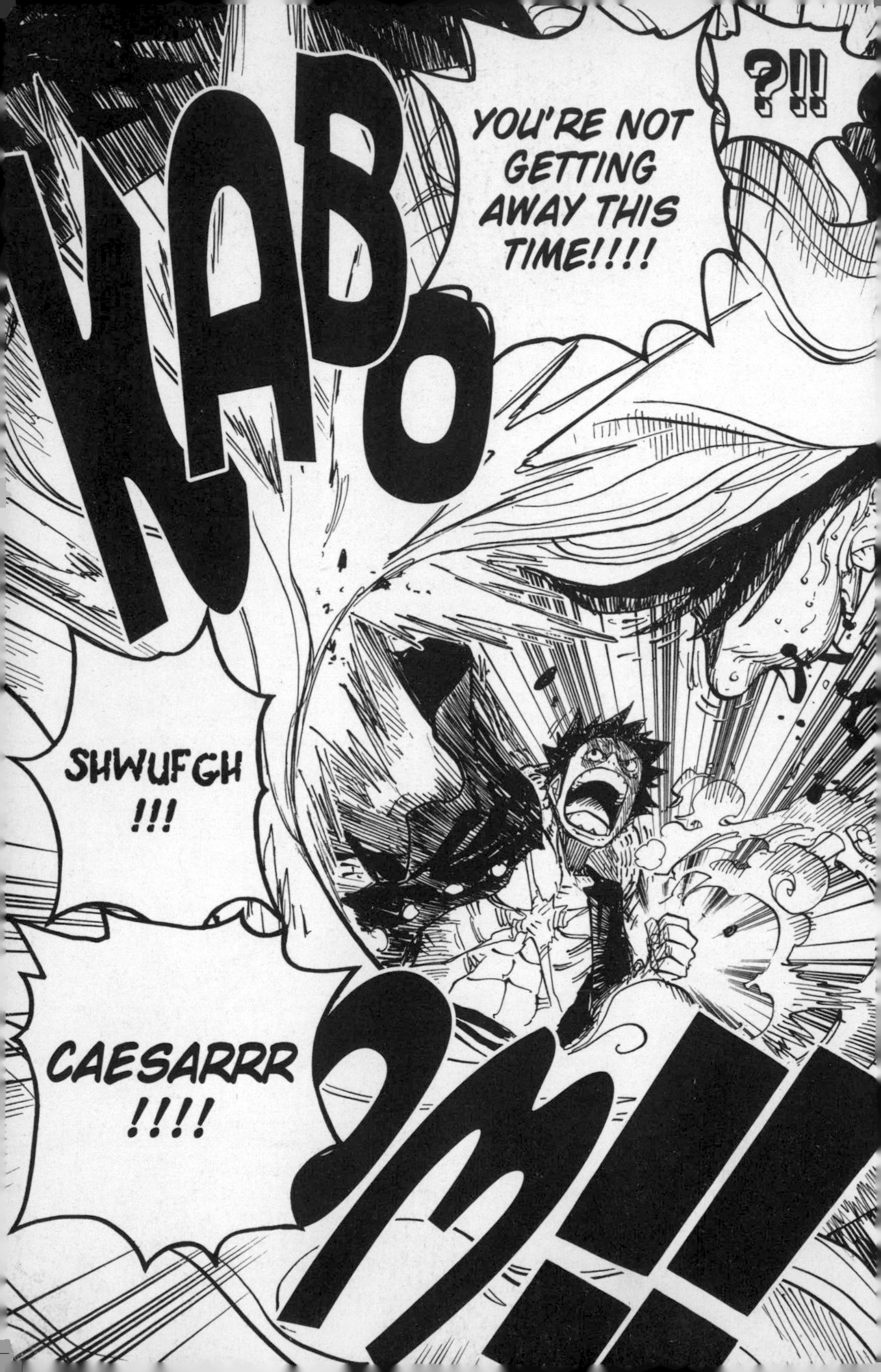
?!!
YOU'RE NOT GETTING AWAY THIS TIME!!!!
KABO
SHWUFGH !!!
CAESARRR !!!!

SBS Question Corner

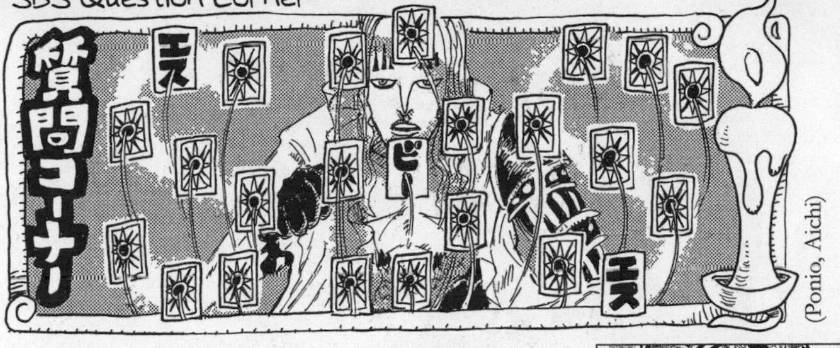
質問コーナー
エス
ビ
エス

(Ponio, Aichi)

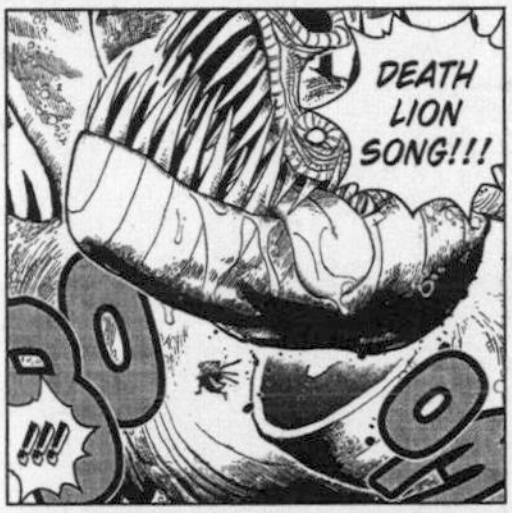
DEATH LION SONG!!!

Q: In Chapter 656, Zolo has a really cool scene killing a dragon with Death Lion Song, and I noticed that it bears a strong resemblance to the scene of Ryuma the samurai beating a dragon in the pre-*One Piece* short manga "Monsters" that appears in your short story collection, *Wanted!* Did that scene hold a lot of meaning for you, Mr. Oda?

--Ono Rose Town People

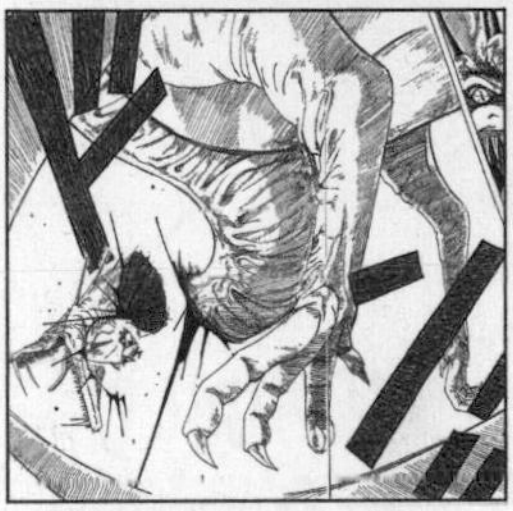

A: Wow! I'm surprised you noticed something from so long ago. When I was doing the dragon-slicing scene in Punk Hazard, it did remind me of the short story "Monsters" that I drew almost twenty years ago. All I really remember is that Ryuma the protagonist was something of an original model for Zolo, and he sliced a dragon in half in a big huge panel. I chose not to re-read the old story, preferring to simply draw another big-panel dragon-slicing scene from scratch. Go ahead and compare my decapitations from age 19 and 38. (haha)

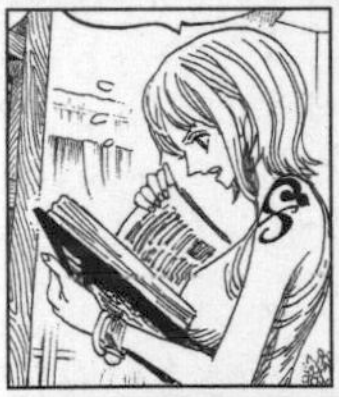

Q: Two years ago (in Volume 61), Nami reads a book in Weatheria and exclaims, "Lightning raining down like rain?!" Is this referring to the island the G-5 ship is moored at on Chapter 655 of Volume 66? Tell us, or I'll go like this! Zzzap!

--P.S. I Love Law

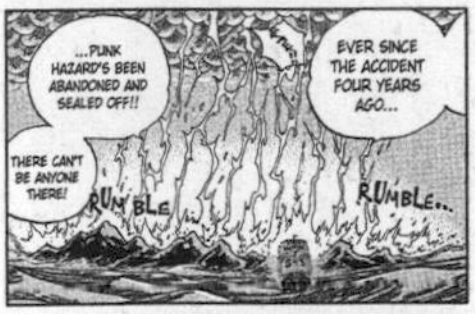
EVER SINCE THE ACCIDENT FOUR YEARS AGO...
...PUNK HAZARD'S BEEN ABANDONED AND SEALED OFF!!
THERE CAN'T BE ANYONE THERE!
RUMBLE
RUMBLE...

A: Zzzap? Don't make fun of lasers!! That's right. When the three needles point out from Fish-Man Island, Luffy wants to go to the middle destination, the shakiest needle. That was Raijin Island, where lightning falls. It's also the place Urouge was headed at the end of Volume 60. Smoker had Luffy's mindset perfectly identified, but the Sunny got caught in the Whiteström and wound up closer to Punk Hazard, which didn't correspond to any of the needles. I wonder what kind of adventures we'd have had if the ship went to Raijin Island?

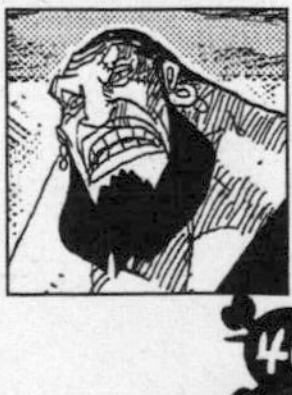

Chapter 681:
LUFFY VS. MASTER

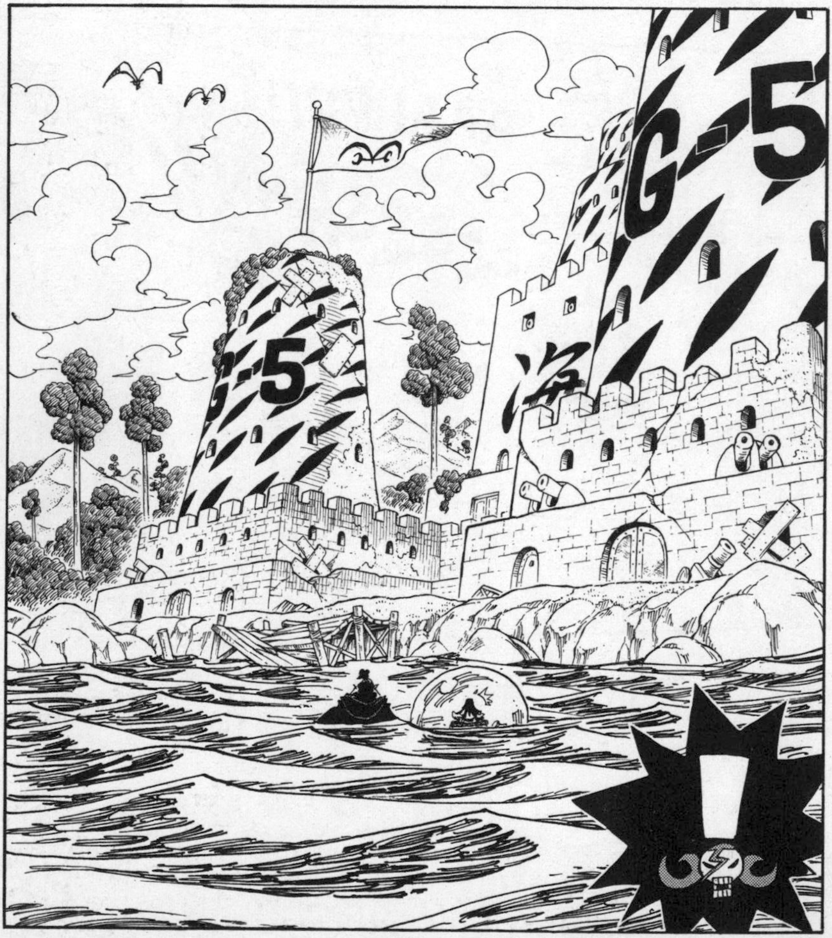
G-5
G-5
海
!

CARIBOU'S NEW WORLD KEE HEE HEE, VOL. 7:
"ARRIVING AT RAMSHACKLE NAVAL BASE G-5"

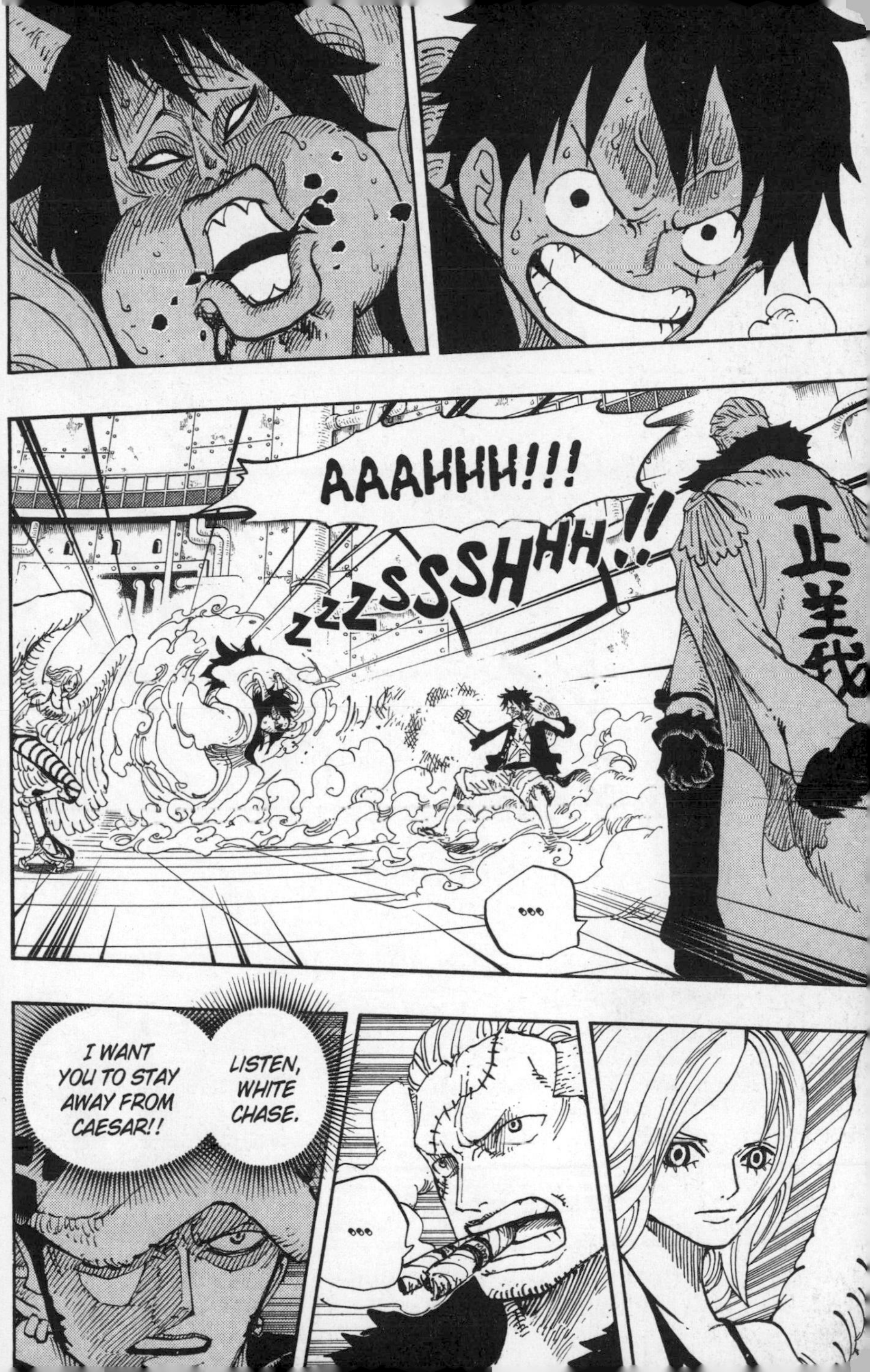
AAAHHH!!!
ZZZSSSHHH!!
...
...
LISTEN, WHITE CHASE.
I WANT YOU TO STAY AWAY FROM CAESAR!!

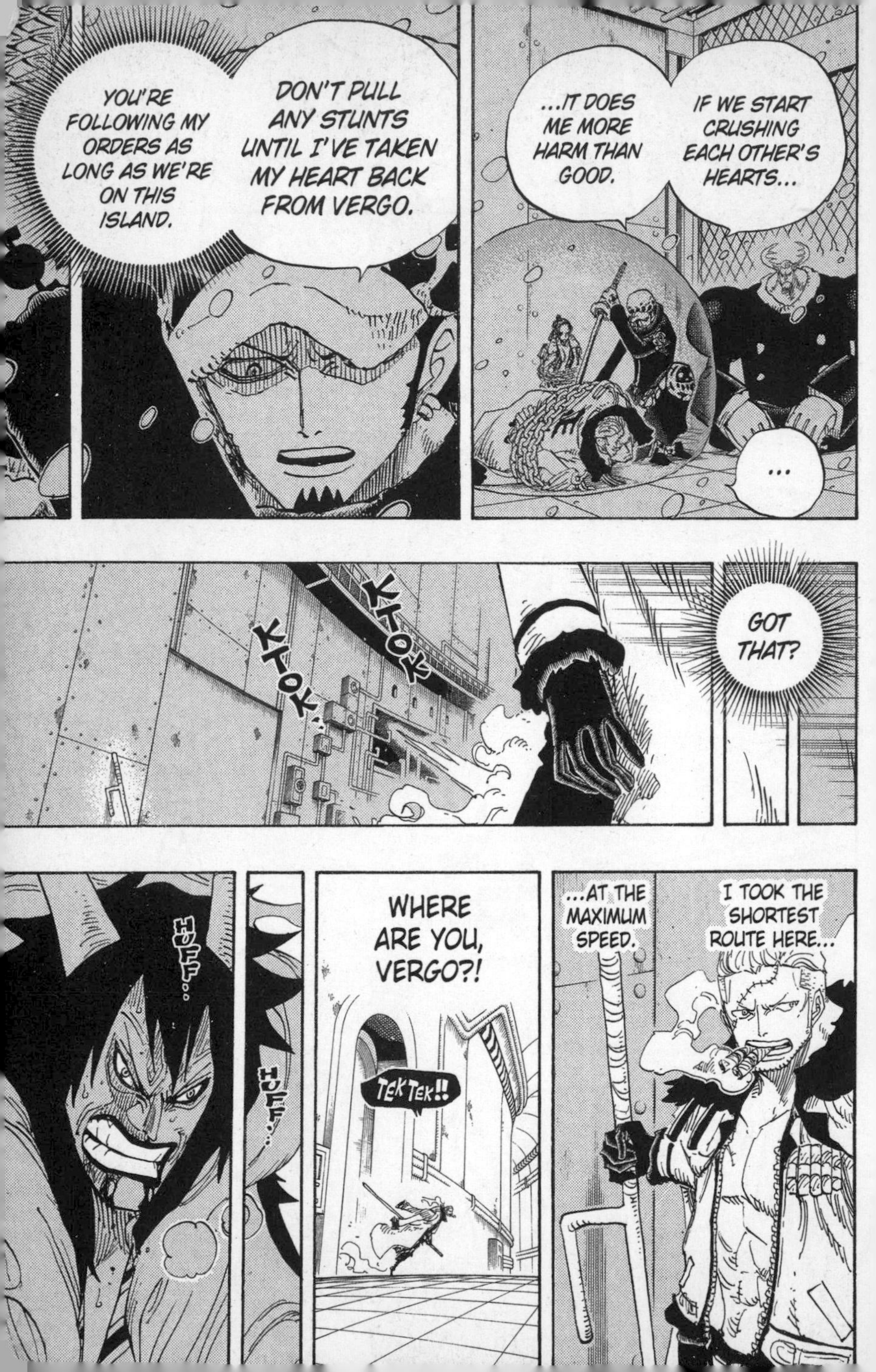
IF WE START CRUSHING EACH OTHER'S HEARTS...
...IT DOES ME MORE HARM THAN GOOD.
...
DON'T PULL ANY STUNTS UNTIL I'VE TAKEN MY HEART BACK FROM VERGO.
YOU'RE FOLLOWING MY ORDERS AS LONG AS WE'RE ON THIS ISLAND.
GOT THAT?
KTOK
KTOK
I TOOK THE SHORTEST ROUTE HERE...
...AT THE MAXIMUM SPEED.
WHERE ARE YOU, VERGO?!
TEK TEK!!
HUFF..
HUFF..

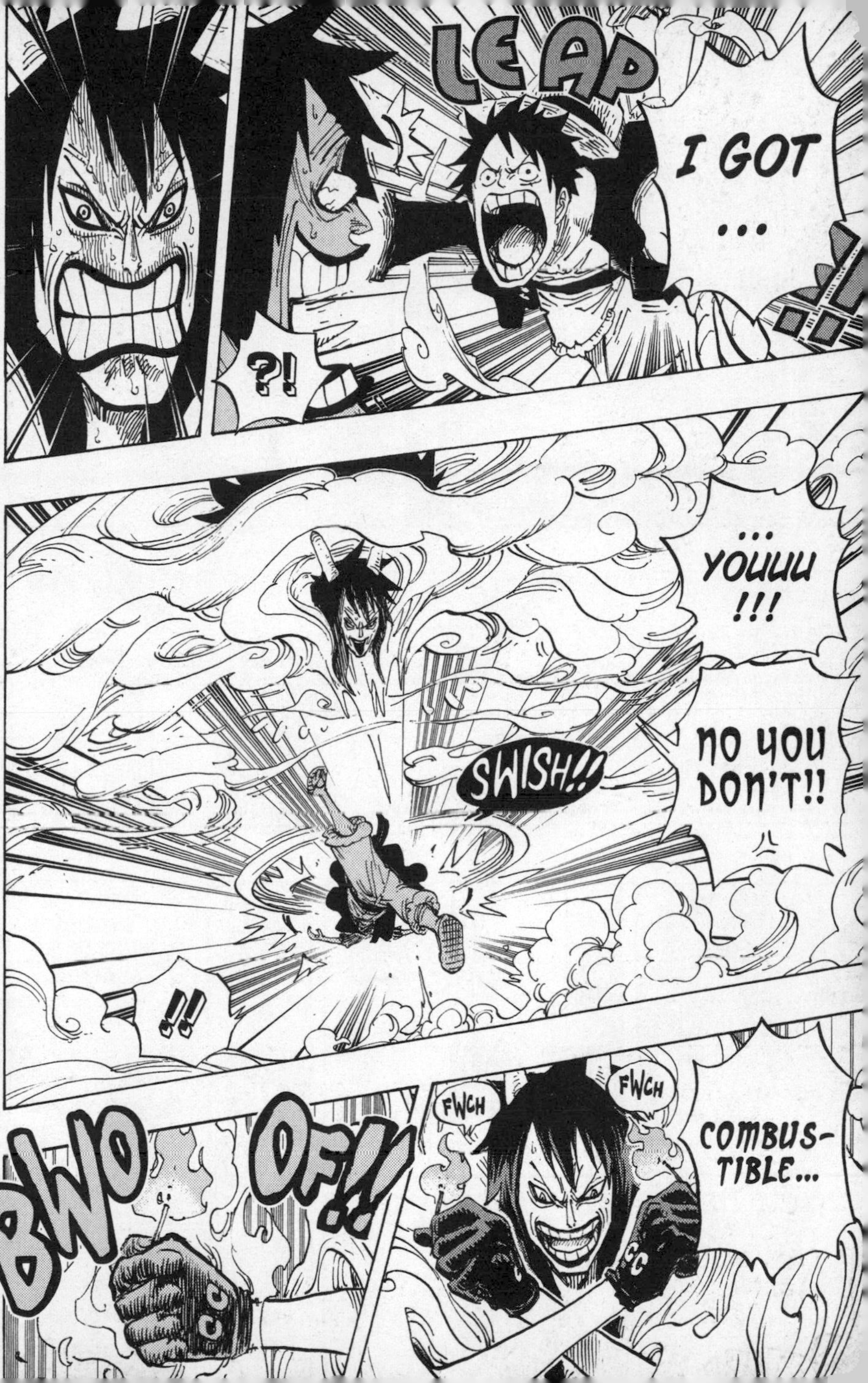
LEAP
I GOT ...
?!
... YOUUU !!!
SWISH!!
NO YOU DON'T!!
!!
FWCH
FWCH
COMBUS-TIBLE...
BWOOF!!

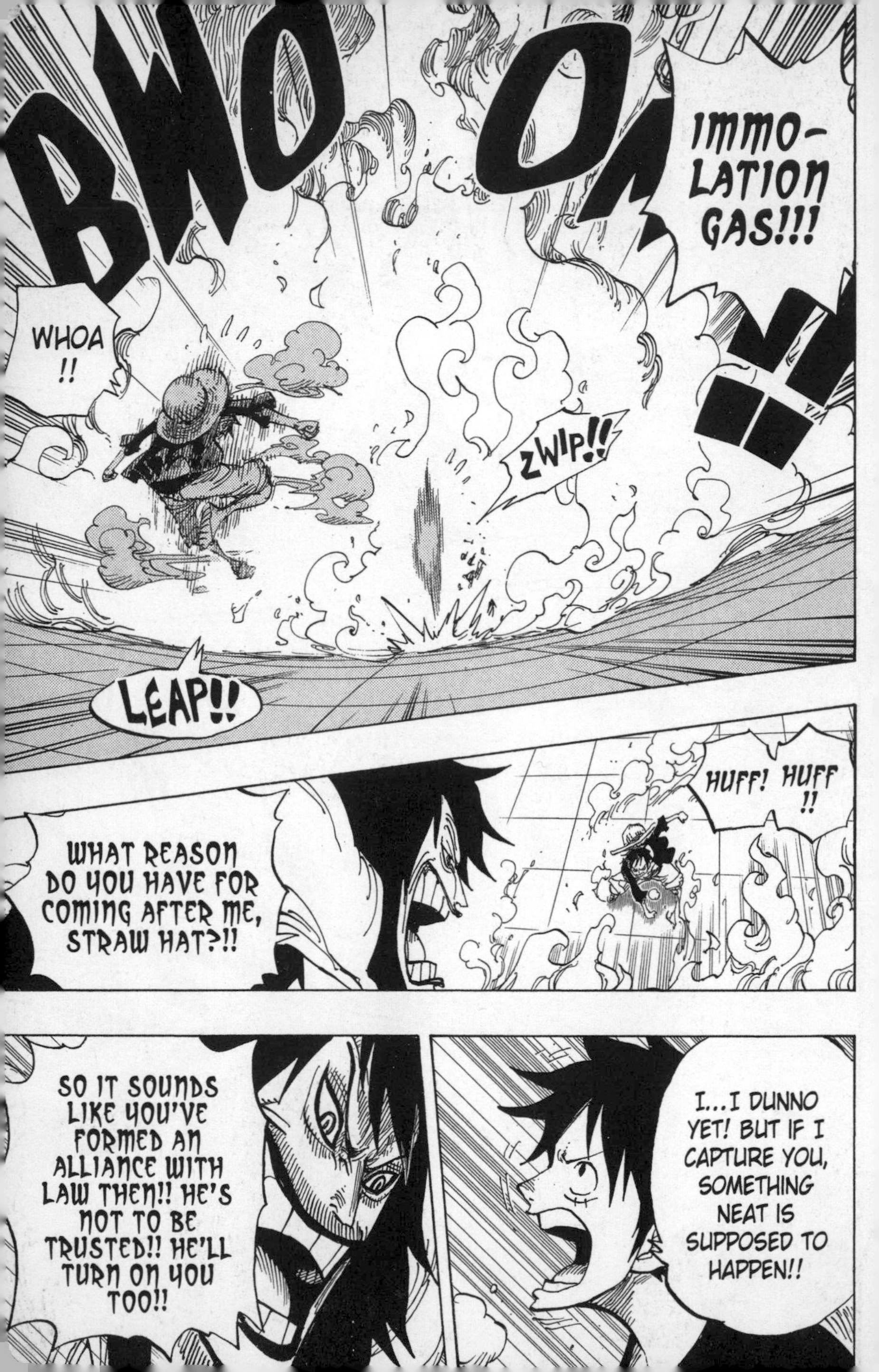
IMMO-
LATION
GAS!!!
WHOA
!!
ZWIP!!
LEAP!!
HUFF! HUFF
!!
WHAT REASON DO YOU HAVE FOR COMING AFTER ME, STRAW HAT?!!
I...I DUNNO YET! BUT IF I CAPTURE YOU, SOMETHING NEAT IS SUPPOSED TO HAPPEN!!
SO IT SOUNDS LIKE YOU'VE FORMED AN ALLIANCE WITH LAW THEN!! HE'S NOT TO BE TRUSTED!! HE'LL TURN ON YOU TOO!!

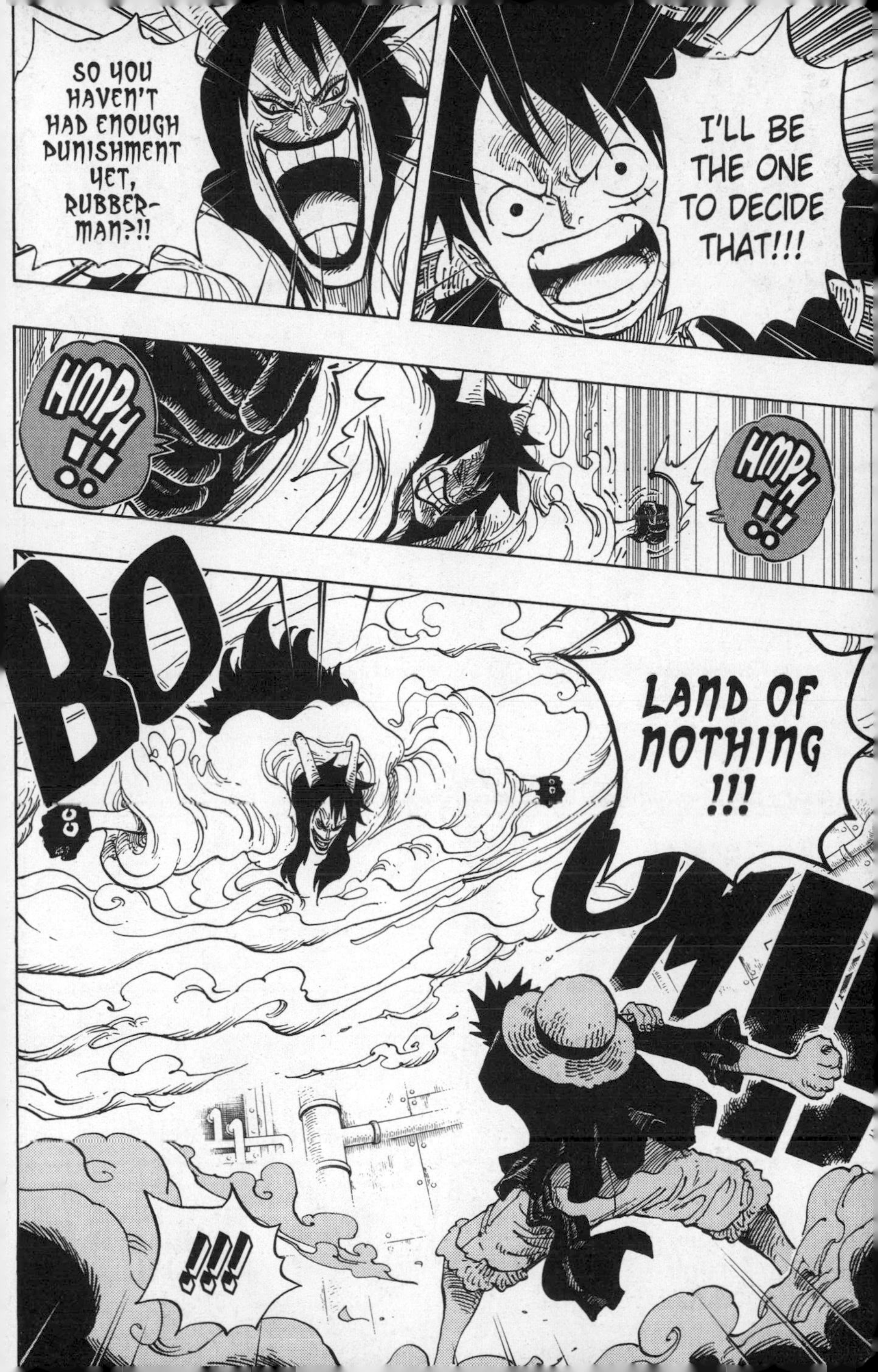
I'LL BE THE ONE TO DECIDE THAT!!!
SO YOU HAVEN'T HAD ENOUGH PUNISHMENT YET, RUBBER-MAN?!!
HMPH!!
HMPH!!
LAND OF NOTHING!!!
BOOM!!
!!!

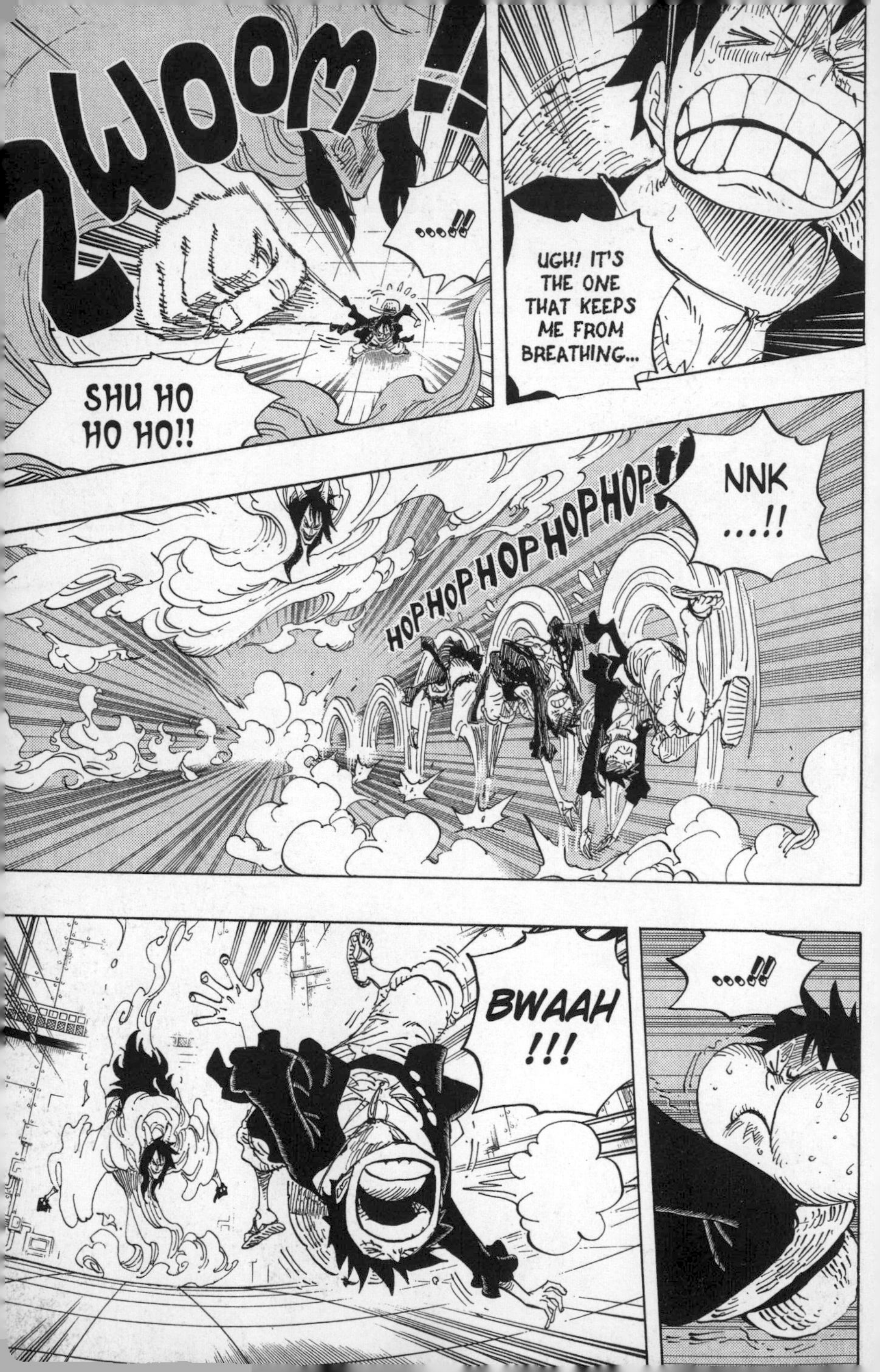
UGH! IT'S THE ONE THAT KEEPS ME FROM BREATHING...
ZWOOM!!
...!!
SHU HO HO HO!!
NNK ...!!
HOP HOP HOP HOP HOP HOP!!
...!!
BWAAH !!!

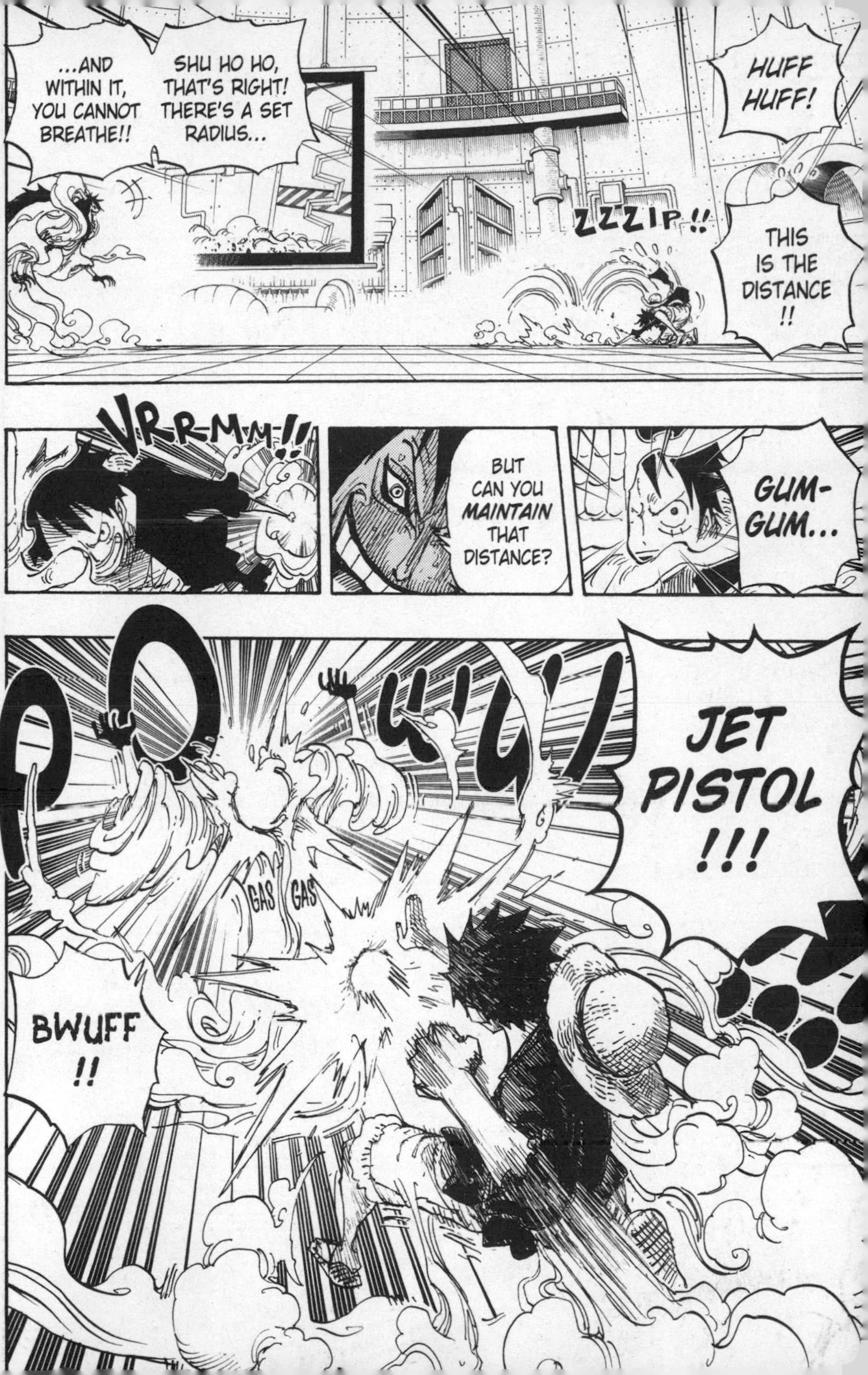
SHU HO HO, THAT'S RIGHT! THERE'S A SET RADIUS...
...AND WITHIN IT, YOU CANNOT BREATHE!!
HUFF HUFF!
ZZZIP!!
THIS IS THE DISTANCE!!
GUM-GUM...
BUT CAN YOU *MAINTAIN* THAT DISTANCE?
VRRMM!!
JET PISTOL!!!
GAS GAS
BWUFF!!

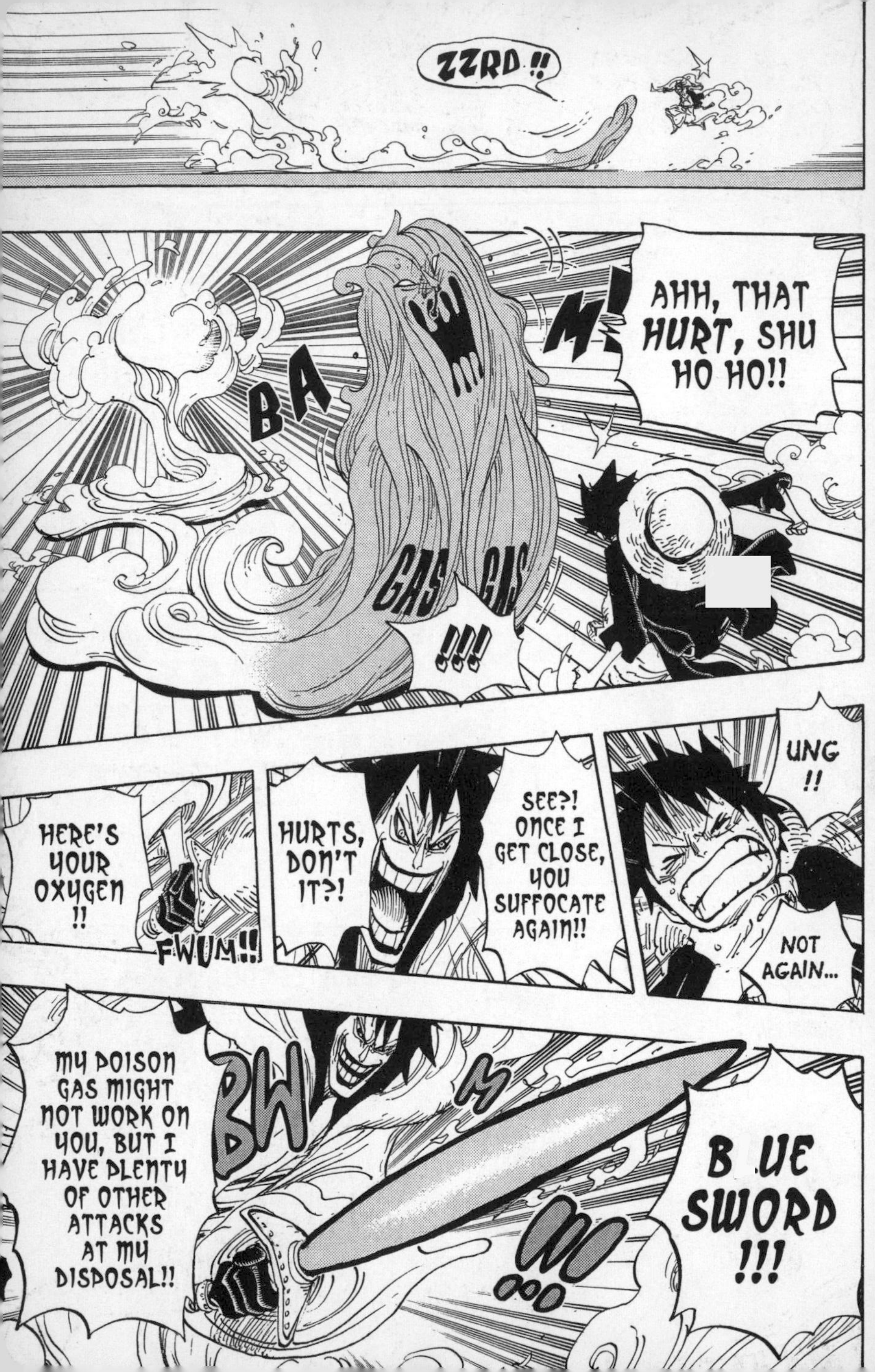
ZZRD!!
AHH, THAT HURT, SHU HO HO!!
BAM!
GAS GAS!!!
UNG!!
NOT AGAIN...
SEE?! ONCE I GET CLOSE, YOU SUFFOCATE AGAIN!!
HURTS, DON'T IT?!
HERE'S YOUR OXYGEN!!
FWUM!!
B UE SWORD!!!
MY POISON GAS MIGHT NOT WORK ON YOU, BUT I HAVE PLENTY OF OTHER ATTACKS AT MY DISPOSAL!!
BWMM!!!

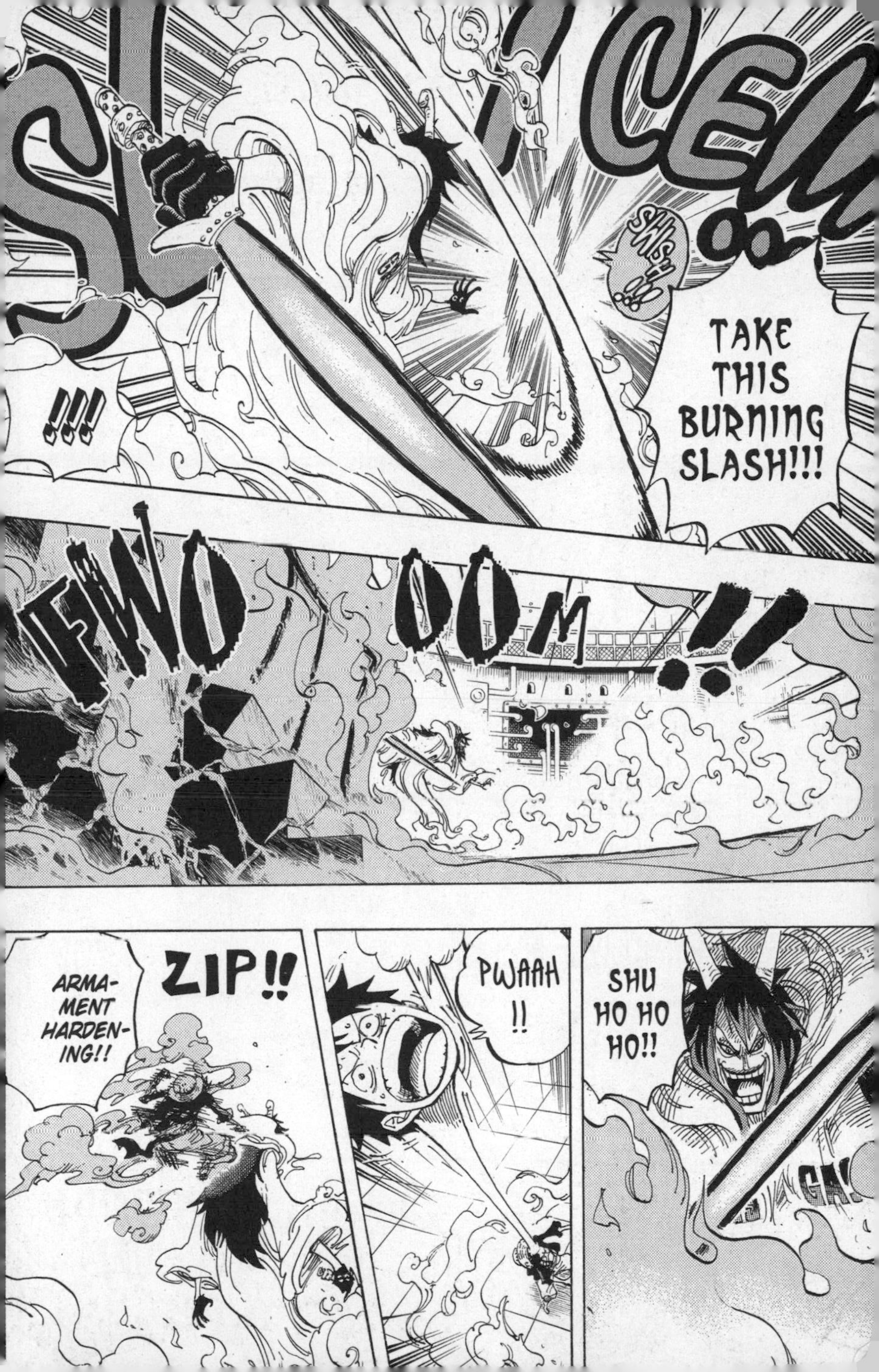
SWISH!!!
TAKE THIS BURNING SLASH!!!
!!!
FWOOOM!!!
SHU HO HO HO!!
PWAAH !!
ZIP!!
ARMA-MENT HARDEN-ING!!

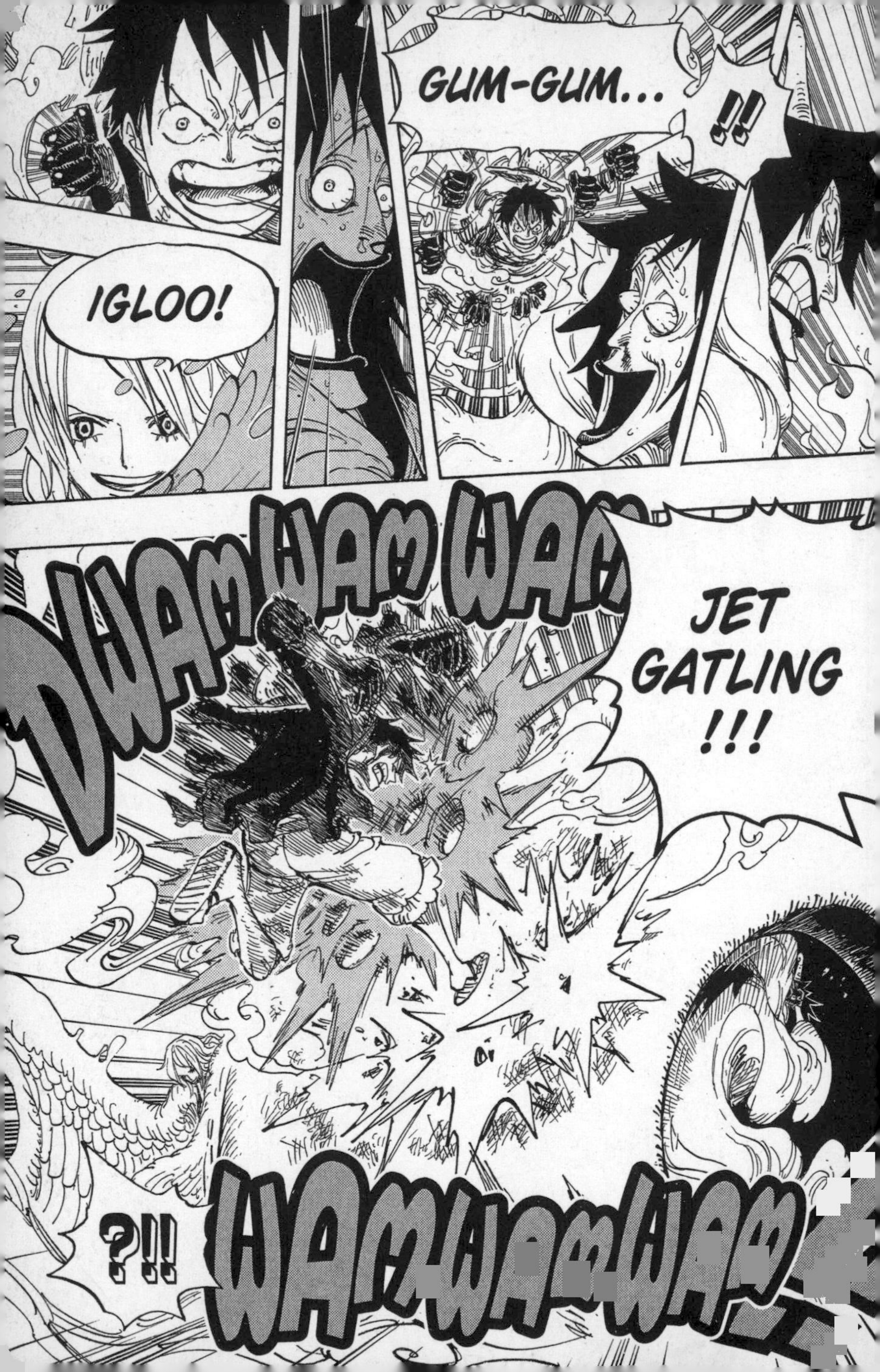
GUM-GUM...
!!
IGLOO!
JET GATLING !!!
DWAM WAM WAM
?!!
WAM WAM WAM

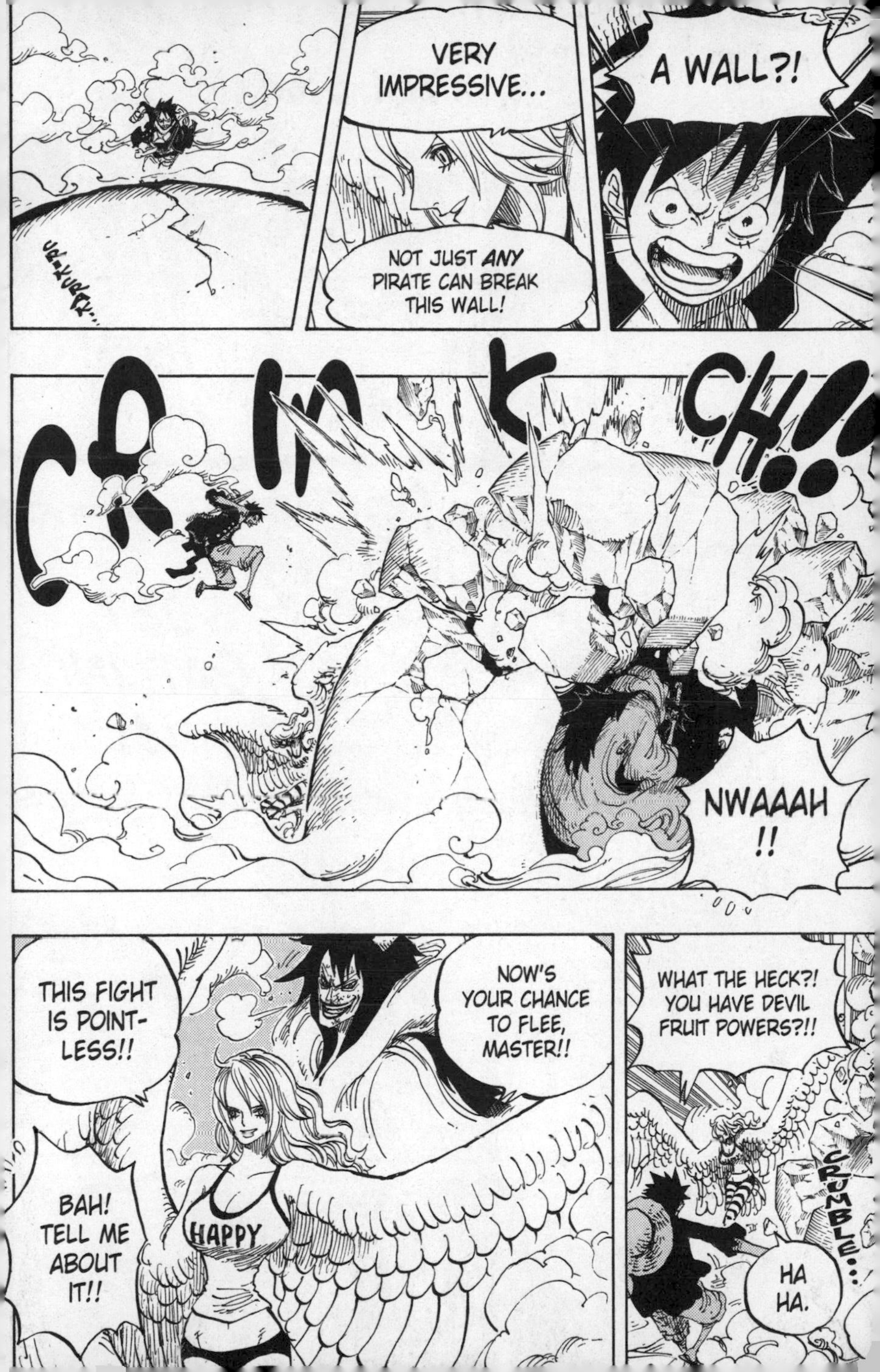
A WALL?!
VERY IMPRESSIVE...
NOT JUST ANY PIRATE CAN BREAK THIS WALL!
NWAAAH!!
WHAT THE HECK?! YOU HAVE DEVIL FRUIT POWERS?!!
CRUMBLE...
HA HA.
NOW'S YOUR CHANCE TO FLEE, MASTER!!
THIS FIGHT IS POINTLESS!!
BAH! TELL ME ABOUT IT!!
HAPPY

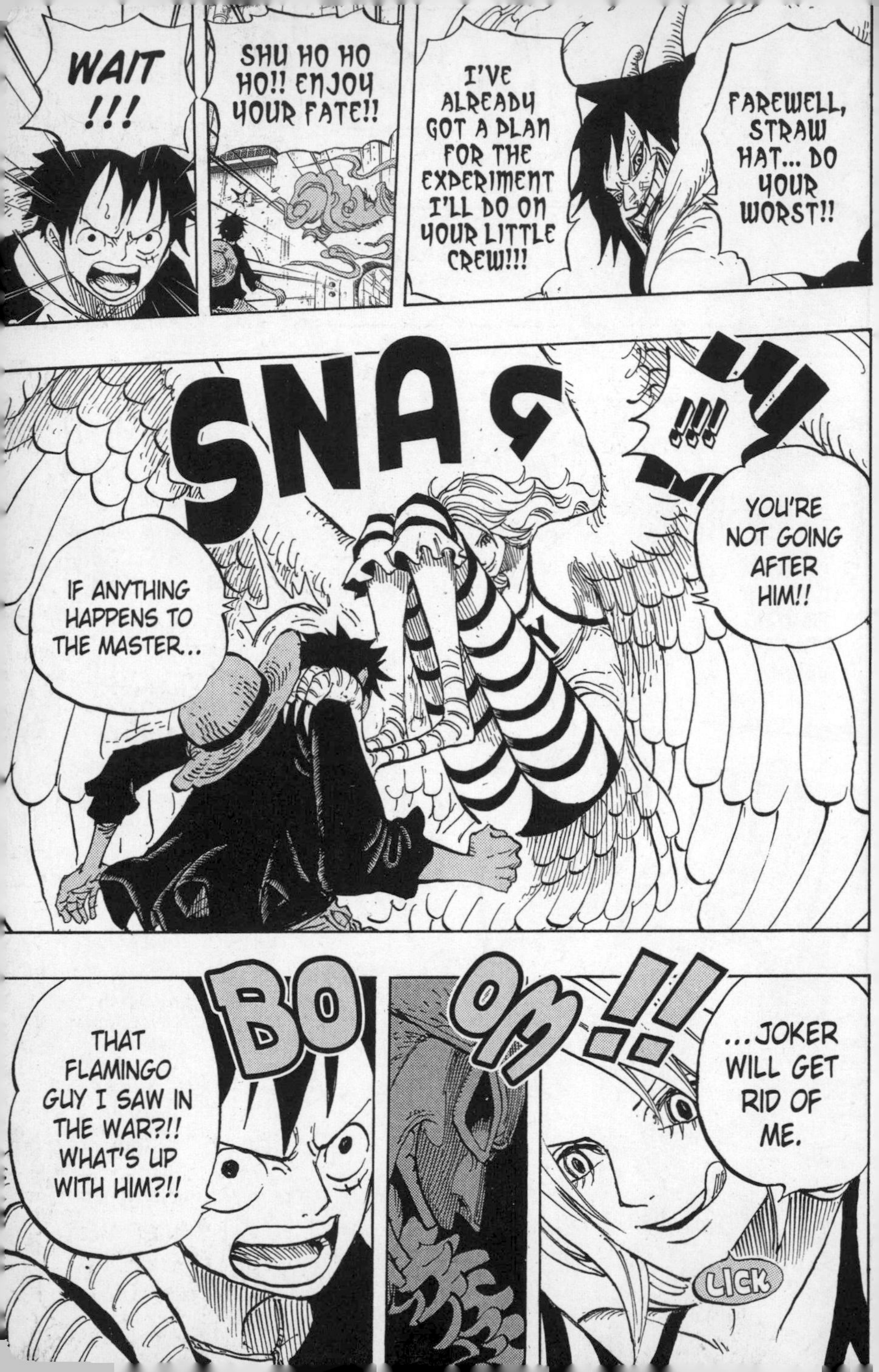
FAREWELL, STRAW HAT... DO YOUR WORST!!
I'VE ALREADY GOT A PLAN FOR THE EXPERIMENT I'LL DO ON YOUR LITTLE CREW!!!
SHU HO HO HO!! ENJOY YOUR FATE!!
WAIT!!!
SNAP!!!
YOU'RE NOT GOING AFTER HIM!!
IF ANYTHING HAPPENS TO THE MASTER...
...JOKER WILL GET RID OF ME.
LICK
BOOM!!
THAT FLAMINGO GUY I SAW IN THE WAR?!! WHAT'S UP WITH HIM?!!

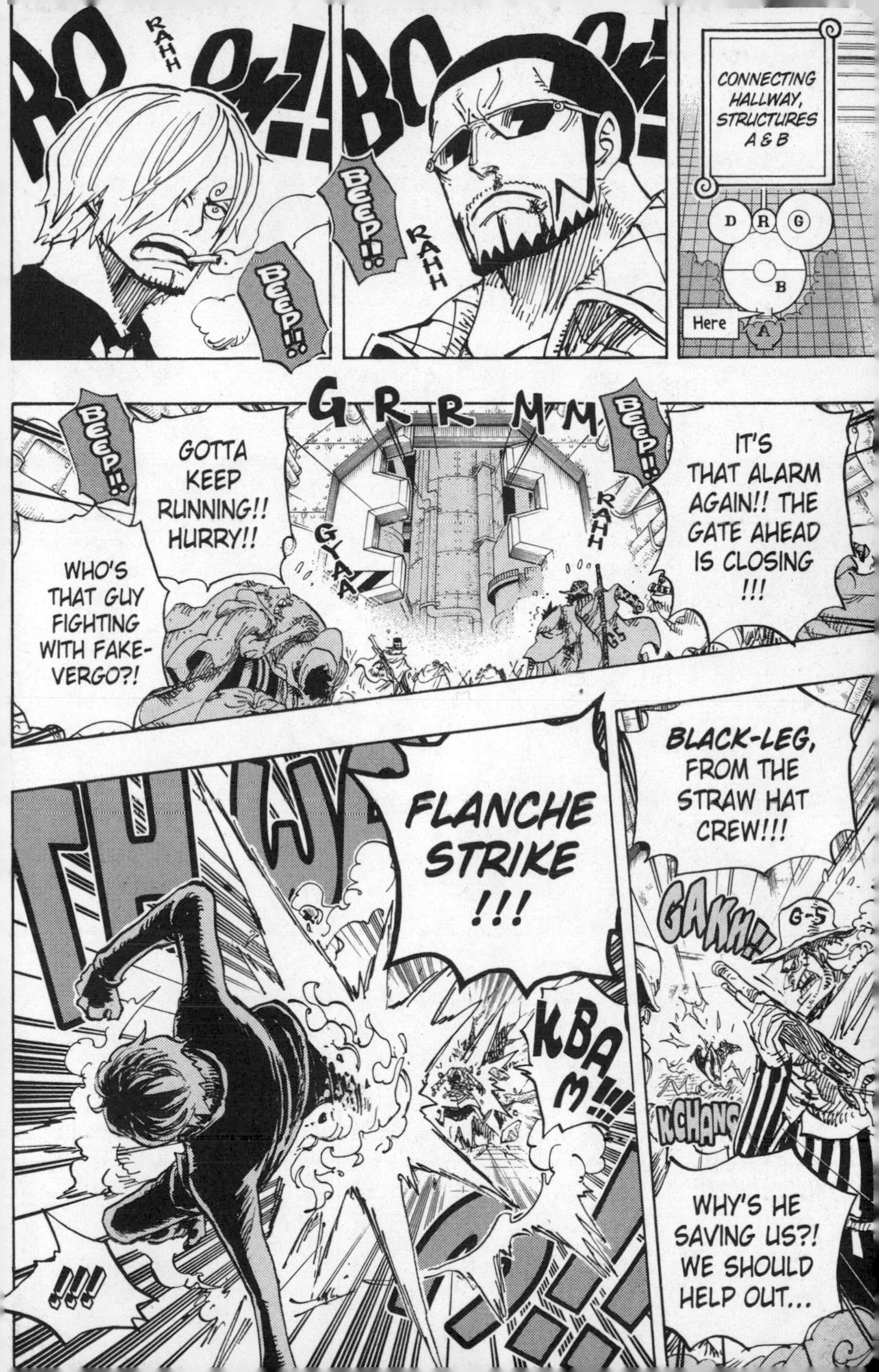

CONNECTING HALLWAY, STRUCTURES A & B
D
R
G
B
Here
A
BEEP!!
RAHH
RAHH
BEEP!!
BEEP!!
IT'S THAT ALARM AGAIN!! THE GATE AHEAD IS CLOSING!!!
BEEP!!
RAHH
GRRRMMM
GYAA
GOTTA KEEP RUNNING!! HURRY!!
BEEP!!
WHO'S THAT GUY FIGHTING WITH FAKE-VERGO?!
BLACK-LEG, FROM THE STRAW HAT CREW!!!
GAKH!!
G-5
KCHANG
WHY'S HE SAVING US?! WE SHOULD HELP OUT...
FLANCHE STRIKE!!!
KBAMM!!!
!!!

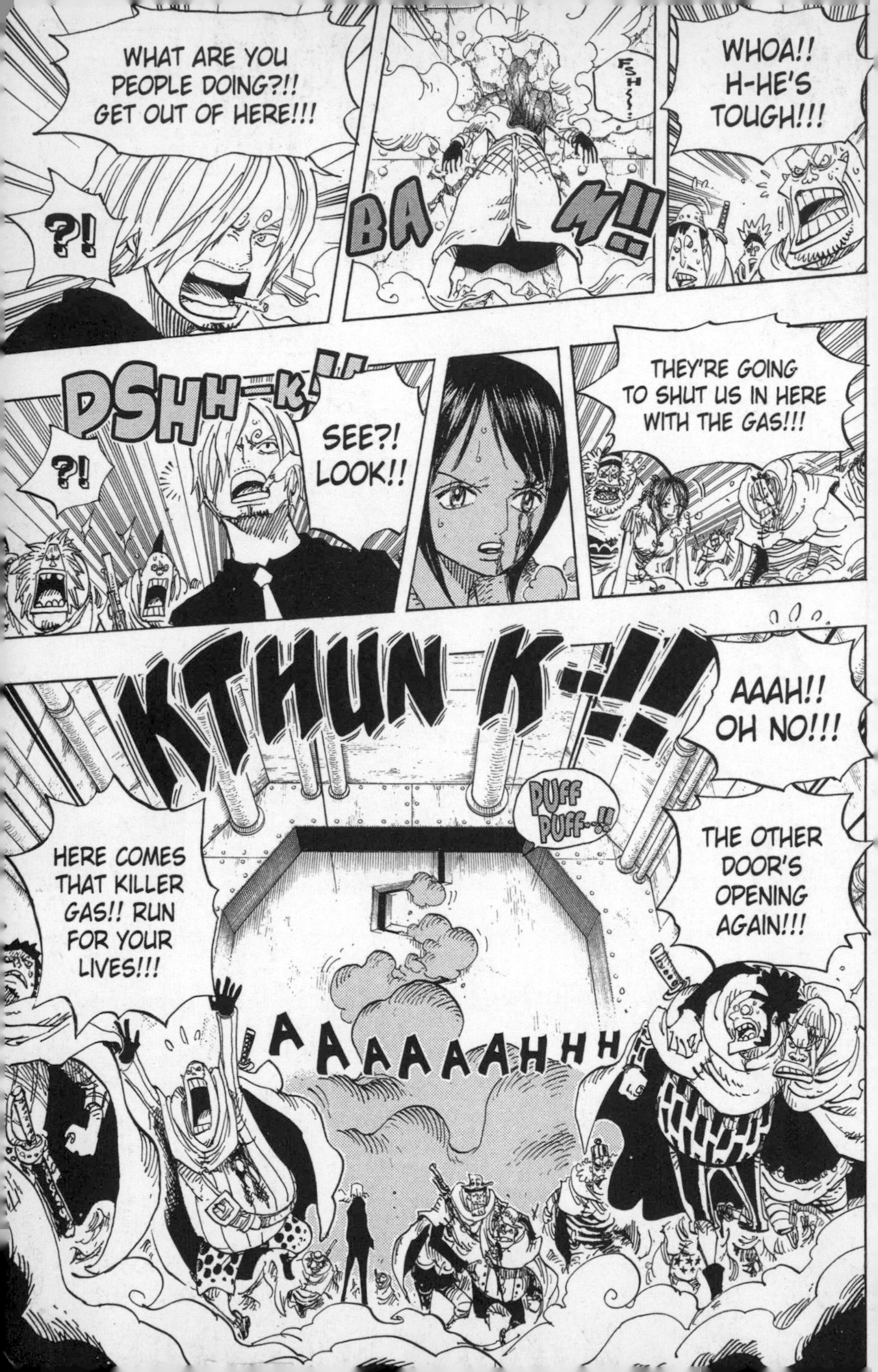
WHOA!! H-HE'S TOUGH!!!
BAM!!
WHAT ARE YOU PEOPLE DOING?!! GET OUT OF HERE!!!
?!
THEY'RE GOING TO SHUT US IN HERE WITH THE GAS!!!
SEE?! LOOK!!
PSHH-K!!
?!
KTHUNK!!
AAAH!! OH NO!!!
THE OTHER DOOR'S OPENING AGAIN!!!
PUFF PUFF!!
HERE COMES THAT KILLER GAS!! RUN FOR YOUR LIVES!!!
AAAAAAAHHH

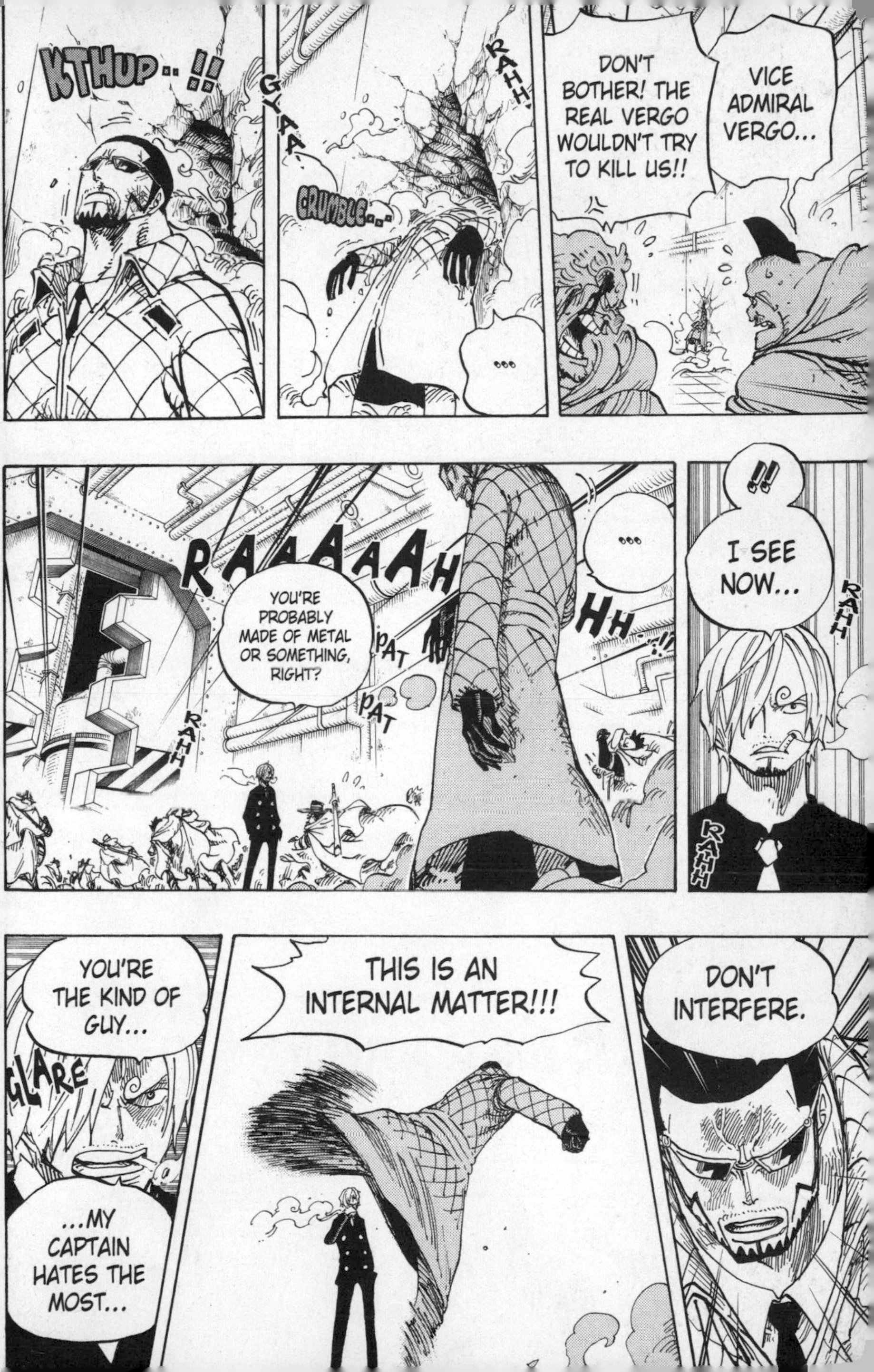
VICE ADMIRAL VERGO...
DON'T BOTHER! THE REAL VERGO WOULDN'T TRY TO KILL US!!
RAHH
GYAA
CRUMBLE...
...
KTHUP..!!
!!
I SEE NOW...
RAHH
RAHH
...
RAAAAAAHH
YOU'RE PROBABLY MADE OF METAL OR SOMETHING, RIGHT?
PAT
PAT
RAHH
DON'T INTERFERE.
THIS IS AN INTERNAL MATTER!!!
YOU'RE THE KIND OF GUY...
GLARE
...MY CAPTAIN HATES THE MOST...

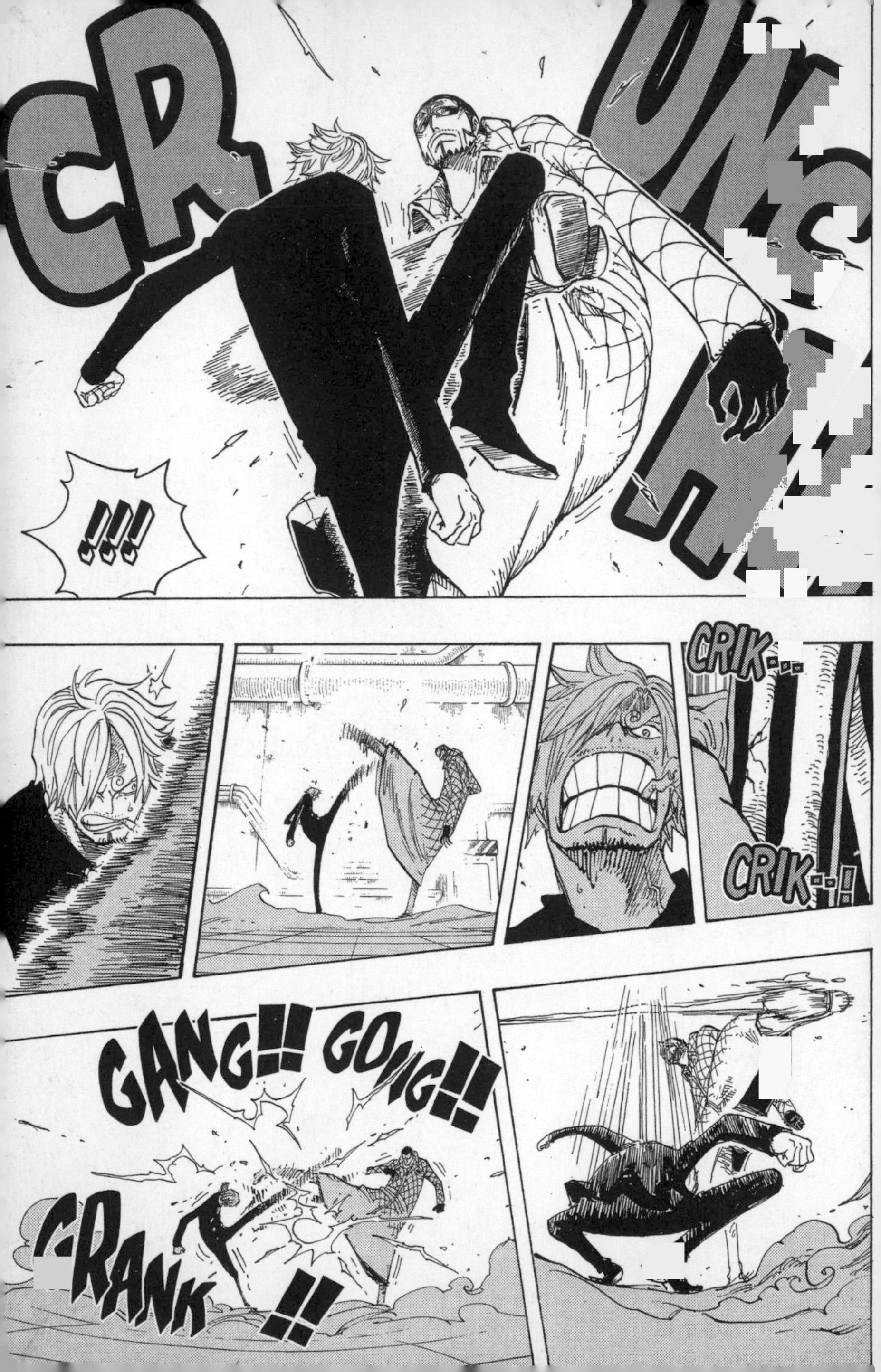

CR
!!!
CRIK...
CRIK..!
GANG!! GONG!!
CRANK!!

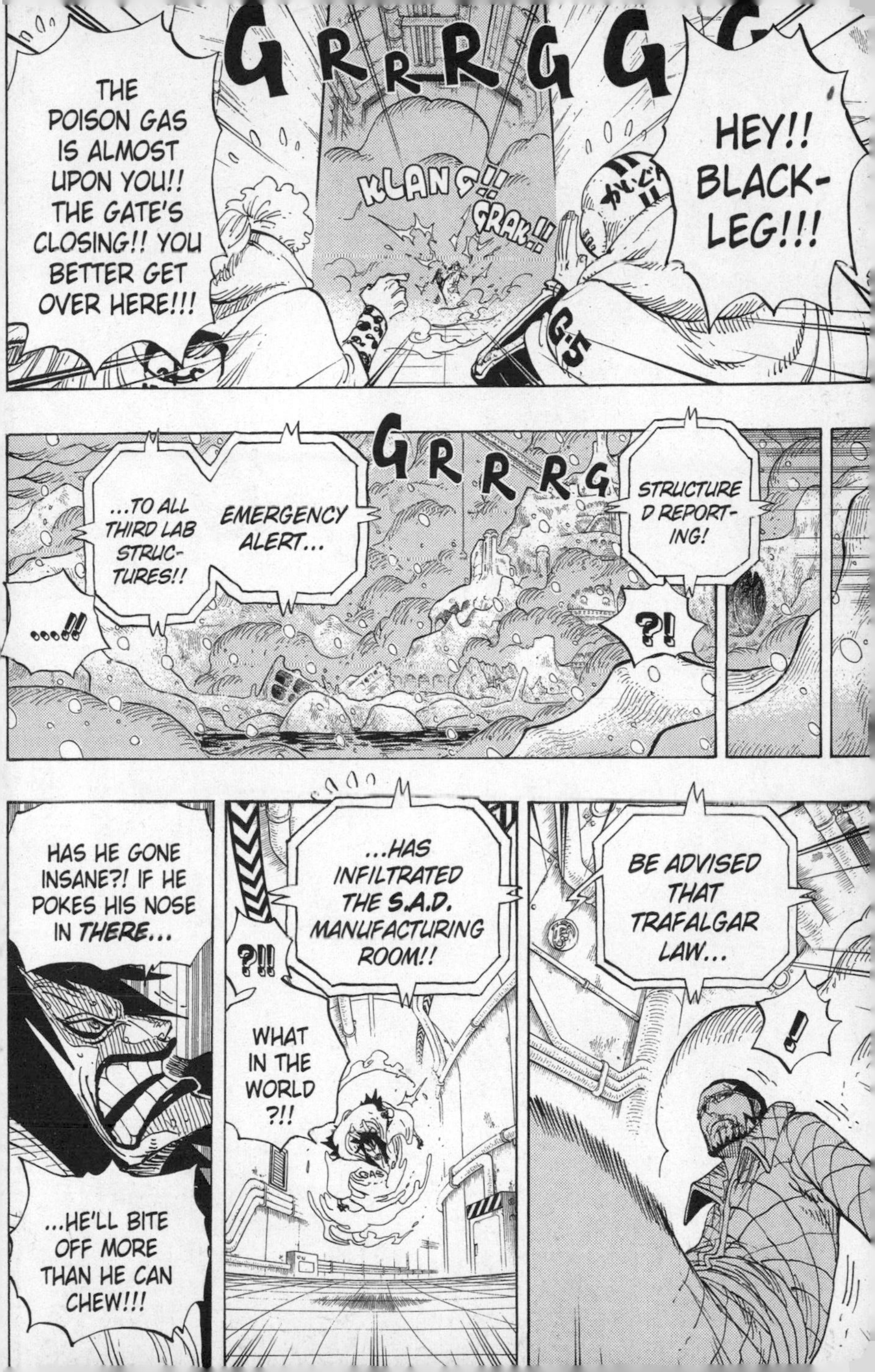
HEY!! BLACK-LEG!!!
GRRRGGG
KLANG!!
GRAK!!
THE POISON GAS IS ALMOST UPON YOU!! THE GATE'S CLOSING!! YOU BETTER GET OVER HERE!!!
G-5
STRUCTURE D REPORTING!
?!
GRRRG
EMERGENCY ALERT...
...TO ALL THIRD LAB STRUCTURES!!
....!!
BE ADVISED THAT TRAFALGAR LAW...
!
...HAS INFILTRATED THE S.A.D. MANUFACTURING ROOM!!
?!!
WHAT IN THE WORLD?!!
HAS HE GONE INSANE?! IF HE POKES HIS NOSE IN *THERE*...
...HE'LL BITE OFF MORE THAN HE CAN CHEW!!!

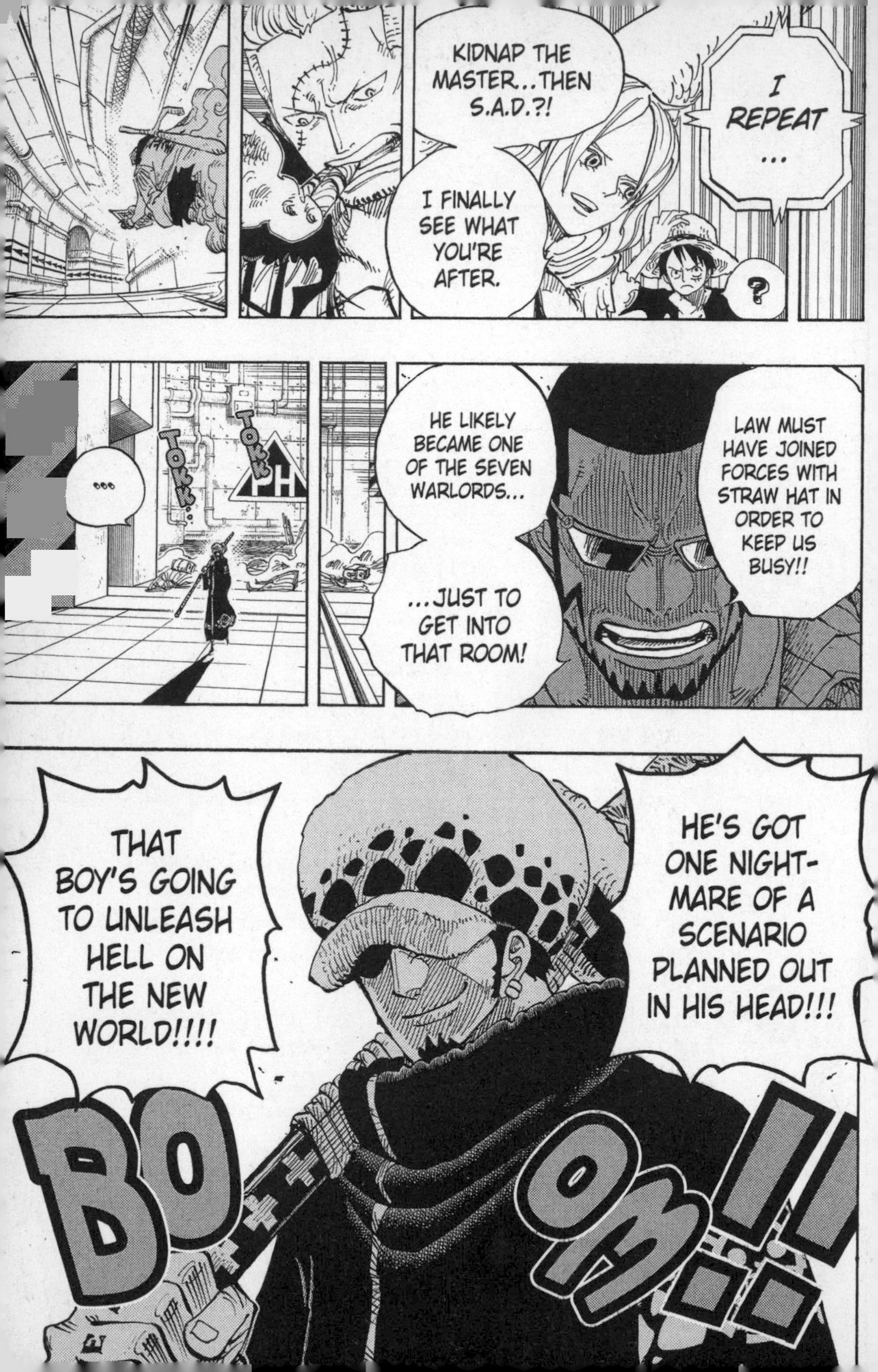
I REPEAT ...
?
KIDNAP THE MASTER...THEN S.A.D.?!
I FINALLY SEE WHAT YOU'RE AFTER.
LAW MUST HAVE JOINED FORCES WITH STRAW HAT IN ORDER TO KEEP US BUSY!!
HE LIKELY BECAME ONE OF THE SEVEN WARLORDS...
...JUST TO GET INTO THAT ROOM!
TOKK
TOKK
PH
...
HE'S GOT ONE NIGHT-MARE OF A SCENARIO PLANNED OUT IN HIS HEAD!!!
THAT BOY'S GOING TO UNLEASH HELL ON THE NEW WORLD!!!!
BOOM!!

SBS Question Corner

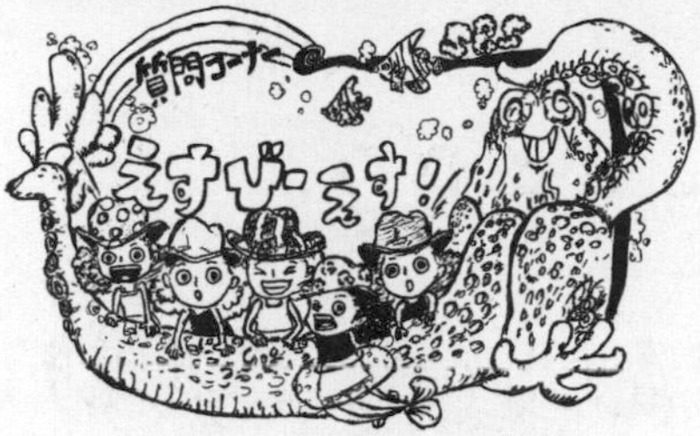

(Ryo, Wakayama)

A: There are two letters to show off here.

Q: I have a question, Mr. Oda. Can you give us profiles (birthday, height, age) of all the Straw Hats with their current information?

--Ma~

Q: Mr. Oda! I have a request! Can you tell me the order that the various Straw Hats joined the crew? Thank you!

--Yoshikawa

A: What a novel idea! Good thinking. After fifteen years of One Piece, you lose track of these things. The sender of the first letter above is just ten years old. When you're older, go back and read how the Straw Hats came together. The number on each picture is the order they joined the crew. The heights listed are the first for the crew after the two-year skip. Oh, and just so you know, before the Thousand Sunny, they rode on a ship called the Merry Go.

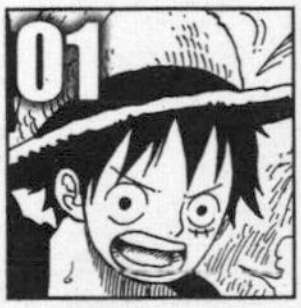
01

Monkey D. Luffy
May 5, Age 19
5'9" (Gum-Gum Fruit)
Appears: Vol. 1 –(E)

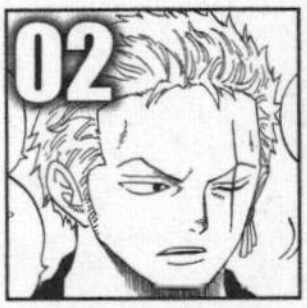
02

Roronoa Zolo
November 11, Age 21
5'11"
Appears: Vol. 1 –(E)

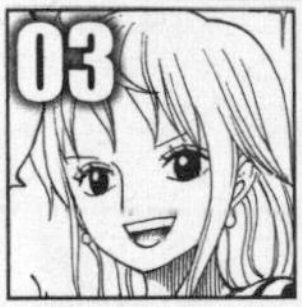
03

Nami
July 3, Age 20
5'7"
Appears: Vol. 1 –(E)

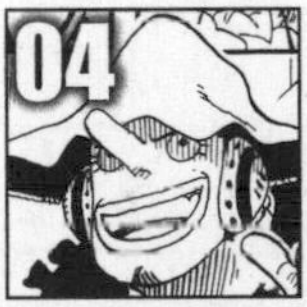
04

Usopp
April 1, Age 19
5'9"
Appears: Vol. 3 –(E)

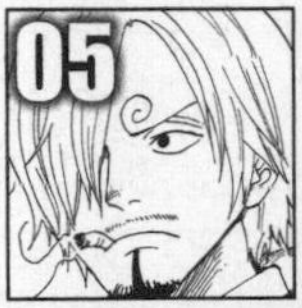
05

Sanji
March 2, Age 21
5'11"
Appears: Vol. 5 –(N)

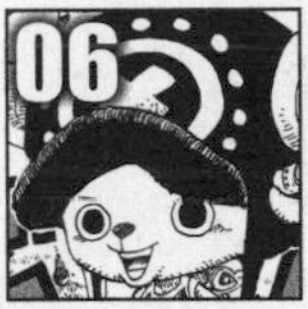
06

TonyTony Chopper
December 24, Age 17
2'11" (Human-Human Fruit)
Appears: Vol. 15 –(G)

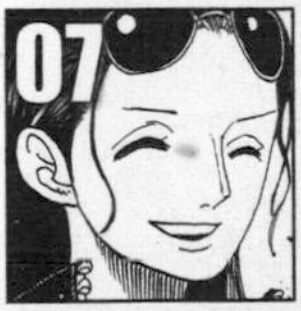
07

Nico Robin
February 6, Age 30
6'2" (Flower-Flower Fruit)
Appears: Vol. 13 –West

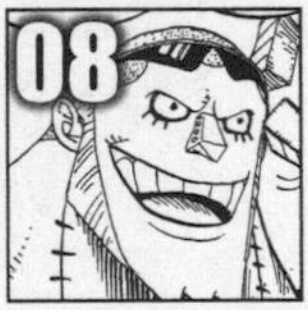
08

Franky (Cutty Flam)
March 9, Age 36
7'11"
Appears: Vol. 35 –(S)

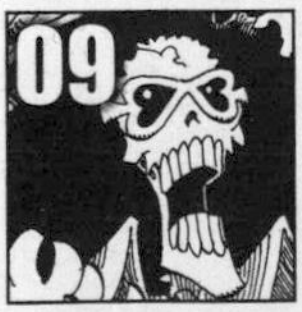
09

Brook
April 3, Age 90
9'1" (Revive-Revive Fruit)
Appears: Vol. 46 –(W)

A: The circled letters next to their first appearance shows what sea they're from.
(E) East Blue (W) West Blue
(S) South Blue (N) North Blue
(G) Grand Line
If you want to know their bounty numbers, go back and check out the character profiles at the beginning of the book.

Chapter 682:
PUPPET MASTER

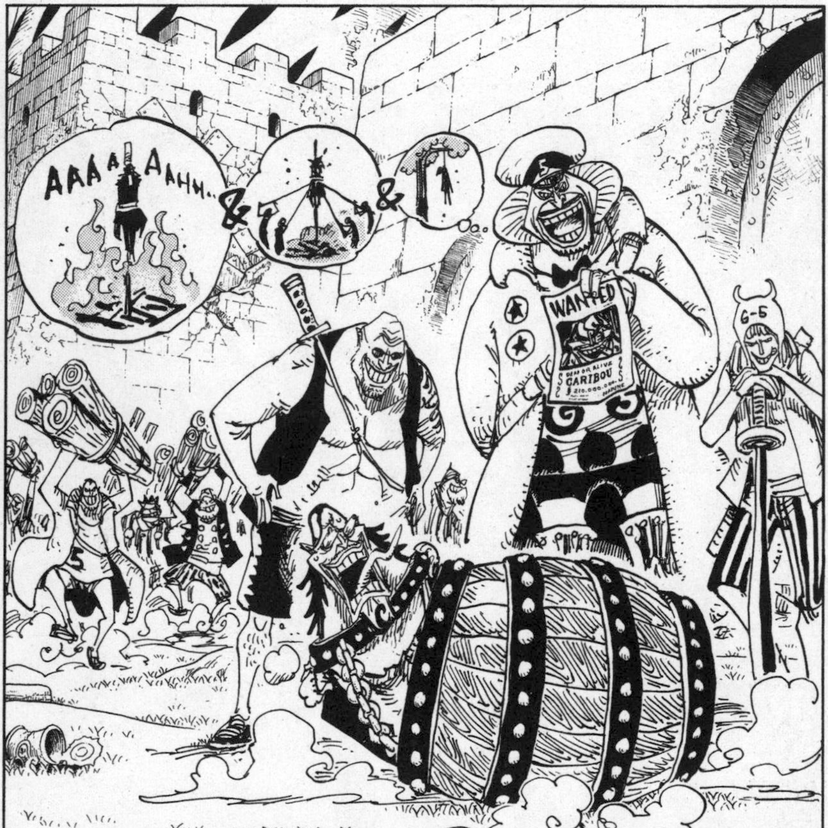
AAAAAAHH...
&
&
WANTED
CARIBOU

CARIBOU'S NEW WORLD KEE HEE HEE, VOL. 8: "COMMODORE YARISUGI HAS FOUND TOO MUCH OF A GOOD THING"

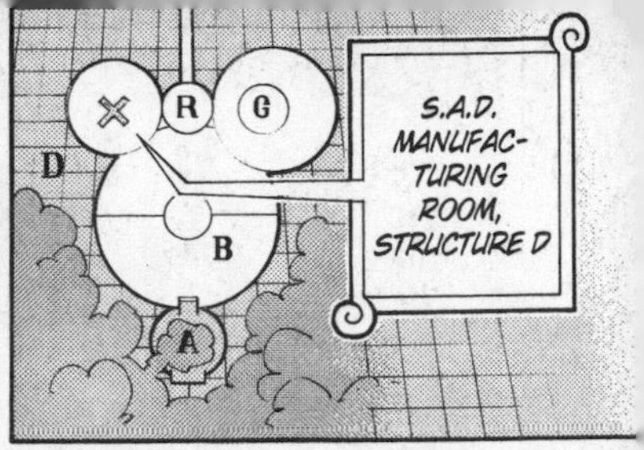
R
G
D
B
A
S.A.D. MANUFAC-TURING ROOM, STRUCTURE D

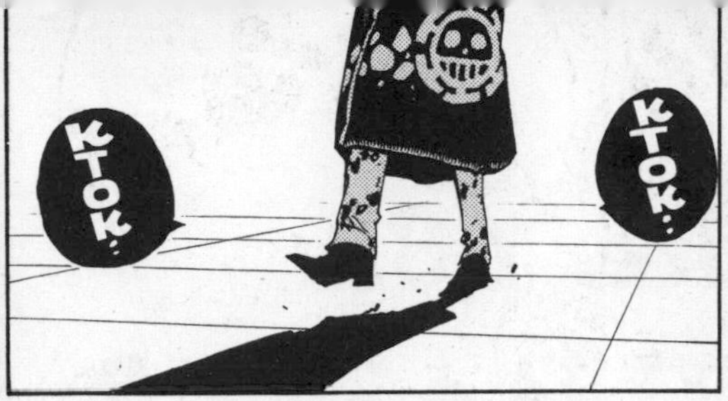
KTOK
KTOK

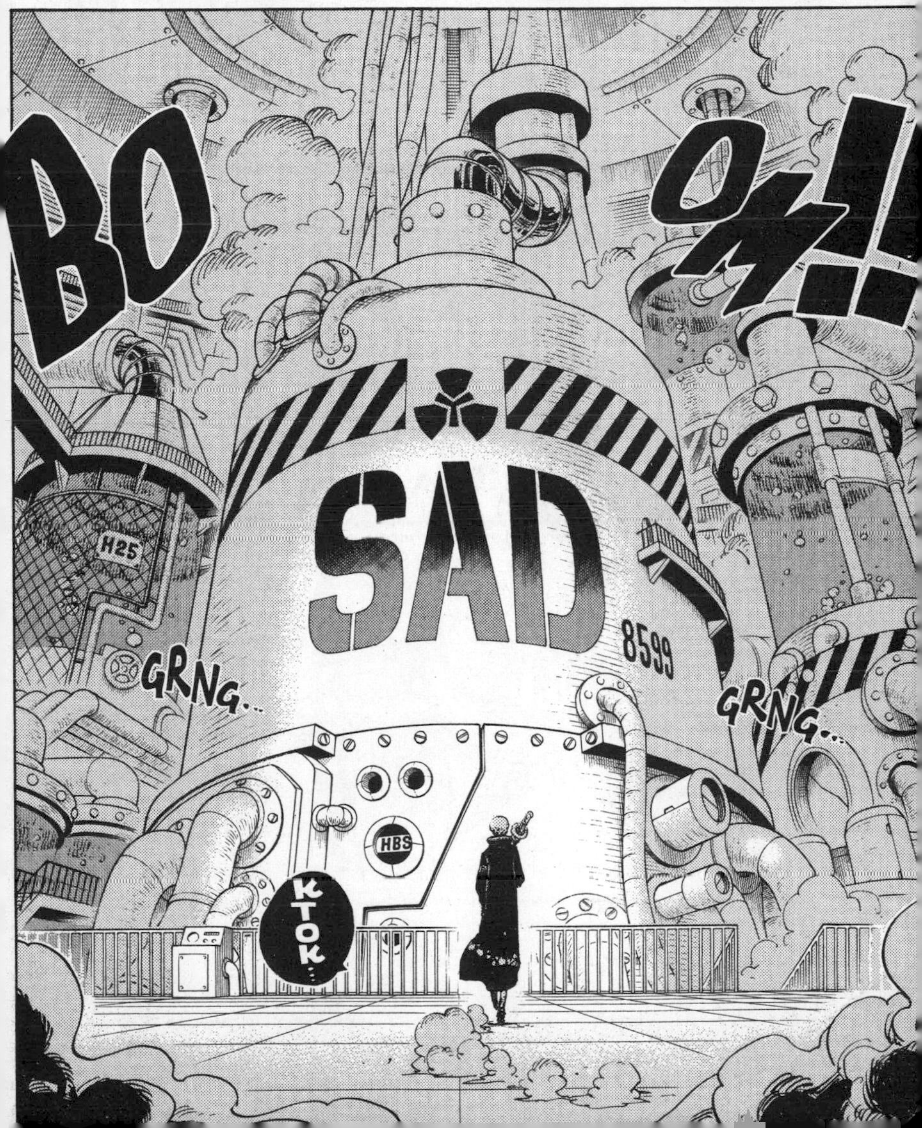
BOOM!!
SAD
8599
H25
GRNG...
GRNG...
HBS
KTOK...

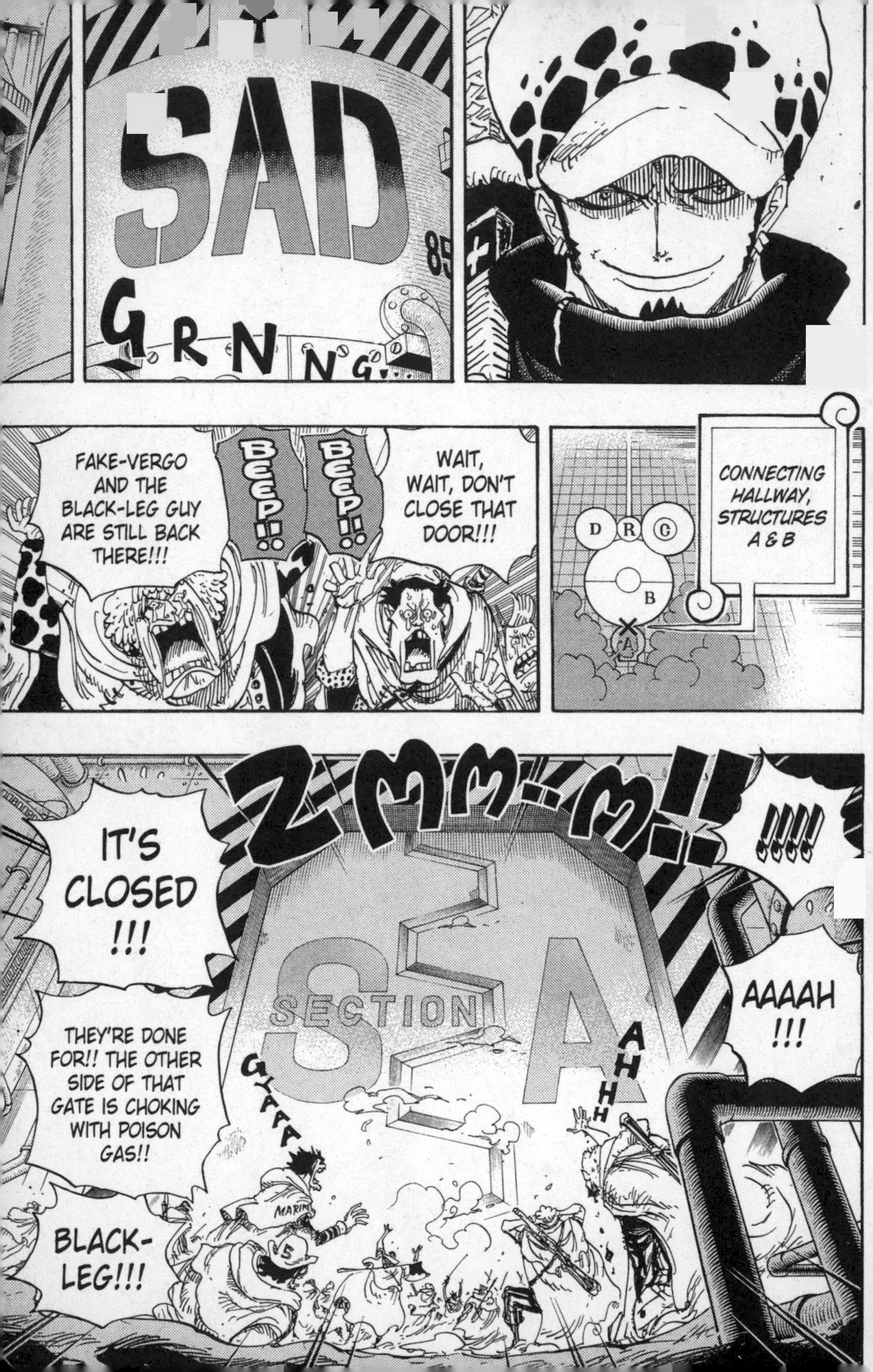
SAD
85
GRNNNG...
CONNECTING HALLWAY, STRUCTURES A & B
D
R
C
B
A
WAIT, WAIT, DON'T CLOSE THAT DOOR!!!
BEEP!!
BEEP!!
FAKE-VERGO AND THE BLACK-LEG GUY ARE STILL BACK THERE!!!
ZMM-M!!
!!!!
AAAAH!!!
IT'S CLOSED!!!
SECTION
SA
AHHH
GYAAA
THEY'RE DONE FOR!! THE OTHER SIDE OF THAT GATE IS CHOKING WITH POISON GAS!!
BLACK-LEG!!!

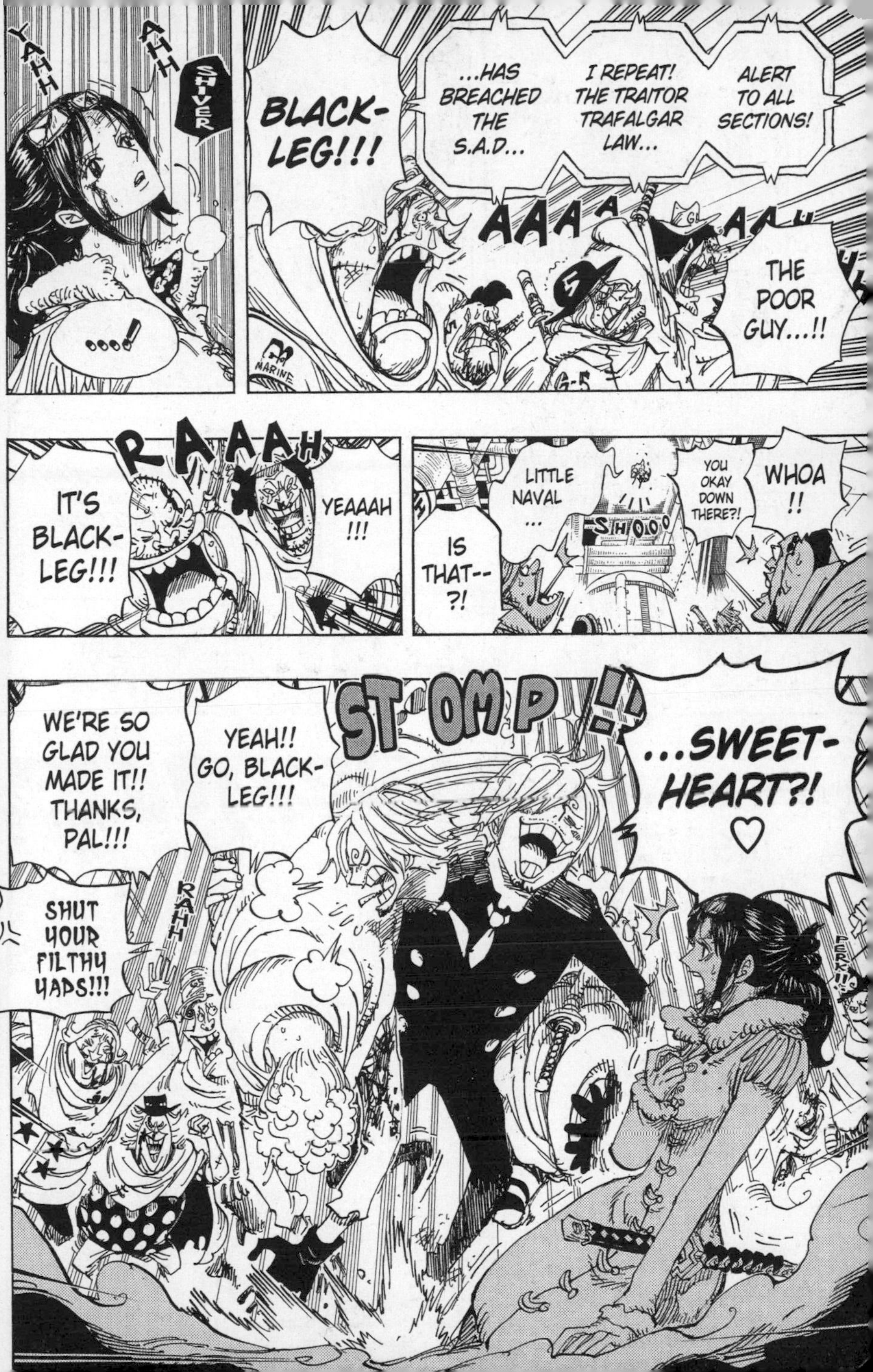
ALERT TO ALL SECTIONS!
I REPEAT! THE TRAITOR TRAFALGAR LAW...
...HAS BREACHED THE S.A.D...
BLACK-LEG!!!
AAAAAAH
THE POOR GUY...!!
MARINE
G-5
AHH
YAHH
SHIVER
....!
WHOA !!
YOU OKAY DOWN THERE?!
LITTLE NAVAL ...
IS THAT--?!
SHOOO
RAAAH
YEAAAH !!!
IT'S BLACK-LEG!!!
...SWEET-HEART?! ♡
STOMP!!
PERK!!
YEAH!! GO, BLACK-LEG!!!
WE'RE SO GLAD YOU MADE IT!! THANKS, PAL!!!
RAHH
SHUT YOUR FILTHY YAPS!!!

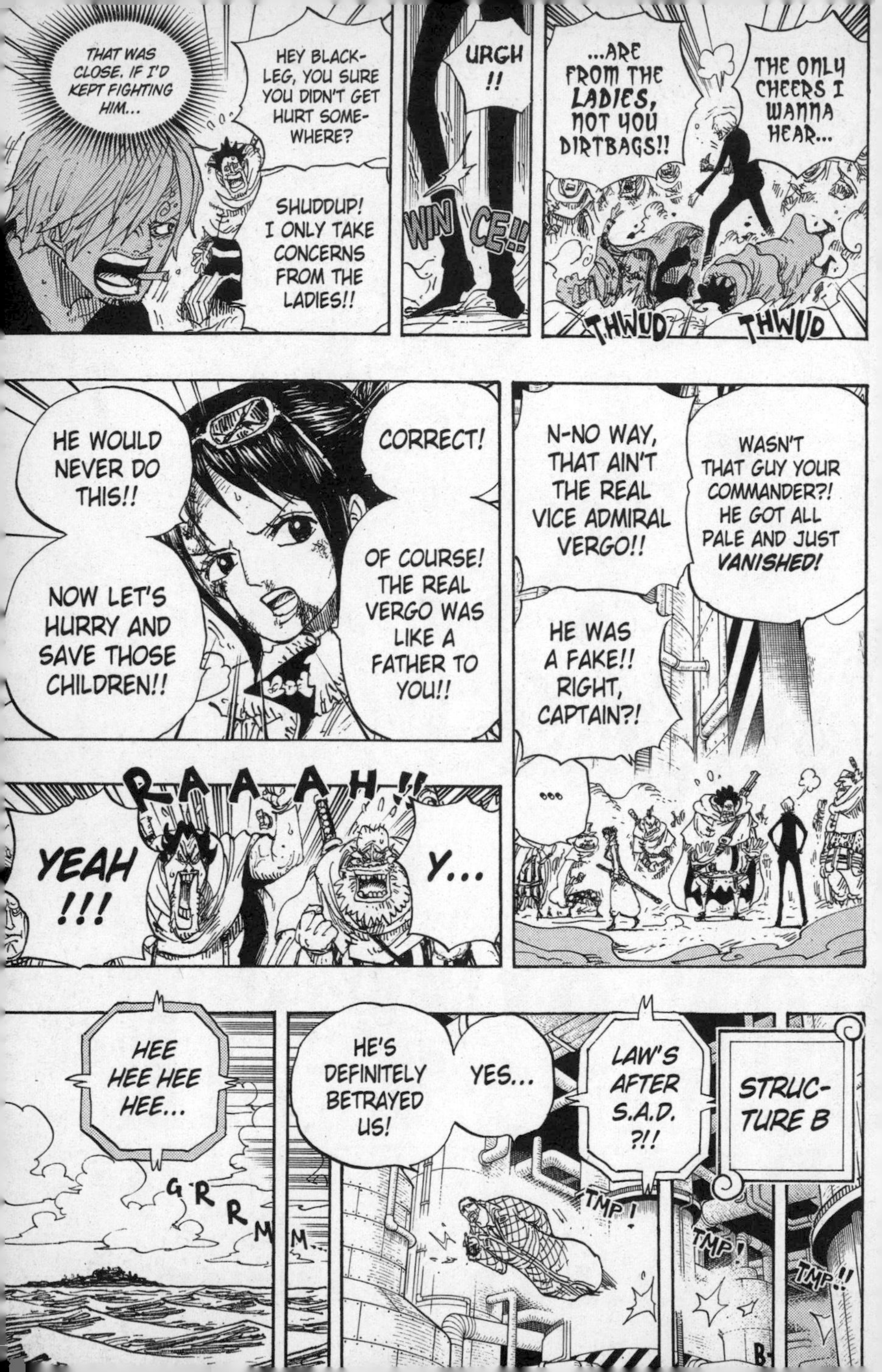
THE ONLY CHEERS I WANNA HEAR...
...ARE FROM THE LADIES, NOT YOU DIRTBAGS!!
THWUD
THWUD
URGH!!
WINCE!!
HEY BLACK-LEG, YOU SURE YOU DIDN'T GET HURT SOMEWHERE?
SHUDDUP! I ONLY TAKE CONCERNS FROM THE LADIES!!
THAT WAS CLOSE. IF I'D KEPT FIGHTING HIM...
WASN'T THAT GUY YOUR COMMANDER?! HE GOT ALL PALE AND JUST VANISHED!
N-NO WAY, THAT AIN'T THE REAL VICE ADMIRAL VERGO!!
HE WAS A FAKE!! RIGHT, CAPTAIN?!
...
CORRECT!
OF COURSE! THE REAL VERGO WAS LIKE A FATHER TO YOU!!
HE WOULD NEVER DO THIS!!
NOW LET'S HURRY AND SAVE THOSE CHILDREN!!
Y...
RAAAH!!
YEAH!!!
STRUCTURE B
LAW'S AFTER S.A.D.?!!
TMP!
TMP!
TMP!!
YES...
HE'S DEFINITELY BETRAYED US!
HEE HEE HEE HEE...
GRRMMM...

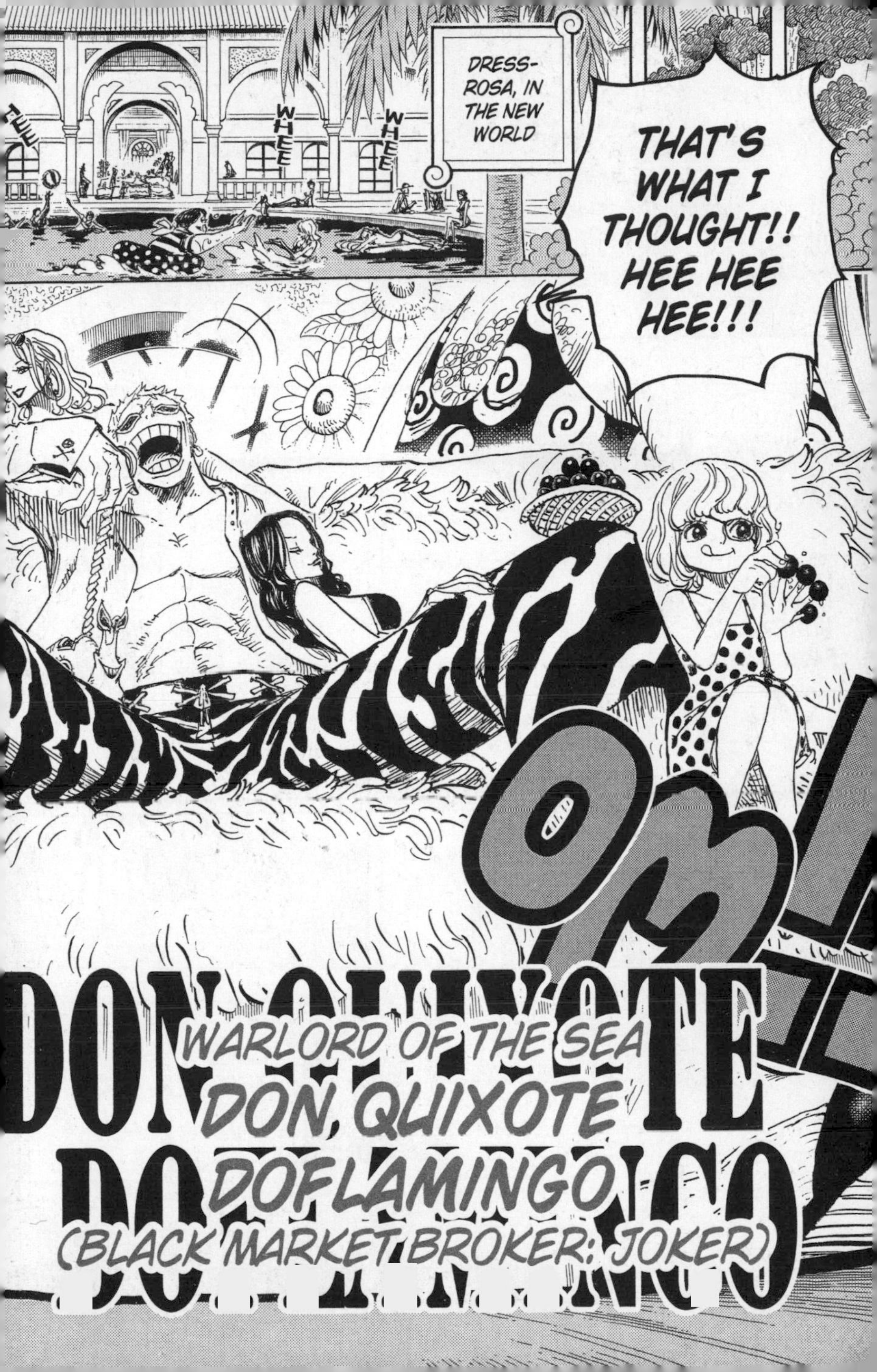
DRESS-ROSA, IN THE NEW WORLD
WHEEE
WHEEE
THAT'S WHAT I THOUGHT!! HEE HEE HEE!!!
WARLORD OF THE SEA
DON QUIXOTE DOFLAMINGO
(BLACK MARKET BROKER: JOKER)

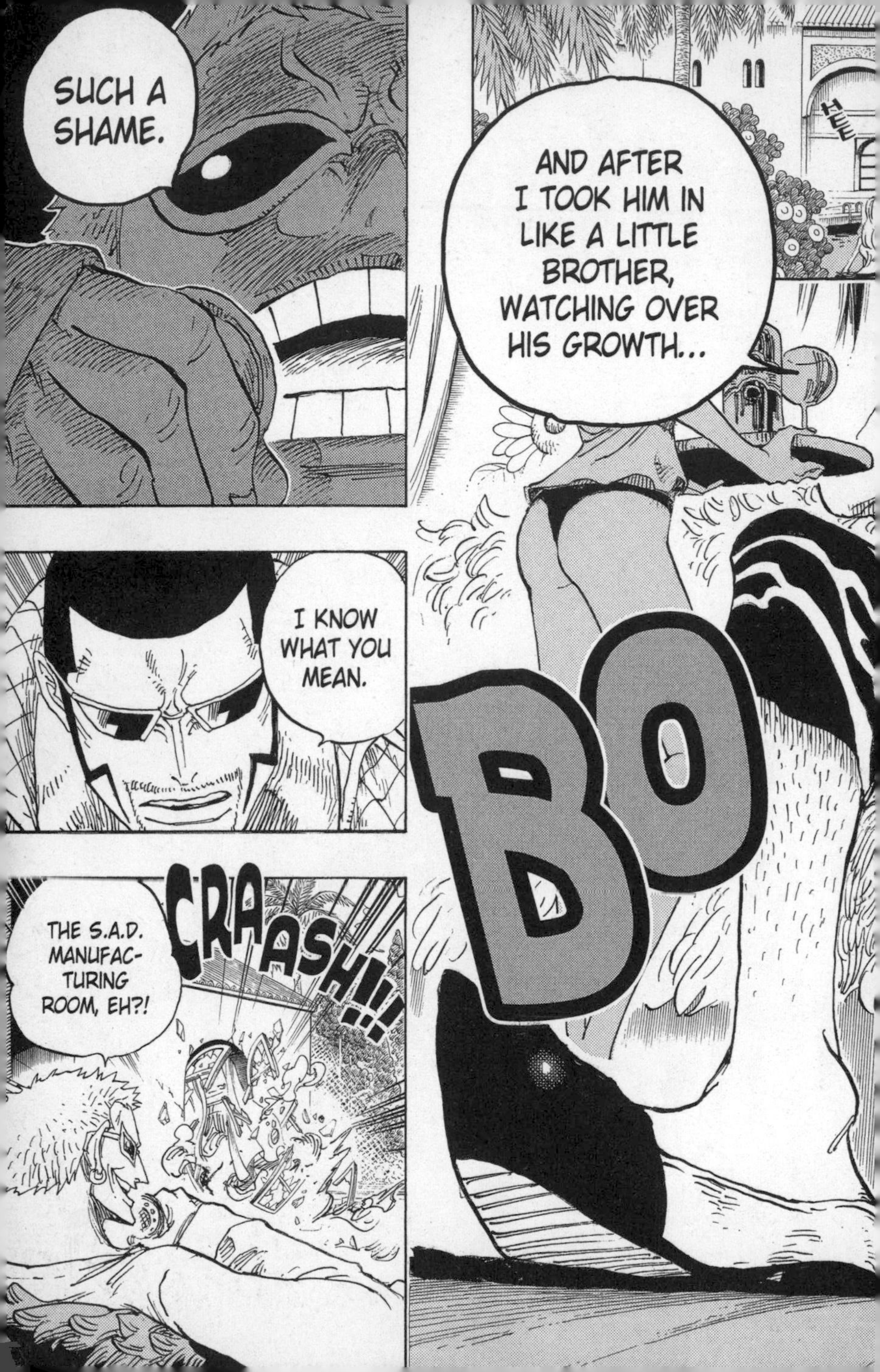
HEE
AND AFTER I TOOK HIM IN LIKE A LITTLE BROTHER, WATCHING OVER HIS GROWTH...
BO
SUCH A SHAME.
I KNOW WHAT YOU MEAN.
CRAASH!!!
THE S.A.D. MANUFAC-TURING ROOM, EH?!

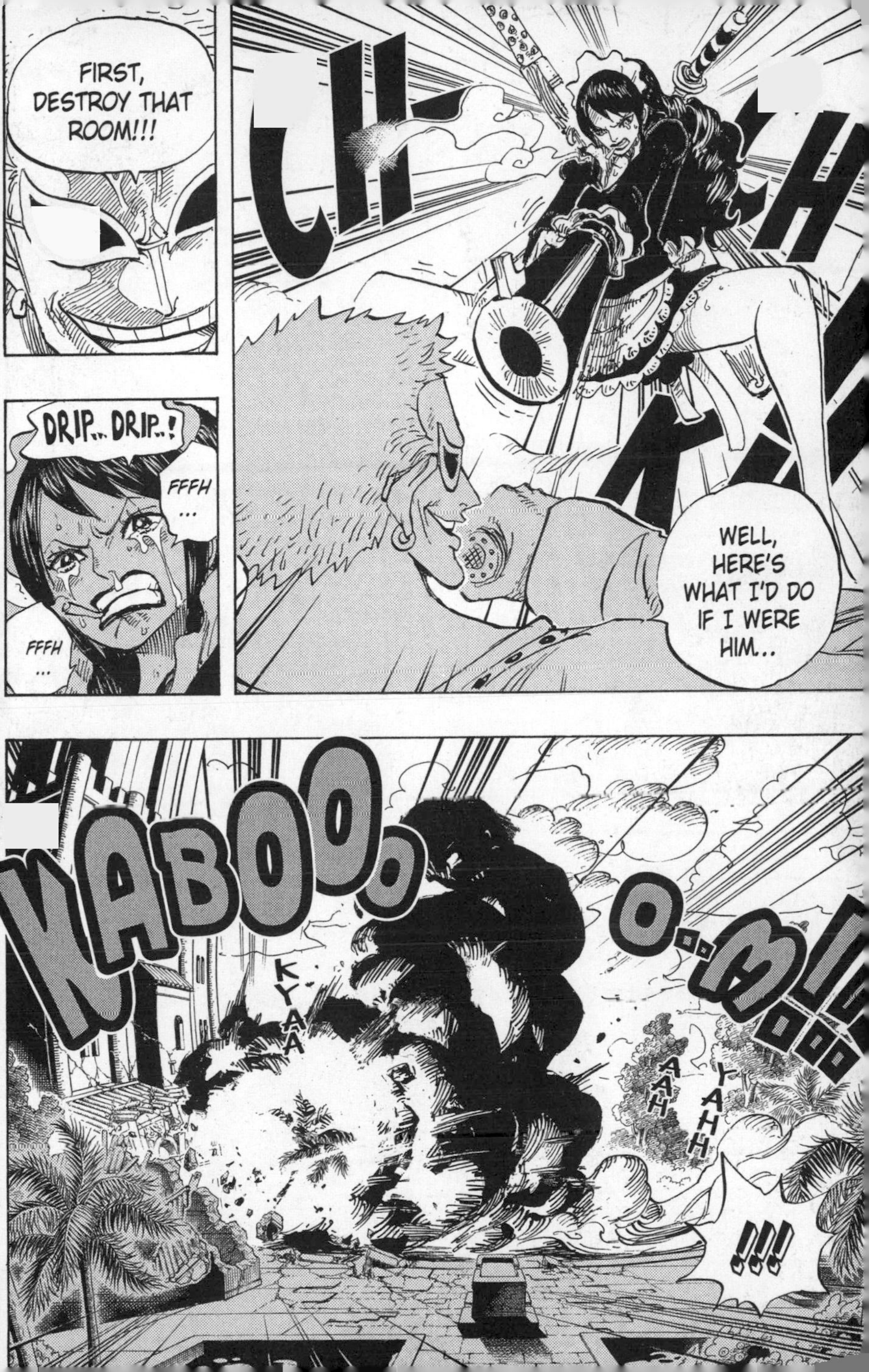
CH
CH
WELL, HERE'S WHAT I'D DO IF I WERE HIM..
FIRST, DESTROY THAT ROOM!!!
DRIP.. DRIP..!
FFFH ...
FFFH ...
KABOOOO-O-OM!!
KYAA
AAH
YAHH
!!!

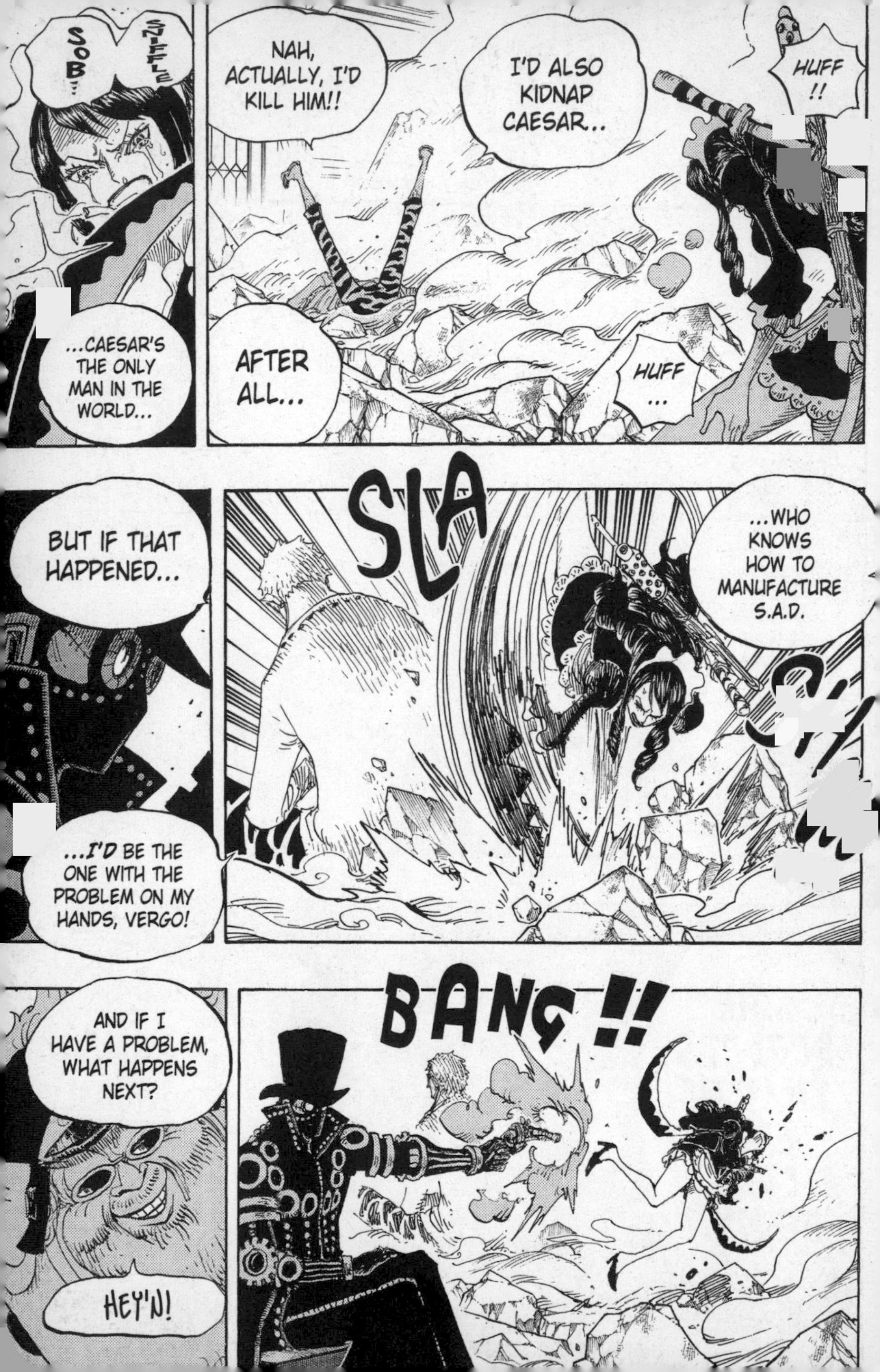
HUFF!!
I'D ALSO KIDNAP CAESAR...
NAH, ACTUALLY, I'D KILL HIM!!
HUFF...
AFTER ALL...
SOB... SNIFFLE
...CAESAR'S THE ONLY MAN IN THE WORLD...
SLA
...WHO KNOWS HOW TO MANUFACTURE S.A.D.
BUT IF THAT HAPPENED...
...I'D BE THE ONE WITH THE PROBLEM ON MY HANDS, VERGO!
BANG!!
AND IF I HAVE A PROBLEM, WHAT HAPPENS NEXT?
HEY'N!

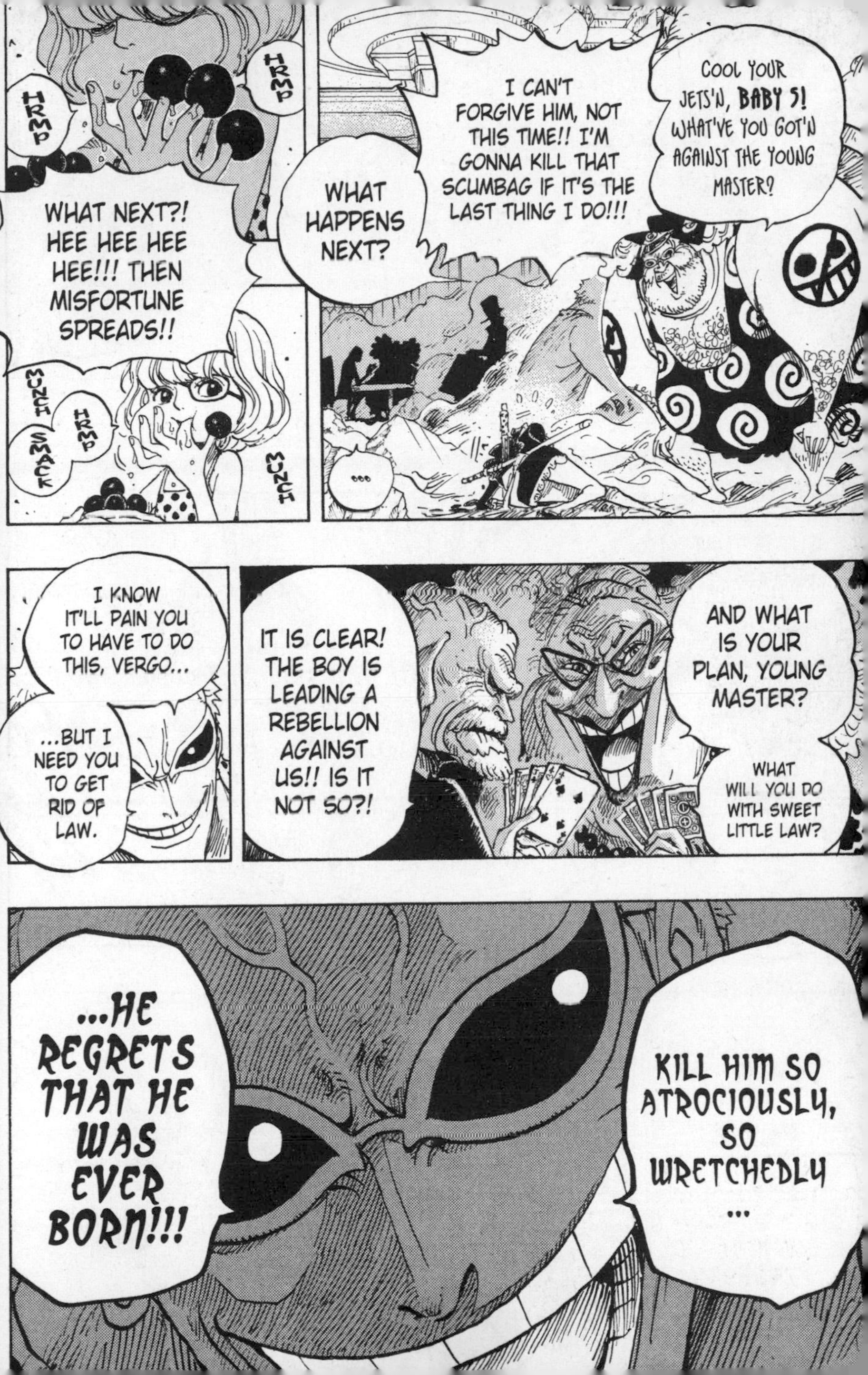
COOL YOUR JETS'N, BABY 5! WHAT'VE YOU GOT'N AGAINST THE YOUNG MASTER?
I CAN'T FORGIVE HIM, NOT THIS TIME!! I'M GONNA KILL THAT SCUMBAG IF IT'S THE LAST THING I DO!!!
WHAT HAPPENS NEXT?
...
HRMP
HRMP
WHAT NEXT?! HEE HEE HEE HEE!!! THEN MISFORTUNE SPREADS!!
MUNCH
HRMP
MUNCH
SMACK
AND WHAT IS YOUR PLAN, YOUNG MASTER?
WHAT WILL YOU DO WITH SWEET LITTLE LAW?
IT IS CLEAR! THE BOY IS LEADING A REBELLION AGAINST US!! IS IT NOT SO?!
I KNOW IT'LL PAIN YOU TO HAVE TO DO THIS, VERGO...
...BUT I NEED YOU TO GET RID OF LAW.
KILL HIM SO ATROCIOUSLY, SO WRETCHEDLY ...
...HE REGRETS THAT HE WAS EVER BORN!!!

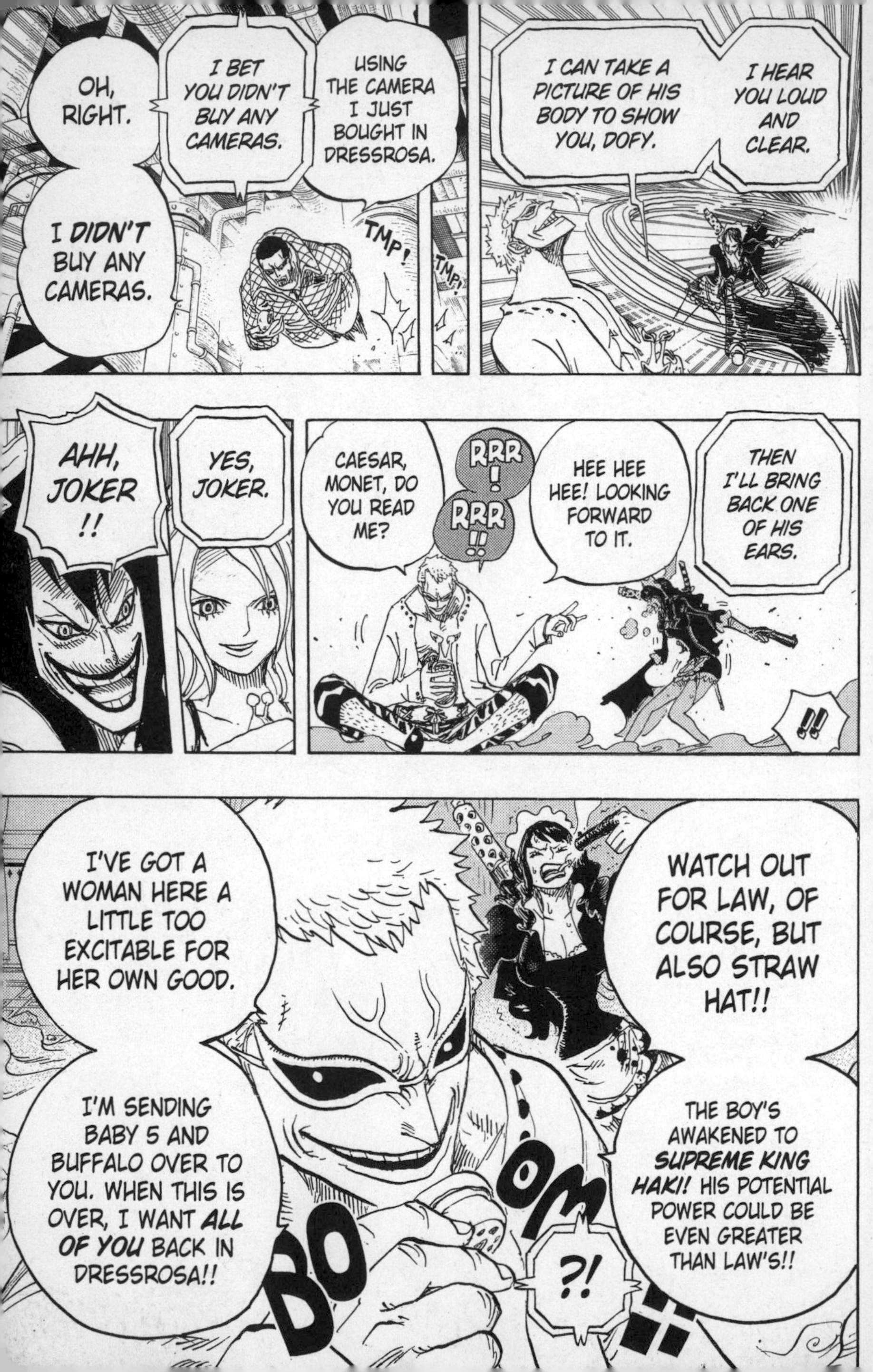
I HEAR YOU LOUD AND CLEAR.
I CAN TAKE A PICTURE OF HIS BODY TO SHOW YOU, DOFY.
USING THE CAMERA I JUST BOUGHT IN DRESSROSA.
I BET YOU DIDN'T BUY ANY CAMERAS.
OH, RIGHT.
TMP!
TMP!
I *DIDN'T* BUY ANY CAMERAS.
THEN I'LL BRING BACK ONE OF HIS EARS.
HEE HEE HEE! LOOKING FORWARD TO IT.
RRR!
RRR!!
CAESAR, MONET, DO YOU READ ME?
!!
YES, JOKER.
AHH, JOKER !!
WATCH OUT FOR LAW, OF COURSE, BUT ALSO STRAW HAT!!
THE BOY'S AWAKENED TO ***SUPREME KING HAKI!*** HIS POTENTIAL POWER COULD BE EVEN GREATER THAN LAW'S!!
?!
I'VE GOT A WOMAN HERE A LITTLE TOO EXCITABLE FOR HER OWN GOOD.
I'M SENDING BABY 5 AND BUFFALO OVER TO YOU. WHEN THIS IS OVER, I WANT ***ALL OF YOU*** BACK IN DRESSROSA!!
BOOM!!

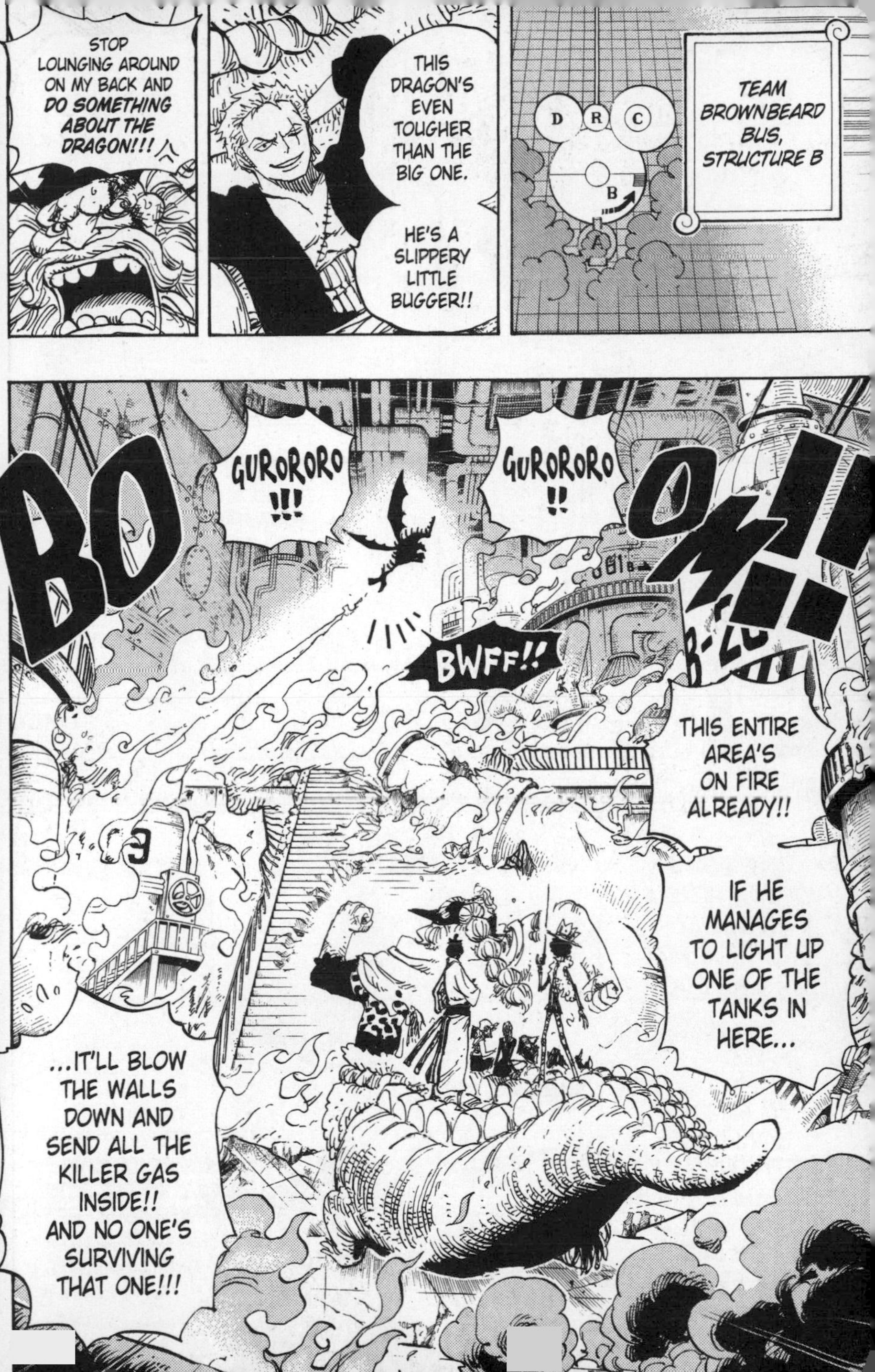
TEAM BROWNBEARD BUS, STRUCTURE B
D
R
C
B
A
THIS DRAGON'S EVEN TOUGHER THAN THE BIG ONE.
HE'S A SLIPPERY LITTLE BUGGER!!
STOP LOUNGING AROUND ON MY BACK AND DO SOMETHING ABOUT THE DRAGON!!!
OM!!
GURORORO!!
GURORORO!!!
BO
BWFF!!
THIS ENTIRE AREA'S ON FIRE ALREADY!!
IF HE MANAGES TO LIGHT UP ONE OF THE TANKS IN HERE...
...IT'LL BLOW THE WALLS DOWN AND SEND ALL THE KILLER GAS INSIDE!! AND NO ONE'S SURVIVING THAT ONE!!!

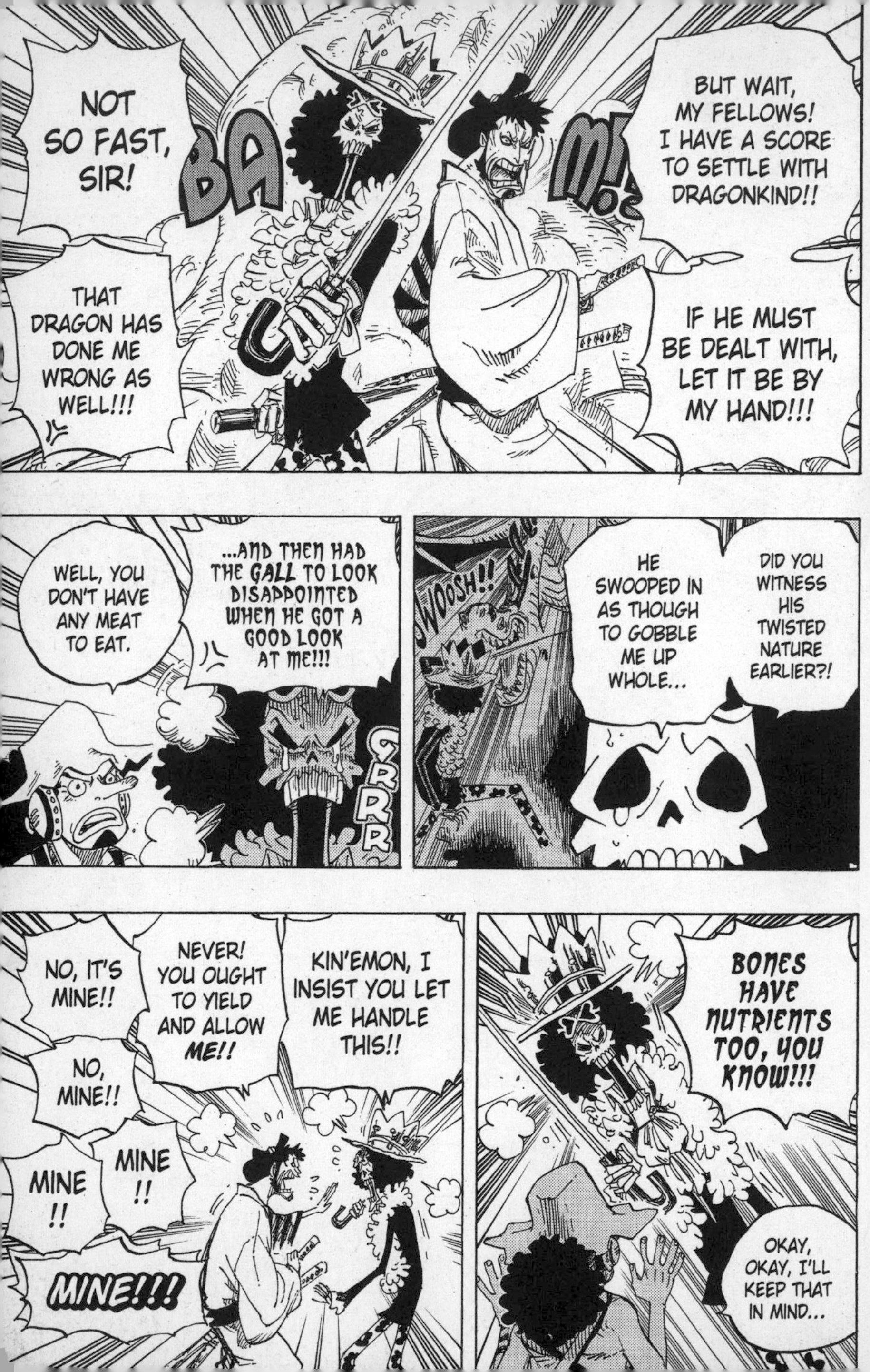
BUT WAIT, MY FELLOWS! I HAVE A SCORE TO SETTLE WITH DRAGONKIND!!
IF HE MUST BE DEALT WITH, LET IT BE BY MY HAND!!!
BAM!
NOT SO FAST, SIR!
THAT DRAGON HAS DONE ME WRONG AS WELL!!!
DID YOU WITNESS HIS TWISTED NATURE EARLIER?!
HE SWOOPED IN AS THOUGH TO GOBBLE ME UP WHOLE...
SWOOSH!!
...AND THEN HAD THE GALL TO LOOK DISAPPOINTED WHEN HE GOT A GOOD LOOK AT ME!!!
GRRR
WELL, YOU DON'T HAVE ANY MEAT TO EAT.
BONES HAVE NUTRIENTS TOO, YOU KNOW!!!
OKAY, OKAY, I'LL KEEP THAT IN MIND...
KIN'EMON, I INSIST YOU LET ME HANDLE THIS!!
NEVER! YOU OUGHT TO YIELD AND ALLOW ME!!
NO, IT'S MINE!!
NO, MINE!!
MINE!!
MINE!!
MINE!!!

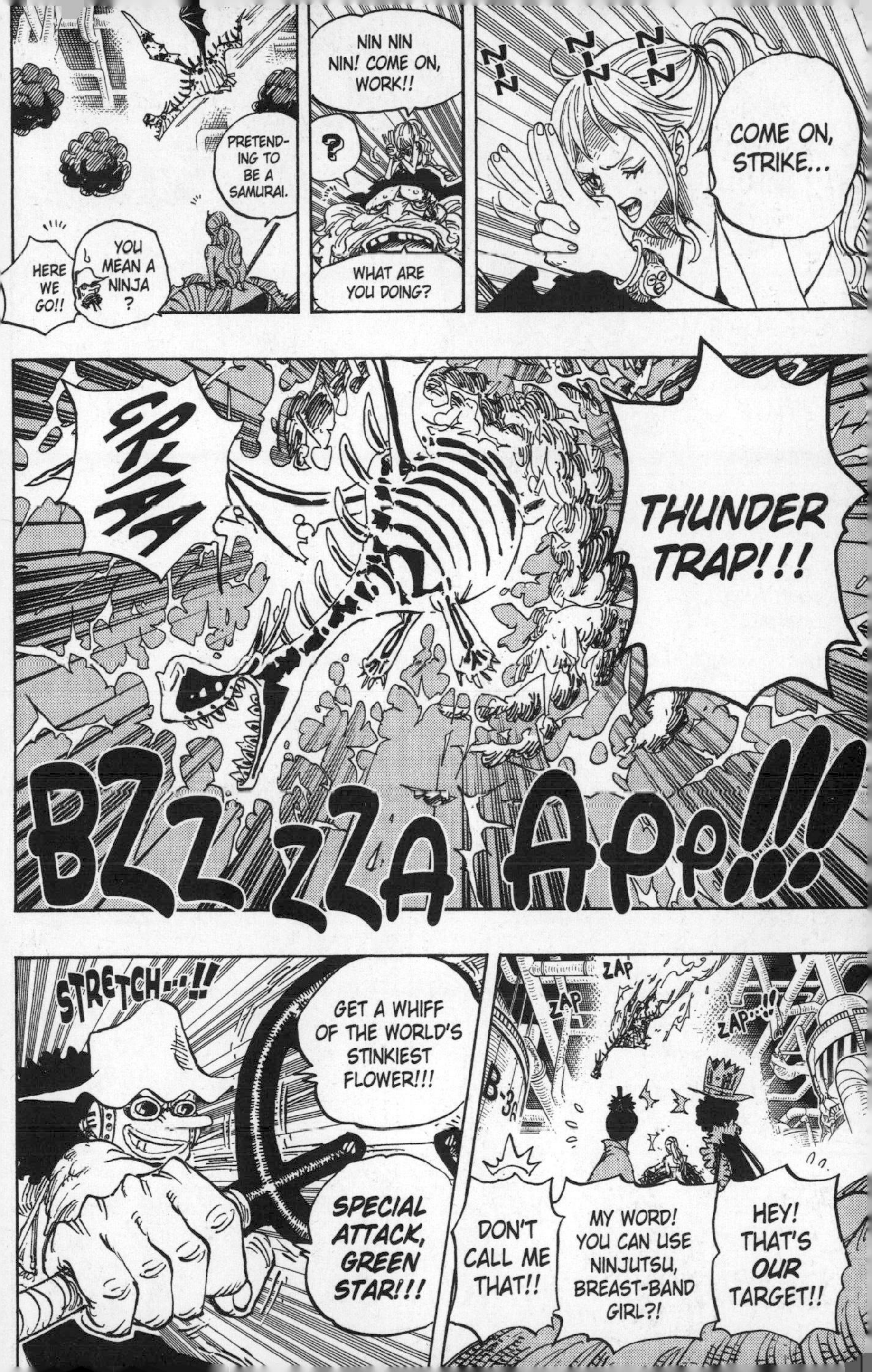
COME ON, STRIKE...
NIN NIN NIN! COME ON, WORK!!
?
WHAT ARE YOU DOING?
PRETENDING TO BE A SAMURAI.
YOU MEAN A NINJA?
HERE WE GO!!
THUNDER TRAP!!!
GRYAAA
BZZzZA APP!!!
ZAP
ZAP
ZAP...!!
HEY! THAT'S OUR TARGET!!
MY WORD! YOU CAN USE NINJUTSU, BREAST-BAND GIRL?!
DON'T CALL ME THAT!!
STRETCH...!!
GET A WHIFF OF THE WORLD'S STINKIEST FLOWER!!!
SPECIAL ATTACK, GREEN STAR!!!

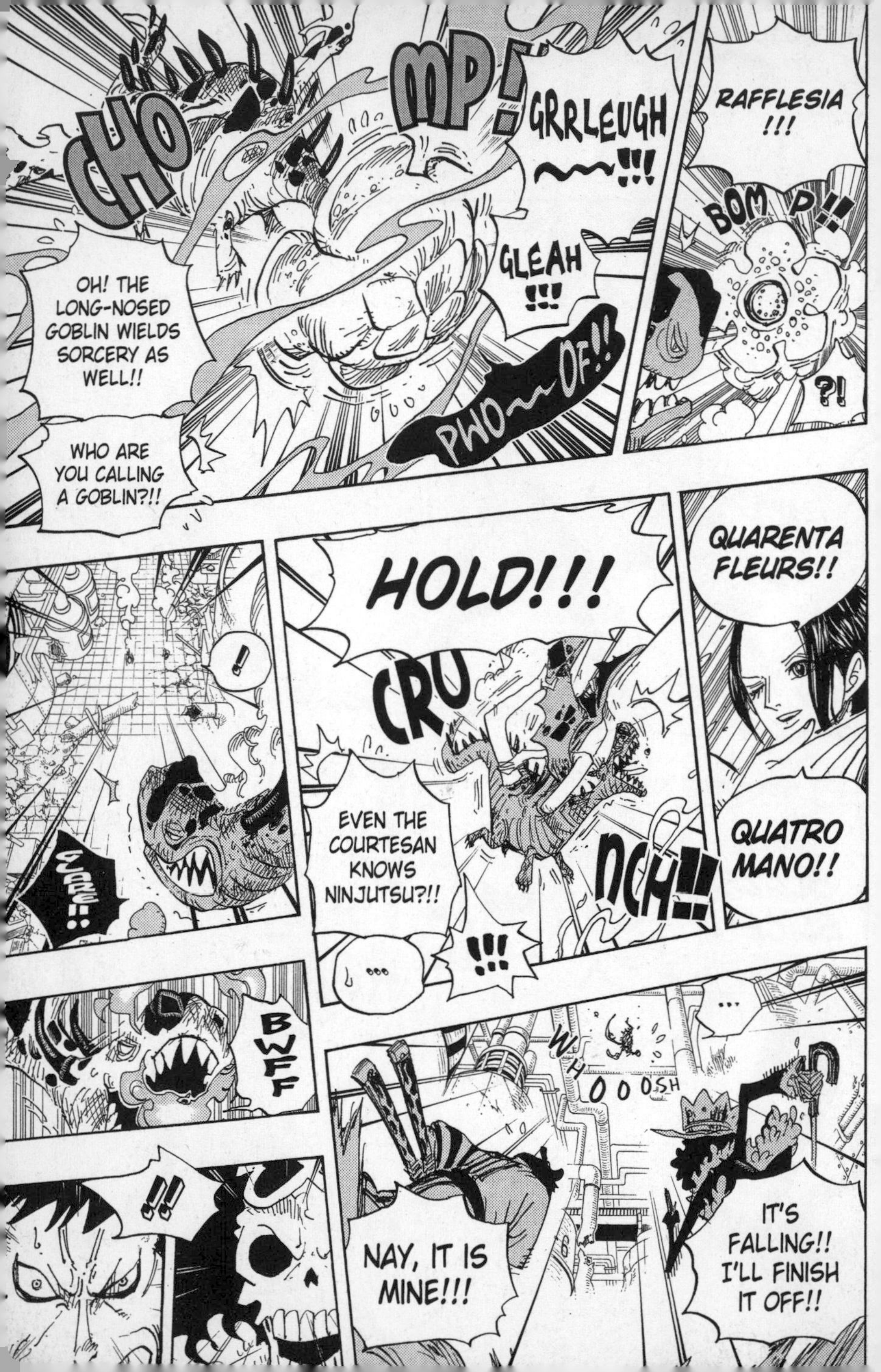
RAFFLESIA!!!
BOMP!!
?!
CHOMP!
GRRLEUGH~~!!!
GLEAH!!!
PWO~OF!!
OH! THE LONG-NOSED GOBLIN WIELDS SORCERY AS WELL!!
WHO ARE YOU CALLING A GOBLIN?!!
QUARENTA FLEURS!!
QUATRO MANO!!
HOLD!!!
CRUNCH!!
EVEN THE COURTESAN KNOWS NINJUTSU?!!
!!!
...
!
GLARE!!
...
WHOOOSH
IT'S FALLING!! I'LL FINISH IT OFF!!
NAY, IT IS MINE!!!
BWFF
!!

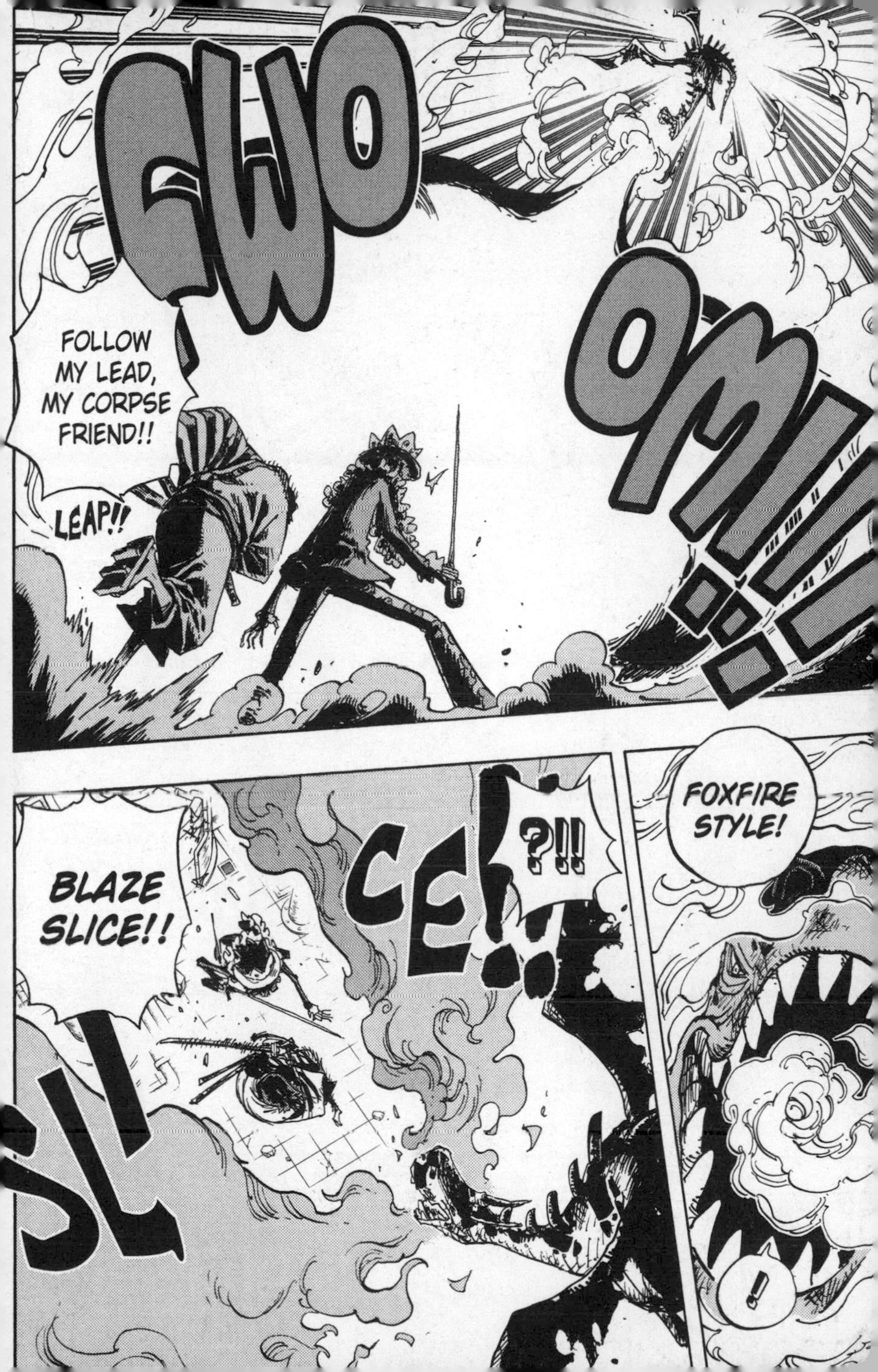
GWO
OM!!
FOLLOW MY LEAD, MY CORPSE FRIEND!!
LEAP!!
FOXFIRE STYLE!
!
?!!
CE!!
BLAZE SLICE!!
SL

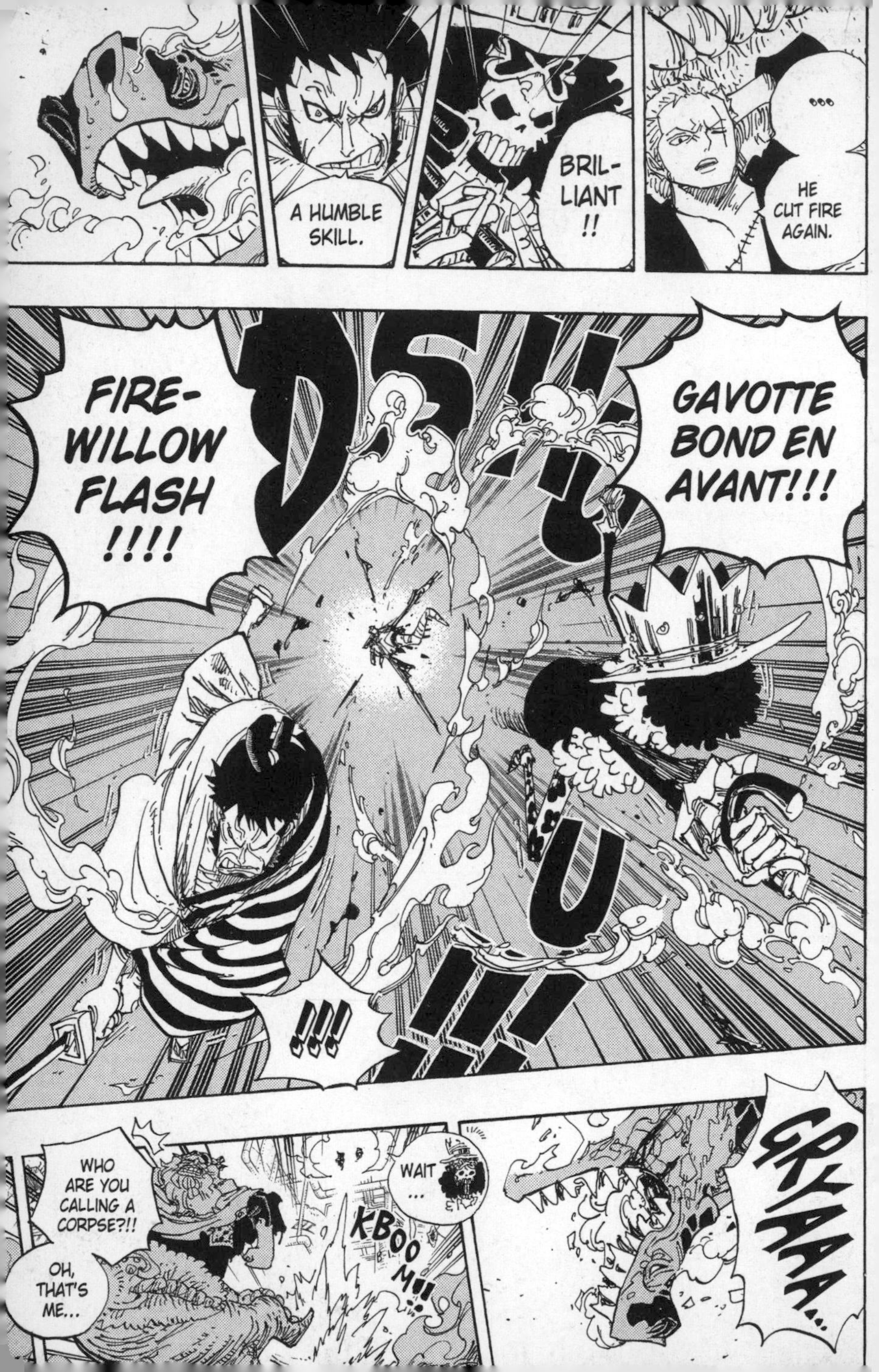
...
HE CUT FIRE AGAIN.
BRIL-LIANT!!
A HUMBLE SKILL.
GAVOTTE BOND EN AVANT!!!
FIRE-WILLOW FLASH!!!!
GRYAAAA...
WAIT ...
KBOOM!!
WHO ARE YOU CALLING A CORPSE?!!
OH, THAT'S ME...

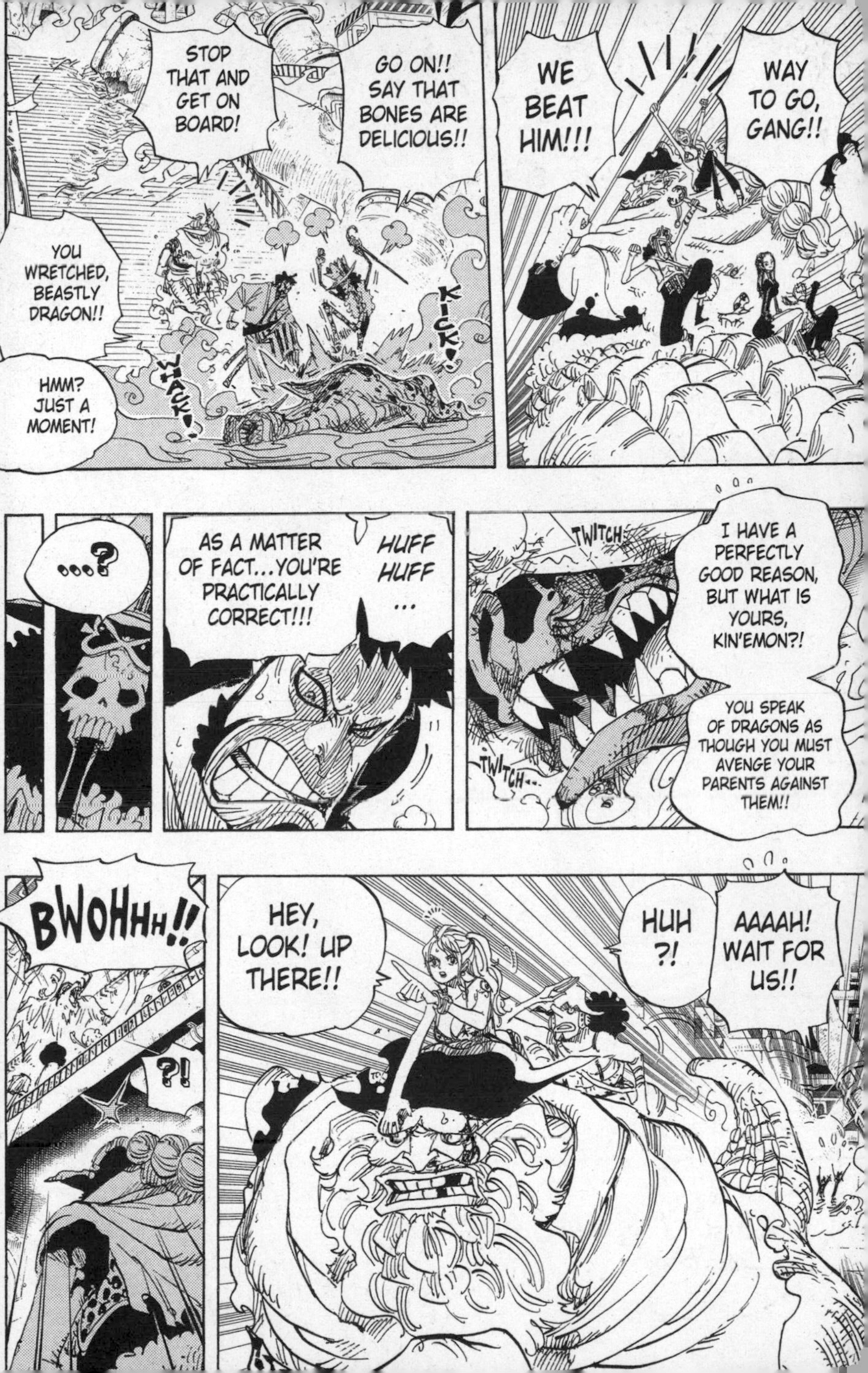
WAY TO GO, GANG!!
WE BEAT HIM!!!
GO ON!! SAY THAT BONES ARE DELICIOUS!!
STOP THAT AND GET ON BOARD!
KICK!
YOU WRETCHED, BEASTLY DRAGON!!
WHACK!
HMM? JUST A MOMENT!
TWITCH
I HAVE A PERFECTLY GOOD REASON, BUT WHAT IS YOURS, KIN'EMON?!
YOU SPEAK OF DRAGONS AS THOUGH YOU MUST AVENGE YOUR PARENTS AGAINST THEM!!
TWITCH...
HUFF HUFF ...
AS A MATTER OF FACT...YOU'RE PRACTICALLY CORRECT!!!
...?
AAAAH! WAIT FOR US!!
HUH ?!
HEY, LOOK! UP THERE!!
BWOHHH!!
?!

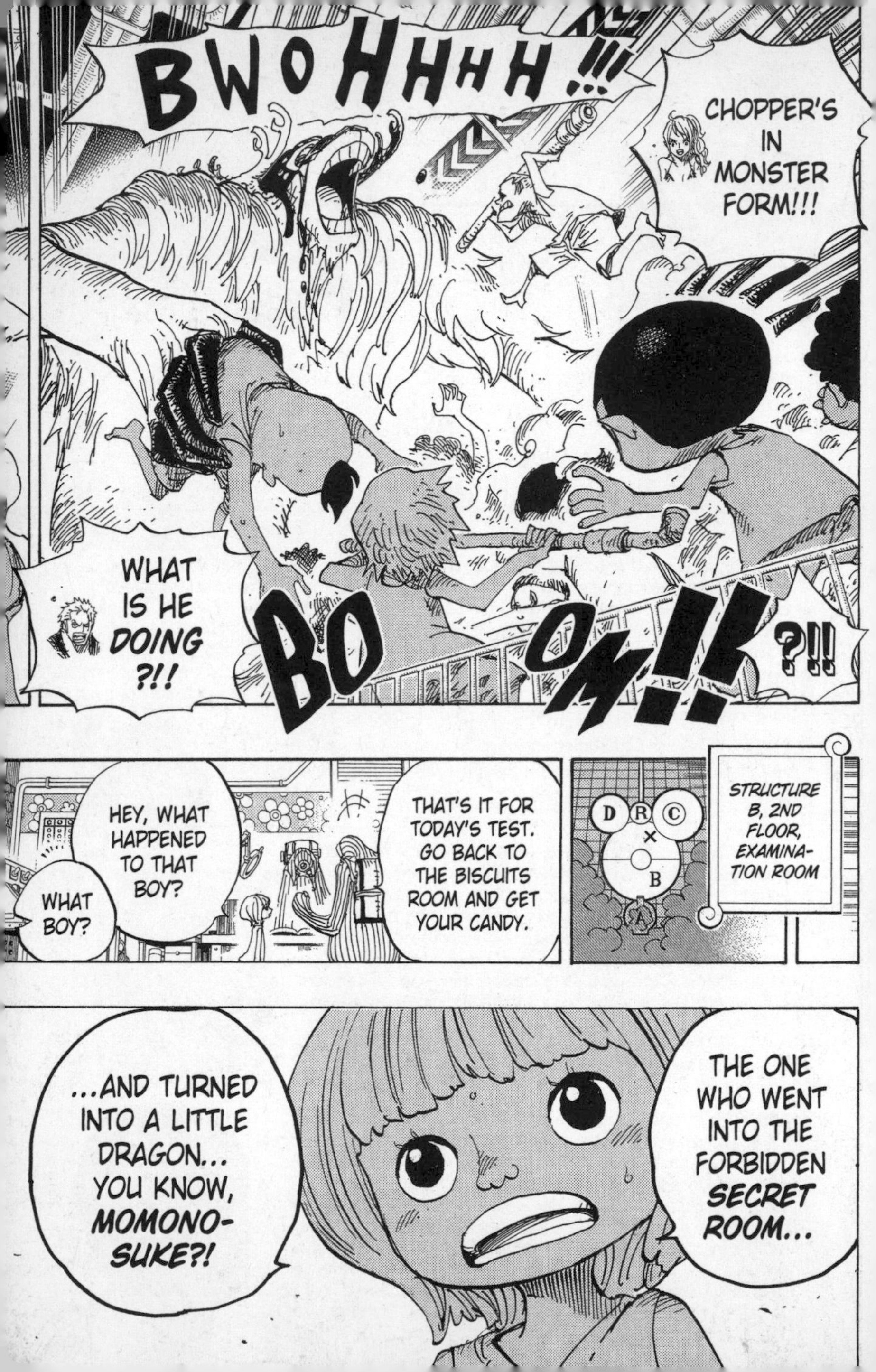
BWOHHHH!!!
CHOPPER'S IN MONSTER FORM!!!
?!!
BOOM!!
WHAT IS HE DOING?!!
STRUCTURE B, 2ND FLOOR, EXAMINATION ROOM
D
R
C
B
A
THAT'S IT FOR TODAY'S TEST. GO BACK TO THE BISCUITS ROOM AND GET YOUR CANDY.
HEY, WHAT HAPPENED TO THAT BOY?
WHAT BOY?
THE ONE WHO WENT INTO THE FORBIDDEN SECRET ROOM...
...AND TURNED INTO A LITTLE DRAGON... YOU KNOW, MOMONOSUKE?!

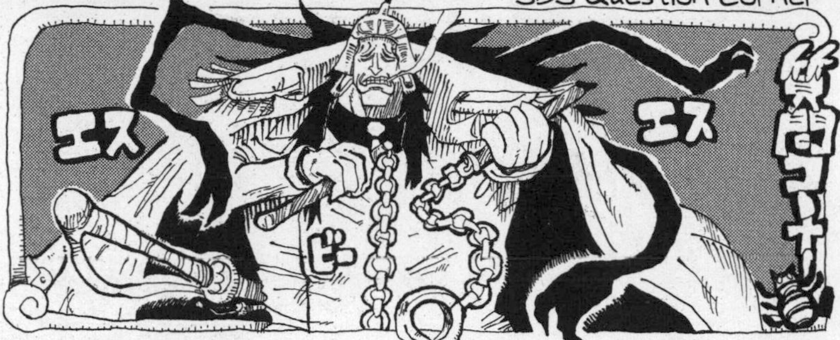
エス
ビー
エス
質問コーナー

(Satomo, Yamanashi)

Q: Hey, Odacchi! Tell me the name and the trick to pulling off the goofy running style that Zolo, Kin'emon, Sanji and Brook are doing!!

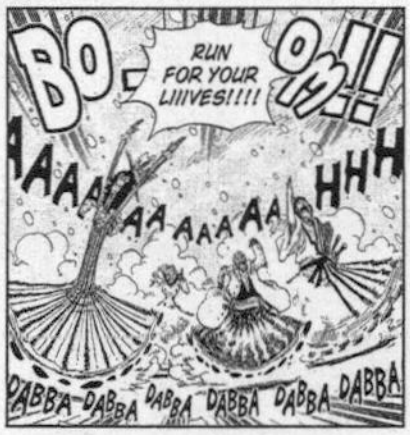
BO-
RUN FOR YOUR LIIIVES!!!!
OM!!
AAAAA
AAAAAA
HHH
DABBA DABBA DABBA DABBA DABBA DABBA

--Macchi and Takeshi

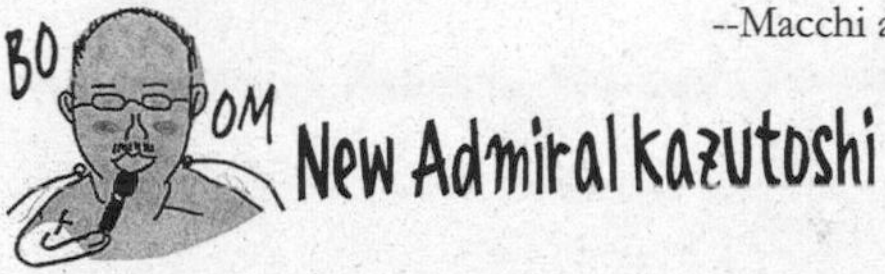
BO
OM
New Admiral kazutoshi

A: Ignoring that "New Admiral Kazutoshi" thing, you're talking about the dabba-dabba run, right? Old-school manga and anime used that effect all the time. You don't see it much these days, though. Basically, you're running so fast that it looks like you have a bunch of legs down there. Let's call it the "Dabba-Dabba-Dash." How do you do it? Just move those legs as fast as they'll go. And when you're running, shout, "Dabbadabbadabba!!" at the top of your lungs. It'll be a big hit at the next World Track & Field Championship.

Q: Odacchi! I've noticed something. Are the names Foxfire Kin'emon and his son Momonosuke taken from the old-time movie star Kinnosuke Nakamura?! Well?!

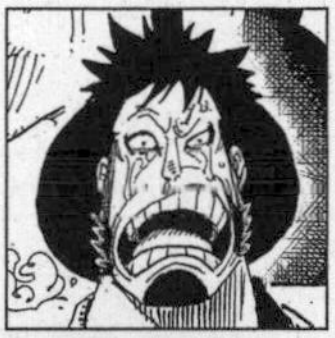

--Kamiki

A: Yes! You're correct. He was a star of period movies, and I'm a huge fan. Isn't it funny how when my little riddles get solved, I'm really excited?! Well, how about I tease a little something coming ahead? Luffy and crew will go to Wano in the future. I've been dying to draw this story for ages. I'll probably slip in a whole lot of my personal interests in that one. Heehee.

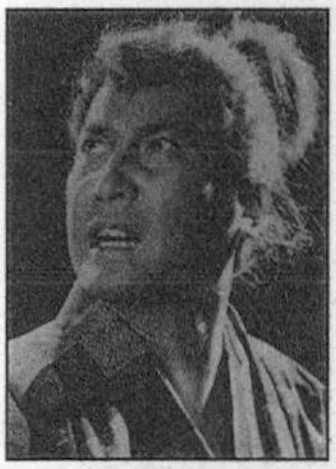

Hangyakuji (1961) © Toei

Q: There are so many characters in the world of *One Piece*. Which one takes the longest to draw?

--Noel

A: Good question. General Franky's kind of a pain. I like designing robots, but I'm not good at drawing the same one many times. But that's a robot. As far as humans go, it takes longer to draw the women. Especially the dark-haired ones. Black hair requires a technique called tsuyabeta. You have to fill in the black with a brush pen, while leaving behind the white reflective streaks. Which means the answer is Hancock. It's very challenging to do justice to the most beautiful woman in the world.

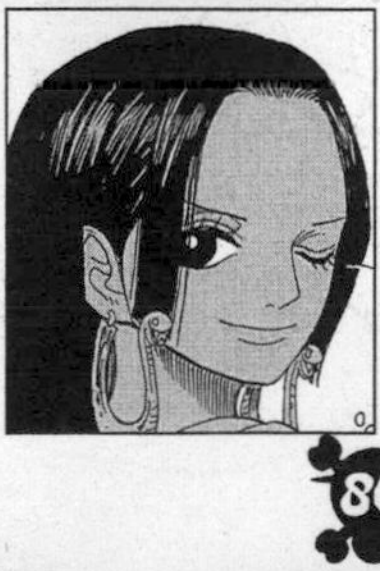

Chapter 683:
AN ICY WOMAN

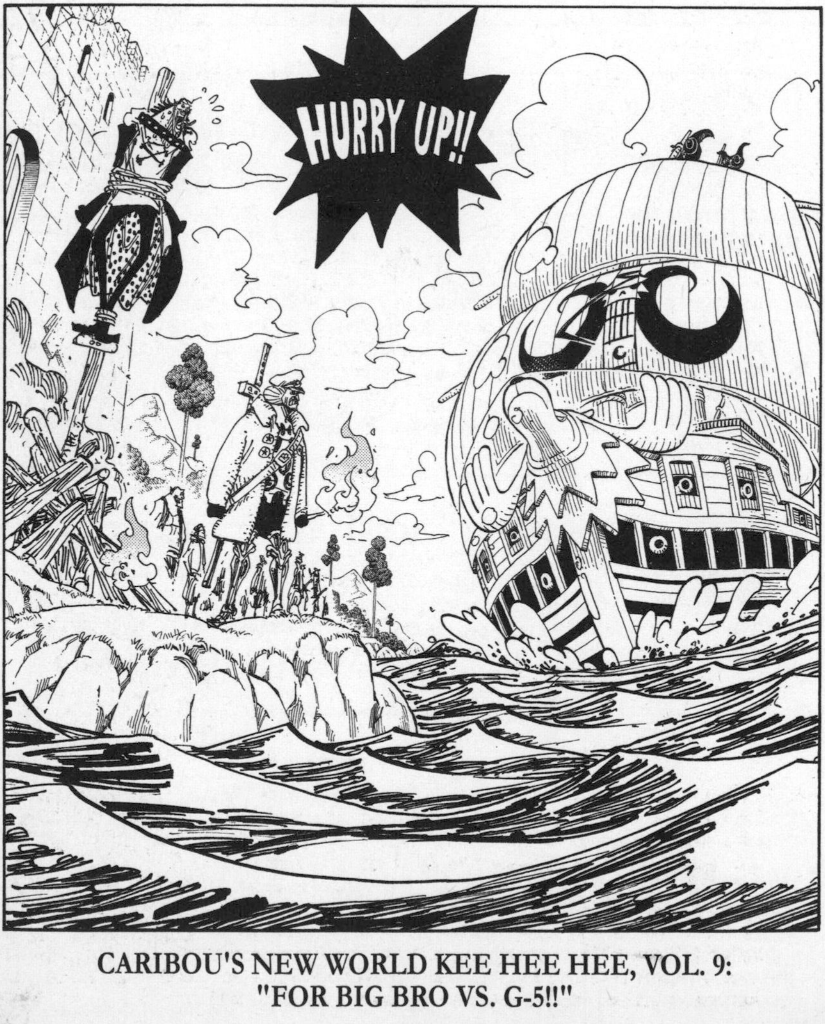
HURRY UP!!

CARIBOU'S NEW WORLD KEE HEE HEE, VOL. 9:
"FOR BIG BRO VS. G-5!!"

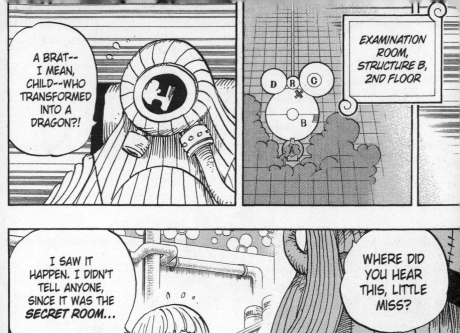

EXAMINATION ROOM, STRUCTURE B, 2ND FLOOR
A BRAT-- I MEAN, CHILD--WHO TRANSFORMED INTO A DRAGON?!
WHERE DID YOU HEAR THIS, LITTLE MISS?
I SAW IT HAPPEN. I DIDN'T TELL ANYONE, SINCE IT WAS THE SECRET ROOM...
...BUT I WAS WORRIED FOR HIM, SINCE WE CAME HERE ON THE SAME BOAT.
AH, I SEE. WELL DON'T WORRY, HE'S FINE...
THIS IS A BIG LABORATORY. WE HAVE MANY MEDICAL ROOMS.
HE'S JUST BEING KEPT IN A DIFFERENT SPOT...
IS HE EATING NOW? WHY WOULDN'T HE EAT ANYTHING?
OF COURSE HE'S EATING WELL... HE'S JUST FINE!
BUT REMEMBER, YOU NEED TO KEEP NEWS ABOUT THE SECRET ROOM HUSH-HUSH FROM THE OTHER KIDS!

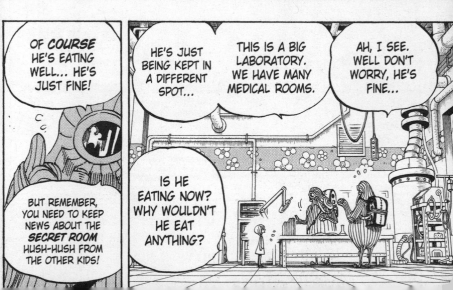

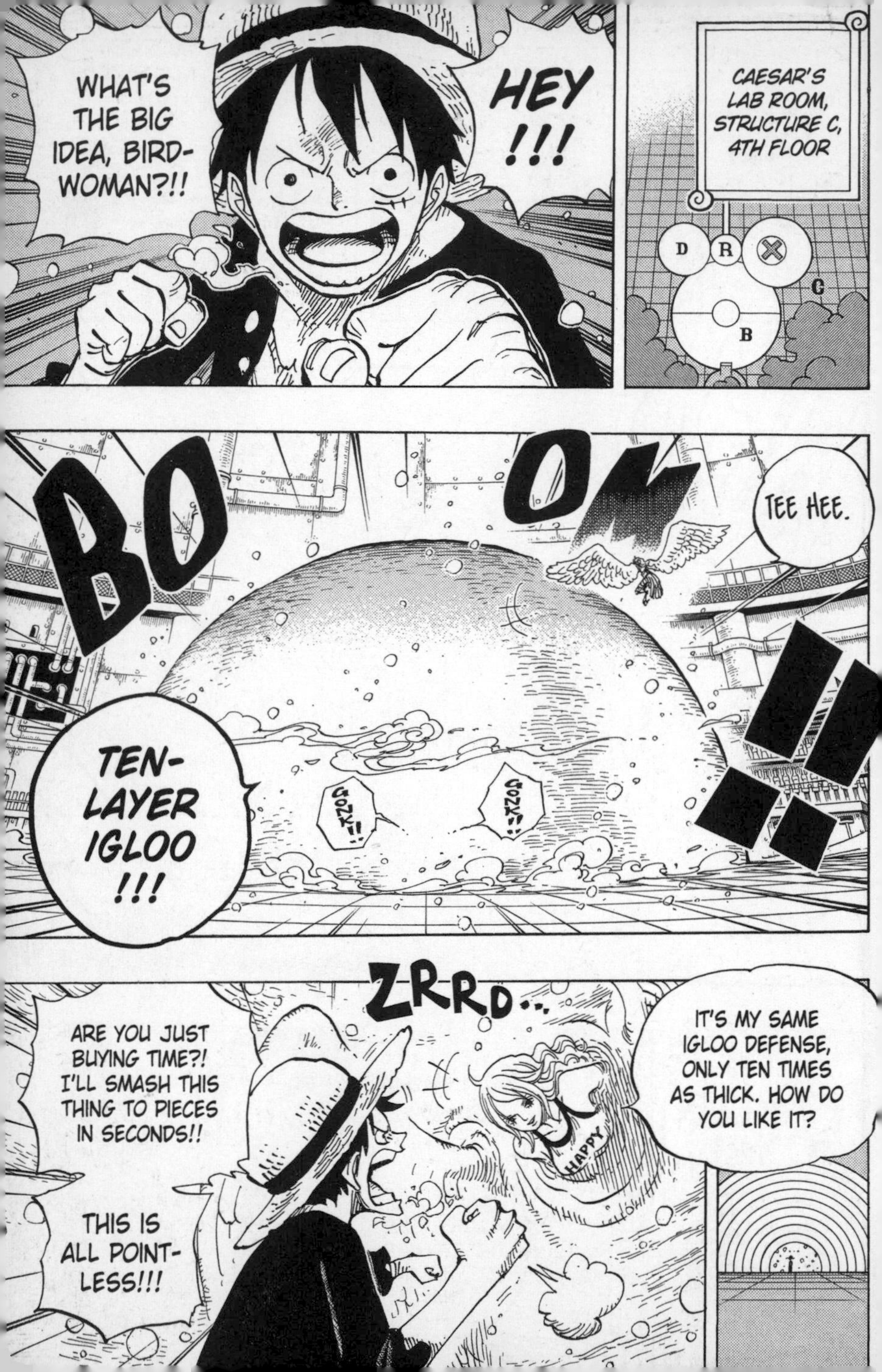
CAESAR'S LAB ROOM, STRUCTURE C, 4TH FLOOR
D
R
C
B
HEY!!!
WHAT'S THE BIG IDEA, BIRD-WOMAN?!!
BOOM
TEE HEE.
!!
GONK!!
GONK!!
TEN-LAYER IGLOO!!!
ZRRD...
IT'S MY SAME IGLOO DEFENSE, ONLY TEN TIMES AS THICK. HOW DO YOU LIKE IT?
HAPPY
ARE YOU JUST BUYING TIME?! I'LL SMASH THIS THING TO PIECES IN SECONDS!!
THIS IS ALL POINTLESS!!!

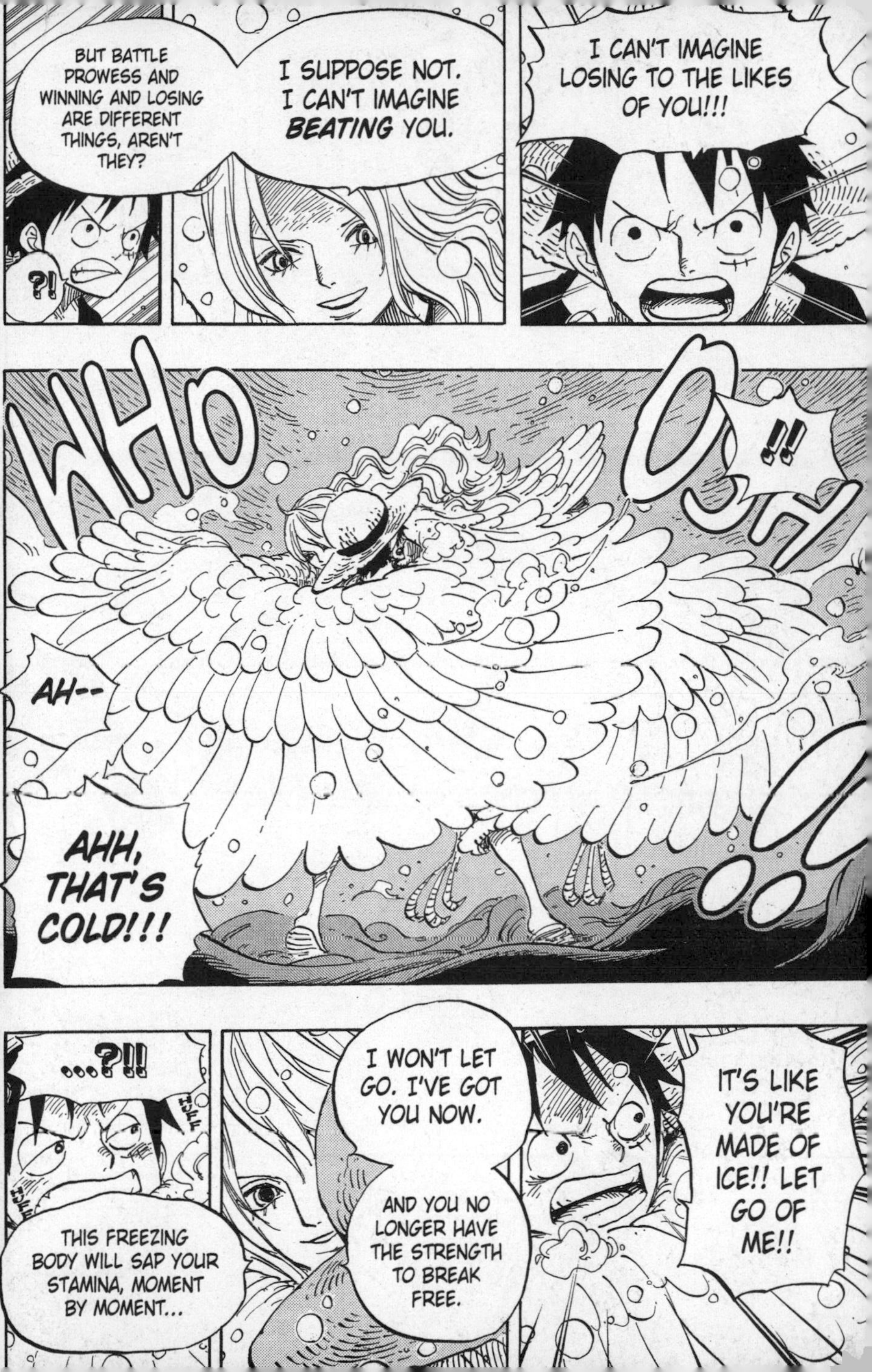
I CAN'T IMAGINE LOSING TO THE LIKES OF YOU!!!
I SUPPOSE NOT. I CAN'T IMAGINE *BEATING* YOU.
BUT BATTLE PROWESS AND WINNING AND LOSING ARE DIFFERENT THINGS, AREN'T THEY?
?!
WHOOSH
!!
AH--
AHH, THAT'S COLD!!!
IT'S LIKE YOU'RE MADE OF ICE!! LET GO OF ME!!
I WON'T LET GO. I'VE GOT YOU NOW.
AND YOU NO LONGER HAVE THE STRENGTH TO BREAK FREE.
...?!!
HUFF
HUFF
THIS FREEZING BODY WILL SAP YOUR STAMINA, MOMENT BY MOMENT...

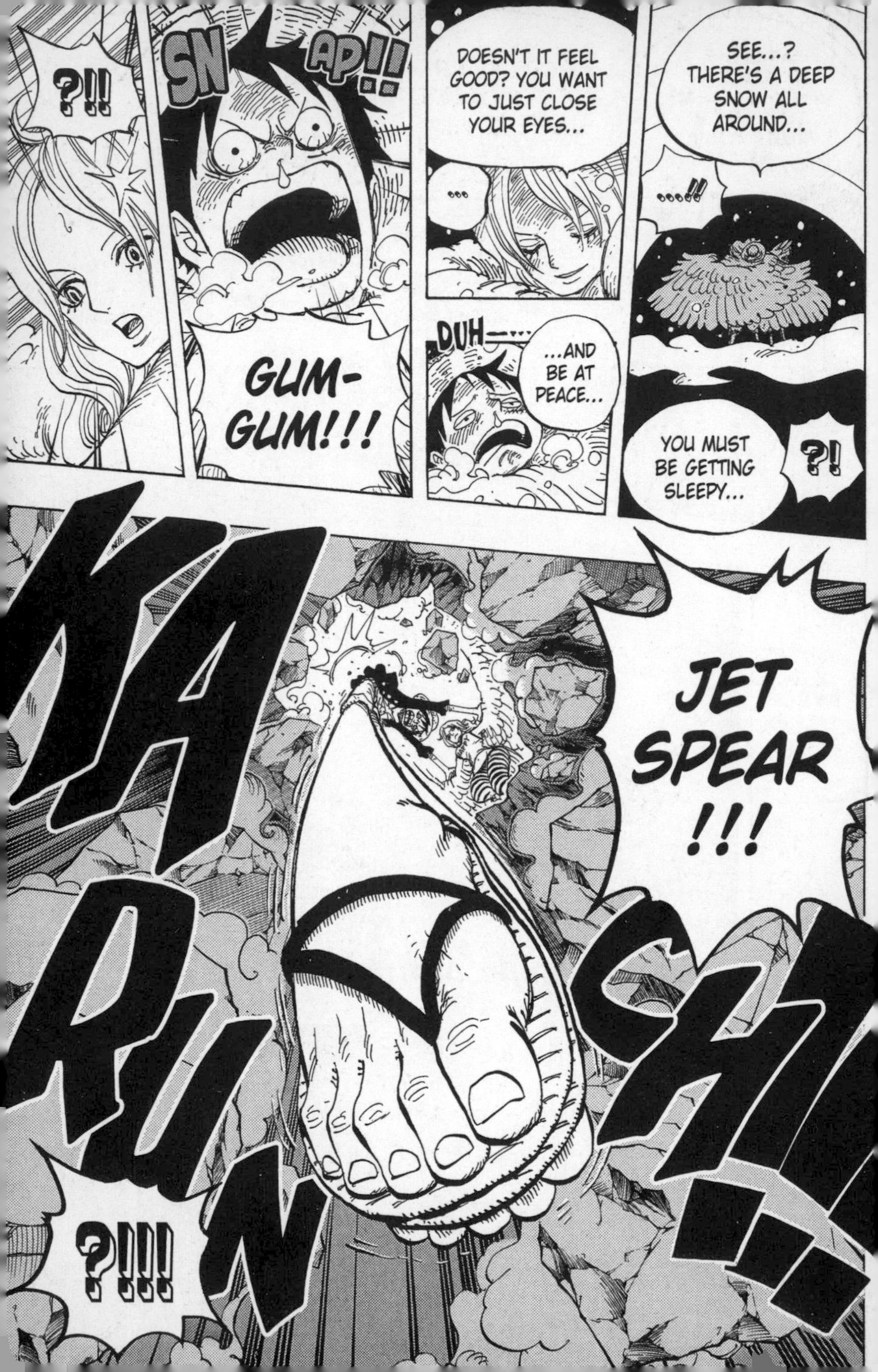
SEE...? THERE'S A DEEP SNOW ALL AROUND...
....!!
YOU MUST BE GETTING SLEEPY...
?!
DOESN'T IT FEEL GOOD? YOU WANT TO JUST CLOSE YOUR EYES...
...
DUH—....
...AND BE AT PEACE...
SN
AP!!
GUM-GUM!!!
?!!
JET SPEAR!!!
?!!!

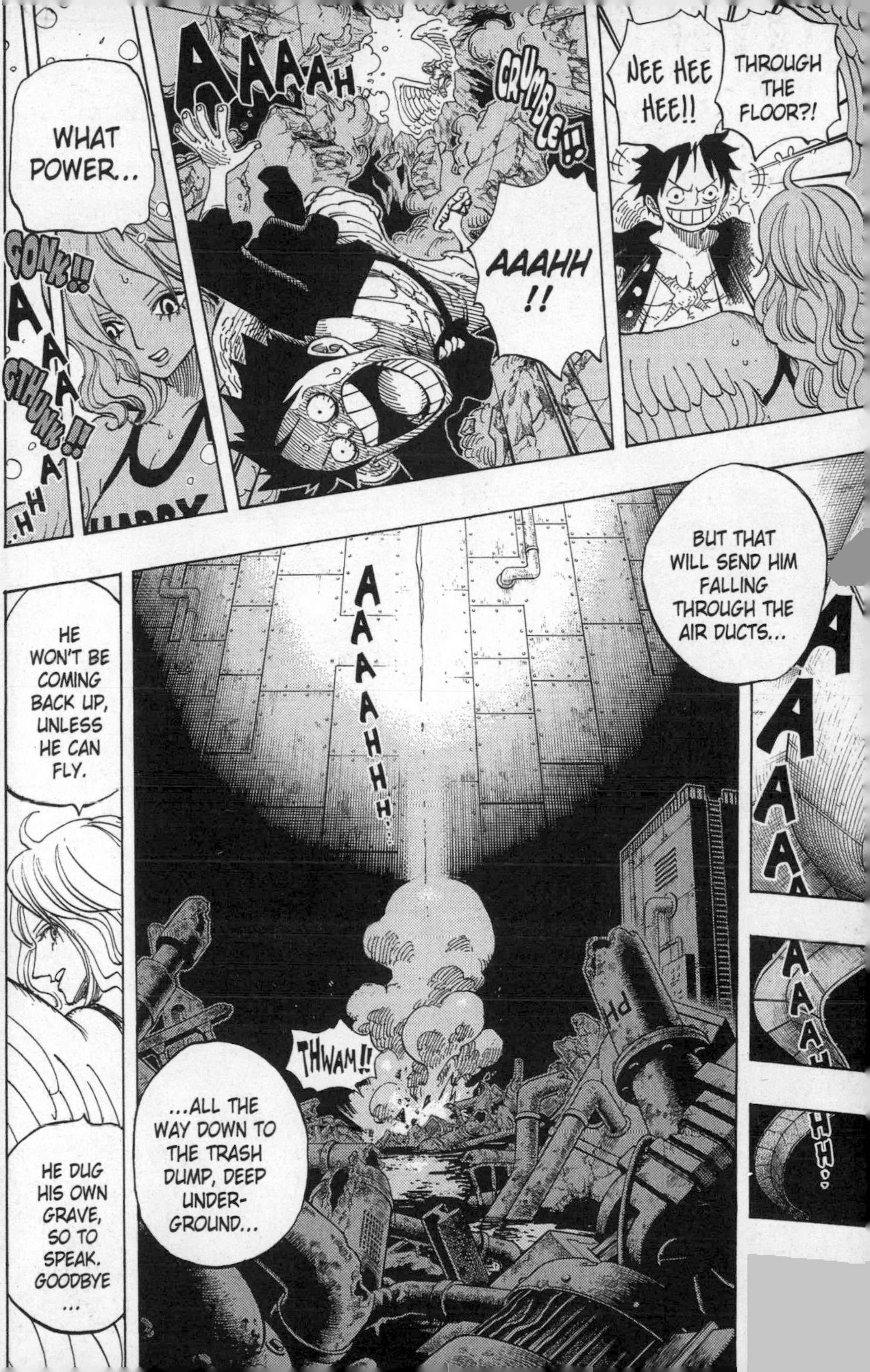
THROUGH THE FLOOR?!
NEE HEE HEE!!
AAAAAH
CRUMBLE!!
AAAHH!!
WHAT POWER...
GONK!!
GTHUNK!!
AAAAAHH
BUT THAT WILL SEND HIM FALLING THROUGH THE AIR DUCTS...
AAAAAAAAAHHH...
THWAM!!
...ALL THE WAY DOWN TO THE TRASH DUMP, DEEP UNDERGROUND...
HE WON'T BE COMING BACK UP, UNLESS HE CAN FLY.
HE DUG HIS OWN GRAVE, SO TO SPEAK. GOODBYE...

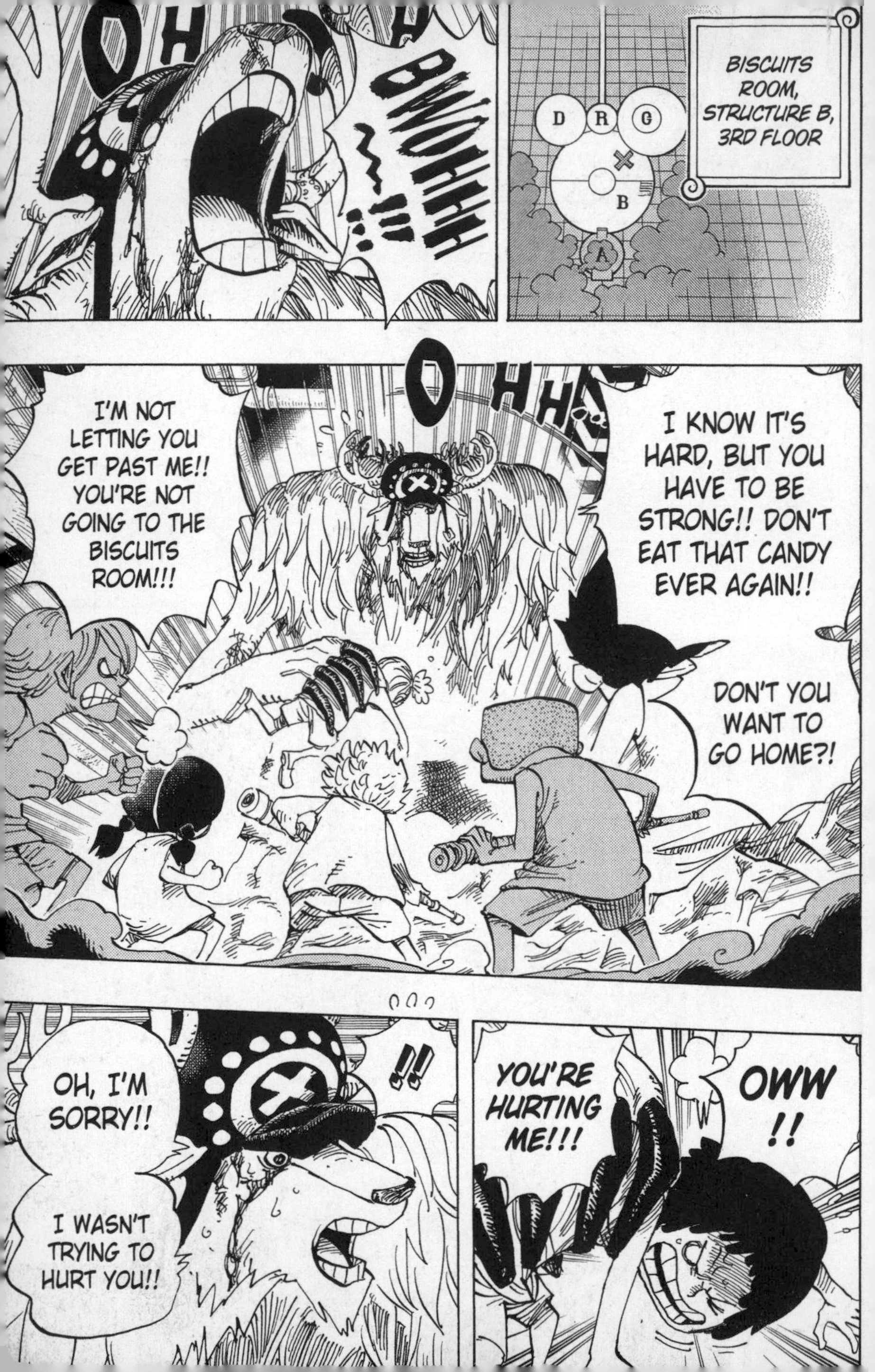

BISCUITS ROOM, STRUCTURE B, 3RD FLOOR
D
R
G
B
A
OH
BWOHHHHH
I KNOW IT'S HARD, BUT YOU HAVE TO BE STRONG!! DON'T EAT THAT CANDY EVER AGAIN!!
OHHH
I'M NOT LETTING YOU GET PAST ME!! YOU'RE NOT GOING TO THE BISCUITS ROOM!!!
DON'T YOU WANT TO GO HOME?!
OWW!!
YOU'RE HURTING ME!!!
!!
OH, I'M SORRY!!
I WASN'T TRYING TO HURT YOU!!

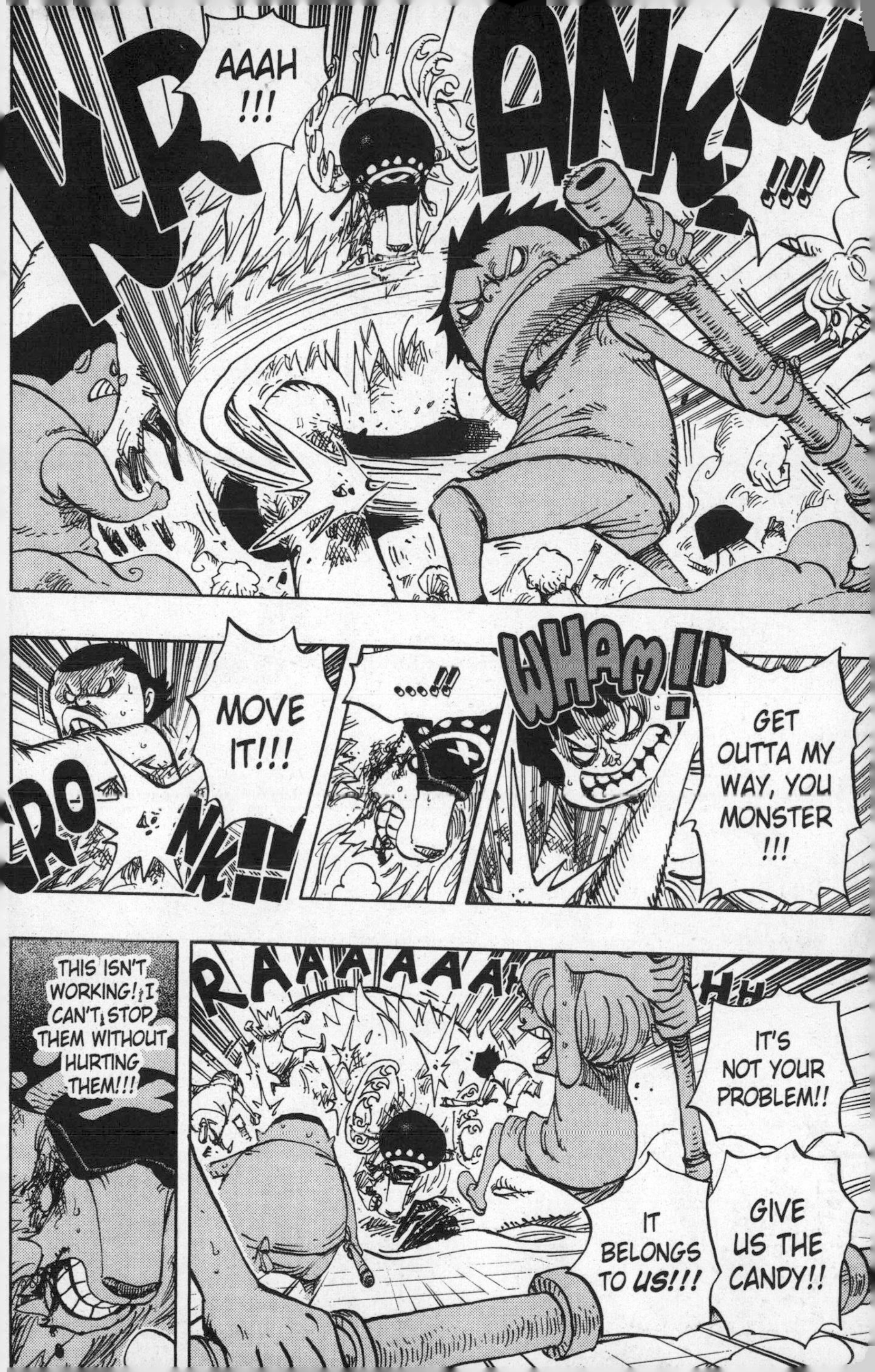

KRANK!!!
AAAH!!!
MOVE IT!!!
...!!
WHAM!!
GET OUTTA MY WAY, YOU MONSTER!!!
CRONK!!
RAAAAAAAHH
IT'S NOT YOUR PROBLEM!!
GIVE US THE CANDY!!
IT BELONGS TO *US*!!!
THIS ISN'T WORKING! I CAN'T STOP THEM WITHOUT HURTING THEM!!!

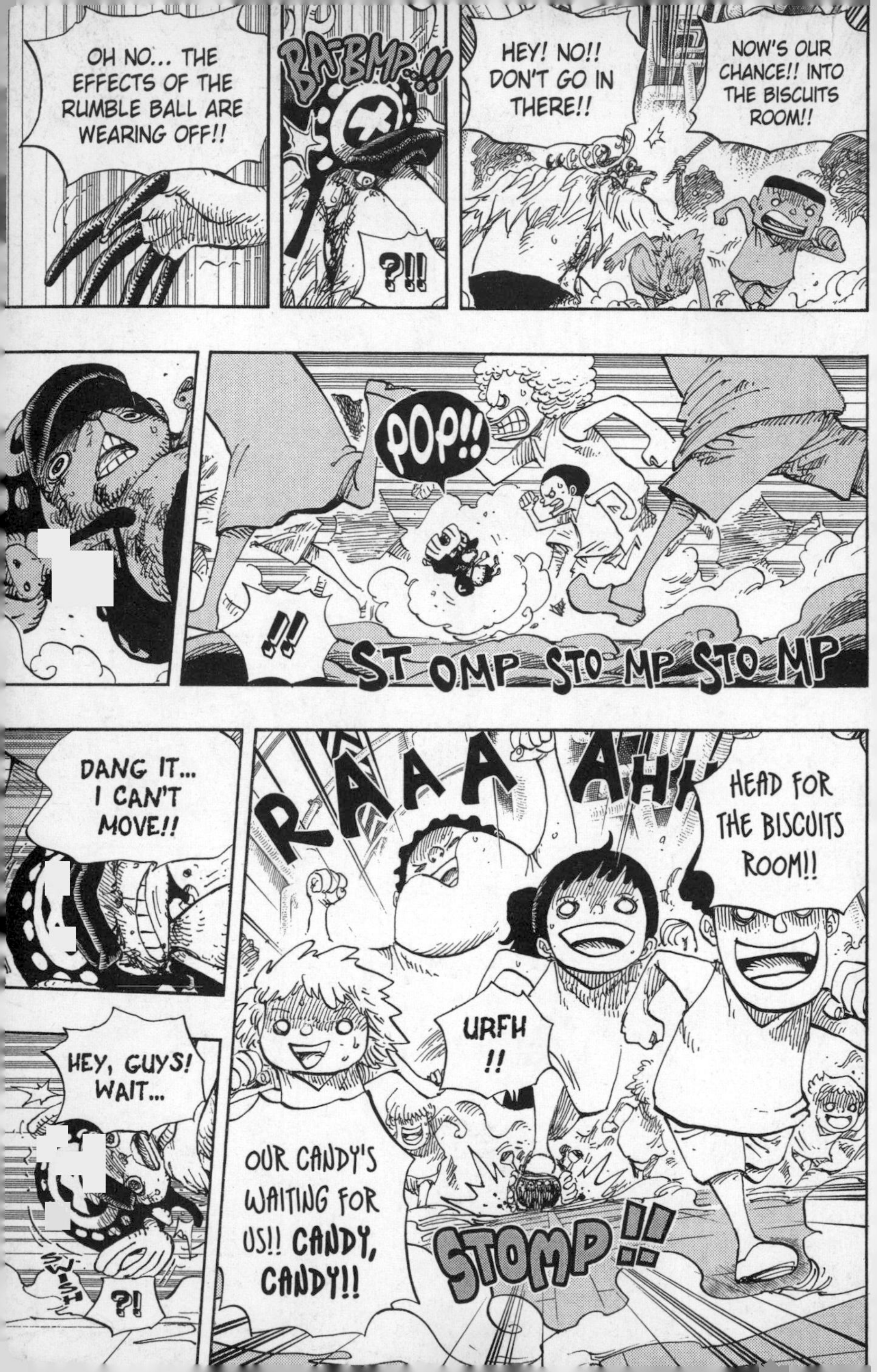
NOW'S OUR CHANCE!! INTO THE BISCUITS ROOM!!
HEY! NO!! DON'T GO IN THERE!!
BA-BMP...!!
?!!
OH NO... THE EFFECTS OF THE RUMBLE BALL ARE WEARING OFF!!
POP!!
!!
STOMP STOMP STOMP
RAAAAHH
HEAD FOR THE BISCUITS ROOM!!
URFH !!
OUR CANDY'S WAITING FOR US!! CANDY, CANDY!!
STOMP!!
DANG IT... I CAN'T MOVE!!
HEY, GUYS! WAIT...
SWISH
?!

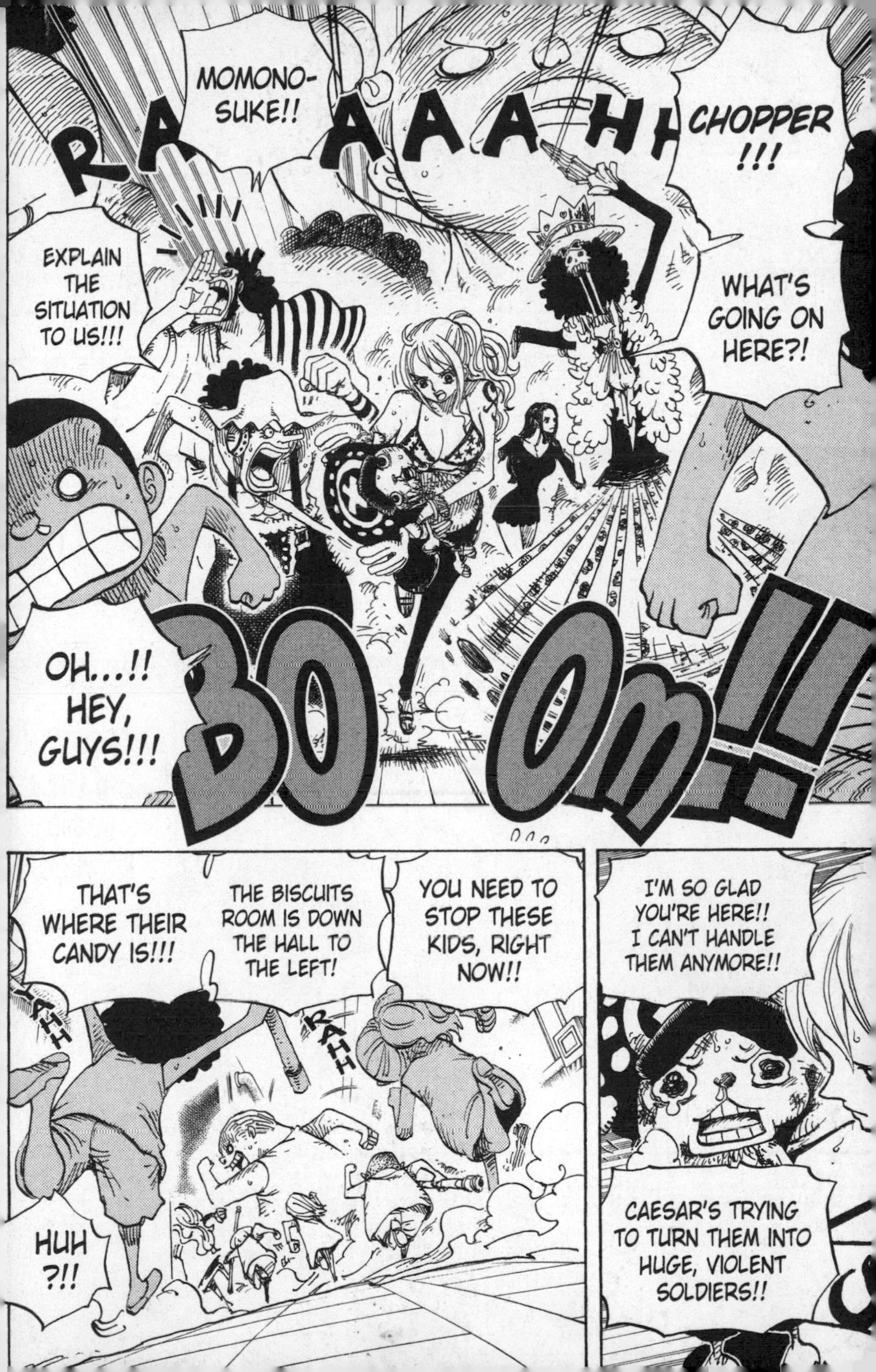
CHOPPER!!!
MOMONOSUKE!!
RAAAAAHH
WHAT'S GOING ON HERE?!
EXPLAIN THE SITUATION TO US!!!
OH...!! HEY, GUYS!!!
BOOM!!
I'M SO GLAD YOU'RE HERE!! I CAN'T HANDLE THEM ANYMORE!!
CAESAR'S TRYING TO TURN THEM INTO HUGE, VIOLENT SOLDIERS!!
YOU NEED TO STOP THESE KIDS, RIGHT NOW!!
THE BISCUITS ROOM IS DOWN THE HALL TO THE LEFT!
THAT'S WHERE THEIR CANDY IS!!!
RAHH
YAHH
HUH ?!!

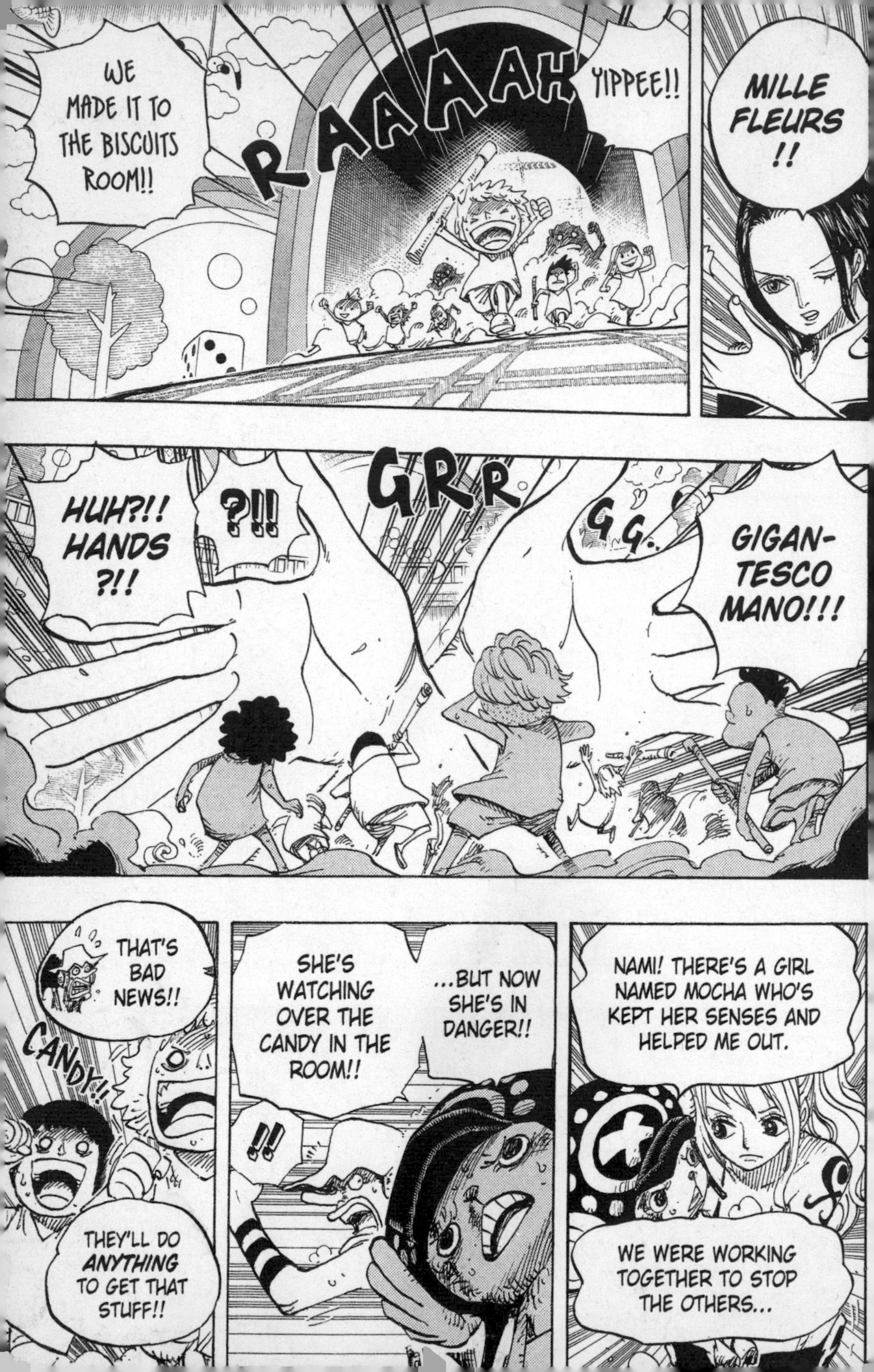
MILLE FLEURS !!
YIPPEE!!
RAAAAAH
WE MADE IT TO THE BISCUITS ROOM!!
GIGAN-TESCO MANO!!!
GG..
GRR
?!!
HUH?!! HANDS ?!!
NAMI! THERE'S A GIRL NAMED MOCHA WHO'S KEPT HER SENSES AND HELPED ME OUT.
WE WERE WORKING TOGETHER TO STOP THE OTHERS...
SHE'S WATCHING OVER THE CANDY IN THE ROOM!!
...BUT NOW SHE'S IN DANGER!!
!!
THAT'S BAD NEWS!!
CANDY!!
THEY'LL DO ANYTHING TO GET THAT STUFF!!

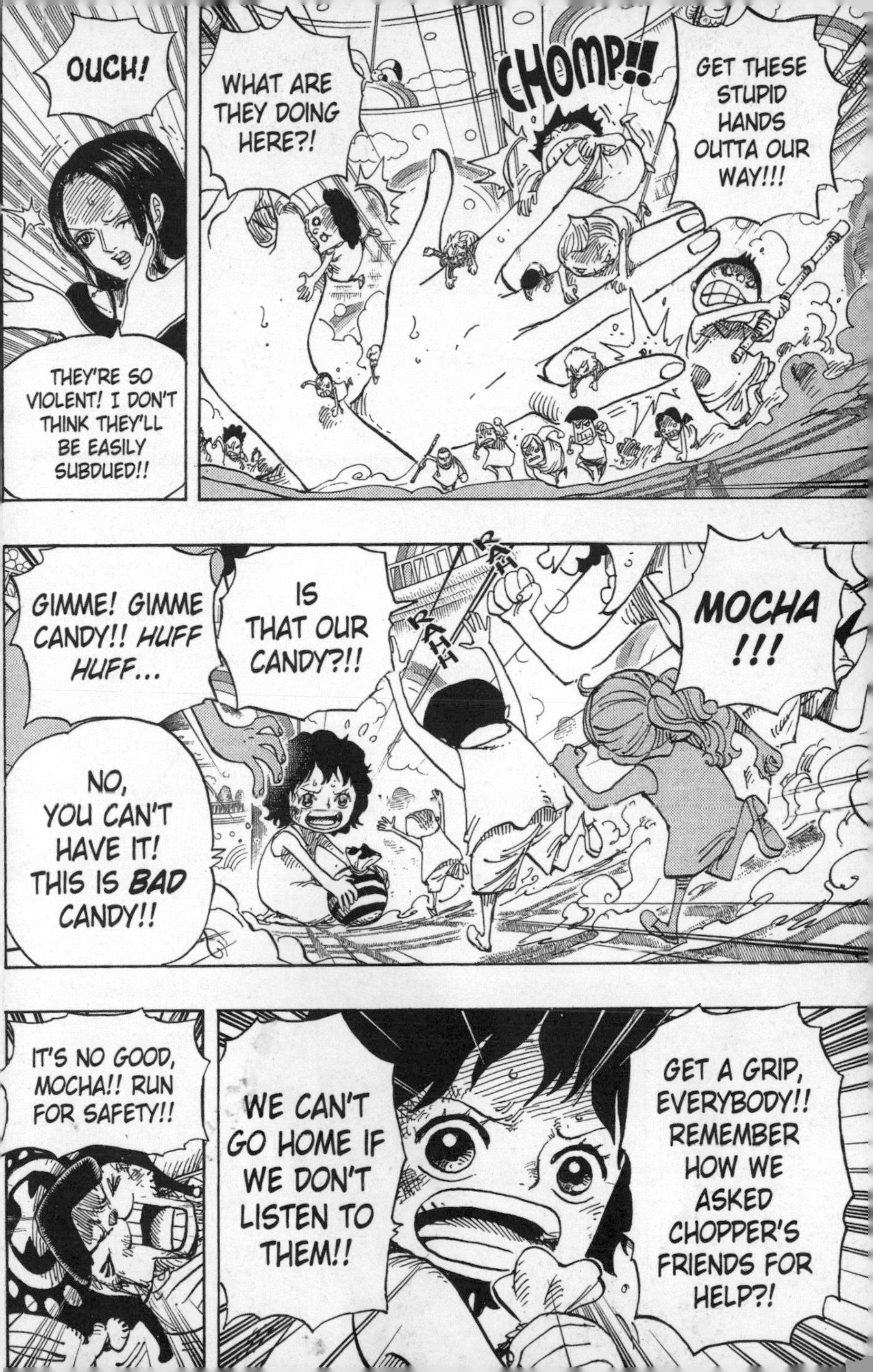

GET THESE STUPID HANDS OUTTA OUR WAY!!!
CHOMP!!
WHAT ARE THEY DOING HERE?!
OUCH!
THEY'RE SO VIOLENT! I DON'T THINK THEY'LL BE EASILY SUBDUED!!
MOCHA!!!
RAHH
RAHH
IS THAT OUR CANDY?!!
GIMME! GIMME CANDY!! HUFF HUFF...
NO, YOU CAN'T HAVE IT! THIS IS BAD CANDY!!
GET A GRIP, EVERYBODY!! REMEMBER HOW WE ASKED CHOPPER'S FRIENDS FOR HELP?!
WE CAN'T GO HOME IF WE DON'T LISTEN TO THEM!!
IT'S NO GOOD, MOCHA!! RUN FOR SAFETY!!

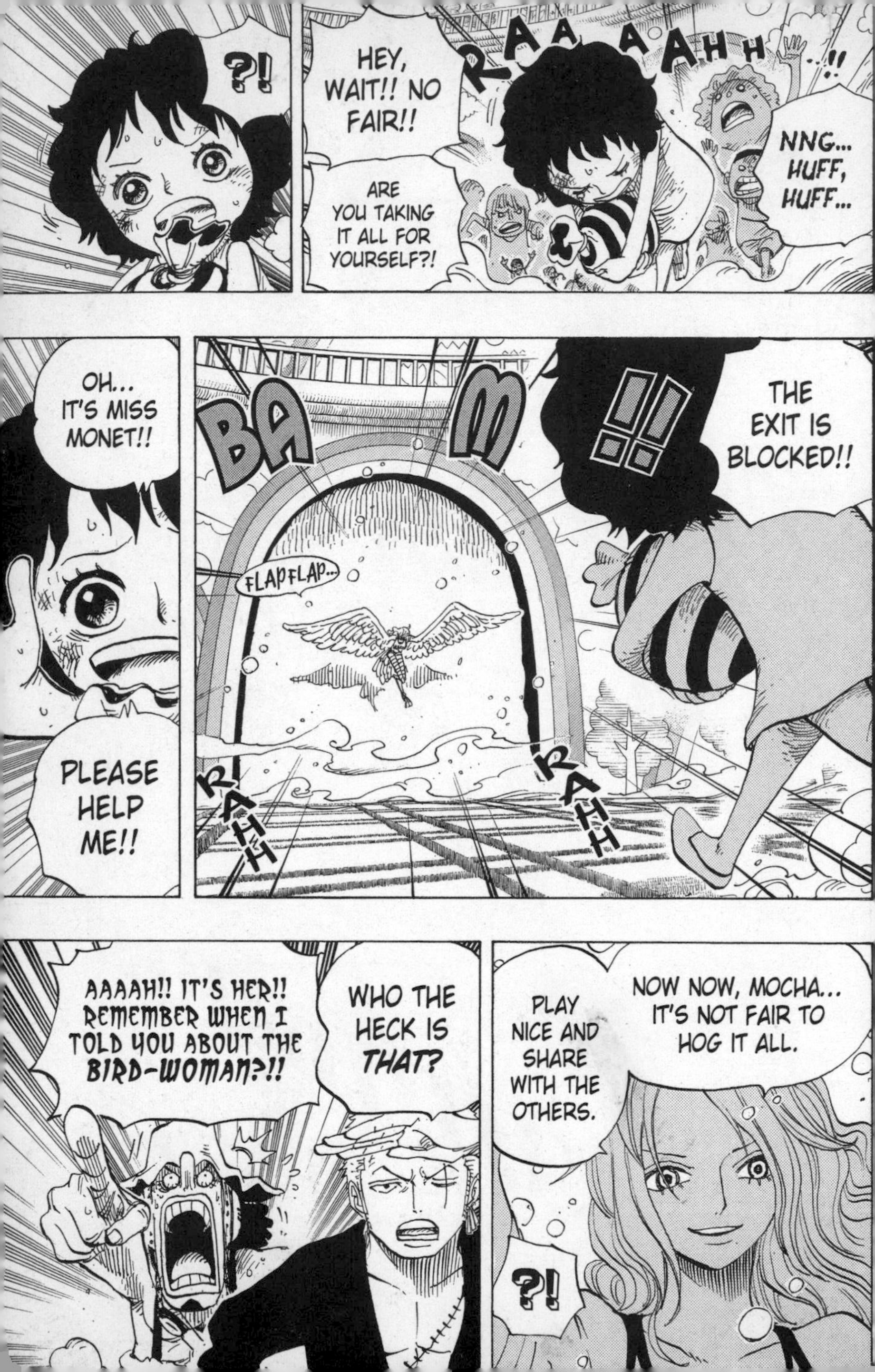
RAAAAAHH..!!
NNG... HUFF, HUFF...
HEY, WAIT!! NO FAIR!!
ARE YOU TAKING IT ALL FOR YOURSELF?!
?!
!!
THE EXIT IS BLOCKED!!
BAM
FLAPFLAP...
RAHH
RAHH
OH... IT'S MISS MONET!!
PLEASE HELP ME!!
NOW NOW, MOCHA... IT'S NOT FAIR TO HOG IT ALL.
PLAY NICE AND SHARE WITH THE OTHERS.
?!
WHO THE HECK IS *THAT?*
AAAAH!! IT'S HER!! REMEMBER WHEN I TOLD YOU ABOUT THE *BIRD-WOMAN?!!*

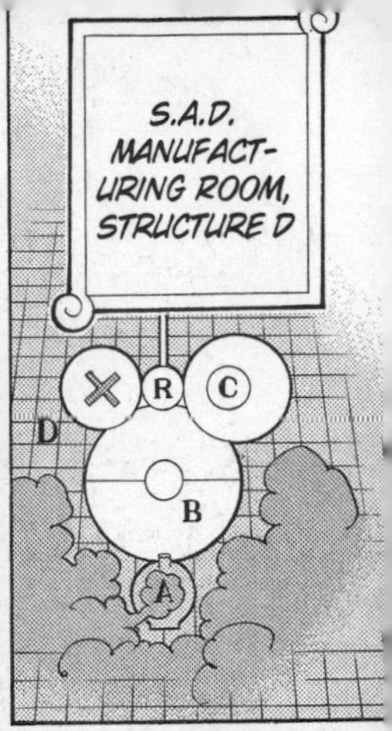
S.A.D. MANUFACTURING ROOM, STRUCTURE D
R
C
D
B
A

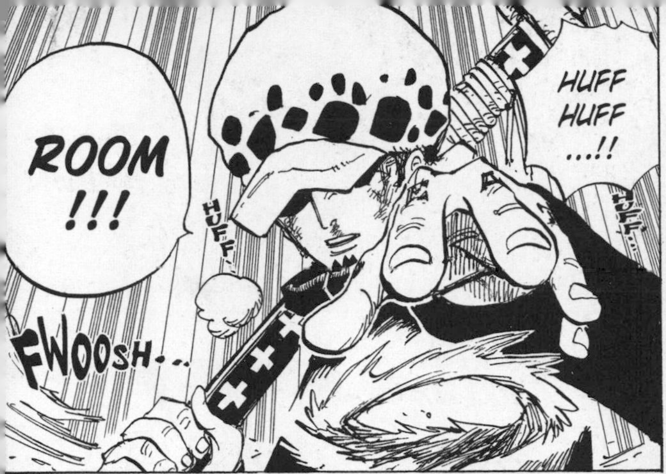
HUFF HUFF ...!!
HUFF...
ROOM !!!
HUFF...
FWOOSH...

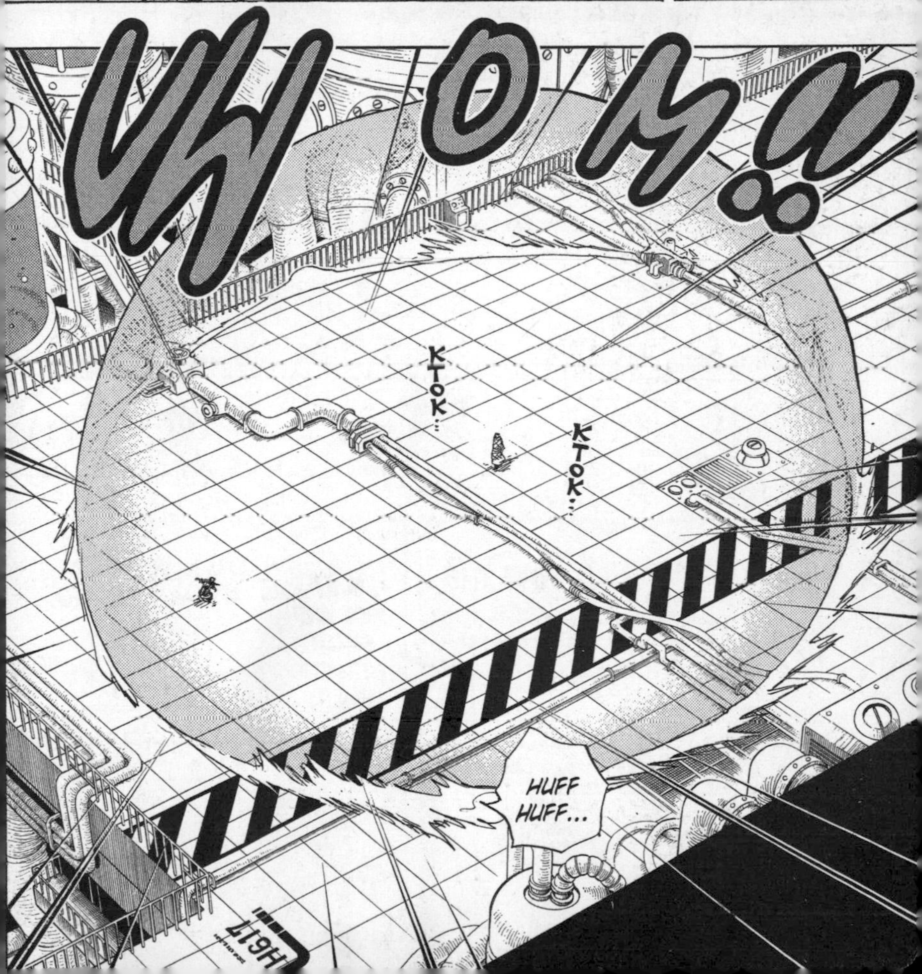
WOMM!!
KTOK...
KTOK...
HUFF HUFF...

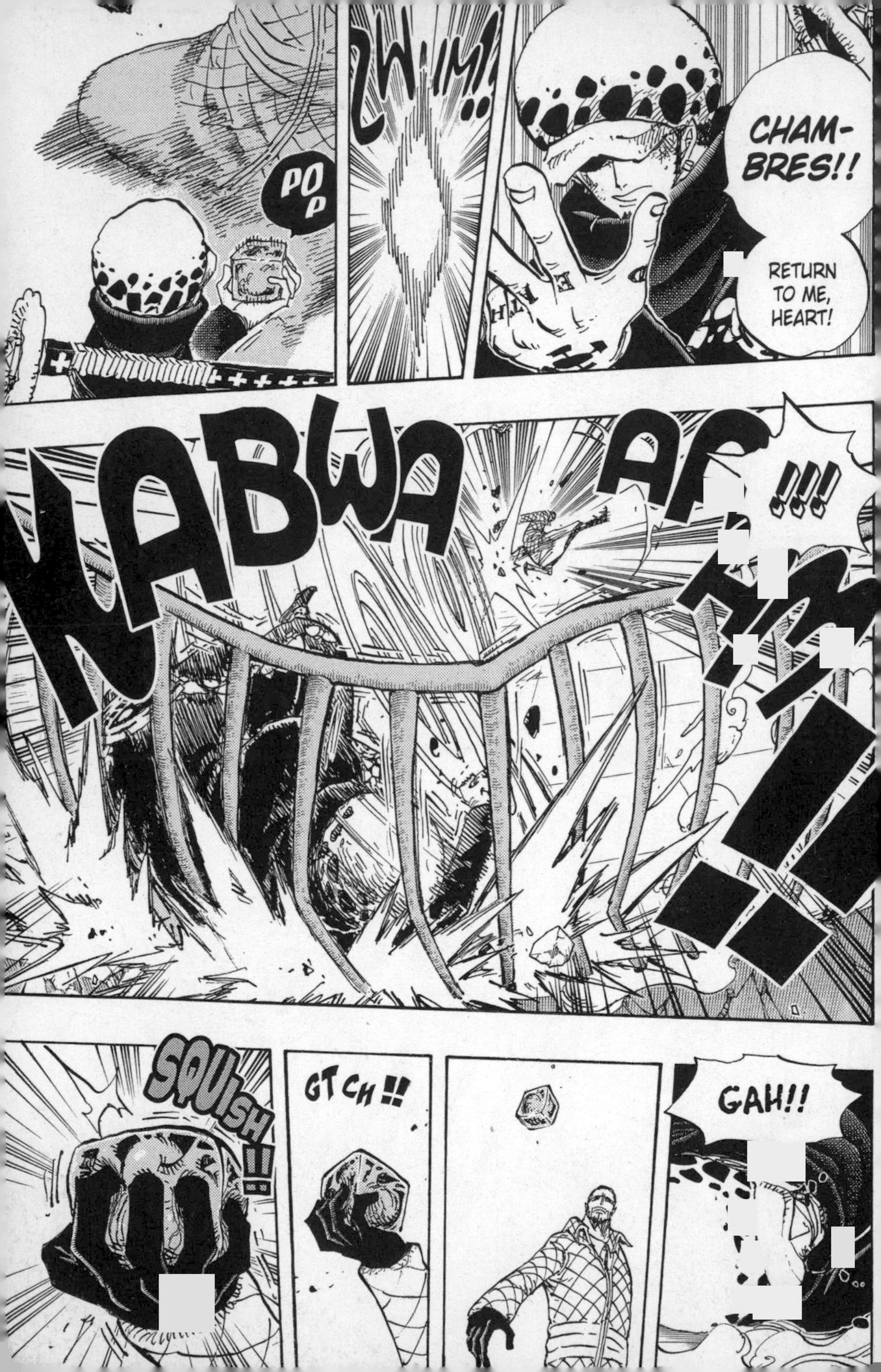
CHAM-
BRES!!
RETURN TO ME, HEART!
ZHWM!!
POP
KABWAAAM!!!
GAH!!
GTCH!!
SQUISH!!

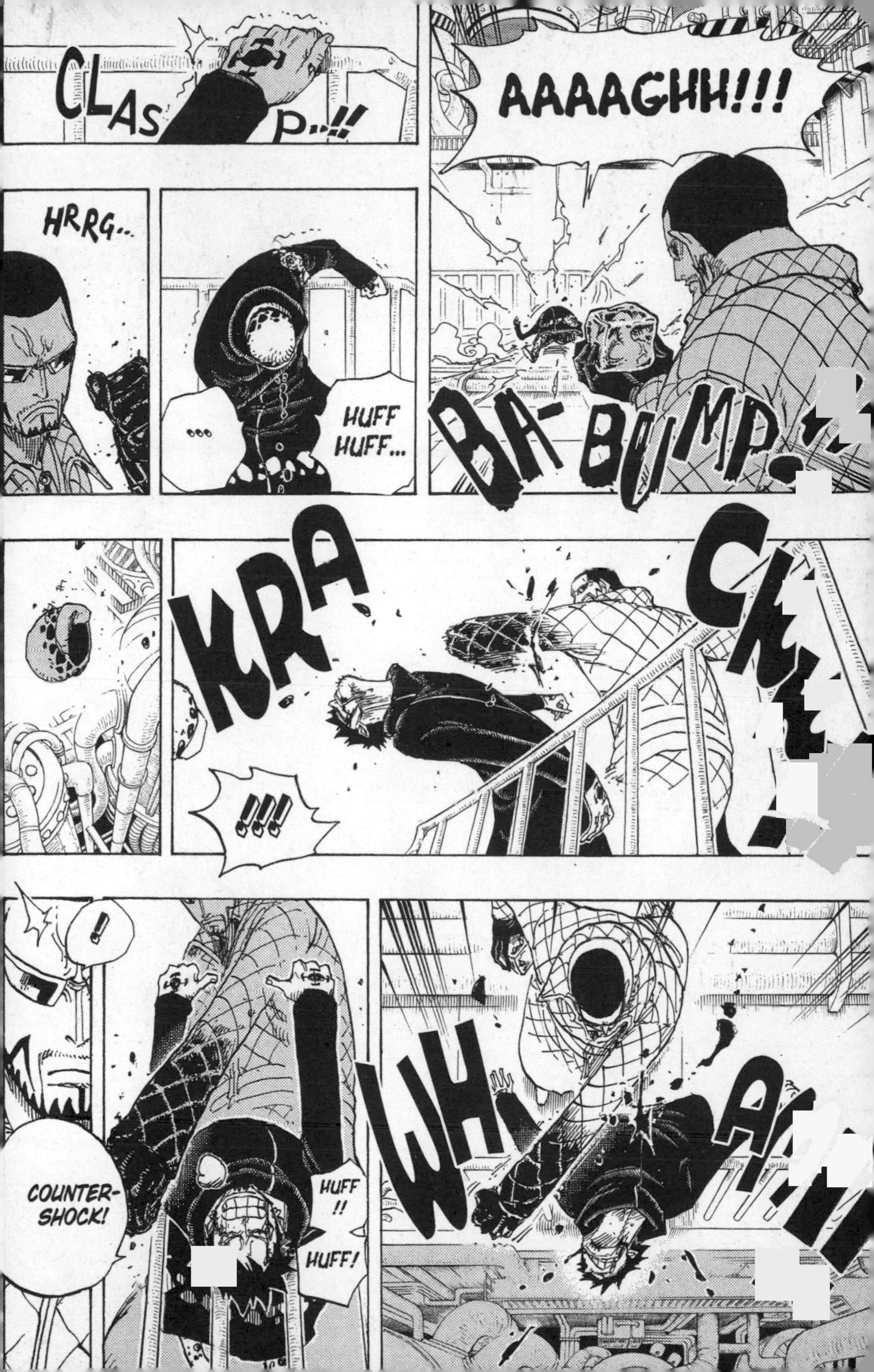
AAAAGHH!!!
BA-BUMP
CLASP..!!
...
HUFF HUFF...
HRRG...
KRA
CK
!!!
WH
!
HUFF !!
HUFF!
COUNTER-SHOCK!

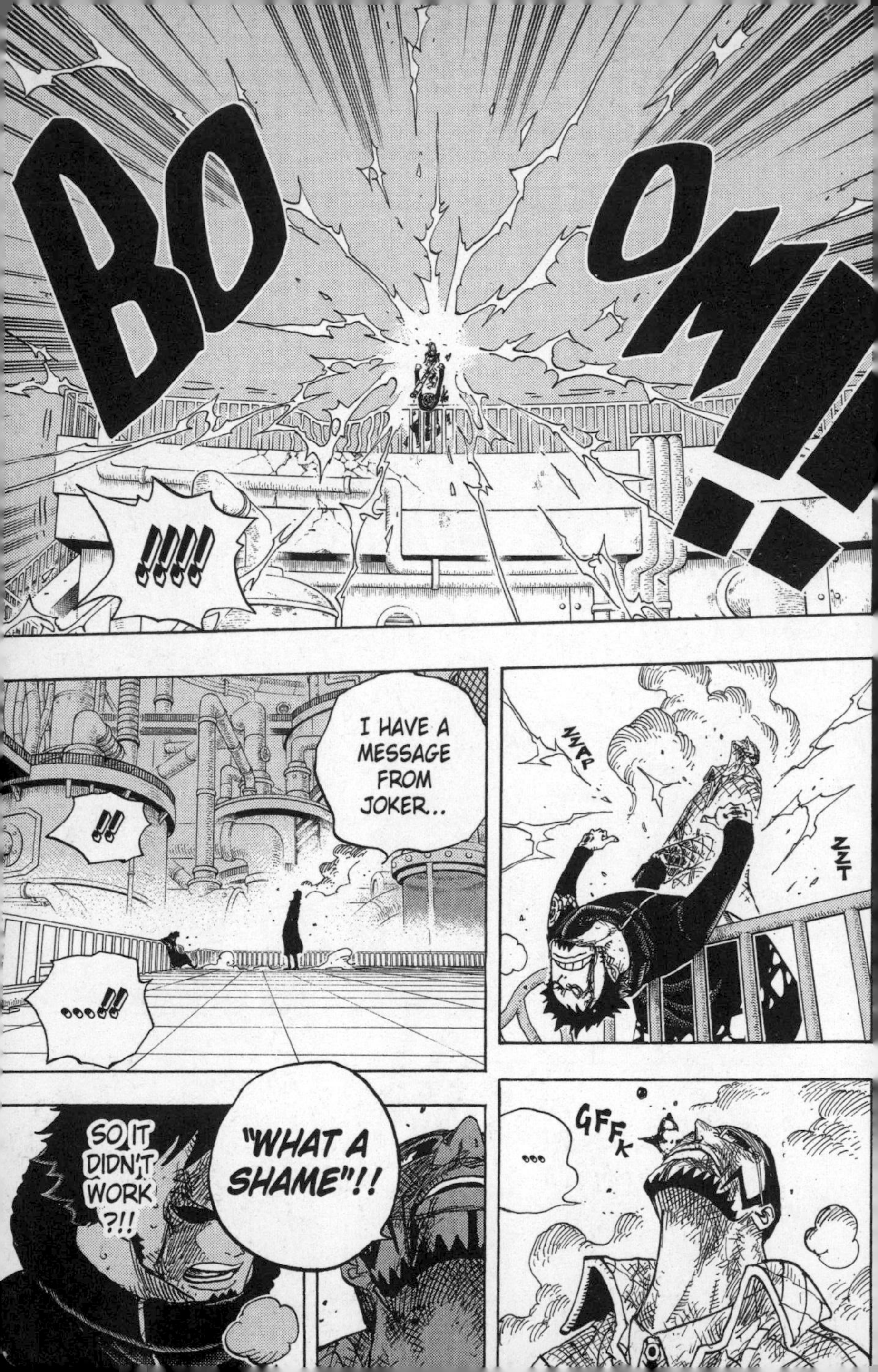
BOOOM!!
!!!!
ZZAP
ZZT
I HAVE A MESSAGE FROM JOKER...
!!
....!!
GFFK
...
"WHAT A SHAME"!!
SO IT DIDN'T WORK?!!

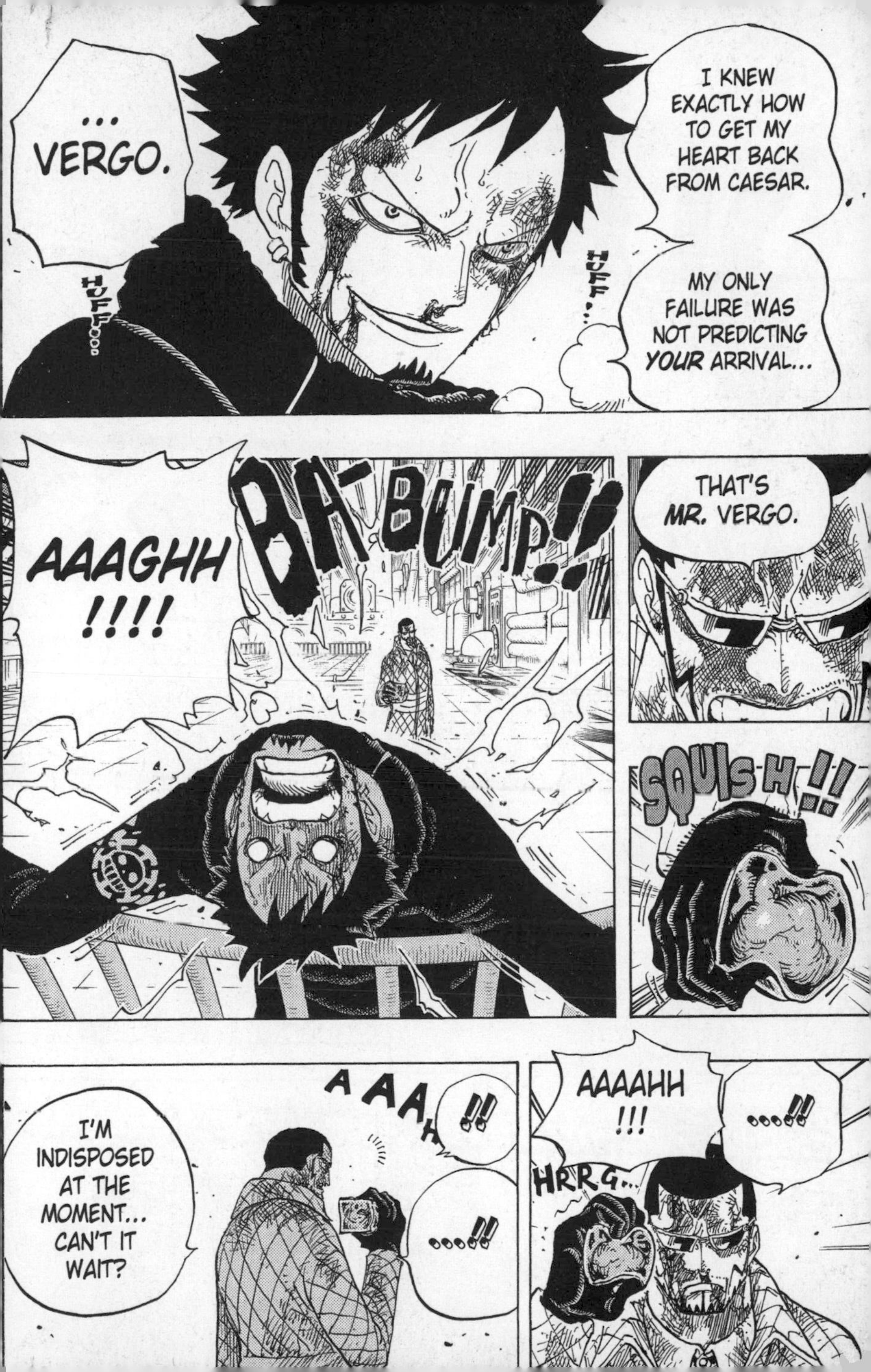

I KNEW EXACTLY HOW TO GET MY HEART BACK FROM CAESAR.
MY ONLY FAILURE WAS NOT PREDICTING *YOUR* ARRIVAL...
HUFF...
...VERGO.
HUFF...
THAT'S *MR.* VERGO.
SQUISH!!
BA-BUMP!!
AAAGHH!!!!
...!!
AAAAHH!!!
HRRG...
AAAH!!
...!!
I'M INDISPOSED AT THE MOMENT... CAN'T IT WAIT?

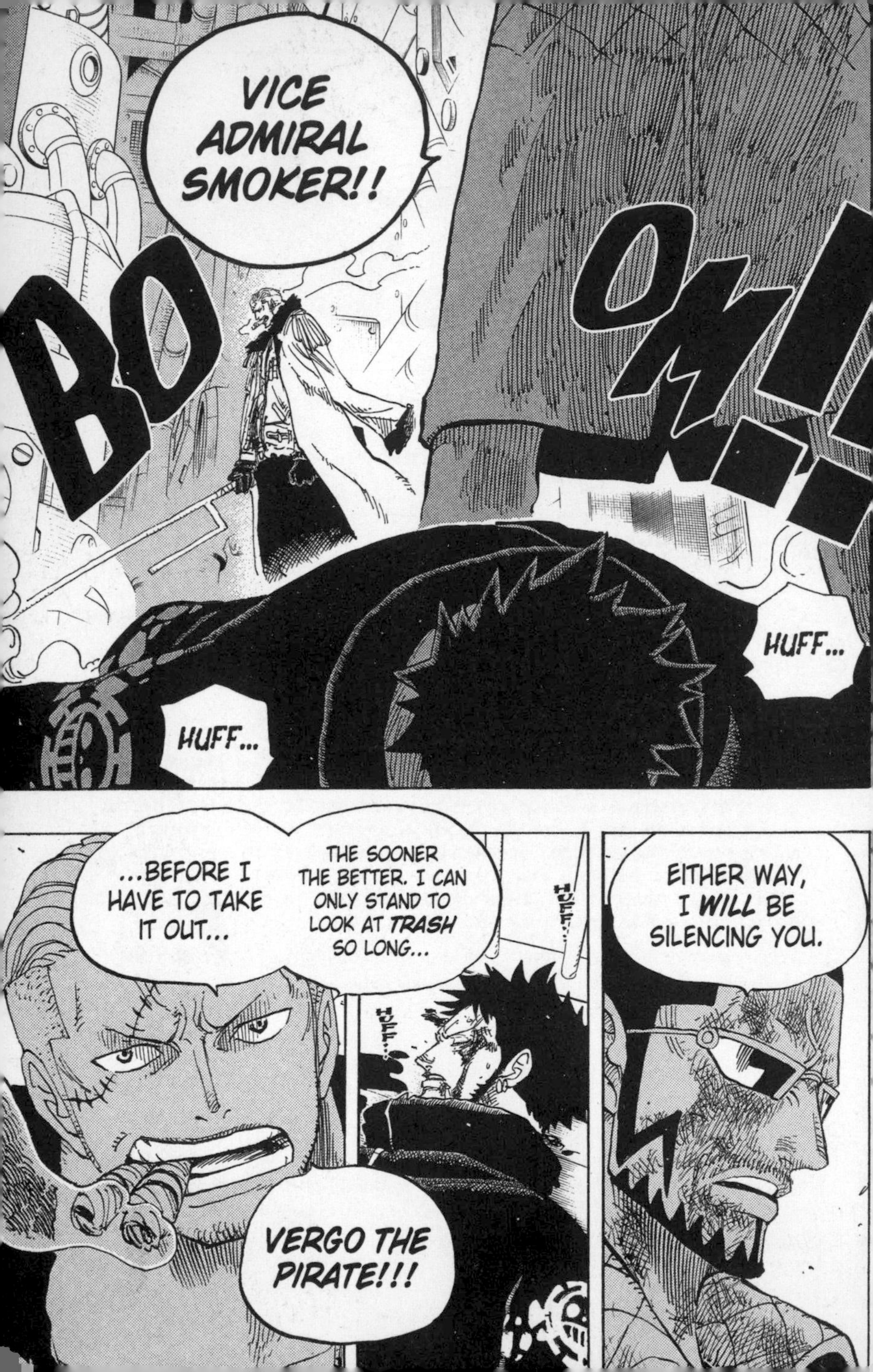
VICE ADMIRAL SMOKER!!
BOOM!!
HUFF...
HUFF...
EITHER WAY, I *WILL* BE SILENCING YOU.
HUFF...
THE SOONER THE BETTER. I CAN ONLY STAND TO LOOK AT *TRASH* SO LONG...
...BEFORE I HAVE TO TAKE IT OUT...
HUFF...
VERGO THE PIRATE!!!

質問コーナー
エス ビー エス
ひーっ

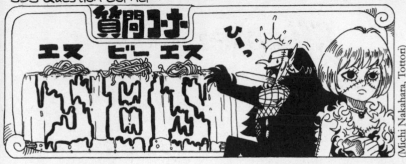

(Michi Nakahara, Tottori)

Q: Warning!

The following segment contains considerable amounts of vulgar content, and reader discretion is advised. Those with weak stomachs are urged to proceed with the story.

--Patan

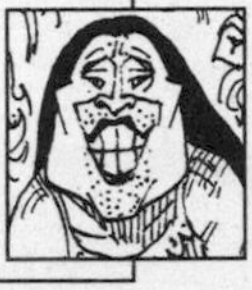

A: Huh...?! We have a warning? This is outrageous! Well, I certainly don't want anyone thinking my work is vulgar, so I'll answer your questions in the most dainty and elegant manner I can. Ahem! Please proceed with your questions...

YOU WILL GIVE YOUR HEART TO ME!!!
DO WE HAVE A DEAL?!!

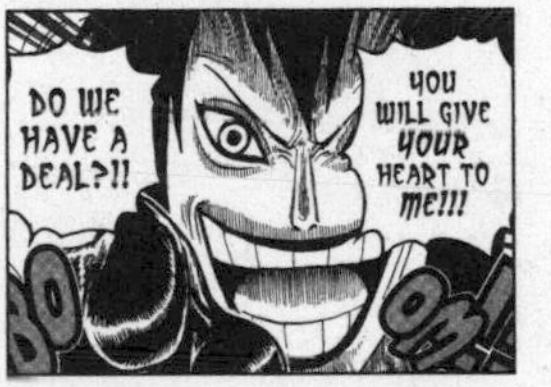

Q: Hello, PervichiroOda. Why did Caesar demand Law's heart? You'd figure that demanding his penis instead would be more damaging to Law.

--Ikeyan

A: Ahem. Indeed, the weenis (daintier term) is more sensitive, shall we say. But what about the visual image? Law holding a weenis, or Law holding a heart. Which one is a more powerful picture? Remember, Law delivered a hundred pirate hearts to Navy HQ in order to be a Warlord of the Sea... If he'd given them a hundred weenises, he'd be more like a Warlord of the Pee.

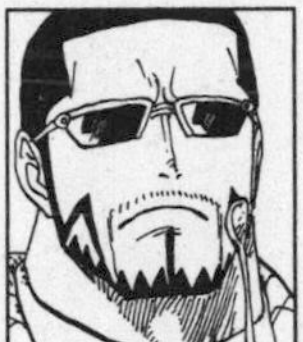

Q: Vergo can cover his whole body with Color of Armament Haki, right? Does that mean he can imbue his penis with Armament Haki too?

--Newcomer

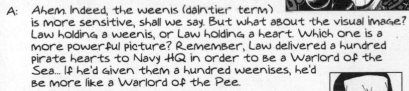

A: Ahem. He can. It certainly would make a man... great.

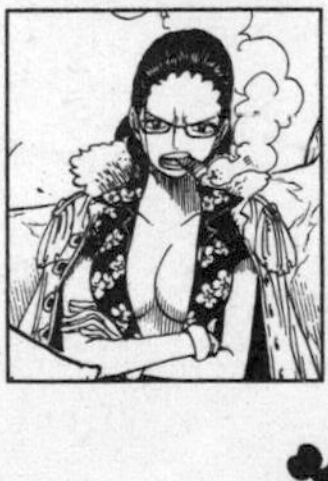

Q: Smoker, how can you just rip a bra off like that?! (See SBS, Vol. 68) It's simply monstrous of you. If it's that constricting, you can just wear it on your head like Mr. Oda does!

--Yusamai

A: Ahem. Care to join me, Smoker?

Chapter 684:

DON'T DO IT, VEGAPUNK

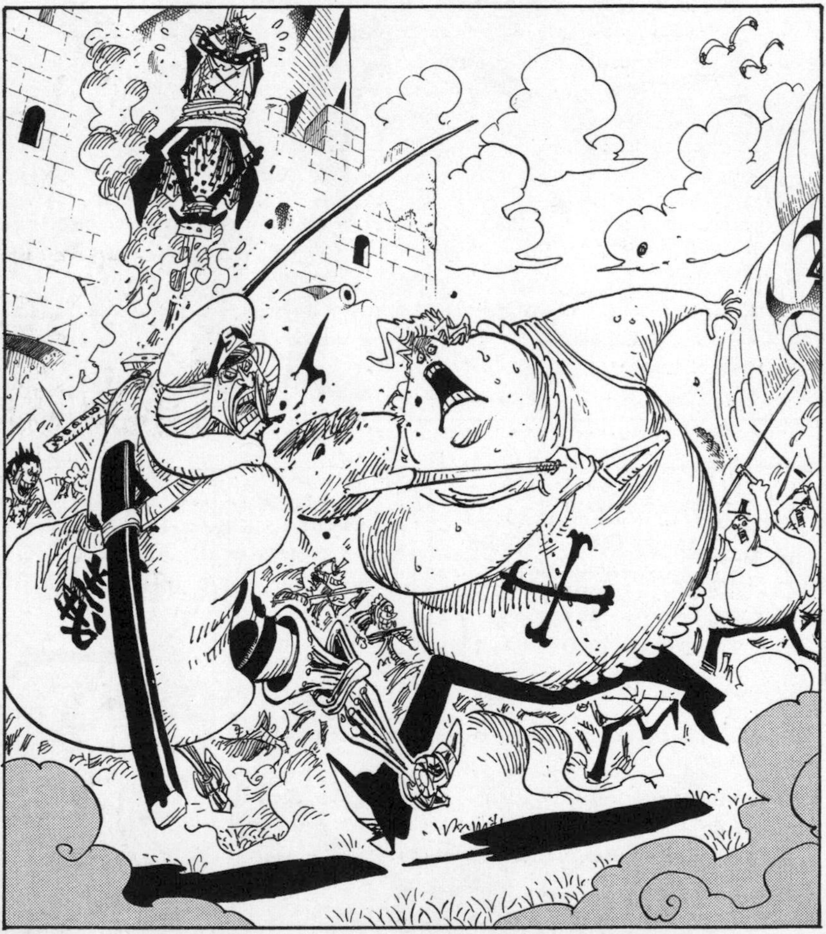

CARIBOU'S NEW WORLD KEE HEE HEE, VOL. 10:
"CARIBOU PIRATES VS. NAVAL G-5"

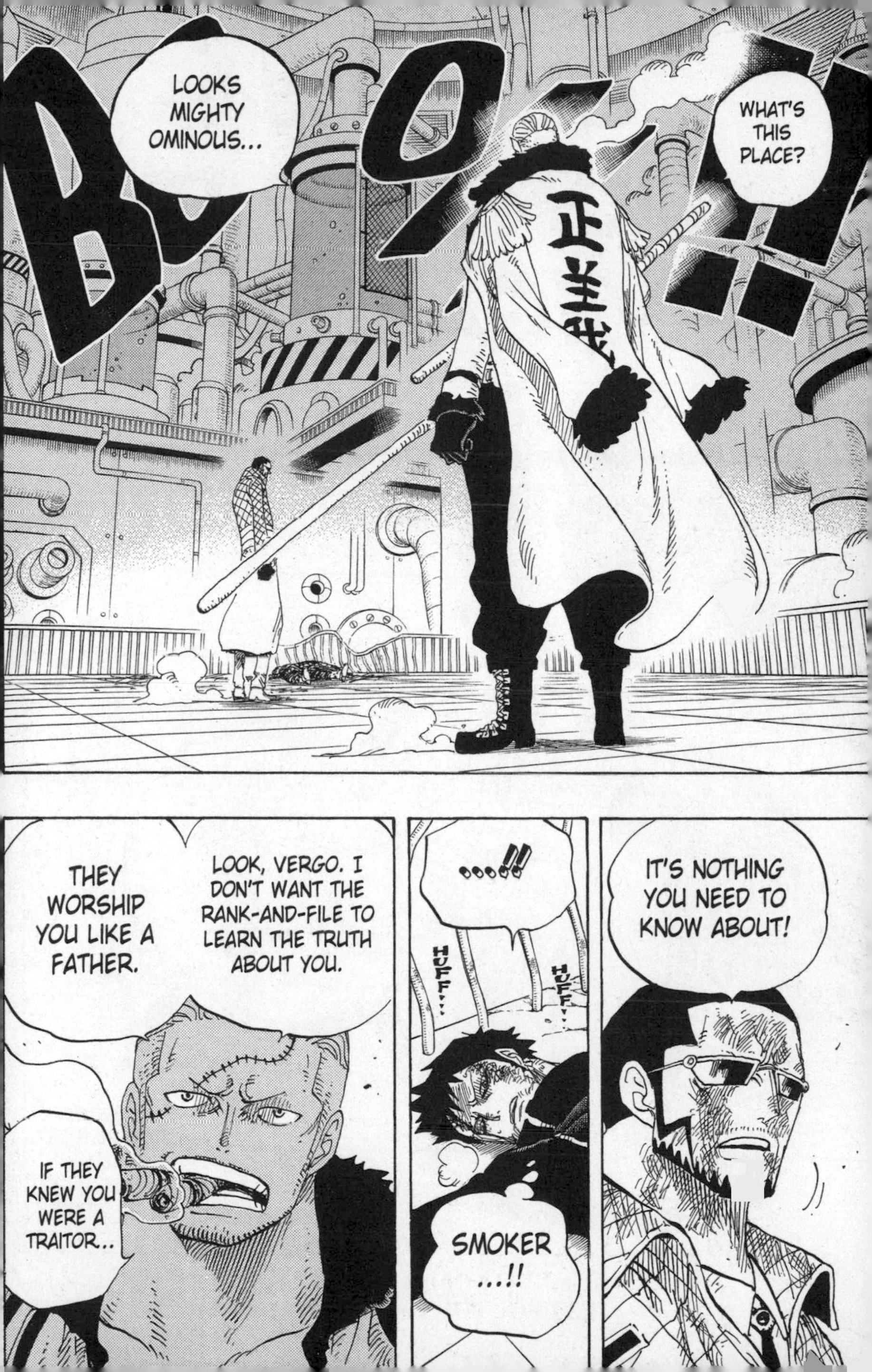
WHAT'S THIS PLACE?
LOOKS MIGHTY OMINOUS...
正義
IT'S NOTHING YOU NEED TO KNOW ABOUT!
....!!
HUFF...
HUFF...
SMOKER ...!!
LOOK, VERGO. I DON'T WANT THE RANK-AND-FILE TO LEARN THE TRUTH ABOUT YOU.
THEY WORSHIP YOU LIKE A FATHER.
IF THEY KNEW YOU WERE A TRAITOR...

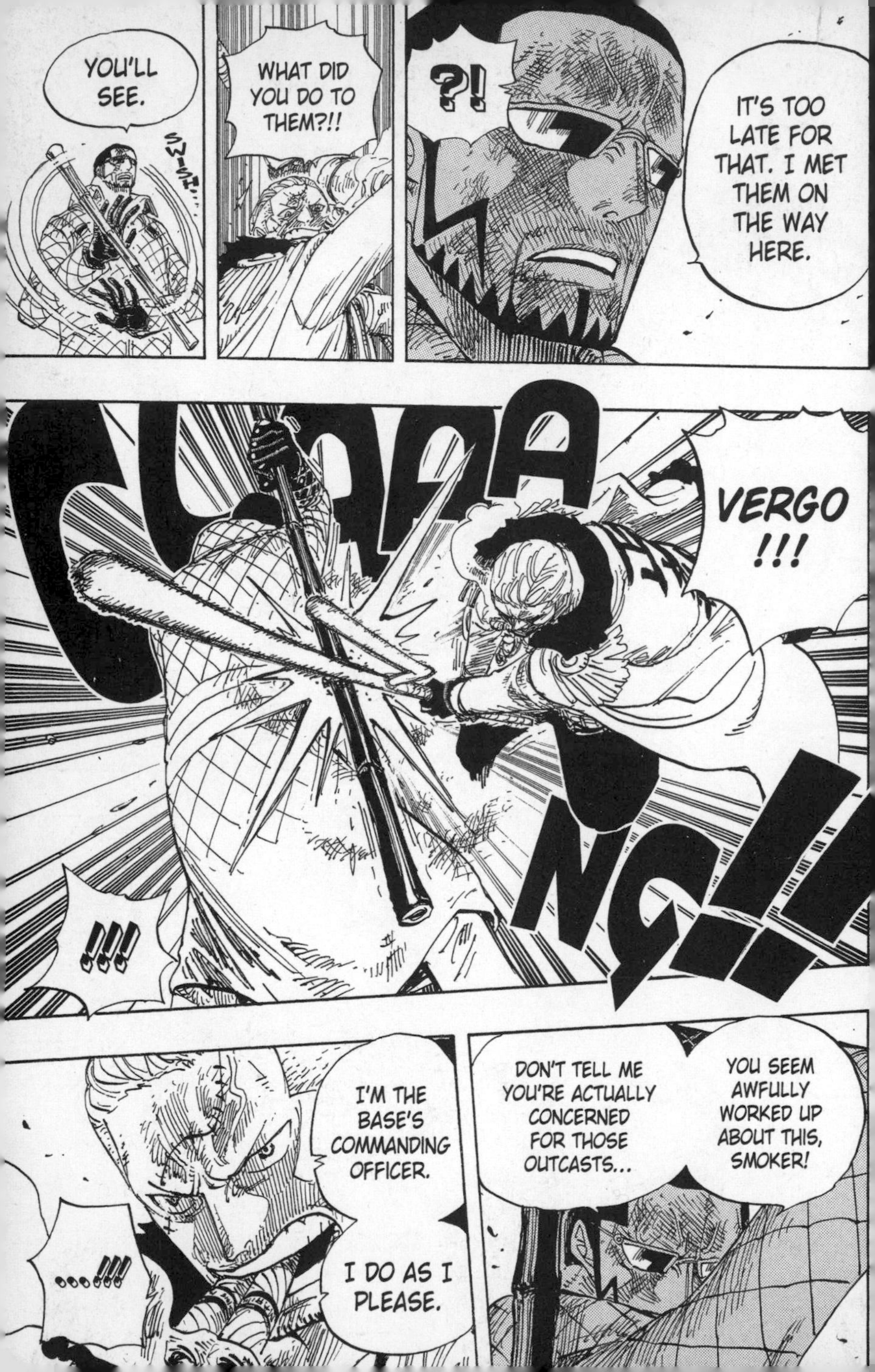
IT'S TOO LATE FOR THAT. I MET THEM ON THE WAY HERE.
?!
WHAT DID YOU DO TO THEM?!!
YOU'LL SEE.
SWISH
VERGO!!!
!!!
YOU SEEM AWFULLY WORKED UP ABOUT THIS, SMOKER!
DON'T TELL ME YOU'RE ACTUALLY CONCERNED FOR THOSE OUTCASTS...
I'M THE BASE'S COMMANDING OFFICER.
I DO AS I PLEASE.
...!!!

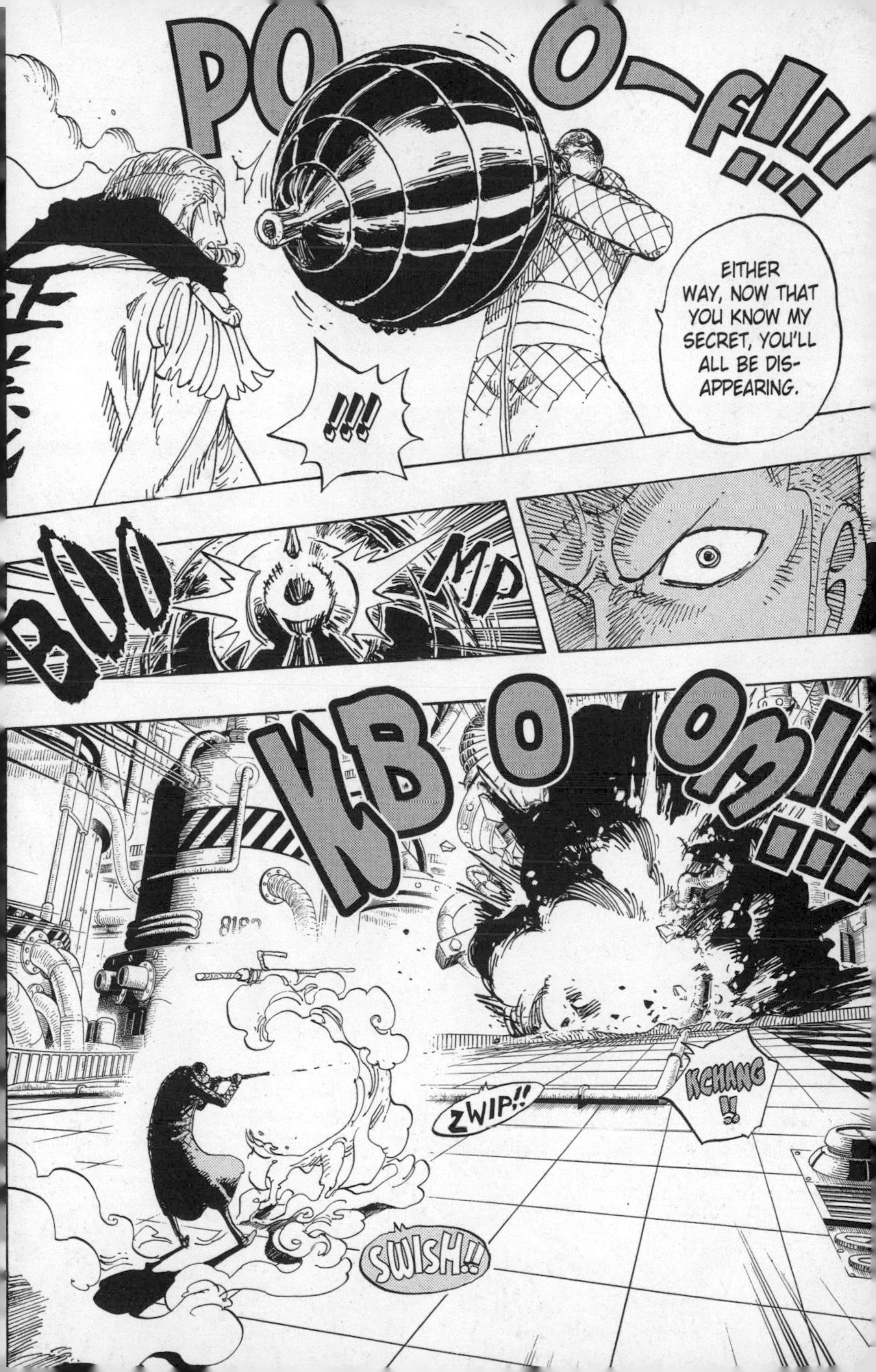

PO O-F!!!
EITHER WAY, NOW THAT YOU KNOW MY SECRET, YOU'LL ALL BE DIS-APPEARING.
!!!
BOOMP
KBOOOM!!
KCHANG!!
ZWIP!!
SWISH!!

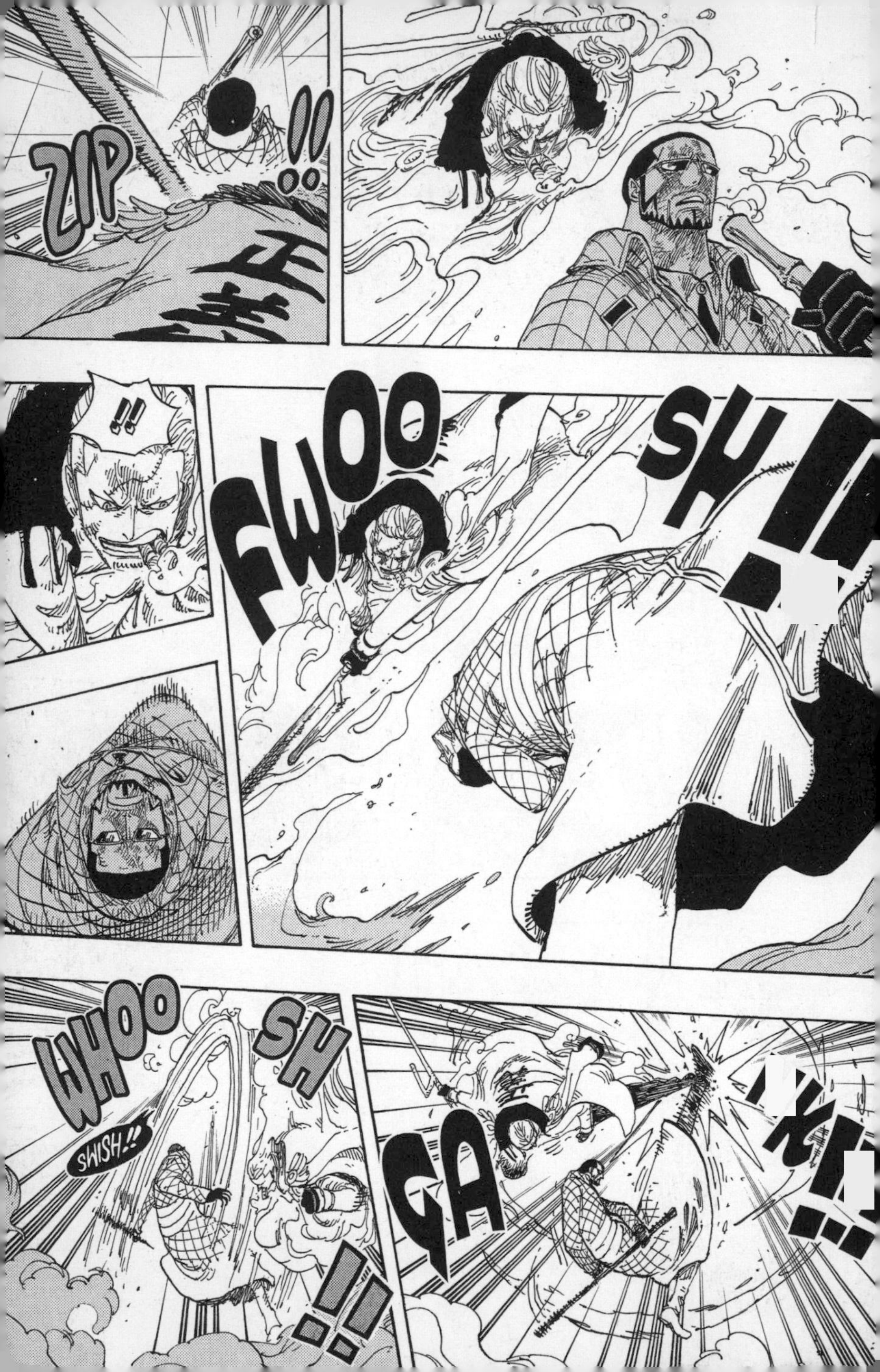
ZIP
!!
SH
FWOO
!!
GA
WHOO
SH
SWISH!!
!!

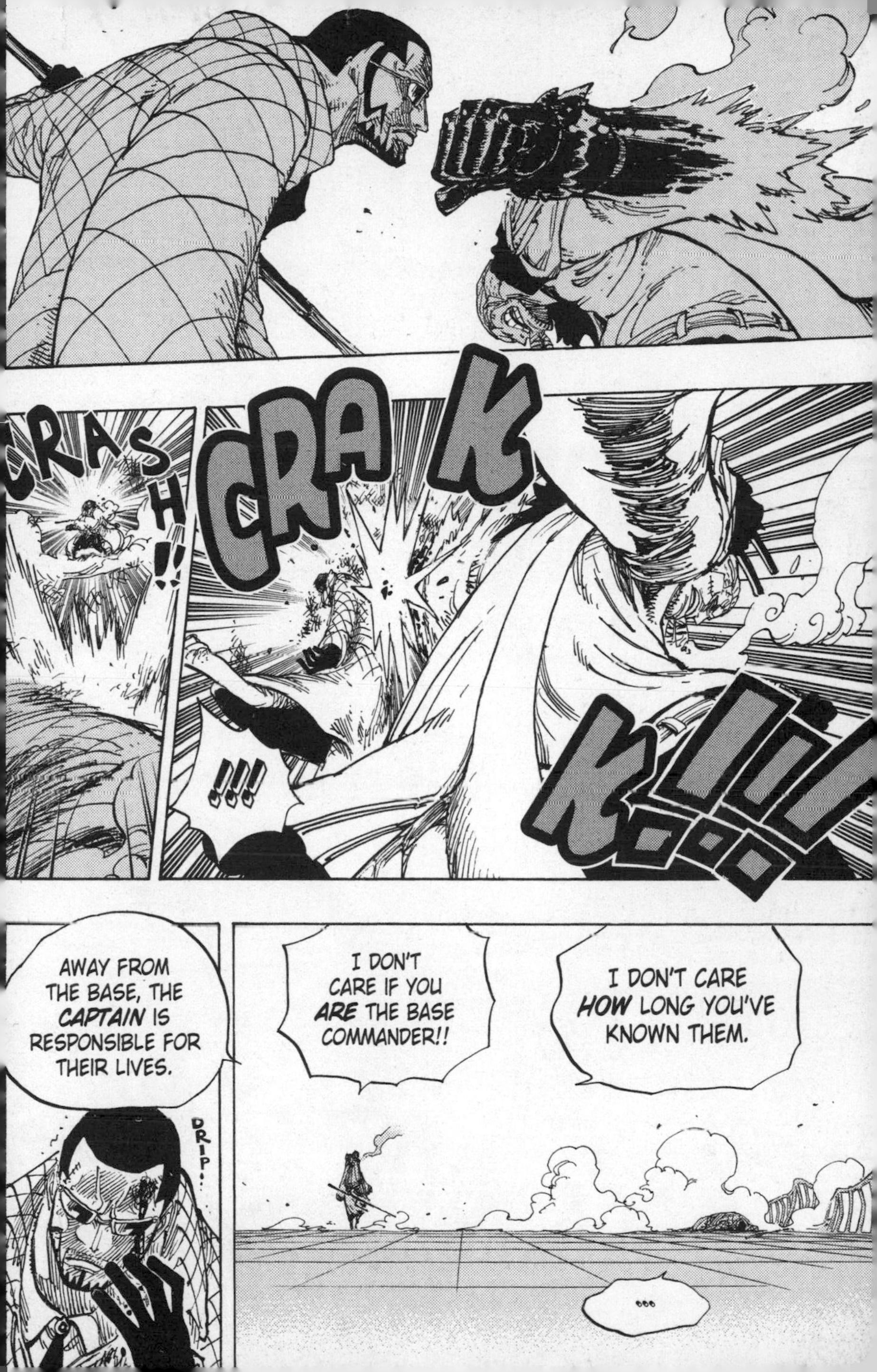
CRAKK!!!!
!!!
CRASH!!
I DON'T CARE HOW LONG YOU'VE KNOWN THEM.
I DON'T CARE IF YOU ARE THE BASE COMMANDER!!
...
AWAY FROM THE BASE, THE CAPTAIN IS RESPONSIBLE FOR THEIR LIVES.
DRIP...

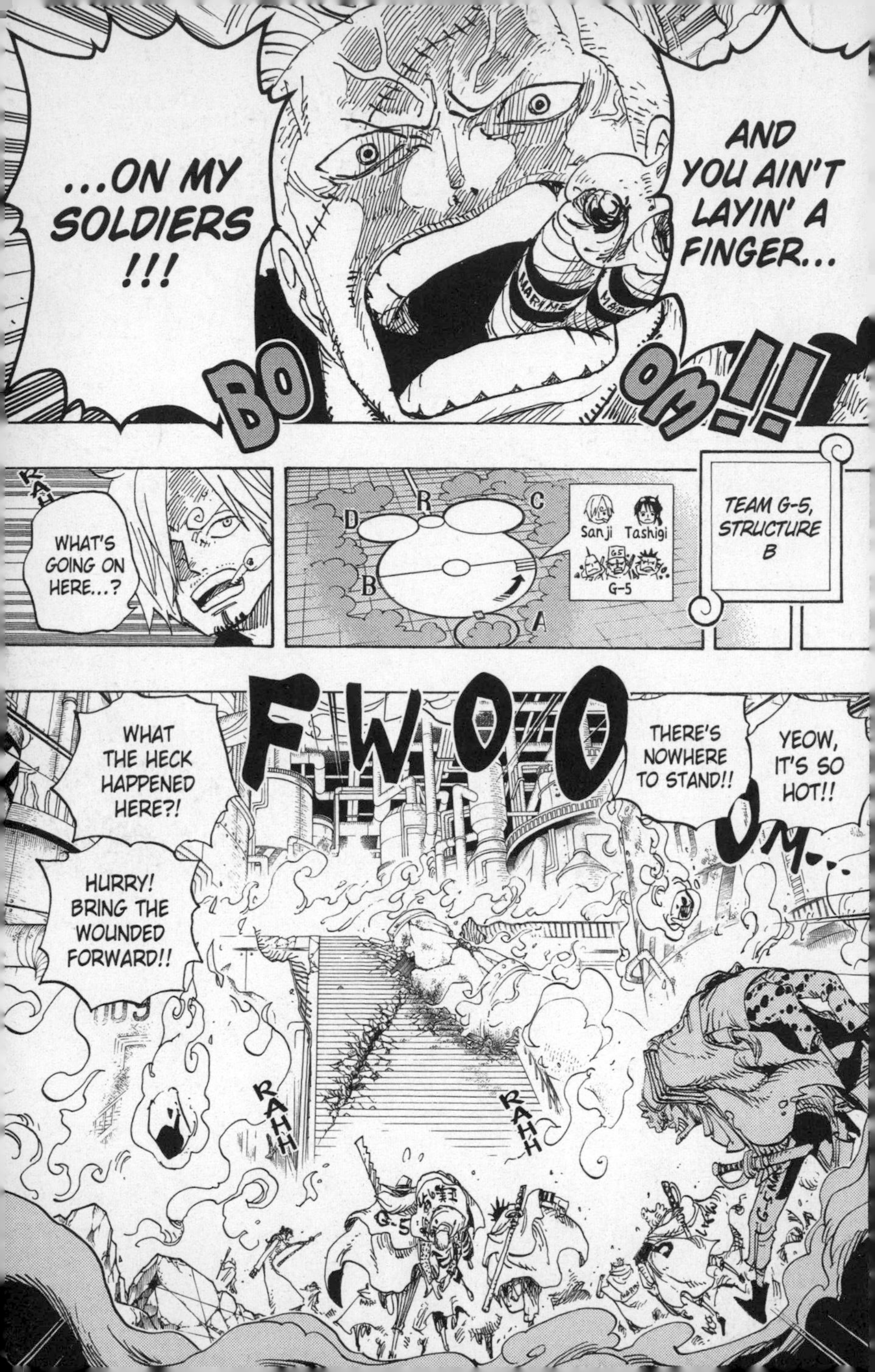

AND YOU AIN'T LAYIN' A FINGER...
...ON MY SOLDIERS!!!
BOOM!!!
TEAM G-5, STRUCTURE B
Sanji
Tashigi
G-5
D
R
C
B
A
RAH
WHAT'S GOING ON HERE...?
FWOOOM...
YEOW, IT'S SO HOT!!
THERE'S NOWHERE TO STAND!!
WHAT THE HECK HAPPENED HERE?!
HURRY! BRING THE WOUNDED FORWARD!!
RAHH
RAHH

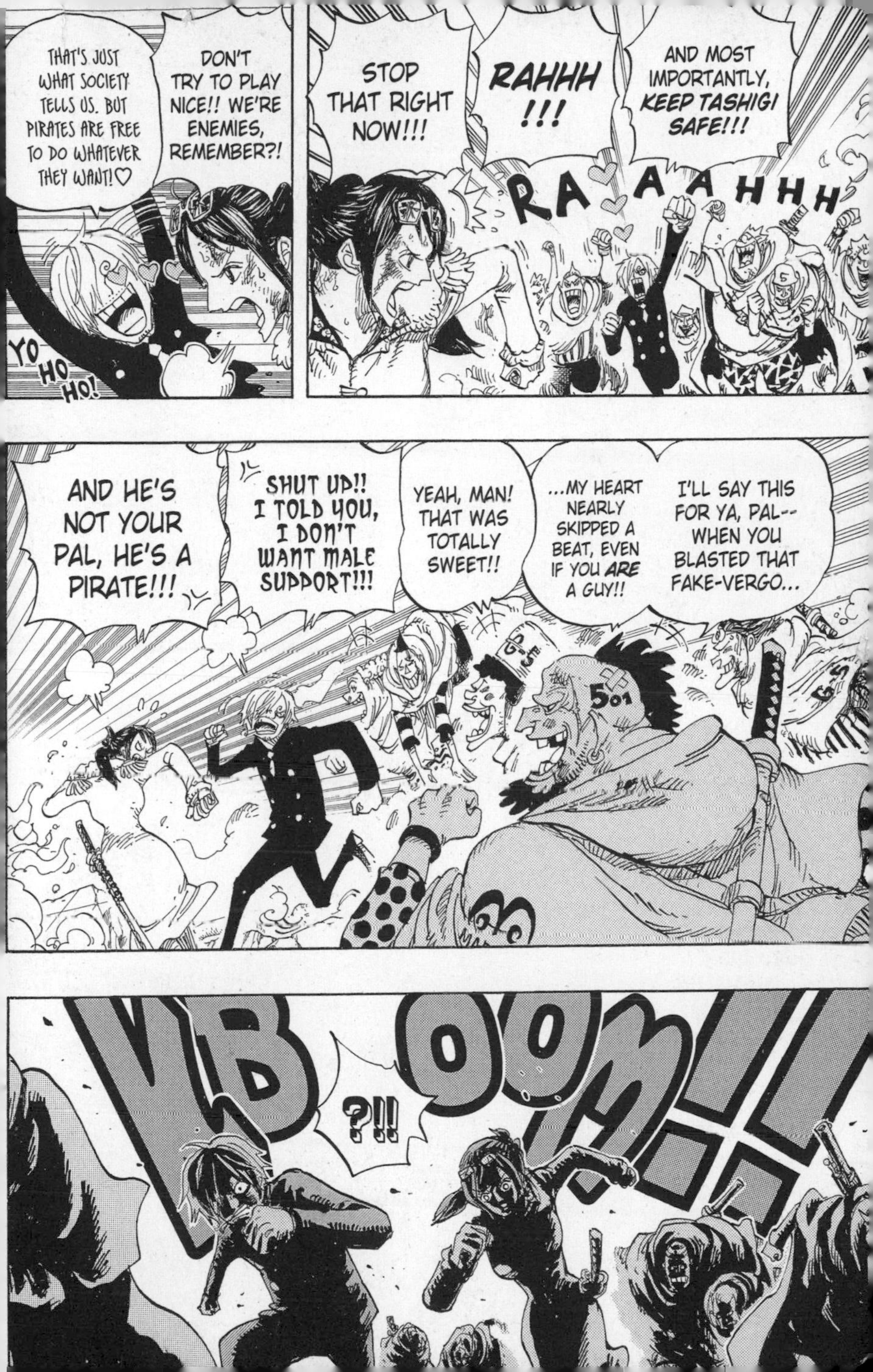
AND MOST IMPORTANTLY, KEEP TASHIGI SAFE!!!
RAHHH!!!
STOP THAT RIGHT NOW!!!
RAAAHHHH
DON'T TRY TO PLAY NICE!! WE'RE ENEMIES, REMEMBER?!
THAT'S JUST WHAT SOCIETY TELLS US. BUT PIRATES ARE FREE TO DO WHATEVER THEY WANT!♡
YO HO HO!
I'LL SAY THIS FOR YA, PAL-- WHEN YOU BLASTED THAT FAKE-VERGO...
...MY HEART NEARLY SKIPPED A BEAT, EVEN IF YOU ARE A GUY!!
YEAH, MAN! THAT WAS TOTALLY SWEET!!
SHUT UP!! I TOLD YOU, I DON'T WANT MALE SUPPORT!!!
AND HE'S NOT YOUR PAL, HE'S A PIRATE!!!
VBOOM!!
?!!

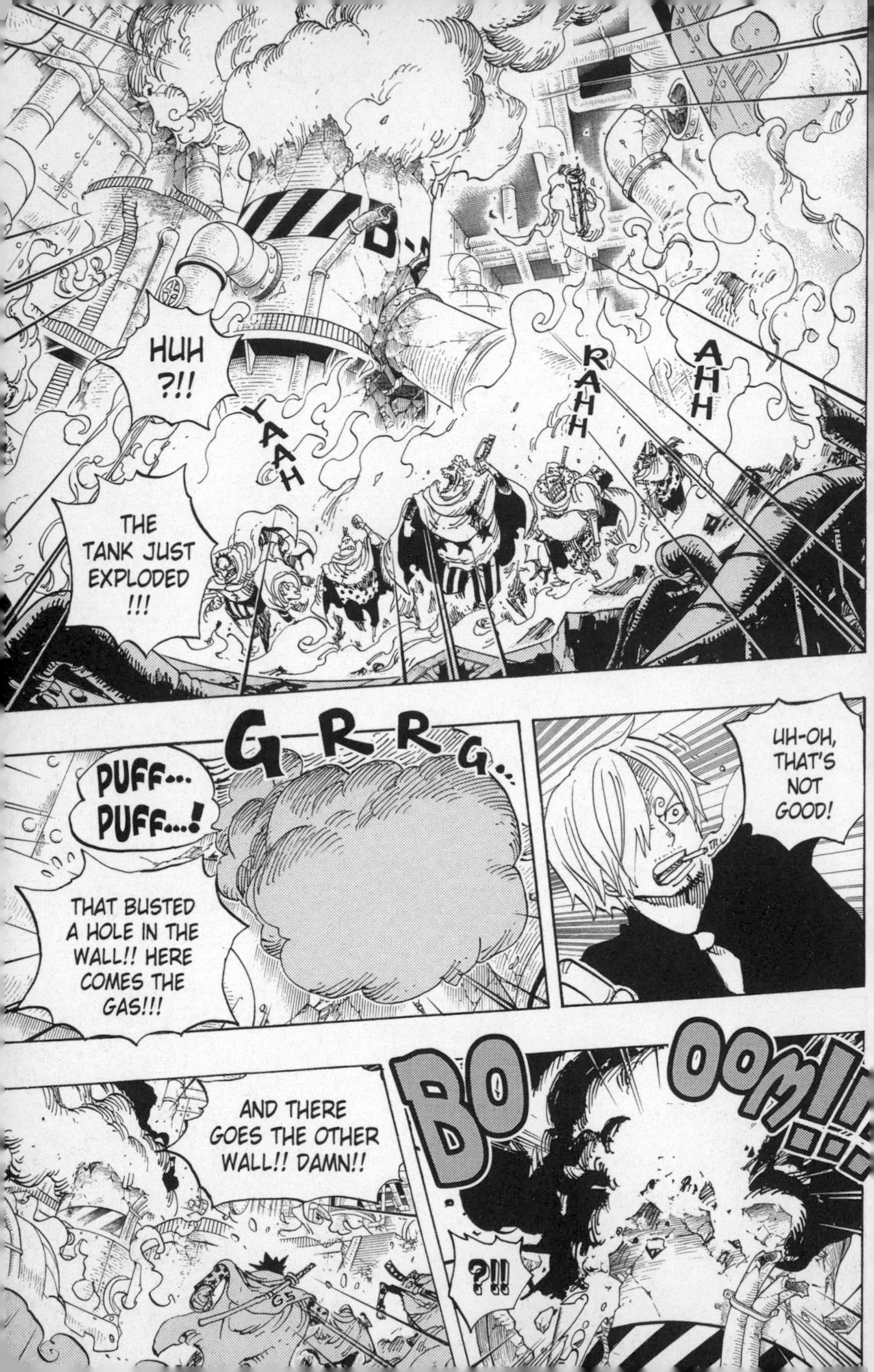
AHH
RAHH
HUH ?!!
YAAH
THE TANK JUST EXPLODED !!!
UH-OH, THAT'S NOT GOOD!
GRRRG...
PUFF... PUFF...!
THAT BUSTED A HOLE IN THE WALL!! HERE COMES THE GAS!!!
BOOOM!!...
AND THERE GOES THE OTHER WALL!! DAMN!!
?!!

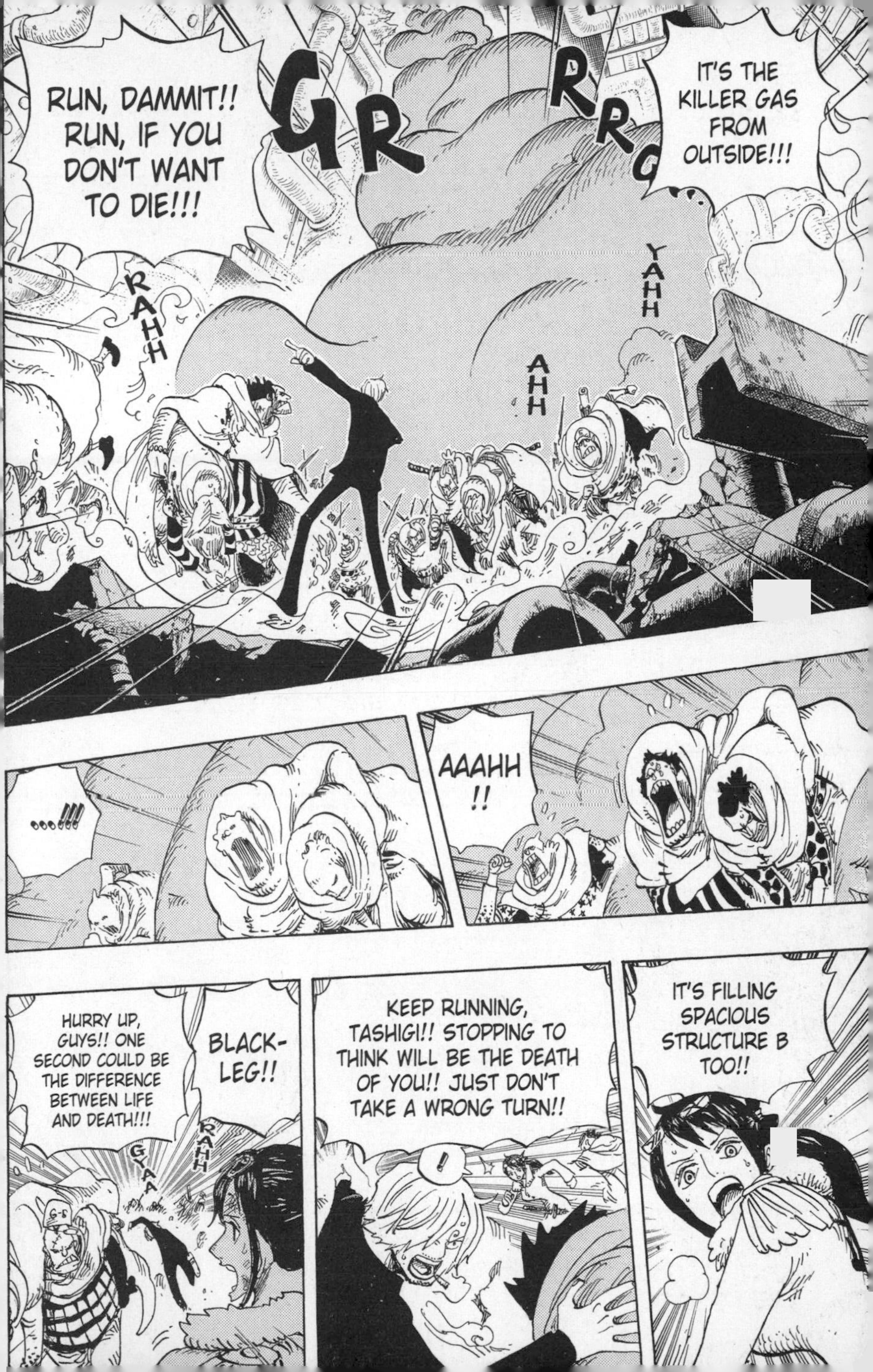
IT'S THE KILLER GAS FROM OUTSIDE!!!
GRRRRG
RUN, DAMMIT!! RUN, IF YOU DON'T WANT TO DIE!!!
YAHH
AHH
RAHH
AAAHH !!
...!!!
IT'S FILLING SPACIOUS STRUCTURE B TOO!!
KEEP RUNNING, TASHIGI!! STOPPING TO THINK WILL BE THE DEATH OF YOU!! JUST DON'T TAKE A WRONG TURN!!
!
BLACK-LEG!!
HURRY UP, GUYS!! ONE SECOND COULD BE THE DIFFERENCE BETWEEN LIFE AND DEATH!!!
RAHH
GYAA

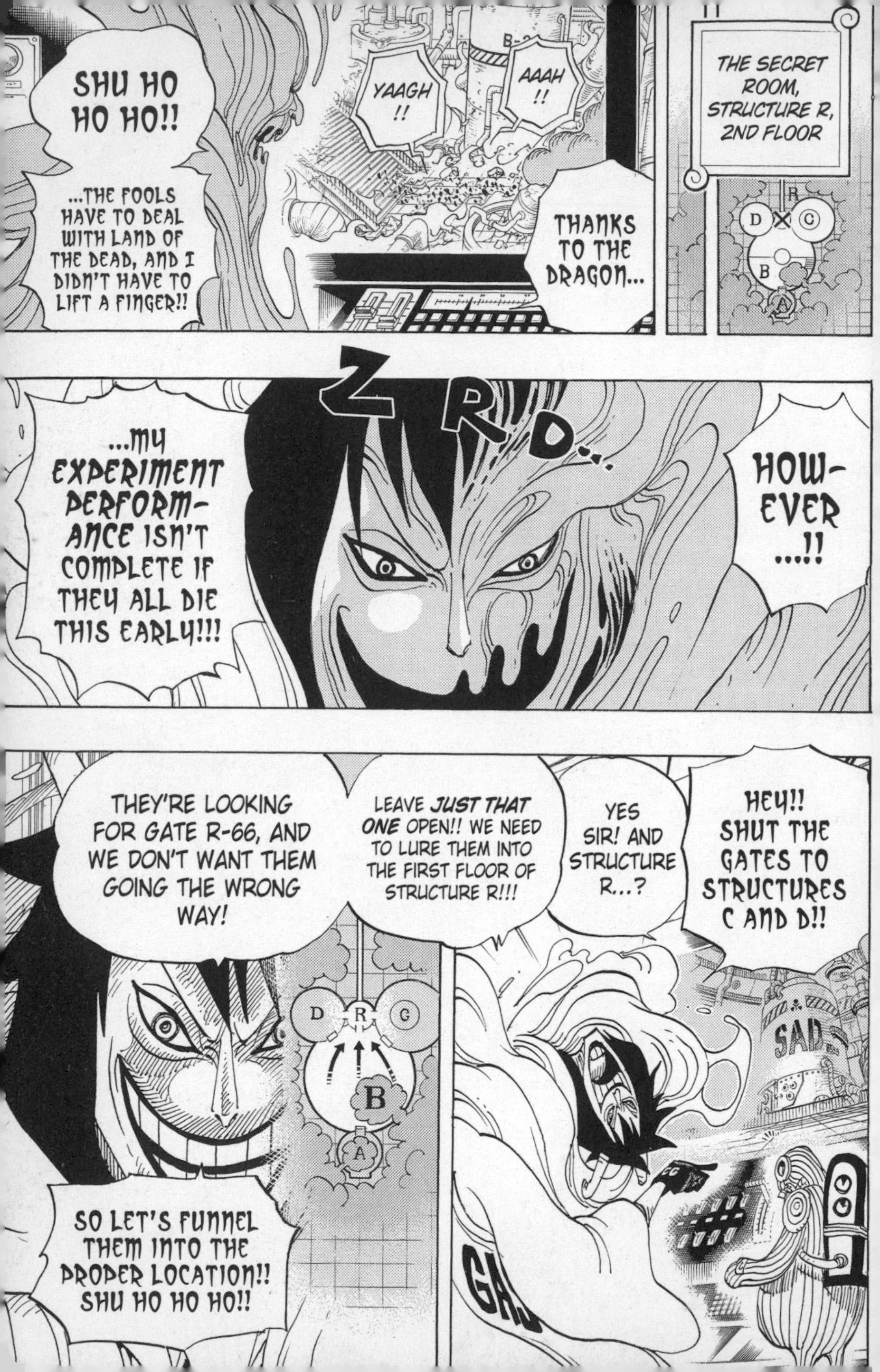
THE SECRET ROOM, STRUCTURE R, 2ND FLOOR
R
D
C
B
A
AAAH!!
YAAGH!!
THANKS TO THE DRAGON...
SHU HO HO HO!!
...THE FOOLS HAVE TO DEAL WITH LAND OF THE DEAD, AND I DIDN'T HAVE TO LIFT A FINGER!!
HOW-EVER ....!!
ZRD...
...MY EXPERIMENT PERFORM-ANCE ISN'T COMPLETE IF THEY ALL DIE THIS EARLY!!!
HEY!! SHUT THE GATES TO STRUCTURES C AND D!!
YES SIR! AND STRUCTURE R...?
SAD
LEAVE JUST THAT ONE OPEN!! WE NEED TO LURE THEM INTO THE FIRST FLOOR OF STRUCTURE R!!!
THEY'RE LOOKING FOR GATE R-66, AND WE DON'T WANT THEM GOING THE WRONG WAY!
D
R
C
B
A
SO LET'S FUNNEL THEM INTO THE PROPER LOCATION!! SHU HO HO HO!!

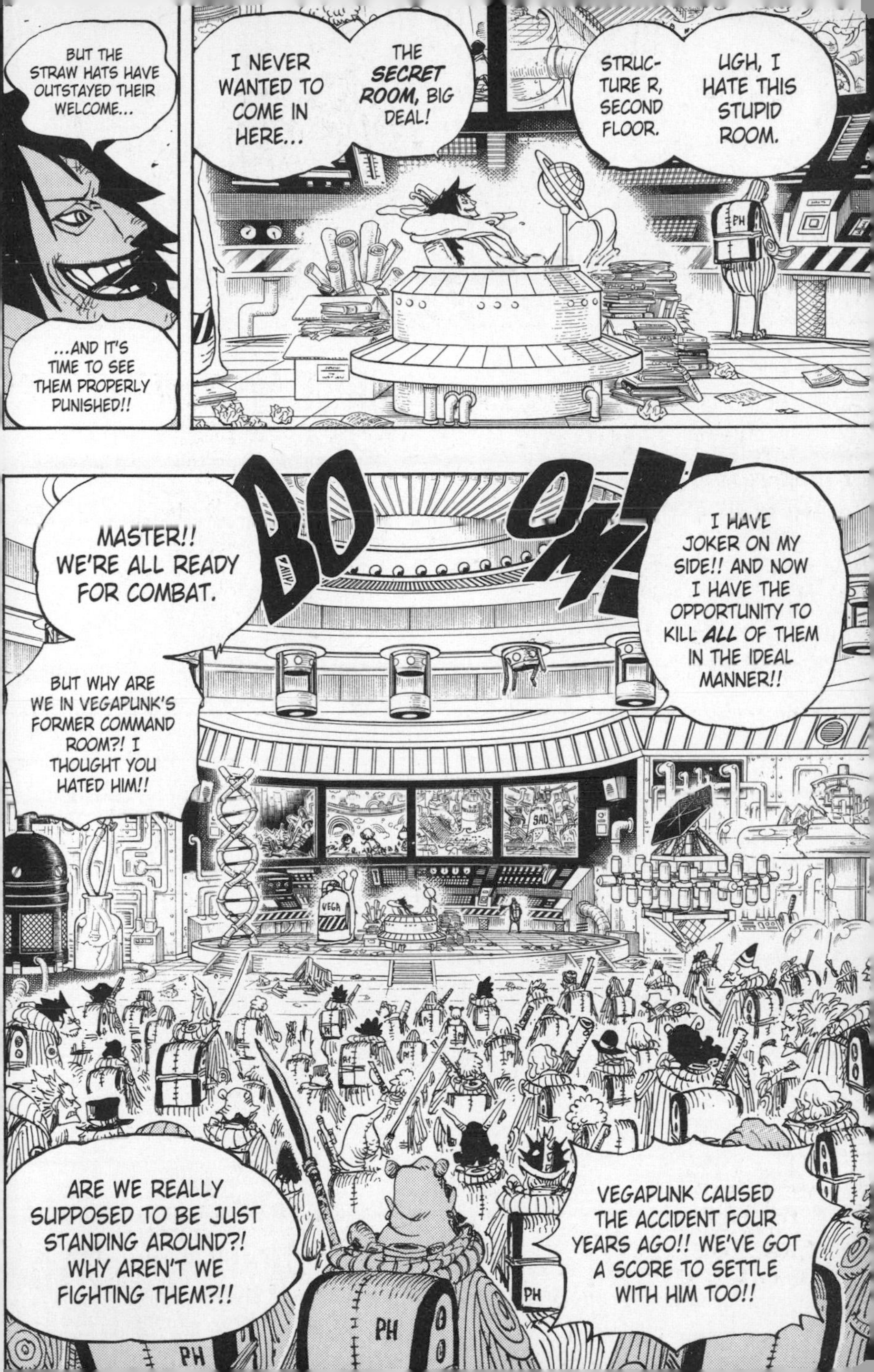
UGH, I HATE THIS STUPID ROOM.
STRUCTURE R, SECOND FLOOR.
THE SECRET ROOM, BIG DEAL!
I NEVER WANTED TO COME IN HERE...
BUT THE STRAW HATS HAVE OUTSTAYED THEIR WELCOME...
...AND IT'S TIME TO SEE THEM PROPERLY PUNISHED!!
BOOM!
I HAVE JOKER ON MY SIDE!! AND NOW I HAVE THE OPPORTUNITY TO KILL ALL OF THEM IN THE IDEAL MANNER!!
MASTER!! WE'RE ALL READY FOR COMBAT.
BUT WHY ARE WE IN VEGAPUNK'S FORMER COMMAND ROOM?! I THOUGHT YOU HATED HIM!!
VEGAPUNK CAUSED THE ACCIDENT FOUR YEARS AGO!! WE'VE GOT A SCORE TO SETTLE WITH HIM TOO!!
ARE WE REALLY SUPPOSED TO BE JUST STANDING AROUND?! WHY AREN'T WE FIGHTING THEM?!!

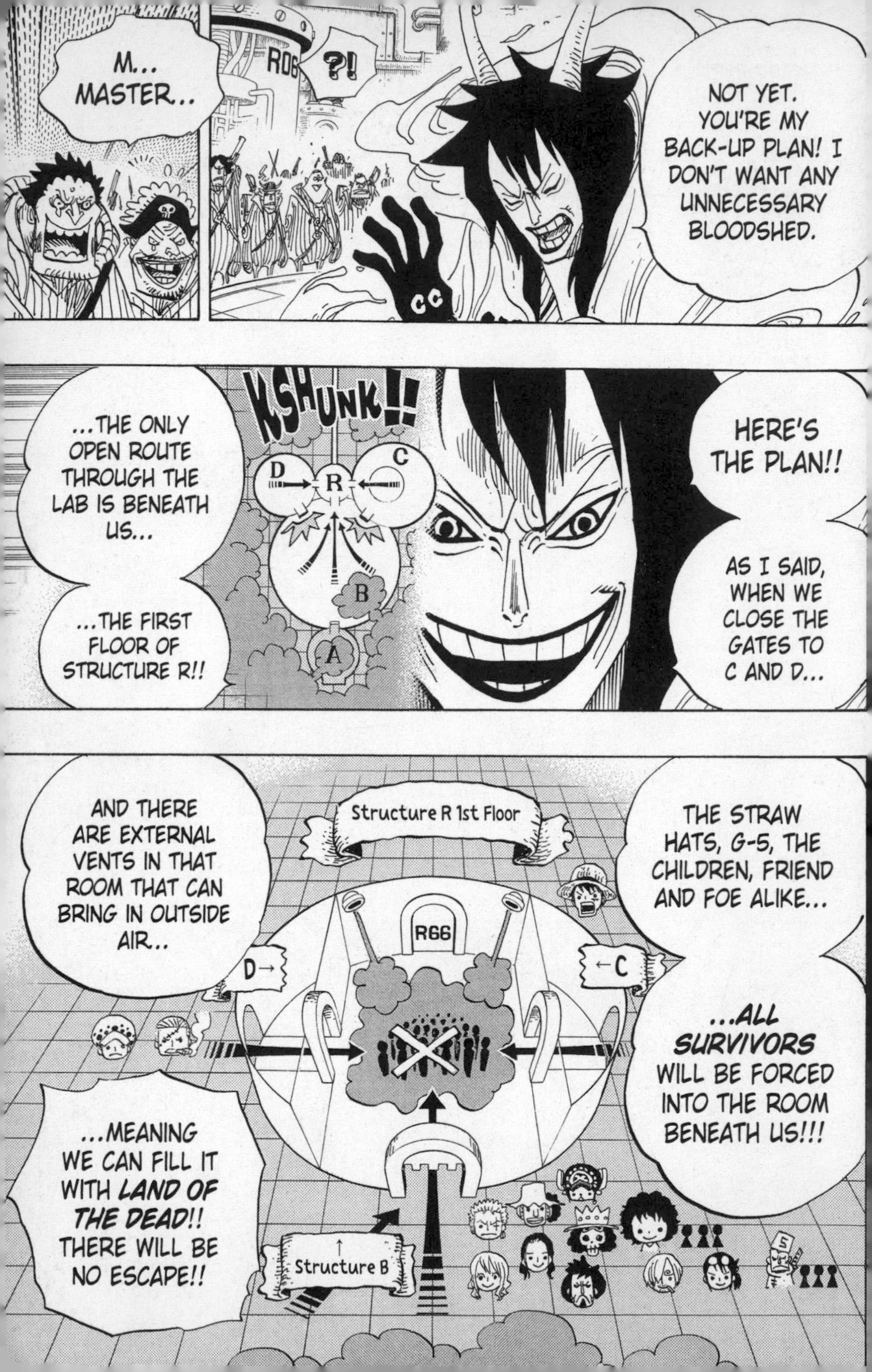
R06
?!
NOT YET. YOU'RE MY BACK-UP PLAN! I DON'T WANT ANY UNNECESSARY BLOODSHED.
M... MASTER...
KSHUNK!!
HERE'S THE PLAN!!
AS I SAID, WHEN WE CLOSE THE GATES TO C AND D...
D
R
C
B
A
...THE ONLY OPEN ROUTE THROUGH THE LAB IS BENEATH US...
...THE FIRST FLOOR OF STRUCTURE R!!
THE STRAW HATS, G-5, THE CHILDREN, FRIEND AND FOE ALIKE...
...*ALL SURVIVORS* WILL BE FORCED INTO THE ROOM BENEATH US!!!
Structure R 1st Floor
R66
←C
D→
↑ Structure B
AND THERE ARE EXTERNAL VENTS IN THAT ROOM THAT CAN BRING IN OUTSIDE AIR...
...MEANING WE CAN FILL IT WITH *LAND OF THE DEAD*!! THERE WILL BE NO ESCAPE!!

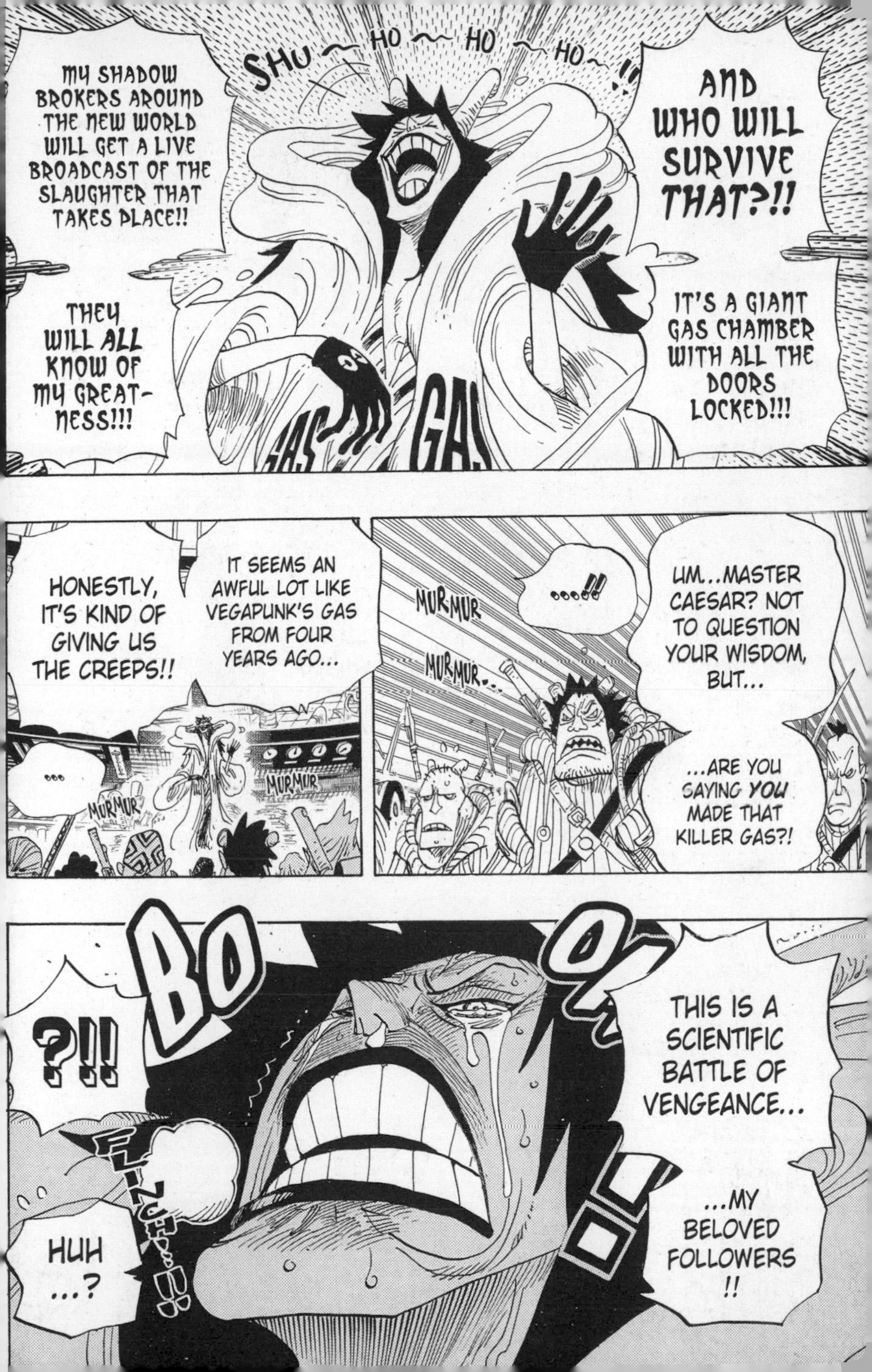
AND WHO WILL SURVIVE THAT?!!
SHU~HO~HO~HO~!!
MY SHADOW BROKERS AROUND THE NEW WORLD WILL GET A LIVE BROADCAST OF THE SLAUGHTER THAT TAKES PLACE!!
IT'S A GIANT GAS CHAMBER WITH ALL THE DOORS LOCKED!!!
THEY WILL ALL KNOW OF MY GREAT-NESS!!!
GAS
GAS
...!!
UM...MASTER CAESAR? NOT TO QUESTION YOUR WISDOM, BUT...
MURMUR
MURMUR...
...ARE YOU SAYING YOU MADE THAT KILLER GAS?!
IT SEEMS AN AWFUL LOT LIKE VEGAPUNK'S GAS FROM FOUR YEARS AGO...
HONESTLY, IT'S KIND OF GIVING US THE CREEPS!!
...
MURMUR
MURMUR
THIS IS A SCIENTIFIC BATTLE OF VENGEANCE...
BO
O
...MY BELOVED FOLLOWERS!!
?!!
FLINCH
HUH...?

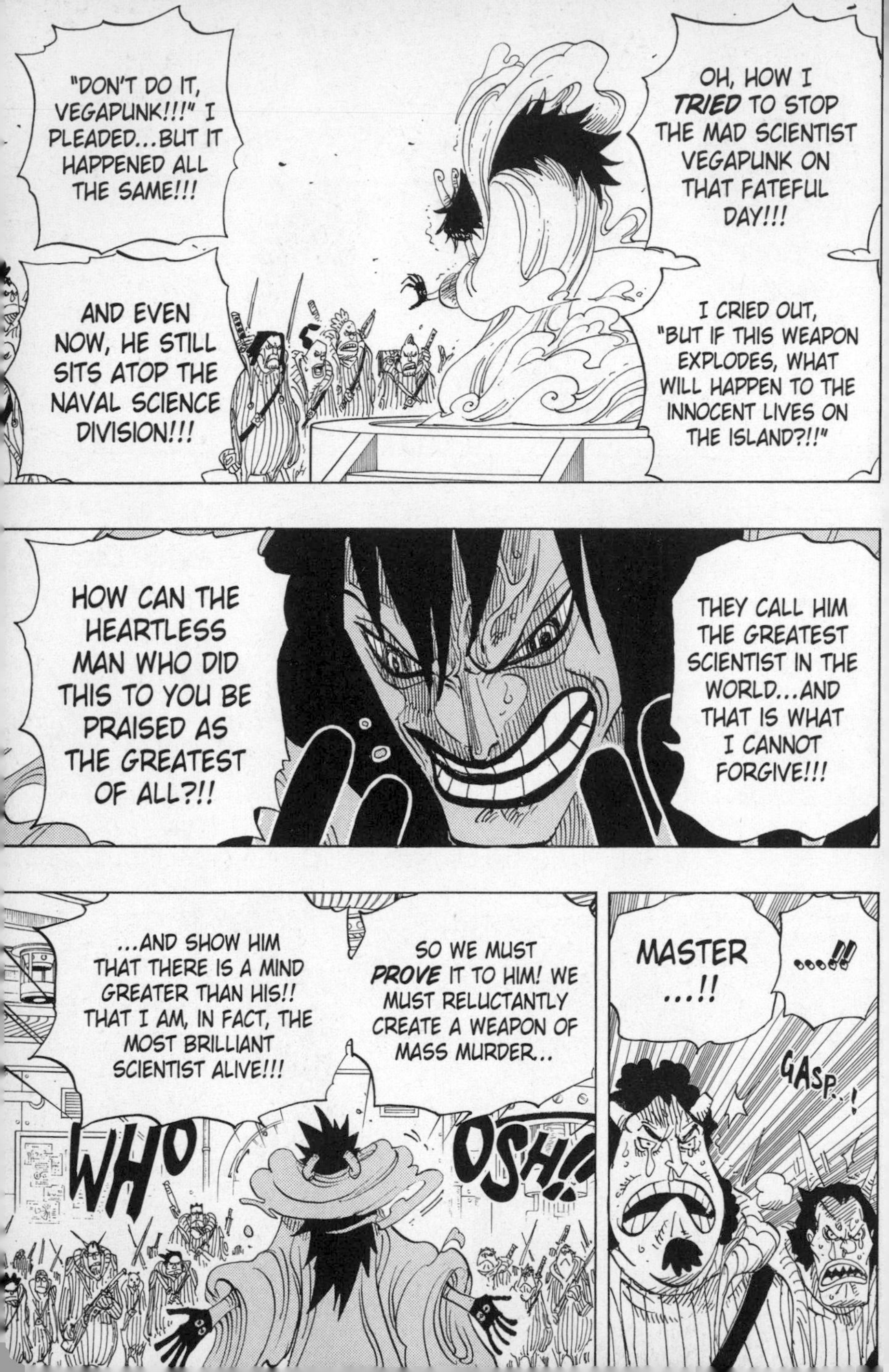
OH, HOW I TRIED TO STOP THE MAD SCIENTIST VEGAPUNK ON THAT FATEFUL DAY!!!
I CRIED OUT, "BUT IF THIS WEAPON EXPLODES, WHAT WILL HAPPEN TO THE INNOCENT LIVES ON THE ISLAND?!!"
"DON'T DO IT, VEGAPUNK!!!" I PLEADED...BUT IT HAPPENED ALL THE SAME!!!
AND EVEN NOW, HE STILL SITS ATOP THE NAVAL SCIENCE DIVISION!!!
THEY CALL HIM THE GREATEST SCIENTIST IN THE WORLD...AND THAT IS WHAT I CANNOT FORGIVE!!!
HOW CAN THE HEARTLESS MAN WHO DID THIS TO YOU BE PRAISED AS THE GREATEST OF ALL?!!
...!!
MASTER ...!!
GASP...!
SO WE MUST PROVE IT TO HIM! WE MUST RELUCTANTLY CREATE A WEAPON OF MASS MURDER...
...AND SHOW HIM THAT THERE IS A MIND GREATER THAN HIS!! THAT I AM, IN FACT, THE MOST BRILLIANT SCIENTIST ALIVE!!!
WHOOSH!!

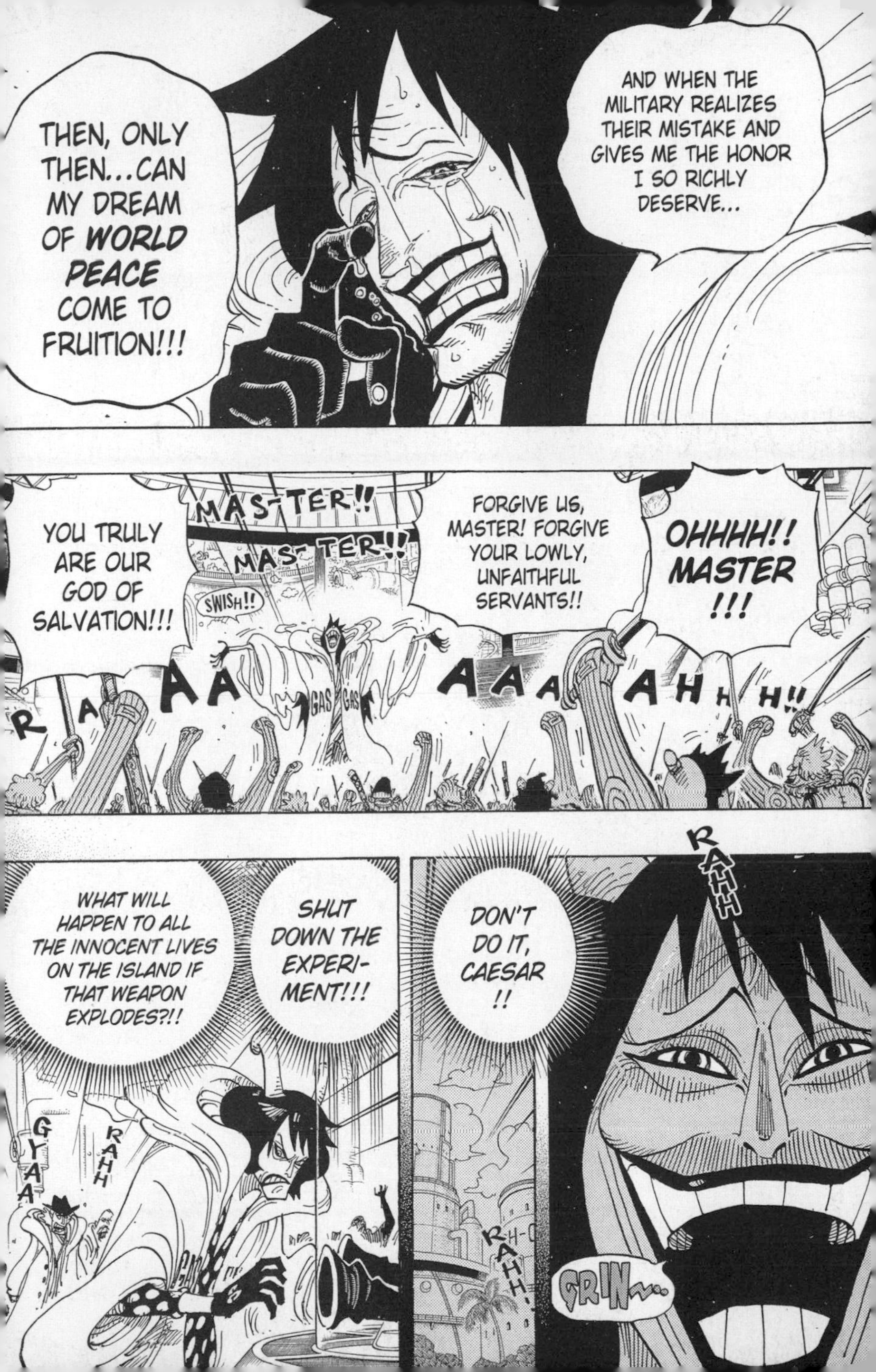

AND WHEN THE MILITARY REALIZES THEIR MISTAKE AND GIVES ME THE HONOR I SO RICHLY DESERVE...
THEN, ONLY THEN...CAN MY DREAM OF **WORLD PEACE** COME TO FRUITION!!!
OHHHH!! MASTER !!!
FORGIVE US, MASTER! FORGIVE YOUR LOWLY, UNFAITHFUL SERVANTS!!
MAS-TER!!
MAS-TER!!
SWISH!!
YOU TRULY ARE OUR GOD OF SALVATION!!!
GAS GAS
RAAAAAAAAHHHH!!
RAHH
DON'T DO IT, CAESAR !!
RAHH
GRIN...
SHUT DOWN THE EXPERI-MENT!!!
WHAT WILL HAPPEN TO ALL THE INNOCENT LIVES ON THE ISLAND IF THAT WEAPON EXPLODES?!!
RAHH
GYAA

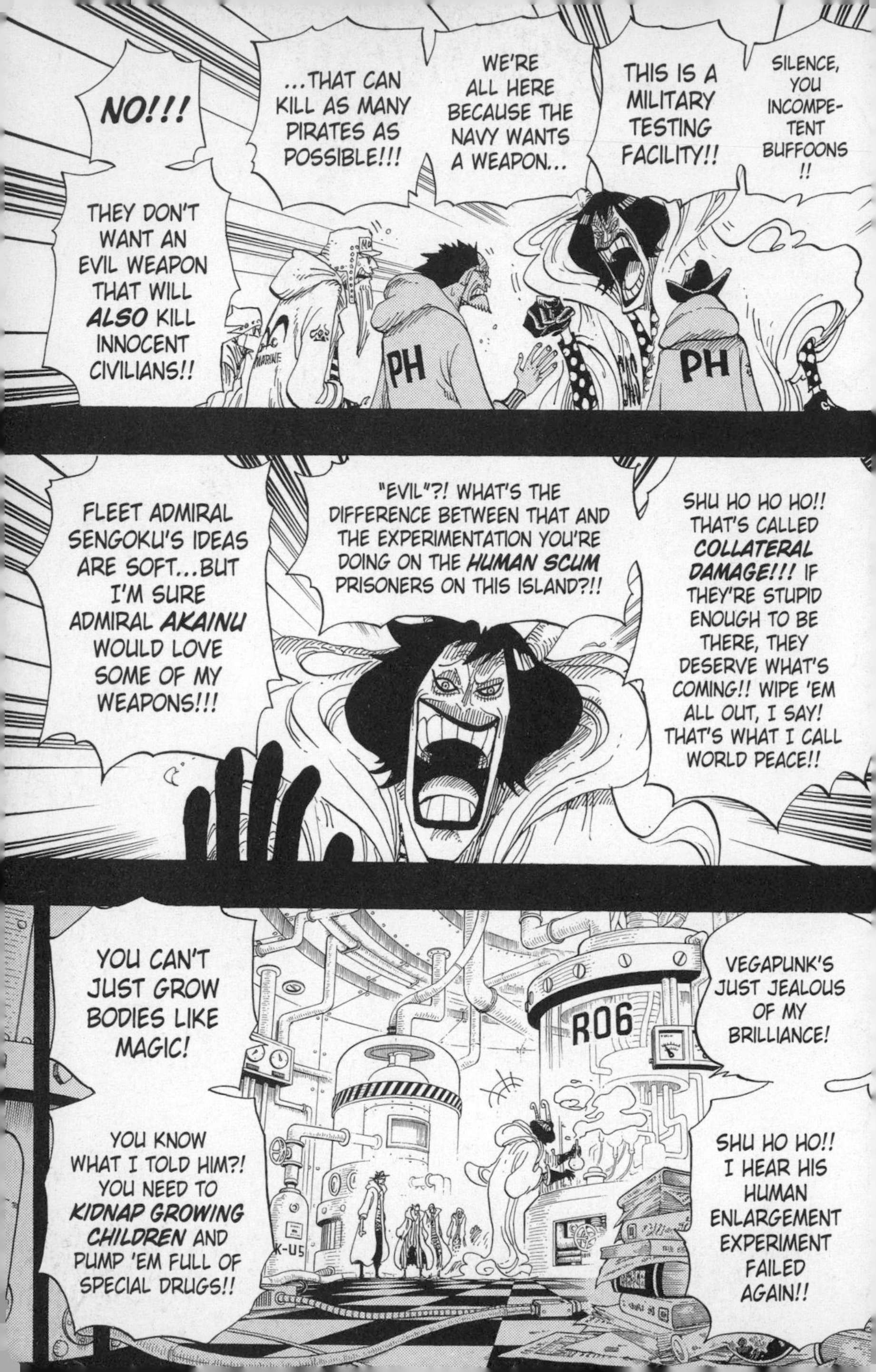
SILENCE, YOU INCOMPETENT BUFFOONS!!
THIS IS A MILITARY TESTING FACILITY!!
WE'RE ALL HERE BECAUSE THE NAVY WANTS A WEAPON...
...THAT CAN KILL AS MANY PIRATES AS POSSIBLE!!!
NO!!!
THEY DON'T WANT AN EVIL WEAPON THAT WILL ALSO KILL INNOCENT CIVILIANS!!
PH
PH
MARINE
SHU HO HO HO!! THAT'S CALLED COLLATERAL DAMAGE!!! IF THEY'RE STUPID ENOUGH TO BE THERE, THEY DESERVE WHAT'S COMING!! WIPE 'EM ALL OUT, I SAY! THAT'S WHAT I CALL WORLD PEACE!!
"EVIL"?! WHAT'S THE DIFFERENCE BETWEEN THAT AND THE EXPERIMENTATION YOU'RE DOING ON THE HUMAN SCUM PRISONERS ON THIS ISLAND?!!
FLEET ADMIRAL SENGOKU'S IDEAS ARE SOFT...BUT I'M SURE ADMIRAL AKAINU WOULD LOVE SOME OF MY WEAPONS!!!
VEGAPUNK'S JUST JEALOUS OF MY BRILLIANCE!
SHU HO HO!! I HEAR HIS HUMAN ENLARGEMENT EXPERIMENT FAILED AGAIN!!
R06
K-U5
YOU CAN'T JUST GROW BODIES LIKE MAGIC!
YOU KNOW WHAT I TOLD HIM?! YOU NEED TO KIDNAP GROWING CHILDREN AND PUMP 'EM FULL OF SPECIAL DRUGS!!

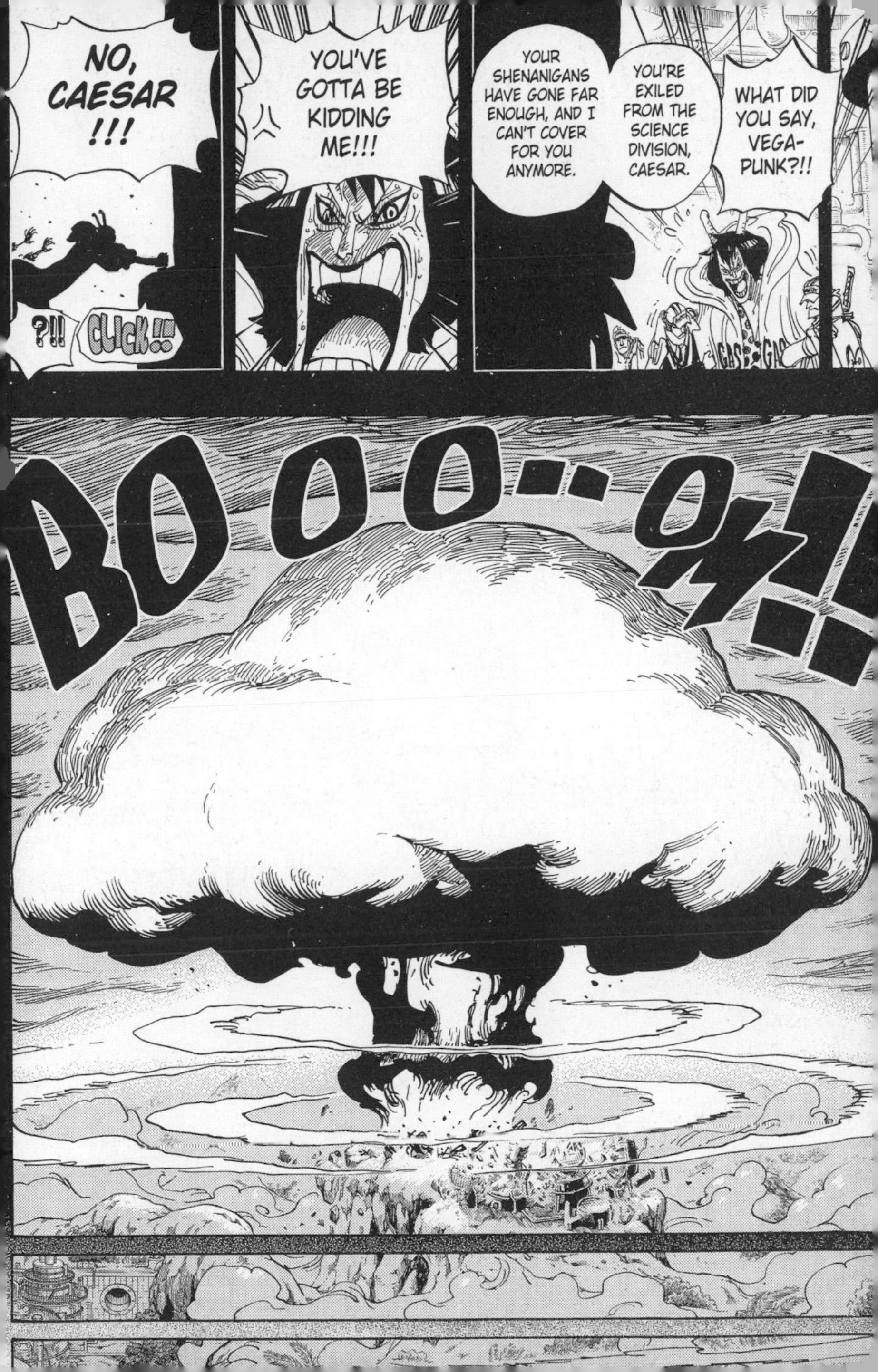
WHAT DID YOU SAY, VEGA-PUNK?!!
YOU'RE EXILED FROM THE SCIENCE DIVISION, CAESAR.
YOUR SHENANIGANS HAVE GONE FAR ENOUGH, AND I CAN'T COVER FOR YOU ANYMORE.
YOU'VE GOTTA BE KIDDING ME!!!
NO, CAESAR!!!
CLICK!!
?!!
BOOOO--OM!!

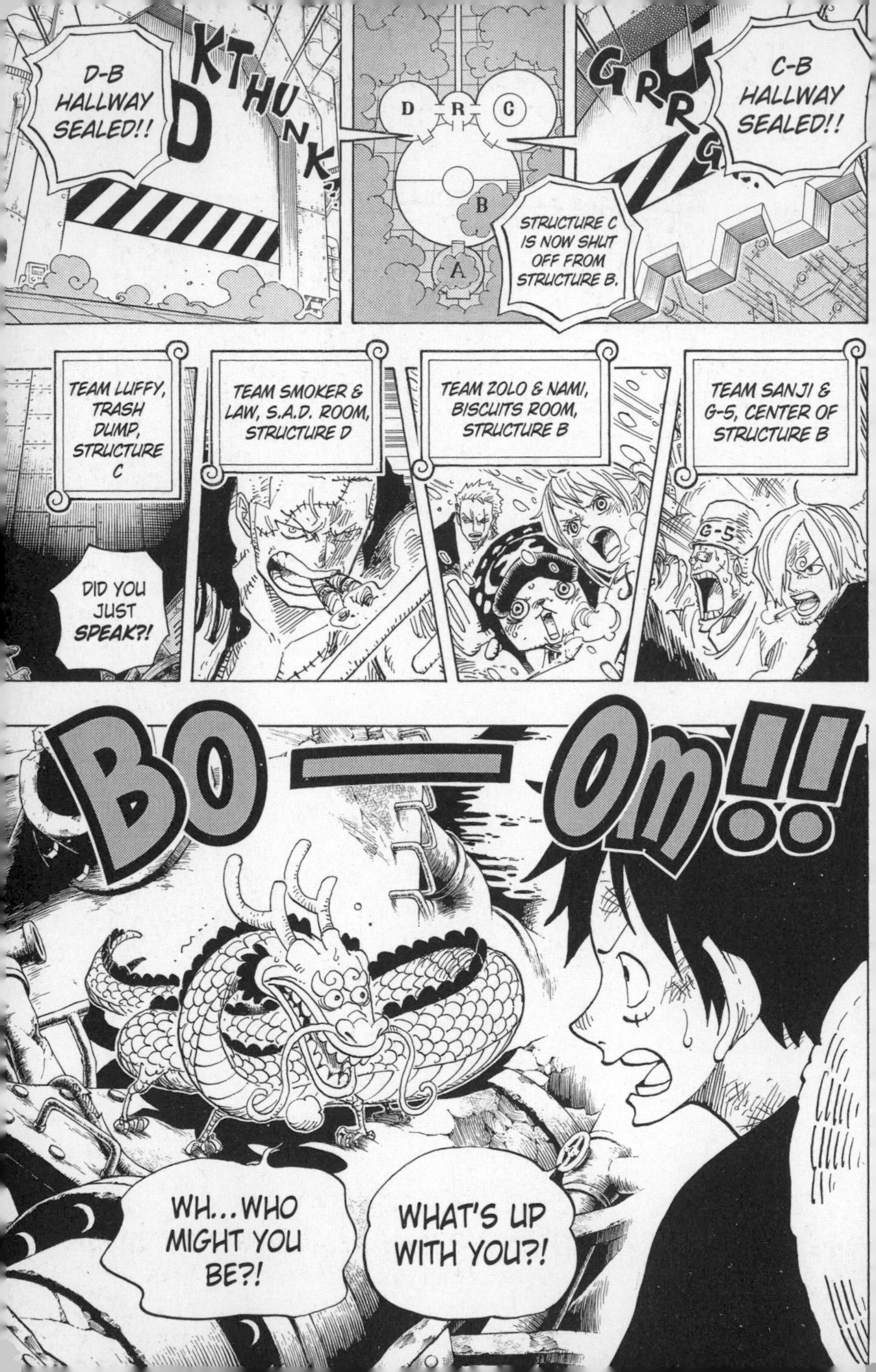
GRRRG
C-B HALLWAY SEALED!!
STRUCTURE C IS NOW SHUT OFF FROM STRUCTURE B.
D R C B A
D-B HALLWAY SEALED!!
DKTHUNK
TEAM SANJI & G-5, CENTER OF STRUCTURE B
G-5
TEAM ZOLO & NAMI, BISCUITS ROOM, STRUCTURE B
TEAM SMOKER & LAW, S.A.D. ROOM, STRUCTURE D
TEAM LUFFY, TRASH DUMP, STRUCTURE C
DID YOU JUST SPEAK?!
BO—OM!!
WHAT'S UP WITH YOU?!
WH...WHO MIGHT YOU BE?!

MY NAME IS MOMONOSUKE

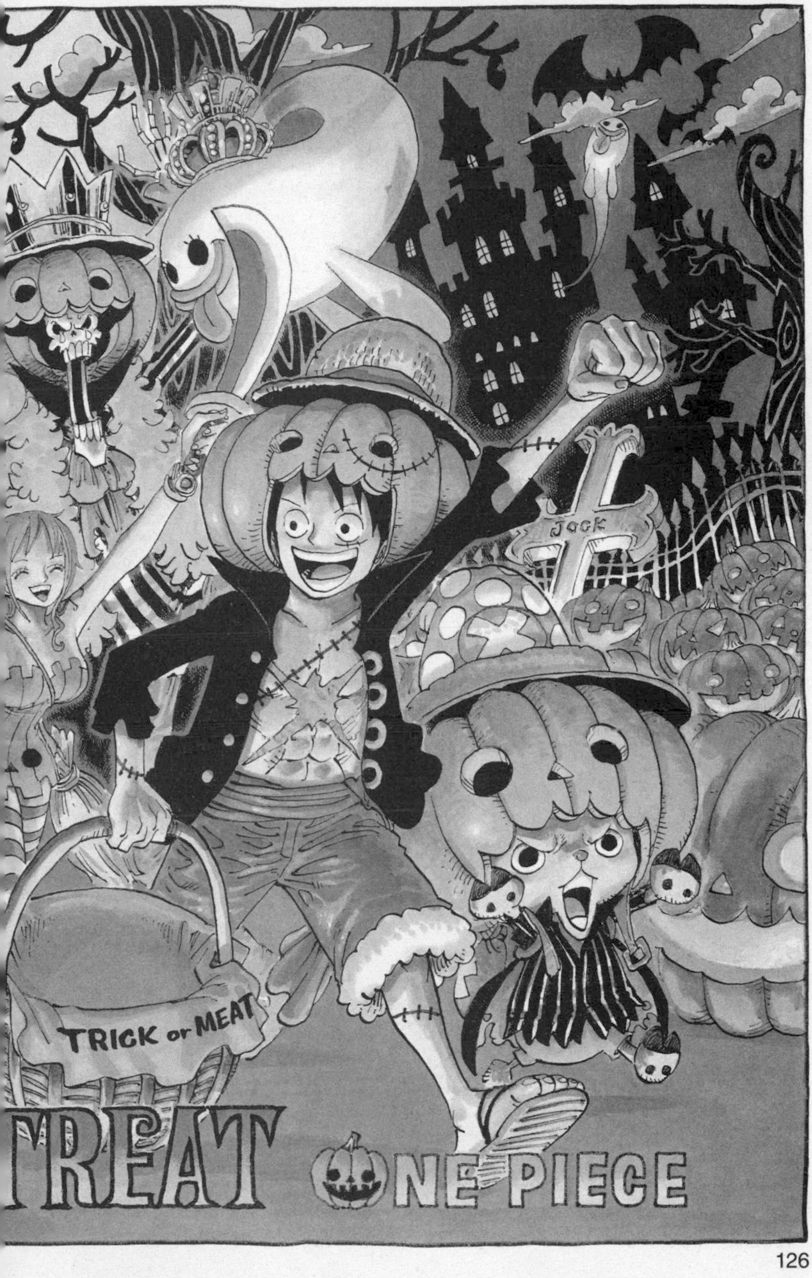

JACK
TRICK or MEAT
TREAT
ONE PIECE

Chapter 685:

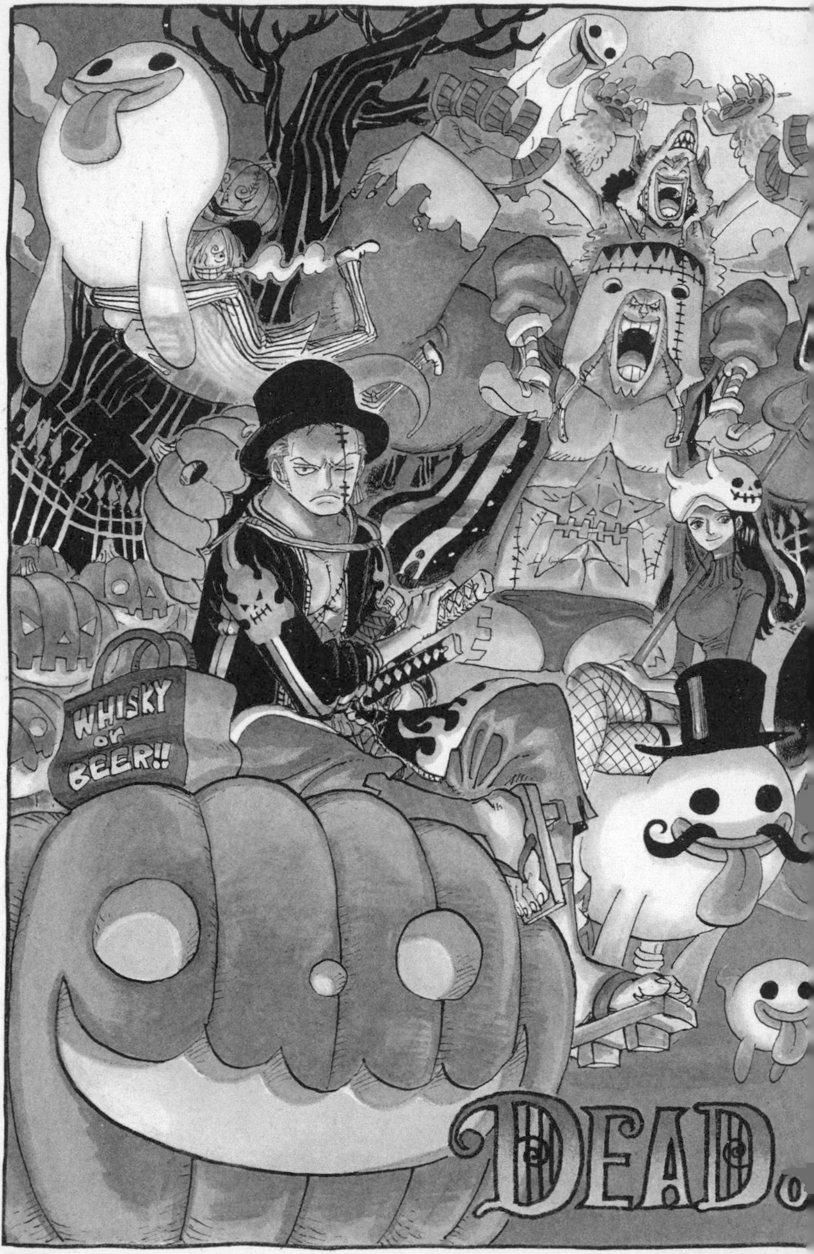
WHISKY or BEER!!
DEAD.

vol.69
ONE PIECE

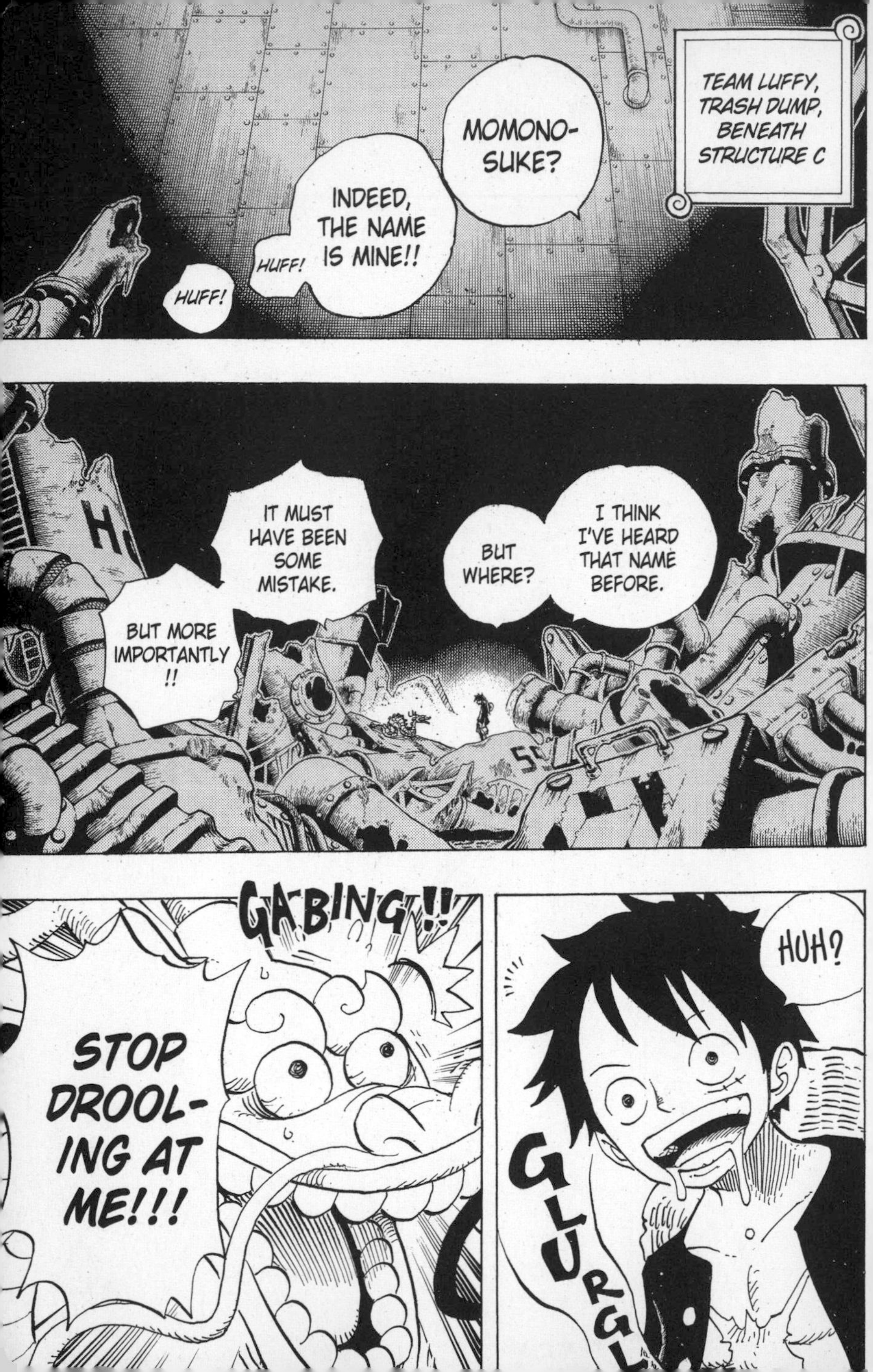
TEAM LUFFY, TRASH DUMP, BENEATH STRUCTURE C
MOMONO-SUKE?
INDEED, THE NAME IS MINE!!
HUFF!
HUFF!
I THINK I'VE HEARD THAT NAME BEFORE.
BUT WHERE?
IT MUST HAVE BEEN SOME MISTAKE.
BUT MORE IMPORTANTLY !!
HUH?
GLURGL
GABING!!
STOP DROOL-ING AT ME!!!

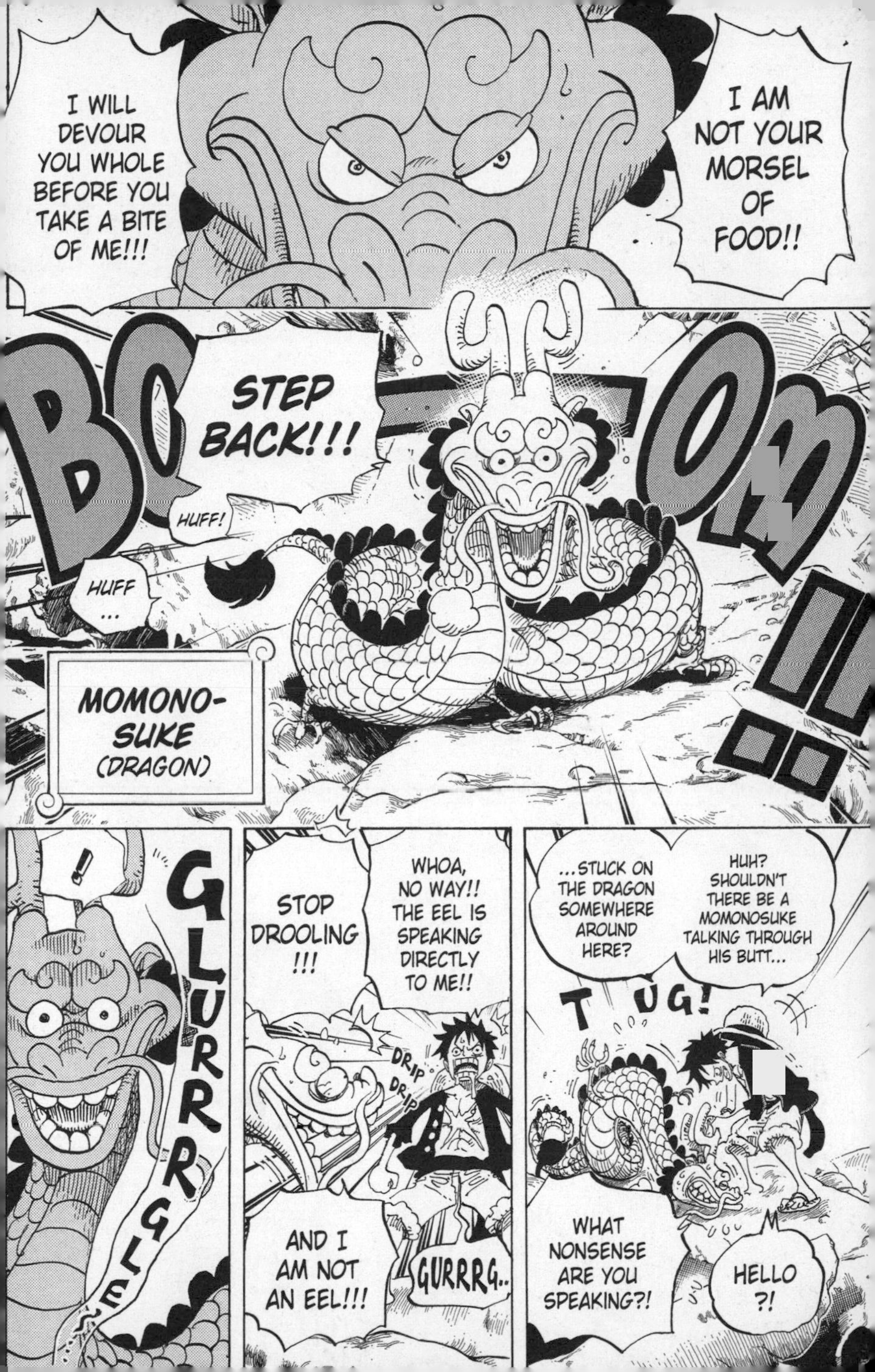

I AM NOT YOUR MORSEL OF FOOD!!
I WILL DEVOUR YOU WHOLE BEFORE YOU TAKE A BITE OF ME!!!
BO
OM!!
STEP BACK!!!
HUFF!
HUFF...
MOMONOSUKE (DRAGON)
HUH? SHOULDN'T THERE BE A MOMONOSUKE TALKING THROUGH HIS BUTT...
...STUCK ON THE DRAGON SOMEWHERE AROUND HERE?
TUG!
HELLO?!
WHAT NONSENSE ARE YOU SPEAKING?!
WHOA, NO WAY!! THE EEL IS SPEAKING DIRECTLY TO ME!!
STOP DROOLING!!!
DRIP
DRIP
AND I AM NOT AN EEL!!!
GURRRG..
!
GLURRRRGLE

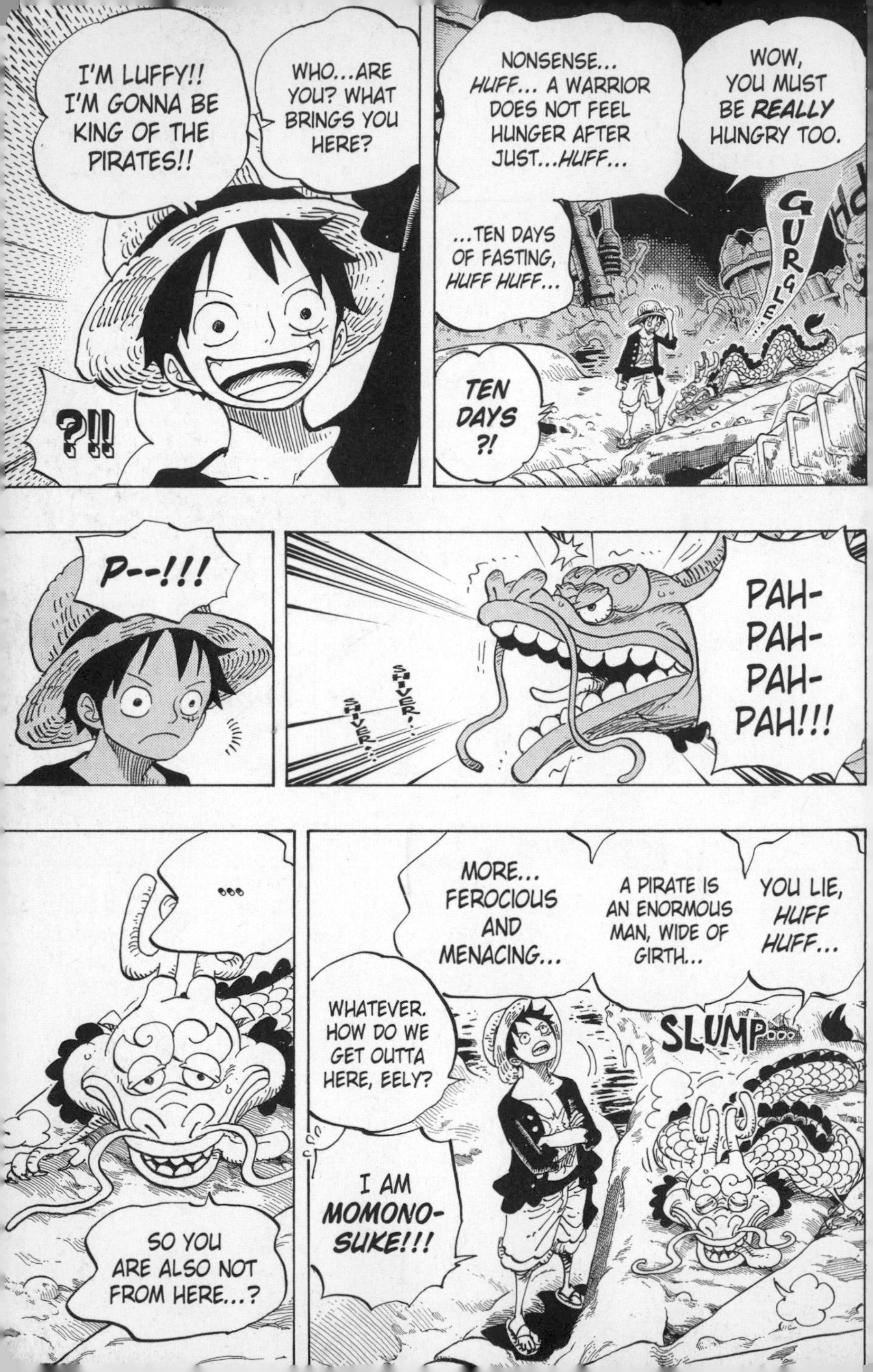

WOW, YOU MUST BE REALLY HUNGRY TOO.
NONSENSE... HUFF... A WARRIOR DOES NOT FEEL HUNGER AFTER JUST...HUFF...
...TEN DAYS OF FASTING, HUFF HUFF...
GURGLE
TEN DAYS?!
WHO...ARE YOU? WHAT BRINGS YOU HERE?
I'M LUFFY!! I'M GONNA BE KING OF THE PIRATES!!
?!!
PAH-PAH-PAH-PAH!!!
SHIVER
SHIVER
P--!!!
YOU LIE, HUFF HUFF...
A PIRATE IS AN ENORMOUS MAN, WIDE OF GIRTH...
MORE... FEROCIOUS AND MENACING...
SLUMP...
WHATEVER. HOW DO WE GET OUTTA HERE, EELY?
I AM MOMONOSUKE!!!
...
SO YOU ARE ALSO NOT FROM HERE...?

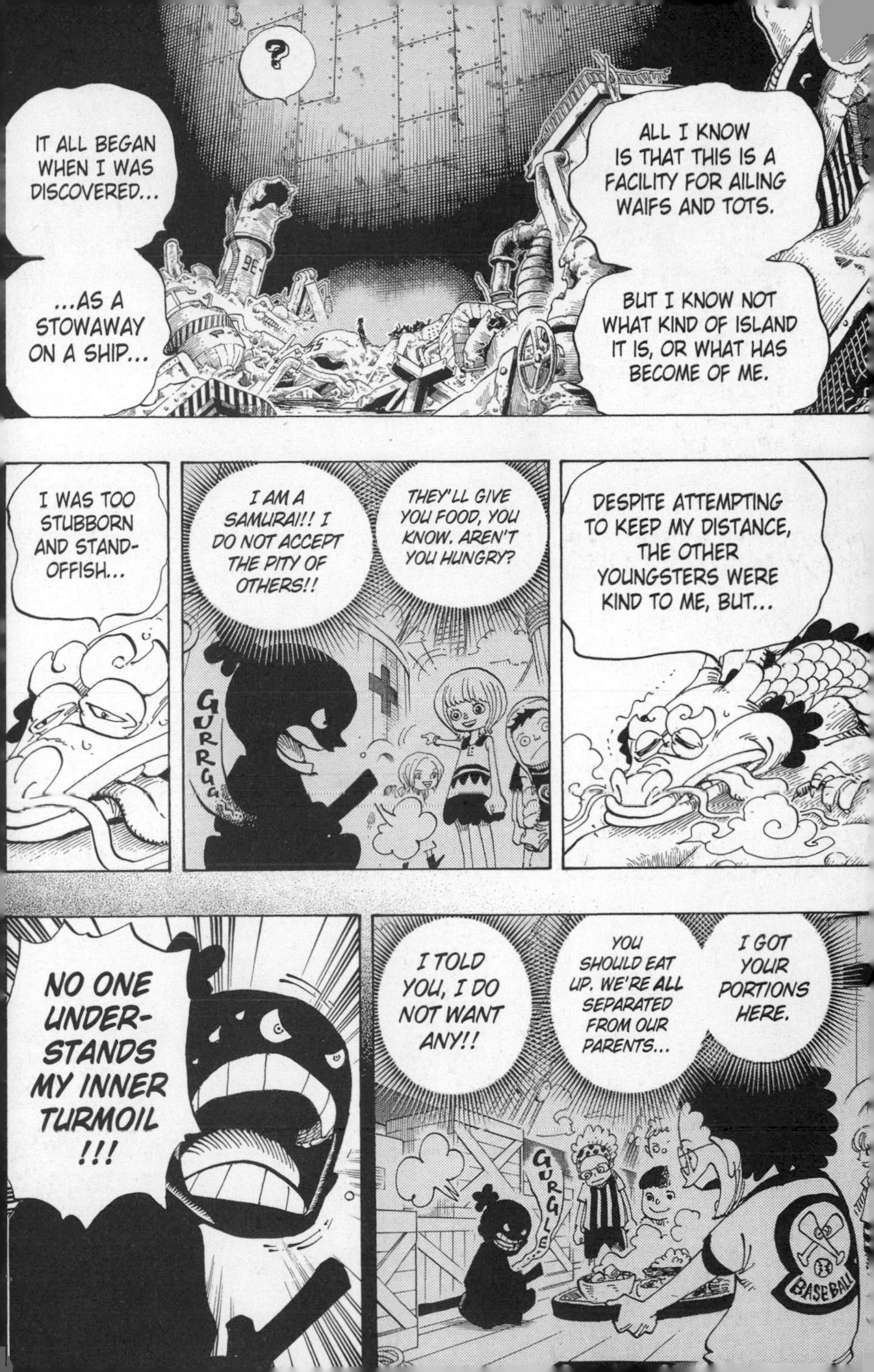
?
ALL I KNOW IS THAT THIS IS A FACILITY FOR AILING WAIFS AND TOTS.
BUT I KNOW NOT WHAT KIND OF ISLAND IT IS, OR WHAT HAS BECOME OF ME.
IT ALL BEGAN WHEN I WAS DISCOVERED...
...AS A STOWAWAY ON A SHIP...
DESPITE ATTEMPTING TO KEEP MY DISTANCE, THE OTHER YOUNGSTERS WERE KIND TO ME, BUT...
THEY'LL GIVE YOU FOOD, YOU KNOW. AREN'T YOU HUNGRY?
I AM A SAMURAI!! I DO NOT ACCEPT THE PITY OF OTHERS!!
GURRGG
I WAS TOO STUBBORN AND STAND-OFFISH...
I GOT YOUR PORTIONS HERE.
YOU SHOULD EAT UP. WE'RE ALL SEPARATED FROM OUR PARENTS...
I TOLD YOU, I DO NOT WANT ANY!!
GURGLE
BASEBALL
NO ONE UNDER-STANDS MY INNER TURMOIL !!!

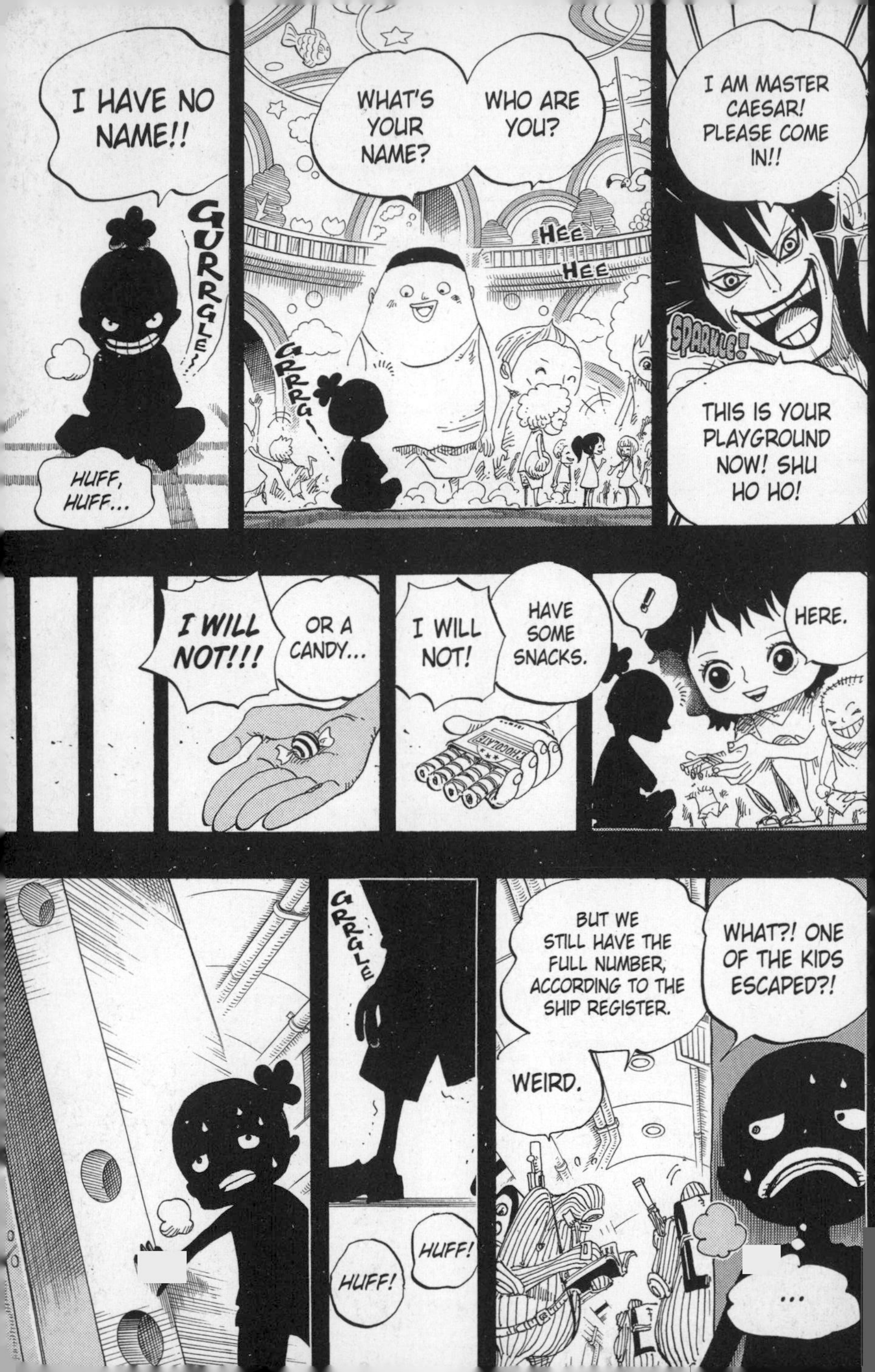
I AM MASTER CAESAR! PLEASE COME IN!!
SPARKLE!
THIS IS YOUR PLAYGROUND NOW! SHU HO HO!
WHO ARE YOU?
WHAT'S YOUR NAME?
HEE HEE
GRRRG
I HAVE NO NAME!!
GURRRGLE
HUFF, HUFF...
!
HERE.
HAVE SOME SNACKS.
I WILL NOT!
CHOCOLATE
OR A CANDY...
I WILL NOT!!!
WHAT?! ONE OF THE KIDS ESCAPED?!
BUT WE STILL HAVE THE FULL NUMBER, ACCORDING TO THE SHIP REGISTER.
WEIRD.
...
GRRGLE
HUFF!
HUFF!

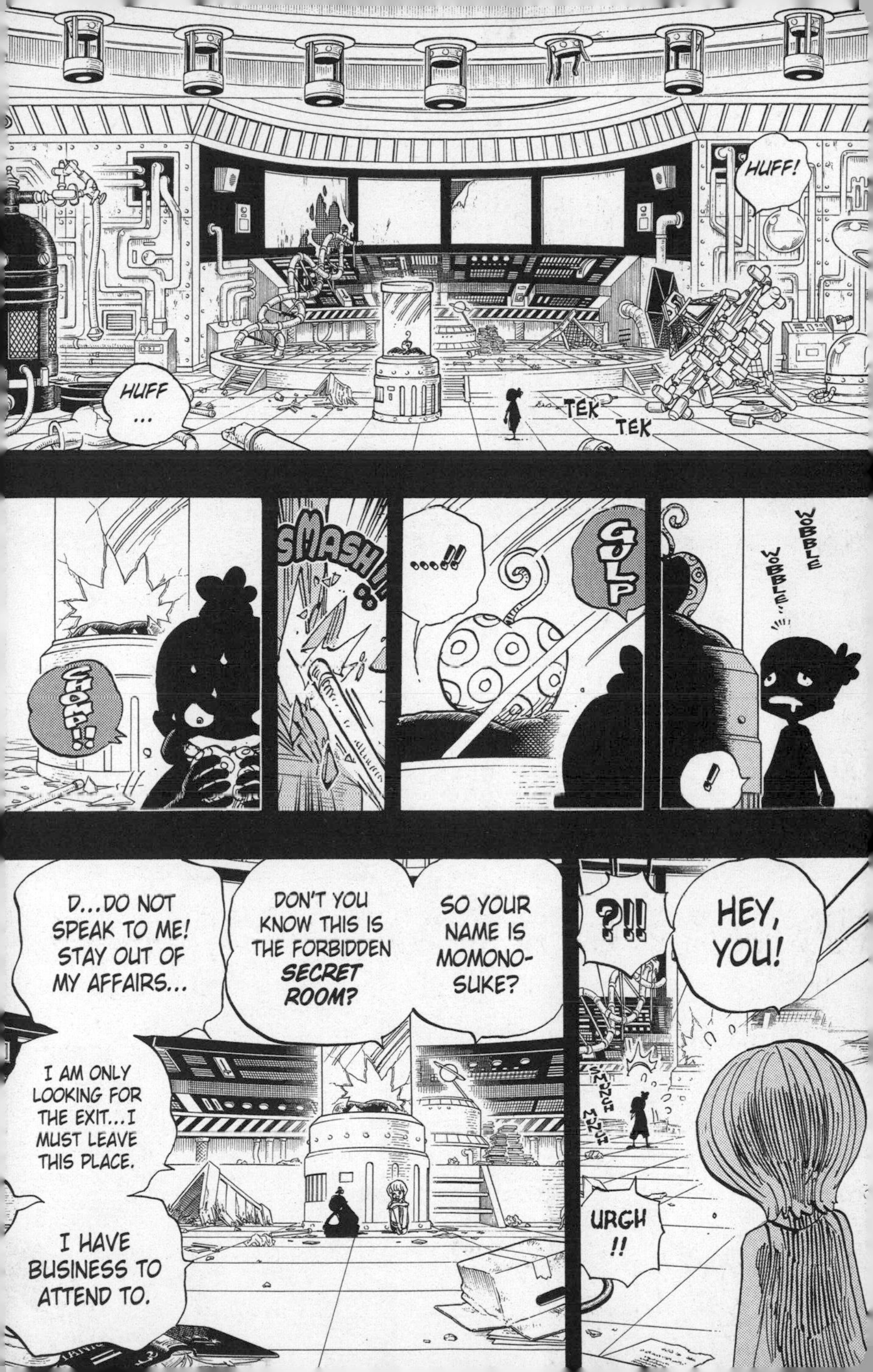
HUFF!
HUFF ...
TEK
TEK
WOBBLE
WOBBLE...
!
GULP
...!!
SMASH!!
CHOMP!!
HEY, YOU!
?!!
MUNCH MUNCH
URGH!!
SO YOUR NAME IS MOMONOSUKE?
DON'T YOU KNOW THIS IS THE FORBIDDEN SECRET ROOM?
D...DO NOT SPEAK TO ME! STAY OUT OF MY AFFAIRS...
I AM ONLY LOOKING FOR THE EXIT...I MUST LEAVE THIS PLACE.
I HAVE BUSINESS TO ATTEND TO.

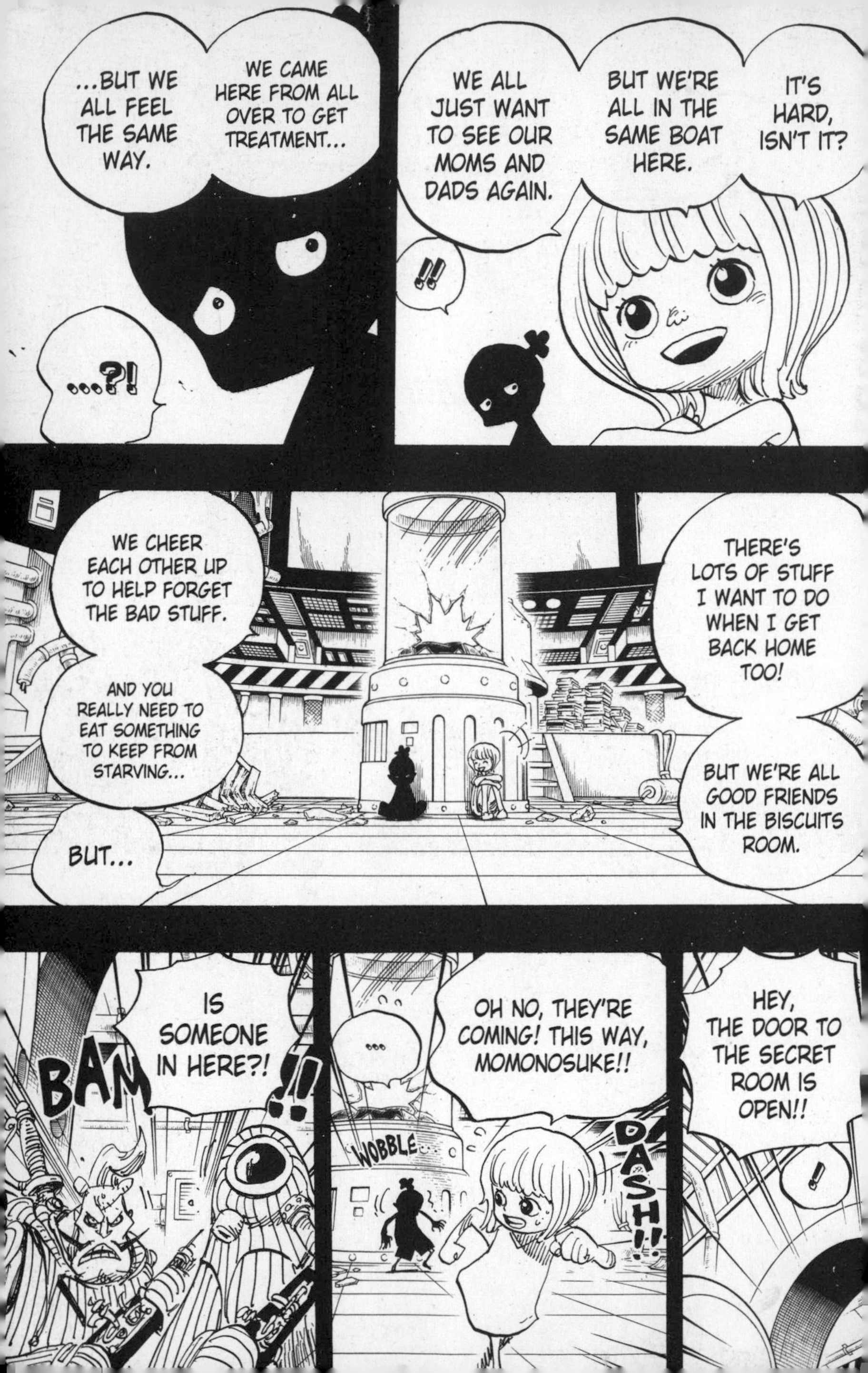
IT'S HARD, ISN'T IT?
BUT WE'RE ALL IN THE SAME BOAT HERE.
WE ALL JUST WANT TO SEE OUR MOMS AND DADS AGAIN.
!!
WE CAME HERE FROM ALL OVER TO GET TREATMENT...
...BUT WE ALL FEEL THE SAME WAY.
...?!
THERE'S LOTS OF STUFF I WANT TO DO WHEN I GET BACK HOME TOO!
BUT WE'RE ALL GOOD FRIENDS IN THE BISCUITS ROOM.
WE CHEER EACH OTHER UP TO HELP FORGET THE BAD STUFF.
AND YOU REALLY NEED TO EAT SOMETHING TO KEEP FROM STARVING...
BUT...
HEY, THE DOOR TO THE SECRET ROOM IS OPEN!!
!
OH NO, THEY'RE COMING! THIS WAY, MOMONOSUKE!!
DASH!!
...
WOBBLE...
IS SOMEONE IN HERE?!
!!
BAM

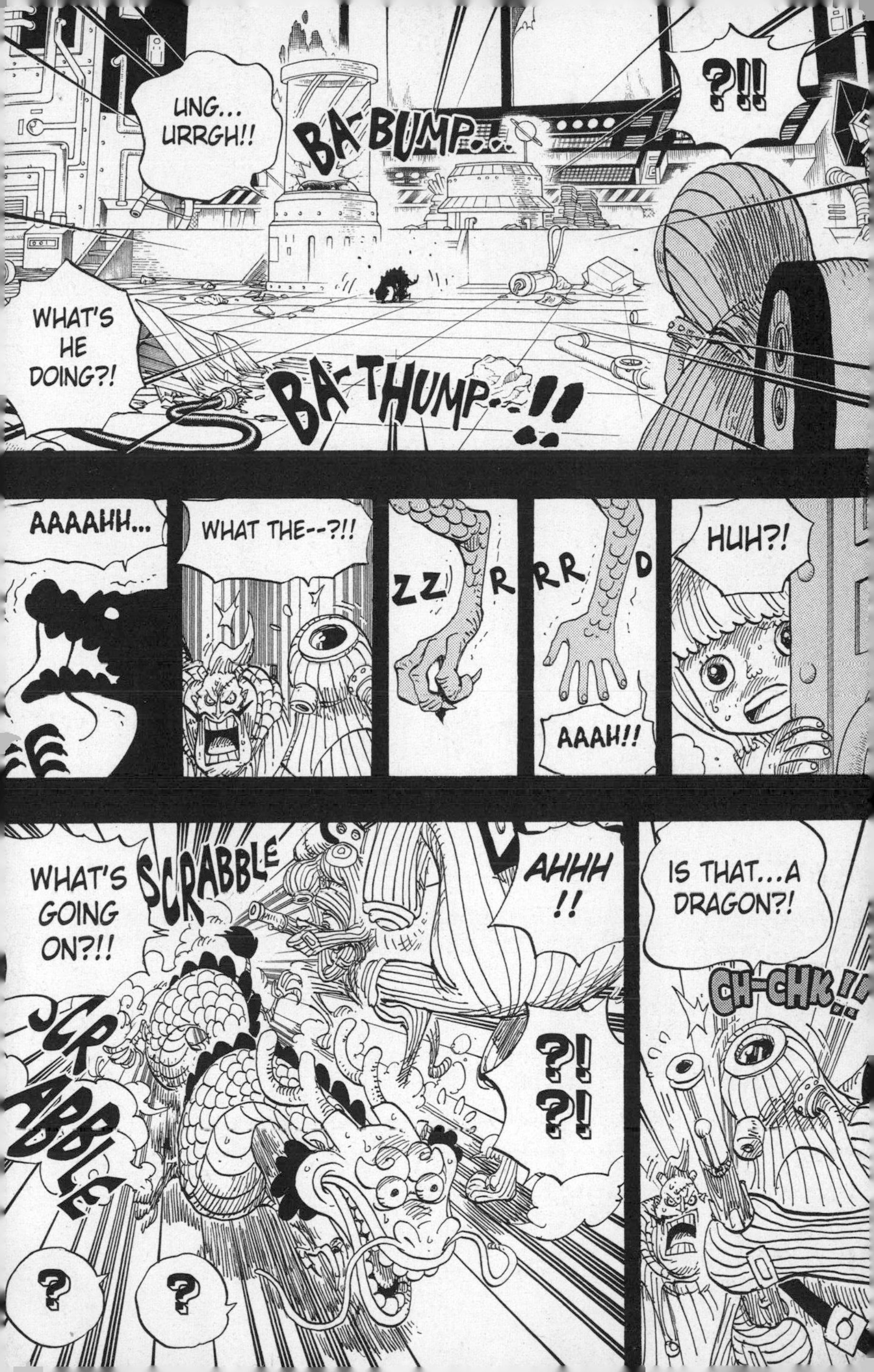
?!!
BA-BUMP...
UNG... URRGH!!
WHAT'S HE DOING?!
BA-THUMP...!!
HUH?!
AAAH!!
ZZ R RR D
WHAT THE--?!!
AAAAHH...
IS THAT...A DRAGON?!
CH-CHK!!
AHHH!!
?! ?!
SCRABBLE
WHAT'S GOING ON?!!
SCRABBLE
?
?

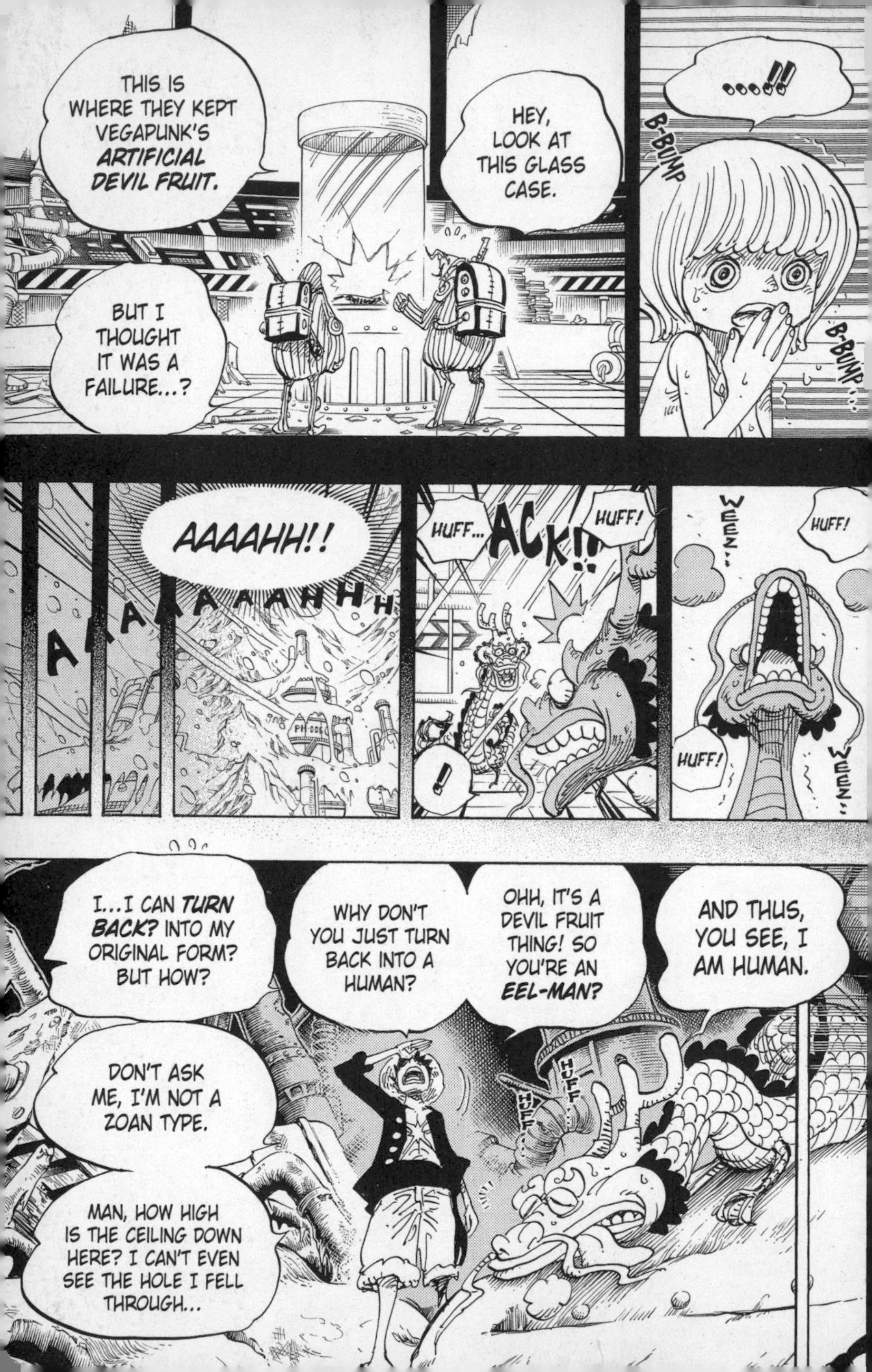
....!!
B-BUMP
B-BUMP...
HEY, LOOK AT THIS GLASS CASE.
THIS IS WHERE THEY KEPT VEGAPUNK'S *ARTIFICIAL DEVIL FRUIT.*
BUT I THOUGHT IT WAS A FAILURE...?
WEEZ..
HUFF!
HUFF!
WEEZ..
HUFF!
HUFF...
ACK!!
!
AAAAHH!!
AAAAAAAAHHH
AND THUS, YOU SEE, I AM HUMAN.
OHH, IT'S A DEVIL FRUIT THING! SO YOU'RE AN *EEL-MAN?*
WHY DON'T YOU JUST TURN BACK INTO A HUMAN?
I...I CAN *TURN BACK?* INTO MY ORIGINAL FORM? BUT HOW?
DON'T ASK ME, I'M NOT A ZOAN TYPE.
HUFF
HUFF
MAN, HOW HIGH IS THE CEILING DOWN HERE? I CAN'T EVEN SEE THE HOLE I FELL THROUGH...

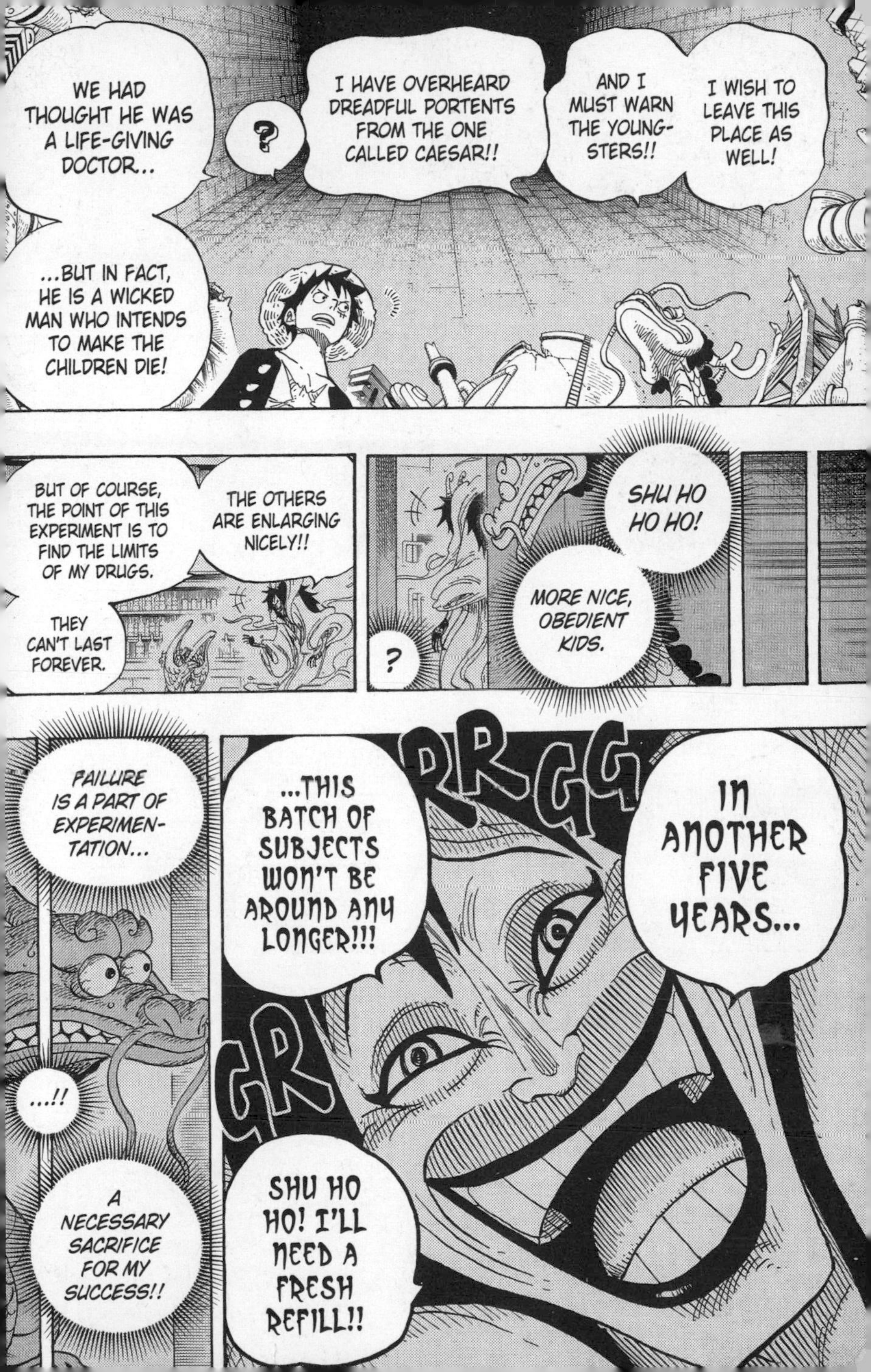
I WISH TO LEAVE THIS PLACE AS WELL!
AND I MUST WARN THE YOUNGSTERS!!
I HAVE OVERHEARD DREADFUL PORTENTS FROM THE ONE CALLED CAESAR!!
?
WE HAD THOUGHT HE WAS A LIFE-GIVING DOCTOR...
...BUT IN FACT, HE IS A WICKED MAN WHO INTENDS TO MAKE THE CHILDREN DIE!
SHU HO HO HO!
MORE NICE, OBEDIENT KIDS.
?
THE OTHERS ARE ENLARGING NICELY!!
BUT OF COURSE, THE POINT OF THIS EXPERIMENT IS TO FIND THE LIMITS OF MY DRUGS.
THEY CAN'T LAST FOREVER.
IN ANOTHER FIVE YEARS...
GRRGG
...THIS BATCH OF SUBJECTS WON'T BE AROUND ANY LONGER!!!
GR
SHU HO HO! I'LL NEED A FRESH REFILL!!
FAILURE IS A PART OF EXPERIMENTATION...
...!!
A NECESSARY SACRIFICE FOR MY SUCCESS!!

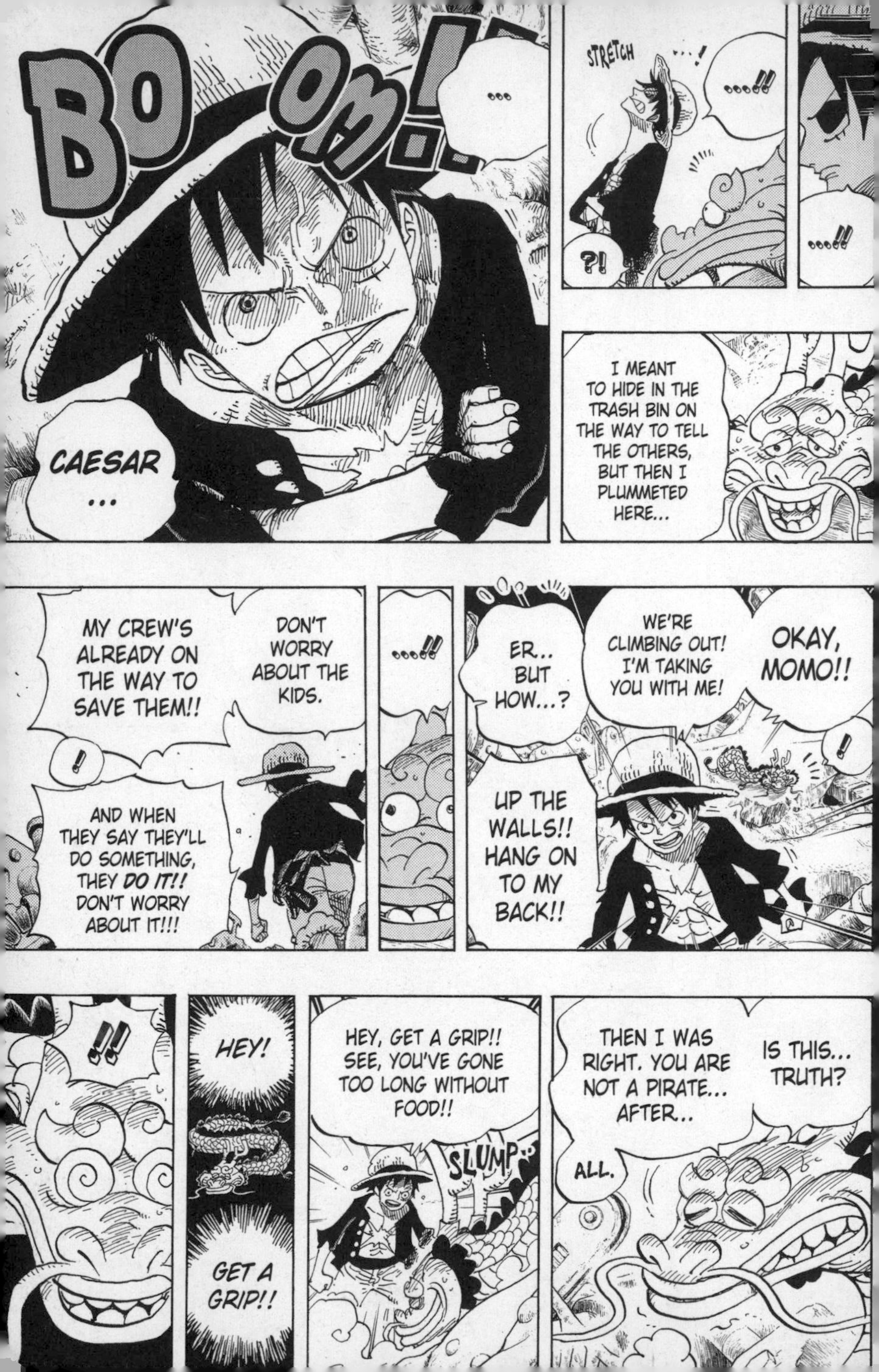
....!!
....!!
STRETCH
...!
?!
I MEANT TO HIDE IN THE TRASH BIN ON THE WAY TO TELL THE OTHERS, BUT THEN I PLUMMETED HERE...
BOOM!!
...
CAESAR ...
OKAY, MOMO!!
WE'RE CLIMBING OUT! I'M TAKING YOU WITH ME!
ER... BUT HOW...?
!
UP THE WALLS!! HANG ON TO MY BACK!!
....!!
DON'T WORRY ABOUT THE KIDS.
MY CREW'S ALREADY ON THE WAY TO SAVE THEM!!
!
AND WHEN THEY SAY THEY'LL DO SOMETHING, THEY *DO IT!!* DON'T WORRY ABOUT IT!!!
IS THIS... TRUTH?
THEN I WAS RIGHT. YOU ARE NOT A PIRATE... AFTER... ALL.
HEY, GET A GRIP!! SEE, YOU'VE GONE TOO LONG WITHOUT FOOD!!
SLUMP
HEY!
GET A GRIP!!
!!

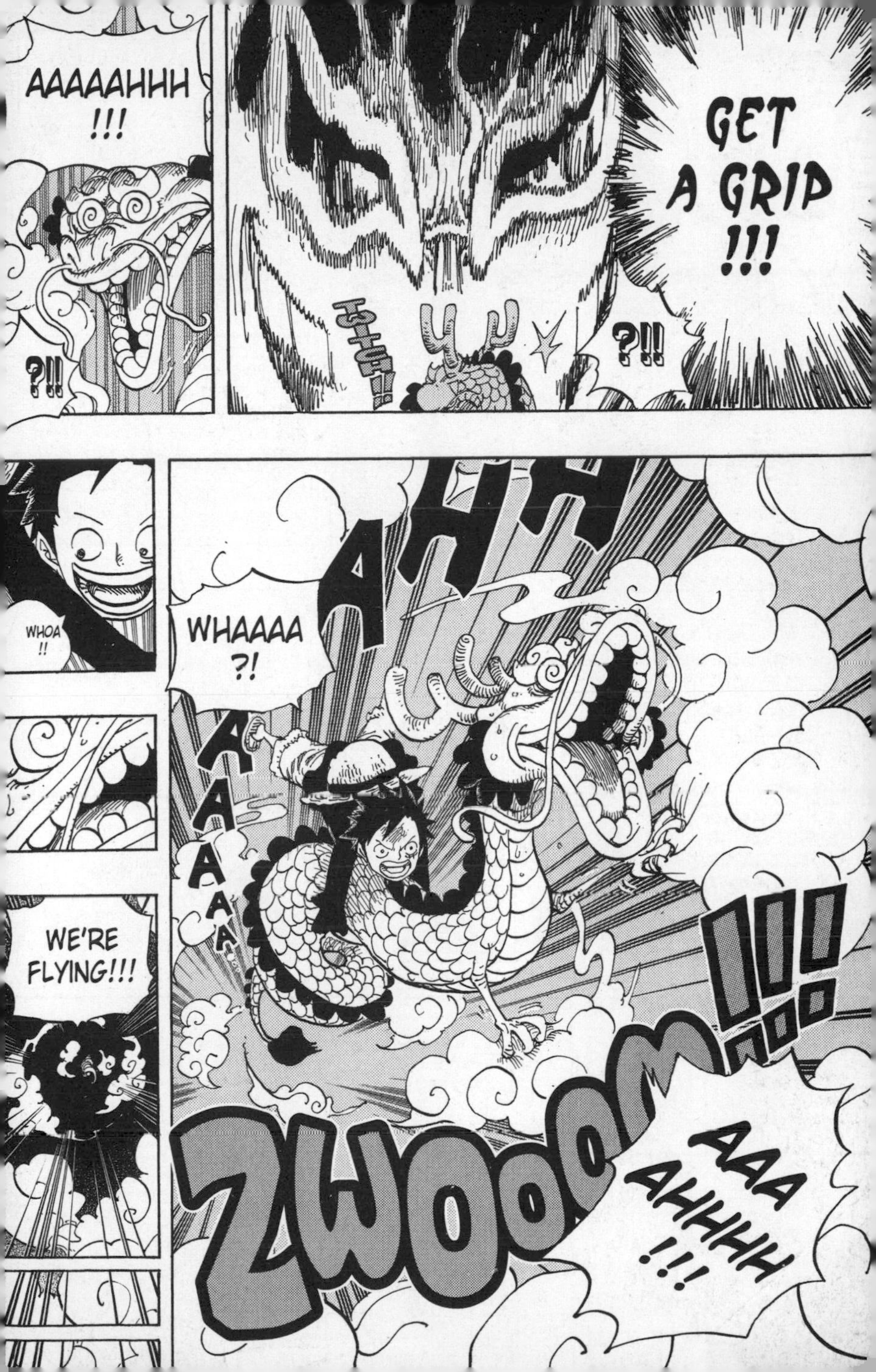
GET A GRIP!!!
?!!
AAAAAHHH!!!
?!!
AHH
WHAAAA?!
AAAAAA
ZWOOOOM!!!
AAAAHHHH!!!
WHOA!!
WE'RE FLYING!!!

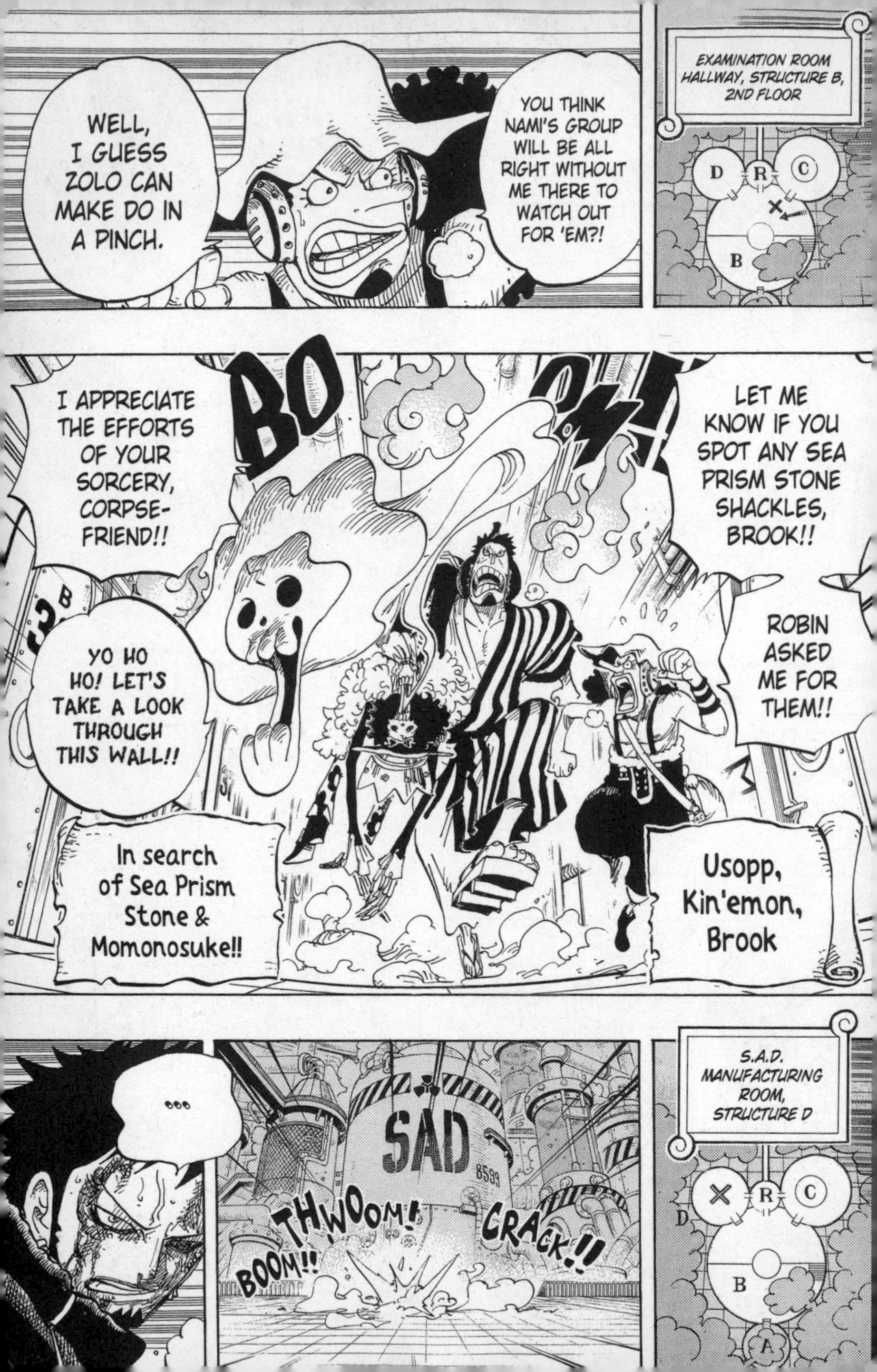
EXAMINATION ROOM HALLWAY, STRUCTURE B, 2ND FLOOR
D
R
C
B
YOU THINK NAMI'S GROUP WILL BE ALL RIGHT WITHOUT ME THERE TO WATCH OUT FOR 'EM?!
WELL, I GUESS ZOLO CAN MAKE DO IN A PINCH.
BOOM
LET ME KNOW IF YOU SPOT ANY SEA PRISM STONE SHACKLES, BROOK!!
I APPRECIATE THE EFFORTS OF YOUR SORCERY, CORPSE-FRIEND!!
ROBIN ASKED ME FOR THEM!!
YO HO HO! LET'S TAKE A LOOK THROUGH THIS WALL!!
Usopp, Kin'emon, Brook
In search of Sea Prism Stone & Momonosuke!!
S.A.D. MANUFACTURING ROOM, STRUCTURE D
D
R
C
B
A
SAD
8599
THWOOM!
CRACK!!
BOOM!!
...

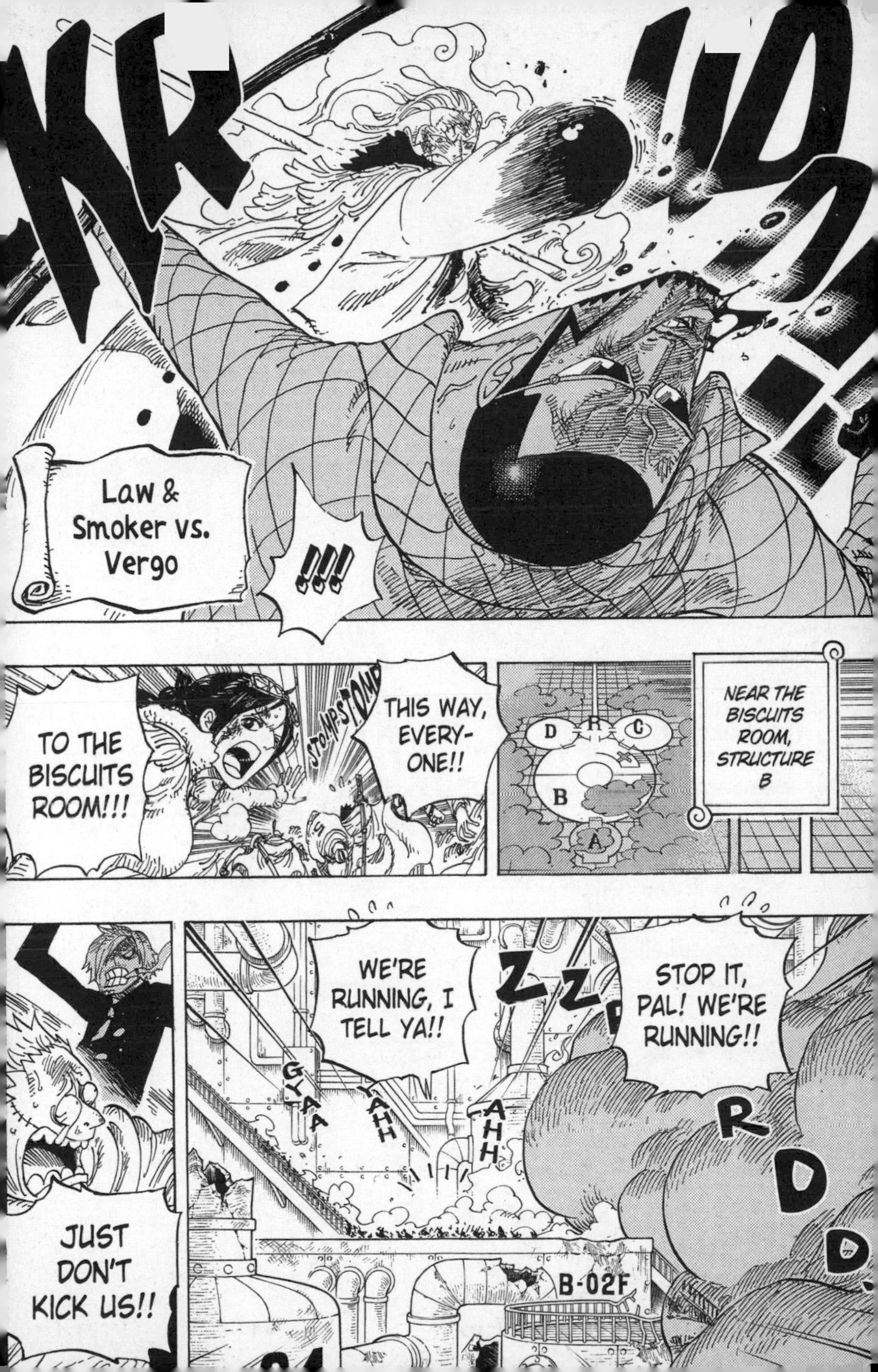

Law &
Smoker vs.
Vergo
!!!
NEAR THE BISCUITS ROOM, STRUCTURE B
D
R
C
B
A
THIS WAY, EVERY-ONE!!
STOMP STOMP
TO THE BISCUITS ROOM!!!
STOP IT, PAL! WE'RE RUNNING!!
WE'RE RUNNING, I TELL YA!!
GYAA
YAHH
AHH
B-02F
JUST DON'T KICK US!!

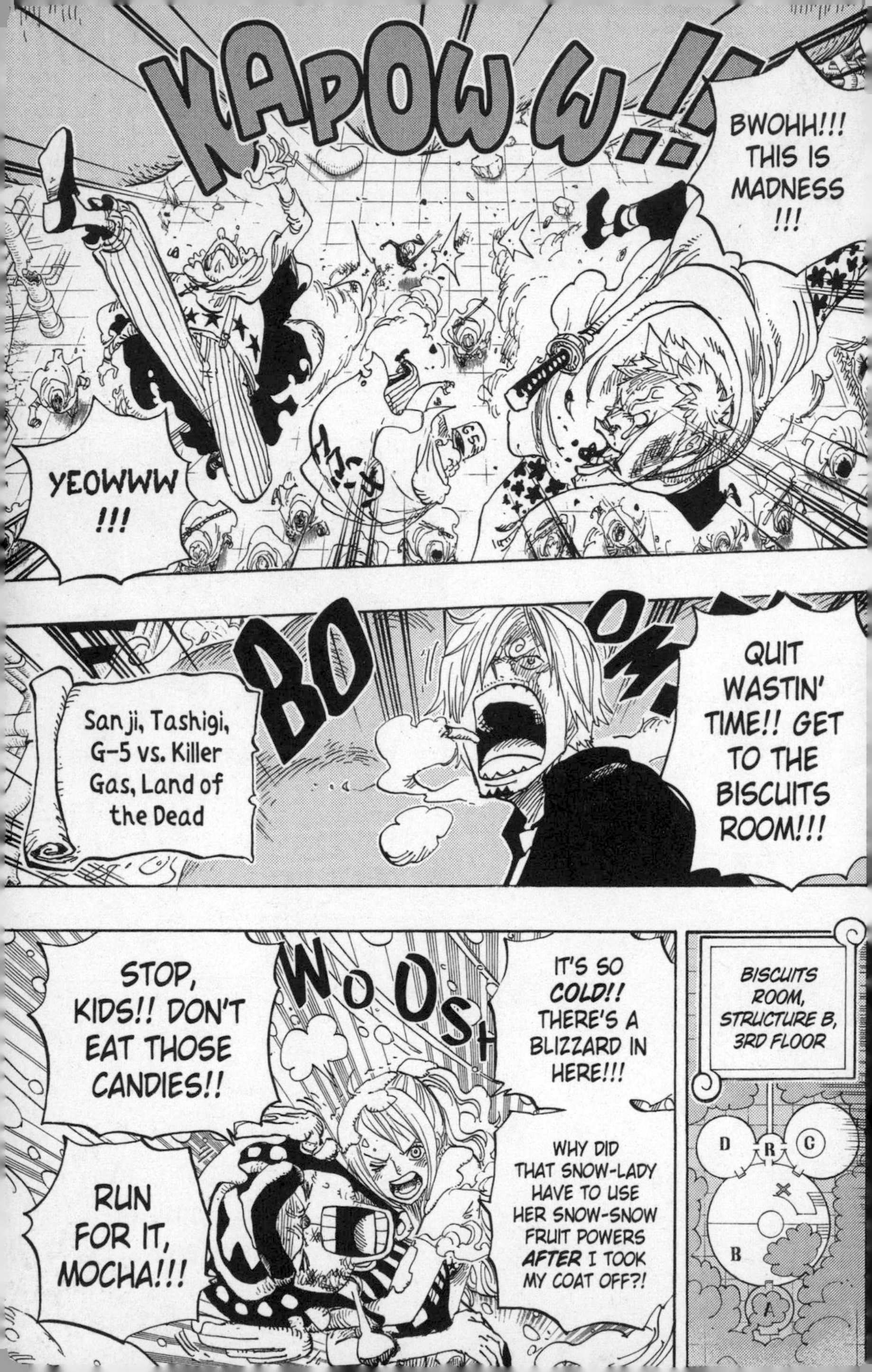
KAPOWW!!
BWOHH!!! THIS IS MADNESS!!!
YEOWWW!!!
QUIT WASTIN' TIME!! GET TO THE BISCUITS ROOM!!!
BOOOM
Sanji, Tashigi, G-5 vs. Killer Gas, Land of the Dead
BISCUITS ROOM, STRUCTURE B, 3RD FLOOR
D
R
C
B
A
IT'S SO COLD!! THERE'S A BLIZZARD IN HERE!!!
WHY DID THAT SNOW-LADY HAVE TO USE HER SNOW-SNOW FRUIT POWERS AFTER I TOOK MY COAT OFF?!
WOOSH
STOP, KIDS!! DON'T EAT THOSE CANDIES!!
RUN FOR IT, MOCHA!!!

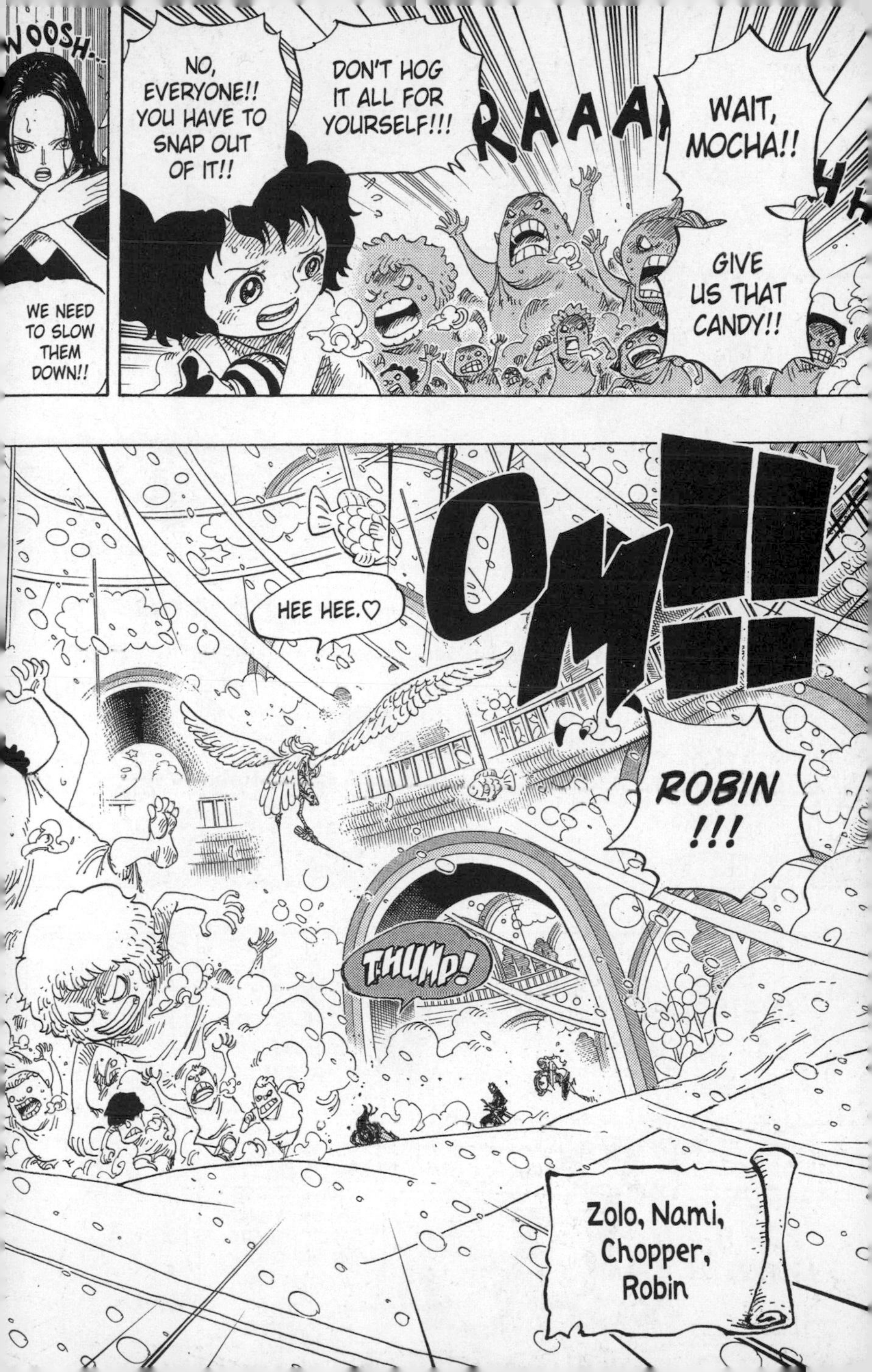
WAIT, MOCHA!!
GIVE US THAT CANDY!!
RAAA
DON'T HOG IT ALL FOR YOURSELF!!!
NO, EVERYONE!! YOU HAVE TO SNAP OUT OF IT!!
WOOSH...
WE NEED TO SLOW THEM DOWN!!
OH!!
ROBIN !!!
HEE HEE.♡
THUMP!
Zolo, Nami, Chopper, Robin

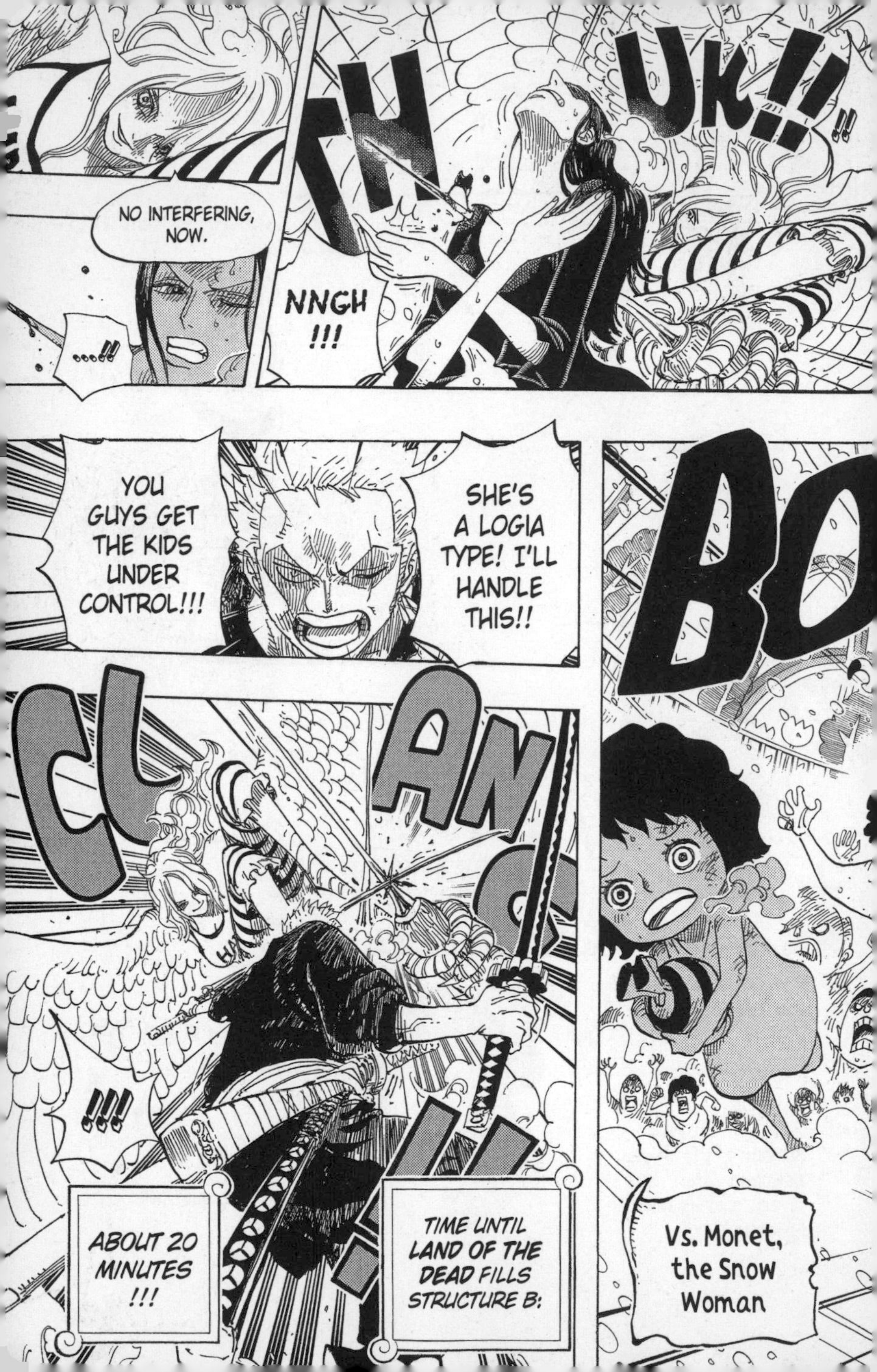

CH
UK!!
!!
NNGH !!!
NO INTERFERING, NOW.
...!!
BO
Vs. Monet, the Snow Woman
SHE'S A LOGIA TYPE! I'LL HANDLE THIS!!
YOU GUYS GET THE KIDS UNDER CONTROL!!!
CL
AN
!!!
TIME UNTIL LAND OF THE DEAD FILLS STRUCTURE B:
ABOUT 20 MINUTES !!!

SBS Question Corner

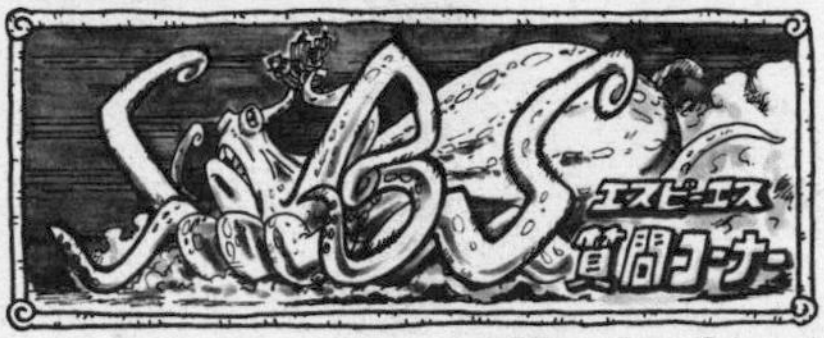
SBS
エスピーエス
質問コーナー

(Hippo Iron, Saitama)

Q: Mr. Oda, can you draw the Impel Down characters--Magellan, Hannyabal, Sadi, Saldeath--as children?

--IjiekAmayot

A: Sure! How about I throw in Domino as well?

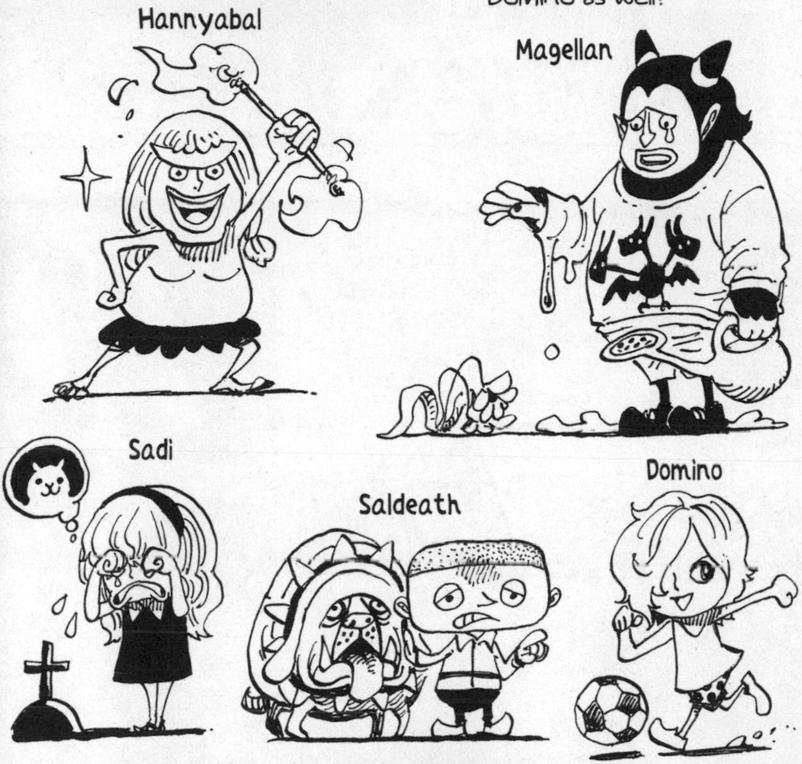
Hannyabal
Magellan
Sadi
Saldeath
Domino

Q: Odacchi x 2!! What if Lola the Proposer ate the Slip-Slip Fruit?

--Nasuo

A: She's not much different, if you ask me. Her skin is certainly much smoother!

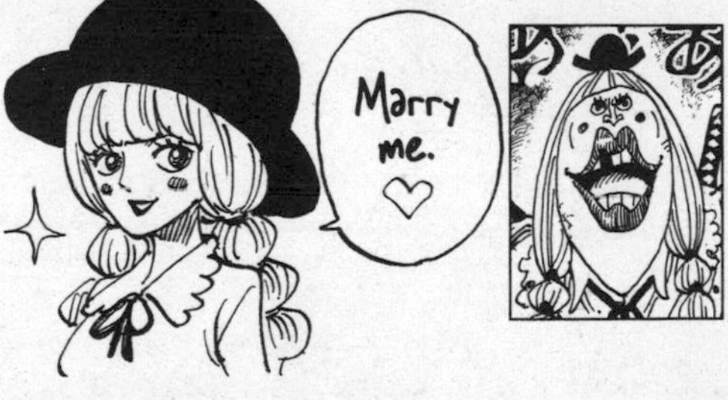
Marry me.

Chapter 686:
THE SNOW-WOMAN IN THE BISCUITS ROOM

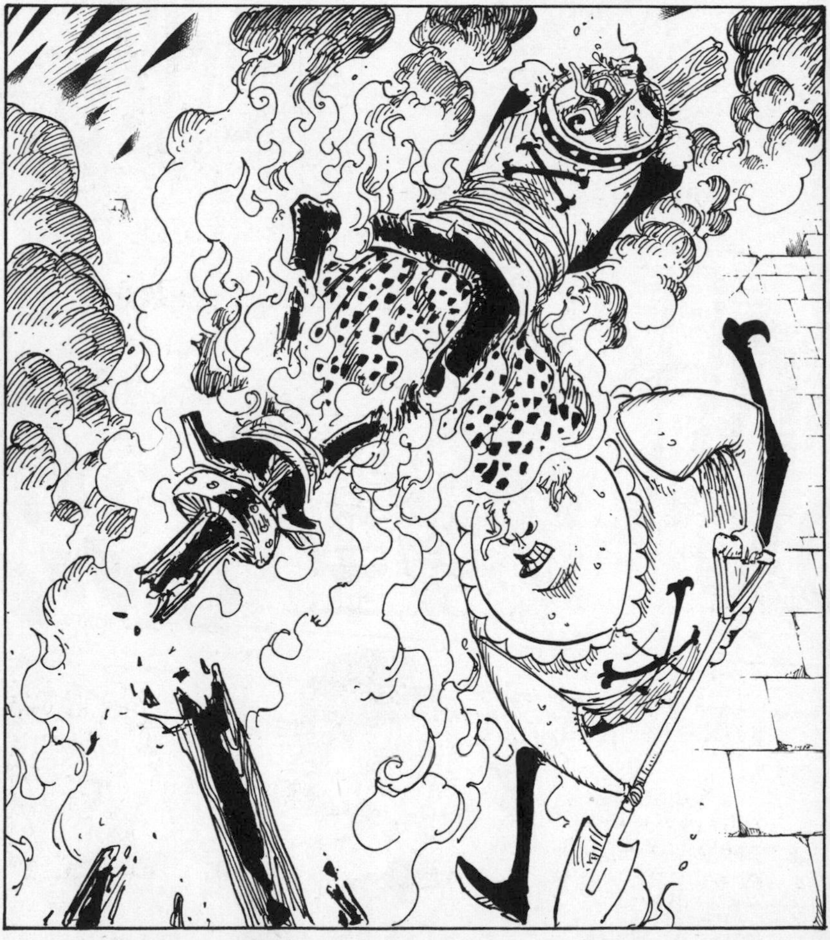

CARIBOU'S NEW WORLD KEE HEE HEE, VOL. 11:
"SAVING BIG BRO!!"

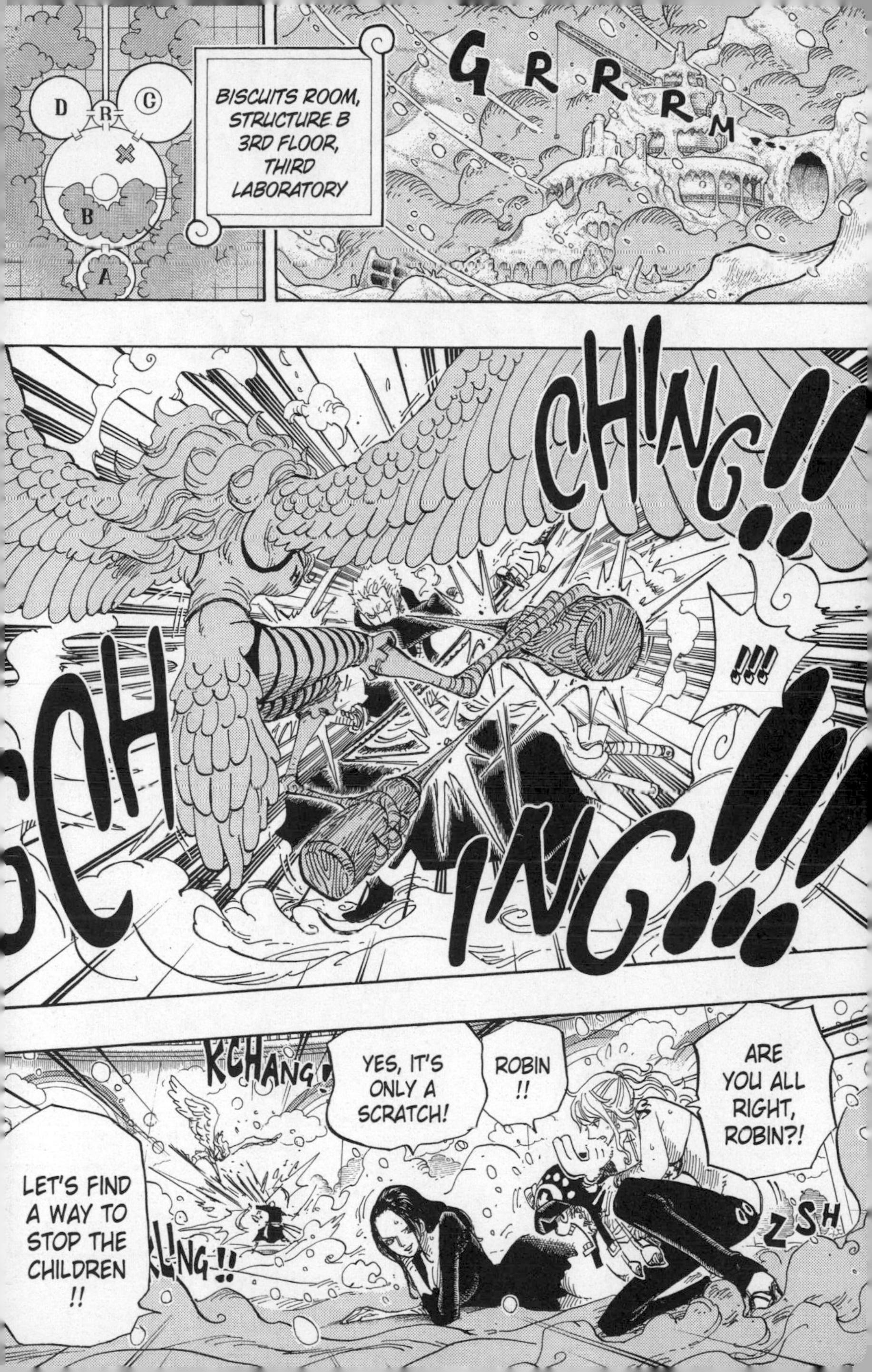
GRRRRM
D
R
C
B
A
BISCUITS ROOM, STRUCTURE B 3RD FLOOR, THIRD LABORATORY
CHING!!
!!!
CHING!!
ARE YOU ALL RIGHT, ROBIN?!
ZSH
ROBIN!!
YES, IT'S ONLY A SCRATCH!
KCHANG
LET'S FIND A WAY TO STOP THE CHILDREN!!

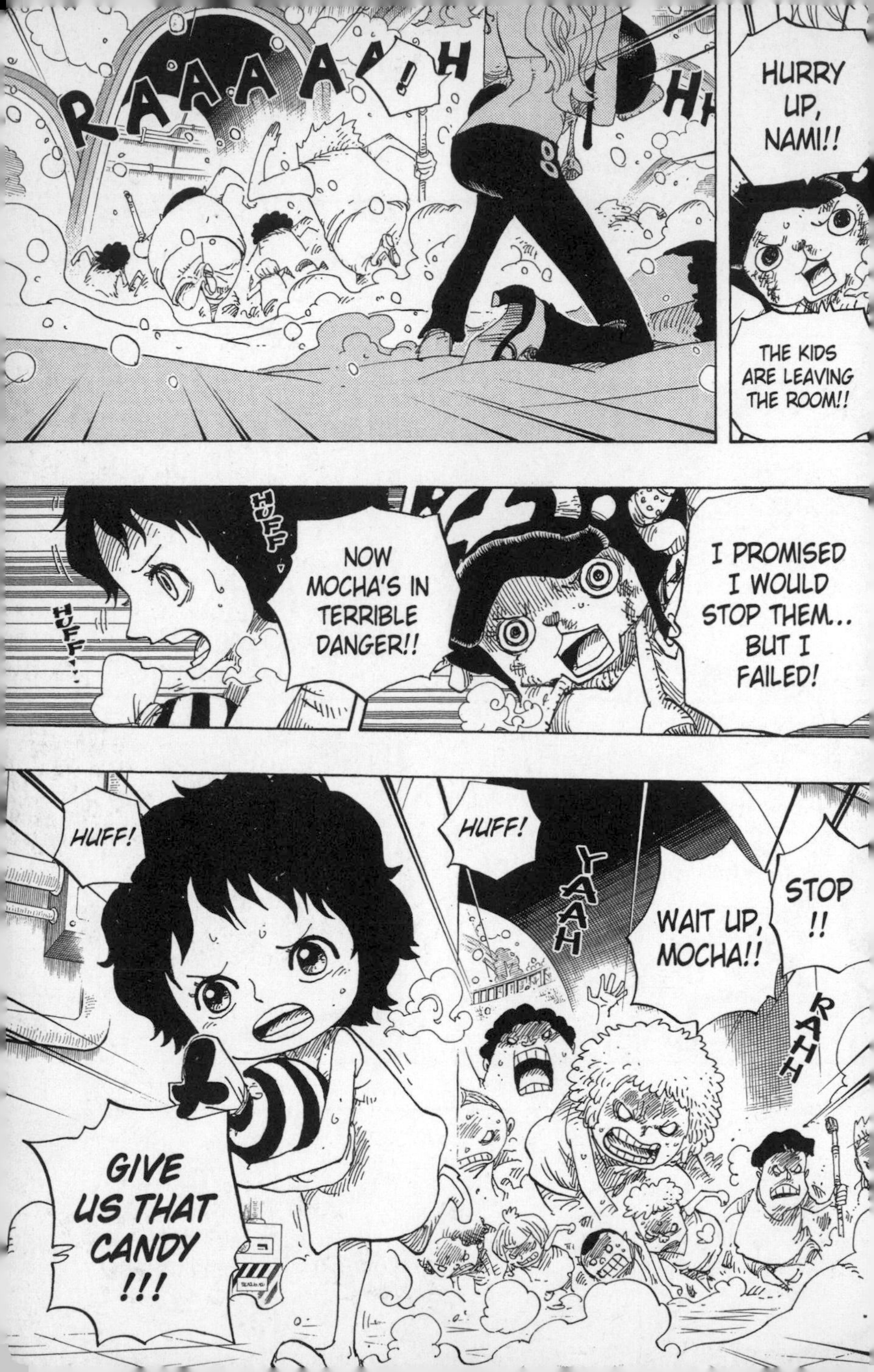
HURRY UP, NAMI!!
THE KIDS ARE LEAVING THE ROOM!!
RAAAAA!H
HH
I PROMISED I WOULD STOP THEM... BUT I FAILED!
NOW MOCHA'S IN TERRIBLE DANGER!!
HUFF
HUFF...
STOP !!
WAIT UP, MOCHA!!
RAHH
YAAAH
HUFF!
HUFF!
GIVE US THAT CANDY !!!

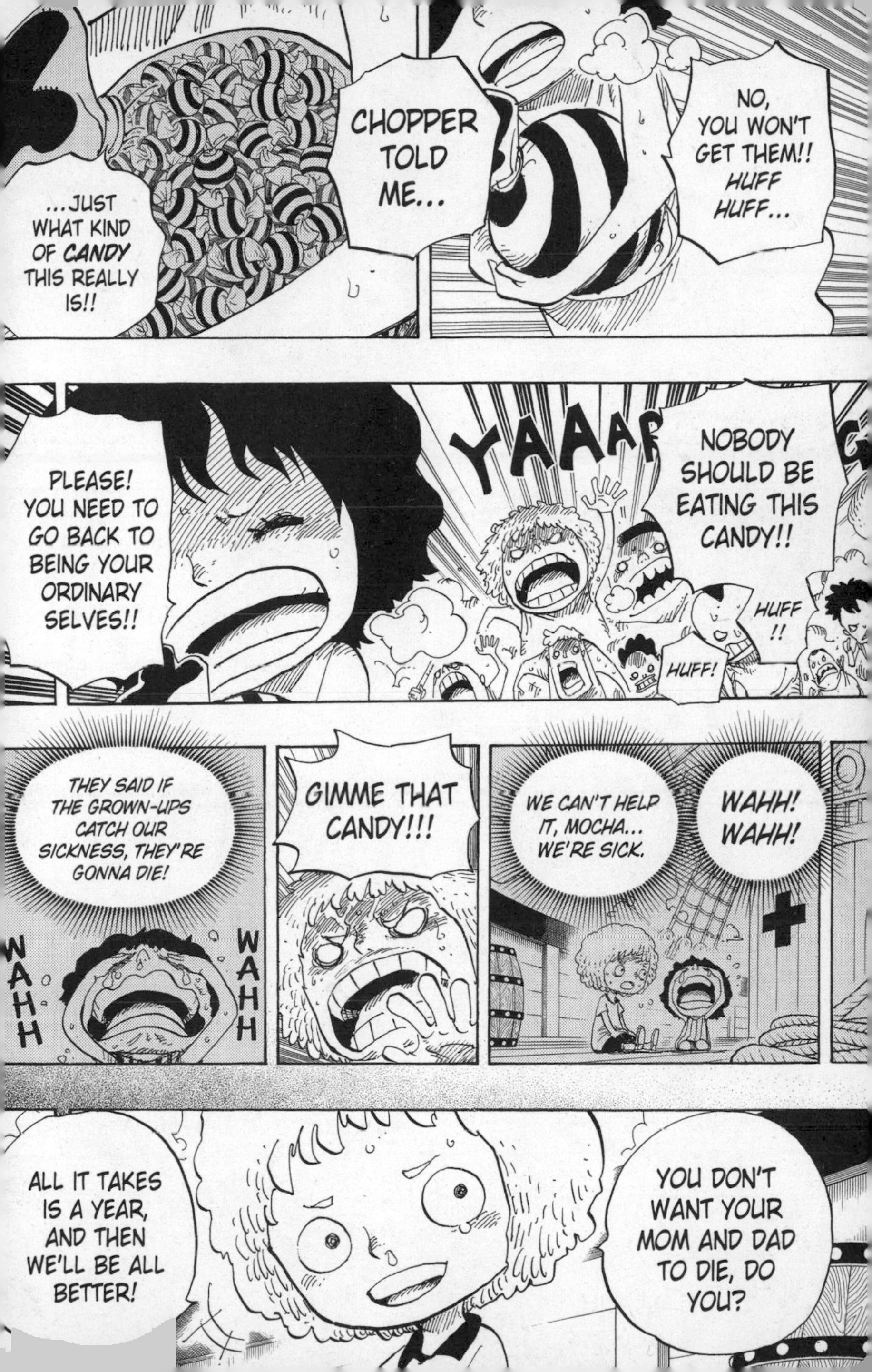
NO, YOU WON'T GET THEM!! HUFF HUFF...
CHOPPER TOLD ME...
...JUST WHAT KIND OF CANDY THIS REALLY IS!!
NOBODY SHOULD BE EATING THIS CANDY!!
YAAAR
HUFF !!
HUFF!
PLEASE! YOU NEED TO GO BACK TO BEING YOUR ORDINARY SELVES!!
WAHH! WAHH!
WE CAN'T HELP IT, MOCHA... WE'RE SICK.
GIMME THAT CANDY!!!
THEY SAID IF THE GROWN-UPS CATCH OUR SICKNESS, THEY'RE GONNA DIE!
WAHH
WAHH
YOU DON'T WANT YOUR MOM AND DAD TO DIE, DO YOU?
ALL IT TAKES IS A YEAR, AND THEN WE'LL BE ALL BETTER!

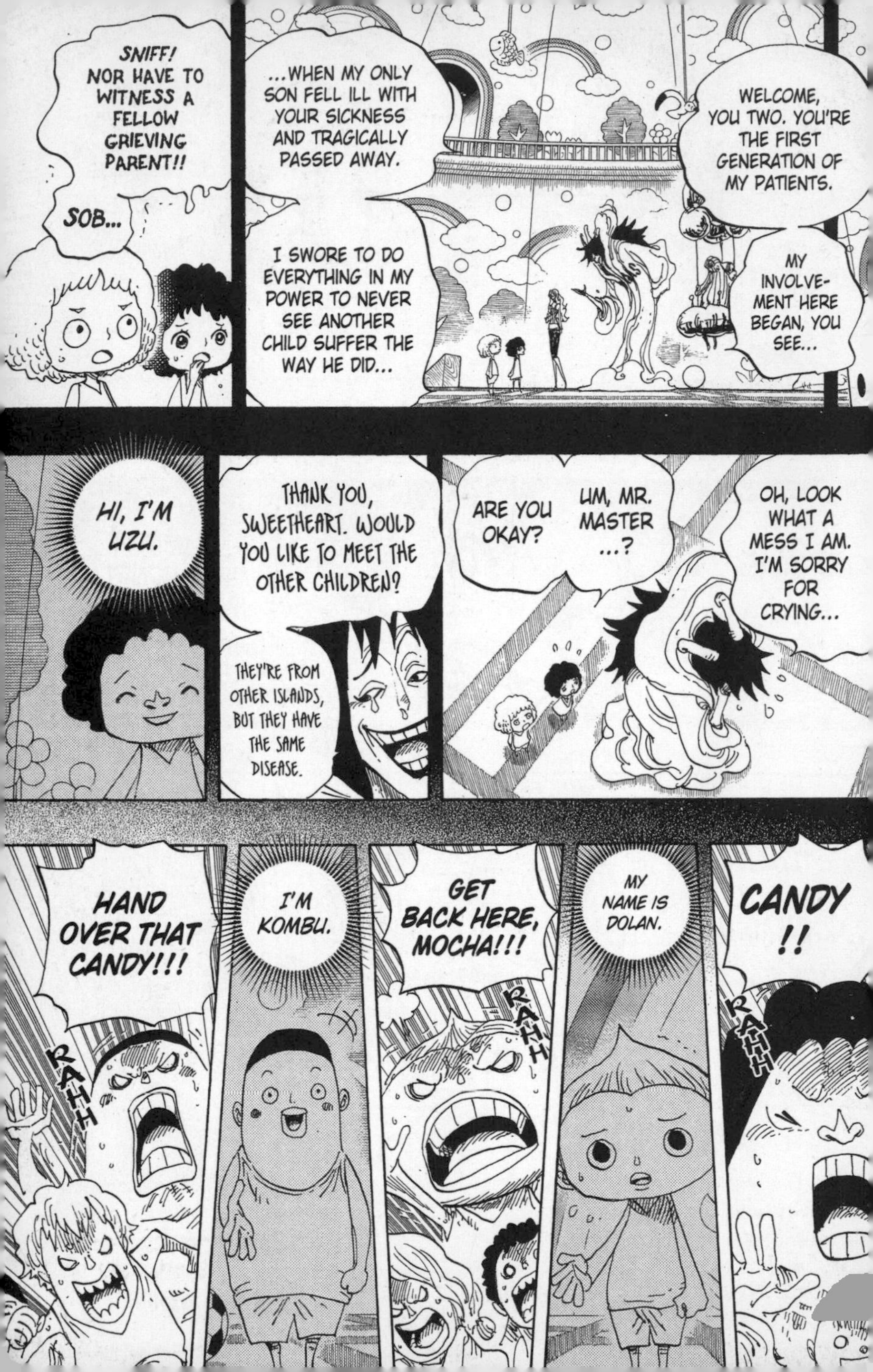
WELCOME, YOU TWO. YOU'RE THE FIRST GENERATION OF MY PATIENTS.
MY INVOLVEMENT HERE BEGAN, YOU SEE...
...WHEN MY ONLY SON FELL ILL WITH YOUR SICKNESS AND TRAGICALLY PASSED AWAY.
I SWORE TO DO EVERYTHING IN MY POWER TO NEVER SEE ANOTHER CHILD SUFFER THE WAY HE DID...
SNIFF! NOR HAVE TO WITNESS A FELLOW GRIEVING PARENT!!
SOB...
OH, LOOK WHAT A MESS I AM. I'M SORRY FOR CRYING...
UM, MR. MASTER ...?
ARE YOU OKAY?
THANK YOU, SWEETHEART. WOULD YOU LIKE TO MEET THE OTHER CHILDREN?
THEY'RE FROM OTHER ISLANDS, BUT THEY HAVE THE SAME DISEASE.
HI, I'M UZU.
CANDY !!
RAHH
MY NAME IS DOLAN.
GET BACK HERE, MOCHA!!!
RAHH
I'M KOMBU.
HAND OVER THAT CANDY!!!
RAHH

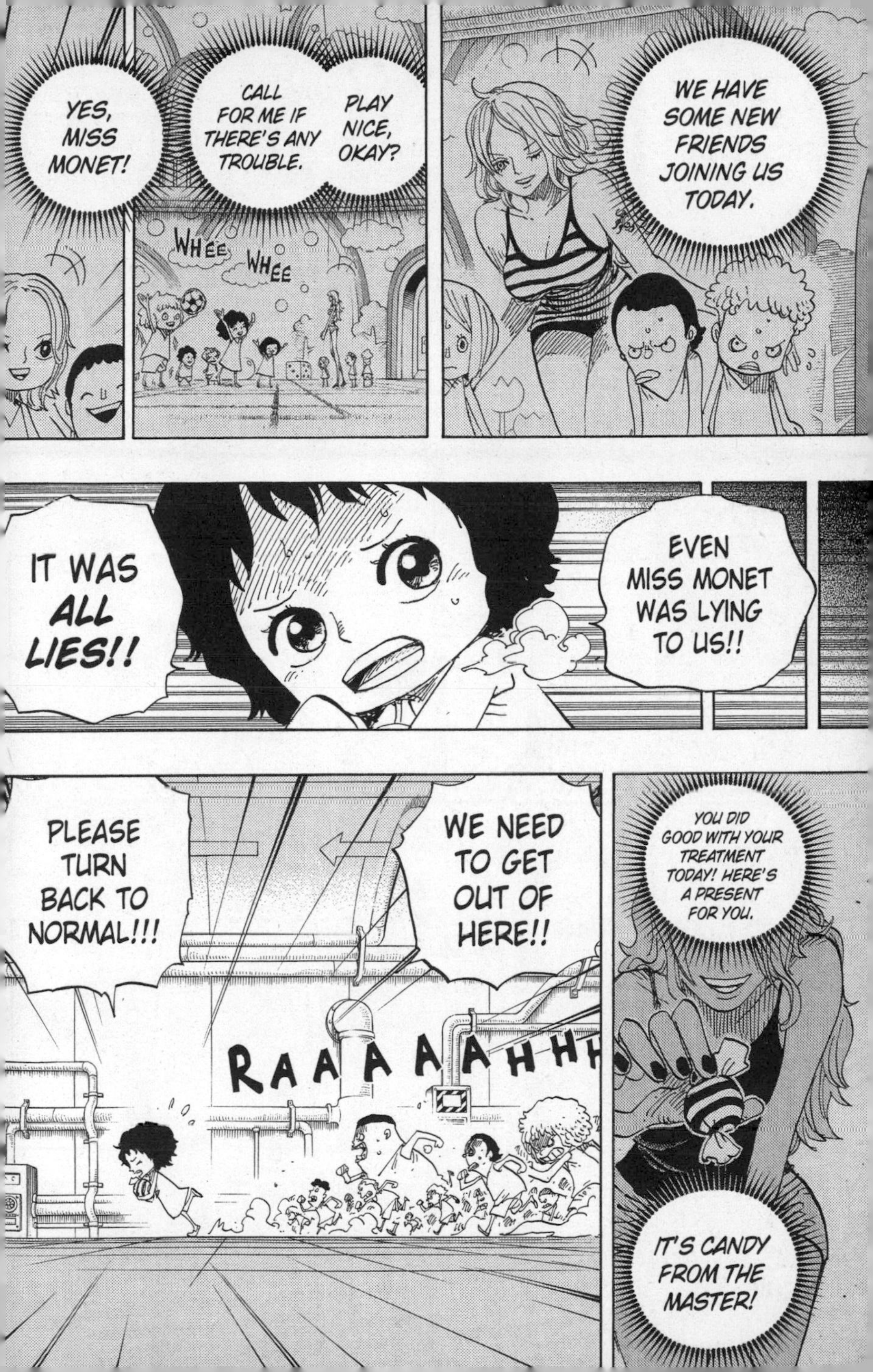
WE HAVE SOME NEW FRIENDS JOINING US TODAY.
PLAY NICE, OKAY?
CALL FOR ME IF THERE'S ANY TROUBLE.
WHEE
WHEE
YES, MISS MONET!
EVEN MISS MONET WAS LYING TO US!!
IT WAS ALL LIES!!
YOU DID GOOD WITH YOUR TREATMENT TODAY! HERE'S A PRESENT FOR YOU.
IT'S CANDY FROM THE MASTER!
WE NEED TO GET OUT OF HERE!!
PLEASE TURN BACK TO NORMAL!!!
RAAAAAHHH

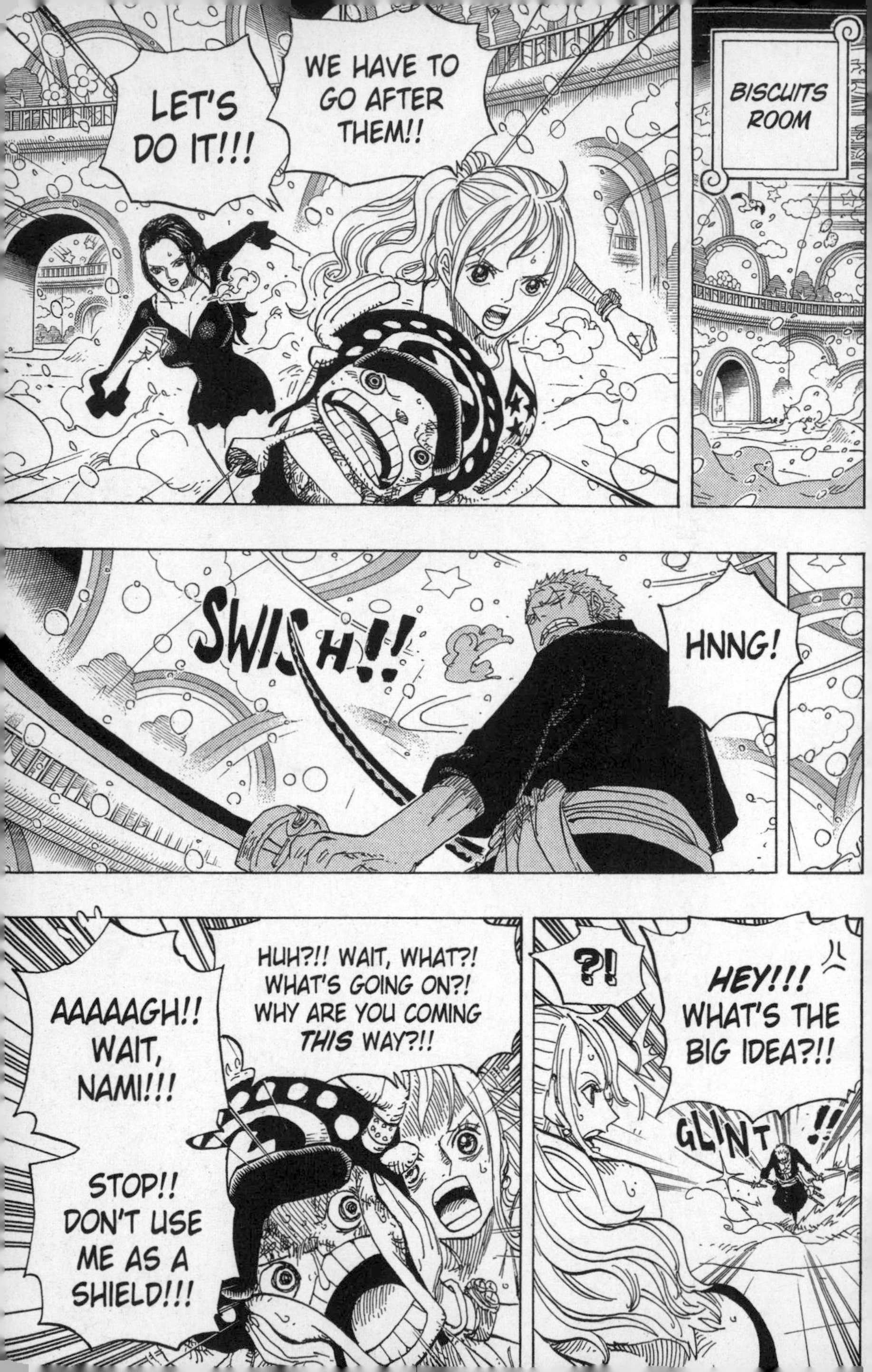
BISCUITS ROOM
WE HAVE TO GO AFTER THEM!!
LET'S DO IT!!!
HNNG!
SWISH!!
?!
HEY!!! WHAT'S THE BIG IDEA?!!
GLINT!!
HUH?!! WAIT, WHAT?! WHAT'S GOING ON?! WHY ARE YOU COMING THIS WAY?!!
AAAAAGH!! WAIT, NAMI!!!
STOP!! DON'T USE ME AS A SHIELD!!!

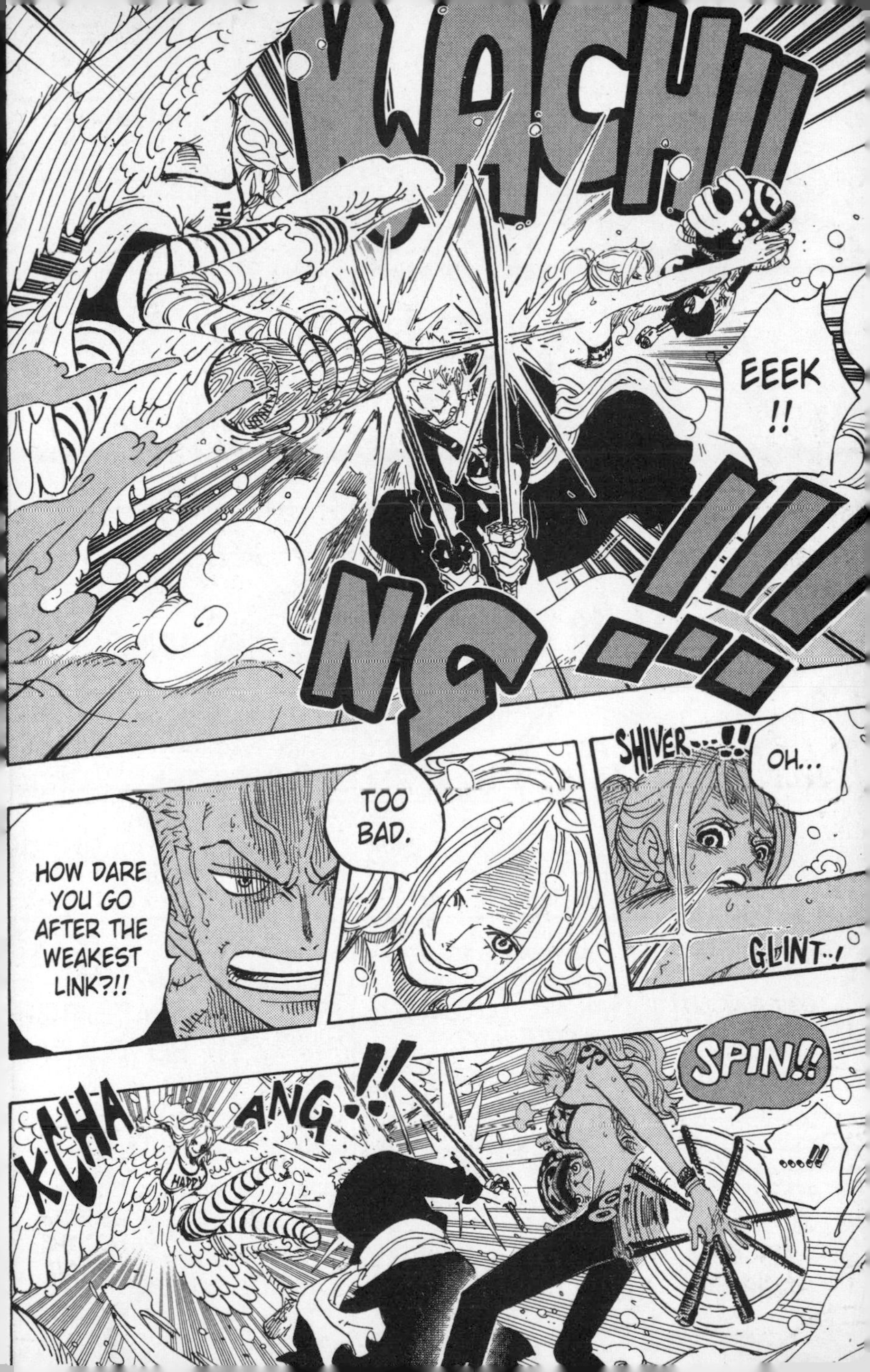
KACHI!!
EEEK !!
NG...!!!
OH...
SHIVER...!!
GLINT..!
TOO BAD.
HOW DARE YOU GO AFTER THE WEAKEST LINK?!!
SPIN!!
...!!
KCHAANG..!!
HAPPY

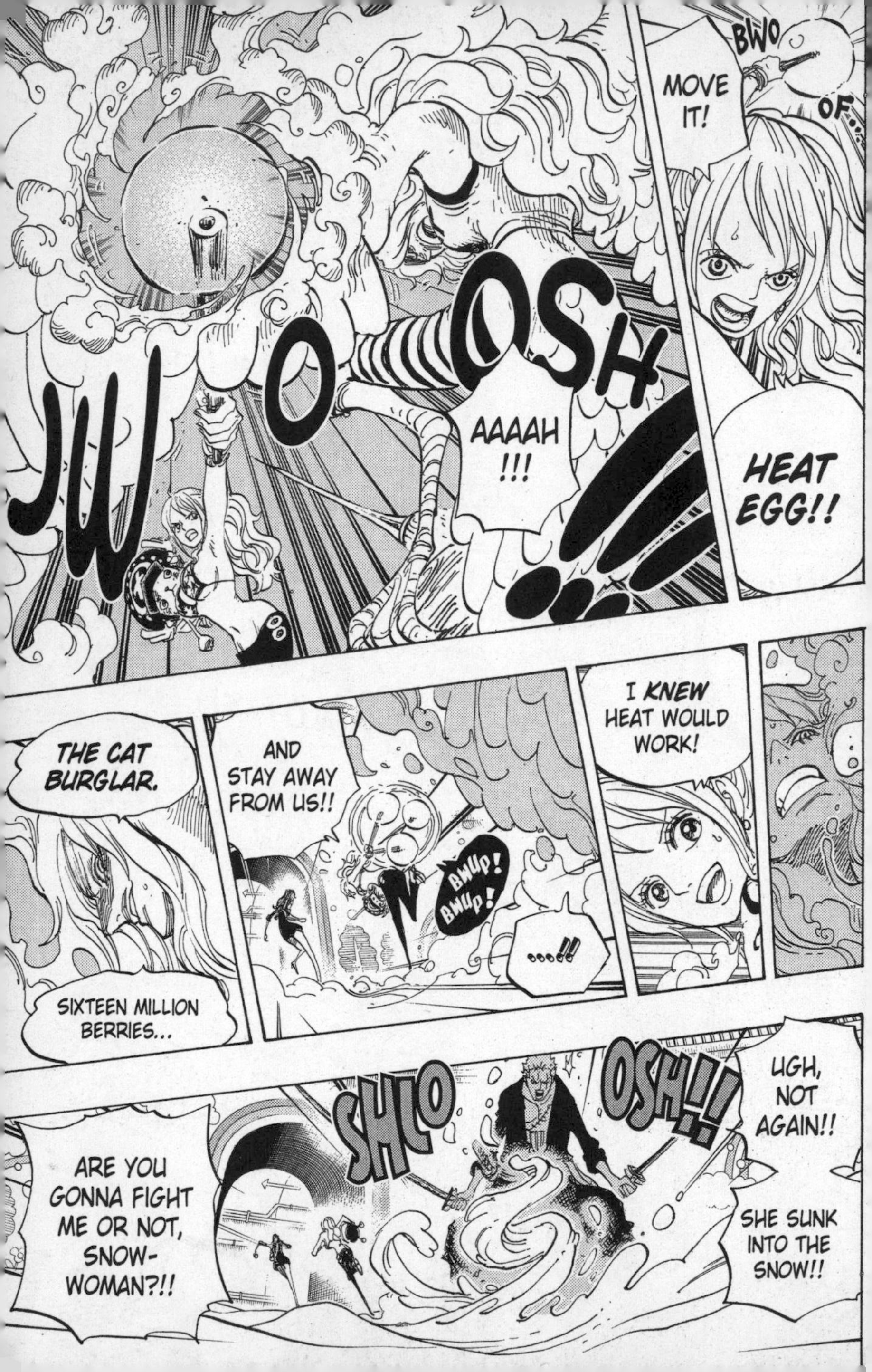
BWO
OF...
MOVE IT!
HEAT EGG!!
JUWOOSH!!
AAAAH!!!
I KNEW HEAT WOULD WORK!
...!!
AND STAY AWAY FROM US!!
BWUP! BWUP!
THE CAT BURGLAR.
SIXTEEN MILLION BERRIES...
UGH, NOT AGAIN!!
SHLOOSH!!!
SHE SUNK INTO THE SNOW!!
ARE YOU GONNA FIGHT ME OR NOT, SNOW-WOMAN?!!

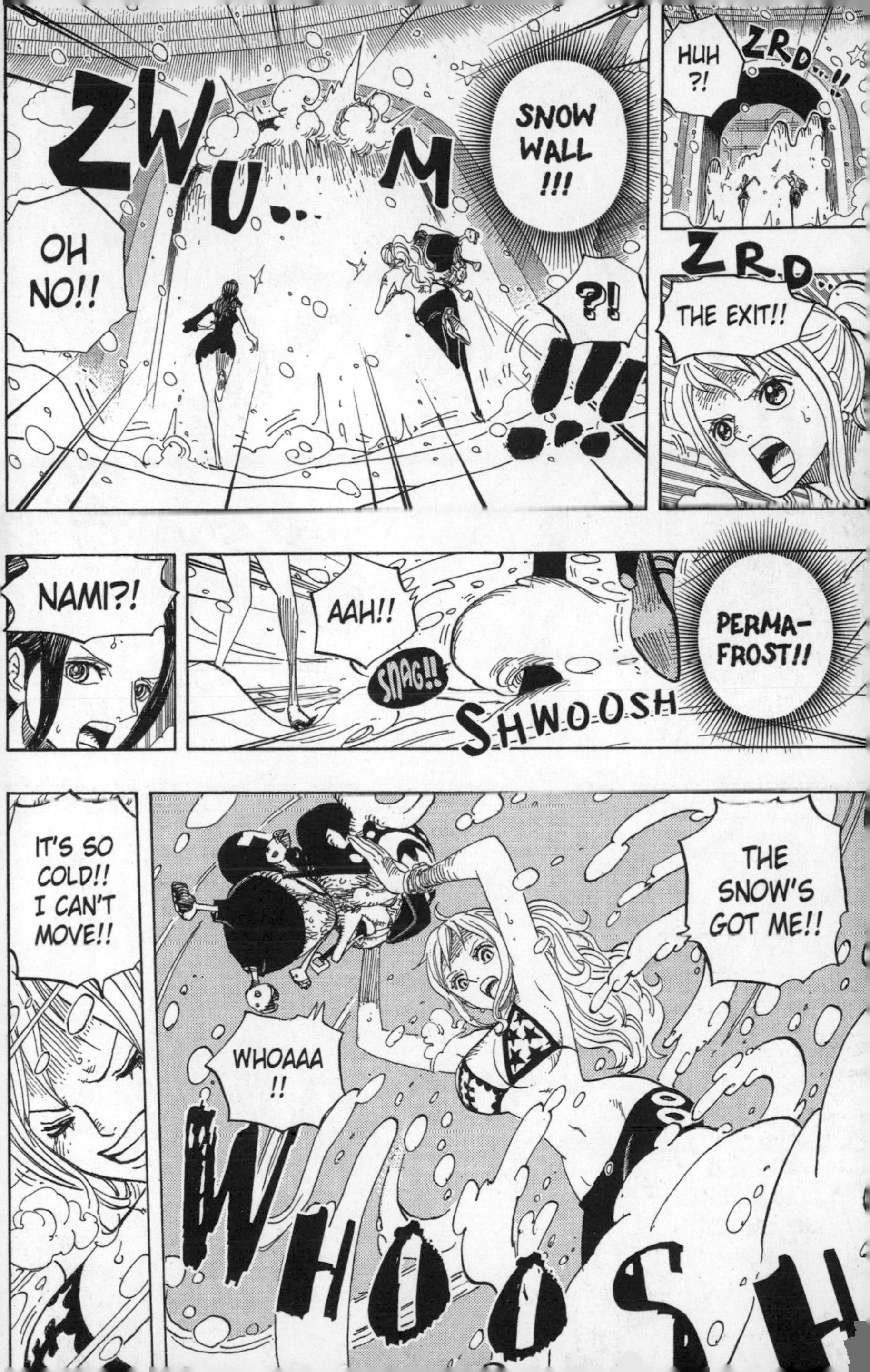
ZRD...!!
HUH ?!
ZRD...
THE EXIT!!
SNOW WALL !!!
ZWUM...
OH NO!!
?!
PERMA-FROST!!
AAH!!
SNAG!!
SHWOOSH
NAMI?!
THE SNOW'S GOT ME!!
WHOAAA !!
WHOOOSH
IT'S SO COLD!! I CAN'T MOVE!!

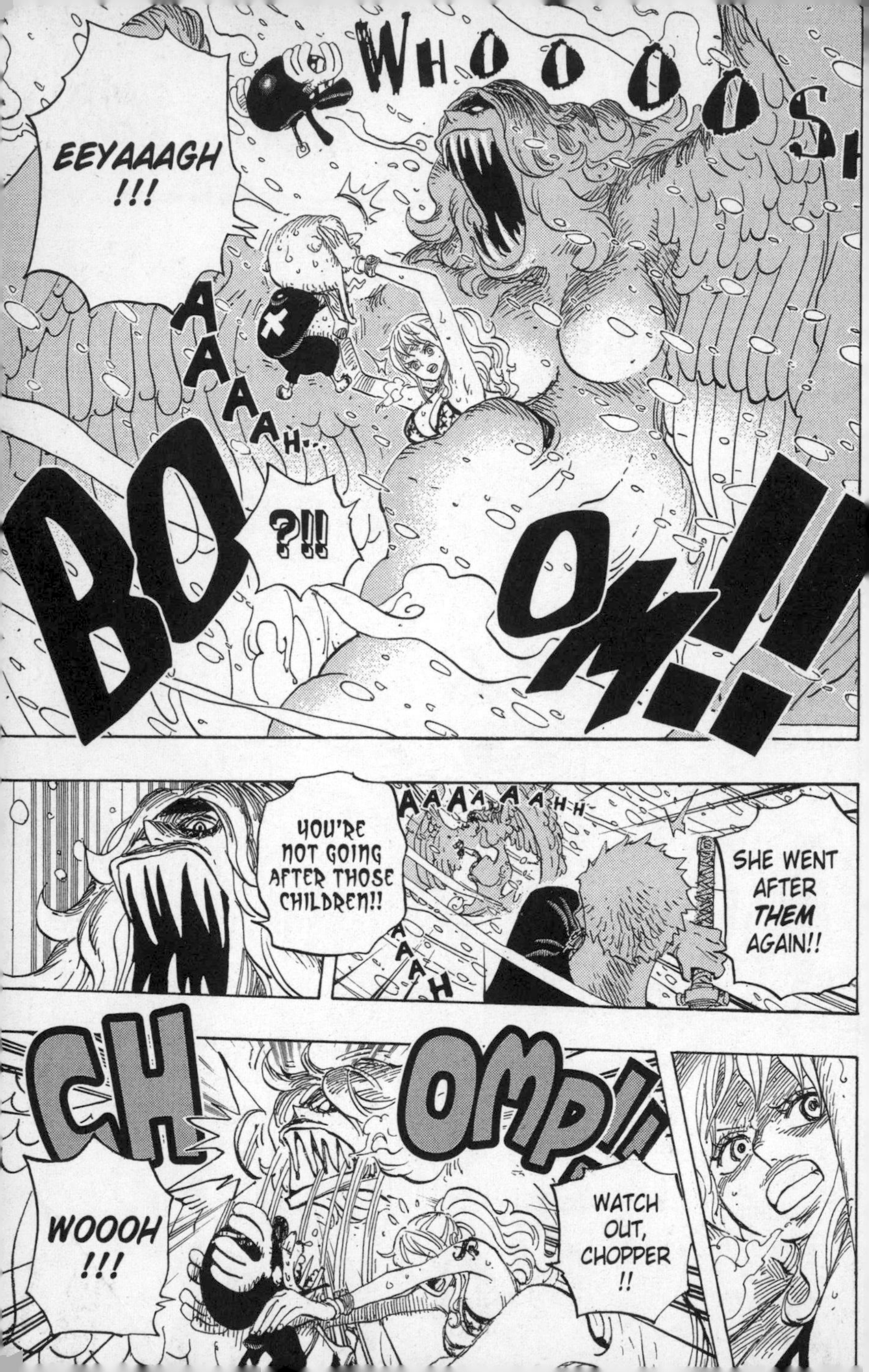
WHOOOOOSH
EEYAAAGH !!!
AAAAAH..
?!!
BOOM!!!
SHE WENT AFTER THEM AGAIN!!
YOU'RE NOT GOING AFTER THOSE CHILDREN!!
AAAAAAAHH
AAAAH
CHOMP!!
WATCH OUT, CHOPPER !!
WOOOH !!!

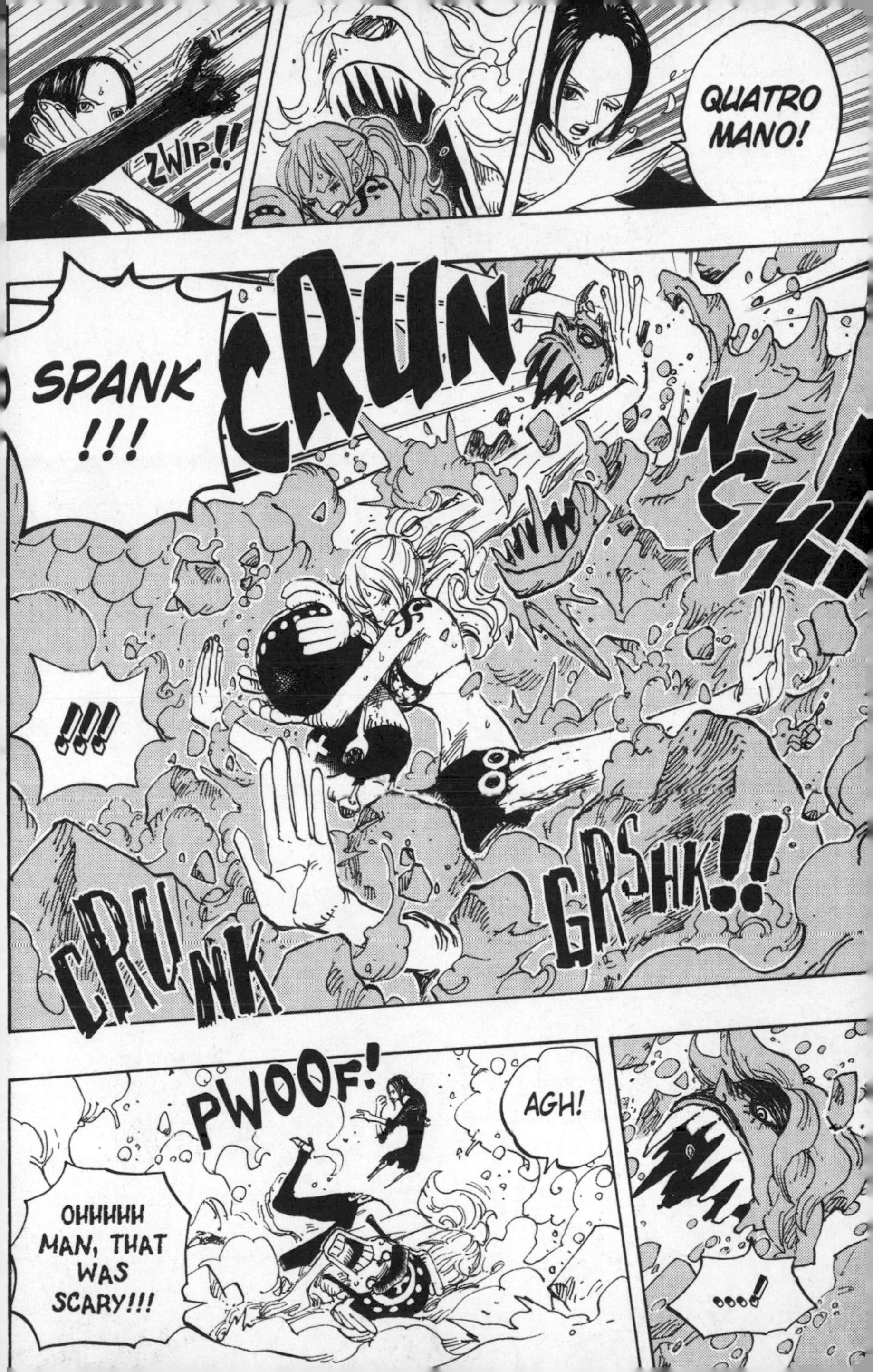
QUATRO MANO!
ZWIP!!
CRUNCH!!
SPANK !!!
!!!
GRSHK!!
CRUNK
...!
AGH!
PWOOF!
OHHHHH MAN, THAT WAS SCARY!!!

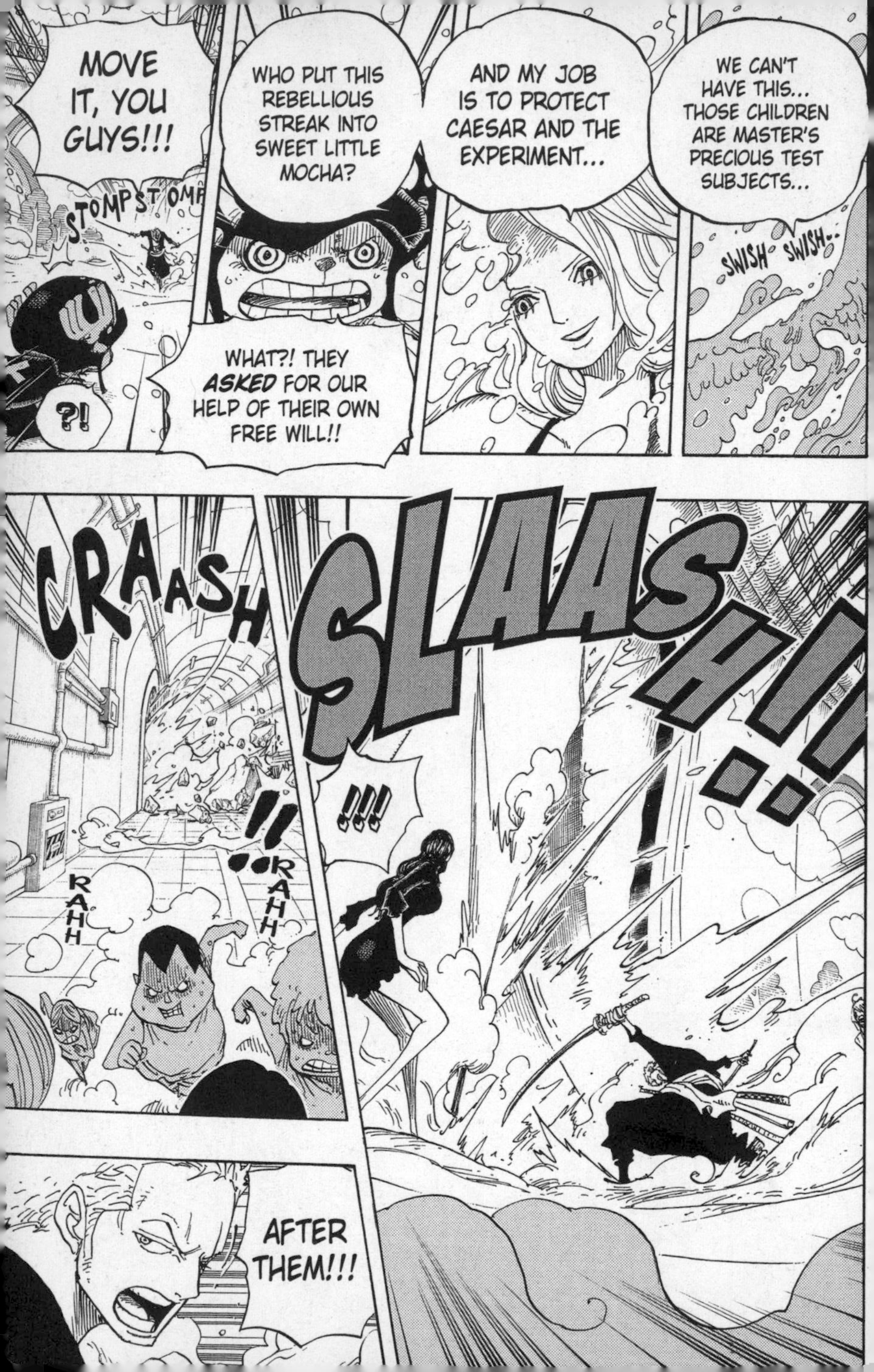
WE CAN'T HAVE THIS... THOSE CHILDREN ARE MASTER'S PRECIOUS TEST SUBJECTS...
SWISH SWISH...
AND MY JOB IS TO PROTECT CAESAR AND THE EXPERIMENT...
WHO PUT THIS REBELLIOUS STREAK INTO SWEET LITTLE MOCHA?
WHAT?! THEY ASKED FOR OUR HELP OF THEIR OWN FREE WILL!!
MOVE IT, YOU GUYS!!!
STOMP STOMP
?!
SLAASH!!
!!!
CRAASH
!!
RAHH
RAHH
AFTER THEM!!!

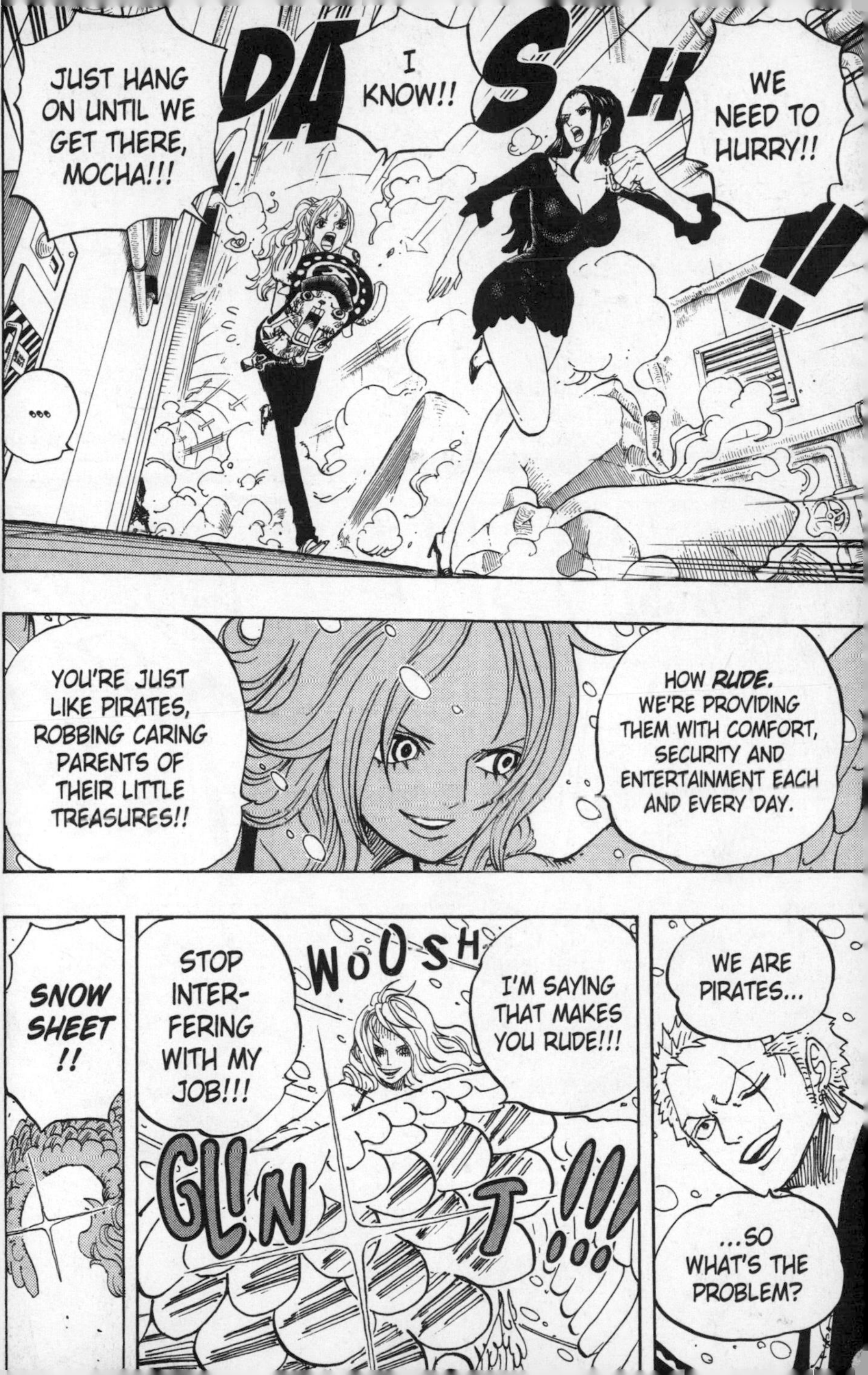
WE NEED TO HURRY!!
!!
DASH
I KNOW!!
JUST HANG ON UNTIL WE GET THERE, MOCHA!!!
...
HOW RUDE. WE'RE PROVIDING THEM WITH COMFORT, SECURITY AND ENTERTAINMENT EACH AND EVERY DAY.
YOU'RE JUST LIKE PIRATES, ROBBING CARING PARENTS OF THEIR LITTLE TREASURES!!
WE ARE PIRATES...
...SO WHAT'S THE PROBLEM?
I'M SAYING THAT MAKES YOU RUDE!!!
WOOSH
STOP INTER-FERING WITH MY JOB!!!
GLINT
SNOW SHEET!!

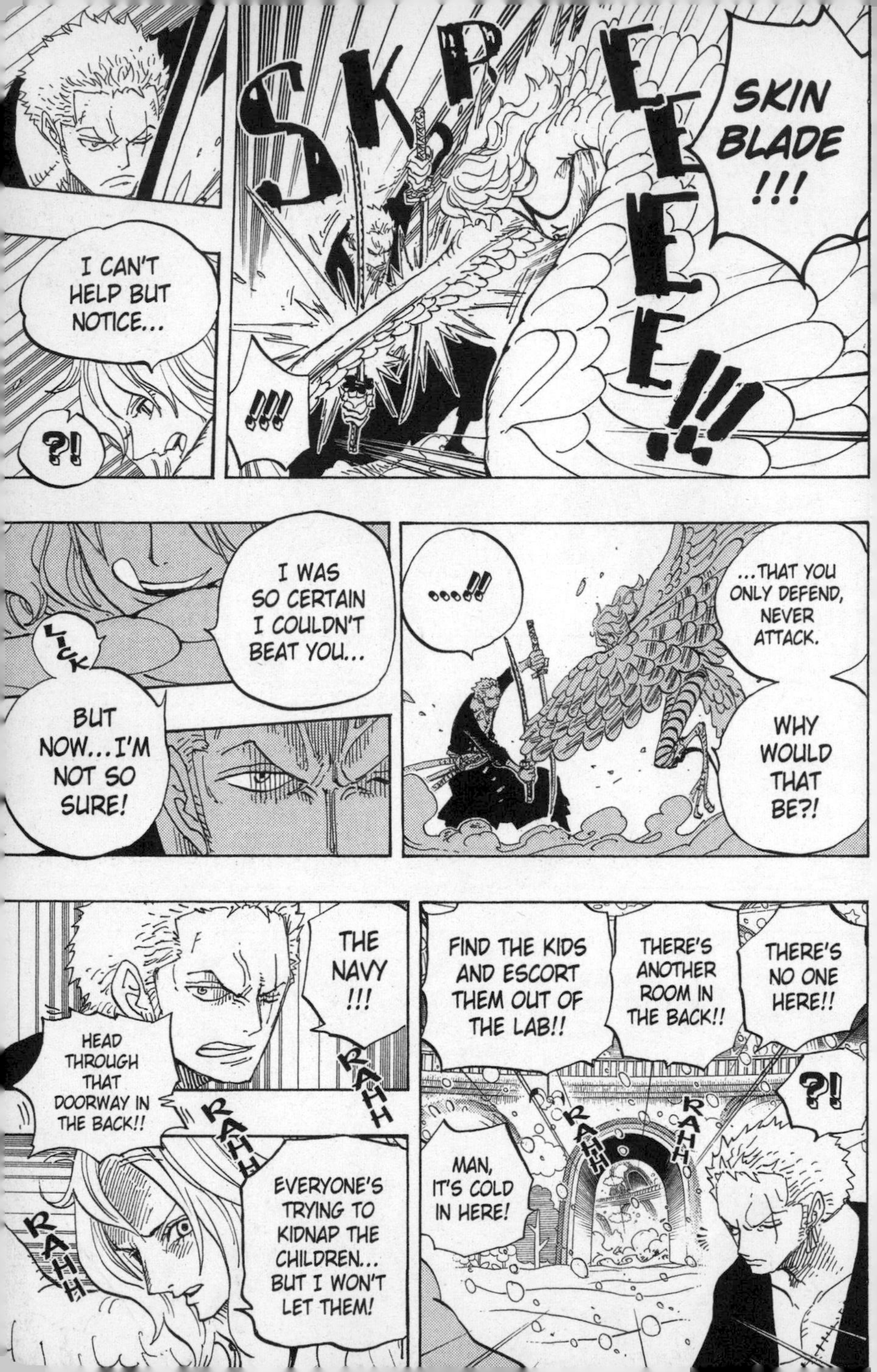
SKREEEE!!!
SKIN BLADE!!!
!!!
I CAN'T HELP BUT NOTICE...
?!
...!!
...THAT YOU ONLY DEFEND, NEVER ATTACK.
WHY WOULD THAT BE?!
I WAS SO CERTAIN I COULDN'T BEAT YOU...
LICK
BUT NOW... I'M NOT SO SURE!
THERE'S NO ONE HERE!!
THERE'S ANOTHER ROOM IN THE BACK!!
FIND THE KIDS AND ESCORT THEM OUT OF THE LAB!!
RAHH
RAHH
MAN, IT'S COLD IN HERE!
?!
THE NAVY!!!
RAHH
HEAD THROUGH THAT DOORWAY IN THE BACK!!
RAHH
RAHH
EVERYONE'S TRYING TO KIDNAP THE CHILDREN... BUT I WON'T LET THEM!

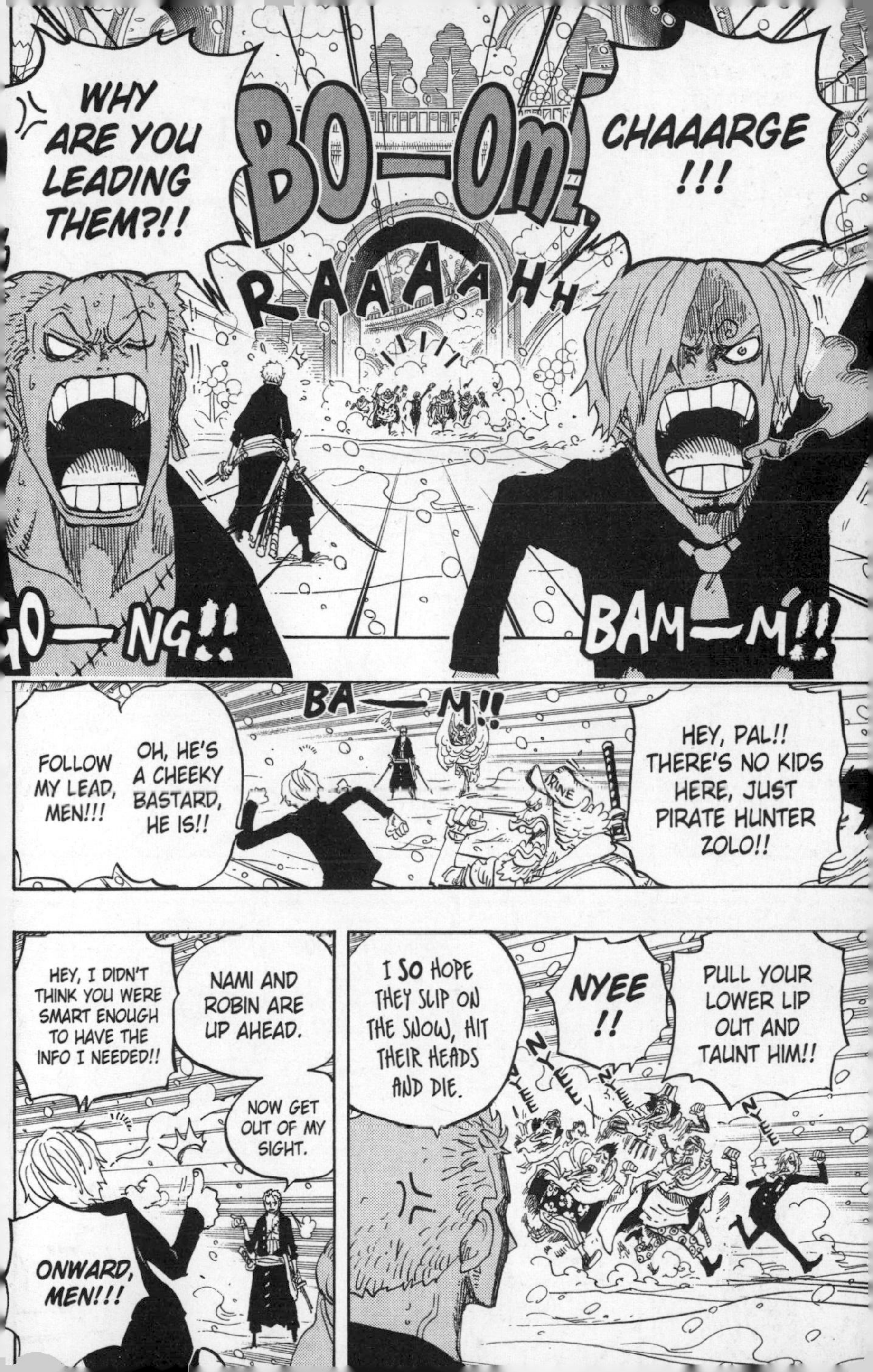
CHAAARGE !!!
BO-OM
RAAAAHH
WHY ARE YOU LEADING THEM?!!
BAM—M!!
O—NG!!
HEY, PAL!! THERE'S NO KIDS HERE, JUST PIRATE HUNTER ZOLO!!
BA—M!!
OH, HE'S A CHEEKY BASTARD, HE IS!!
FOLLOW MY LEAD, MEN!!!
PULL YOUR LOWER LIP OUT AND TAUNT HIM!!
NYEE !!
I SO HOPE THEY SLIP ON THE SNOW, HIT THEIR HEADS AND DIE.
NYEE
NYEE
NYEE
NAMI AND ROBIN ARE UP AHEAD.
HEY, I DIDN'T THINK YOU WERE SMART ENOUGH TO HAVE THE INFO I NEEDED!!
NOW GET OUT OF MY SIGHT.
ONWARD, MEN!!!

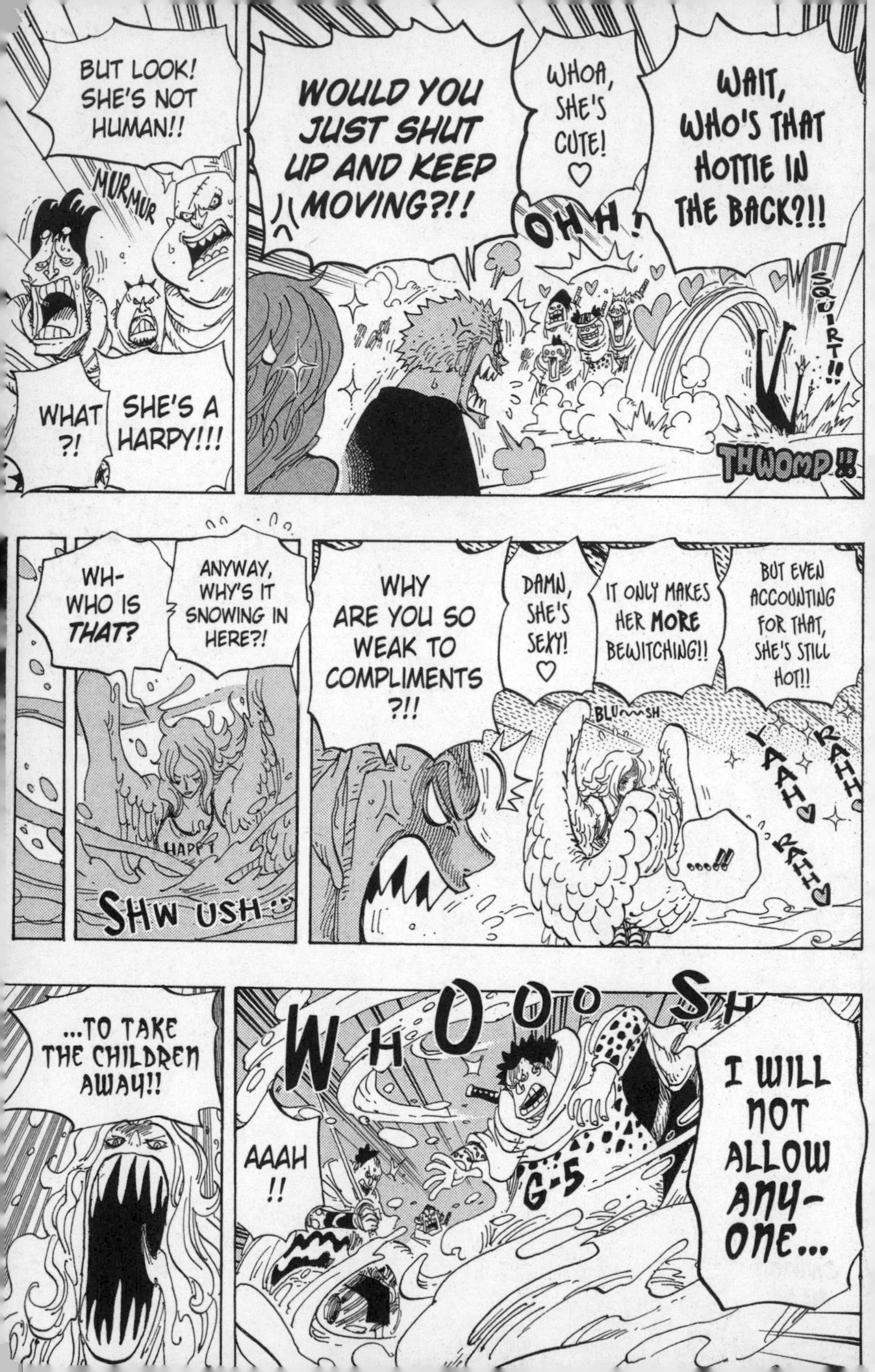
WAIT, WHO'S THAT HOTTIE IN THE BACK?!!
WHOA, SHE'S CUTE! ♡
OHHH!
SQUIRT!!
THWOMP!!
WOULD YOU JUST SHUT UP AND KEEP MOVING?!!
BUT LOOK! SHE'S NOT HUMAN!!
MURMUR
SHE'S A HARPY!!!
WHAT?!
BUT EVEN ACCOUNTING FOR THAT, SHE'S STILL HOT!!
IT ONLY MAKES HER MORE BEWITCHING!!
DAMN, SHE'S SEXY! ♡
WHY ARE YOU SO WEAK TO COMPLIMENTS?!!
BLU~SH
YAAAH♡
RAHH
RAHH♡
...!!
ANYWAY, WHY'S IT SNOWING IN HERE?!
WH- WHO IS THAT?
HAPPY
SHWUSH
I WILL NOT ALLOW ANYONE...
WHOOOSH
G-5
AAAH!!
...TO TAKE THE CHILDREN AWAY!!

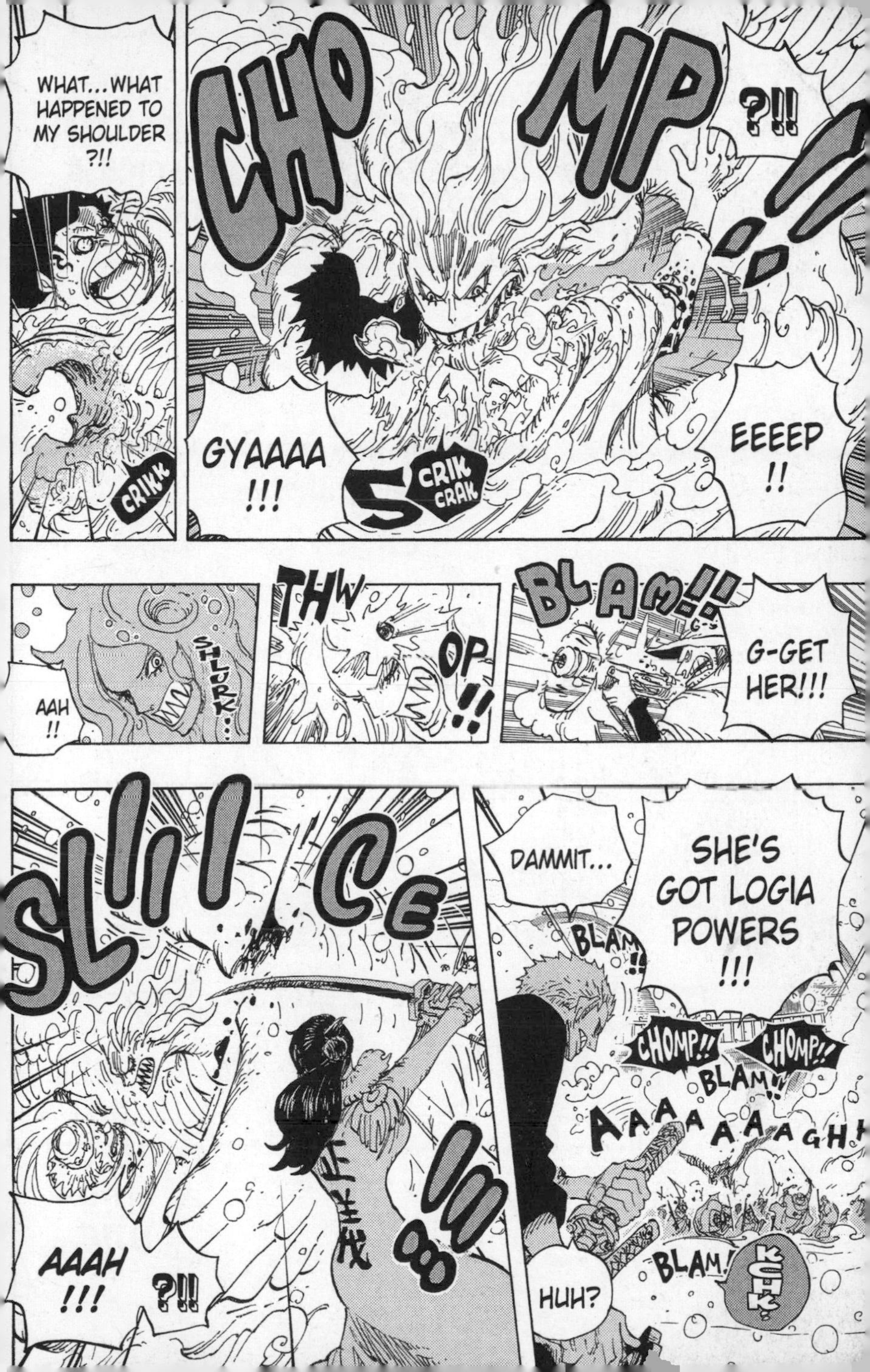
?!!
CHOMP!!
EEEEP !!
GYAAAA !!!
CRIK CRAK
WHAT...WHAT HAPPENED TO MY SHOULDER ?!!
CRIKK
BLAM!!
G-GET HER!!!
THWOP!!
SHLURK...
AAH !!
SHE'S GOT LOGIA POWERS !!!
DAMMIT...
BLAM!!
CHOMP!!
CHOMP!!
BLAM!!
AAAAAAAAGH!
BLAM!
KCHK
HUH?
SLIIICE!!!
AAAH !!!
?!!

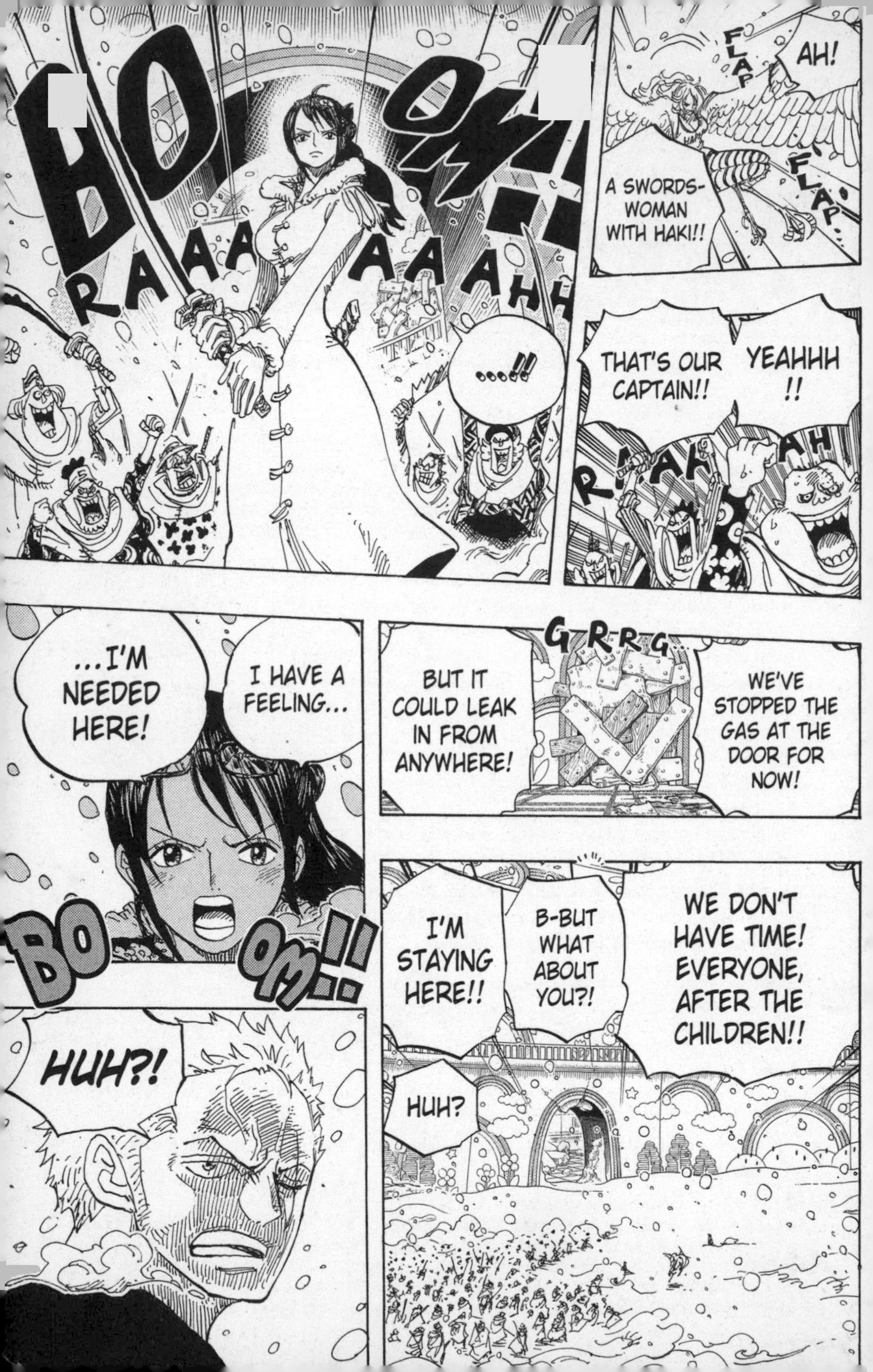
AH!
FLAP
FLAP
A SWORDS-WOMAN WITH HAKI!!
YEAHHH!!
THAT'S OUR CAPTAIN!!
RAAH
BOOOM!!
RAAAAAAHH
....!!
WE'VE STOPPED THE GAS AT THE DOOR FOR NOW!
GRRG
BUT IT COULD LEAK IN FROM ANYWHERE!
I HAVE A FEELING...
...I'M NEEDED HERE!
BOOM!!
WE DON'T HAVE TIME! EVERYONE, AFTER THE CHILDREN!!
B-BUT WHAT ABOUT YOU?!
I'M STAYING HERE!!
HUH?
HUH?!

SBS Question Corner

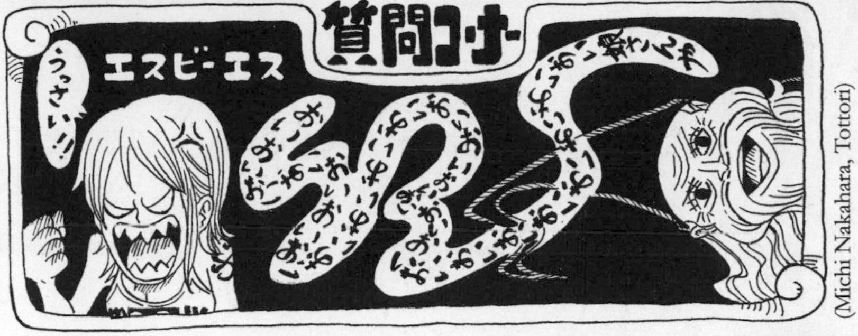

うっさい!!
エスピーエス
質問コーナー

(Michi Nakahara, Tottori)

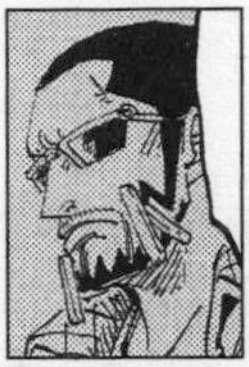

Q: Odacchi!! Odacchi… What did you have for breakfast? Your face is shining and sparkling. Speaking of breakfast, on p.106 of Volume 68, did Vergo happen to have french fries that morning…? Well?

--I Had Barbecue This Morning Dude

A: Man, everything sticks to him, doesn't it? I think he probably had your typical hamburger combo meal. Hamburger, fries, shake (strawberry). That's Vergo's typical breakfast. Also, my face is shining from the leftover colored lights I had for breakfast.

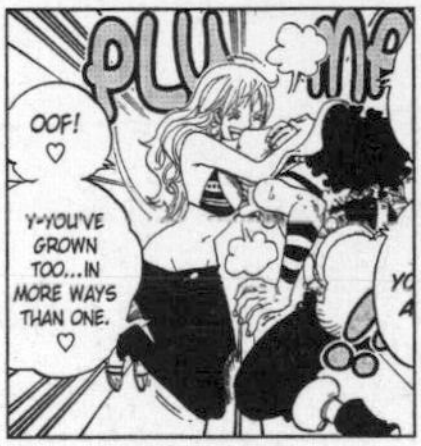

OOF! ♡
Y-YOU'VE GROWN TOO...IN MORE WAYS THAN ONE. ♡

Q: I noticed people were curious about Nami's New World bust size in Volume 66. Well, as an employee of a ladies' underwear store, I'll give you an answer: I think Nami's a J-cup, perhaps even more... My eyeball estimate says she measures 25 inches underneath, 38 and a half on top. That would actually make her a K-cup, but there isn't even a K measurement in Japan. You'd have to import a bra. Yes, she's literally off the charts!!! Personally, my answer is that she's a "Nami-cup." (boiiing)

--Secret ChageroKiyomizu Fan

A: Yes. This day has finally come, young men. I thrust this assignment upon the readers in Volume 66. Thank you for all your answers. Sanji! Has your nose stopped bleeding?! Read the results!

Sanji: **Ah... Sorry about that other time. So, you want Nami and Robin's current measurements? Yes, the numbers are higher, but don't be mistaken! What's really increased is their overall sexiness!!**

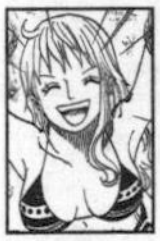

Bust: 38.5 (J-cup)
Waist: 23
Hip: 34.5

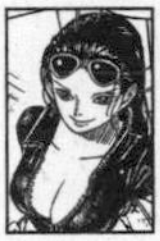

Bust: 39.5 (J-cup)
Waist: 23.5
Hip: 35.5

A: Ah, nice! Very nice! Easy to remember! Thanks, Sanji! So this is what constitutes a Nami-cup. Incredible.

Nami: **What are you doing over here? If you want to use our bodies for your segment, you'd better pay up. ✧**

A: Run away!! Dabbadabbadabba...
Huff huff... Well, folks... huff huff... that's it for this volume. No extras at the end, because I pushed for twelve chapters this time. The big shots at Shueisha told me it will never happen again. But I really wanted everyone to see until Chapter 690 in this book... I'll work on my ability to wrap things into a smaller package... See you next volume!!

Chapter 687:
WILD BEAST

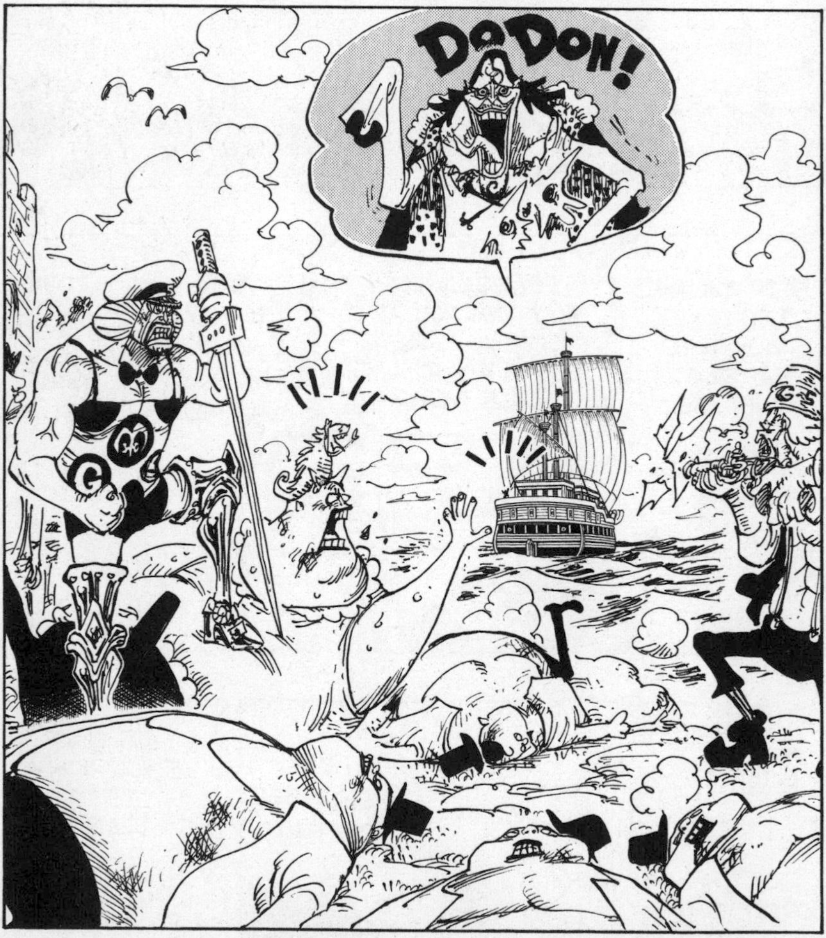
DADON!

CARIBOU'S NEW WORLD KEE HEE HEE, VOL. 12:
"CARIBOU ON THE LAM"

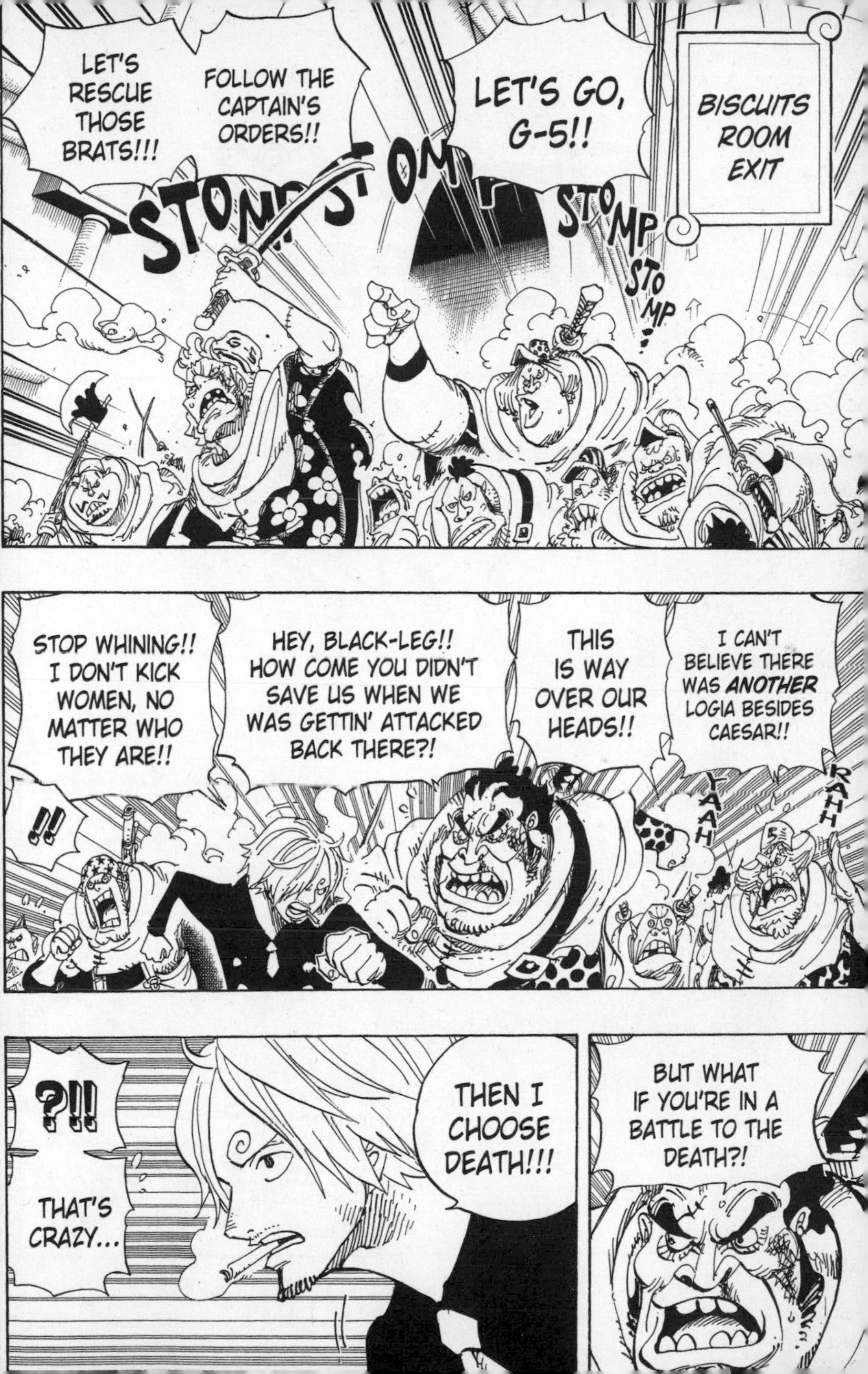
BISCUITS ROOM EXIT
LET'S GO, G-5!!
FOLLOW THE CAPTAIN'S ORDERS!!
LET'S RESCUE THOSE BRATS!!!
STOMP STOMP
STOMP
STOMP
RAHH
YAAAH
I CAN'T BELIEVE THERE WAS ***ANOTHER*** LOGIA BESIDES CAESAR!!
THIS IS WAY OVER OUR HEADS!!
HEY, BLACK-LEG!! HOW COME YOU DIDN'T SAVE US WHEN WE WAS GETTIN' ATTACKED BACK THERE?!
STOP WHINING!! I DON'T KICK WOMEN, NO MATTER WHO THEY ARE!!
!!
BUT WHAT IF YOU'RE IN A BATTLE TO THE DEATH?!
THEN I CHOOSE DEATH!!!
?!!
THAT'S CRAZY...

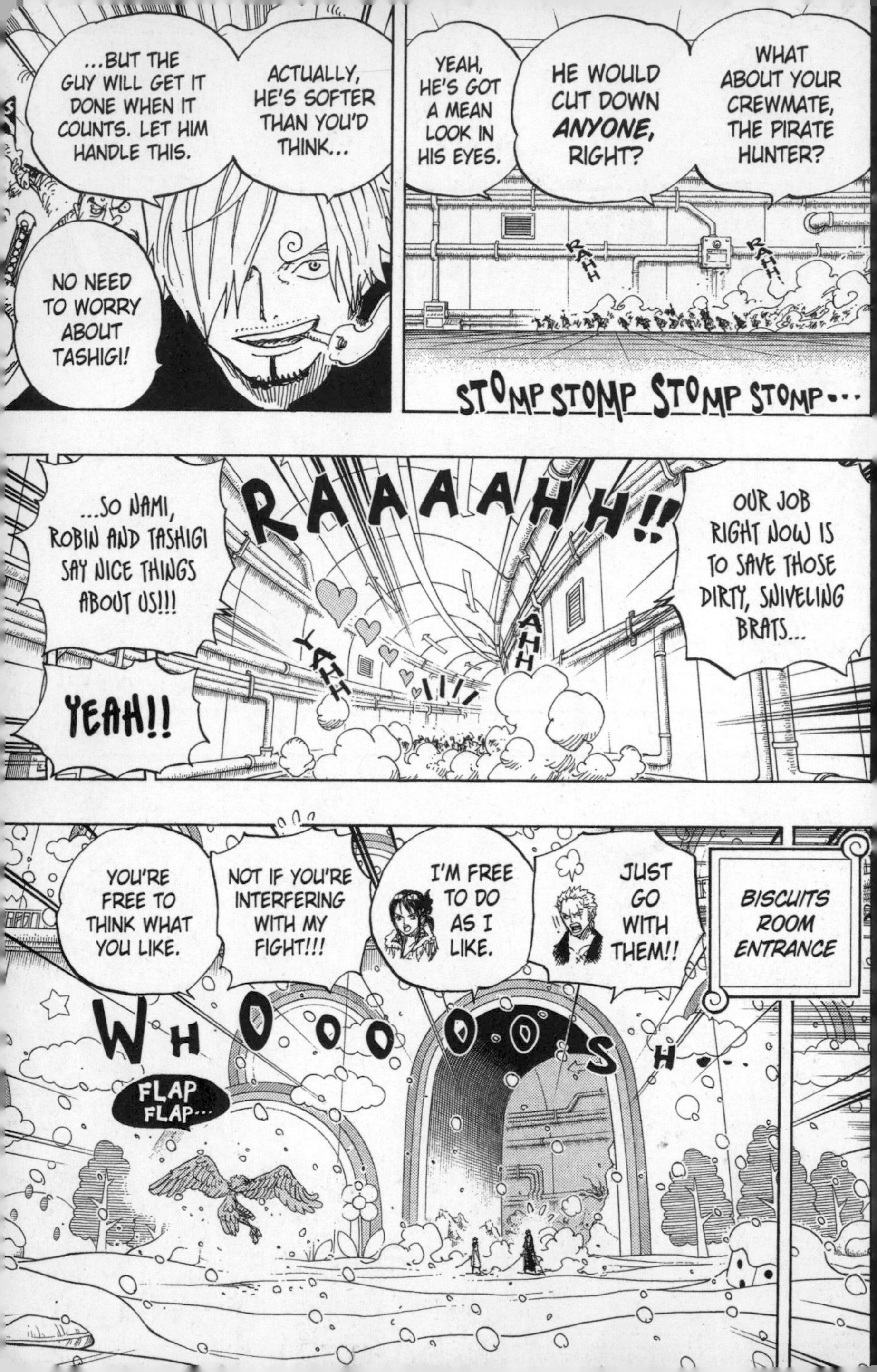
WHAT ABOUT YOUR CREWMATE, THE PIRATE HUNTER?
HE WOULD CUT DOWN ANYONE, RIGHT?
YEAH, HE'S GOT A MEAN LOOK IN HIS EYES.
RAHH
RAHH
STOMP STOMP STOMP STOMP...
ACTUALLY, HE'S SOFTER THAN YOU'D THINK...
...BUT THE GUY WILL GET IT DONE WHEN IT COUNTS. LET HIM HANDLE THIS.
NO NEED TO WORRY ABOUT TASHIGI!
OUR JOB RIGHT NOW IS TO SAVE THOSE DIRTY, SNIVELING BRATS...
RAAAAHH!!
AHH
YAHH
...SO NAMI, ROBIN AND TASHIGI SAY NICE THINGS ABOUT US!!!
YEAH!!
BISCUITS ROOM ENTRANCE
JUST GO WITH THEM!!
I'M FREE TO DO AS I LIKE.
NOT IF YOU'RE INTERFERING WITH MY FIGHT!!!
YOU'RE FREE TO THINK WHAT YOU LIKE.
WHOOOOOSH...
FLAP FLAP...

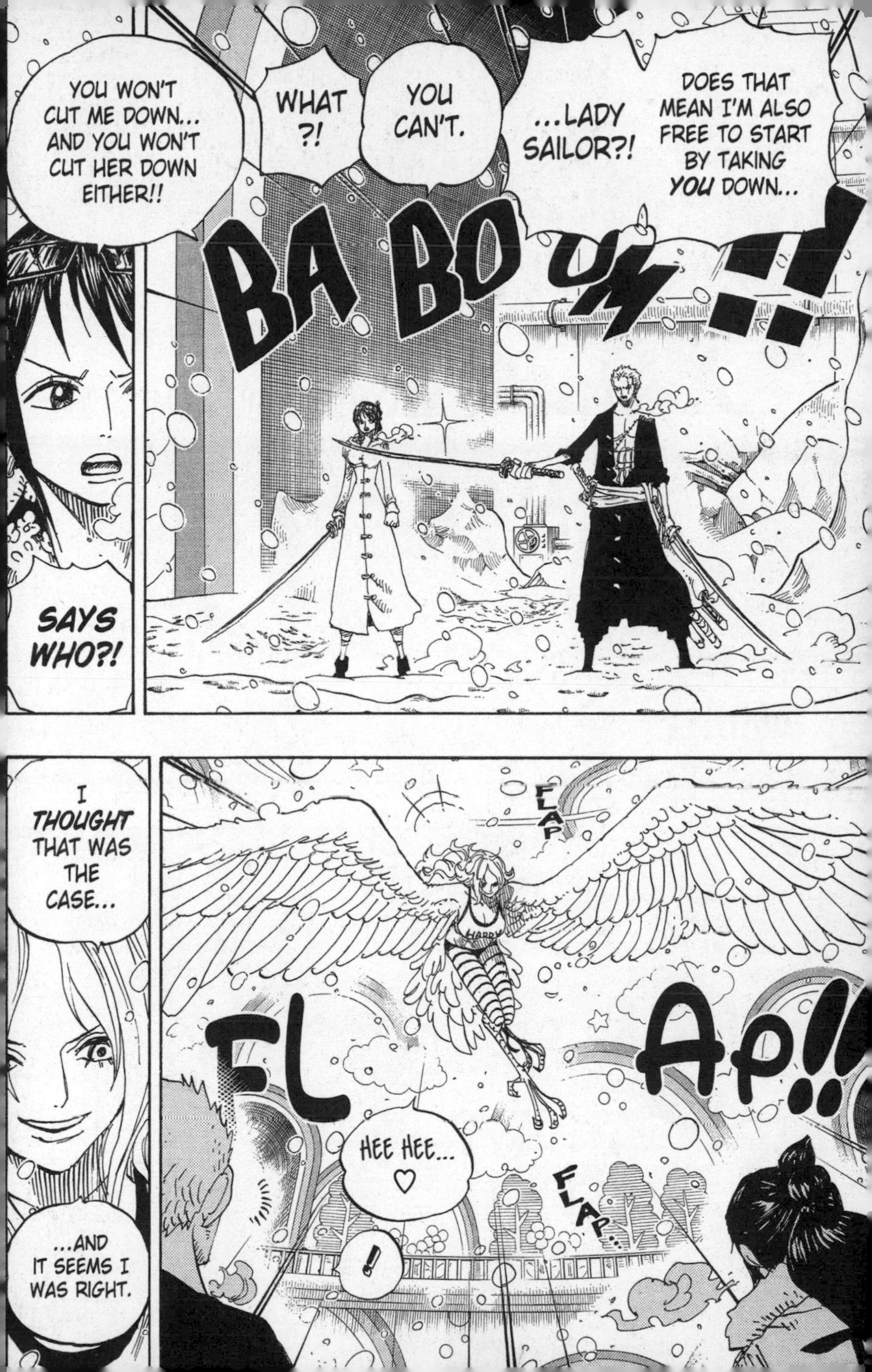
DOES THAT MEAN I'M ALSO FREE TO START BY TAKING YOU DOWN...
...LADY SAILOR?!
YOU CAN'T.
WHAT ?!
YOU WON'T CUT ME DOWN... AND YOU WON'T CUT HER DOWN EITHER!!
BA BOOM!!
SAYS WHO?!
FLAP
FLAP!!
HEE HEE... ♡
FLAP...
!
I THOUGHT THAT WAS THE CASE...
...AND IT SEEMS I WAS RIGHT.

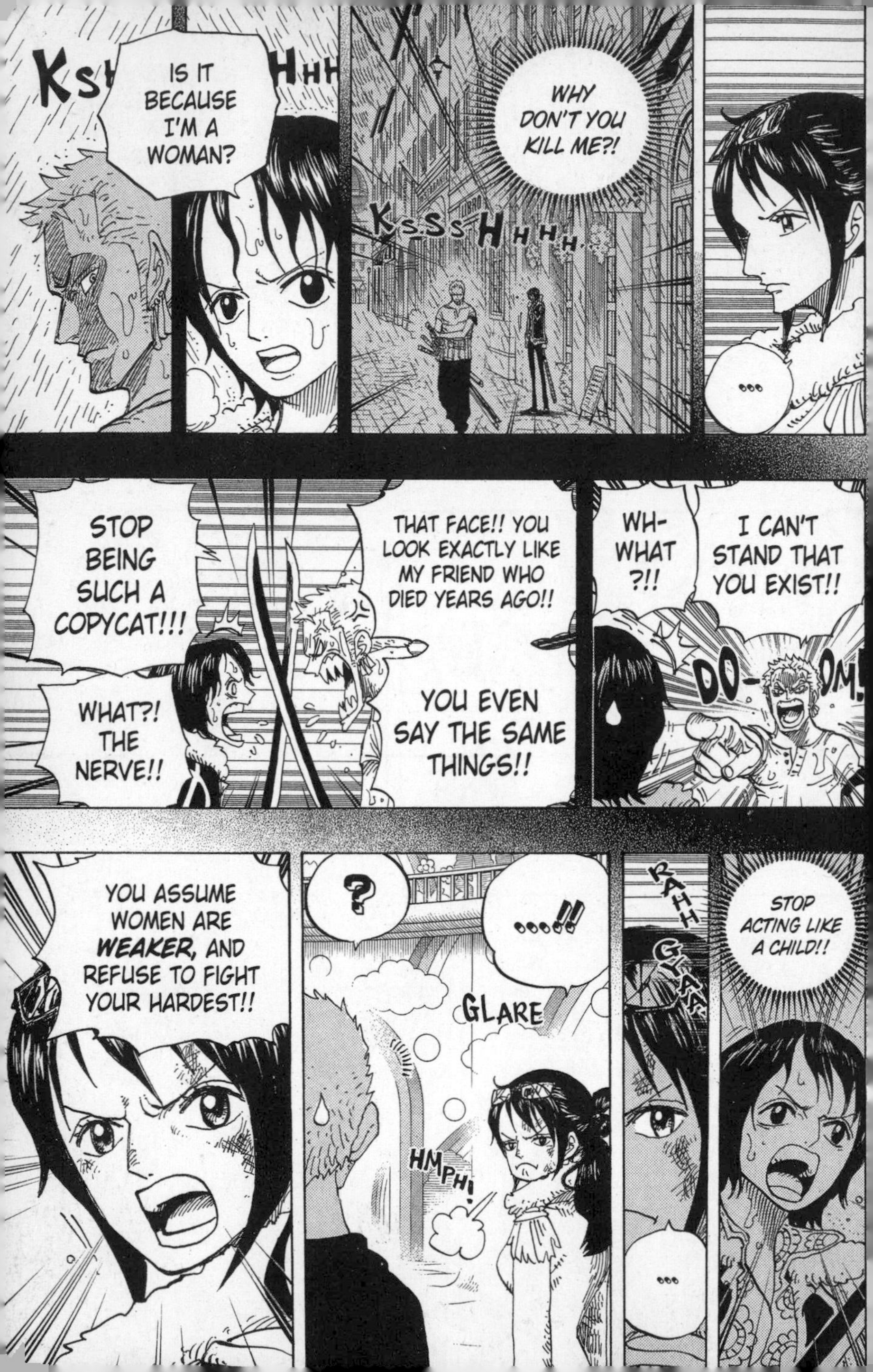
...
WHY DON'T YOU KILL ME?!
KSSSHHHH
IS IT BECAUSE I'M A WOMAN?
KSHHH
I CAN'T STAND THAT YOU EXIST!!
WH-WHAT?!!
DO-OM!
THAT FACE!! YOU LOOK EXACTLY LIKE MY FRIEND WHO DIED YEARS AGO!!
YOU EVEN SAY THE SAME THINGS!!
STOP BEING SUCH A COPYCAT!!!
WHAT?! THE NERVE!!
STOP ACTING LIKE A CHILD!!
RAHH
GYAA
...
...!!
?
GLARE
HMPH!
YOU ASSUME WOMEN ARE *WEAKER,* AND REFUSE TO FIGHT YOUR HARDEST!!

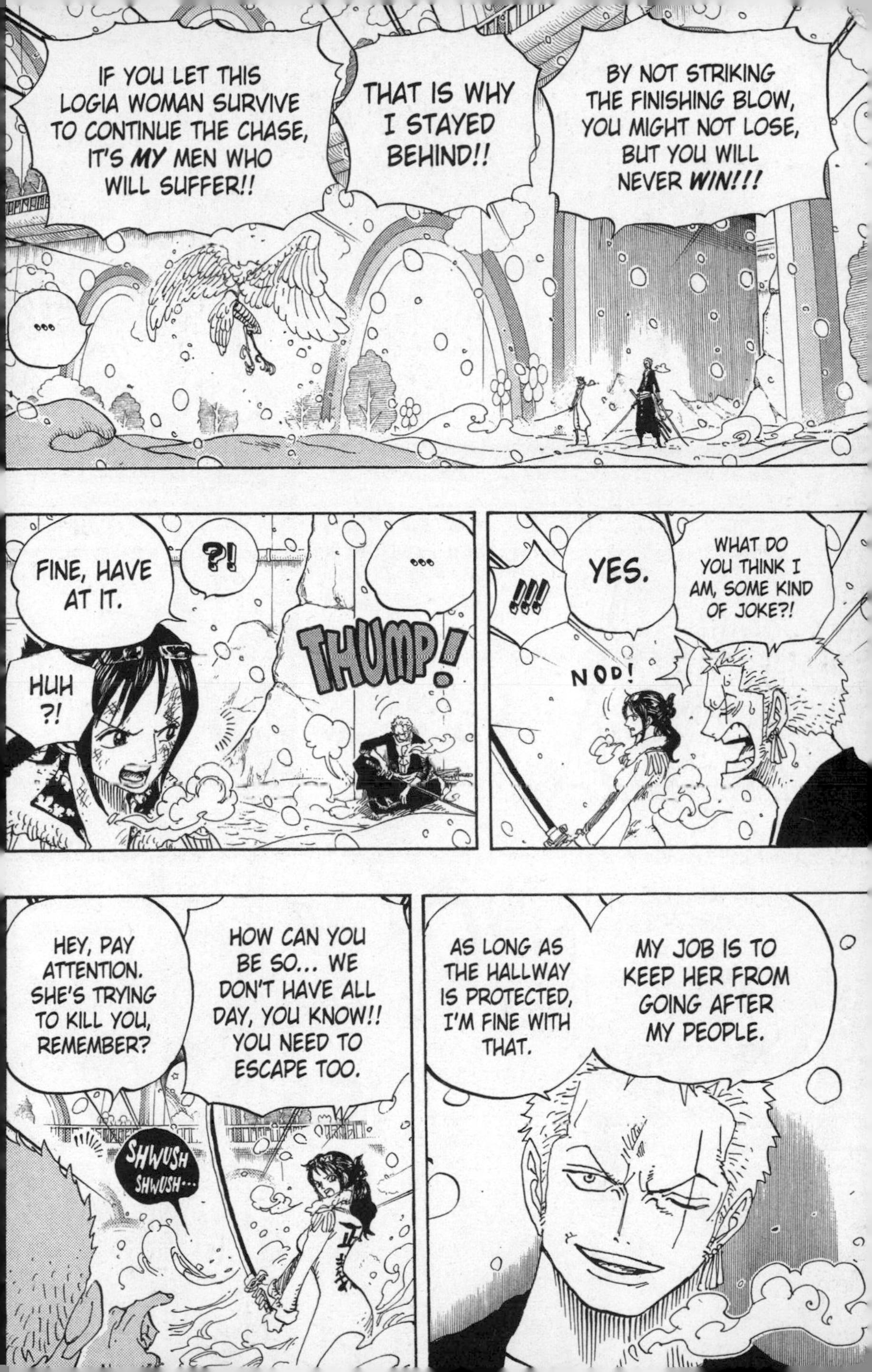
BY NOT STRIKING THE FINISHING BLOW, YOU MIGHT NOT LOSE, BUT YOU WILL NEVER *WIN!!!*
THAT IS WHY I STAYED BEHIND!!
IF YOU LET THIS LOGIA WOMAN SURVIVE TO CONTINUE THE CHASE, IT'S *MY* MEN WHO WILL SUFFER!!
...
WHAT DO YOU THINK I AM, SOME KIND OF JOKE?!
YES.
!!!
NOD!
...
THUMP!
?!
FINE, HAVE AT IT.
HUH ?!
MY JOB IS TO KEEP HER FROM GOING AFTER MY PEOPLE.
AS LONG AS THE HALLWAY IS PROTECTED, I'M FINE WITH THAT.
HOW CAN YOU BE SO... WE DON'T HAVE ALL DAY, YOU KNOW!! YOU NEED TO ESCAPE TOO.
HEY, PAY ATTENTION. SHE'S TRYING TO KILL YOU, REMEMBER?
SHWUSH SHWUSH...

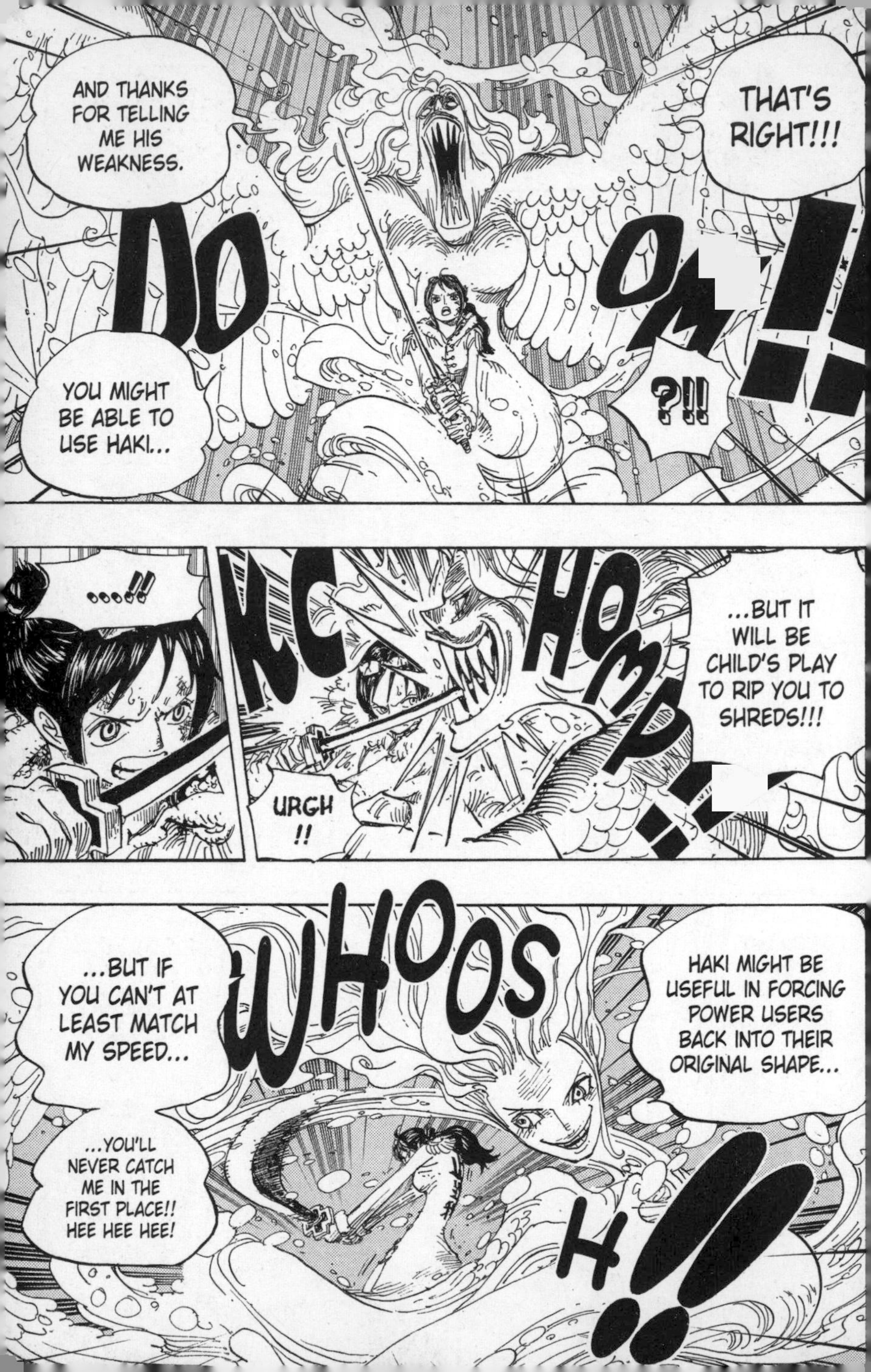
THAT'S RIGHT!!!
DOOM!!
?!!
AND THANKS FOR TELLING ME HIS WEAKNESS.
YOU MIGHT BE ABLE TO USE HAKI...
...BUT IT WILL BE CHILD'S PLAY TO RIP YOU TO SHREDS!!!
KCHOMP!!
URGH !!
...!!
HAKI MIGHT BE USEFUL IN FORCING POWER USERS BACK INTO THEIR ORIGINAL SHAPE...
WHOOSH!!
...BUT IF YOU CAN'T AT LEAST MATCH MY SPEED...
...YOU'LL NEVER CATCH ME IN THE FIRST PLACE!! HEE HEE HEE!

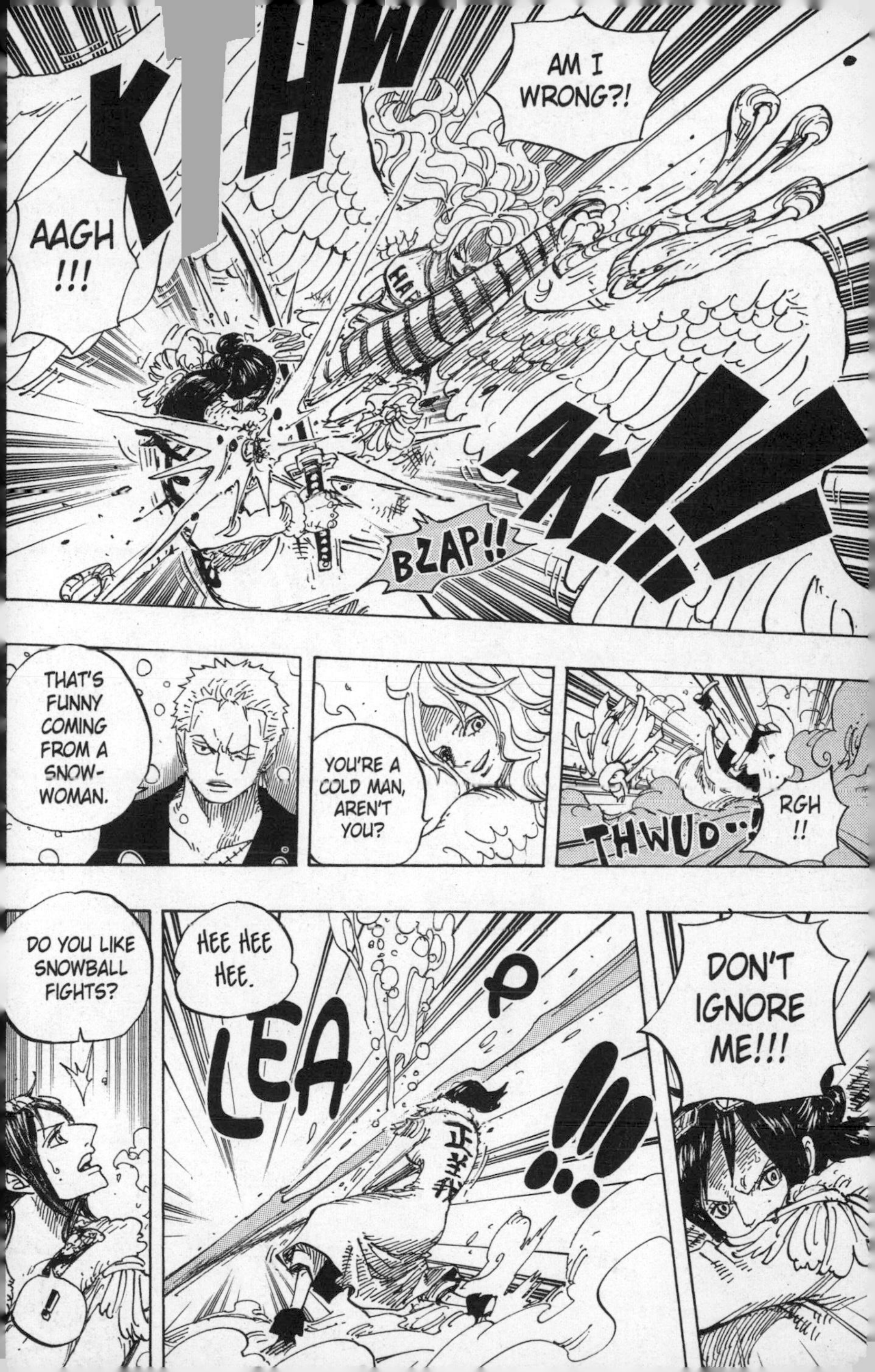
AM I WRONG?!
KHW
AK!!!
AAGH!!!
BZAP!!
RGH!!
THWUD..!
YOU'RE A COLD MAN, AREN'T YOU?
THAT'S FUNNY COMING FROM A SNOW-WOMAN.
DON'T IGNORE ME!!!
HEE HEE HEE.
LEAP!!!
DO YOU LIKE SNOWBALL FIGHTS?
!

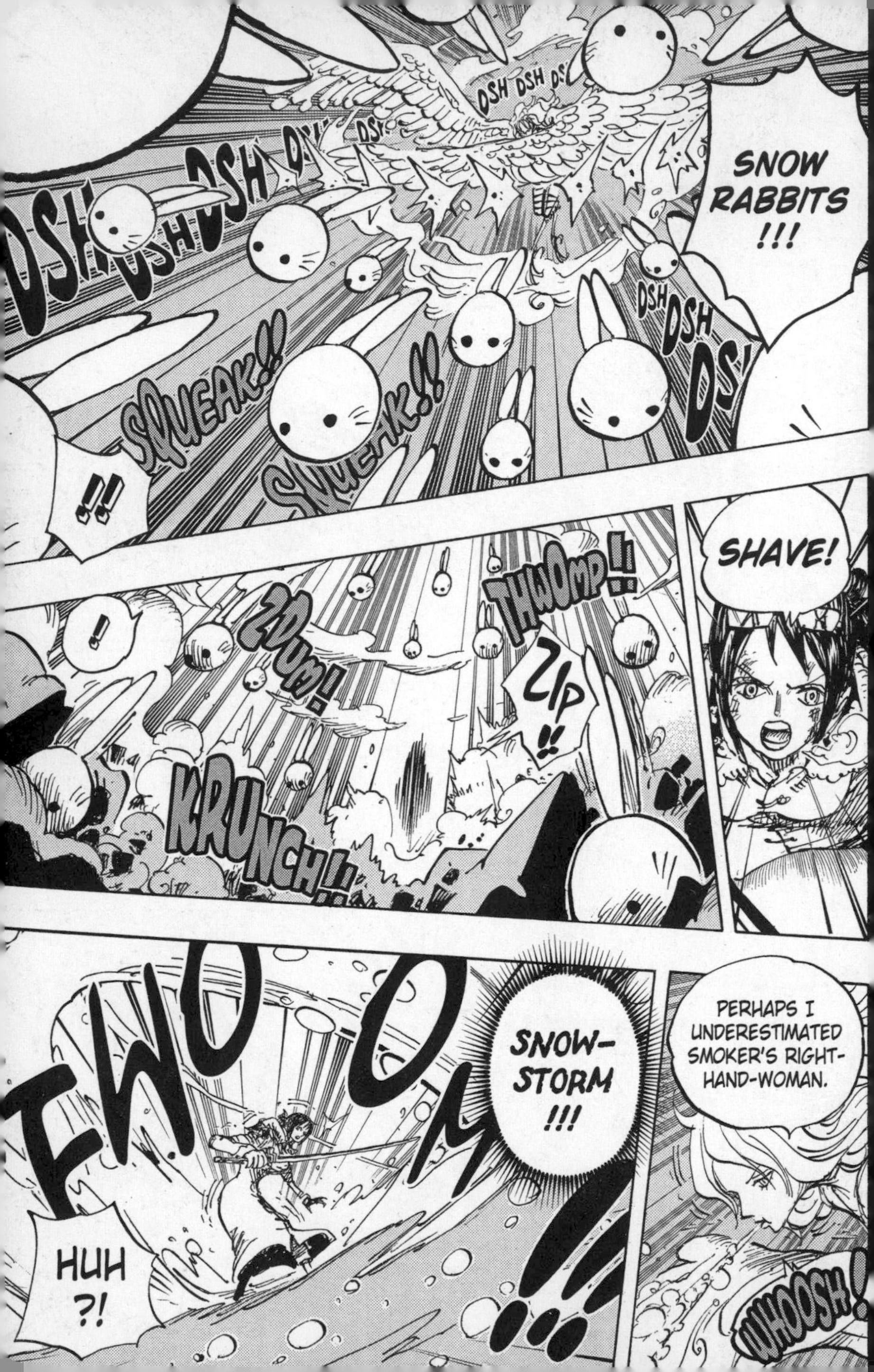
SNOW RABBITS!!!
DSH DSH DS
DSH DSH DSH DSH DS
SQUEAK!!
SQUEAK!!
DSH DSH DS!
!!
SHAVE!
THWOMP!!
ZIP!!
ZOOM!
KRUNCH!!
!
PERHAPS I UNDERESTIMATED SMOKER'S RIGHT-HAND-WOMAN.
WHOOSH!
SNOW-STORM!!!
FWOOM!!
HUH?!

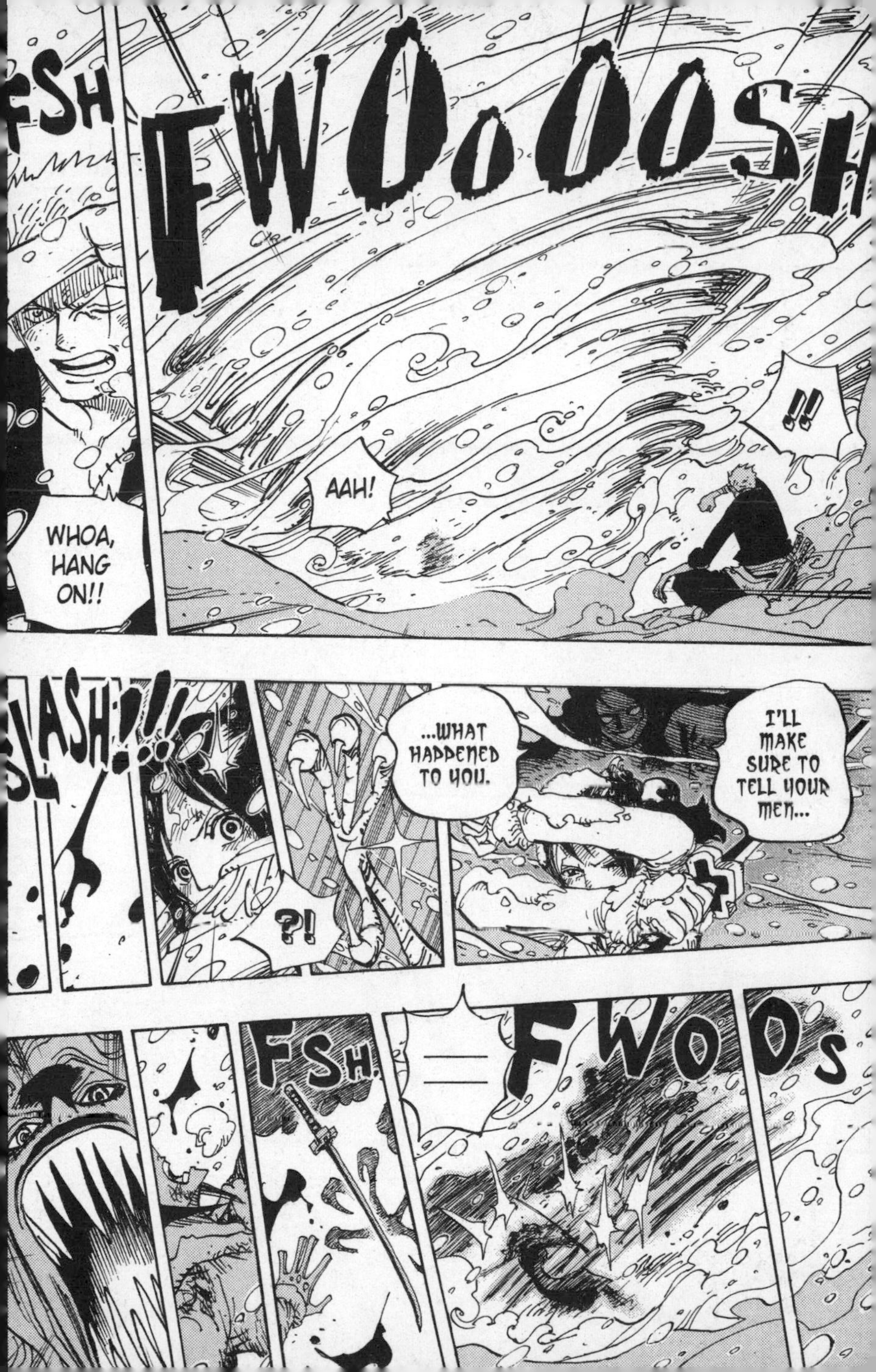
FWOOOOSH
!!
AAH!
FSH
WHOA, HANG ON!!
I'LL MAKE SURE TO TELL YOUR MEN...
...WHAT HAPPENED TO YOU.
?!
SLASH!!!
FWOOS
FSH

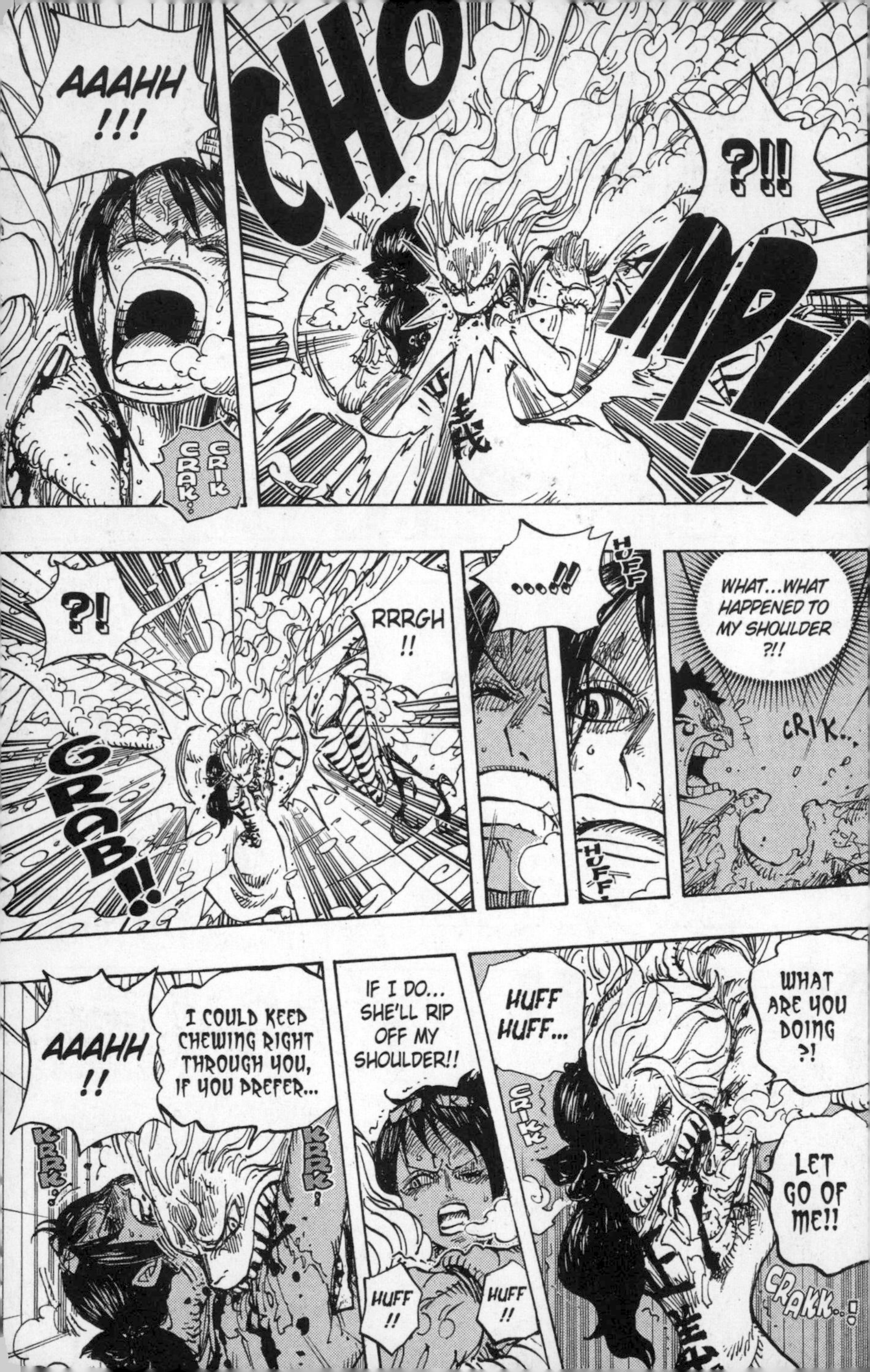
?!!
CHOMP!!
AAAHH !!!
CRIK
CRAK
WHAT...WHAT HAPPENED TO MY SHOULDER ?!!
CRIK...
HUFF
....!!
HUFF
RRRGH !!
?!
GRAB!!
WHAT ARE YOU DOING ?!
LET GO OF ME!!
HUFF HUFF...
CRIK
CRAKK..!
IF I DO... SHE'LL RIP OFF MY SHOULDER!!
HUFF !!
HUFF !!
I COULD KEEP CHEWING RIGHT THROUGH YOU, IF YOU PREFER...
AAAHH !!
KRRK
KRRK

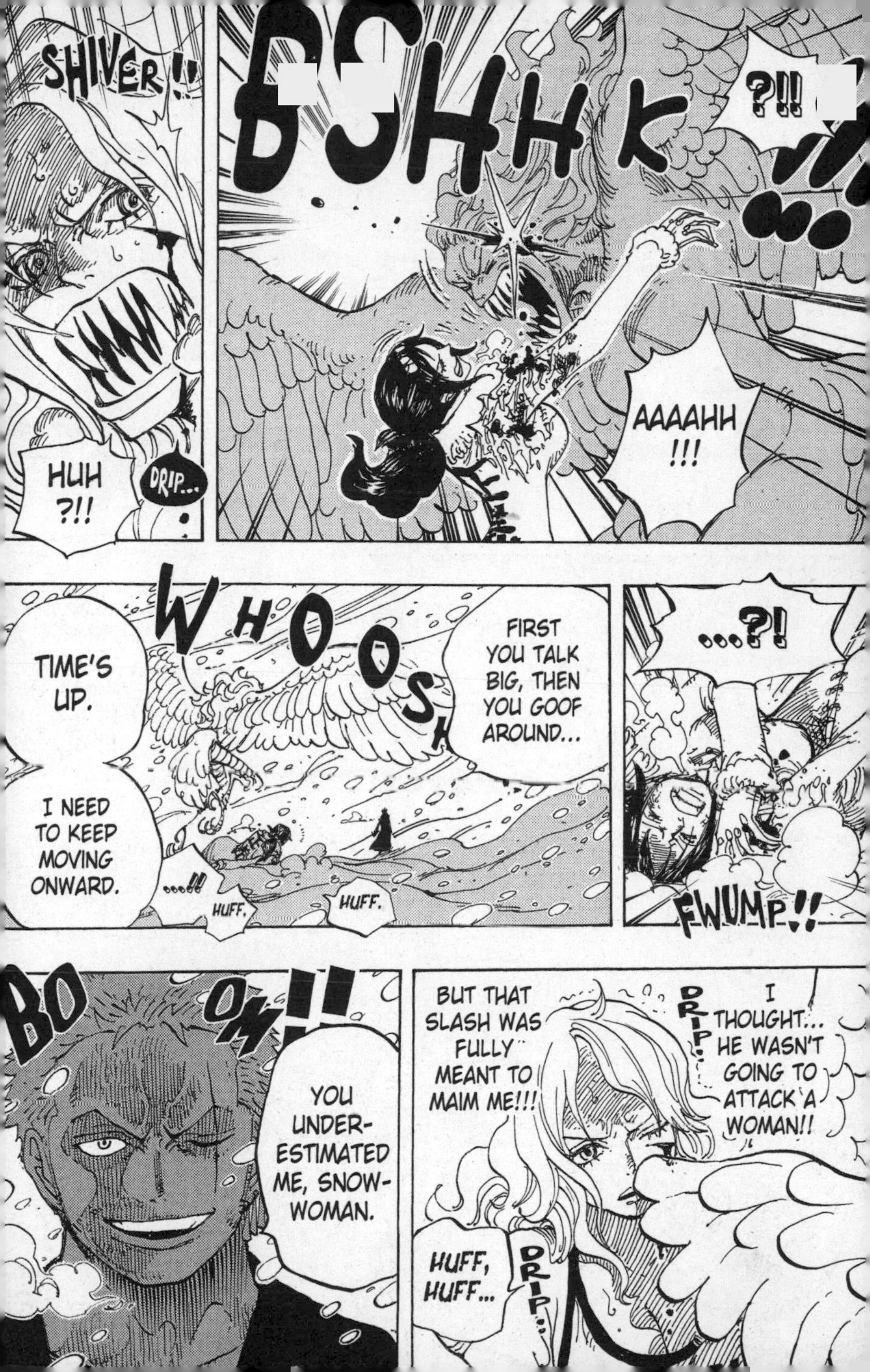
BSHHK
?!!
AAAAHH !!!
SHIVER !!
HUH ?!!
DRIP...
...?!
FWUMP!!
WHOOSH
FIRST YOU TALK BIG, THEN YOU GOOF AROUND...
TIME'S UP.
I NEED TO KEEP MOVING ONWARD.
HUFF.
...!!
HUFF.
I THOUGHT... HE WASN'T GOING TO ATTACK A WOMAN!!
DRIP
BUT THAT SLASH WAS FULLY MEANT TO MAIM ME!!!
DRIP...
HUFF, HUFF...
BOOM!!
YOU UNDER-ESTIMATED ME, SNOW-WOMAN.

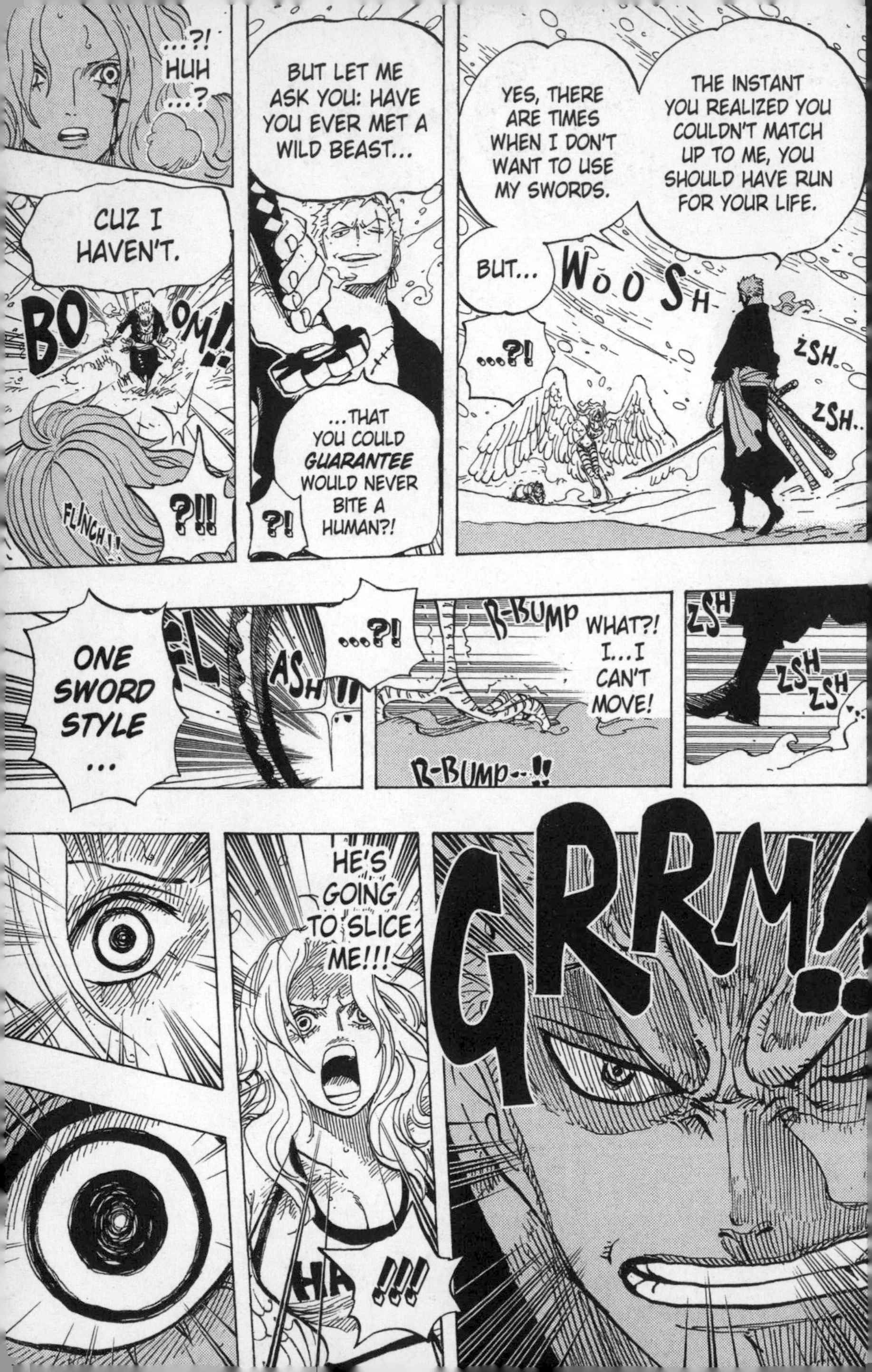

...?! HUH ...?
CUZ I HAVEN'T.
BOOM!!
FLINCH!!
?!!
BUT LET ME ASK YOU: HAVE YOU EVER MET A WILD BEAST...
...THAT YOU COULD GUARANTEE WOULD NEVER BITE A HUMAN?!
?!
YES, THERE ARE TIMES WHEN I DON'T WANT TO USE MY SWORDS.
THE INSTANT YOU REALIZED YOU COULDN'T MATCH UP TO ME, YOU SHOULD HAVE RUN FOR YOUR LIFE.
BUT...
WOOSH
...?!
ZSH...
ZSH...
ONE SWORD STYLE ...
FLASH!!
...?!
R-BUMP
WHAT?! I...I CAN'T MOVE!
R-BUMP...!!
ZSH
ZSH
ZSH
HE'S GOING TO SLICE ME!!!
HA!!!
GRRM!!

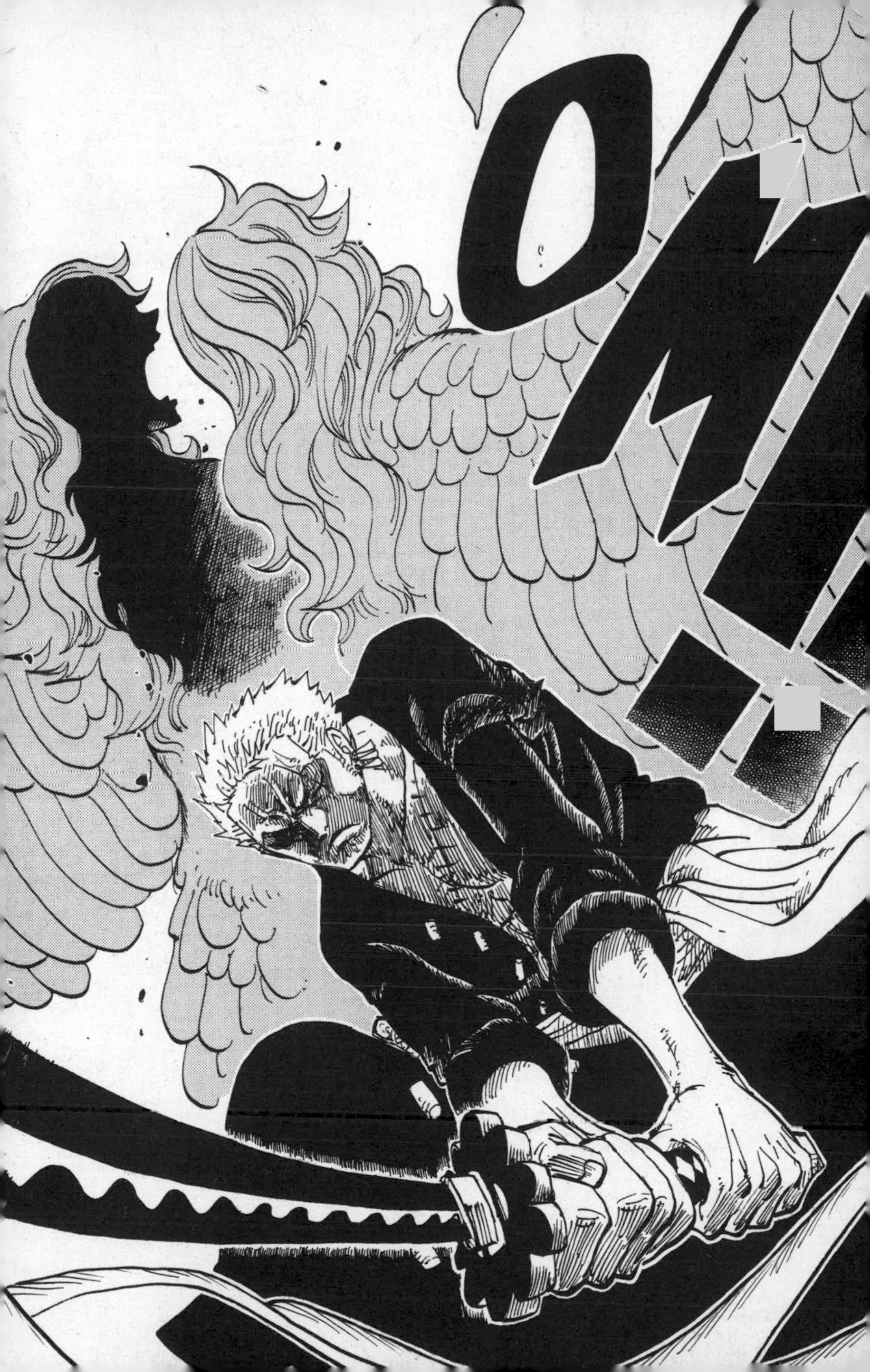

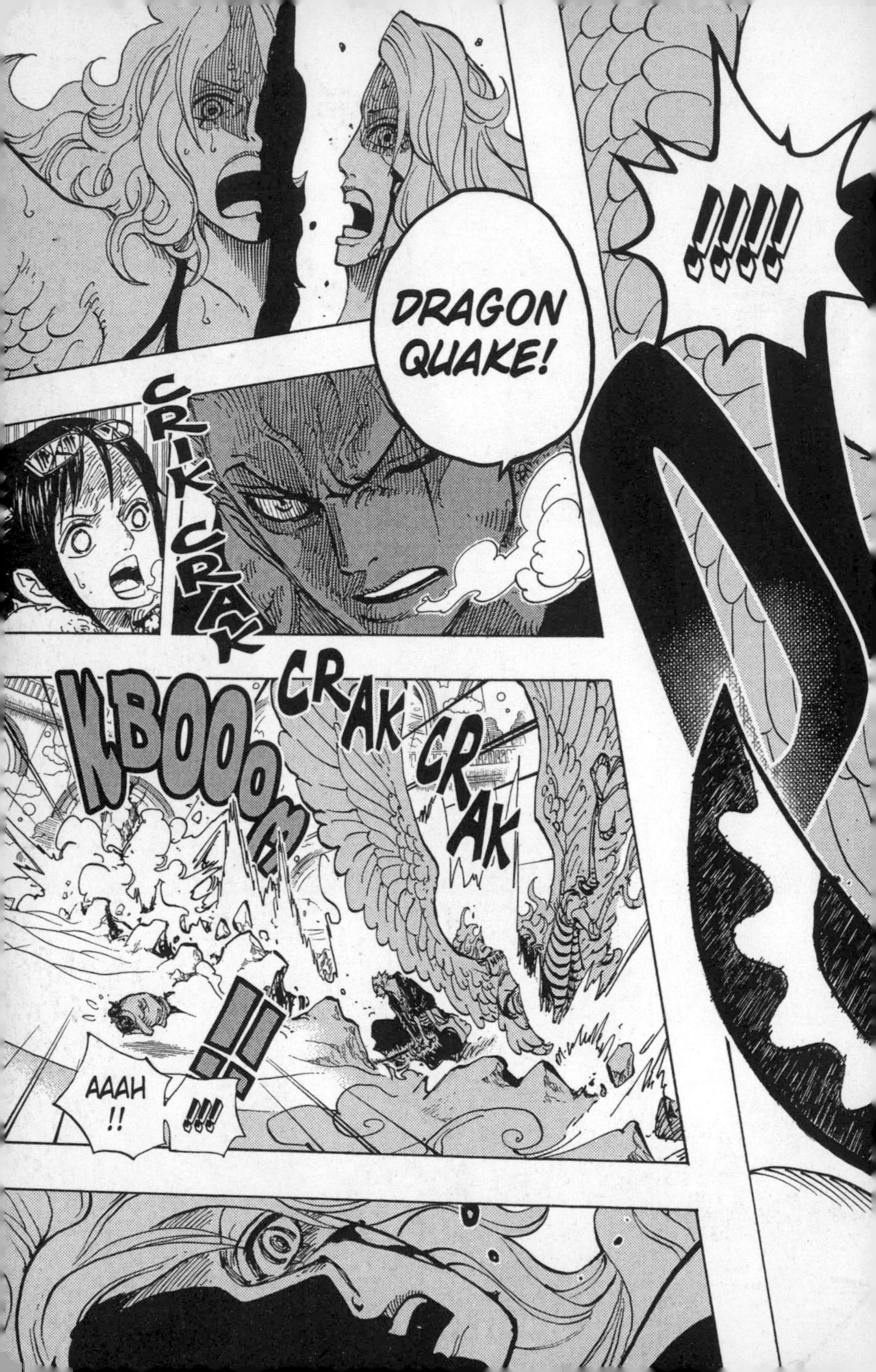
!!!!
DRAGON QUAKE!
CRIK CRACK
CRAK CRAK
KBOOOOM
AAAH !!
!!!

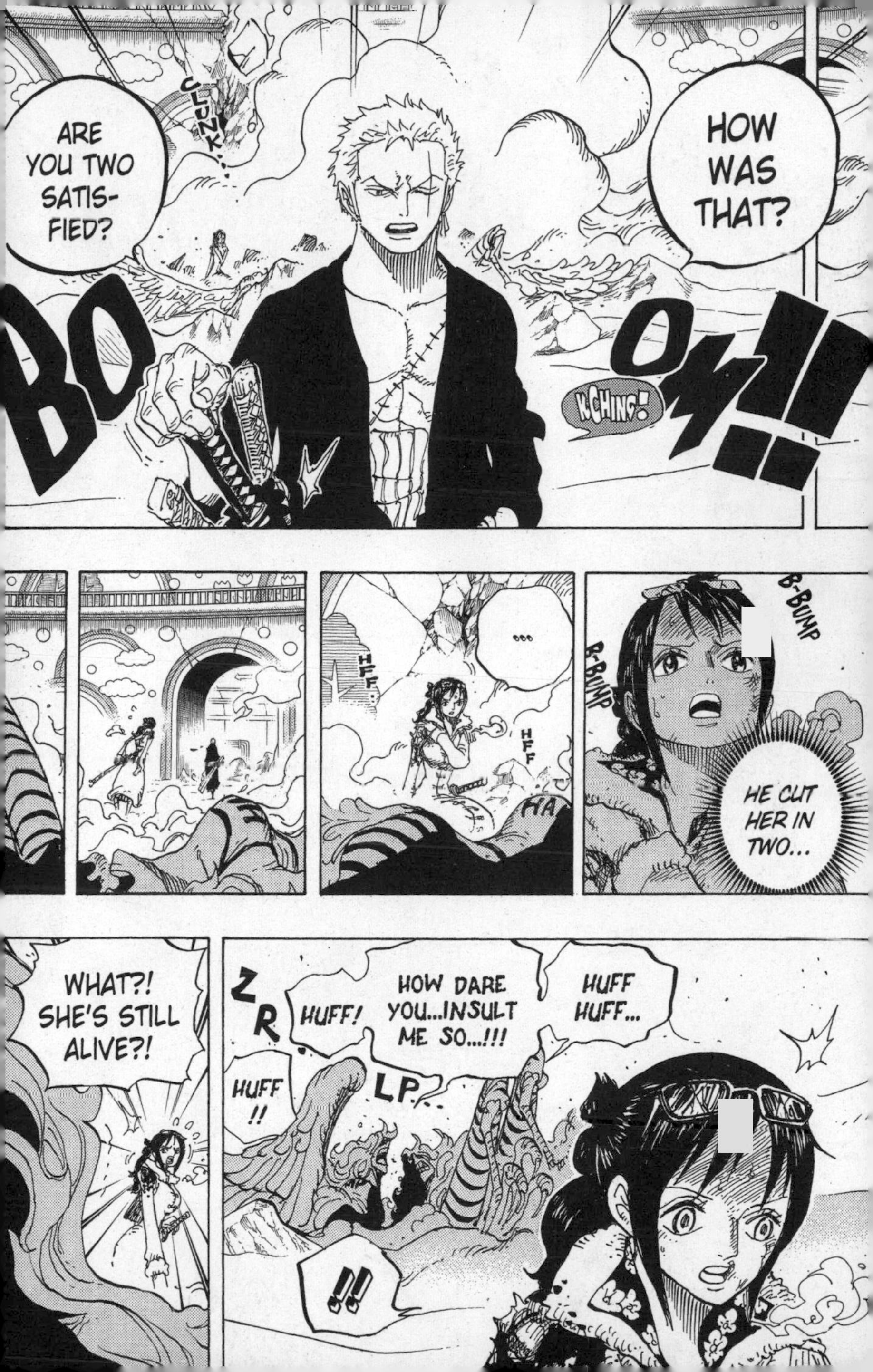
HOW WAS THAT?
CLUNK...
ARE YOU TWO SATIS-FIED?
K'CHING!
BOOM!!
B-BUMP
B-BUMP
HE CUT HER IN TWO...
...
HFF
HFF
HA
HUFF HUFF...
HOW DARE YOU...INSULT ME SO...!!!
HUFF!
HUFF !!
ZRLP...
!!
WHAT?! SHE'S STILL ALIVE?!

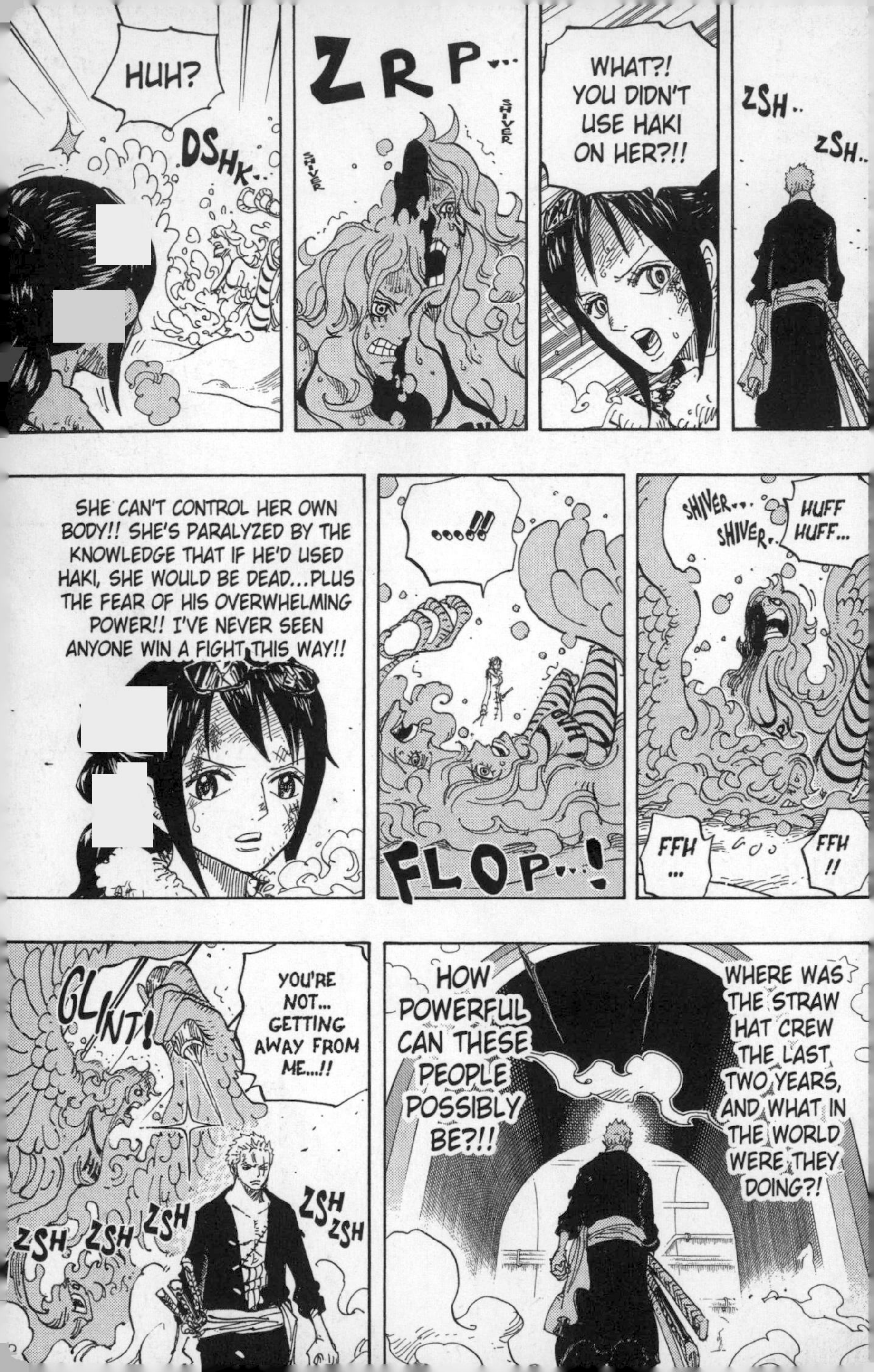
ZSH..
ZSH..
WHAT?! YOU DIDN'T USE HAKI ON HER?!!
ZRP...
SHIVER
SHIVER
HUH?
DSHK..
HUFF HUFF...
SHIVER... SHIVER..
FFH!!
FFH...
....!!
FLOP..!
SHE CAN'T CONTROL HER OWN BODY!! SHE'S PARALYZED BY THE KNOWLEDGE THAT IF HE'D USED HAKI, SHE WOULD BE DEAD...PLUS THE FEAR OF HIS OVERWHELMING POWER!! I'VE NEVER SEEN ANYONE WIN A FIGHT THIS WAY!!
WHERE WAS THE STRAW HAT CREW THE LAST TWO YEARS, AND WHAT IN THE WORLD WERE THEY DOING?!
HOW POWERFUL CAN THESE PEOPLE POSSIBLY BE?!!
YOU'RE NOT... GETTING AWAY FROM ME...!!
GLINT!
ZSH
ZSH
ZSH
ZSH
ZSH
ZSH

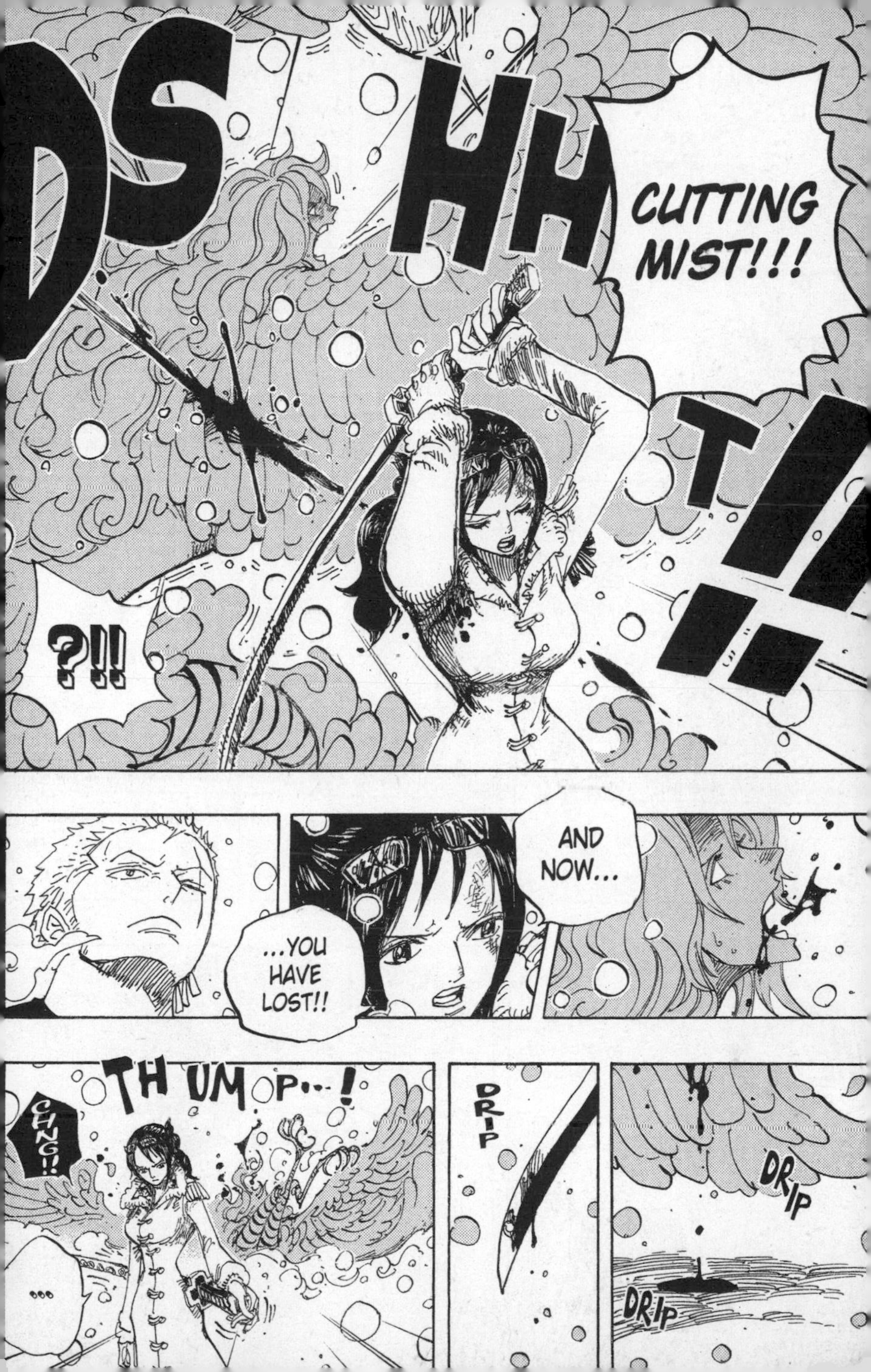
CUTTING MIST!!!
DSHHT!!
?!!
AND NOW...
...YOU HAVE LOST!!
DRIP
DRIP
DRIP
THUMP..!
CHNG!!
...

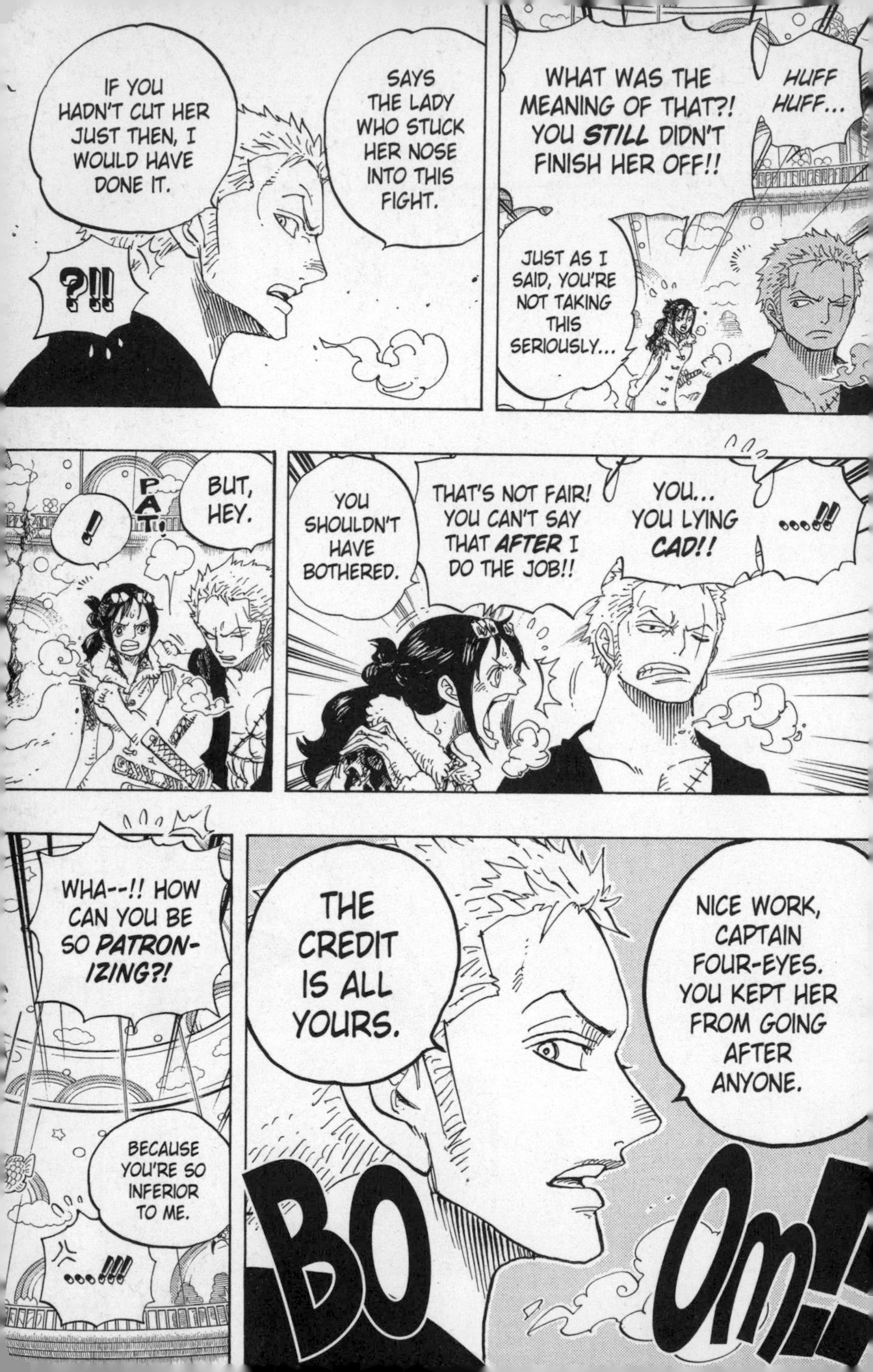
HUFF HUFF...
WHAT WAS THE MEANING OF THAT?! YOU STILL DIDN'T FINISH HER OFF!!
JUST AS I SAID, YOU'RE NOT TAKING THIS SERIOUSLY...
SAYS THE LADY WHO STUCK HER NOSE INTO THIS FIGHT.
IF YOU HADN'T CUT HER JUST THEN, I WOULD HAVE DONE IT.
?!!
...!!
YOU... YOU LYING CAD!!
THAT'S NOT FAIR! YOU CAN'T SAY THAT AFTER I DO THE JOB!!
YOU SHOULDN'T HAVE BOTHERED.
BUT, HEY.
PAT
!
NICE WORK, CAPTAIN FOUR-EYES. YOU KEPT HER FROM GOING AFTER ANYONE.
THE CREDIT IS ALL YOURS.
BOOM!!
WHA--!! HOW CAN YOU BE SO PATRON-IZING?!
BECAUSE YOU'RE SO INFERIOR TO ME.
...!!!

Chapter 688:
MOCHA

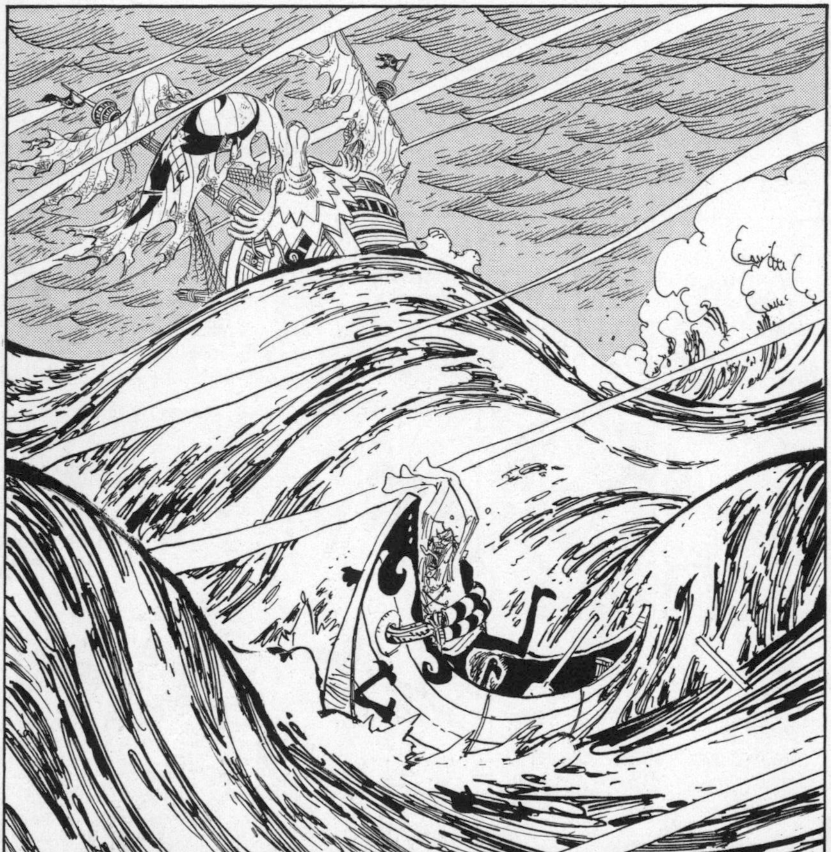

CARIBOU'S NEW WORLD KEE HEE HEE, VOL. 13:
"DIVINE RETRIBUTION"

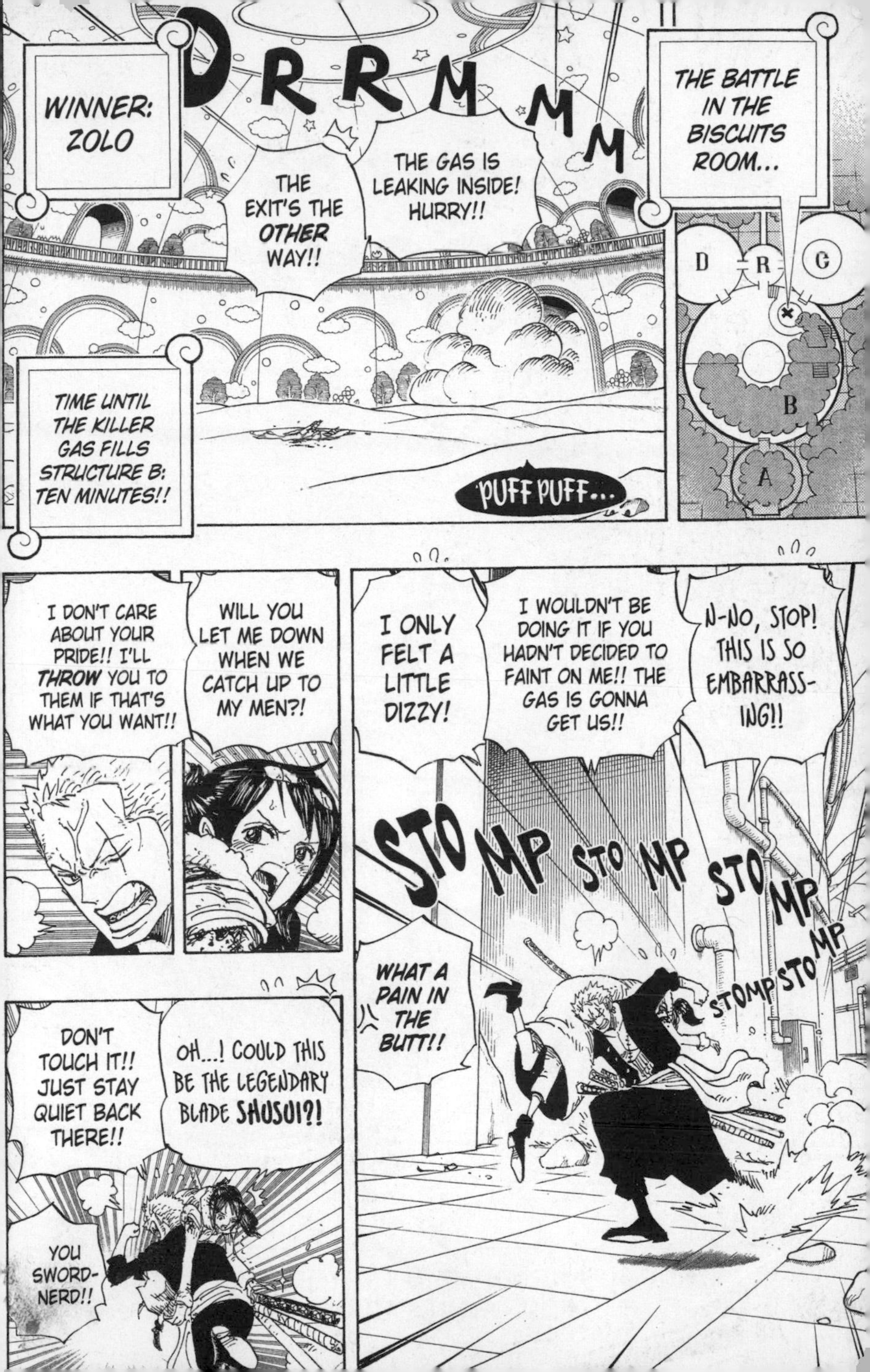
THE BATTLE IN THE BISCUITS ROOM...
D
R
C
B
A
WINNER: ZOLO
DRRMMM
THE GAS IS LEAKING INSIDE! HURRY!!
THE EXIT'S THE *OTHER* WAY!!
TIME UNTIL THE KILLER GAS FILLS STRUCTURE B: TEN MINUTES!!
PUFF PUFF...
N-NO, STOP! THIS IS SO EMBARRASS-ING!!
I WOULDN'T BE DOING IT IF YOU HADN'T DECIDED TO FAINT ON ME!! THE GAS IS GONNA GET US!!
I ONLY FELT A LITTLE DIZZY!
STOMP STOMP STOMP
STOMP STOMP
WHAT A PAIN IN THE BUTT!!
WILL YOU LET ME DOWN WHEN WE CATCH UP TO MY MEN?!
I DON'T CARE ABOUT YOUR PRIDE!! I'LL *THROW* YOU TO THEM IF THAT'S WHAT YOU WANT!!
OH...! COULD THIS BE THE LEGENDARY BLADE **SHUSUI**?!
DON'T TOUCH IT!! JUST STAY QUIET BACK THERE!!
YOU SWORD-NERD!!

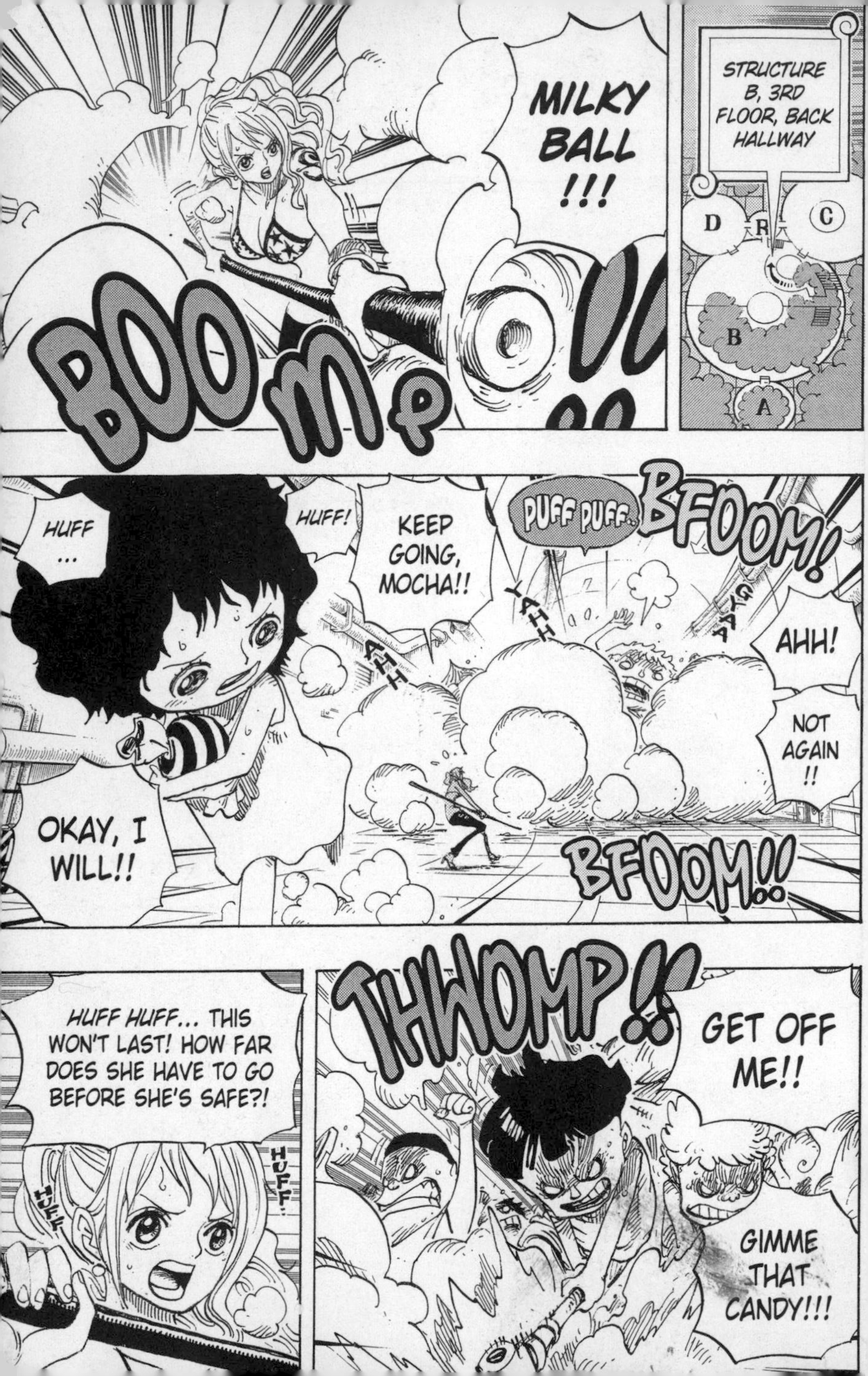
STRUCTURE B, 3RD FLOOR, BACK HALLWAY
D
R
C
B
A
MILKY BALL !!!
BOOMP!!
BFOOM!
PUFF PUFF..
AHH!
NOT AGAIN !!
KEEP GOING, MOCHA!!
HUFF!
HUFF ...
OKAY, I WILL!!
BFOOM!!
THWOMP!!
GET OFF ME!!
GIMME THAT CANDY!!!
HUFF HUFF... THIS WON'T LAST! HOW FAR DOES SHE HAVE TO GO BEFORE SHE'S SAFE?!
HUFF
HUFF

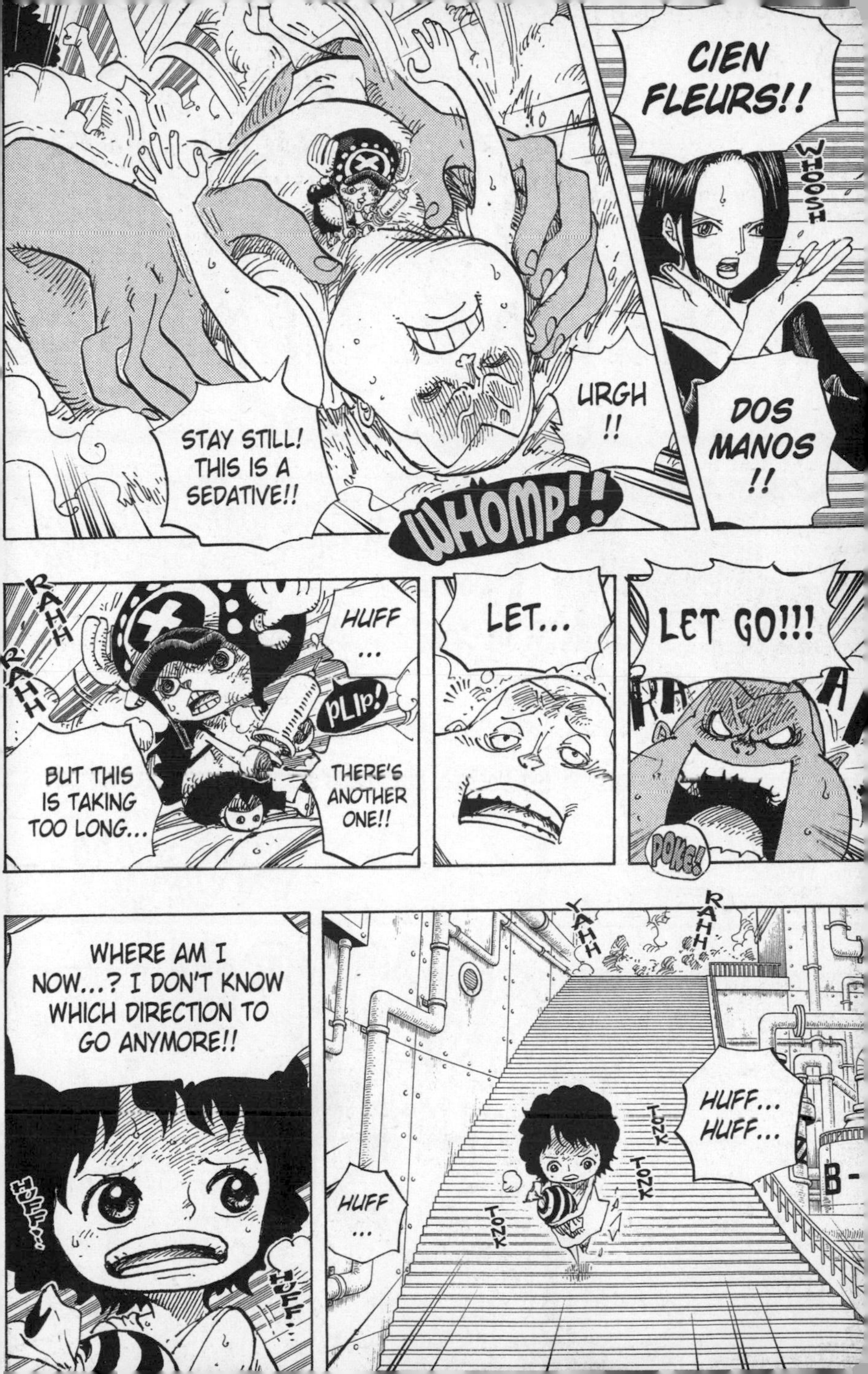
CIEN FLEURS!!
WHOOSH
DOS MANOS !!
URGH !!
STAY STILL! THIS IS A SEDATIVE!!
WHOMP!!
LET GO!!!
POKE!
LET...
HUFF ...
pLIp!
THERE'S ANOTHER ONE!!
BUT THIS IS TAKING TOO LONG...
RAHH
RAHH
RAHH
YAHH
HUFF... HUFF...
TONK
TONK
TONK
HUFF ...
B-
WHERE AM I NOW...? I DON'T KNOW WHICH DIRECTION TO GO ANYMORE!!
HUFF...
HUFF...

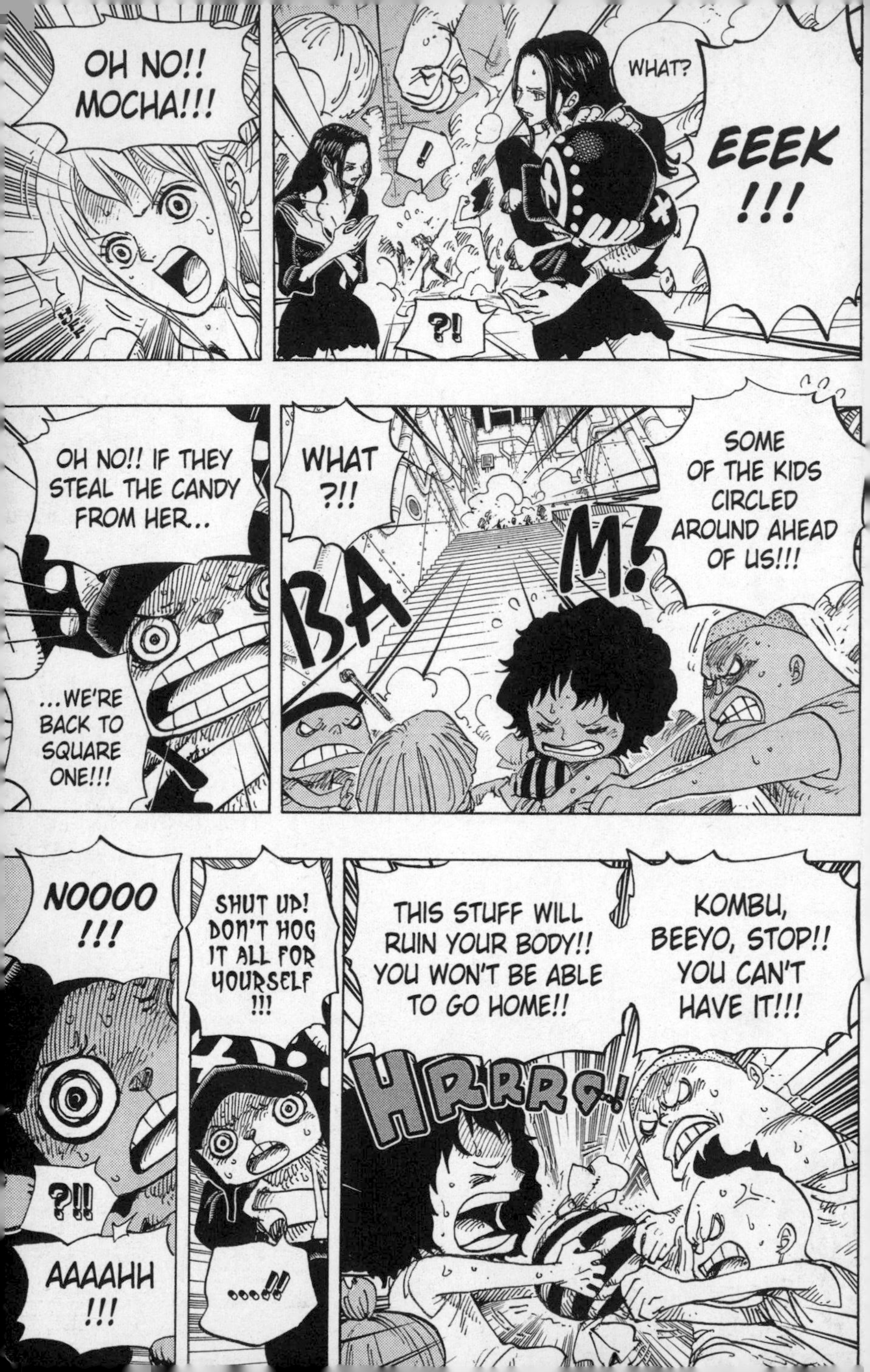
WHAT?
EEEK!!!
!
?!
OH NO!! MOCHA!!!
SOME OF THE KIDS CIRCLED AROUND AHEAD OF US!!!
WHAT?!!
BAM!
OH NO!! IF THEY STEAL THE CANDY FROM HER...
...WE'RE BACK TO SQUARE ONE!!!
KOMBU, BEEYO, STOP!! YOU CAN'T HAVE IT!!!
THIS STUFF WILL RUIN YOUR BODY!! YOU WON'T BE ABLE TO GO HOME!!
HRRRG..!
SHUT UP! DON'T HOG IT ALL FOR YOURSELF!!!
....!!
NOOOO!!!
?!!
AAAAHH!!!

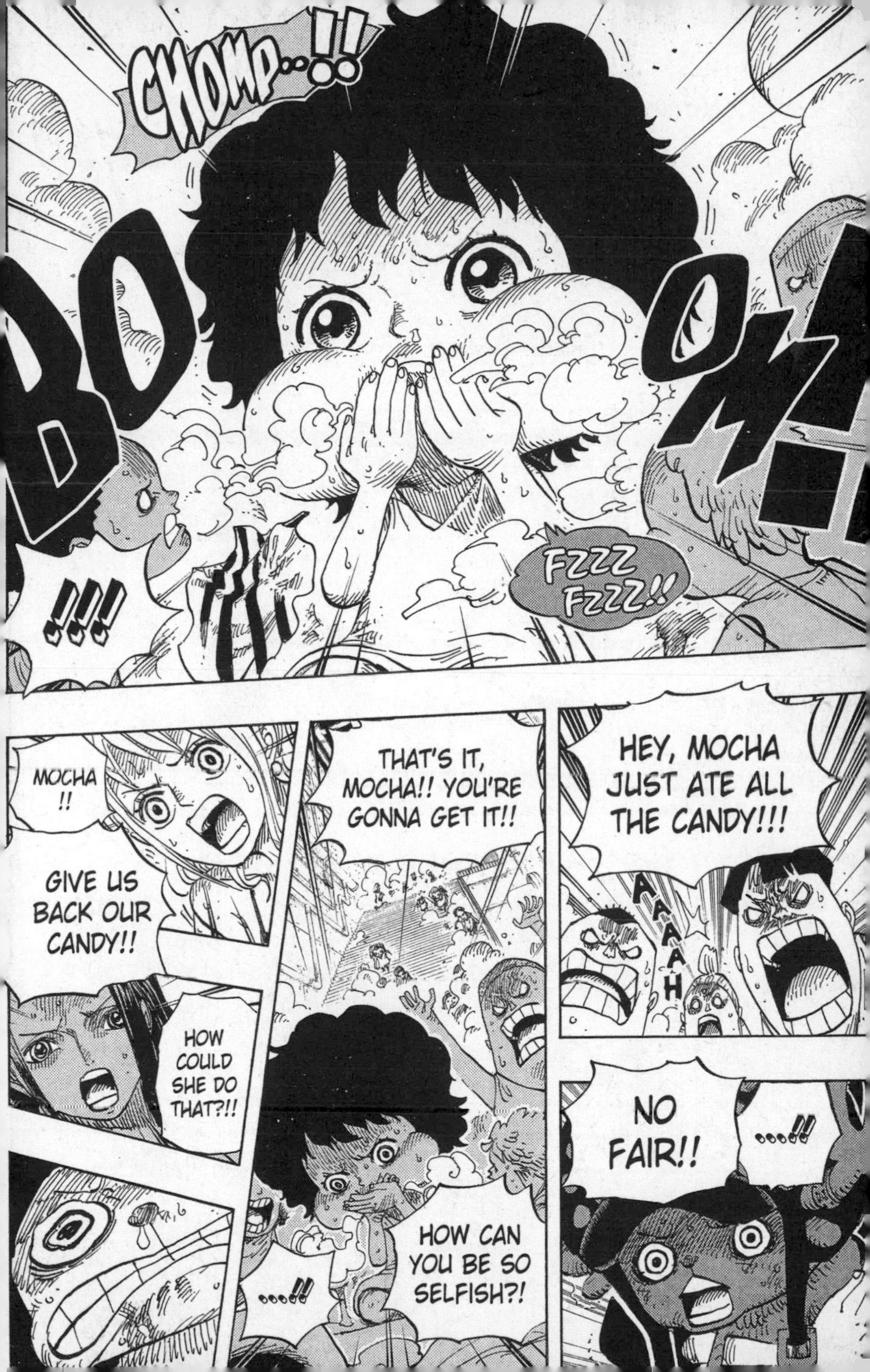
CHOMP..!!
BOOM!!
!!!
FZZZ FZZZ!!
HEY, MOCHA JUST ATE ALL THE CANDY!!!
AAAAH
THAT'S IT, MOCHA!! YOU'RE GONNA GET IT!!
MOCHA !!
GIVE US BACK OUR CANDY!!
HOW COULD SHE DO THAT?!!
NO FAIR!!
...!!
HOW CAN YOU BE SO SELFISH?!
...!!

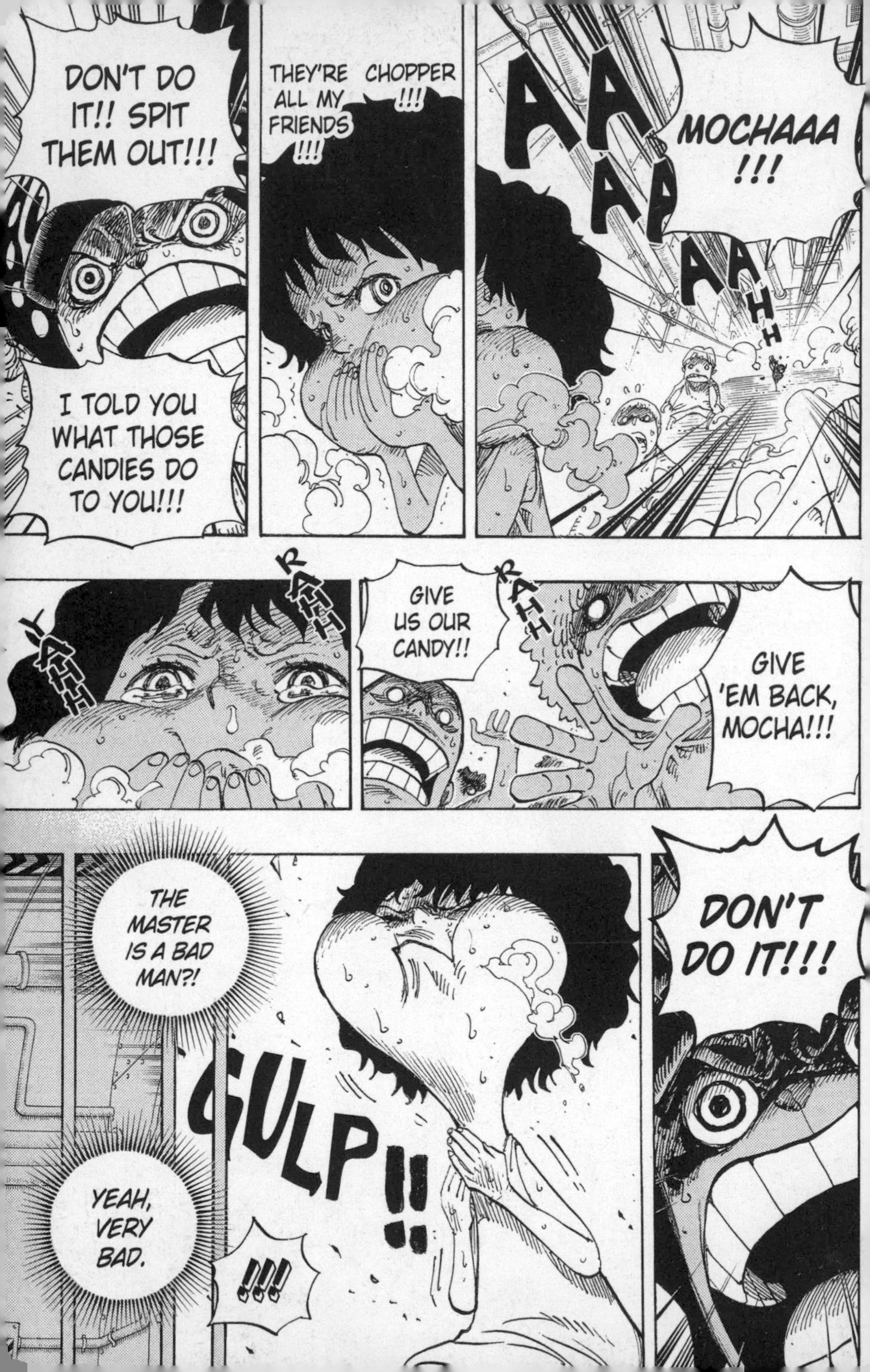
MOCHAAA !!!
AAAAAAHH
CHOPPER !!!
THEY'RE ALL MY FRIENDS !!!
DON'T DO IT!! SPIT THEM OUT!!!
I TOLD YOU WHAT THOSE CANDIES DO TO YOU!!!
GIVE 'EM BACK, MOCHA!!!
RAHH
GIVE US OUR CANDY!!
RAHH
YAHH
DON'T DO IT!!!
GULP!!
!!!
THE MASTER IS A BAD MAN?!
YEAH, VERY BAD.

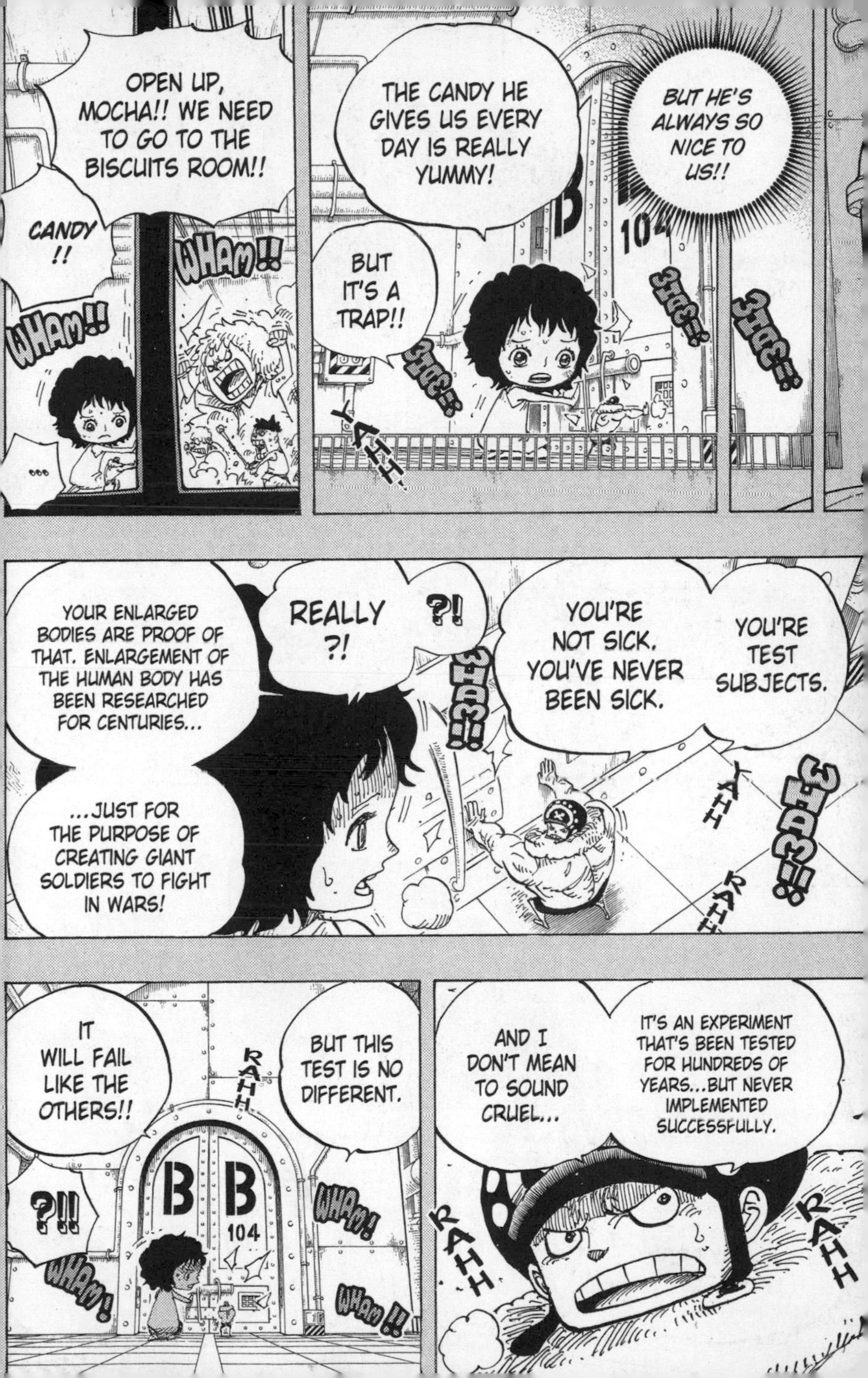
BUT HE'S ALWAYS SO NICE TO US!!
THE CANDY HE GIVES US EVERY DAY IS REALLY YUMMY!
BUT IT'S A TRAP!!
104
OPEN UP, MOCHA!! WE NEED TO GO TO THE BISCUITS ROOM!!
CANDY!!
WHAM!!
WHAM!!
...
YOU'RE TEST SUBJECTS.
YOU'RE NOT SICK. YOU'VE NEVER BEEN SICK.
RAHH
RAHH
REALLY?!
?!
YOUR ENLARGED BODIES ARE PROOF OF THAT. ENLARGEMENT OF THE HUMAN BODY HAS BEEN RESEARCHED FOR CENTURIES...
...JUST FOR THE PURPOSE OF CREATING GIANT SOLDIERS TO FIGHT IN WARS!
IT'S AN EXPERIMENT THAT'S BEEN TESTED FOR HUNDREDS OF YEARS...BUT NEVER IMPLEMENTED SUCCESSFULLY.
AND I DON'T MEAN TO SOUND CRUEL...
RAHH
RAHH
BUT THIS TEST IS NO DIFFERENT.
IT WILL FAIL LIKE THE OTHERS!!
RAHH
WHAM!
WHAM!!
?!!
B B
104
WHAM!

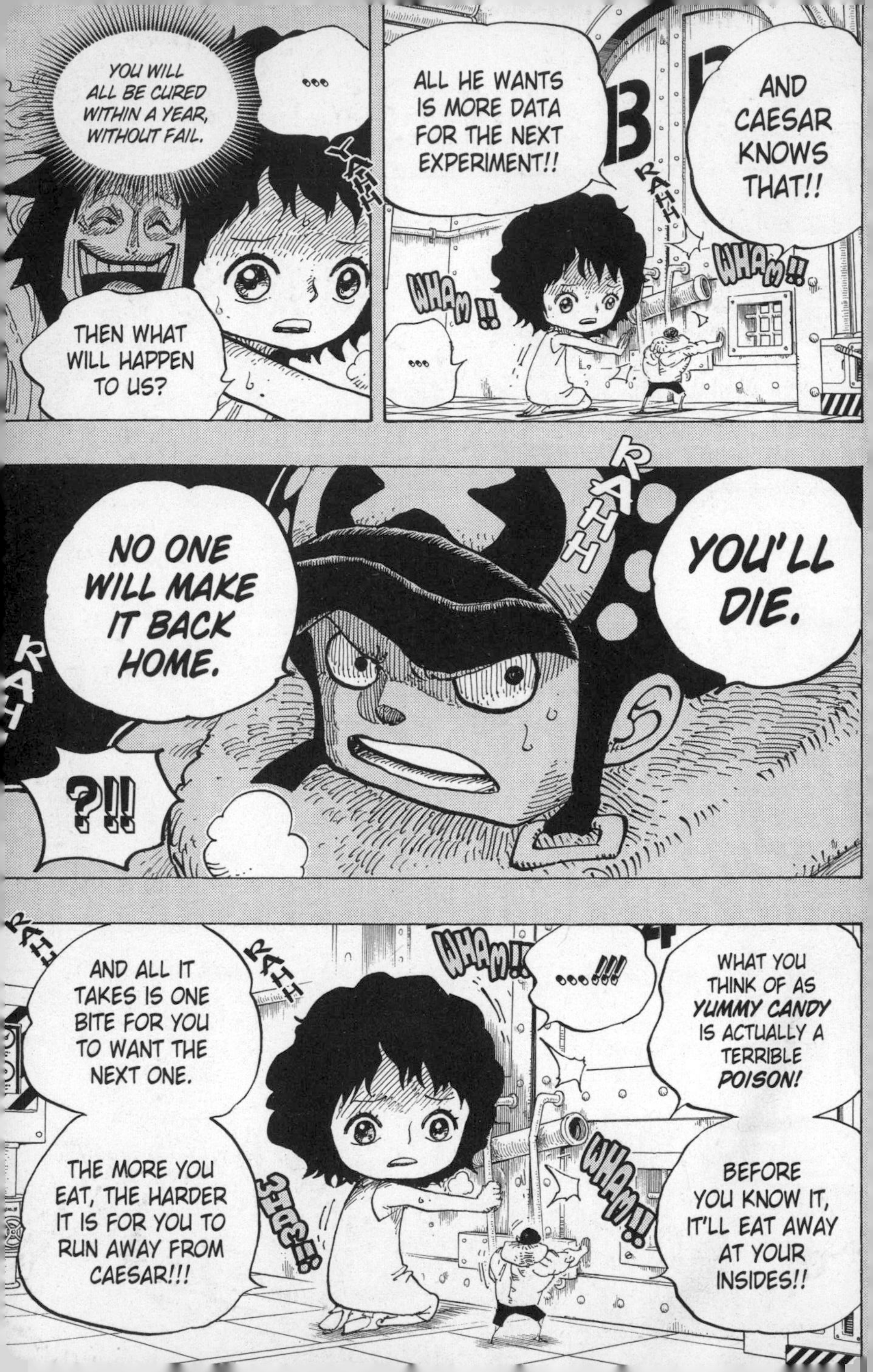
AND CAESAR KNOWS THAT!!
ALL HE WANTS IS MORE DATA FOR THE NEXT EXPERIMENT!!
RAHH
WHAM!!
WHAM!!
...
...
YOU WILL ALL BE CURED WITHIN A YEAR, WITHOUT FAIL.
THEN WHAT WILL HAPPEN TO US?
RAHH
YOU'LL DIE.
NO ONE WILL MAKE IT BACK HOME.
RAH
?!!
WHAT YOU THINK OF AS YUMMY CANDY IS ACTUALLY A TERRIBLE POISON!
...!!!
WHAM!!
RAHH
AND ALL IT TAKES IS ONE BITE FOR YOU TO WANT THE NEXT ONE.
BEFORE YOU KNOW IT, IT'LL EAT AWAY AT YOUR INSIDES!!
WHAM!!
THE MORE YOU EAT, THE HARDER IT IS FOR YOU TO RUN AWAY FROM CAESAR!!!

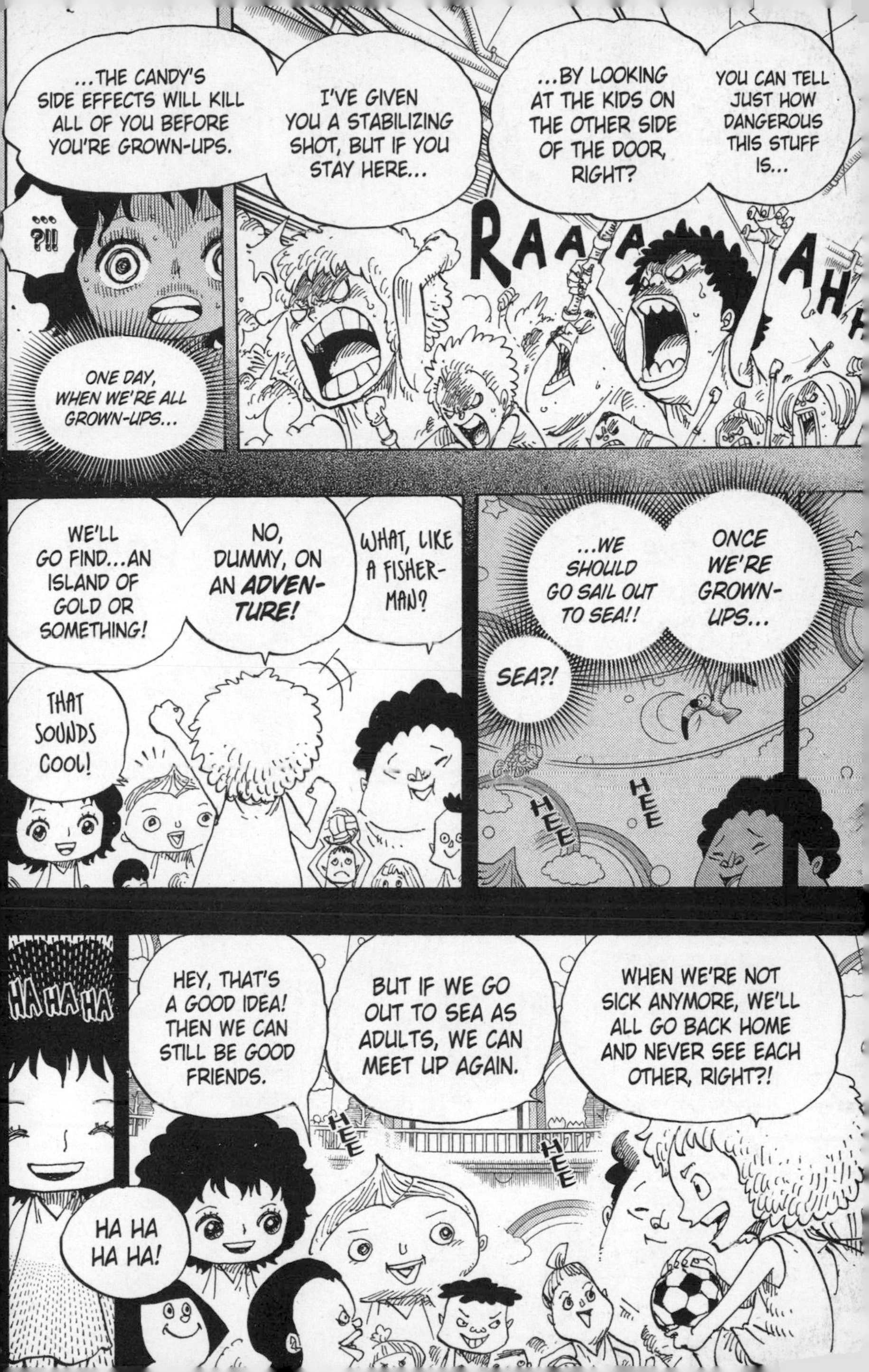
YOU CAN TELL JUST HOW DANGEROUS THIS STUFF IS...
...BY LOOKING AT THE KIDS ON THE OTHER SIDE OF THE DOOR, RIGHT?
I'VE GIVEN YOU A STABILIZING SHOT, BUT IF YOU STAY HERE...
...THE CANDY'S SIDE EFFECTS WILL KILL ALL OF YOU BEFORE YOU'RE GROWN-UPS.
RAAAAHH
...?!!
ONE DAY, WHEN WE'RE ALL GROWN-UPS...
ONCE WE'RE GROWN-UPS...
...WE SHOULD GO SAIL OUT TO SEA!!
SEA?!
HEE
HEE
WHAT, LIKE A FISHERMAN?
NO, DUMMY, ON AN *ADVENTURE!*
WE'LL GO FIND...AN ISLAND OF GOLD OR SOMETHING!
THAT SOUNDS COOL!
WHEN WE'RE NOT SICK ANYMORE, WE'LL ALL GO BACK HOME AND NEVER SEE EACH OTHER, RIGHT?!
BUT IF WE GO OUT TO SEA AS ADULTS, WE CAN MEET UP AGAIN.
HEY, THAT'S A GOOD IDEA! THEN WE CAN STILL BE GOOD FRIENDS.
HEE
HEE
HA HA HA
HA HA HA HA!

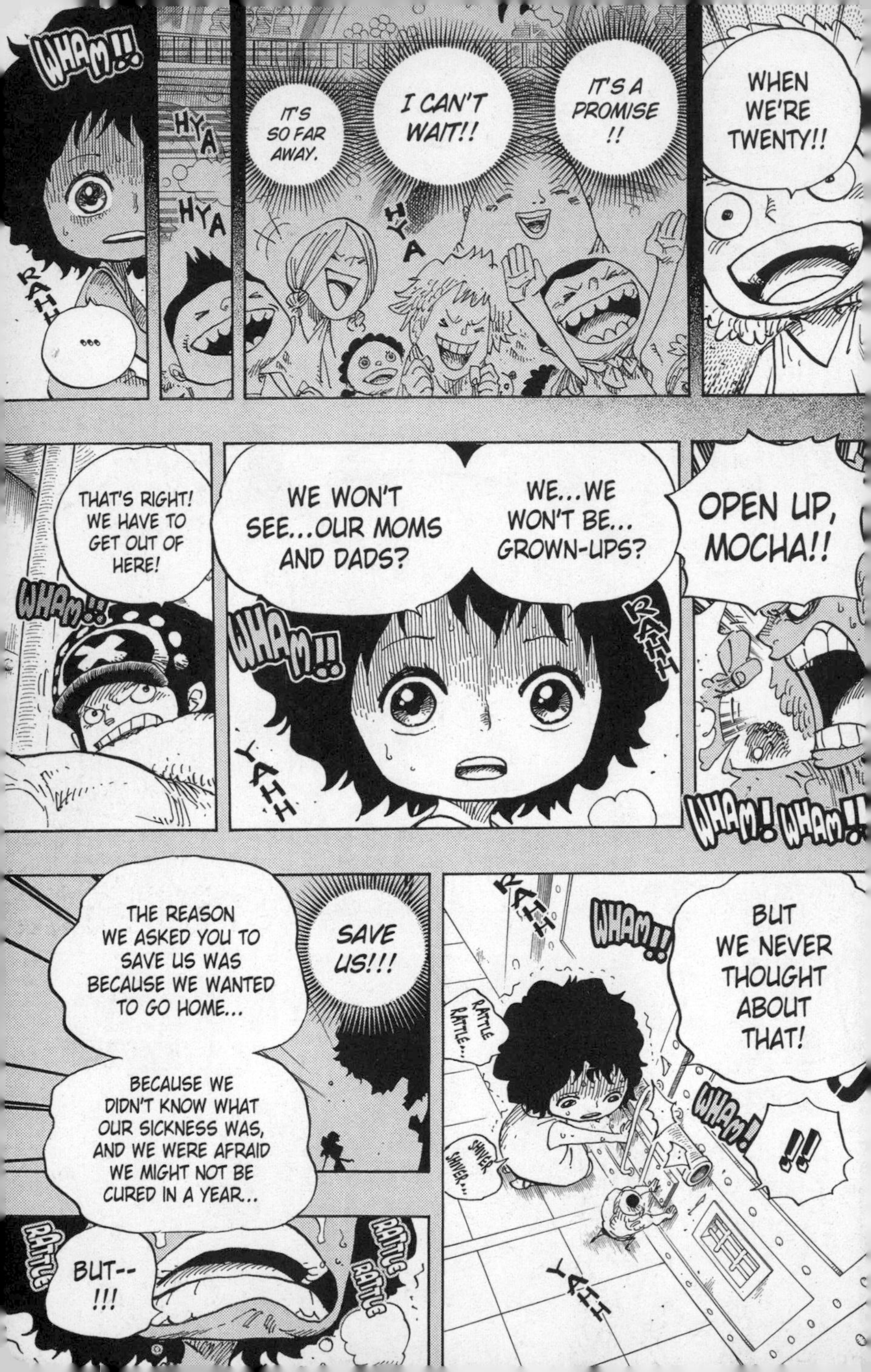
WHEN WE'RE TWENTY!!
IT'S A PROMISE !!
I CAN'T WAIT!!
IT'S SO FAR AWAY.
HYA
HYA
HYA
WHAM!!
RAHH
...
OPEN UP, MOCHA!!
WHAM! WHAM!!
WE...WE WON'T BE... GROWN-UPS?
WE WON'T SEE...OUR MOMS AND DADS?
RAHH
WHAM!!
YAHH
THAT'S RIGHT! WE HAVE TO GET OUT OF HERE!
WHAM!!
BUT WE NEVER THOUGHT ABOUT THAT!
WHAM!!
RAHH
RATTLE RATTLE...
SHIVER SHIVER...
WHAM!
!!
YAHH
SAVE US!!!
THE REASON WE ASKED YOU TO SAVE US WAS BECAUSE WE WANTED TO GO HOME...
BECAUSE WE DIDN'T KNOW WHAT OUR SICKNESS WAS, AND WE WERE AFRAID WE MIGHT NOT BE CURED IN A YEAR...
RATTLE RATTLE
BUT-- !!!
RATTLE

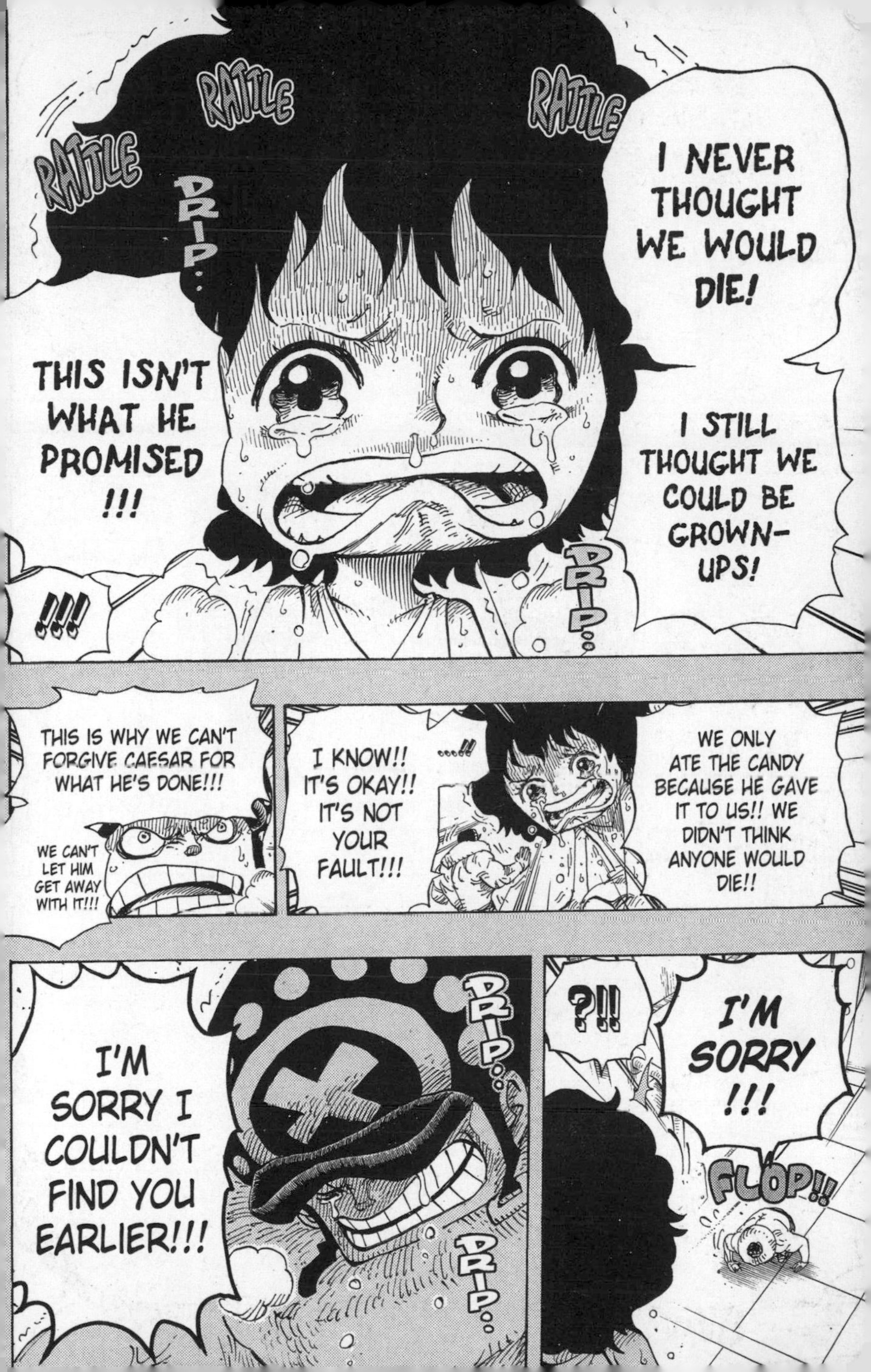
RATTLE
RATTLE
RATTLE
I NEVER THOUGHT WE WOULD DIE!
I STILL THOUGHT WE COULD BE GROWN-UPS!
DRIP...
DRIP...
THIS ISN'T WHAT HE PROMISED!!!
!!!
WE ONLY ATE THE CANDY BECAUSE HE GAVE IT TO US!! WE DIDN'T THINK ANYONE WOULD DIE!!
...!!
I KNOW!! IT'S OKAY!! IT'S NOT YOUR FAULT!!!
THIS IS WHY WE CAN'T FORGIVE CAESAR FOR WHAT HE'S DONE!!!
WE CAN'T LET HIM GET AWAY WITH IT!!!
?!!
I'M SORRY!!!
FLOP!!
DRIP...
I'M SORRY I COULDN'T FIND YOU EARLIER!!!
DRIP...

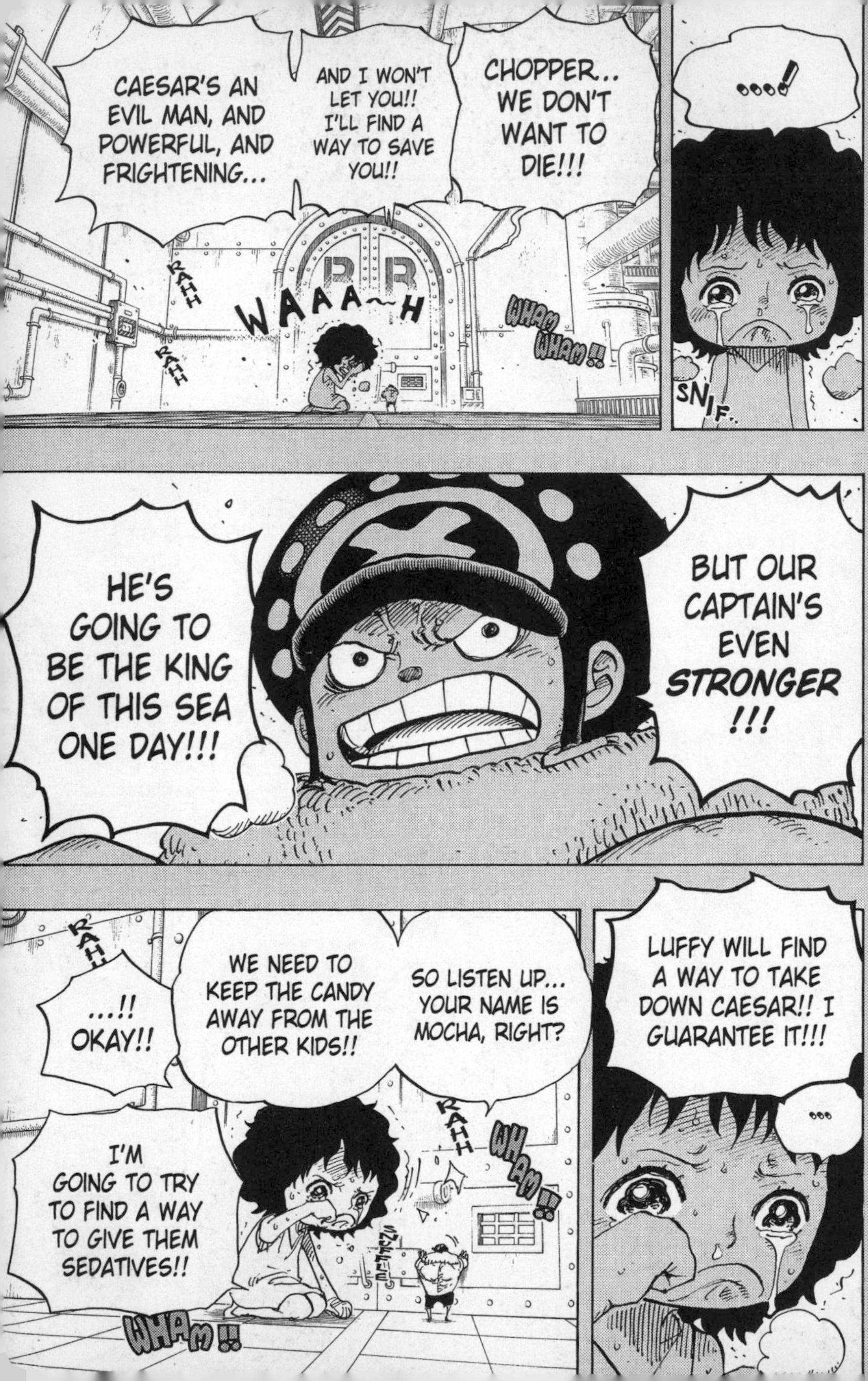
...!
SNIF...
CHOPPER... WE DON'T WANT TO DIE!!!
AND I WON'T LET YOU!! I'LL FIND A WAY TO SAVE YOU!!
CAESAR'S AN EVIL MAN, AND POWERFUL, AND FRIGHTENING...
WHAM WHAM!!
WAAA~H
RAHH
RAHH
BUT OUR CAPTAIN'S EVEN STRONGER!!!
HE'S GOING TO BE THE KING OF THIS SEA ONE DAY!!!
LUFFY WILL FIND A WAY TO TAKE DOWN CAESAR!! I GUARANTEE IT!!!
...
SO LISTEN UP... YOUR NAME IS MOCHA, RIGHT?
WE NEED TO KEEP THE CANDY AWAY FROM THE OTHER KIDS!!
...!! OKAY!!
RAHH
WHAM!!
RAHH
I'M GOING TO TRY TO FIND A WAY TO GIVE THEM SEDATIVES!!
SNUFFLE
WHAM!!

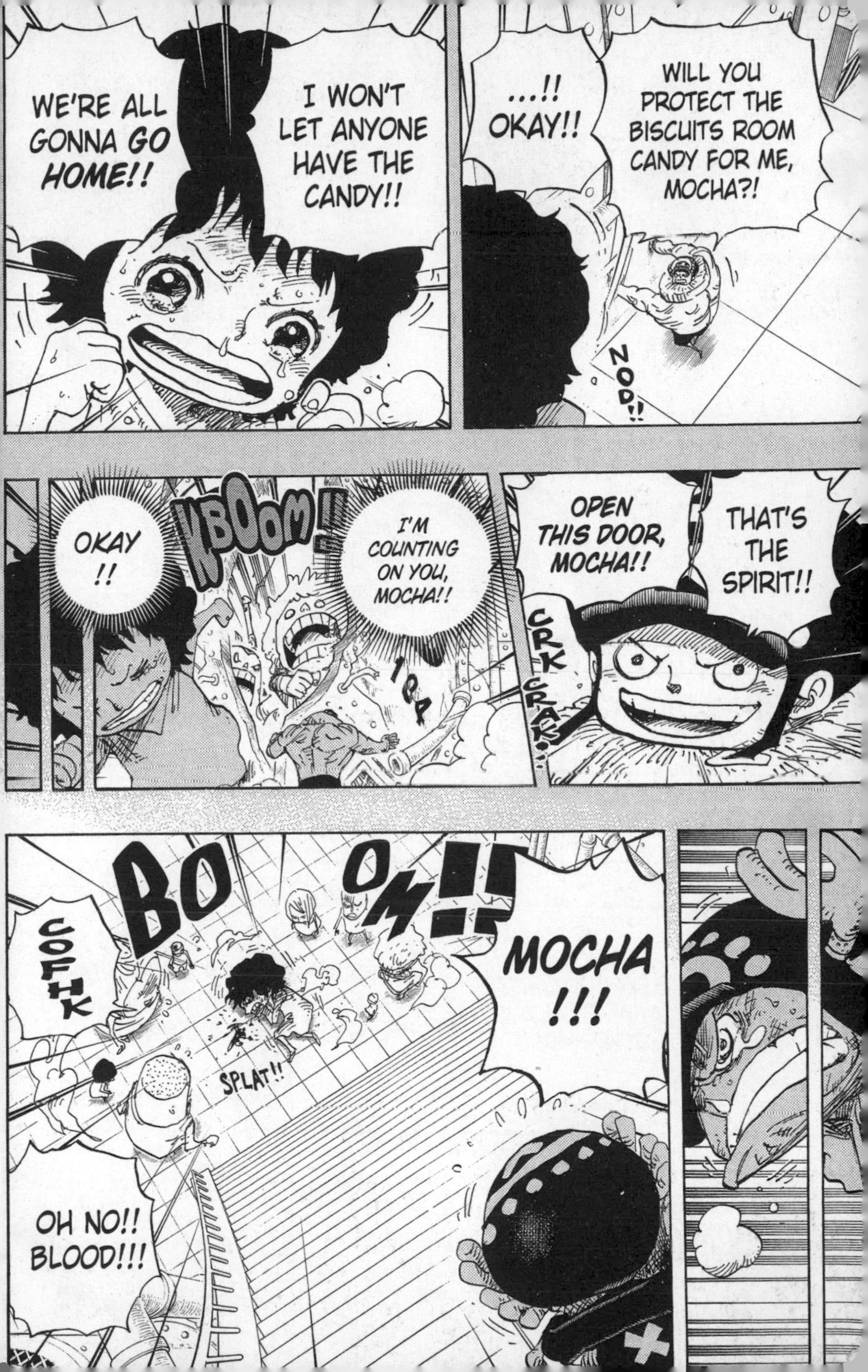
WILL YOU PROTECT THE BISCUITS ROOM CANDY FOR ME, MOCHA?!
...!! OKAY!!
NOD!!
I WON'T LET ANYONE HAVE THE CANDY!!
WE'RE ALL GONNA GO HOME!!
THAT'S THE SPIRIT!!
OPEN THIS DOOR, MOCHA!!
CRK CRAK
I'M COUNTING ON YOU, MOCHA!!
KBOOM!!
OKAY !!
MOCHA !!!
BOOM!!
COFHK
SPLAT!!
OH NO!! BLOOD!!!

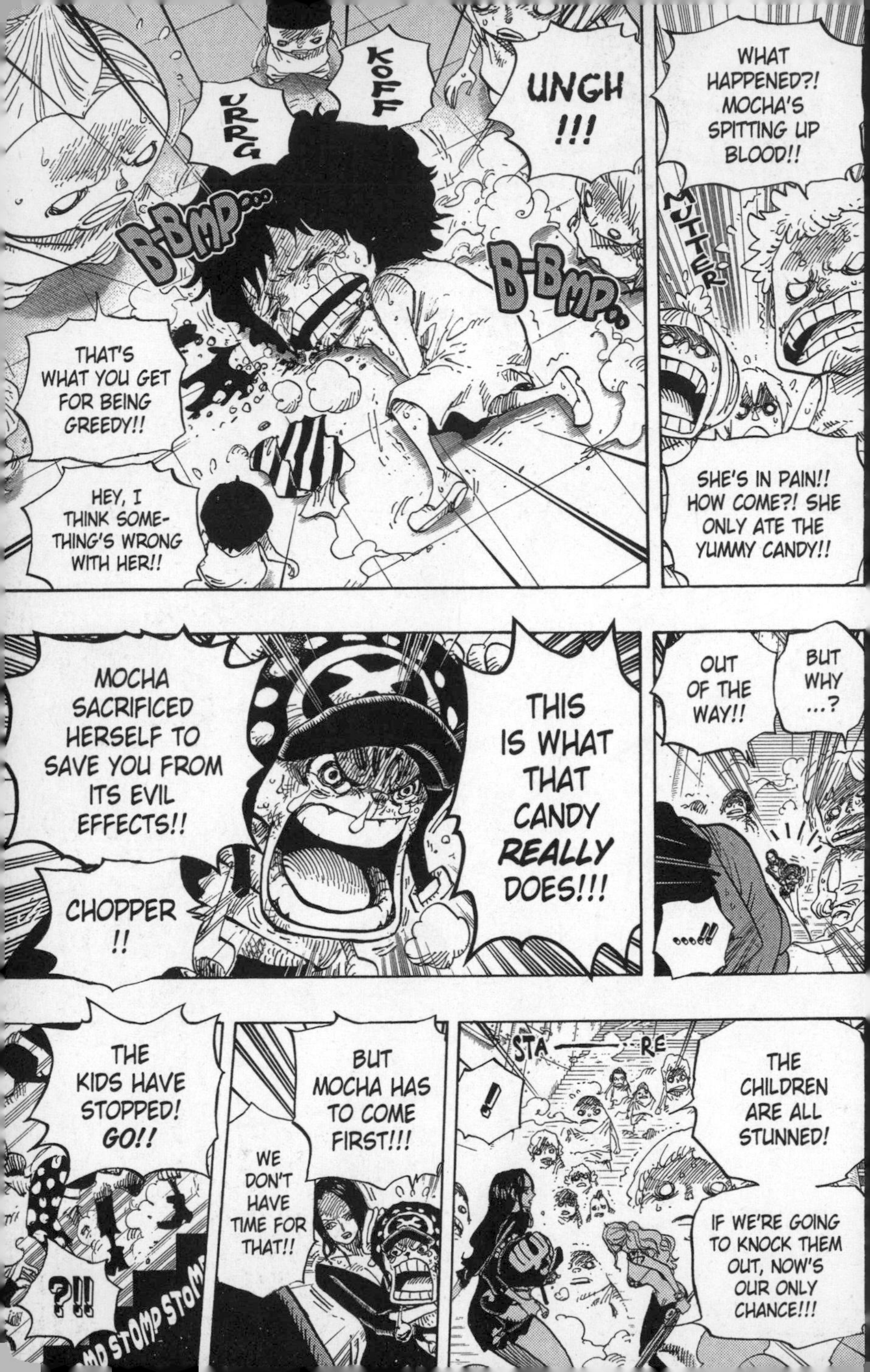
WHAT HAPPENED?! MOCHA'S SPITTING UP BLOOD!!
MUTTER
SHE'S IN PAIN!! HOW COME?! SHE ONLY ATE THE YUMMY CANDY!!
UNGH !!!
KOFF
URRG
B-BMP...
B-BMP...
THAT'S WHAT YOU GET FOR BEING GREEDY!!
HEY, I THINK SOME-THING'S WRONG WITH HER!!
BUT WHY ...?
OUT OF THE WAY!!
...!!
THIS IS WHAT THAT CANDY *REALLY* DOES!!!
MOCHA SACRIFICED HERSELF TO SAVE YOU FROM ITS EVIL EFFECTS!!
CHOPPER !!
STA————RE
!
THE CHILDREN ARE ALL STUNNED!
IF WE'RE GOING TO KNOCK THEM OUT, NOW'S OUR ONLY CHANCE!!!
BUT MOCHA HAS TO COME FIRST!!!
WE DON'T HAVE TIME FOR THAT!!
THE KIDS HAVE STOPPED! *GO!!*
?!!
STOMP STOMP

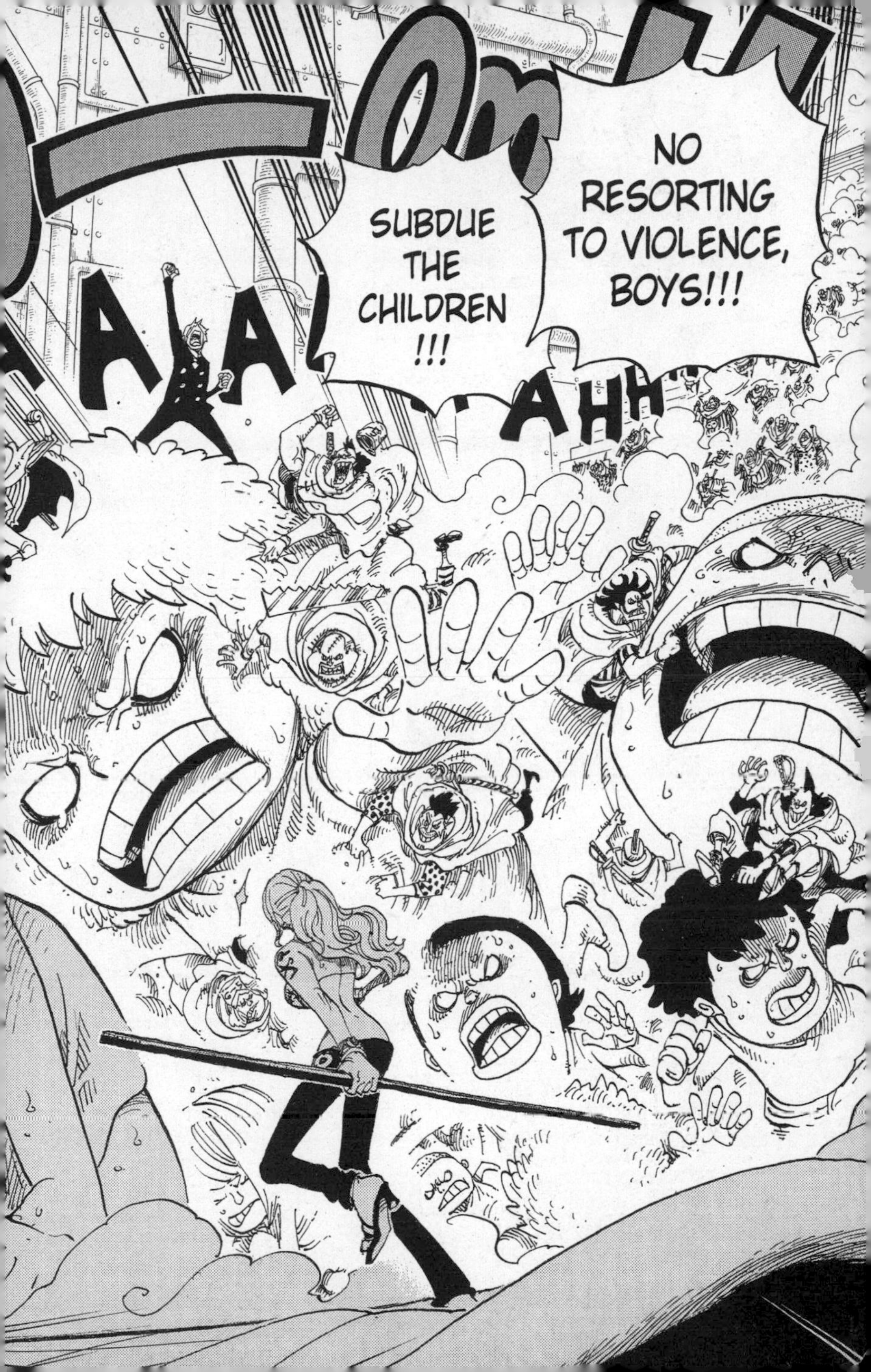
NO RESORTING TO VIOLENCE, BOYS!!!
SUBDUE THE CHILDREN !!!
AHH

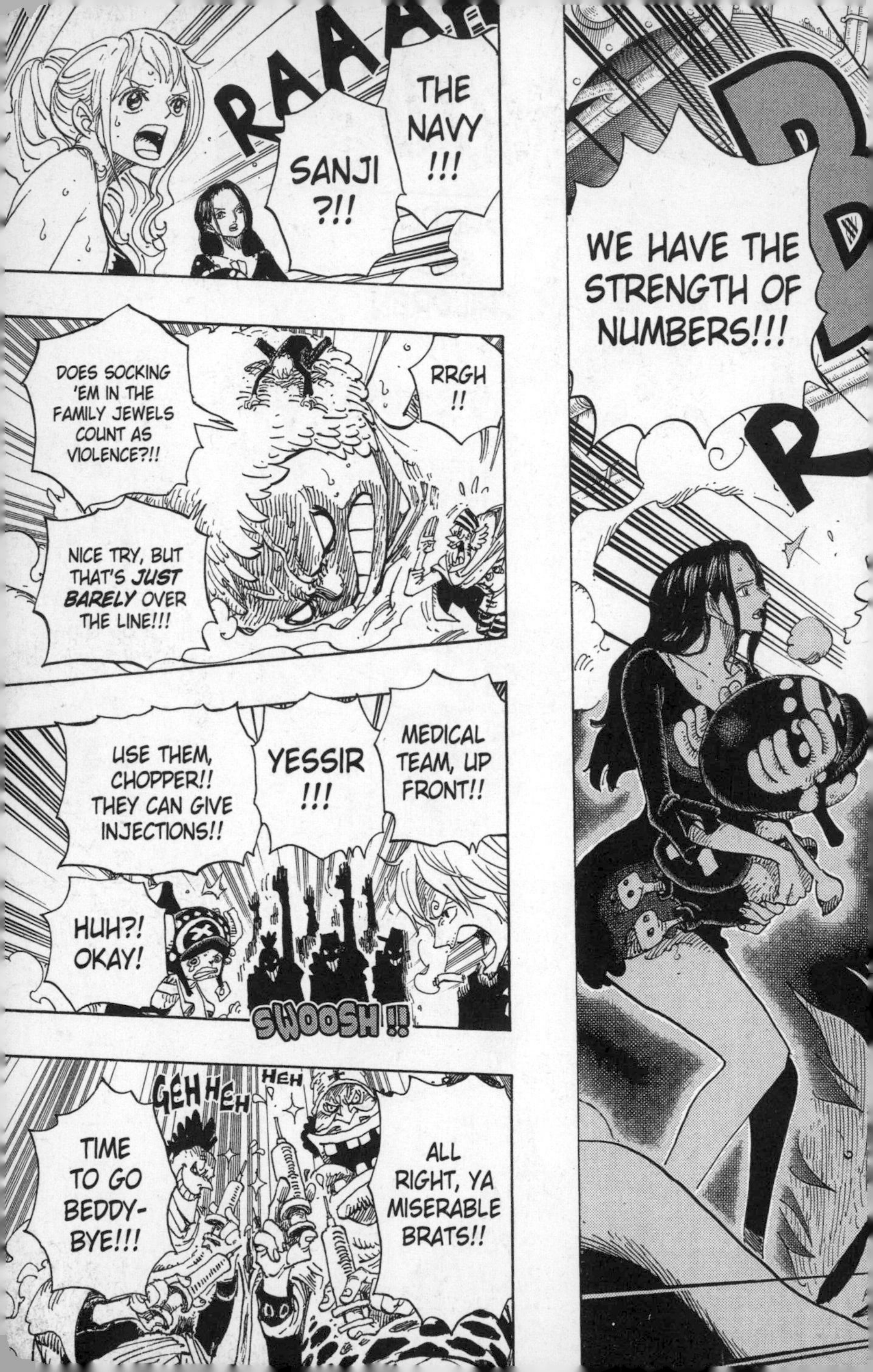
WE HAVE THE STRENGTH OF NUMBERS!!!
THE NAVY!!!
SANJI?!!
RRGH!!
DOES SOCKING 'EM IN THE FAMILY JEWELS COUNT AS VIOLENCE?!!
NICE TRY, BUT THAT'S *JUST BARELY* OVER THE LINE!!!
MEDICAL TEAM, UP FRONT!!
YESSIR!!!
USE THEM, CHOPPER!! THEY CAN GIVE INJECTIONS!!
HUH?! OKAY!
SWOOSH!!
GEH HEH HEH
ALL RIGHT, YA MISERABLE BRATS!!
TIME TO GO BEDDY-BYE!!!

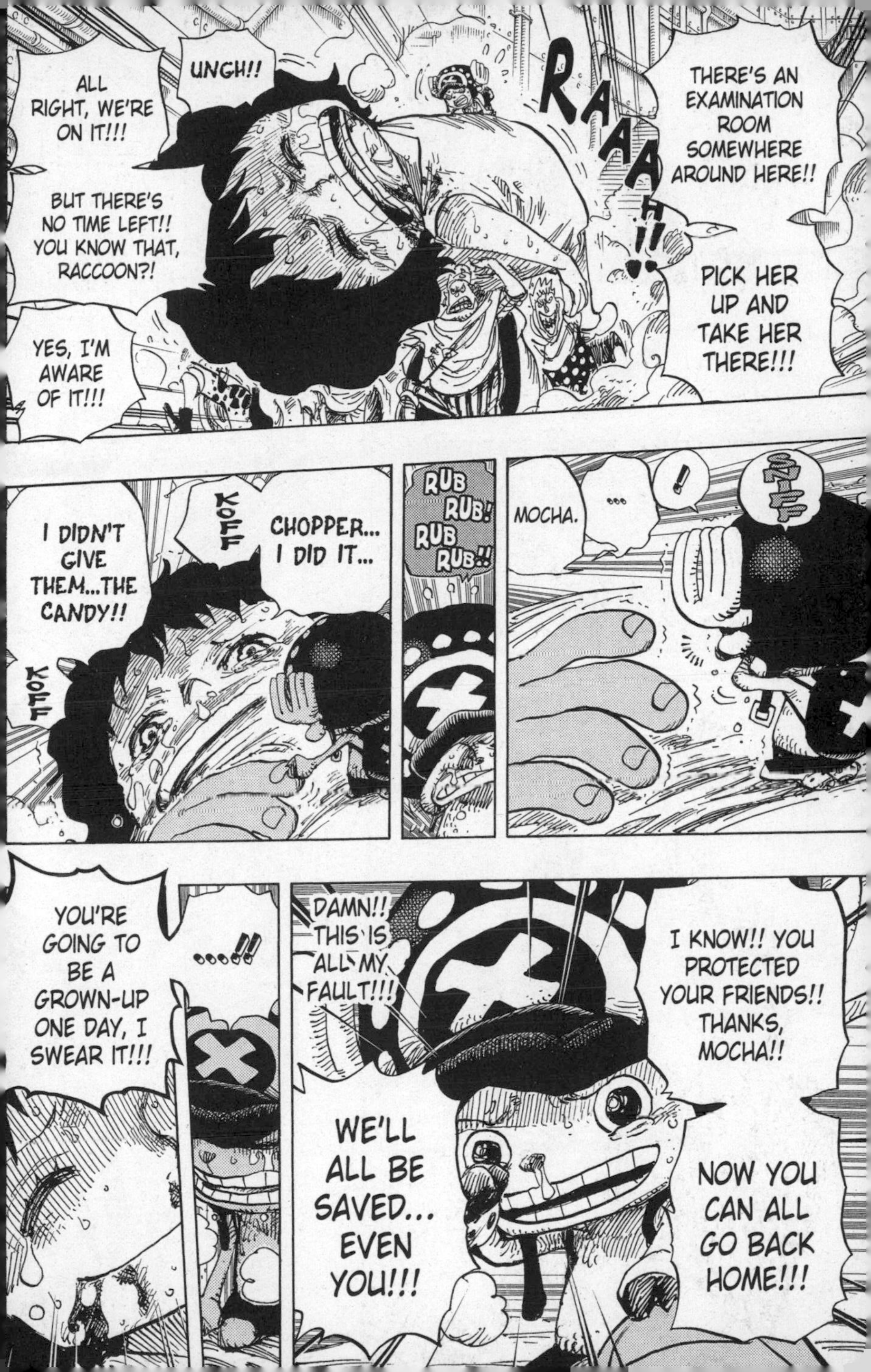
THERE'S AN EXAMINATION ROOM SOMEWHERE AROUND HERE!!
RAAAH!!
PICK HER UP AND TAKE HER THERE!!!
UNGH!!
ALL RIGHT, WE'RE ON IT!!!
BUT THERE'S NO TIME LEFT!! YOU KNOW THAT, RACCOON?!
YES, I'M AWARE OF IT!!!
SNIFF
!
...
MOCHA.
RUB RUB! RUB RUB!!
CHOPPER... I DID IT...
KOFF
I DIDN'T GIVE THEM...THE CANDY!!
KOFF
I KNOW!! YOU PROTECTED YOUR FRIENDS!! THANKS, MOCHA!!
DAMN!! THIS IS ALL MY FAULT!!!
NOW YOU CAN ALL GO BACK HOME!!!
WE'LL ALL BE SAVED... EVEN YOU!!!
.....!!
YOU'RE GOING TO BE A GROWN-UP ONE DAY, I SWEAR IT!!!

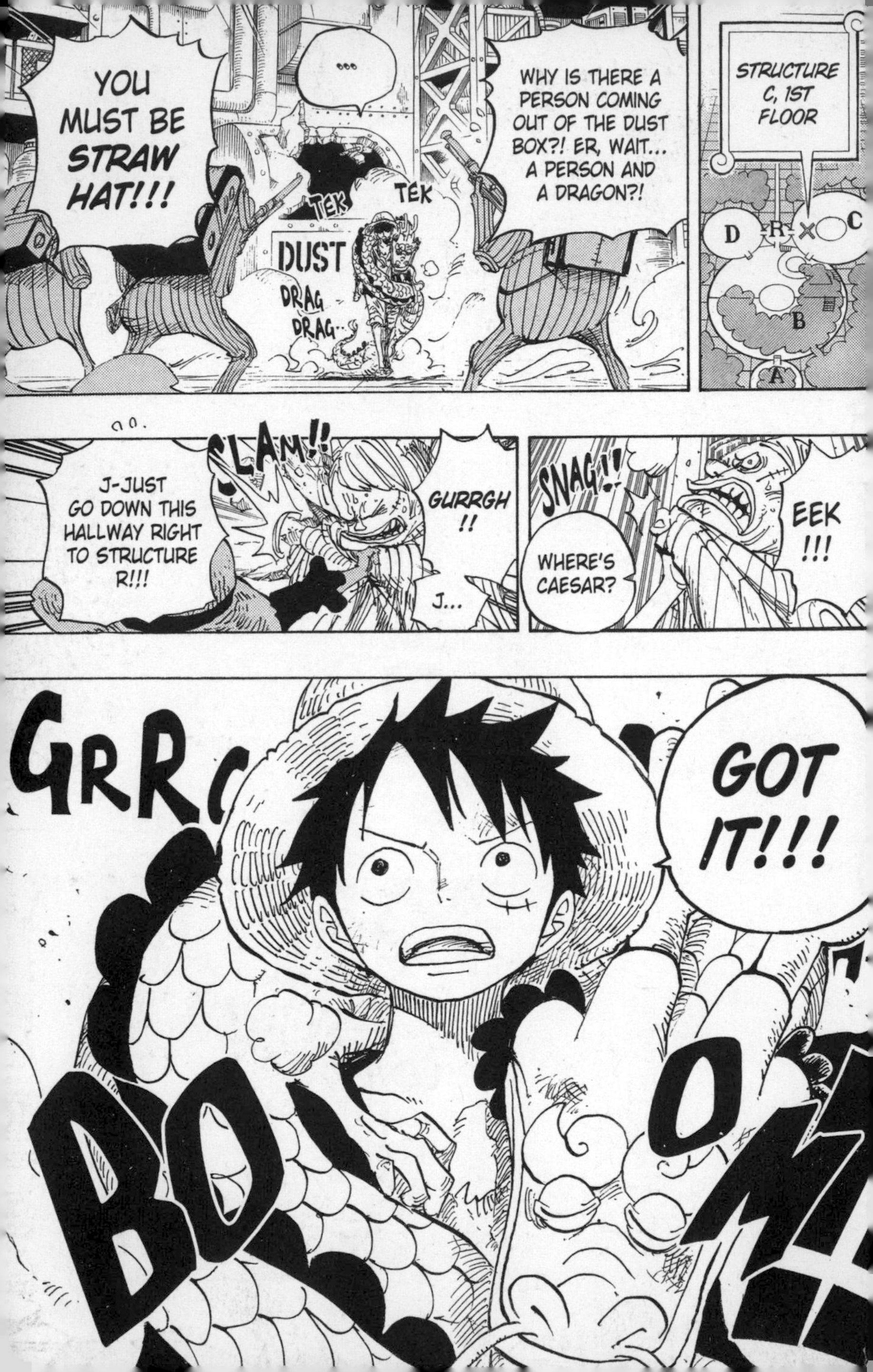
STRUCTURE C, 1ST FLOOR
D
R
C
B
A
WHY IS THERE A PERSON COMING OUT OF THE DUST BOX?! ER, WAIT... A PERSON AND A DRAGON?!
...
YOU MUST BE STRAW HAT!!!
TEK
TEK
DUST
DRAG DRAG...
SNAG!!
EEK!!!
WHERE'S CAESAR?
GURRGH!!
SLAM!!
J-JUST GO DOWN THIS HALLWAY RIGHT TO STRUCTURE R!!!
J...
GOT IT!!!
GRR
BOOM!!

ZIP
!!

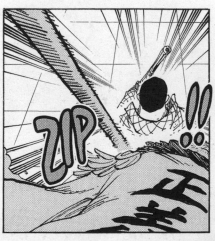

Chapter 689:
THE ISLAND THAT'S THERE BUT ISN'T THERE

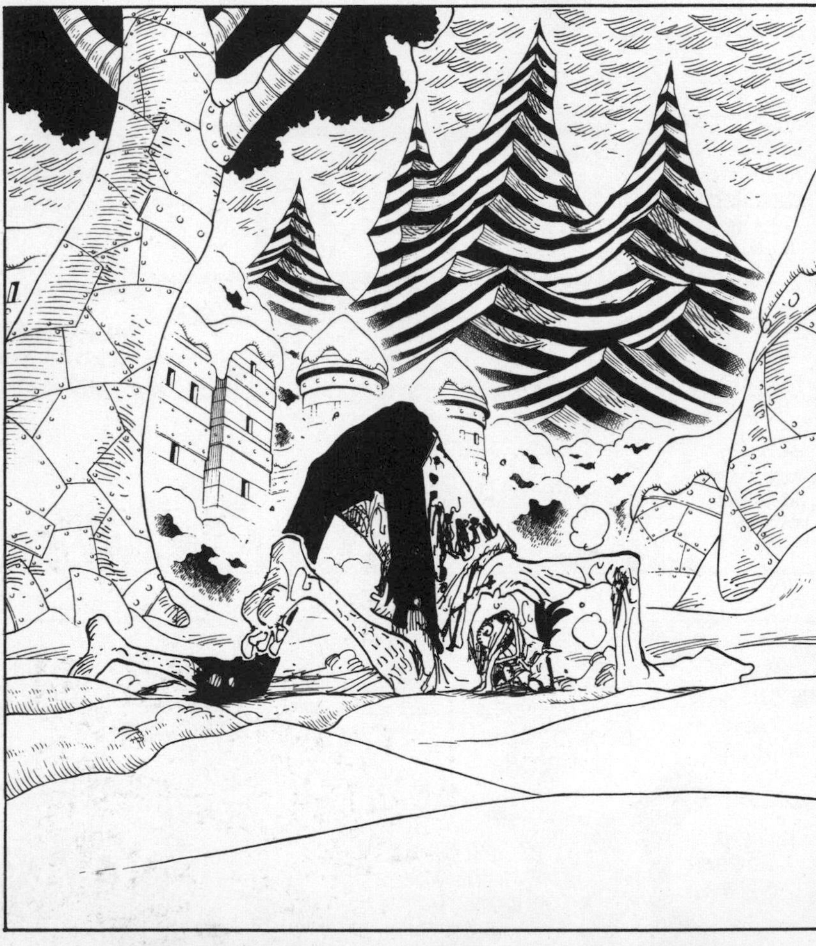

CARIBOU'S NEW WORLD KEE HEE HEE, VOL. 14:
"ALIVE ON SOME NEW ISLAND SOMEWHERE"

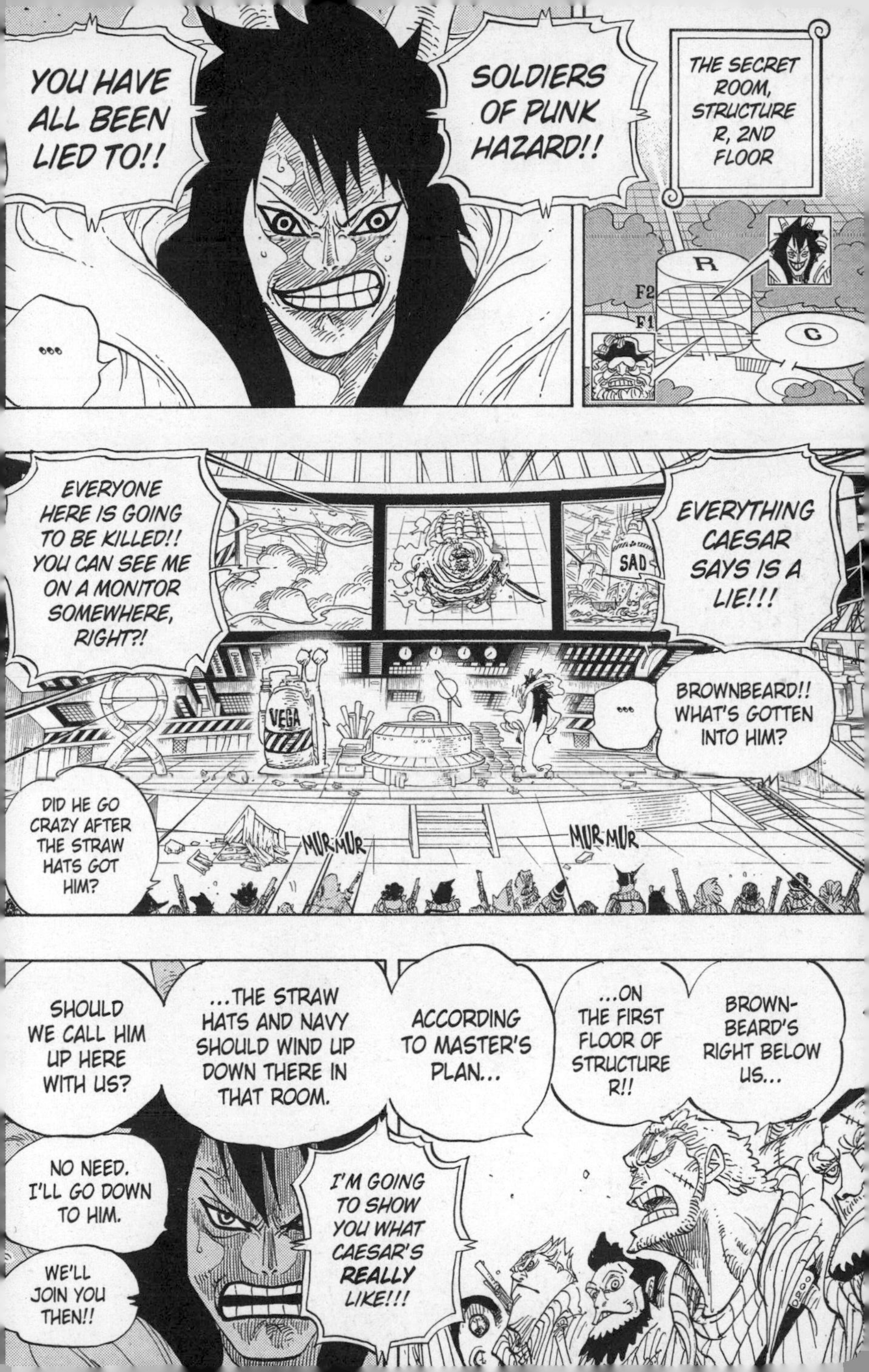
THE SECRET ROOM, STRUCTURE R, 2ND FLOOR
R
F2
F1
C
SOLDIERS OF PUNK HAZARD!!
YOU HAVE ALL BEEN LIED TO!!
...
EVERYTHING CAESAR SAYS IS A LIE!!!
EVERYONE HERE IS GOING TO BE KILLED!! YOU CAN SEE ME ON A MONITOR SOMEWHERE, RIGHT?!
SAD
VEGA
...
BROWNBEARD!! WHAT'S GOTTEN INTO HIM?
MUR MUR
MUR MUR
DID HE GO CRAZY AFTER THE STRAW HATS GOT HIM?
BROWN-BEARD'S RIGHT BELOW US...
...ON THE FIRST FLOOR OF STRUCTURE R!!
ACCORDING TO MASTER'S PLAN...
...THE STRAW HATS AND NAVY SHOULD WIND UP DOWN THERE IN THAT ROOM.
SHOULD WE CALL HIM UP HERE WITH US?
I'M GOING TO SHOW YOU WHAT CAESAR'S REALLY LIKE!!!
NO NEED. I'LL GO DOWN TO HIM.
WE'LL JOIN YOU THEN!!

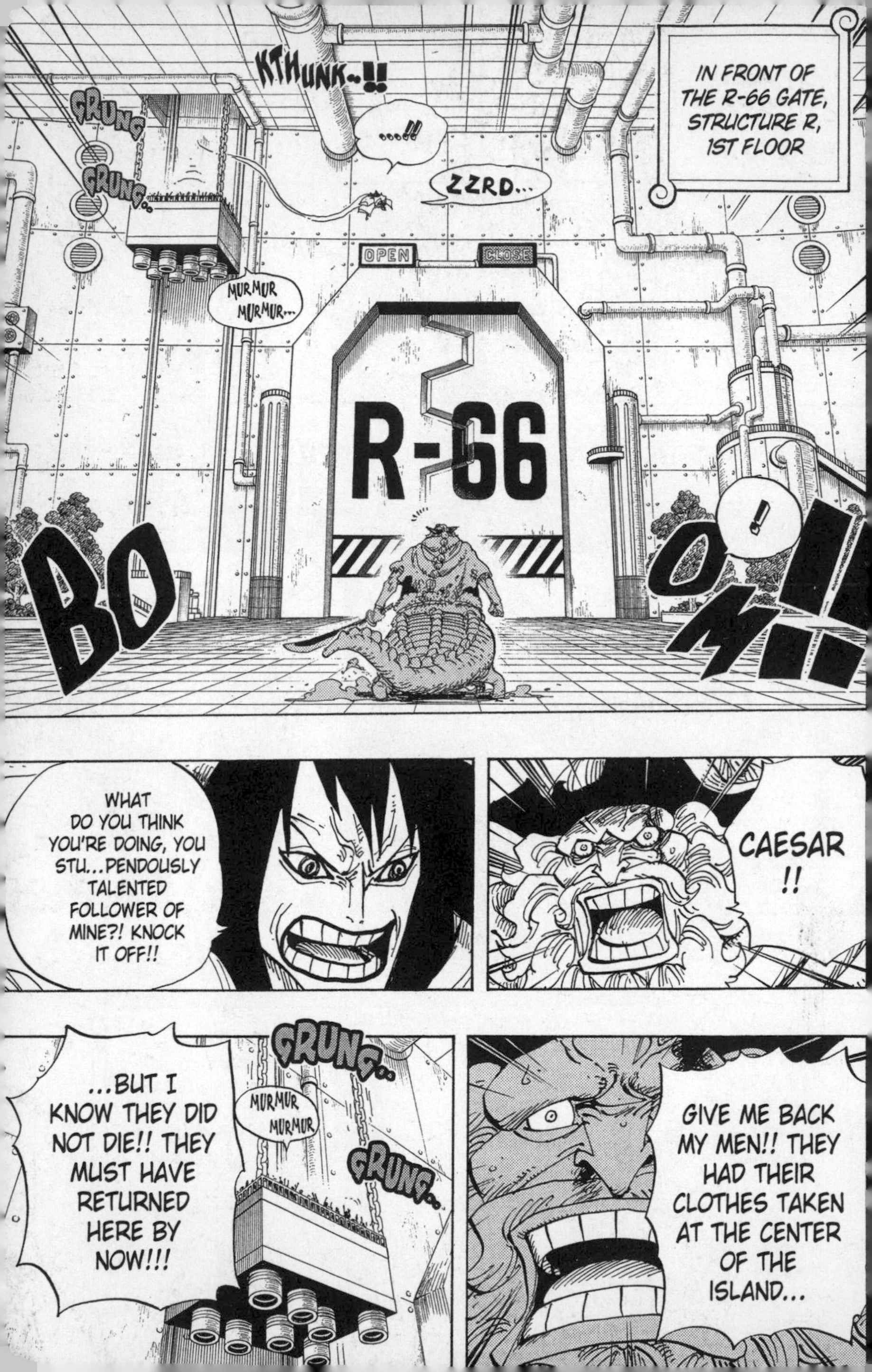
IN FRONT OF THE R-66 GATE, STRUCTURE R, 1ST FLOOR
KTHUNK..!!
....!!
ZZRD...
GRUNG
GRUNG..
OPEN
CLOSE
MURMUR MURMUR...
R-66
!
BOOM!!
CAESAR !!
WHAT DO YOU THINK YOU'RE DOING, YOU STU...PENDOUSLY TALENTED FOLLOWER OF MINE?! KNOCK IT OFF!!
GIVE ME BACK MY MEN!! THEY HAD THEIR CLOTHES TAKEN AT THE CENTER OF THE ISLAND...
GRUNG..
MURMUR MURMUR
GRUNG..
...BUT I KNOW THEY DID NOT DIE!! THEY MUST HAVE RETURNED HERE BY NOW!!!

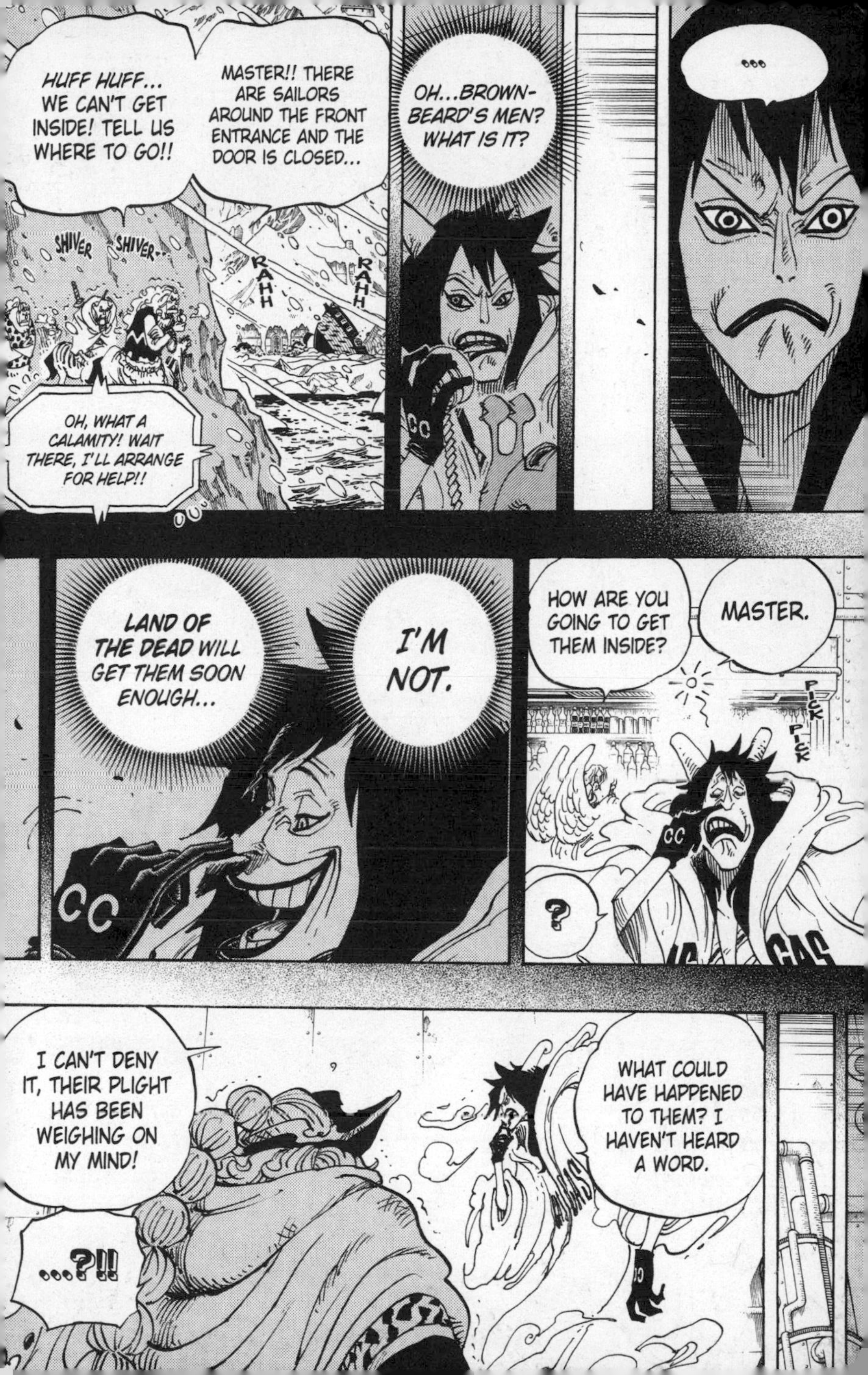
...
OH...BROWN-BEARD'S MEN? WHAT IS IT?
MASTER!! THERE ARE SAILORS AROUND THE FRONT ENTRANCE AND THE DOOR IS CLOSED...
HUFF HUFF... WE CAN'T GET INSIDE! TELL US WHERE TO GO!!
RAHH
RAHH
SHIVER
SHIVER...
OH, WHAT A CALAMITY! WAIT THERE, I'LL ARRANGE FOR HELP!!
MASTER.
HOW ARE YOU GOING TO GET THEM INSIDE?
PICK
PICK
?
I'M NOT.
LAND OF THE DEAD WILL GET THEM SOON ENOUGH...
WHAT COULD HAVE HAPPENED TO THEM? I HAVEN'T HEARD A WORD.
I CAN'T DENY IT, THEIR PLIGHT HAS BEEN WEIGHING ON MY MIND!
...?!!

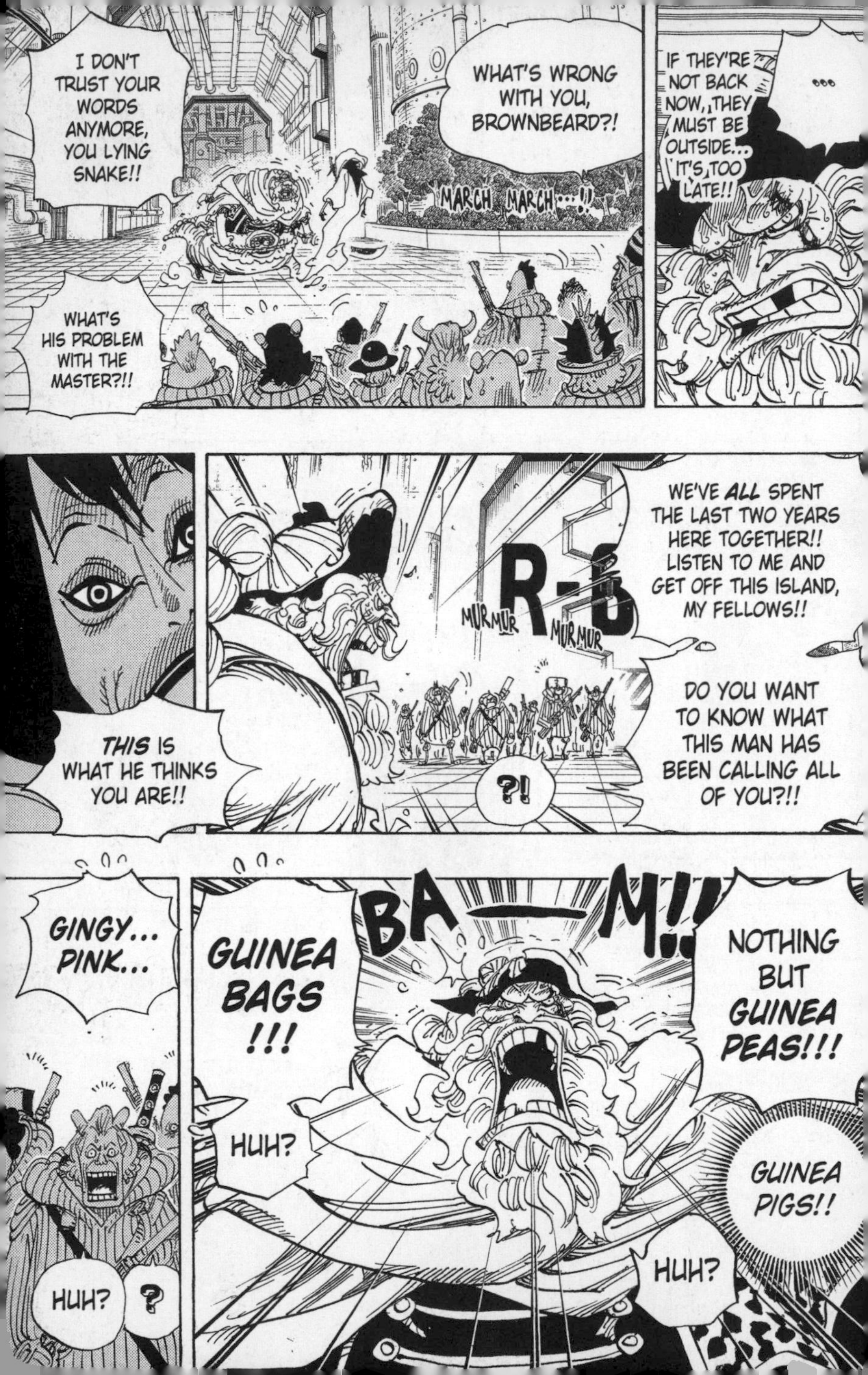
...
IF THEY'RE NOT BACK NOW, THEY MUST BE OUTSIDE... IT'S TOO LATE!!
WHAT'S WRONG WITH YOU, BROWNBEARD?!
I DON'T TRUST YOUR WORDS ANYMORE, YOU LYING SNAKE!!
MARCH MARCH...!!
WHAT'S HIS PROBLEM WITH THE MASTER?!!
WE'VE *ALL* SPENT THE LAST TWO YEARS HERE TOGETHER!! LISTEN TO ME AND GET OFF THIS ISLAND, MY FELLOWS!!
DO YOU WANT TO KNOW WHAT THIS MAN HAS BEEN CALLING ALL OF YOU?!!
R-6
MURMUR MURMUR
?!
THIS IS WHAT HE THINKS YOU ARE!!
NOTHING BUT *GUINEA PEAS!!!*
BA—M!!
GUINEA BAGS!!!
HUH?
GUINEA PIGS!!
HUH?
GINGY... PINK...
HUH?
?

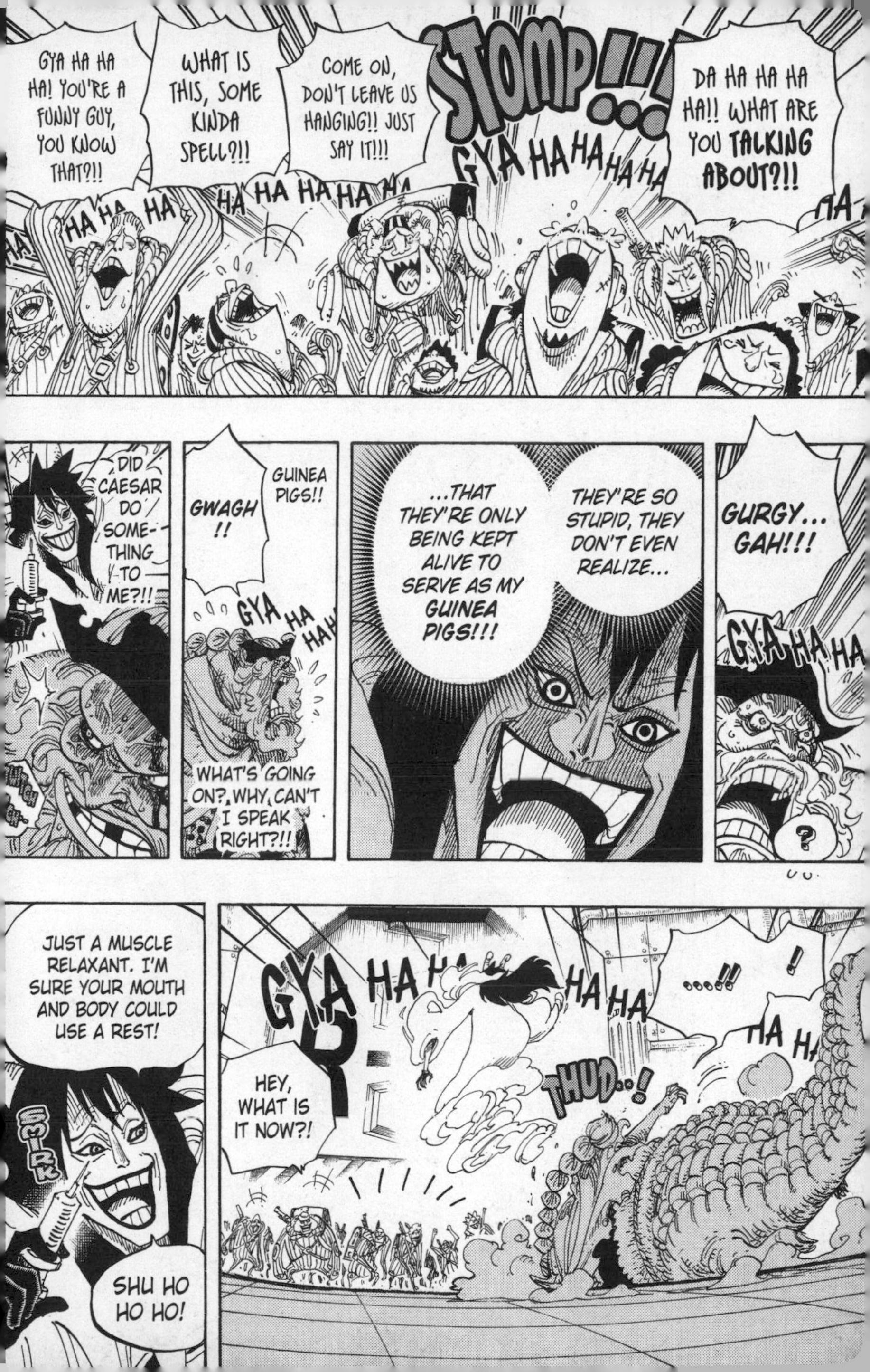
DA HA HA HA HA!! WHAT ARE YOU TALKING ABOUT?!!
STOMP!!!...
GYA HA HA HA HA
COME ON, DON'T LEAVE US HANGING!! JUST SAY IT!!!
HA HA HA HA HA
WHAT IS THIS, SOME KINDA SPELL?!!
HA HA HA
GYA HA HA HA! YOU'RE A FUNNY GUY, YOU KNOW THAT?!!
GURGY... GAH!!!
GYA HA HA
?
THEY'RE SO STUPID, THEY DON'T EVEN REALIZE...
...THAT THEY'RE ONLY BEING KEPT ALIVE TO SERVE AS MY GUINEA PIGS!!!
GUINEA PIGS!!
GWAGH!!
GYA HA HA
WHAT'S GOING ON?! WHY CAN'T I SPEAK RIGHT?!!
DID CAESAR DO SOMETHING TO ME?!!
...!!
!
HA HA
THUD..!
GYA HA HA HA HA
HEY, WHAT IS IT NOW?!
JUST A MUSCLE RELAXANT. I'M SURE YOUR MOUTH AND BODY COULD USE A REST!
SMIRK
SHU HO HO HO!

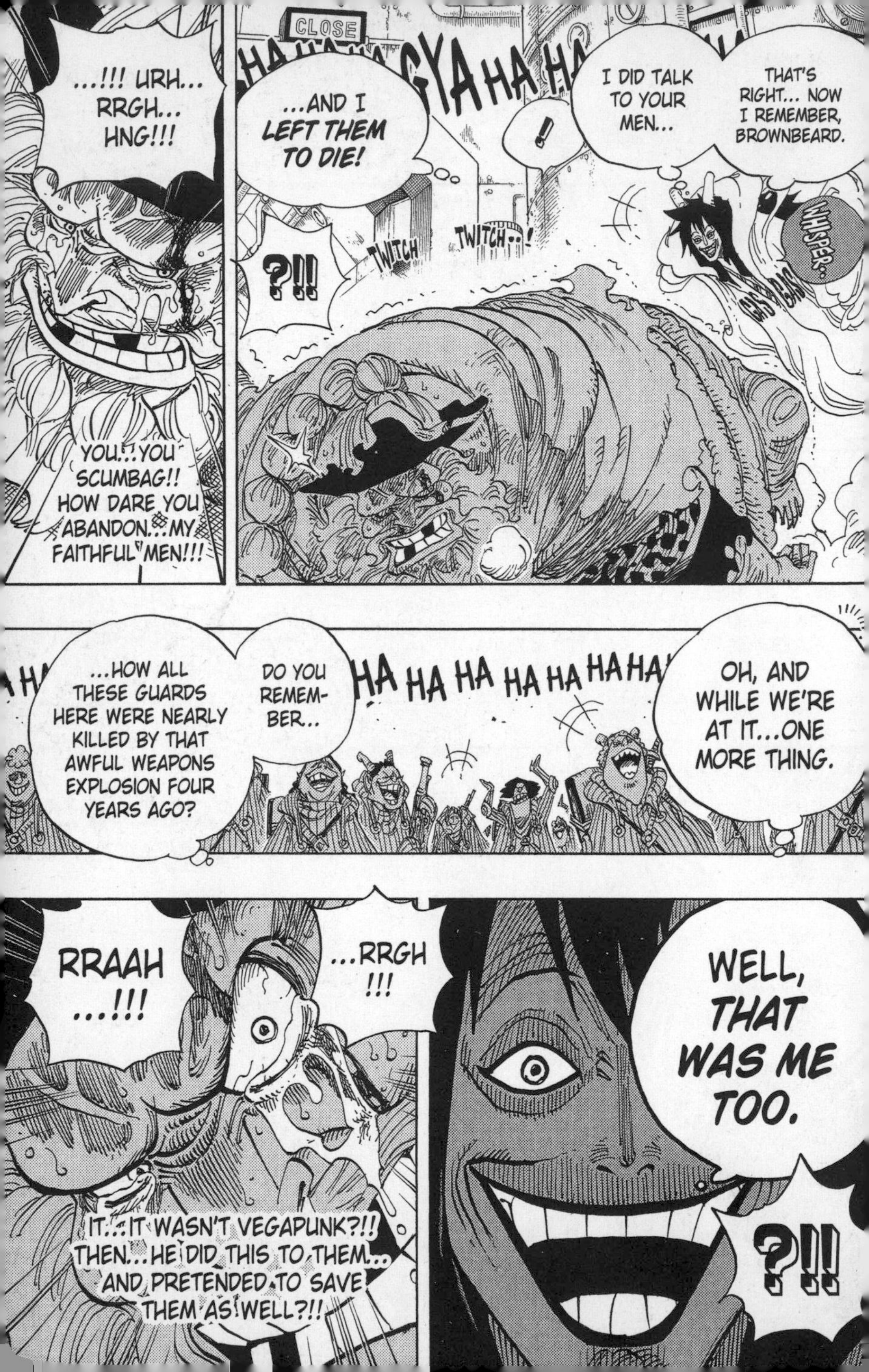
CLOSE
HA HA HA GYA HA HA HA
THAT'S RIGHT... NOW I REMEMBER, BROWNBEARD.
I DID TALK TO YOUR MEN...
WHISPER
!
...AND I LEFT THEM TO DIE!
TWITCH TWITCH
?!!
...!!! URH... RRGH... HNG!!!
YOU... YOU SCUMBAG!! HOW DARE YOU ABANDON... MY FAITHFUL MEN!!!
OH, AND WHILE WE'RE AT IT...ONE MORE THING.
HA HA HA HA HA HA HA HA HA
DO YOU REMEMBER...
...HOW ALL THESE GUARDS HERE WERE NEARLY KILLED BY THAT AWFUL WEAPONS EXPLOSION FOUR YEARS AGO?
WELL, THAT WAS ME TOO.
?!!
...RRGH !!!
RRAAH ...!!!
IT... IT WASN'T VEGAPUNK?!! THEN... HE DID THIS TO THEM... AND PRETENDED TO SAVE THEM AS WELL?!!

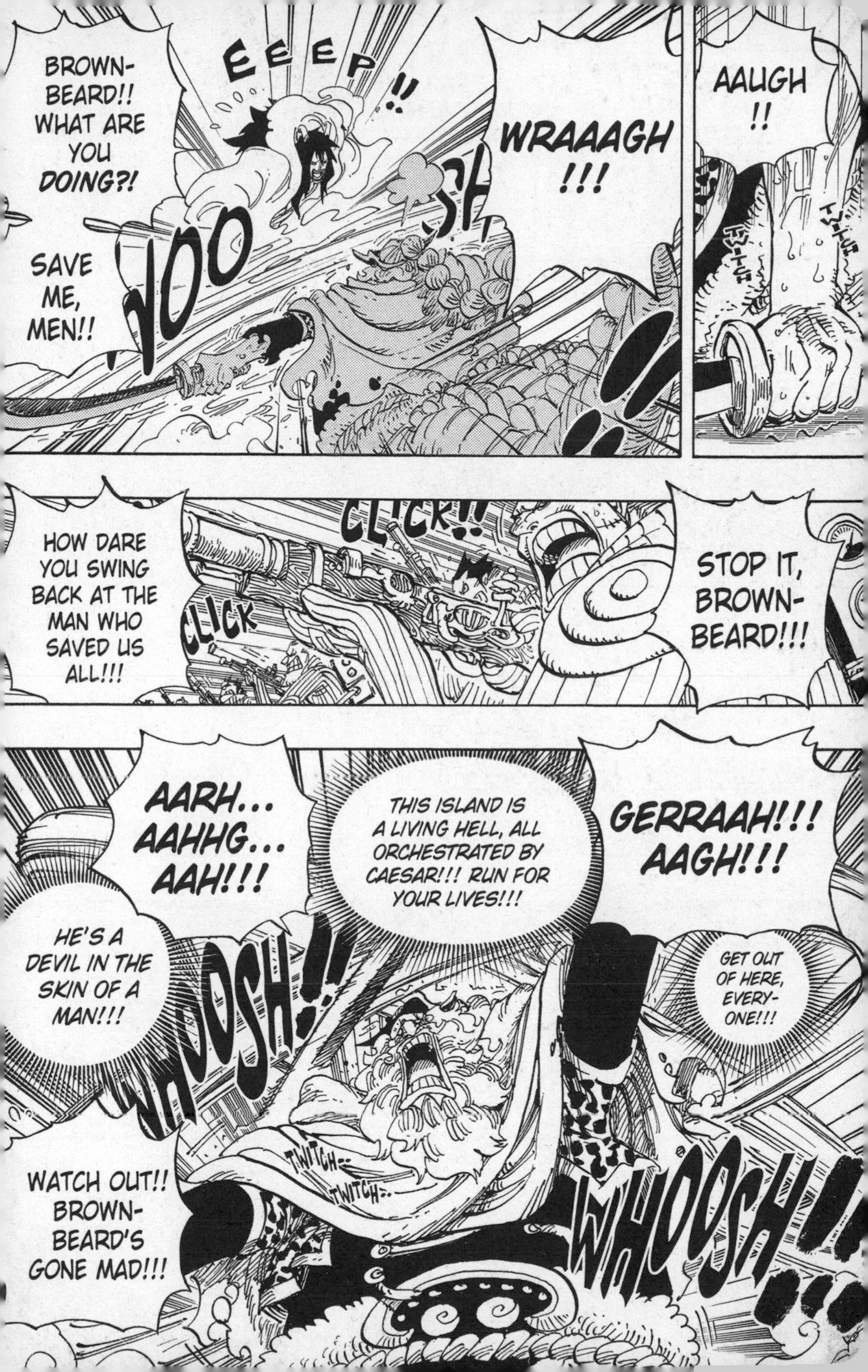
AAUGH!!
TWITCH
TWITCH
WRAAAGH!!!
EEEP!!
BROWN-BEARD!! WHAT ARE YOU DOING?!
SAVE ME, MEN!!
VOOSH
STOP IT, BROWN-BEARD!!!
CLICK!!
CLICK
HOW DARE YOU SWING BACK AT THE MAN WHO SAVED US ALL!!!
GERRAAH!!! AAGH!!!
THIS ISLAND IS A LIVING HELL, ALL ORCHESTRATED BY CAESAR!!! RUN FOR YOUR LIVES!!!
AARH... AAHHG... AAH!!!
GET OUT OF HERE, EVERY-ONE!!!
HE'S A DEVIL IN THE SKIN OF A MAN!!!
WHOOSH!!
TWITCH
TWITCH
WHOOSH!!
WATCH OUT!! BROWN-BEARD'S GONE MAD!!!

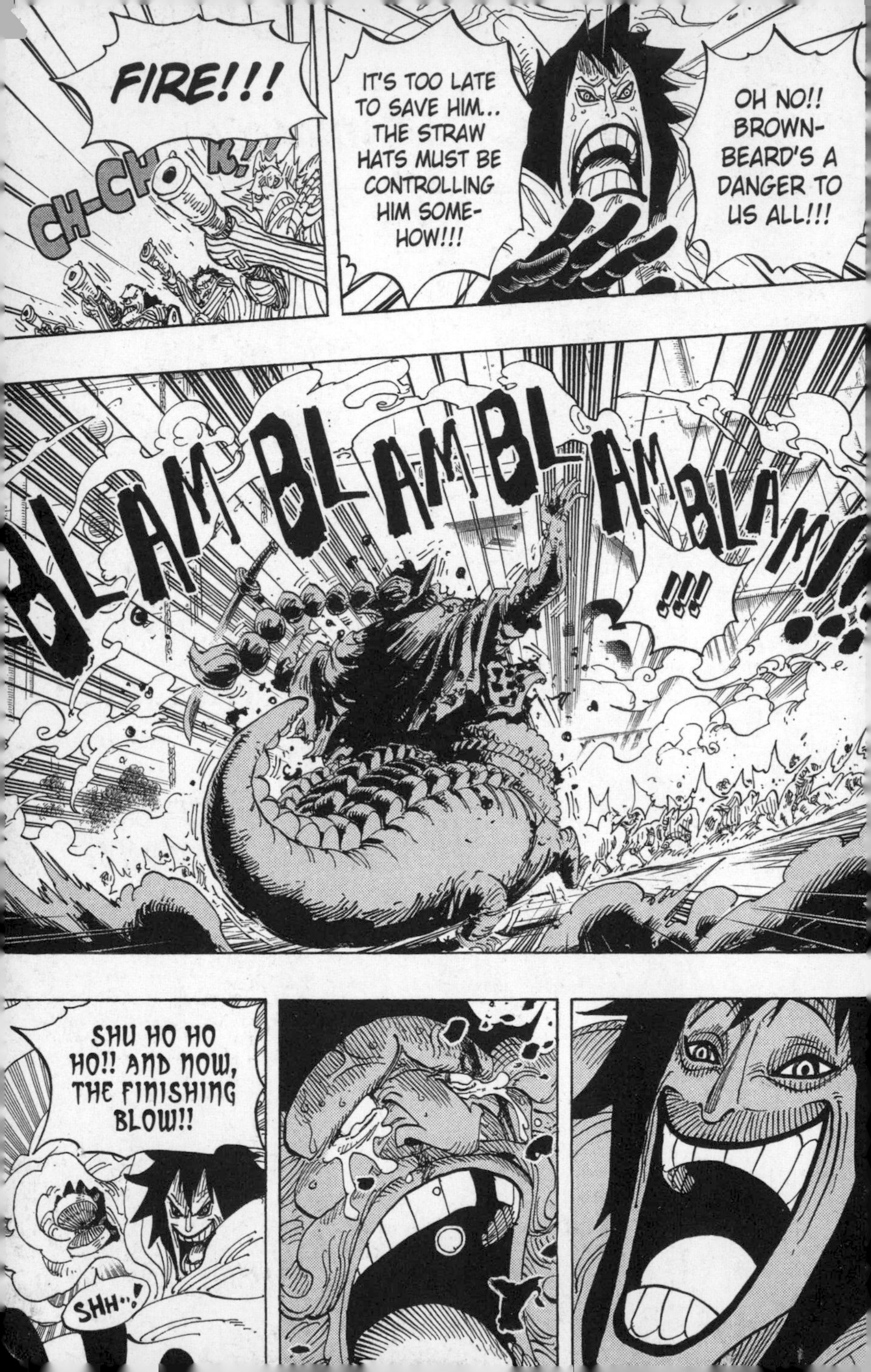
OH NO!! BROWN-BEARD'S A DANGER TO US ALL!!!
IT'S TOO LATE TO SAVE HIM... THE STRAW HATS MUST BE CONTROLLING HIM SOME-HOW!!!
FIRE!!!
CH-CHOK!!
BLAM BLAM BLAM BLAM BLAM!!!
SHU HO HO HO!! AND NOW, THE FINISHING BLOW!!
SHH..!

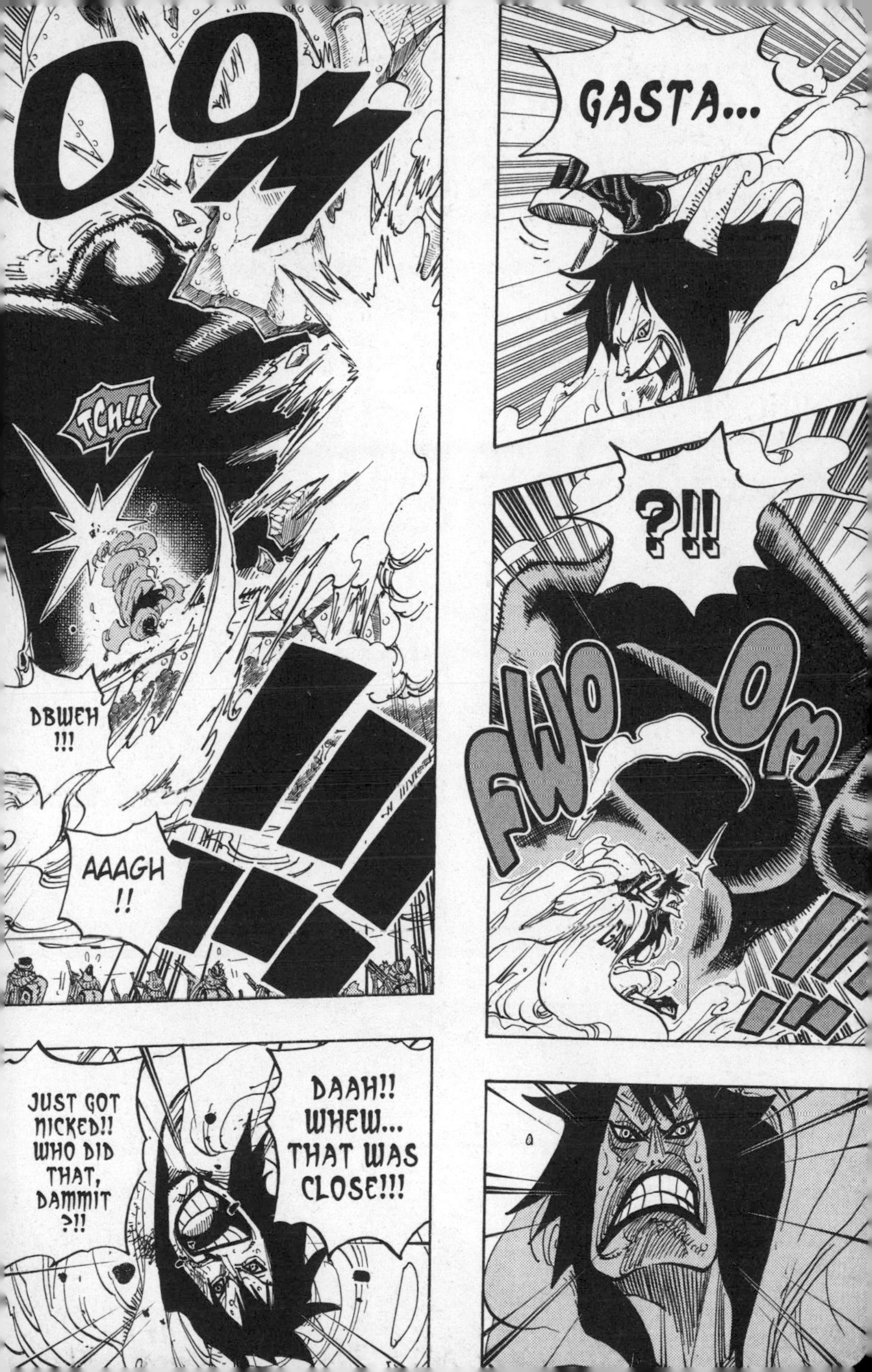
GASTA...
?!!
FWOOM
OOK
TCH!!
DBWEH!!!
AAAGH!!
DAAH!! WHEW... THAT WAS CLOSE!!!
JUST GOT NICKED!! WHO DID THAT, DAMMIT?!!

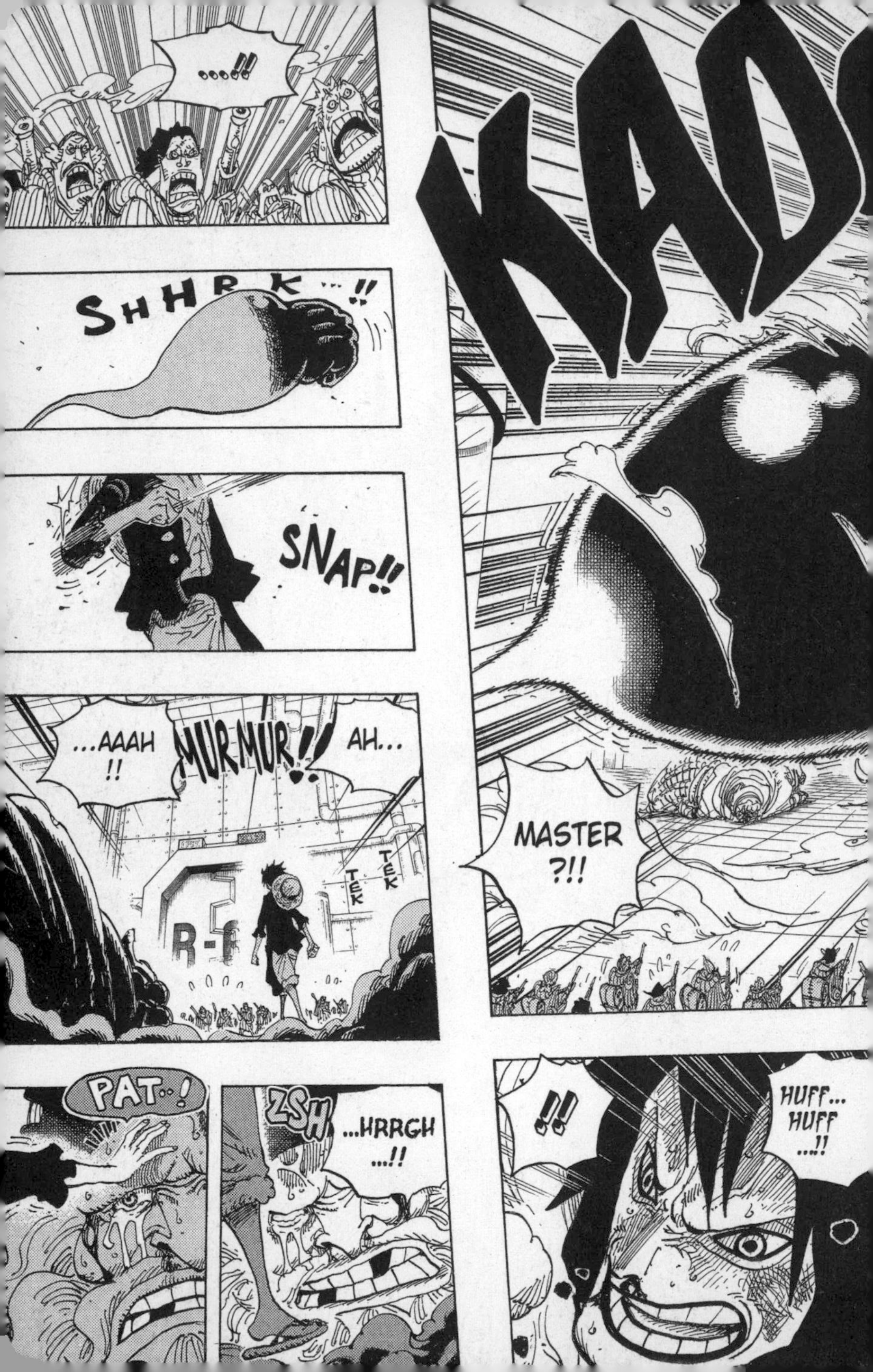

MASTER ?!!
....!!
SHHRK...!!
SNAP!!
AH...
MURMUR!!
...AAAH !!
TEK TEK
HUFF... HUFF ...!!
!!
...HRRGH ...!!
ZSH
PAT..!

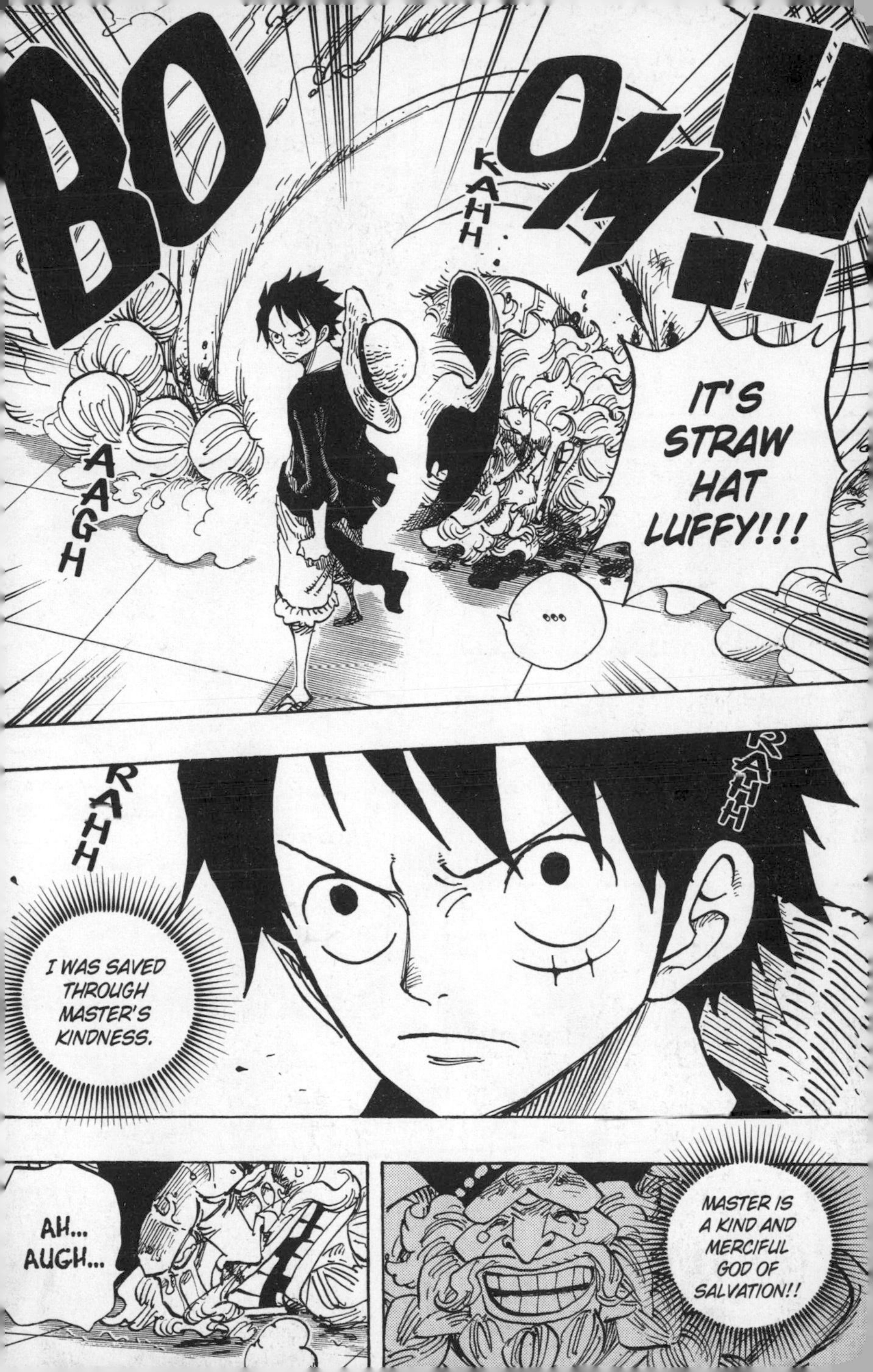
BOOM!!
KAHH
IT'S STRAW HAT LUFFY!!!
AAGH
...
RAHH
RAHH
I WAS SAVED THROUGH MASTER'S KINDNESS.
MASTER IS A KIND AND MERCIFUL GOD OF SALVATION!!
AH... AUGH...

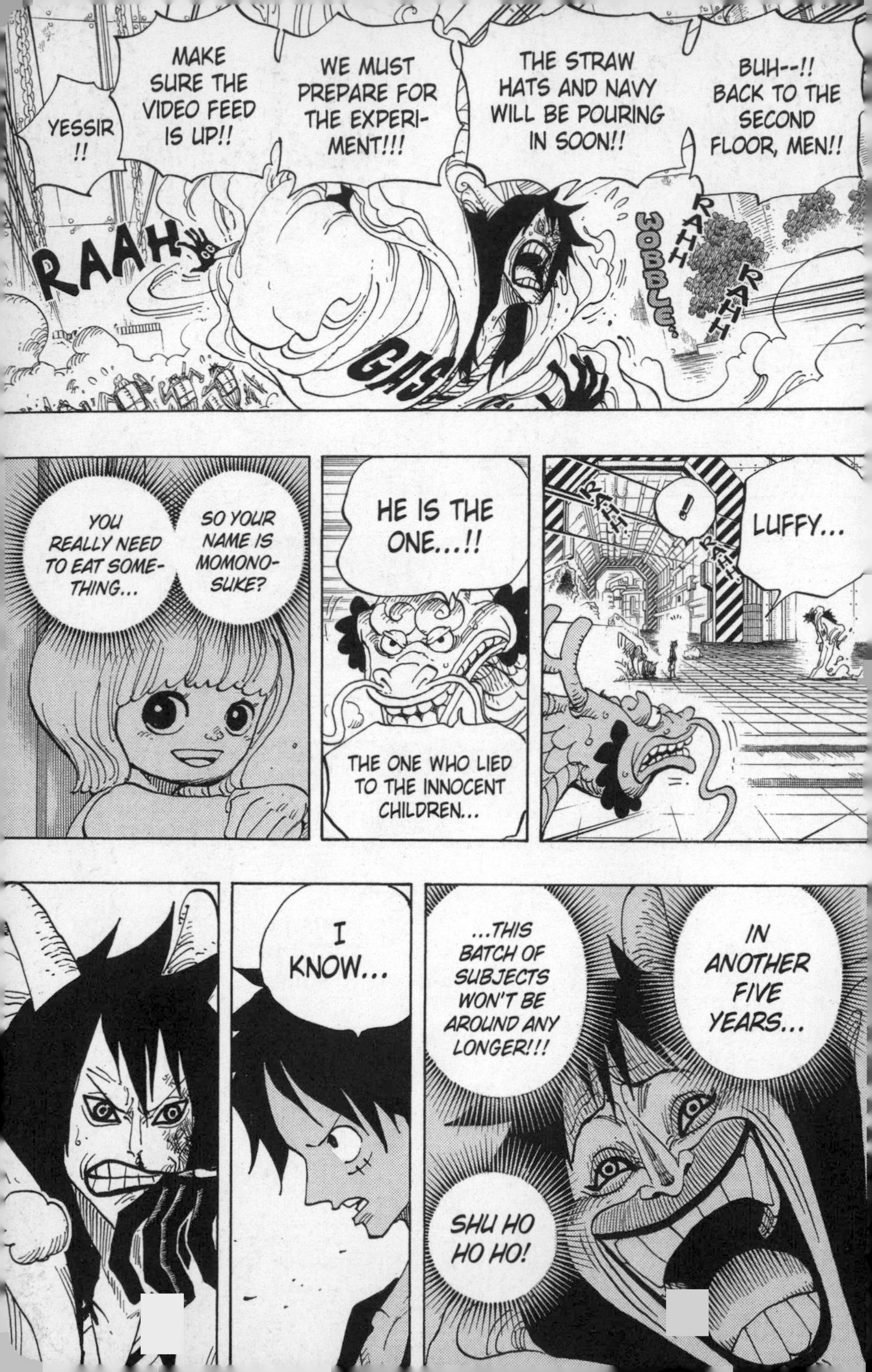
BUH--!! BACK TO THE SECOND FLOOR, MEN!!
THE STRAW HATS AND NAVY WILL BE POURING IN SOON!!
WE MUST PREPARE FOR THE EXPERI- MENT!!!
MAKE SURE THE VIDEO FEED IS UP!!
YESSIR !!
RAHH
RAHH
WOBBLE
GASH
RAAH
!
LUFFY...
RAHH
RAHH
HE IS THE ONE...!!
THE ONE WHO LIED TO THE INNOCENT CHILDREN...
SO YOUR NAME IS MOMONO- SUKE?
YOU REALLY NEED TO EAT SOME- THING...
IN ANOTHER FIVE YEARS...
...THIS BATCH OF SUBJECTS WON'T BE AROUND ANY LONGER!!!
SHU HO HO HO!
I KNOW...

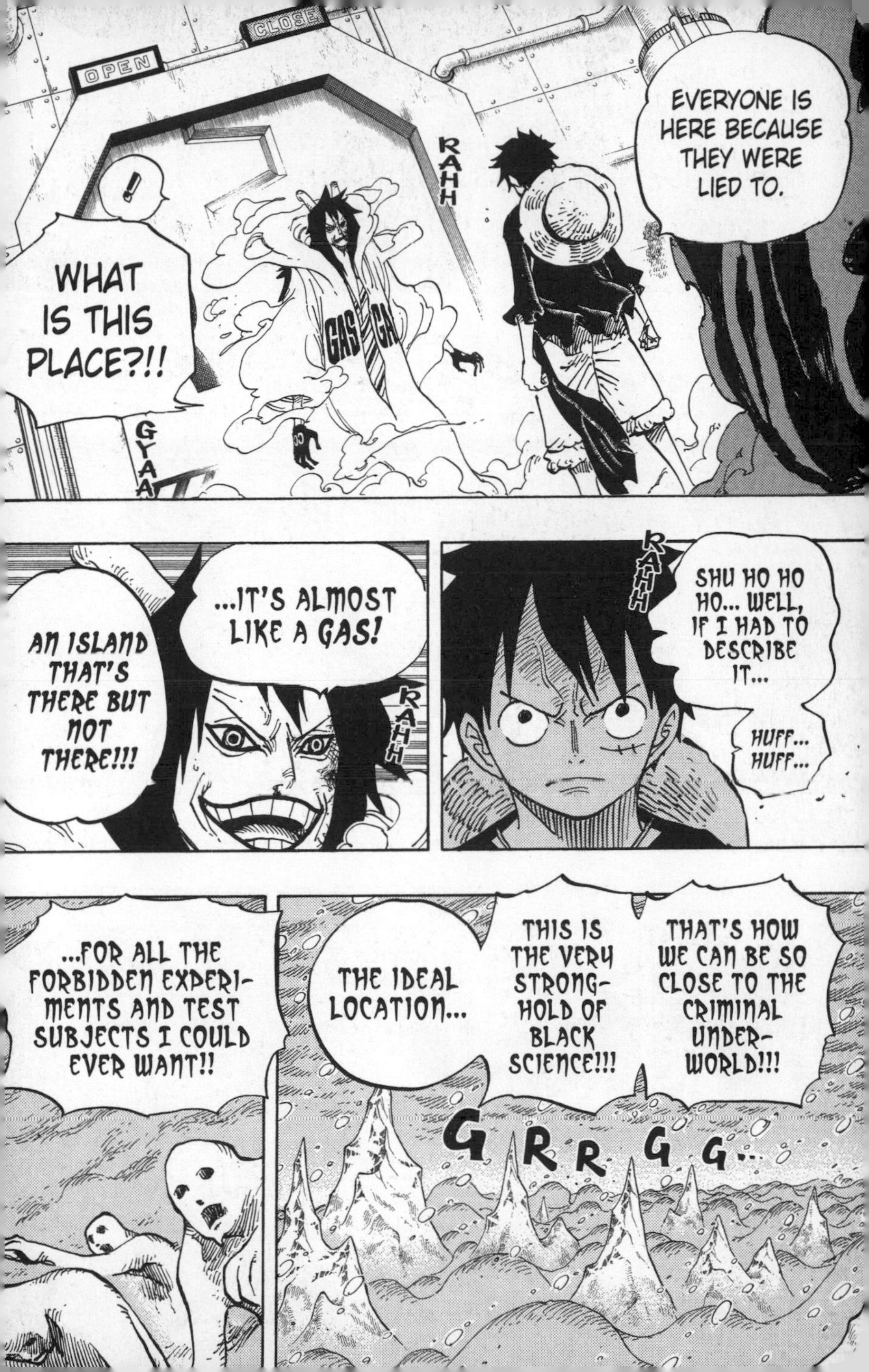
CLOSE
OPEN
EVERYONE IS HERE BECAUSE THEY WERE LIED TO.
RAHH
!
WHAT IS THIS PLACE?!!
GAS GA
GYAA
RAHH
SHU HO HO HO... WELL, IF I HAD TO DESCRIBE IT...
HUFF... HUFF...
...IT'S ALMOST LIKE A GAS!
RAHH
AN ISLAND THAT'S THERE BUT NOT THERE!!!
THAT'S HOW WE CAN BE SO CLOSE TO THE CRIMINAL UNDER-WORLD!!!
THIS IS THE VERY STRONG-HOLD OF BLACK SCIENCE!!!
THE IDEAL LOCATION...
GRRGG...
...FOR ALL THE FORBIDDEN EXPERI-MENTS AND TEST SUBJECTS I COULD EVER WANT!!

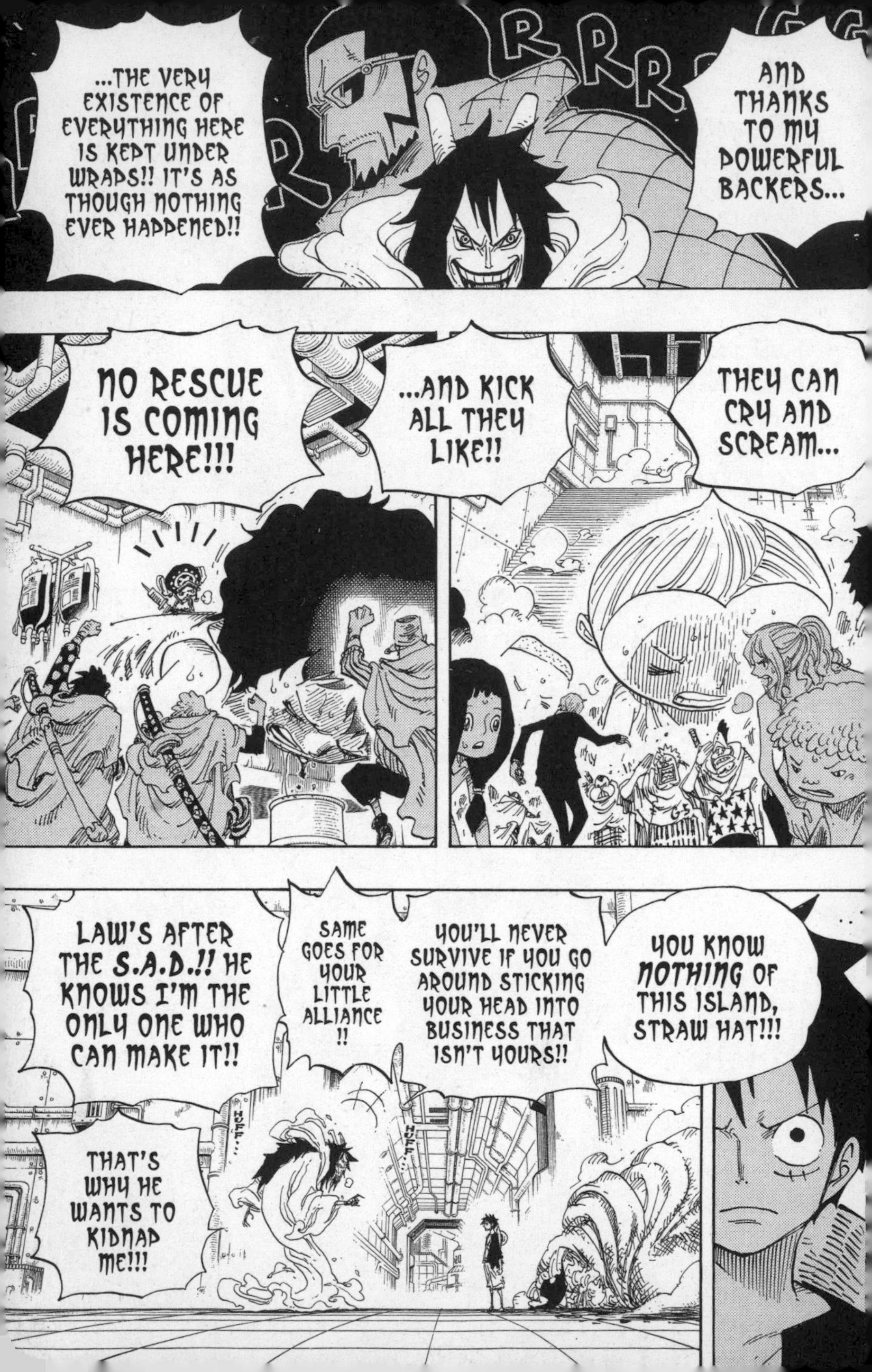
AND THANKS TO MY POWERFUL BACKERS...
...THE VERY EXISTENCE OF EVERYTHING HERE IS KEPT UNDER WRAPS!! IT'S AS THOUGH NOTHING EVER HAPPENED!!
THEY CAN CRY AND SCREAM...
...AND KICK ALL THEY LIKE!!
NO RESCUE IS COMING HERE!!!
YOU KNOW *NOTHING* OF THIS ISLAND, STRAW HAT!!!
YOU'LL NEVER SURVIVE IF YOU GO AROUND STICKING YOUR HEAD INTO BUSINESS THAT ISN'T YOURS!!
SAME GOES FOR YOUR LITTLE ALLIANCE!!
LAW'S AFTER THE *S.A.D.!!* HE KNOWS I'M THE ONLY ONE WHO CAN MAKE IT!!
THAT'S WHY HE WANTS TO KIDNAP ME!!!
HUFF...
HUFF...

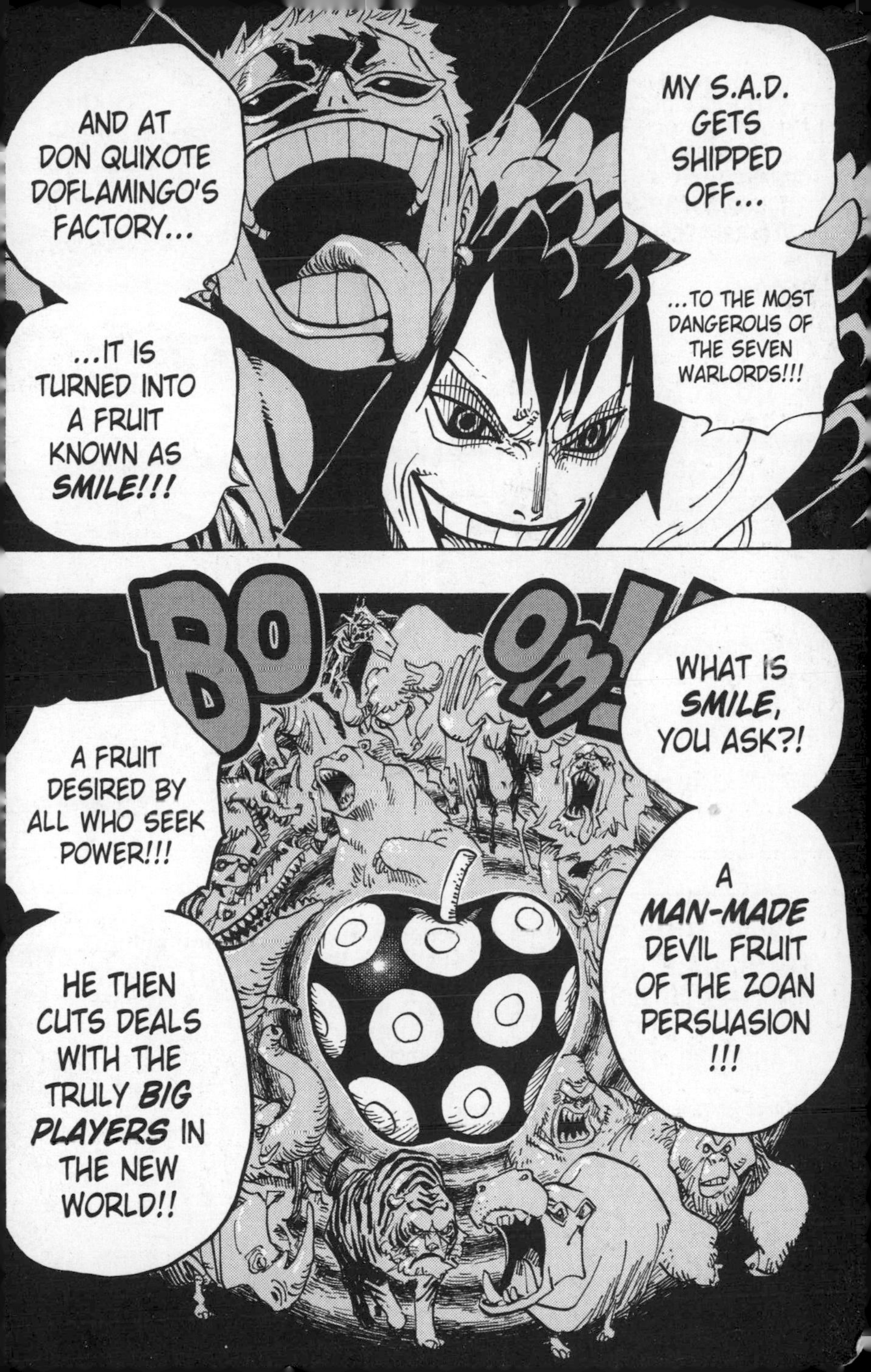
MY S.A.D. GETS SHIPPED OFF...
...TO THE MOST DANGEROUS OF THE SEVEN WARLORDS!!!
AND AT DON QUIXOTE DOFLAMINGO'S FACTORY...
...IT IS TURNED INTO A FRUIT KNOWN AS *SMILE!!!*
BOOM
WHAT IS *SMILE,* YOU ASK?!
A *MAN-MADE* DEVIL FRUIT OF THE ZOAN PERSUASION !!!
A FRUIT DESIRED BY ALL WHO SEEK POWER!!!
HE THEN CUTS DEALS WITH THE TRULY *BIG PLAYERS* IN THE NEW WORLD!!

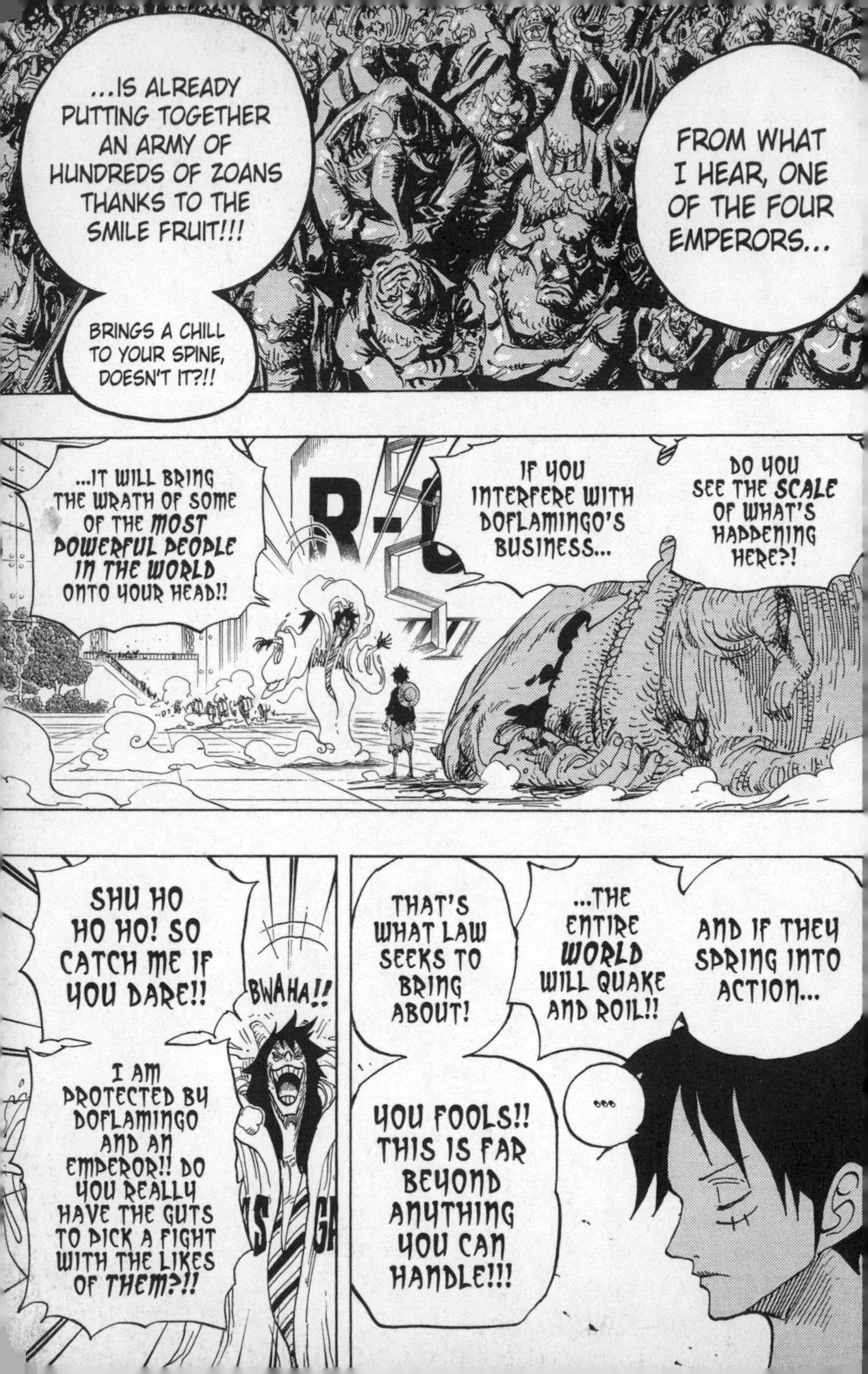
FROM WHAT I HEAR, ONE OF THE FOUR EMPERORS...
...IS ALREADY PUTTING TOGETHER AN ARMY OF HUNDREDS OF ZOANS THANKS TO THE SMILE FRUIT!!!
BRINGS A CHILL TO YOUR SPINE, DOESN'T IT?!!
DO YOU SEE THE SCALE OF WHAT'S HAPPENING HERE?!
IF YOU INTERFERE WITH DOFLAMINGO'S BUSINESS...
...IT WILL BRING THE WRATH OF SOME OF THE MOST POWERFUL PEOPLE IN THE WORLD ONTO YOUR HEAD!!
AND IF THEY SPRING INTO ACTION...
...THE ENTIRE WORLD WILL QUAKE AND ROIL!!
THAT'S WHAT LAW SEEKS TO BRING ABOUT!
...
YOU FOOLS!! THIS IS FAR BEYOND ANYTHING YOU CAN HANDLE!!!
SHU HO HO HO! SO CATCH ME IF YOU DARE!!
BWAHA!!
I AM PROTECTED BY DOFLAMINGO AND AN EMPEROR!! DO YOU REALLY HAVE THE GUTS TO PICK A FIGHT WITH THE LIKES OF THEM?!!

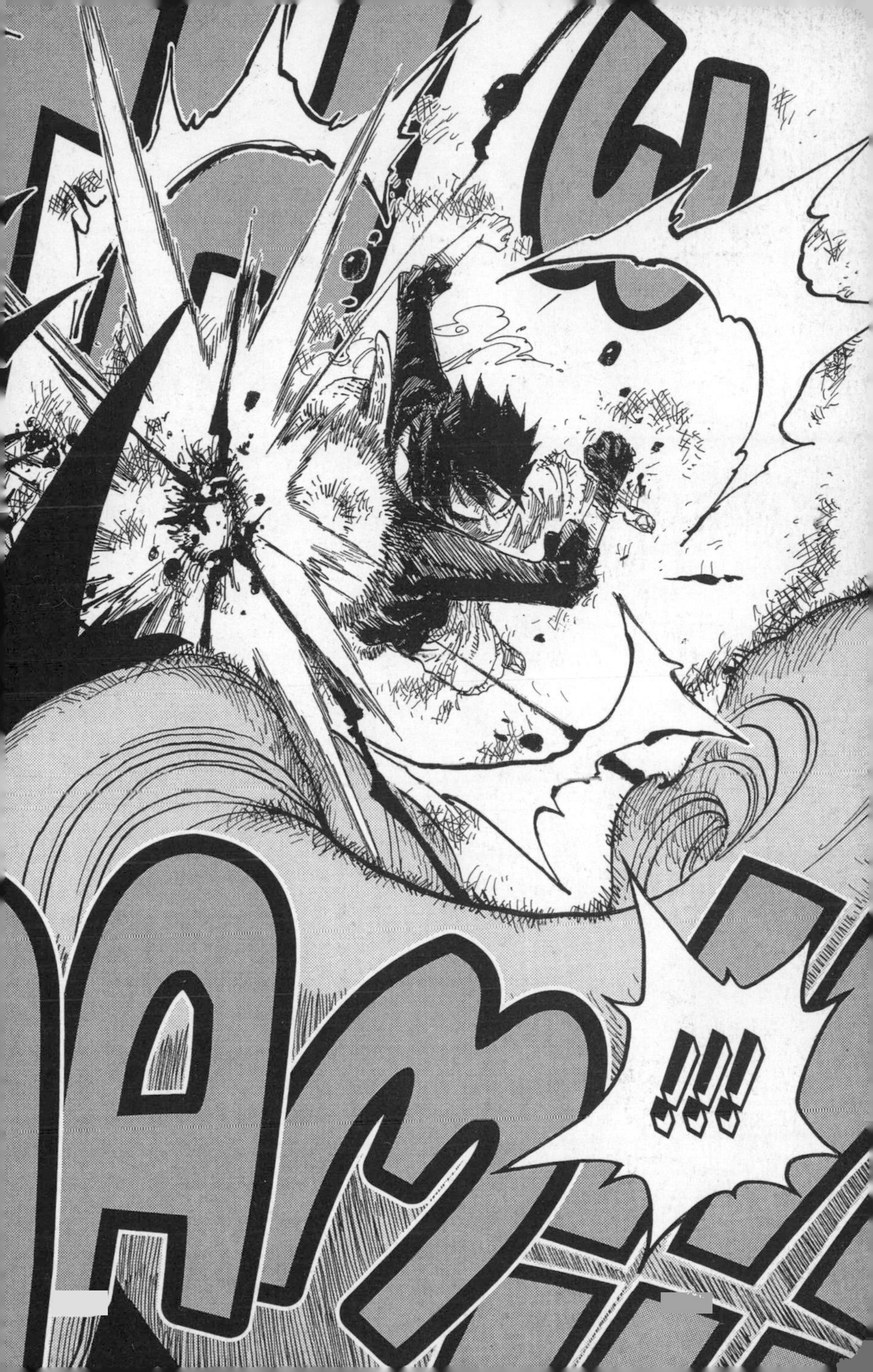

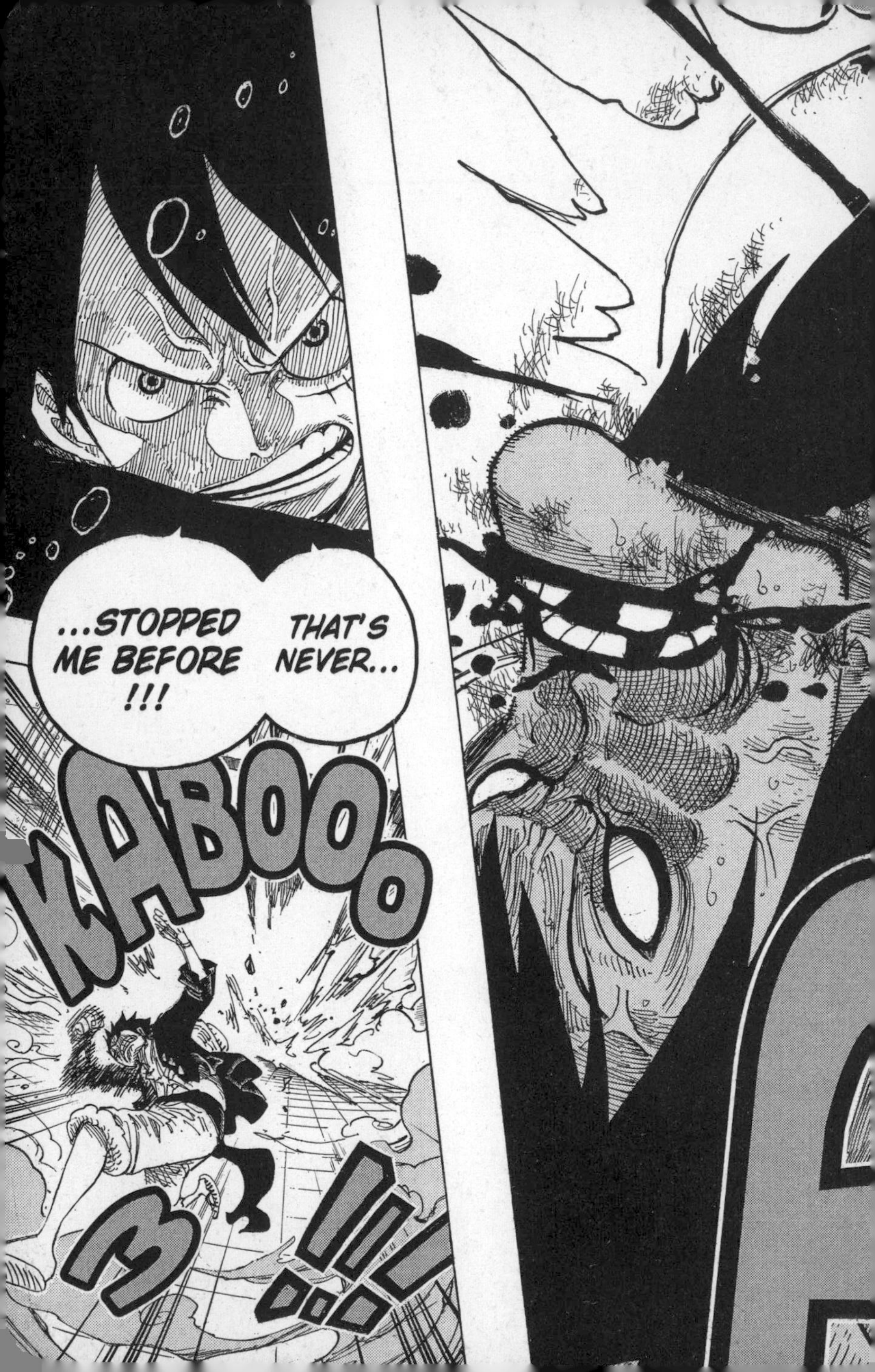
THAT'S NEVER...
...STOPPED ME BEFORE !!!
KABOOOM!!

Chapter 690:
S.A.D.

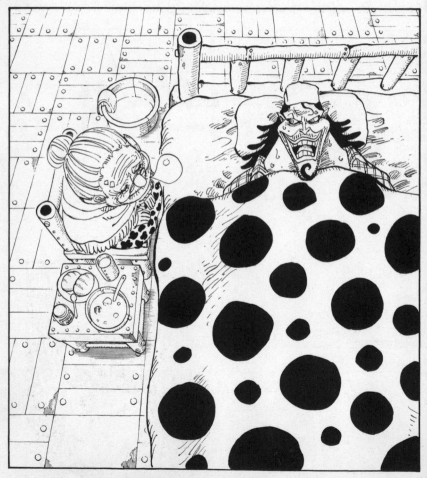

CARIBOU'S NEW WORLD KEE HEE HEE, VOL. 15:
"WAKING UP NEXT TO AN OLD HAG"

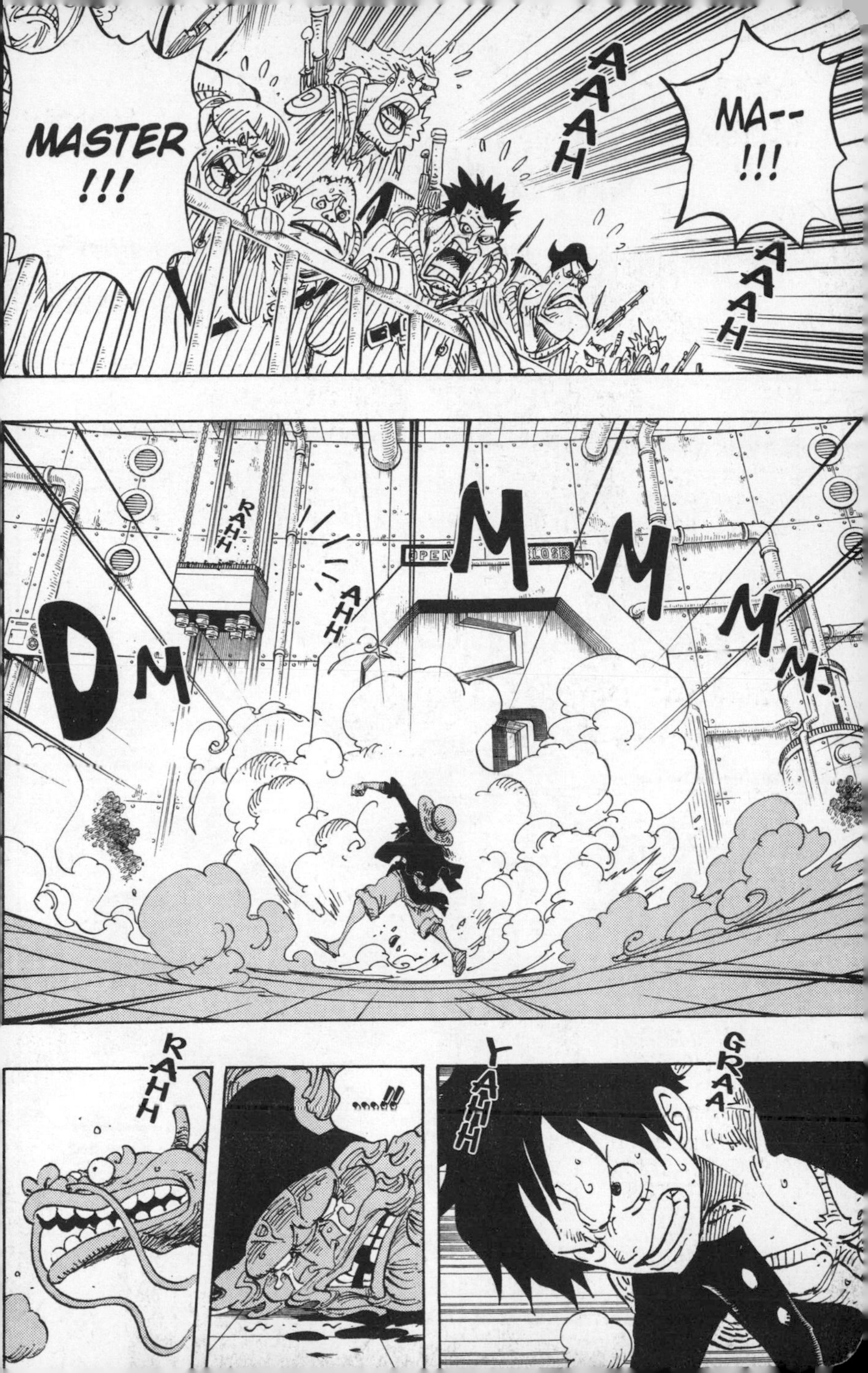
MA-- !!!
AAAAH
AAAAH
MASTER !!!
RAHH
AHH
DMMMMM.
OPEN
CLOSE
GRAA
YAHHH
......!!
RAHH

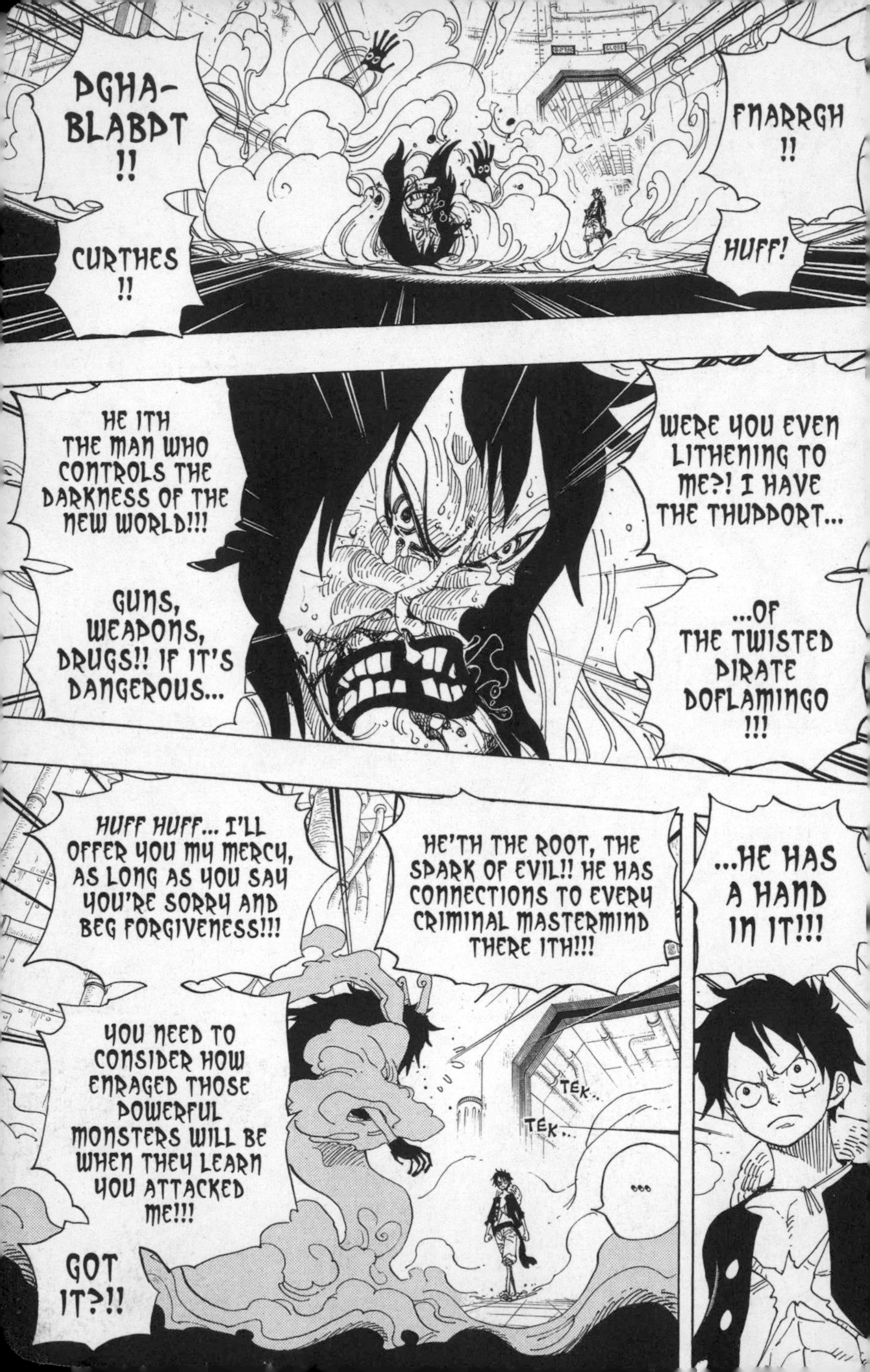
FNARRGH!!
PGHA-BLABPT!!
HUFF!
CURTHES!!
WERE YOU EVEN LITHENING TO ME?! I HAVE THE THUPPORT...
...OF THE TWISTED PIRATE DOFLAMINGO!!!
HE ITH THE MAN WHO CONTROLS THE DARKNESS OF THE NEW WORLD!!!
GUNS, WEAPONS, DRUGS!! IF IT'S DANGEROUS...
...HE HAS A HAND IN IT!!!
HE'TH THE ROOT, THE SPARK OF EVIL!! HE HAS CONNECTIONS TO EVERY CRIMINAL MASTERMIND THERE ITH!!!
HUFF HUFF... I'LL OFFER YOU MY MERCY, AS LONG AS YOU SAY YOU'RE SORRY AND BEG FORGIVENESS!!!
TEK...
TEK...
...
YOU NEED TO CONSIDER HOW ENRAGED THOSE POWERFUL MONSTERS WILL BE WHEN THEY LEARN YOU ATTACKED ME!!!
GOT IT?!!

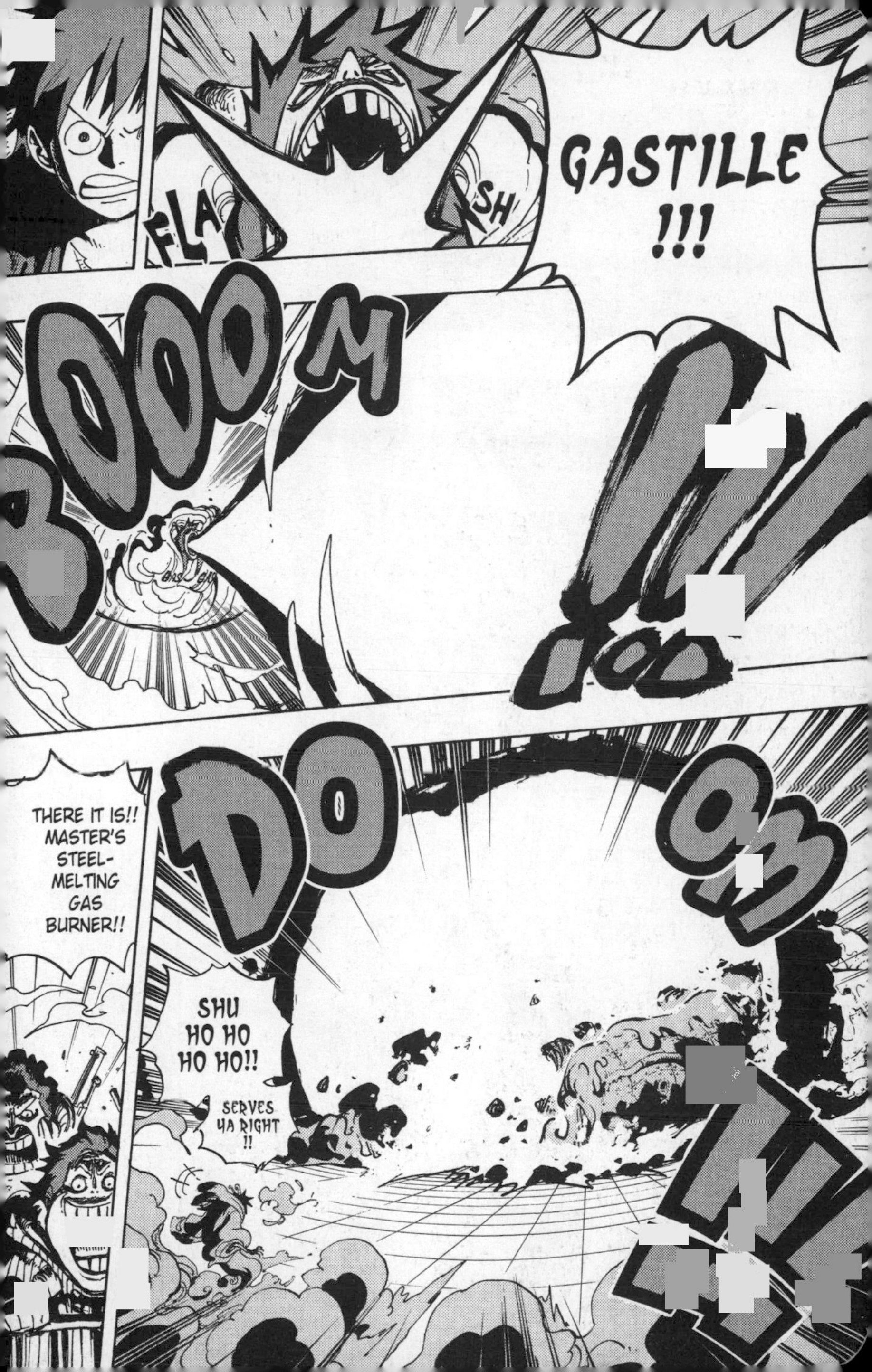
GASTILLE !!!
FLASH
BOOOM!!
DOOM
THERE IT IS!! MASTER'S STEEL-MELTING GAS BURNER!!
SHU HO HO HO HO!!
SERVES YA RIGHT !!

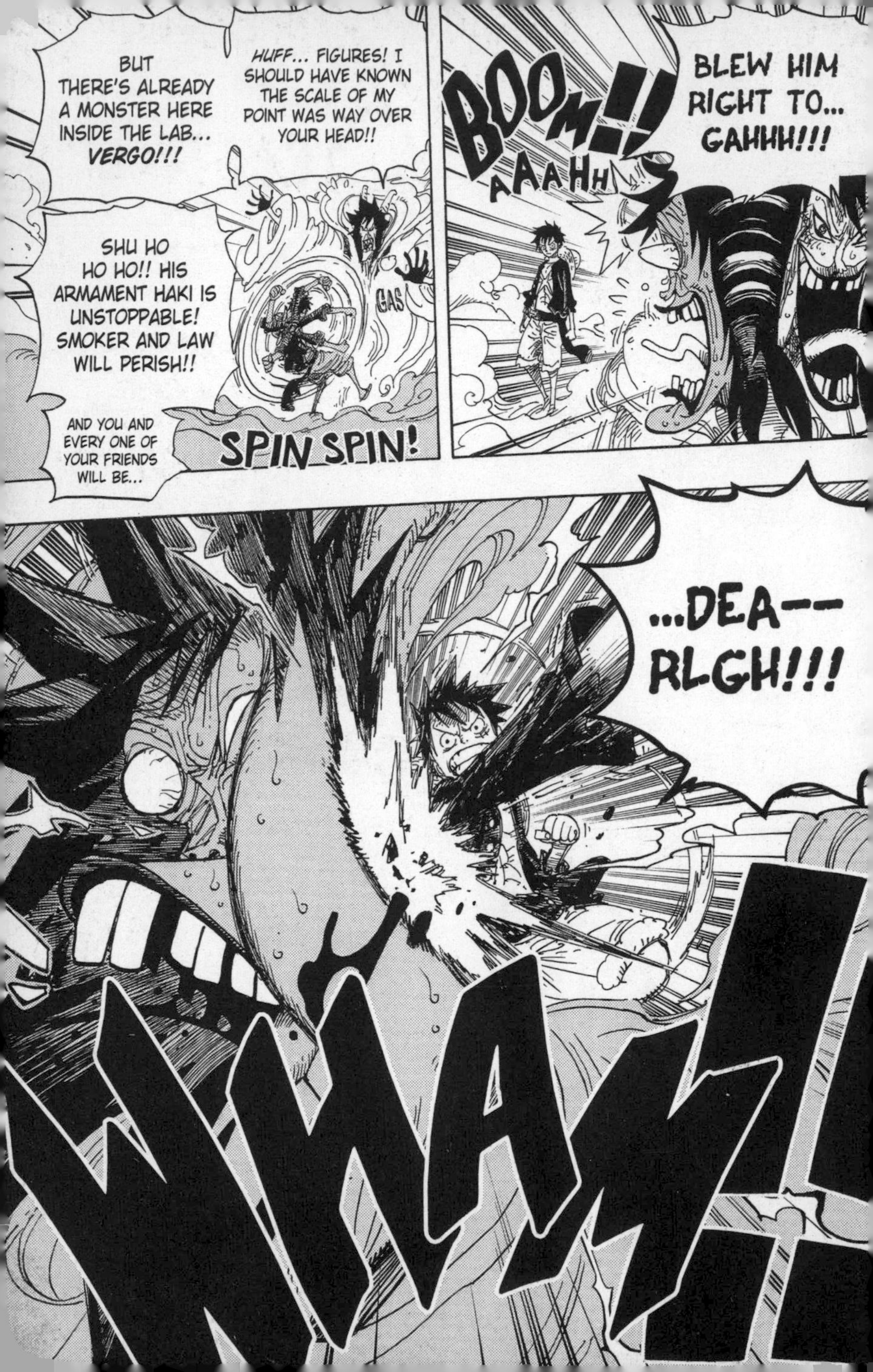
BOOM!!
AAAHH
BLEW HIM RIGHT TO... GAHHH!!!
HUFF... FIGURES! I SHOULD HAVE KNOWN THE SCALE OF MY POINT WAS WAY OVER YOUR HEAD!!
BUT THERE'S ALREADY A MONSTER HERE INSIDE THE LAB... VERGO!!!
GAS
SHU HO HO HO!! HIS ARMAMENT HAKI IS UNSTOPPABLE! SMOKER AND LAW WILL PERISH!!
AND YOU AND EVERY ONE OF YOUR FRIENDS WILL BE...
SPIN SPIN!
...DEA-- RLGH!!!
WHAM!!

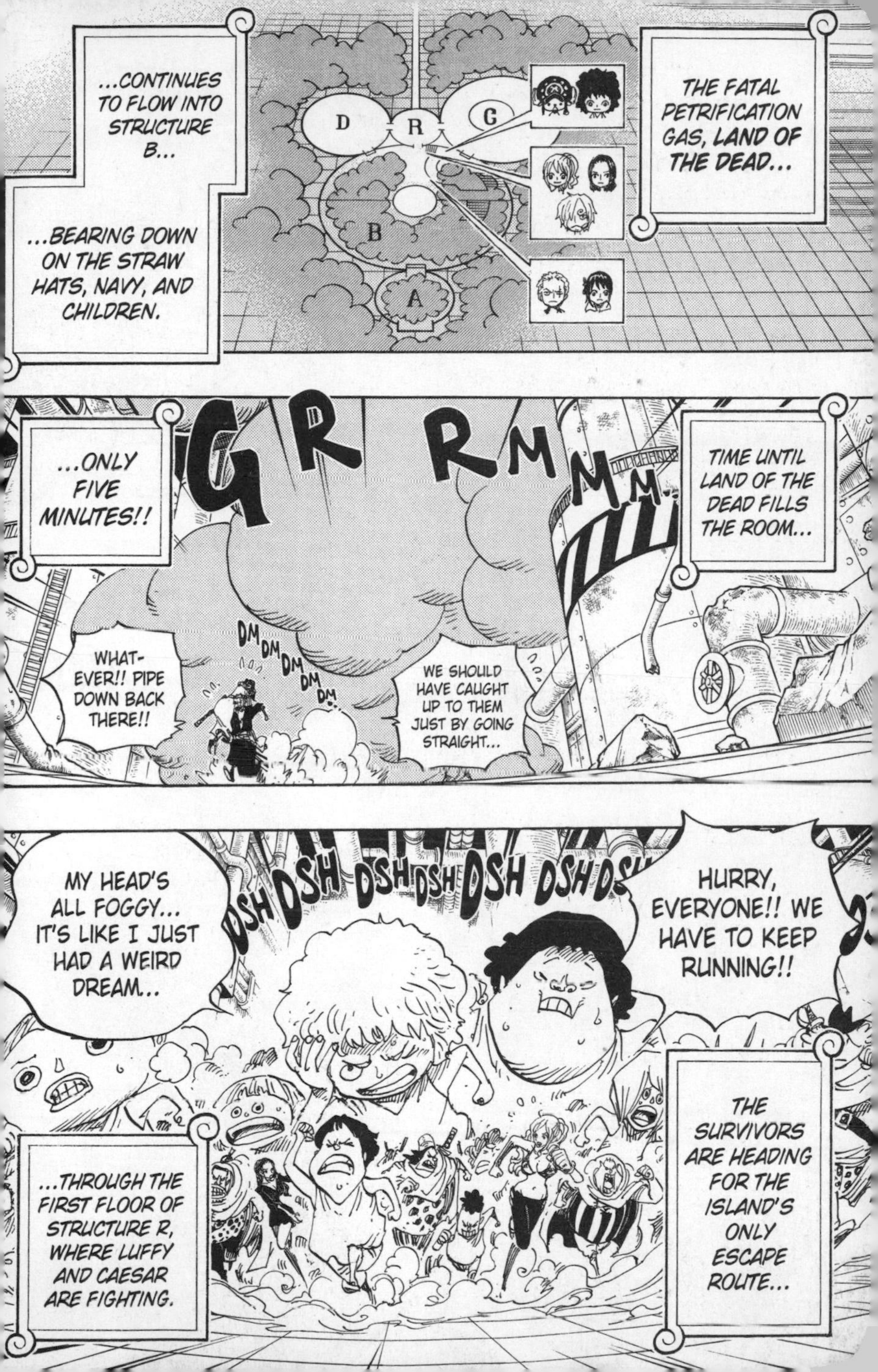
THE FATAL PETRIFICATION GAS, LAND OF THE DEAD...
...CONTINUES TO FLOW INTO STRUCTURE B...
...BEARING DOWN ON THE STRAW HATS, NAVY, AND CHILDREN.
D
R
G
B
A
TIME UNTIL LAND OF THE DEAD FILLS THE ROOM...
...ONLY FIVE MINUTES!!
GRRMMM
WE SHOULD HAVE CAUGHT UP TO THEM JUST BY GOING STRAIGHT...
DM DM DM DM DM
WHAT-EVER!! PIPE DOWN BACK THERE!!
THE SURVIVORS ARE HEADING FOR THE ISLAND'S ONLY ESCAPE ROUTE...
HURRY, EVERYONE!! WE HAVE TO KEEP RUNNING!!
DSH DSH DSH DSH DSH DSH DSH
MY HEAD'S ALL FOGGY... IT'S LIKE I JUST HAD A WEIRD DREAM...
...THROUGH THE FIRST FLOOR OF STRUCTURE R, WHERE LUFFY AND CAESAR ARE FIGHTING.

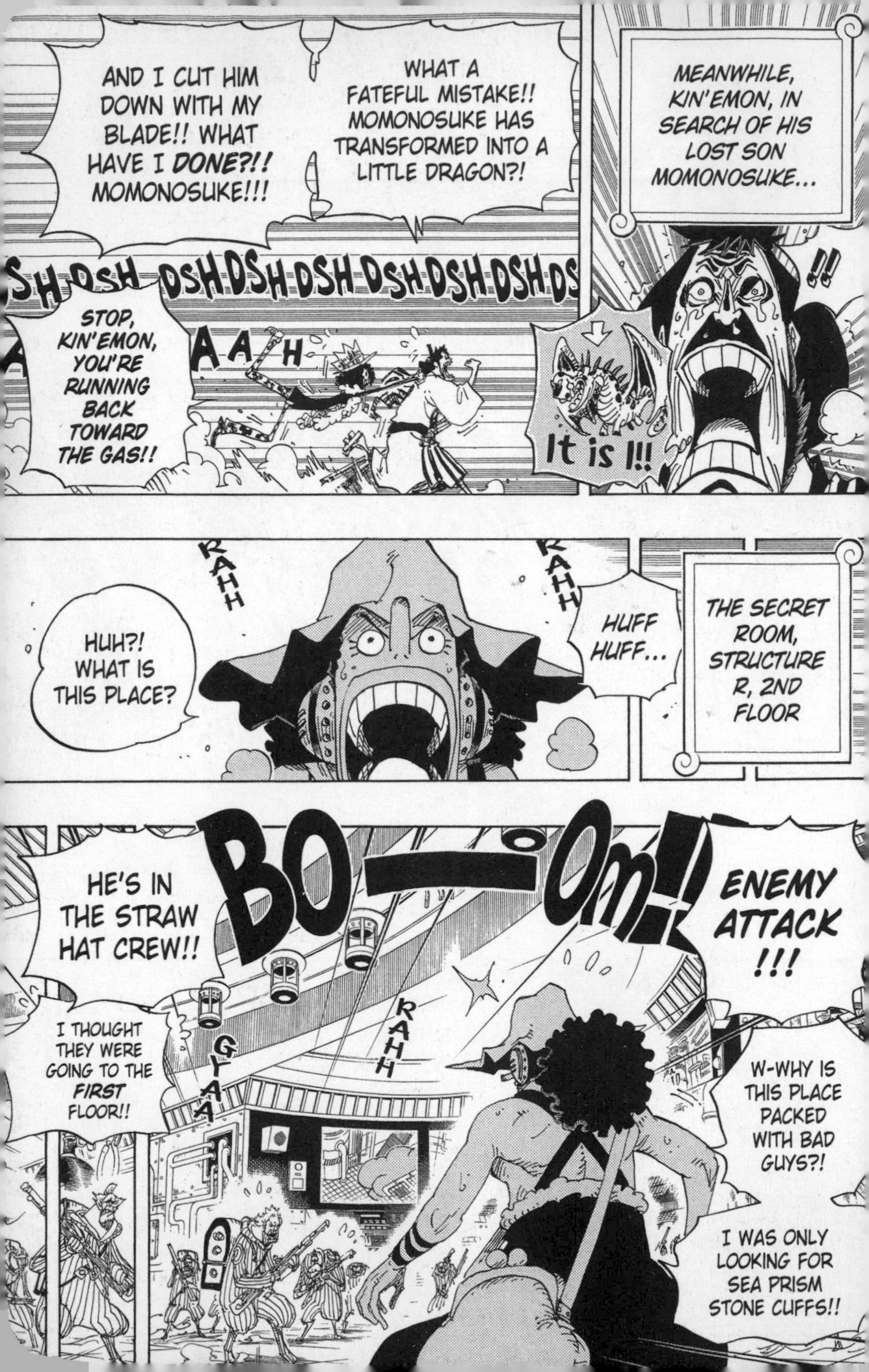
MEANWHILE, KIN'EMON, IN SEARCH OF HIS LOST SON MOMONOSUKE...
!!
It is I!!
WHAT A FATEFUL MISTAKE!! MOMONOSUKE HAS TRANSFORMED INTO A LITTLE DRAGON?!
AND I CUT HIM DOWN WITH MY BLADE!! WHAT HAVE I *DONE?!!* MOMONOSUKE!!!
SHDSH DSHDSH DSHDSH DSHDSH DSHDSHDS
AAAH
STOP, KIN'EMON, YOU'RE RUNNING BACK TOWARD THE GAS!!
THE SECRET ROOM, STRUCTURE R, 2ND FLOOR
RAHH
HUFF HUFF...
RAHH
HUH?! WHAT IS THIS PLACE?
ENEMY ATTACK!!!
BO—OM!!
HE'S IN THE STRAW HAT CREW!!
W-WHY IS THIS PLACE PACKED WITH BAD GUYS?!
I WAS ONLY LOOKING FOR SEA PRISM STONE CUFFS!!
RAHH
GYAAA
I THOUGHT THEY WERE GOING TO THE *FIRST* FLOOR!!

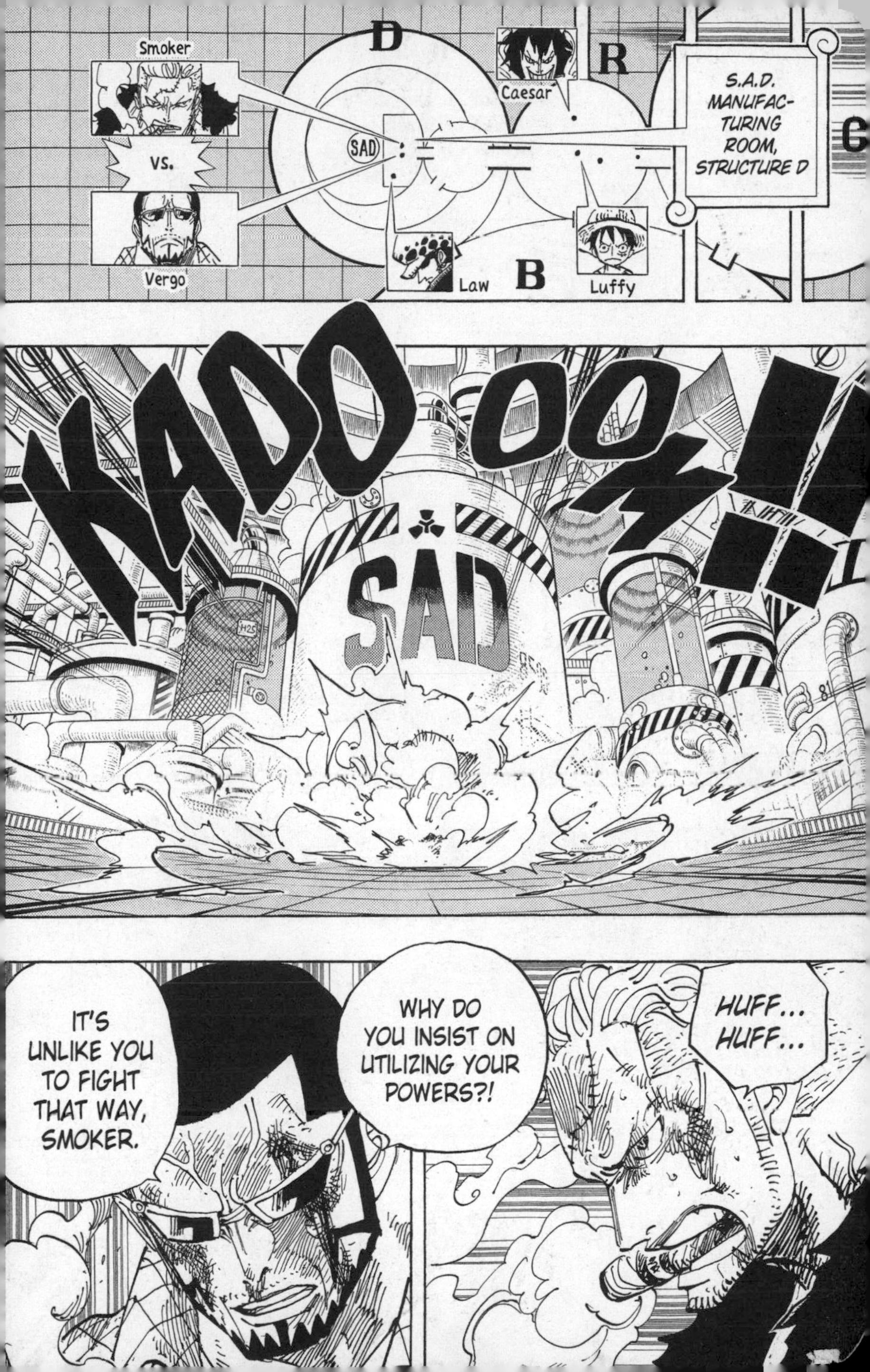
S.A.D. MANUFAC-TURING ROOM, STRUCTURE D
G
R
Caesar
D
Smoker
vs.
Vergo
SAD
Luffy
B
Law
KADOOM!!!
SAD
HUFF... HUFF...
WHY DO YOU INSIST ON UTILIZING YOUR POWERS?!
IT'S UNLIKE YOU TO FIGHT THAT WAY, SMOKER.

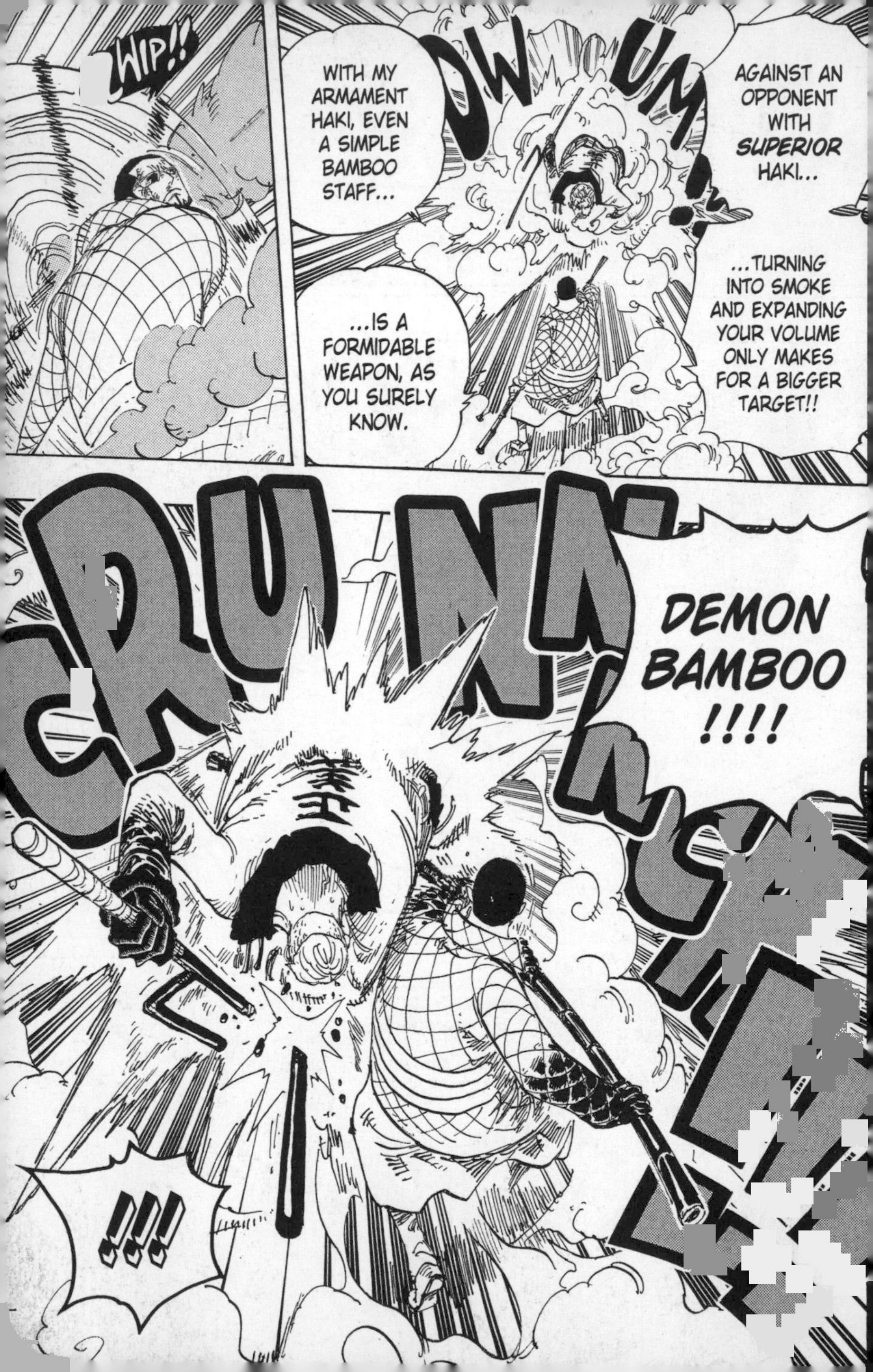
AGAINST AN OPPONENT WITH SUPERIOR HAKI...
...TURNING INTO SMOKE AND EXPANDING YOUR VOLUME ONLY MAKES FOR A BIGGER TARGET!!
WITH MY ARMAMENT HAKI, EVEN A SIMPLE BAMBOO STAFF...
...IS A FORMIDABLE WEAPON, AS YOU SURELY KNOW.
WIP!!
DEMON BAMBOO !!!!
!!!

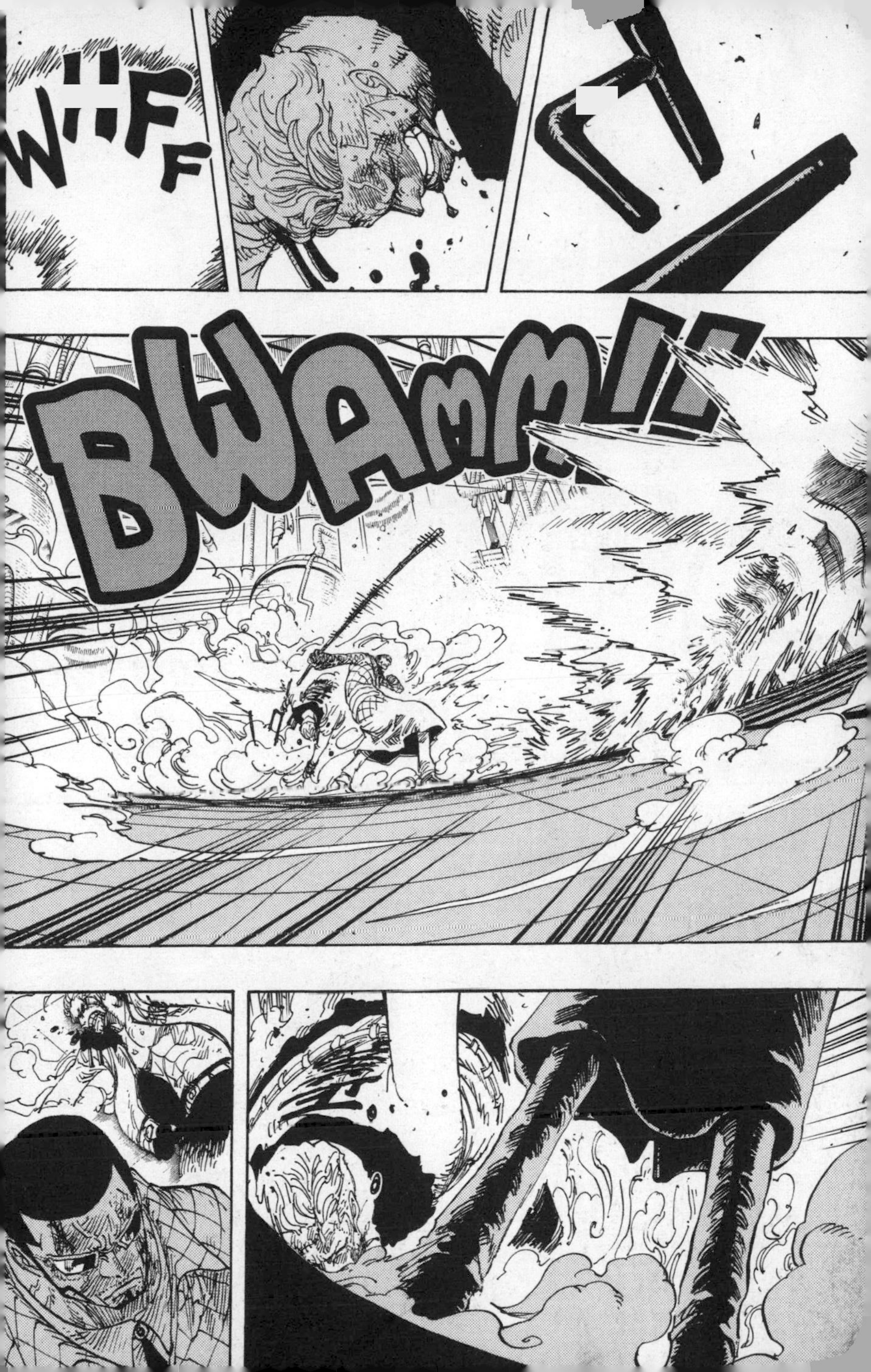
WHIFF
BWAMM!!

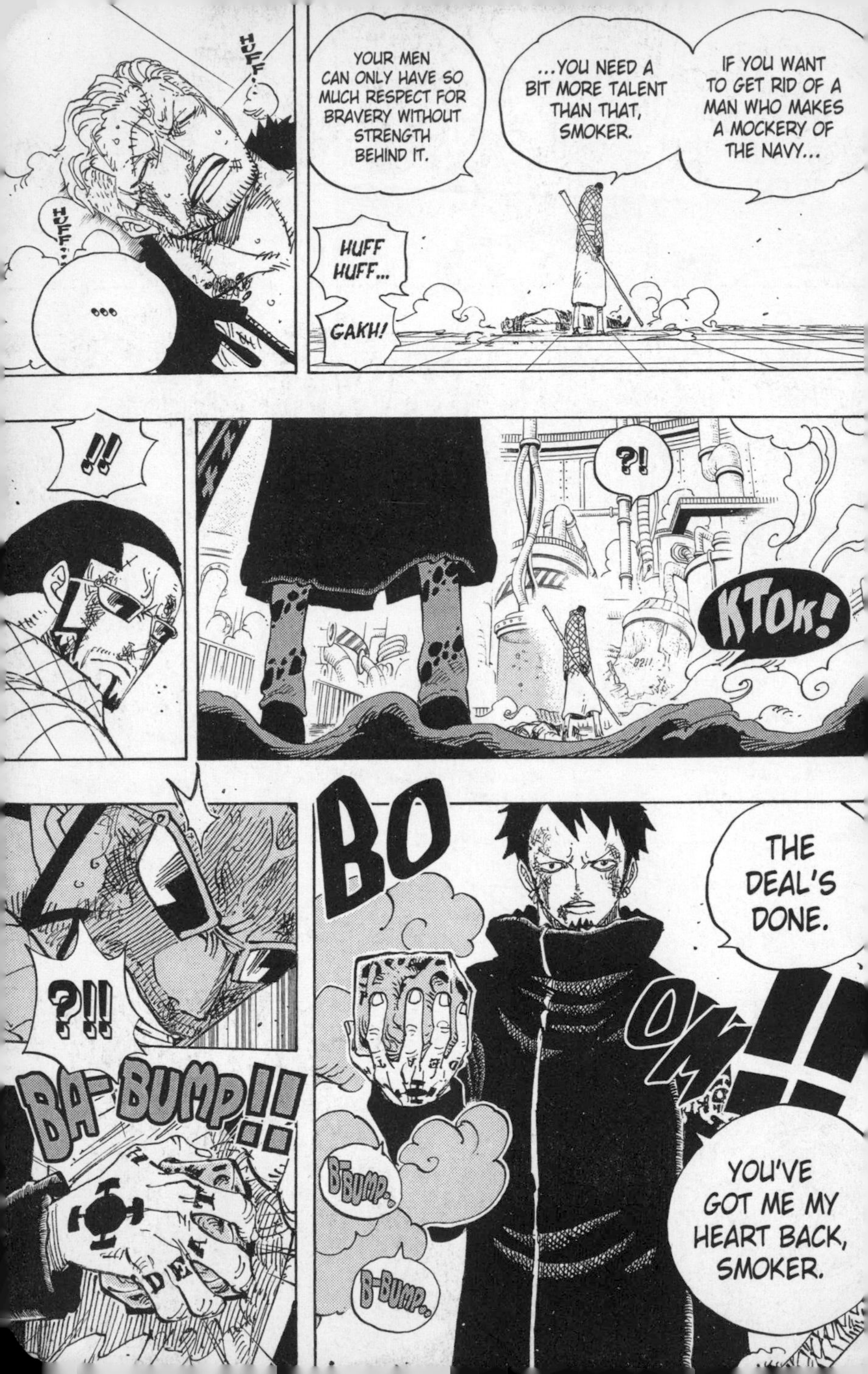
IF YOU WANT TO GET RID OF A MAN WHO MAKES A MOCKERY OF THE NAVY...
...YOU NEED A BIT MORE TALENT THAN THAT, SMOKER.
YOUR MEN CAN ONLY HAVE SO MUCH RESPECT FOR BRAVERY WITHOUT STRENGTH BEHIND IT.
HUFF HUFF...
GAKH!
HUFF...
HUFF...
...
?!
KTOK!
!!
BOOM!!
THE DEAL'S DONE.
YOU'VE GOT ME MY HEART BACK, SMOKER.
B-BUMP..
B-BUMP..
?!!
BA-BUMP!!

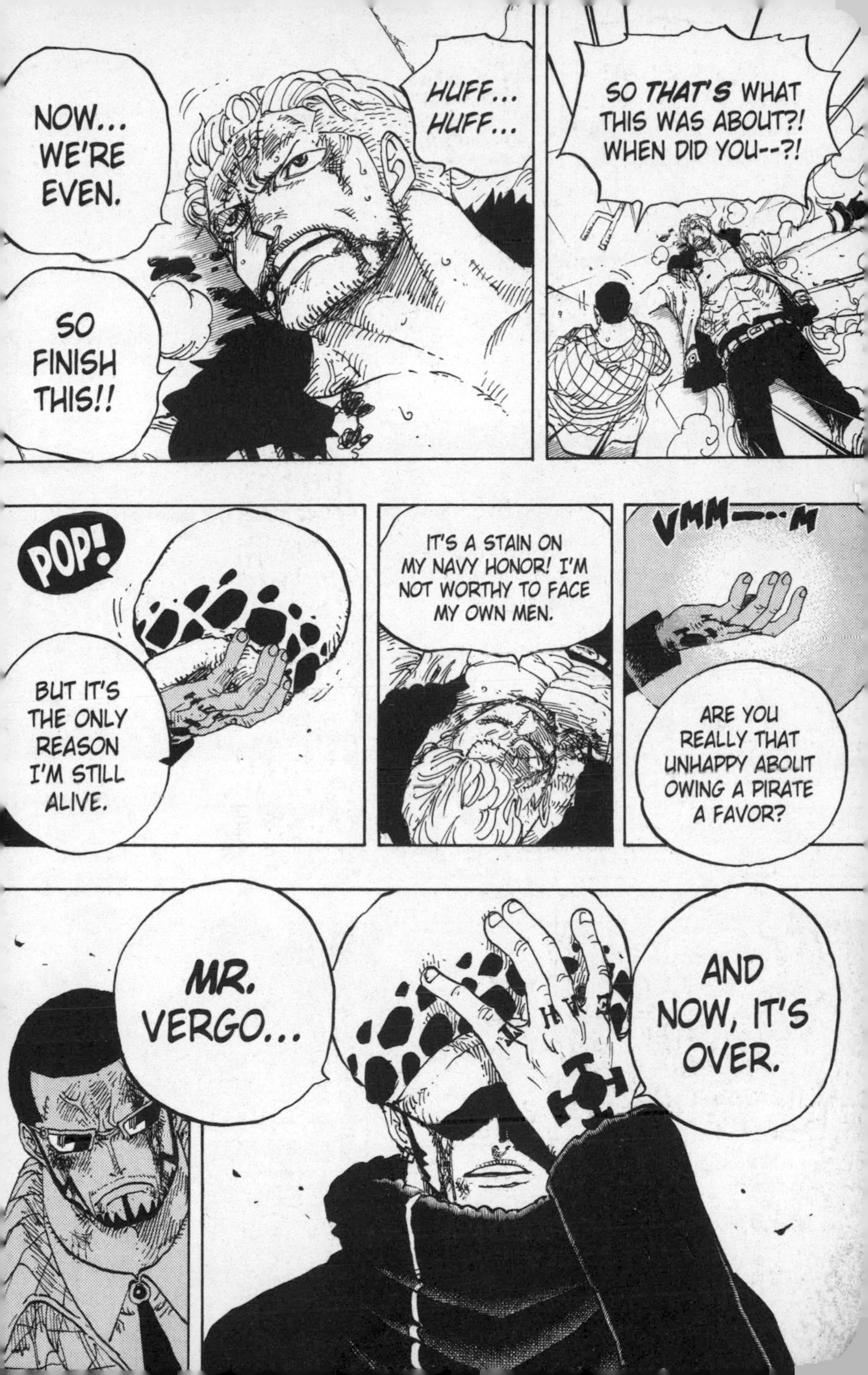
SO *THAT'S* WHAT THIS WAS ABOUT?! WHEN DID YOU--?!
HUFF... HUFF...
NOW... WE'RE EVEN.
SO FINISH THIS!!
VMM---M
ARE YOU REALLY THAT UNHAPPY ABOUT OWING A PIRATE A FAVOR?
IT'S A STAIN ON MY NAVY HONOR! I'M NOT WORTHY TO FACE MY OWN MEN.
POP!
BUT IT'S THE ONLY REASON I'M STILL ALIVE.
AND NOW, IT'S OVER.
MR. VERGO...

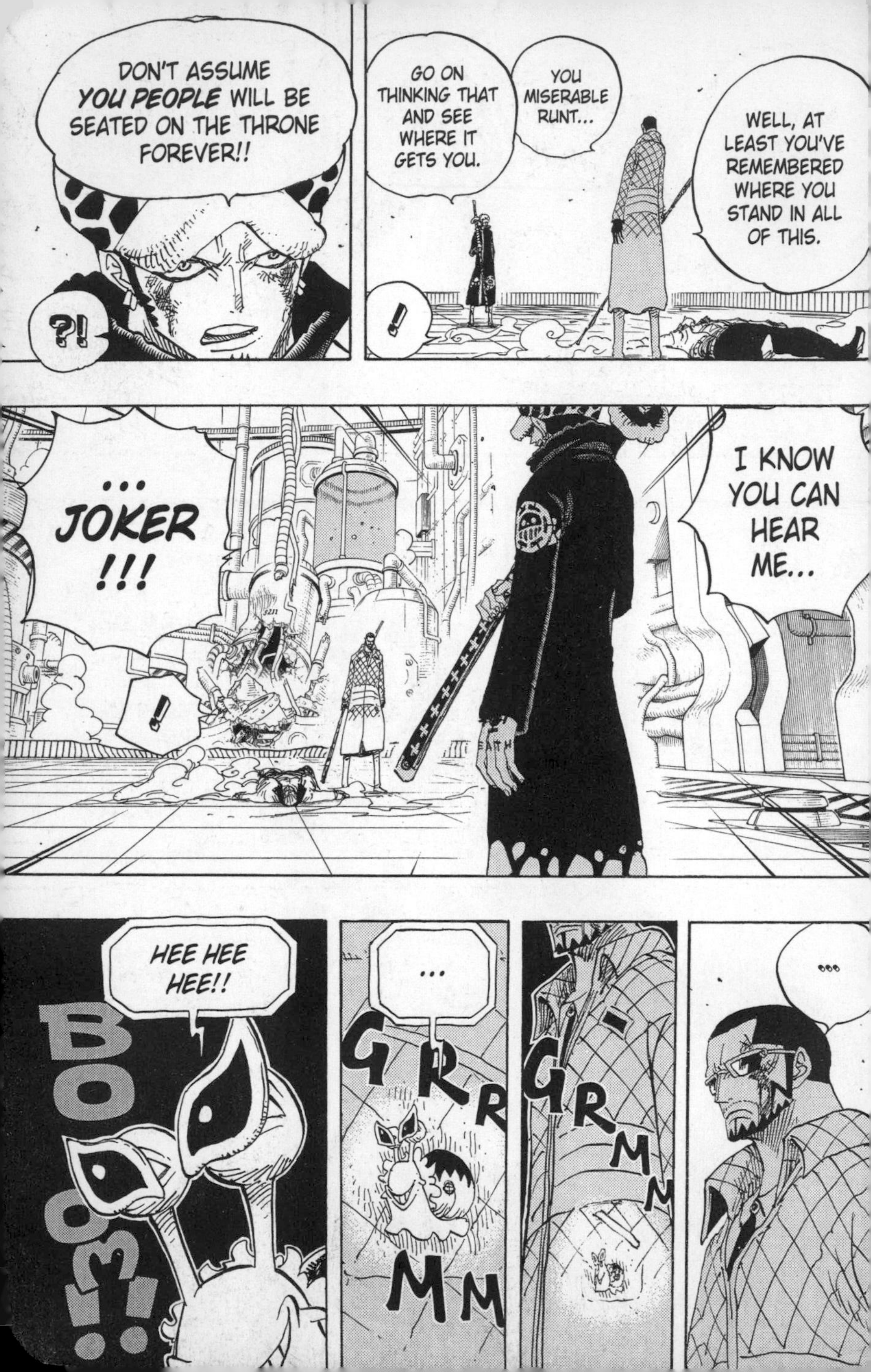
WELL, AT LEAST YOU'VE REMEMBERED WHERE YOU STAND IN ALL OF THIS.
YOU MISERABLE RUNT...
GO ON THINKING THAT AND SEE WHERE IT GETS YOU.
!
DON'T ASSUME *YOU PEOPLE* WILL BE SEATED ON THE THRONE FOREVER!!
?!
I KNOW YOU CAN HEAR ME...
... JOKER !!!
!
...
GRRMMM
...
GRRR
MM
HEE HEE HEE!!
BOOM!!

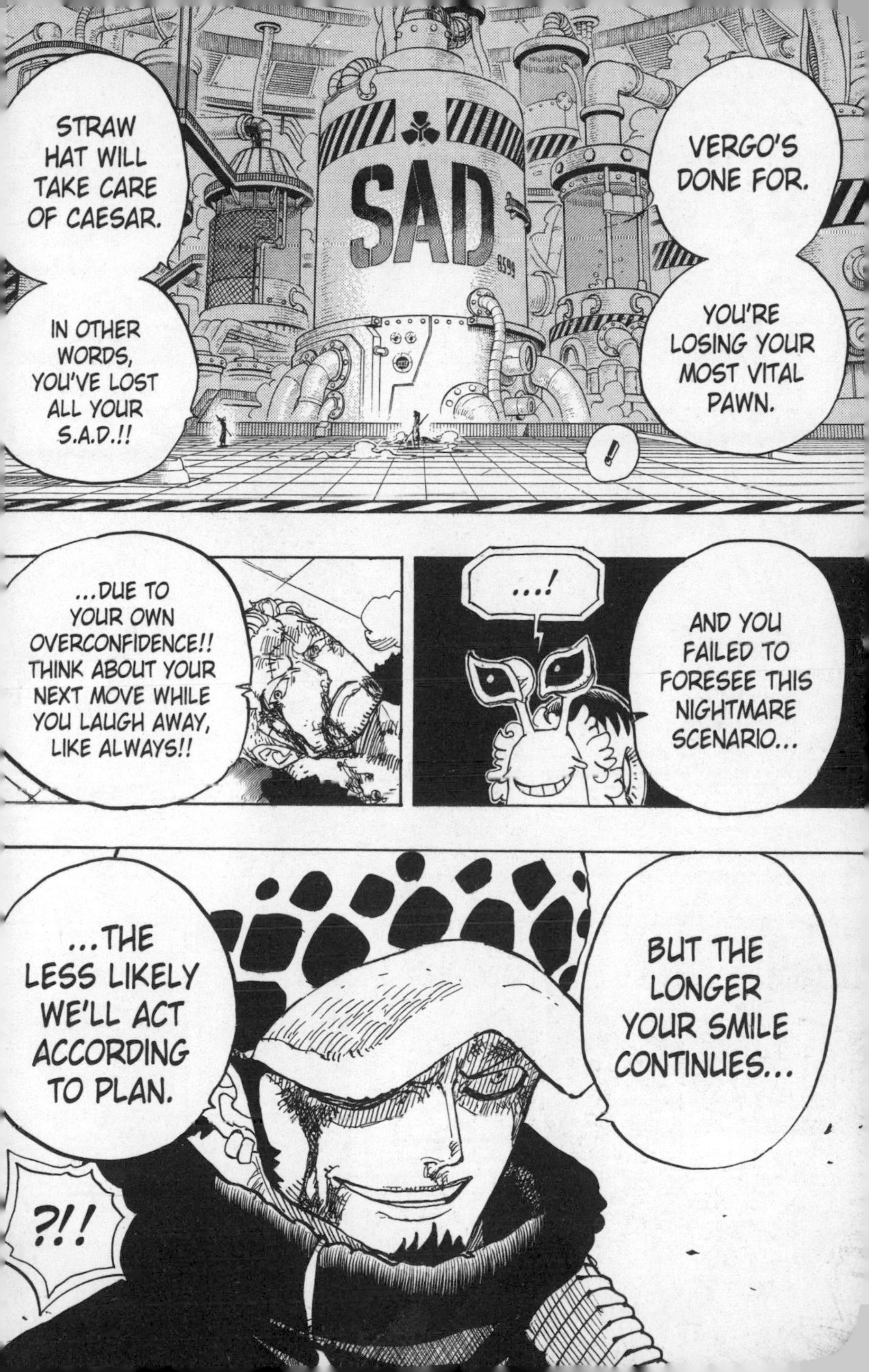
SAD
VERGO'S DONE FOR.
YOU'RE LOSING YOUR MOST VITAL PAWN.
!
STRAW HAT WILL TAKE CARE OF CAESAR.
IN OTHER WORDS, YOU'VE LOST ALL YOUR S.A.D.!!
...!
AND YOU FAILED TO FORESEE THIS NIGHTMARE SCENARIO...
...DUE TO YOUR OWN OVERCONFIDENCE!! THINK ABOUT YOUR NEXT MOVE WHILE YOU LAUGH AWAY, LIKE ALWAYS!!
BUT THE LONGER YOUR SMILE CONTINUES...
...THE LESS LIKELY WE'LL ACT ACCORDING TO PLAN.
?!!

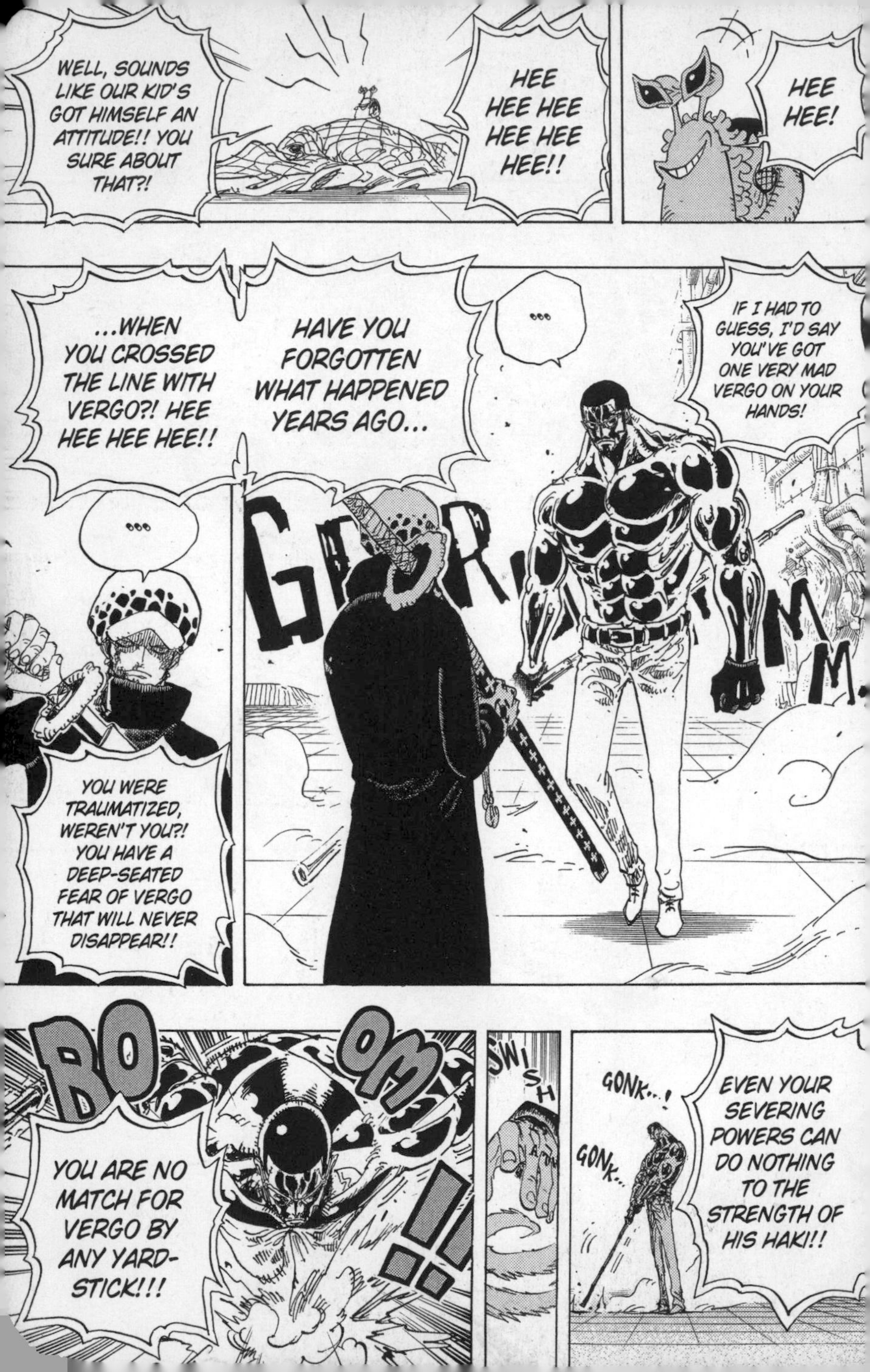
HEE HEE!
HEE HEE HEE HEE HEE!!
WELL, SOUNDS LIKE OUR KID'S GOT HIMSELF AN ATTITUDE!! YOU SURE ABOUT THAT?!
IF I HAD TO GUESS, I'D SAY YOU'VE GOT ONE VERY MAD VERGO ON YOUR HANDS!
...
HAVE YOU FORGOTTEN WHAT HAPPENED YEARS AGO...
...WHEN YOU CROSSED THE LINE WITH VERGO?! HEE HEE HEE HEE!!
...
YOU WERE TRAUMATIZED, WEREN'T YOU?! YOU HAVE A DEEP-SEATED FEAR OF VERGO THAT WILL NEVER DISAPPEAR!!
GONK...!
GONK...
EVEN YOUR SEVERING POWERS CAN DO NOTHING TO THE STRENGTH OF HIS HAKI!!
SWISH
BOOM
YOU ARE NO MATCH FOR VERGO BY ANY YARD-STICK!!!

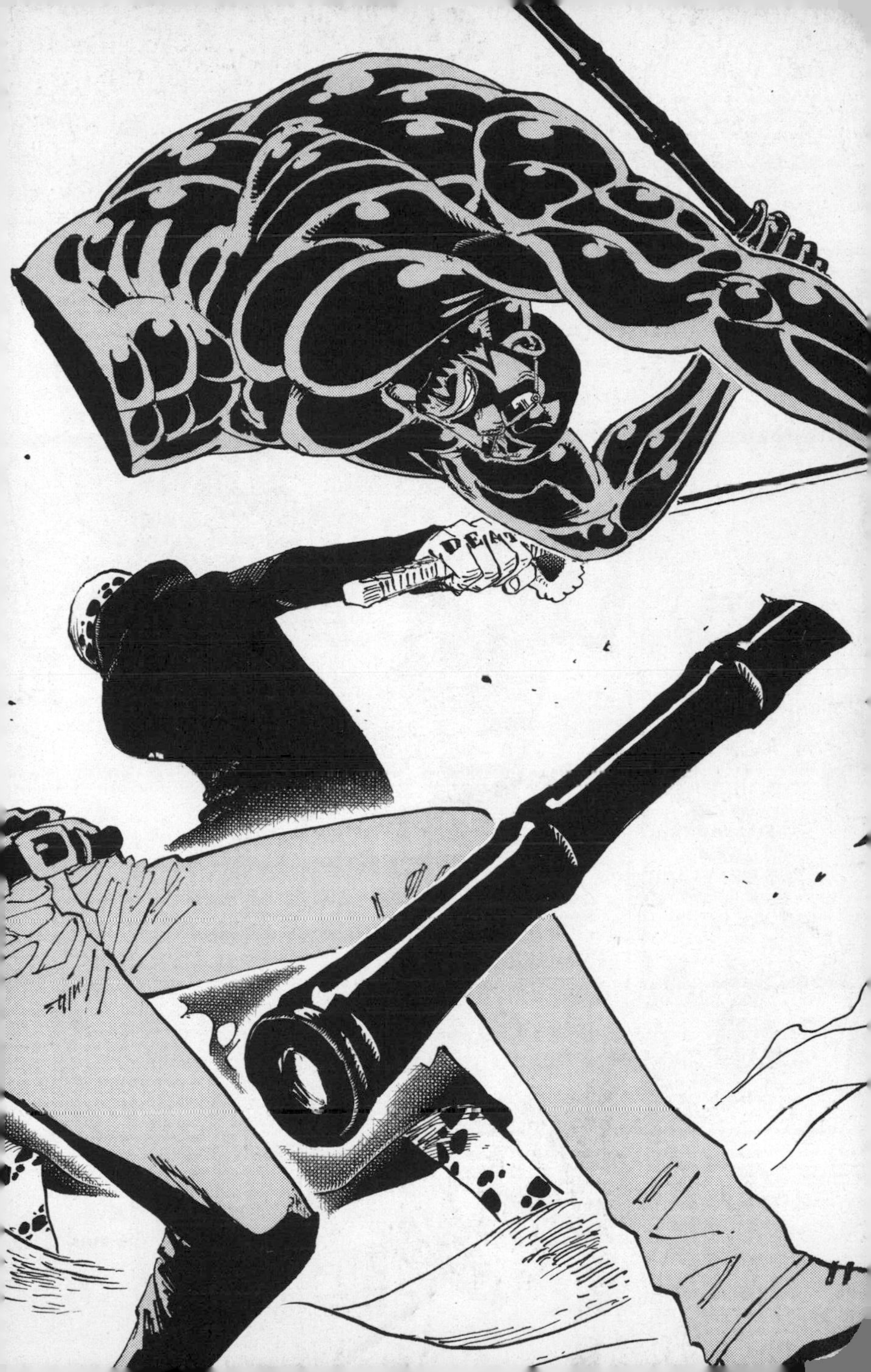

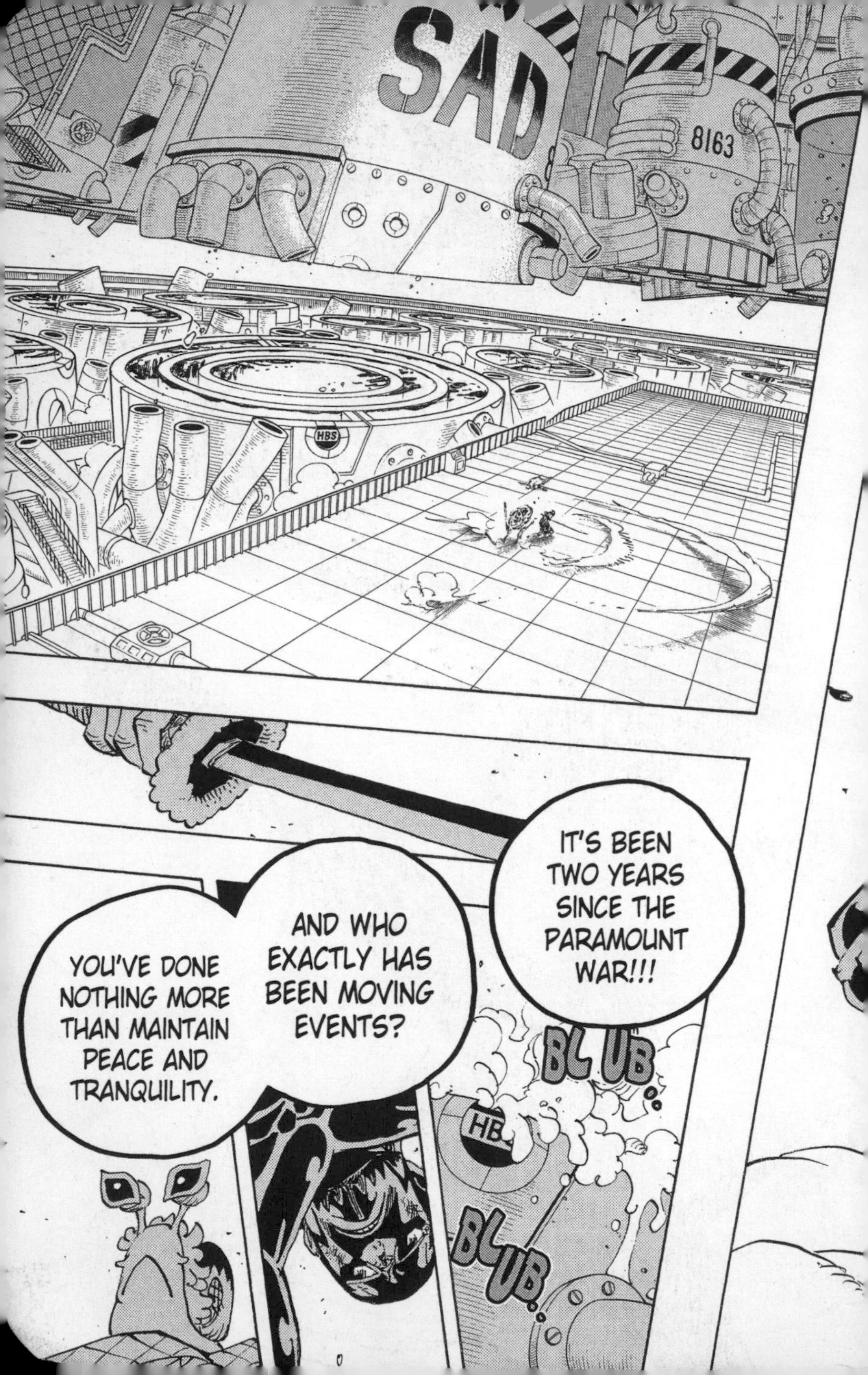
SAD
8163
HBS
IT'S BEEN TWO YEARS SINCE THE PARAMOUNT WAR!!!
AND WHO EXACTLY HAS BEEN MOVING EVENTS?
YOU'VE DONE NOTHING MORE THAN MAINTAIN PEACE AND TRANQUILITY.
BLUB
HB
BLUB

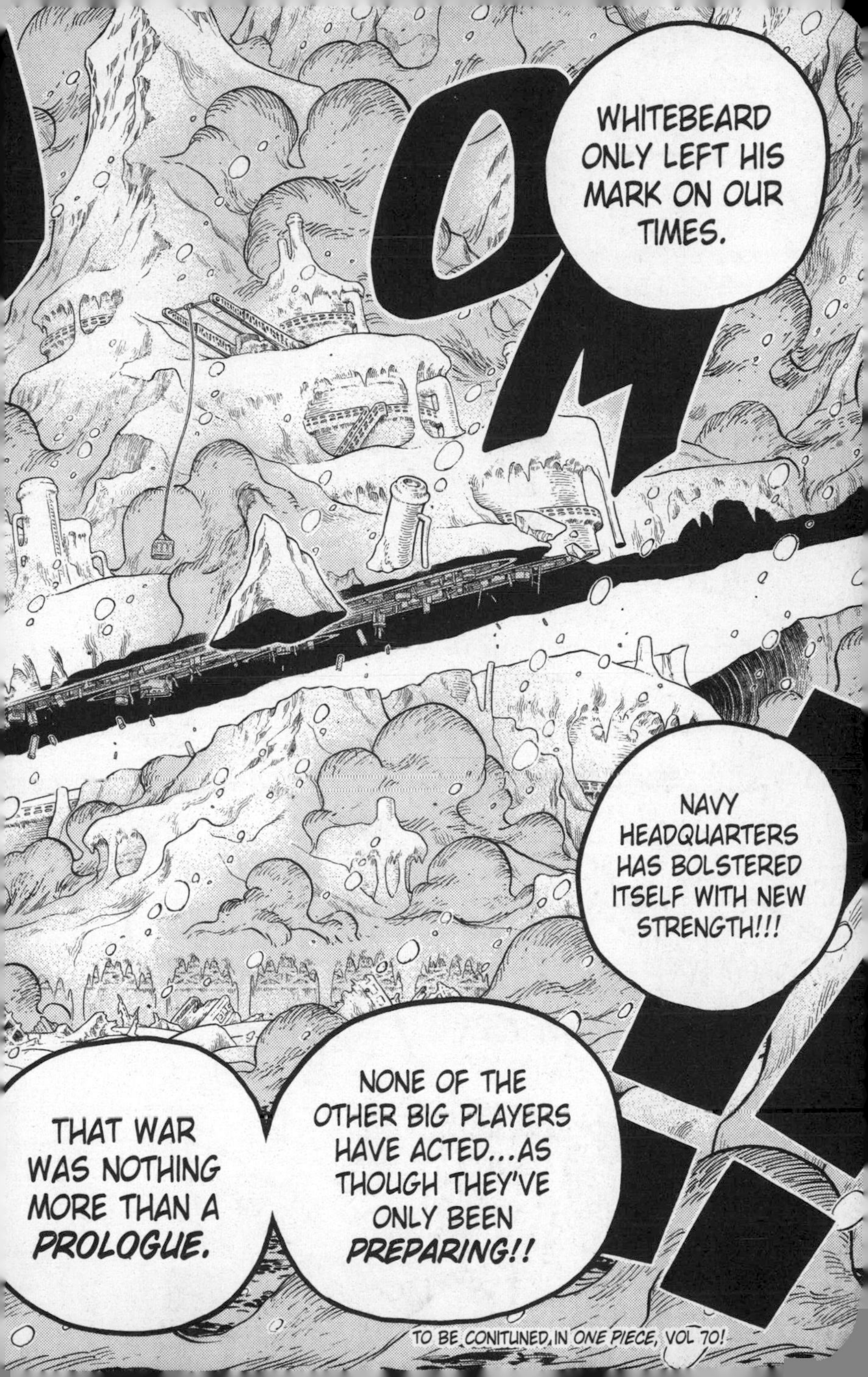
WHITEBEARD ONLY LEFT HIS MARK ON OUR TIMES.
NAVY HEADQUARTERS HAS BOLSTERED ITSELF WITH NEW STRENGTH!!!
NONE OF THE OTHER BIG PLAYERS HAVE ACTED...AS THOUGH THEY'VE ONLY BEEN *PREPARING*!!
THAT WAR WAS NOTHING MORE THAN A *PROLOGUE*.
TO BE CONITUNED IN ONE PIECE, VOL 70!

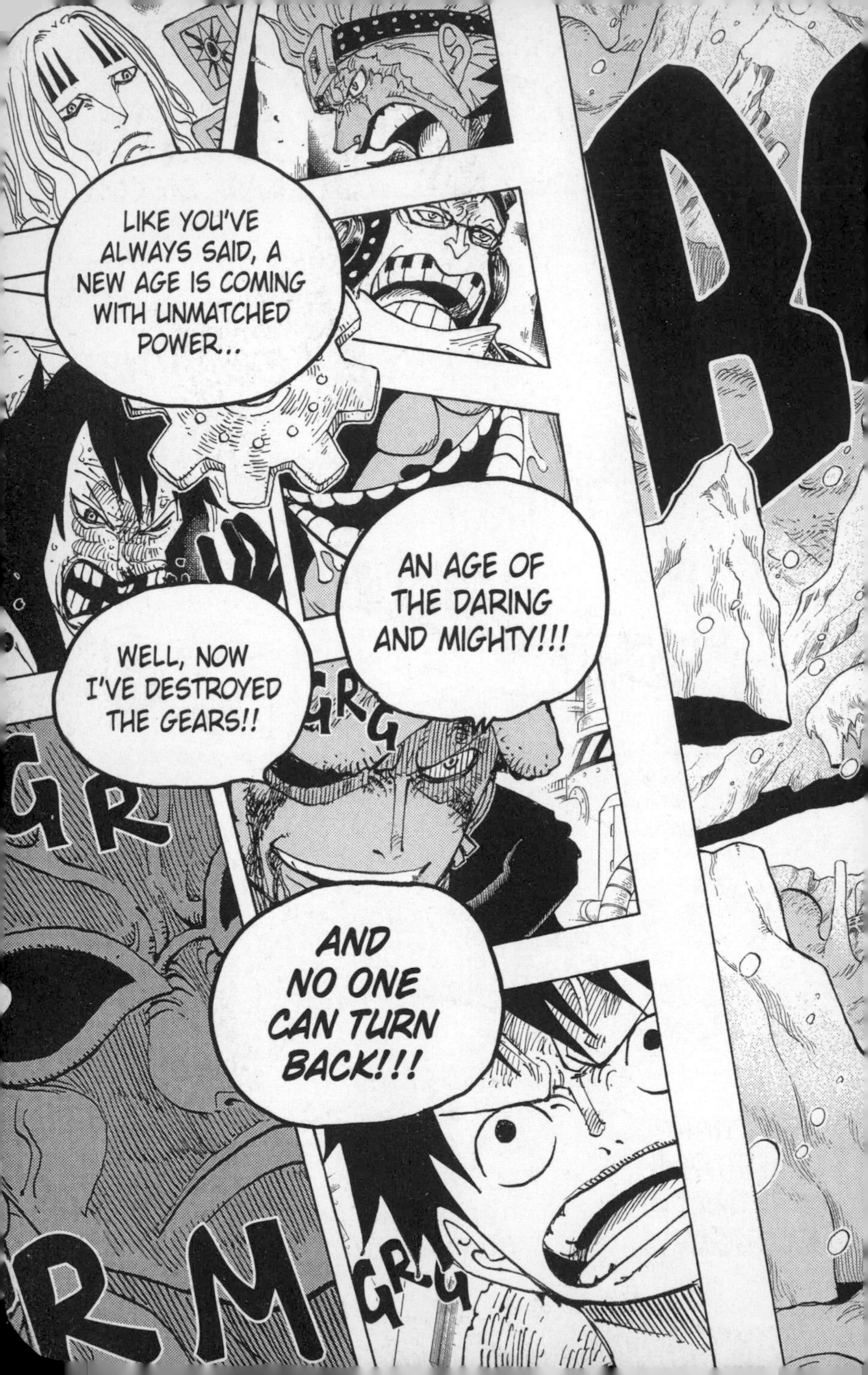
LIKE YOU'VE ALWAYS SAID, A NEW AGE IS COMING WITH UNMATCHED POWER...
AN AGE OF THE DARING AND MIGHTY!!!
WELL, NOW I'VE DESTROYED THE GEARS!!
GRG
GR
AND NO ONE CAN TURN BACK!!!
RM
GRG

COMING NEXT VOLUME:

QUIT THE SEVEN WARLORDS !!!

With Luffy and Law seemingly landing decisive blows against their respective opponents, is the trouble on Punk Hazard now over? Or will the peace be short-lived when an even darker figure heads for the island to join in on the fun...?

ON SALE MARCH 2014!

You're Reading in the Wrong Direction!!

1
3
2
1
2
3
4
5
6

Whoops! Guess what? You're starting at the wrong end of the comic!

...It's true! In keeping with the original Japanese format, **One Piece** is meant to be read from right to left, starting in the upper-right corner.

Unlike English, which is read from left to right, Japanese is read from right to left, meaning that action, sound effects and word-balloon order are completely reversed...something which can make readers unfamiliar with Japanese feel pretty backwards themselves. For this reason, manga or Japanese comics published in the U.S. in English have sometimes been published "flopped"—that is, printed in exact reverse order, as though seen from the other side of a mirror.

By flopping pages, U.S. publishers can avoid confusing readers, but the compromise is not without its downside. For one thing, a character in a flopped manga series who once wore in the original Japanese version a T-shirt emblazoned with "M A Y" (as in "the merry month of") now wears one which reads "Y A M"! Additionally, many manga creators in Japan are themselves unhappy with the process, as some feel the mirror-imaging of their art skews their original intentions.

We are proud to bring you Eiichiro Oda's **One Piece** in the original unflopped format. For now, though, turn to the other side of the book and let the journey begin...!

—Editor

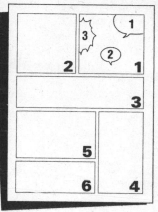